MUNICIPAL
AND GOVERNMENTAL
ACCOUNTING

PRENTICE-HALL ACCOUNTING SERIES

H. A. Finney, Editor

IRVING TENNER, M.B.A., Ph.D., C.P.A.

Associate Professor of Accounting, Roosevelt University; Consultant to the National Committee on Governmental Accounting, to Various Agencies of the Federal Government, and to State and Local Governments

MUNICIPAL
AND GOVERNMENTAL
ACCOUNTING

Third Edition

New York   PRENTICE-HALL, INC.

1955

PREFACE

THE SCOPE of this book has been enlarged to cover not only governments but also certain institutions. The accounting principles and procedures applicable to both state and local governments, including counties, townships, cities and villages, school districts, and special districts, are described. The institutions are hospitals and colleges and universities.

The present book discusses the audit of governmental accounts, with emphasis on those auditing principles and procedures peculiar to governments. The chapter dealing with the classification of accounts has been expanded to cover not only revenue and expenditure accounts, but also the typical balance sheet accounts of each fund. The classification is presented in such a way as to enable the reader to get a bird's-eye view of the accounts which go to make up each fund. Finally, the chapter which formerly dealt with utilities (water and electric plants) now also discusses other enterprises (municipal markets).

Some of the chapters have been combined and others rearranged to bring together discussions of those procedures which are common to certain funds. Many of the questions and problems carried in the preceding edition have been replaced with new questions and problems; also, extensive revisions have been made in most of those retained.

As in the past, the book is consistent with the principles established by the National Committee on Governmental Accounting and the Municipal Finance Officers Association. Moreover, the present book embodies the many important changes in accounting principles, classification of accounts, and terminology which have been made by the National Committee on Governmental Accounting since the publication of the second edition.

Grateful acknowledgment is hereby made to H. A. Finney, Professor Arthur N. Lorig of the University of Washington, Professor C. Aubrey Smith of the University of Texas, and Professor Max Zimering of the

College of the City of New York, who reviewed the material and made many constructive comments, as well as to the many instructors who contributed valuable suggestions. Thanks are extended also to Asher Tenner for his competent assistance throughout the revision of the book.

IRVING TENNER

TABLE OF CONTENTS

vii

several bond issues—Balance sheet for consolidated sinking fund—Accounting for groups of sinking funds—Accounting for utility or other enterprise sinking funds.

and bank acounts—Inter-fund settlements—Choosing the depository—
Accounting for petty cash and change funds—Reconciliations—Summary.

15. General Property Taxes 234

Assessment of property—Levying the tax—Determining the tax rate—
Determining the amount due from each taxpayer—Setting up taxes receivable and billing taxpayers—Collection of a government's taxes by
another unit—Enforcing the collection of taxes—Recording taxes on the
books—Recording discounts on taxes—Recording interest and penalties on
taxes—Accounting for tax sales—Accounting for nonrevenue taxes—Accounting for taxes collected in advance—General property tax statements.

16. Fixed Assets 257

ALL FIXED ASSETS: Classifying fixed assets—Valuing assets acquired
through foreclosure or gifts—Establishing property records—Classifying
individual property records—Additions to fixed assets—Transfer of fixed
assets—Inventory of fixed assets—Asset retirements and replacements.
GENERAL FIXED ASSETS: Depreciation not computed—Asset retirements—
Sale of general fixed assets—Property damaged or destroyed—Statements
of general fixed assets. FIXED ASSETS OF SELF-SUPPORTING ENTERPRISES: Accounting for depreciation—Determining periodic depreciation charges—
Recording depreciation—Re-examining the allowance for depreciation—
Retirement of assets—Replacements—Accounting for replacement fund—
Making replacements out of the fund—Statement of fixed assets–electric
utility.

17. Liabilities 282

LIABILITIES OTHER THAN BONDS: Vouchers payable—Warrants payable—
Tax anticipation notes—Bond anticipation notes—Judgments payable—
Accrued liabilities. BONDS: Classification of bonds—Steps in the accounting procedure for bonds—Authorization of bonds—Sale of bonds—Meeting debt service charges—Recording matured bonds payable and their
payment—Paying matured bonds and interest through fiscal agent—
Subsidiary debt statements.

18. Auditing and Financial Reporting 304

AUDITING STANDARDS AND PROCEDURES: Standards and procedures distinguished—Classifications of audits—Classification of auditors—Purpose of
audit—Preliminary steps—Audit procedure—Revenues—Expenditures—
Assets—Liabilities—Other credits—Surplus. THE AUDIT REPORT: Letter
of transmittal—Financial statements—Arrangement of financial statements. THE ANNUAL FINANCIAL REPORT: Letter of transmittal—Financial
statements—Statistical tables—Arrangement of statistical tables. COM-
BINED FINANCIAL AND AUDIT REPORT. THE MONTHLY FINANCIAL REPORT.

LIST OF FIGURES

LIST OF TABLES

MUNICIPAL
AND GOVERNMENTAL
ACCOUNTING

1

<<<<<<<<<<<<<<<<<<<<<<<<<<<<<<<<<<<<<<<<<<<<<<<<<<<<<<<<<<<<<<<<

PRINCIPLES AND STANDARDS OF GOVERNMENTAL ACCOUNTING

THIS BOOK deals with accounting principles, standards, and procedures applicable to state and local governments, including counties, townships, cities, and villages, and to institutions such as universities and hospitals. It is logical to deal with the accounting for governmental units and certain institutions in the same volume because they have the following characteristics in common: their object is to render service without profit; their assets and liabilities and revenues and expenditures appertain to separately established funds which constitute separate accounting entities; and their operations are controlled by budgets.

The first part of this book deals with governmental accounting, the latter part with institutional accounting.

The National Committee on Governmental Accounting. Since this book embodies the principles developed by the National Committee on Governmental Accounting, a brief description of this organization is in order. The Committee was organized in 1934 for the purpose of developing and helping put into effect sound principles of governmental budgeting, accounting, and reporting. It is composed of representatives of the following organizations: American Accounting Association, American Institute of Accountants, American Municipal Association, Canadian Institute of Chartered Accountants, International City Managers Association, Municipal Finance Officers Association, National Association of Cost Accountants, National Association of State Auditors, Comptrollers, and Treasurers, National Association of State Budget Officers, and National Municipal League. In addition, the United States Government, the Canadian Government, and the Association of School Business Officials are each represented in a liaison capacity. The Committee has issued several publications[1] and has in other ways been instrumental in promoting uniformity and in raising the standards of governmental accounting and auditing.

Purpose of governmental accounting. The purpose of governmental accounting is to supply information concerning governments. At least six groups are interested in the information: the governmental unit's administrators, its legislative body, investors, students of public finance, political scientists, and the general public. While these groups are not mutually exclusive (for example, an investor constitutes part of the general public) there are points at which their interests diverge. For example, the administrator may be concerned with certain minor details of expenditure which would be of little value to anyone else. The political scientist may be interested in the distribution of expenditures by functions,[2] whereas such a distribution may not concern the investor. We may say then that the purpose of governmental accounting is *to produce financial information in a form that is readily useful to all of the parties concerned.*

Commercial vs. governmental accounting. Many accounting principles and standards apply to both commercial and governmental accounting. To illustrate, the accrual basis of accounting under which revenues are recorded when earned even though not collected, and expenditures are considered as such as soon as the liability is incurred applies to both the commercial and governmental accounting fields. In view of the fact, however, that financial statements of a government (except for municipal utilities and other self-supported enterprises) are not intended to show whether the government is being operated at a profit or a loss, there may be justification for omitting from governmental statements some minor items which would ordinarily be included in a balance sheet or an operating statement prepared for a business. The double entry system is applicable to both commercial and governmental accounting.

The mechanics of governmental and commercial accounting procedures are the same: Transactions are recorded from data contained in the accounting documents. The information is first placed in the books of original entry, from which it is posted to the general ledger and subsidiary ledgers. Postings may, however, be made directly from the original documents to the subsidiary ledger accounts, just as they frequently are in commercial accounting. The accounting records of a government, like those of a commercial concern, may be said to consist of (1) the documents forming the basis of and giving details concerning the accounting

---

[1] The Committee's two principal publications are *Municipal Accounting and Auditing* (Chicago: The Committee, 1951) and *A Standard Classification of Municipal Accounts* (Chicago: The Committee, 1953).

[2] For an example of a classification of expenditures by function, see page 13.

transactions, (2) the books of original entry, and (3) the books of final entry, or ledgers.

A proper classification of accounts is essential to good accounting— commercial or governmental. In each case the accounts must be so classified that they will facilitate the preparation of the financial statements. Similarly, uniform accounting terminology is highly desirable in both fields.

Although there are many similarities between commercial and governmental accounting, there are also certain basic differences which necessitate treating governmental accounting in a separate book. These differences are due to (1) the lack of the profit motive in government and (2) the necessity of complying with legal provisions. Although the accounting system of a business must provide the information that may be called for by various governmental agencies, legal provisions do not affect a business as greatly as a government. An accounting system of a business is designed primarily to show the financial position of the business and the results of its operation, the latter in terms of profit or loss. An accounting system of a governmental unit is designed to show not only financial position and operations but also the extent of compliance with legal provisions. The two most important legal provisions affecting governmental accounting are those relating to (1) budgeting and (2) funds.

Compliance with budgetary provisions. The preparation and execution of the budget and the related accounting procedures are governed by legal provisions. The records should help guarantee that expenditures will be made in accordance with legislative intent as expressed in the appropriation acts or ordinances. The methods of accomplishing this will be described later.

Proper budgetary accounting involves not only the control of expenditures in accordance with budgetary provisions but also the compilation of revenue data to serve as a guide in the preparation of future budgets. Revenues must be recorded in such manner and under such classifications as will make possible a comparison of estimated revenues with actual revenues. Such a comparison will reveal to what extent estimates were in error, may prevent the repetition of such errors, and will permit a more accurate planning of expenditures. The recording of revenue estimates on the books of account deserves special mention because it is frequently not required by law and therefore in many instances is neglected.

Funds. Every governmental body must raise and spend its revenues in accordance with special regulations, restrictions, or limitations. To insure that money will be expended for designated purposes, governments establish funds. A fund has therefore been defined as "a sum of money or other resources segregated for the purpose of carrying on specific activities or attaining certain objectives in accordance with special regulations, restrictions, or limitations and constituting an independent fiscal and accounting entity." [3] A separate group of accounts must be provided for each fund to show its assets, liabilities, reserves, and surplus, as well as its revenues and expenditures.

The accounting for governmental funds differs radically from the accounting for funds of a commercial enterprise. The records of a governmental fund include a complete, self-balancing, double entry set of accounts showing the assets, liabilities, reserves, revenues, expenditures, and net worth of the fund. On the other hand, a fund of a commercial enterprise is not regarded as a distinct accounting entity; the fund asset accounts and any related income and expense accounts are not a self-balancing group but are mere elements of the general ledger of the business as a whole.

Establishment of funds. Funds are established in accordance with the requirements of constitutions, statutes, and charters, or pursuant to action by the legislative body or the chief executive.[4] State funds are established by constitution or statute, although certain state funds may be set up by the governor's order. Local-government funds are established by statute, but in municipalities they may also be established in pursuance of charter requirements. Local governments may set up funds by direction of the local legislative body or by order of the chief executive.

On the basis of the authority for their establishment, a distinction must be made between the various funds. The resources of a fund must be expended solely for the purposes specified by the authority. A government may not ordinarily make even a temporary loan from one fund to another without specific authorization.

The funds created by the state constitution, the state legislature, and municipal charters appear, in view of these restrictions, to be the least flexible, because they can be changed only by the state legislature or

---

[3] National Committee on Governmental Accounting, *Municipal Accounting and Auditing* (Chicago: The Committee, 1951), p. 234.

[4] The names assigned to the legislative body and chief executive vary in different governmental units. The following are some examples:

Governmental Unit	Legislative Body	Chief Executive
State	Legislature	Governor
County	Board of County Commissioners or County Court	County Clerk, or County Manager, or Chairman of County Board
Township	Township Commissioners	Township Clerk
City	City Council, or Board of Alderman, or Board of Commissioners	Mayor, or City Manager
Park District	Board of Commissioners or Park Board	Superintendent of Parks
School District	School Board, or Board of Education	Superintendent of Schools

the voters. Funds which are established by a local government's legislative body are more flexible, because changes can be more easily authorized. The most flexible funds are those established by executive authority, since the executive is free to make changes. This does not imply that the latter type of fund is most satisfactory, however, because the purpose of a fund is to act as a restrictive device.

Funds and appropriations distinguished. A distinction must also be made between a fund and an appropriation. An appropriation is an authorization by the legislative body to make expenditures and incur liabilities for specific purposes. Whereas an appropriation is always made by the legislative body, funds may be established by executive order. A fund requires an identification of the assets, liabilities, reserves, surplus, revenues, and expenditures applicable to it, whereas an appropriation merely authorizes an expenditure and does not necessarily provide any one particular revenue source for financing the expenditure. An appropriation specifies in detail the exact purposes for which expenditures may be made, the amount to be spent, and the period of time during which the expenditures are to be made, whereas these detailed restrictions do not apply to funds. No expenditures may be made out of certain funds —the general fund, for example—without an appropriation. Finally, a single appropriation may be made out of several funds.

Number and kinds of funds to be established. The number and kinds of funds employed by governments vary. It is evident, however, that, in view of the restrictions involved, the greater the number of funds the more rigid the financial administration becomes. In the absence of statutory or other legal requirements, therefore, a government should establish as few funds as possible. To permit effective budgetary control and to establish uniformity in financial reports, the National Committee on Governmental Accounting has recommended the following classification of funds:

1. *General fund.* The general fund is used to account for revenues not allocated to specific purposes by law or contractual agreement. That is, any activities not financed from other funds are automatically financed from the general fund.

2. *Special revenue funds.* Special revenue funds are of the same nature as the general fund, the only distinction being that they are usually limited to a single purpose. Examples of special revenue funds are those established for the purpose of financing schools or parks.

3. *Bond funds.* Bond funds are used to account for the proceeds from the sale of bonds.

4. *Special assessment funds.* Special assessment funds are employed to account for charges levied against properties or persons benefiting from special services rendered by the governmental unit.

5. *Sinking funds.* Sinking funds are used to account for the accumulation of resources to retire term bonds.

6. *Trust and agency funds.* Trust and agency funds are set up to account

for assets received by a governmental unit in the capacity of trustee or agent.

7. *Working capital funds.* Working capital funds are established to account for service activities performed by a department or bureau for other departments or bureaus of the same governmental unit.

8. *Utility or other enterprise. funds.* Utility or other enterprise funds are used to account for self-supporting enterprises rendering services primarily for the public.

In addition to the self-balancing accounts for the above-mentioned funds, there are:

The general fixed assets group of accounts, which is used to account for all fixed assets of a governmental unit other than those carried in a working capital fund, a trust fund, or a utility or other enterprise fund.

The general bonded debt and interest group of accounts, which is used to account for the principal of and interest on all unmatured bonds except those payable from (and therefore reflected by the accounts of) a special assessment fund or a utility or other enterprise fund.

Every governmental unit must have a general fund but may not need all of the other funds or groups of accounts. The extent to which they will be used will depend on the kinds of activities carried on by a particular governmental unit, the means of financing them, and the legal restrictions imposed.

Bases of accounting. There are three principal bases of accounting—cash, accrual, and modified cash. Under a strict cash basis, revenues are accounted for only when received in cash and expenditures are taken into account only when money is paid out. Under a strict accrual basis, revenues are taken into account when earned, regardless of the fiscal period in which they are collected, and expenditures are considered as such as soon as liabilities are incurred, regardless of the period in which they are paid. It should be noted, however, that even under the cash basis, not all receipts are revenues; the receipt of cash from the sale of notes is not a revenue because it gives rise to a liability. Similarly, even under the cash basis not all disbursements are expenditures; the payment of the notes is not an expenditure because it results in the reduction of a liability.

In actual practice the accrual basis is modified in several ways. Some governmental units, although on an accrual basis as far as their taxes are concerned, are on a cash basis with respect to their less important revenues. Again, even though a governmental unit may record most of its expenditures on an accrual basis, it may be forced by legal requirements to record some of them on a cash basis. For example, even a governmental unit which accounts for most of its transactions on an accrual basis may find it undesirable to record accrued interest expenses at the end of the fiscal year. This occurs when these expenses are to be included in the budget of the following year and money is to be appropriated for them at that time. If, therefore, they were included as expenditures of the present year, the governmental unit would be violating the law, which usually provides that no expenditure may be incurred until an appropriation for it has been made.

Finally, as indicated in Chapter 13, the degree of accrual varies in different funds. However, even if a governmental unit does not accrue all of its revenues and expenditures, it is usually considered to be on an accrual basis provided it accrues the more important ones.

A third basis of accounting is the modified cash basis (sometimes referred to as the modified accrual basis) under which revenues are not taken into account until collected in cash, but expenditures are considered as such as soon as the liabilities are incurred.

Assuming that legal provisions permit it, the accrual basis should be followed because it is the most accurate in that it recognizes both revenue and expenditure transactions when they take place. For example, under the accrual basis it is possible to make an accurate comparison between the revenues and expenditures of a particular period, whereas such a comparison is not possible under either the cash or the modified cash basis. Again, the accrual basis, by providing for the accrual of revenues and the setting up of the related control accounts in the general ledger for receivables, creates better control over revenues than either the cash or modified cash basis.

If the choice is between the cash and the modified cash bases, the latter is to be preferred because under it expenditures are treated the same as under the accrual basis. For example, under either the accrual or the modified cash basis, it is possible to compare the expenditures for a period with the services rendered during that period and to arrive at actual or standard unit costs. Moreover, under both of these bases accurate comparisons can be made between expenditures of different years, whereas no inter-year comparisons can ordinarily be made with the expenditure data compiled under the cash basis of accounting.

In summary, it may be said that while the modified cash basis is to be preferred over the cash basis, it is inferior to the accrual basis. Accordingly, the use of the accrual basis will be assumed throughout this book unless the other bases are specifically mentioned.

2

<<<<<<<<<<<<<<<<<<<<<<<<<<<<<<<<<<<<<<<<<<<<<<<<<<<<<<<<<<<<

CLASSIFICATION OF ACCOUNTS

Accounts are the media through which financial data are collected for use in the financial statements. To facilitate the accounting work and the preparation of financial statements, accounts are classified into certain well-defined groups. For example, accounts may be classified or grouped according to funds. Within each fund, accounts may be classified according to whether they show the *financial condition* of the fund or indicate *changes* in condition—that is, whether they go to make up the balance sheet or the revenue and expenditure statements. This chapter is divided into three parts, the first part dealing with the classification of balance sheet accounts, the second part with the classification of revenue accounts, and the third with the classification of expenditure accounts.

Classification of Balance Sheet Accounts

A classification of selected balance sheet accounts is illustrated in Figure 1. The following facts should be noted about this classification:

1. As the title of the chart indicates, the illustration is confined to selected balance sheet accounts and is not a complete list of balance sheet accounts.

2. The classification is a master list from which accounts would be selected as needed for the different funds. As Figure 1 shows, some of the accounts apply to one fund only while others apply to more than one fund.

3. The accounts are classified into three principal groups: (a) assets and other debits, (b) liabilities and other credits, and (c) surplus. *Assets* include items actually owned by the government, such as cash and taxes receivable. *Other debits* consist principally of items which are not assets at the date of the balance sheet but which are eventually expected to be converted into assets, such as estimated revenues. *Liabilities* consist of debts or other legal obligations. *Other credits* include items which are

8

not liabilities at the balance sheet date but which may become liabilities at some future date (for example, appropriations), as well as accounts which show fund equities other than surplus (for example, the Reserve for Retirement of Sinking Fund Bonds account and the Trust and Agency Fund Balances account). *Surplus* is the excess of assets and other debits over liabilities and other credits.

4. Assets are classified into two groups, namely, (a) assets other than fixed and (b) fixed assets. Fixed assets have been defined as "assets of a long-term character which are intended to be held or used, such as land, buildings, machinery, furniture, and other equipment." All other assets may, for practical purposes, be designated as nonfixed assets.

5. Liabilities are classified into two groups, namely, (a) long-term liabilities and (b) liabilities other than long-term. Long-term liabilities are those which mature within more than one year from the balance sheet date and which are not payable from the present resources of a fund. Examples are bonds and interest payable more than one year from the date of the balance sheet or those payable within one year, but for the retirement of which no resources have been provided in the particular fund at the balance sheet date. All other liabilities are classified as non-long-term.

6. Balance sheet accounts may be classified on still another basis, namely, according to whether they are budgetary accounts or proprietary accounts. Budgetary accounts are those which show the condition of the budget. Examples are to be found listed under "Other Debits" and "Other Credits" in the chart. For instance, the Estimated Revenues account listed under "Other Debits" is a budgetary account because it does not represent an asset at the balance sheet date but rather represents an item which is expected to become an asset. Similarly, the Appropriations account shown under "Other Credits" is a budgetary account because it reflects estimated liabilities provided for in the budget. In contrast with the budgetary accounts are the proprietary accounts, which represent actual assets, such as cash or taxes receivable, and actual liabilities, such as vouchers payable or matured bonds payable. It must be recognized, however, that some proprietary accounts are also used to show the condition of the budget. For example, the Revenues account (shown under "Other Debits") is a proprietary account because it reflects revenues actually earned. But it also reflects the condition of the budget because, on the balance sheet prepared during the fiscal year, it is deducted from the Estimated Revenues account to arrive at the amount of estimated revenues remaining to be realized.

Classification of Revenue Accounts

Revenues are increases in assets or decreases in liabilities which increase ownership equity. Revenue accounts are classified for the purpose of (1)

Figure 1

Chart of Selected Balance Sheet Accounts

A. Assets and Other Debits	General Fund	Special Revenue Funds	Bond Funds	Special Assessment Funds	Sinking Funds	Trust and Agency Funds	Working Capital Funds	Utility or Other Enterprise Funds	General Fixed Assets	General Bonded Debt and Interest
Assets										
Assets—Other Than Fixed:										
Cash	x	x	x	x	x	x	x	x		
Taxes Receivable—Current	x	x			x					
Estimated Uncollectible Current Taxes (Credit)	x	x			x					
Taxes Receivable—Delinquent	x	x			x					
Estimated Uncollectible Delinquent Taxes (Credit)	x	x			x					
Tax Liens Receivable	x	x			x					
Estimated Uncollectible Tax Liens (Credit)	x	x			x					
Accounts Receivable	x	x	x					x		
Estimated Uncollectible Accounts (Credit)	x	x	x					x		
Due from Other Funds	x	x	x	x	x	x	x	x		
Due from Other Governmental Units	x									
Special Assessments Receivable				x						
Investments	x	x			x	x		x		
Interest Receivable on Investments					x	x		x		
Taxes Levied for Other Governmental Units						x				
Inventory of Materials and Supplies	x	x					x	x		
Fixed Assets:										
Land							x	x	x	
Buildings							x	x	x	
Allowance for Depreciation—Buildings							x	x		
Improvements Other Than Buildings							x	x	x	
Allowance for Depreciation—Improvements Other Than Buildings							x	x		
Machinery and Equipment							x	x	x	
Allowance for Depreciation—Machinery and Equipment							x	x		
Other Debits										
Estimated Revenues	x	x								
Revenues (Credit)	x	x								
Bonds Authorized—Unissued			x							
Improvements Authorized				x						
Required Sinking Fund Contribution					x					
Sinking Fund Contribution Revenues (Credit)					x					
Amount to be Provided for Payment of Bonds										x
Amount to be Provided for Payment of Interest										x

B. Liabilities and Other Credits

Liabilities

	General Fund	Special Revenue Funds	Bond Funds	Special Assessment Funds	Sinking Funds	Trust and Agency Funds	Working Capital Funds	Utility or Other Enterprise Funds	General Fixed Assets	General Bonded Debt and Interest
Liabilities—Other Than Long-Term:										
Vouchers Payable	x	x	x	x			x	x		
Unaudited Accounts Payable	x	x	x	x			x	x		
Judgments Payable	x	x	x	x						
Pensions Payable						x				
Contracts Payable—Uncompleted Contracts			x	x				x		
Contracts Payable—Retained Percentage			x	x				x		
Due to Other Funds	x	x	x	x	x	x	x	x		
Due to Other Governmental Units	x									
Matured Bonds Payable	x									
Matured Interest Payable	x									
Taxes Collected in Advance	x	x			x					
Long-Term Liabilities:										
Bonds Payable								x		x
Interest Payable on Bonds in Future Years										x

Other Credits

	General Fund	Special Revenue Funds	Bond Funds	Special Assessment Funds	Sinking Funds	Trust and Agency Funds	Working Capital Funds	Utility or Other Enterprise Funds	General Fixed Assets	General Bonded Debt and Interest
Appropriations	x	x	x	x						
Appropriation Expenditures (Debit)	x	x	x	x						
Encumbrances (Debit)	x	x	x	x						
Reserve for Encumbrances	x	x	x	x						
Contributions from Other Funds							x			
Reserve for Retirement of Sinking Fund Bonds					x					
Reserve for Retirements							x			
Reserve for Rebates				x						
Trust and Agency Fund Balances							x			

C. Surplus

	General Fund	Special Revenue Funds	Bond Funds	Special Assessment Funds	Sinking Funds	Trust and Agency Funds	Working Capital Funds	Utility or Other Enterprise Funds	General Fixed Assets	General Bonded Debt and Interest
Unappropriated Surplus	x	x	x	x	x	x	x			
Earned Surplus								x		
Reserve for Inventories	x	x								
Investment in General Fixed Assets									x	

preparing and controlling the budget, (2) controlling revenues, (3) preparing financial statements, and (4) preparing comparative financial statistics. A classification of revenue accounts by source of revenue will furnish the necessary data for all these purposes.

General fund revenues. The following are the main revenue classes of the general fund:

Taxes
Licenses and permits
Fines, forfeits, and other penalties
Revenue from use of money and property
Revenue from other agencies
Charges for current services
Sales, and compensation for loss, of fixed assets
Transfers from other funds

In actual practice, accounts would not usually be set up for the above classes of revenue. That is, these classes are broad group headings, which are useful for reporting purposes. For example, no account entitled Revenue from Use of Money and Property would be set up. Instead, individual accounts would be provided for each type of revenue falling within this class, as follows:

Interest on Bank Deposits
Interest on Investments
Rents and Concessions
Royalties

To arrive at the total revenue accrued or received from the use of money and property, it would be necessary to combine the balances of these accounts. The detailed revenue sources applicable to each class are discussed in Chapter 5.

Revenues of other funds. Some of the above revenues apply to the other funds. For example, taxes may also be a revenue source of special revenue funds and sinking funds. Moreover, some of the funds also have other sources of revenue. To cite one example, special assessment fund revenues consist for the most part of special assessments levied against property owners, the governmental unit's share of the cost of the improvement, and interest on assessments receivable.

Distinction between revenues of a fund and revenues of a governmental unit. A distinction must be made between the revenues of a fund and the revenues of the governmental unit as a whole. Some receipts or accruals may constitute fund revenues but may not be revenues of the governmental unit because they increase the ownership equity of the fund but not of the unit. To illustrate, proceeds from the sale of bonds are revenues of the bond fund because they increase its ownership equity and do not create any liability in that fund. They are not, however, revenues of the governmental unit, since they are a liability of the unit. Similarly, charges to departments for services are revenues of the working capital fund but not of the governmental unit as a whole, because these charges must be paid by other departments.

In classifying revenues for the purpose of state-wide or national financial statistics, only those of the governmental unit as a whole are included. These usually consist of the revenues of the general fund, revenues of special revenue funds, special assessments collected from property owners, and the revenues of utilities or other enterprises operated by the governmental unit.

Classification of Expenditure Accounts

Expenditures are classified for the purpose of (1) securing information to be used in estimating the expenditures for a fiscal period and in controlling appropriations, (2) insuring that money is expended economically, (3) preparing financial statements, and (4) compiling comparative financial statistics. To obtain all the required information, the accounts are classified by (1) function, (2) activity, (3) organization unit, (4) character, and (5) object. Each of these classifications is discussed below.

Classification by function. The functional classification is useful primarily in the compilation of financial statistics. Since the organization structures of even the same units of government (for example, cities) vary, it would be practically impossible to secure comparable financial data if some common classifications were not followed. Since all governments have some functions in common (although some have more functions than others), comparable statistics are secured by classifying expenditures *by function.*

The following is a classification of expenditures by function:

General government
Public safety
Highways
Sanitation and waste removal
Health and hospitals
Public welfare
Schools
Libraries
Recreation
Public service enterprises
Interest
Retirement of bonds

Classification by activity. Each function consists of a group of activities. For example, the function of sanitation and waste removal may include the following:

Supervision
Operation of sewer system
Sewage treatment and disposal
Street cleaning
Dust prevention
Collection of garbage and ashes
Operation of comfort stations

The classification of expenditures by activity is needed in securing accurate comparative cost data and in the preparation of the budget. Unit cost accounting is possible only if expenditures are classified by activities. Again, because comparable activities can be found in various governmental units, the classification of expenditures by activity makes it possible to compare costs for similar activities in different governmental units. Through comparing the cost of an activity with the expected benefit, it is possible to make an intelligent decision as to whether the scope of the activity should be increased, decreased, or left unaltered.

Classification by organization unit. The classification of expenditures by organization unit is important because it provides the means whereby expenditures can be controlled and responsibility can be definitely allocated. Sound budgetary control is not possible without responsibility on the part of the officials carrying on the operations of the government. The allocation of appropriations and their related expenditures to organization units is essential if officials are to be held responsible for staying within the appropriation, and if they are to know the amount which they may spend. The estimates of expenditures submitted by heads of organization units form in part the basis of appropriations. The classification of expenditures by organization units is thus essential for both budget preparation and budget control.

Since the form of organization varies, it is not possible to present any one typical organization structure. The following is an example of a classification of accounts by organization unit for a department of public works of one municipality:

DEPARTMENT OF PUBLIC WORKS
Bureau of Administration
Bureau of Construction and Design
Bureau of Maintenance
Division of Streets and Sewers
Division of Mechanical Equipment
Bureau of Waste Collection and Disposal
Division of Sewage Disposal

Division of Waste Collection
Division of Waste Disposal
Bureau of Building Inspection
Bureau of Weights and Measures
Bureau of Street Lighting

Classification by character. Expenditures may be classified in accordance with whether they represent current expenses, capital outlays, or the retirement of bonds. The distinction between an expense and a capital outlay is that the latter results in the acquisition of a fixed asset. The distinction between expenses and capital outlays, on the one hand, and the retirement of bonds on the other, is self-evident.

Classification by object. To classify expenditures *by object* is to group them according to the article purchased or the service obtained. Current expenses may be classified into the following main objects: personal services, contractual services, materials and supplies, and other charges. Fixed assets may be classified as land, structures and improvements, and equipment. In turn, structures and improvements and equipment constructed (as distinguished from those purchased) may be further classified according to the amount of personal services, contractual services, materials and supplies, and other charges incurred in their construction. The objects of expenditures incident to the liquidation of long-term indebtedness are (1) the retirement of serial bonds and (2) the creation of sinking funds by periodical contributions. The following is an example of a heading for a combined character and object classification, as it is frequently found in financial statements:

Character

CURRENT EXPENSES				CAPITAL OUTLAYS			RETIREMENT OF BONDED DEBT	
Objects				Objects			Objects	
Personal Services	Contractual Services	Materials and Supplies	Other Charges	Land	Structures and Improvements	Equipment	Serial Bonds	Contributions to Sinking Funds

It should be noted that this heading does not show the amount of personal services, contractual services, and so forth under structures and improvements or equipment. While this information is usually compiled for each fixed asset constructed, it is not usually reported except in special financial statements. The reason is that the municipality also acquires many of its fixed assets by purchase and this information could obviously not be presented for such assets. If the objects of expenditure were reported for some of the fixed assets (those constructed) but not for others (those purchased) confusion would result.

Each of the objects of expenditure listed under current expenses in the above heading may in turn be divided into sub-objects as indicated by the examples which follow. In examining these sub-objects, it will be seen that contractual services themselves may require the use of personal services, materials and supplies, and so forth. The governmental unit is not directly concerned with these. Its only concern is to see that the contractor complies with the terms of the contract.

PERSONAL SERVICES
    Regular Salaries and Wages
    Temporary Salaries and Wages
    Other Personal Services
CONTRACTUAL SERVICES
    Heat, Light, and Power
    Postage
    Telephone and Telegraph
    Traveling Expenses
    Subsistence and Support of Persons
    Storage and Care of Vehicles
    Printing, Binding, and Advertising
    Repairs to Buildings and Equipment
    Other Contractual Services
MATERIALS AND SUPPLIES
    Agricultural and Horticultural Supplies
    Chemicals, Drugs, and Laboratory Supplies
    Clothing
    Food
    Fuel
    Motor Fuels
    Office Supplies
    Construction Materials
    Parts for Equipment
    Other Materials and Supplies
OTHER CHARGES
    Rents
    Insurance
    Official Bonds
    Workmen's Compensation
    Refunds, Awards, and Indemnities
    Subscriptions and Memberships
    Pension and Retirement Contributions
    Grants and Subsidies
    Taxes
    Interest

The object classifications indicated above are sometimes subdivided still further. Thus, Traveling Expenses, shown under Contractual Services, might be divided as follows:

Local Traveling Expenses
Long-Distance Traveling Expenses (including board and lodging)
Mileage Allowance

On the other hand, many governments restrict the object classification to the main titles previously mentioned—namely, personal services, contractual services, materials and supplies, and other charges. The extent to which the object classification should be detailed will depend on the information which is deemed necessary for budgetary or cost purposes.

Classification by function, organization unit, character, and object. The statement heading illustrated on page 15 reflected a classification of expenditures by character and object. It is, of course, also necessary to show the organization unit by which these expenditures were incurred and frequently also the function accomplished by each organization unit. In other words, it is important to prepare a statement classifying the expenditures by function, organization unit, character, and object. Such a statement is illustrated on page 86.

Coding expenditure accounts. To facilitate the accounting work and the preparation of financial statistics, accounts are coded—that is, are assigned numbers and symbols which can be used in the place of the account titles. In actual practice, all accounts are coded, but for our purpose it will be sufficient to illustrate merely the codification of expenditure accounts because the coding of these accounts presents more difficult problems than the coding of other accounts. The coding system shown here represents only one type; several other types are in use.

Account coding is especially helpful in the classification of expenditures. Through a combination of code numbers, it is possible to tell at a glance the function and organization unit under which a particular expenditure is to be classified, as well as the character and object of the particular expenditure. As an illustration, let us take again the functions and departments previously illustrated. Assume that all accounts pertaining to the general government function are assigned the numbers 1000-1999, all accounts pertaining to the public safety function are assigned the numbers 2000-2999, and so on. In that case, the code numbers assigned to the accounts designating functions and organization units would be as indicated below:

1000-1999 GENERAL GOVERNMENT
    1000 Council
    1100 Executive Department

1200 Courts
1300 Board of Elections
1400 Department of Finance
   1410 Administration
   1420 Bureau of Accounts
   1430 Bureau of Treasury
   1440 Bureau of Purchases
   1450 Bureau of Assessments
1500 Department of Law
1600 City Clerk's Office
1700 Board of Zoning Appeals
1800 Civil Service Commission
1900 City Historian
2000- 2999 PUBLIC SAFETY
2000 Department of Police
2100 Department of Fire
2200 Department of Correction
2300 Board of Examiners—Plumbers
2400 Board of Examiners—Electricians
3000- 3999 HIGHWAYS
4000- 4999 SANITATION AND WASTE REMOVAL
5000- 5999 HEALTH AND HOSPITALS
6000- 6999 PUBLIC WELFARE
7000- 7999 SCHOOLS
8000- 8999 LIBRARIES
9000- 9999 RECREATION
10000-10999 INTEREST
11000-11999 RETIREMENT OF BONDS

Let us assume further that the character classification is coded as follows:

A-D Current Expenses[1]
E-G Capital Outlays
H-I Retirement of Bonds

A separate letter would be assigned in turn to each object coming within the Current Expenses group, as in the following list:

A Personal Services
B Contractual Services
C Materials and Supplies
D Other Charges

---

[1] Where tabulating equipment is used, numbers would have to be substituted for letters.

The Capital Outlays account might similarly be divided thus:

E Land
F Structures and Improvements
G Equipment

Similarly, Retirement of Bonds might be divided as follows:

H Serial Bonds
I Contributions to Sinking Funds

Each of the objects of expenditure listed above may be subdivided still further, and the numbering system must therefore be expanded to take care of the subdivision. Thus, Personal Services would be coded as follows:

A1 Regular Salaries and Wages
A2 Temporary Salaries and Wages
A3 Other Personal Services

As we have seen, it may be necessary to use a combination of classifications. In that case, the codes for functions and organization units are combined with the codes for the other classifications in such a manner that it is possible to tell at a glance to which class a particular expenditure belongs. For example, on the basis of the code numbers here illustrated, the code number for an expenditure for regular salaries made by the city council would be 1000-A1. The following are a few examples of the information which may be derived from certain codes.

Assume that the following expenditures were incurred:

1. Salaries were paid to regular employees of the bureau of accounts.
2. Traveling expenses for a long-distance trip taken by the head of the bureau of purchases are to be charged against that bureau.
3. New benches were purchased for the city court.

The expenditures would be coded, respectively, as follows:

1. Code No. 1420-A1
     Function—General Government (1000-1999 group)
       Organization Unit—Department of Finance (1400)
                         Bureau of Accounts (1420)
         Character—Current Expenses (A-D)
           Object—Personal Services (A)
                   Regular Salaries and Wages (A1)
2. Code No. 1440-B4
     Function—General Government (1000-1999 group)
       Organization Unit—Department of Finance (1400)
                         Bureau of Purchases (1440)
         Character—Current Expenses (A-D)
           Object—Contractual Services (B)
                   Traveling Expenses (B4)

3. Code No. 1200-G2
        Function—General Government (1000-1999 group)
        Organization Unit—Courts (1200)
            Character—Capital Outlays (E-G)
                Equipment (G)
                Benches (G2)

No special provision is made in the above code for designating the name of the fund. The latter can usually be identified from the series of numbers in the classification. For example, in the case of the above classification, all accounts bearing numbers between 1,000 and 11,999 may be designated as general fund accounts. Special revenue fund expenditure accounts might be assigned a series of numbers beginning with 12,000 and ending, let us say, with 19,999.

Media for classifying expenditure data. As indicated subsequently, the same subsidiary account may be used to record both the appropriation and the related expenditures. A separate account is established for each object, but the account is coded to show also the function, organization unit, and, where applicable, the activity to which it applies. The following is an example of part of the heading of a ledger sheet:

Code No. 1420-A
Function: General Government
Organization Unit: Department
    of Finance—Bureau of Accounts
Activity: Accounting
Character: Current Expenses
Object: Personal Services

The total *current expenses* for the bureau of accounts are determined by adding the balances for each of the objects of current expense listed under the bureau. The bureau's *total expenditures* are obtained by adding current expenses and capital outlays. Total expenses for the finance department are arrived at by adding the balances of each of the bureaus making up the department. Finally, total expenditures for general government are obtained by adding the expenditures of the organization units performing the function.

From the examples illustrated on page 19 it is evident that the classification can be carried even further. Thus, Personal Services may be subdivided into Regular Salaries and Wages, Temporary Salaries and Wages, and Other Personal Services. Separate accounts would in that case be established for each of these sub-objects. The balances of these accounts would, when added together, give the total for personal services and the procedure would thereafter be the same as that outlined in the preceding paragraph.

3

≪≪

BUDGETING

A BUDGET is a plan dealing with the proposed expenditures for a given period or purpose and with the means of financing them. Budgets may be classified as long-term and current. The long-term budget covers a period of at least five years, while the current budget generally is prepared for a period of one year.[1] In this chapter, we shall be concerned primarily with the current budget.

Relationship between funds and the budget. Even though expenditures of governmental money are already restricted through the establishment of funds, a budget is necessary. Legal provisions governing the funds merely insure use of the money for the purposes for which the fund was set up, and do not indicate the amount to be expended for each activity financed out of the fund. These amounts are detailed in the budget. In discussing budgetary procedure, a distinction must be made between the general budget and special budgets. The general budget deals primarily with the general fund and special revenue funds. Special budgets are prepared, in addition, for some other funds. The first part of this chapter is devoted to the general budget—that is, the budget for the general fund and special revenue funds. In the second part, we shall indicate the modifications that are necessary in the preparation and execution of special budgets.

The General Budget

Budgetary procedure may be divided into three steps: (1) preparation of the budget, (2) adoption of the budget, and (3) execution of the budget. Each of these steps will be discussed.

Preparation of the budget. The agencies charged with the preparation

---

[1] The current budgets of most state governments cover a period of two years. But there is no great difference in budgetary principles for state and local governments or for budgets prepared annually and biennially.

of the budget vary. In some cases the legislative body itself, or a committee of its members, takes charge of budget preparation. Under a centralized form of financial organization, however, the budget is prepared under the supervision of the chief executive. The technical work may be performed either by a member of the department of finance or by a budget officer appointed by the chief executive and responsible to him. It will be assumed throughout this chapter that the budget is prepared under the supervision of the chief executive and that a budget officer is charged with the technical work.

The budget calendar. Sound financial planning requires that preparation of the budget be started in time for its adoption before the beginning of the period to which it applies. To insure that adequate time will be allowed, a budget calendar similar to the one illustrated in Figure 2 is frequently prepared, listing each step in the budgetary procedure and the time allowed for its completion.

Call for departmental estimates. A call by the chief executive for departmental estimates is one of the first steps in the preparation of the budget. Forms for departmental estimates are illustrated in Figures 3-6. Figure 3 illustrates a form used in estimating expenses for personal services. The first eight columns of this schedule are usually filled in by the finance officer; columns 9-11 are filled in by the head of the department. The columns headed "Recommended by Chief Executive" are filled in by the chief executive before he presents the budget to the legislative body. Amounts are placed in the remaining columns after the legislative body has made the appropriation. If, however, appropriations are not made for each class of position but in a lump sum for the total personal service expenses of each organization unit, only the total amount appropriated is shown. For example, in the schedule illustrated (Figure 3) it is assumed that the legislative body made an appropriation for the total amount to be spent by the police department for personal services and did not specify separately the amount appropriated for the chief of police, deputy chief, chief of detectives, and so on. Accordingly, only one amount ($26,000) is shown as the appropriation for the personal service expenses of the police department.

Figure 4 illustrates a form used for estimating expenditures other than those to be made for personal services and Figure 5 illustrates a form used to estimate capital outlays. The data in these schedules may be further summarized in another schedule, which is illustrated in Figure 6. This schedule is especially valuable if appropriations are made by main classes of expenditures. If such a summary is prepared, and if appropriations are made to the classes of expenditure listed in the summary, the "Appropriation by Legislative Body" column is omitted from the other three schedules.

Figure **2**

A GOVERNMENTAL UNIT

Budget Calendar
For Budget Year Beginning January 1, 1956

Date	Steps in Budget Procedure
Prior to October 1, 1955..............	Budget officer prepares estimate forms and instructions.
October 1..........................	Budget officer distributes estimate forms and instructions among departments.
October 1 to October 21..............	Departments prepare estimates. Budget officer prepares estimates of fixed charges and other nondepartmental items. Budget officer also prepares estimates of taxes and other nondepartmental revenues.
October 22.........................	Filled-in departmental estimate forms are returned to the budget officer by departments.
October 22 to November 1............	Budget officer consolidates estimates.
November 2 to November 30..........	Budget officer conducts departmental hearings. Budget officer confers with chief executive, and the latter determines amounts to be finally recommended to the legislative body. Chief executive also determines amounts to be adopted as the official revenue estimates of the municipality for the budget year. Chief executive prepares budget message. Budget officer prepares final budget document for submission to legislative body.
December 1.........................	Budget document, including message of chief executive, is turned over to legislative body.
December 2.........................	Legislative body turns budget document over to its budget committee.
December 2 to December 15..........	Budget committee conducts public hearings and makes recommendations concerning the amounts to be appropriated.
December 16........................	Budget committee turns its recommendations over to the legislative body.
December 16 to December 23..........	Legislative body considers the committee's recommendations.
December 23........................	Legislative body adopts the budget by passing an appropriation ordinance. Legislative body levies taxes by passing a tax levy ordinance.
December 27........................	Request for allotments is sent out by chief executive through budget officer.
January 2, 1956....................	Adopted budget is recorded on the books.
January 6..........................	Departments submit work programs and allotment schedules to budget officer.
January 6 to January 15..............	Budget officer consolidates allotment schedules and presents them with recommendations to chief executive.
January 15.........................	Chief executive makes final revisions.
January 16.........................	Department heads are informed of the amounts alloted to them. Allotments are recorded on the books.

Figure 3

Figure 3

Fund: General
Function: Public Safety
Department: Police
Submitted by: A. Johnson, Chief
Date: October 10, 1955

A GOVERNMENTAL UNIT
Departmental Estimate
Personal Services
1956

Departmental Code: 2000

Code No.	Classification	ACTUAL						PROPOSED, 1956			RECOMMENDED BY CHIEF EXECUTIVE			APPROPRIATION BY LEGISLATIVE BODY
		January 1, 1955			October 1, 1955									
		No.	Rate	Amount	No.	Rate	Amount	No.	Rate	Amount	No.	Rate	Amount	Amount
1	2	3	4	5	6	7	8	9	10	11	12	13	14	15
A-1.1	Chief of Police	1	$6,500	$6,500	1	$6,500	$6,500	1	$6,500	$6,500	1	$6,500	$6,500	
A-1.2	Depty Chief	1	5,500	5,500	1	5,500	5,500	1	5,500	5,500	1	5,500	5,500	
A-1.9	Policewoman	1	2,800	2,800	1	2,800	2,800	1	2,800	2,800	1	2,800	2,800	
	Total	11	—	$26,000	11	—	$26,000	11	—	$26,000	11	—	$26,000	$26,000

Figure 4

Departmental Code: 2000

A GOVERNMENTAL UNIT
Departmental Estimate
Current Expenses—Other Than Personal Services
1956

Fund: General
Function: Public Safety
Department: Police
Submitted by: A. Johnson, Chief
Date: October 10, 1955

| Code No. | Classification | ACTUAL EXPENDITURES | | | Estimated Expenditures Balance of 1955 | Total Columns 5 and 6 | 1956 | | |
| | | 1953 | 1954 | 1955 (First Nine Months) | | | Proposed by Department | Recommended by Chief Executive | Appropriation by Legislative Body |
1	2	3	4	5	6	7	8	9	10
B	CONTRACTUAL SERVICES:								
B-1	Printing	$ 247	$ 255	$ 195	$ 65	$ 260	$ 280	$ 275	
B-2	Gas	74	73	55	20	75	80	75	
B-3	Electricity	158	161	126	43	169	177	175	
B-4	Water	56	53	41	14	55	60	55	
B-19	Motorcycle Repairs	1,045	980	745	250	995	1,150	1,000	
B-20	Auto Repairs	1,197	1,260	960	315	1,275	1,400	1,300	
B-21	Repairs to Office Equipment	293	300	235	80	315	363	320	
	Total	$3,070	$3,082	$2,357	$ 787	$3,144	$3,510	$3,200	$3,200
C	MATERIALS AND SUPPLIES:								
C-1	Janitor Supplies	$ 95	$ 96	$ 77	$ 25	$ 102	$ 120	$ 120	
C-6	Clothing	1,011	1,200	785	260	1,045	1,300	1,100	
C-7	Gasoline	1,587	1,570	1,259	420	1,679	1,800	1,700	
C-8	Lubricants	278	281	220	70	290	330	290	
C-45	Record Supplies	100	115	95	30	125	150	120	
C-50	Ammunition	427	431	335	115	450	500	470	
	Total	$3,498	$3,693	$2,771	$ 920	$3,691	$4,200	$3,800	$3,800
D	OTHER CHARGES:								
D-1	Rent	$1,800	$1,800	$1,405	$ 470	$1,875	$1,900	$1,900	
D-2	Surety Bond Premiums	80	80	60	20	80	100	100	
	Total	$1,880	$1,880	$1,465	$ 490	$1,955	$2,000	$2,000	$2,000
	Grand Total	$8,448	$8,655	$6,593	$2,197	$8,790	$9,710	$9,000	$9,000

Figure 5

A GOVERNMENTAL UNIT

Departmental Code: 2000

Departmental Estimate
Capital Outlays
1956

Fund: General
Function: Public Safety
Department: Police
Submitted by: A. Johnson, Chief
Date: October 10, 1955

Code No.	Classification	Explanation	PROPOSED BY DEPARTMENT			Recommended by Chief Executive	Appropriation by Legislative Body
			Quantity	Unit Price	Cost		
1	2	3	4	5	6	7	8
G-1	Office Equipment	Desks	1	$ 90	$ 90	$ 90	
G-2	Automotive Equipment	Sedans	2	1,500	3,000	3,000	
G-6	Automotive Equipment	Motorcycles	2	900	1,800	1,800	
G-20	Firearms	Sub-Machine Guns	2	400	800	800	
		Total	—	—	$10,000	$10,000	$10,000

Figure 6

Departmental Code: 2000

A GOVERNMENTAL UNIT
Departmental Estimate
Summary
1956

Fund: General
Function: Public Safety
Department: Police
Submitted by: A. Johnson, Chief
Date: October 10, 1955

Code No.	Classification	Actual Expenditures 1953	1954	1955 (First Nine Months)	Estimated Expenditures Balance of 1955	Total Columns 5 and 6	Proposed by Department	1956 Recommended by Chief Executive	Appropriation by Legislative Body
1	2	3	4	5	6	7	8	9	10
A	Personal Services	$22,000	$24,000	$19,000	$ 7,000	$26,000	$26,000	$26,000	$26,000
B	Contractual Services	3,070	3,082	2,357	787	3,144	3,510	3,200	3,200
C	Materials and Supplies	3,498	3,693	2,771	920	3,691	4,200	3,800	3,800
D	Other Charges	1,880	1,880	1,465	490	1,955	2,000	2,000	2,000
	Total Current Expenses	$30,448	$32,655	$25,593	$ 9,197	$34,790	$35,710	$35,000	$35,000
E-G	Capital Outlays	$13,000	$12,000	$ 9,000	$ 2,000	$11,000	$10,000	$10,000	$10,000
	Total	$43,448	$44,655	$34,593	$11,197	$45,790	$45,710	$45,000	$45,000

The foregoing schedules are essential even if a performance budget is to be prepared. A performance budget is one which classifies actual and estimated expenditures by organization units, activities, and units of work. Under a performance budget, it is possible to make estimates on the basis of what is expected to be accomplished rather than solely on the basis of what has been spent by a particular organization unit in the past. If activities are susceptible to unit cost measurement, the estimates can be based on work programs, similar to the one illustrated in Figure 7. But even if units of measurement cannot be used, it is possible to correlate expenditures with performance by classifying them by activities. The foregoing schedules are needed even under a performance budget, because even under such a budget it is essential to know which organization unit or units have been or are going to be responsible for carrying out each activity.

Estimating other charges. Some expenditures are not allocated to any function or organization unit. Examples are interest, contributions to pension funds, retirement of serial bonds, and contributions to sinking funds. These expenditure estimates are therefore prepared by the budget officer who also reports estimated deficits.

Revenue estimates. The amount of revenue which will accrue or will be received during the year must be kept in mind. Accordingly, even before the department heads begin to prepare their estimates, the budget officer will estimate the amount of revenues which will be available. Figure 8 illustrates a statement of actual and estimated general fund revenues. In order to save space, only a few revenues have been listed.

If the governmental unit expects to have, at the end of the year, an unappropriated surplus represented by cash, and this surplus is not set aside as a reserve, the surplus may be taken into account in estimating the resources available to finance expenditures of the coming year. This is true even though the surplus comes from *past* years' revenues.

Revision of departmental estimates. As soon as department heads have filled out the budget estimate forms, and at any rate not later than the date designated in the budget calendar, they transmit the forms, together with work programs and other supporting data, to the budget officer. The latter notes whether the estimates have been properly prepared, summarizes the information received, and presents the schedules, together with the summaries and revenue estimates, to the chief excutive, who then begins to prepare his recommendations to the legislative body.

Both the departmental estimate schedules and the work programs are of great help to the chief executive in preparing his recommendations. In addition, he confers with department heads, whom he may ask to justify estimates of expenditures. In larger governmental units, the chief executive may employ efficiency engineers to make special investigations to determine whether departmental requests are justified.

Figure 7

A GOVERNMENTAL UNIT
Work Program
1956

Departmental Code: 4000

Fund: General
Function: Sanitation and Waste Removal
Department: Public Works
Bureau: Sanitation
Submitted by: M. A. Downs, Chief
Date: October 10, 1955

Operation	Work Unit	ACTUAL 1954			ESTIMATED 1955			ESTIMATED 1956		
		No. of Units	Unit Cost	Total	No. of Units	Unit Cost	Total	No. of Units	Unit Cost	Total
Garbage Collection	Tons	158,319	$1.45	$229,562.55	168,000	$1.46	$245,280.00	170,000	$1.44	$244,800.00
Incineration	Tons	170,350	1.18	201,013.00	180,000	1.18	212,400.00	182,000	1.19	216,580.00

29

Figure 8

A GOVERNMENTAL UNIT

General Fund

Statement of Actual and Estimated Revenues

	Actual 1954	Actual First Nine Months of 1955	Estimated Remainder of 1955	Total Columns 2 and 3	Estimated 1956
TAXES:					
General Property Taxes	$294,000	$291,000	—	$291,000	$288,000
Interest and Penalties on Taxes	1,100	800	$ 250	1,050	1,000
Total Taxes	$295,100	$291,800	$ 250	$292,050	$289,000
LICENSES AND PERMITS:					
Motor Vehicle Licenses	$ 31,000	$ 25,500	$ 7,000	$ 32,500	$ 34,000
Parking Meters	1,500	1,450	450	1,900	2,000
Beer and Liquor Licenses	11,000	9,000	3,000	12,000	13,000
Amusement Licenses	6,200	4,650	1,225	5,875	6,000
Newsdealers' Licenses	1,350	990	300	1,290	1,300
Total Licenses and Permits	$ 51,050	$ 41,590	$11,975	$ 53,565	$ 56,300
CHARGES FOR CURRENT SERVICES:					
Election Fee Revenues	$ 1,100	$ 1,000	$ 200	$ 1,200	$ 1,000
Sale of Ordinances	1,200	925	250	1,175	1,000
Charges for Private Police Service	5,100	3,000	1,050	4,050	4,000
Fees for Inspection of Dairy Products	375	465	135	600	800
Total Charges for Current Services	$ 7,775	$ 5,390	$ 1,635	$ 7,025	$ 6,800
SALE OF FIXED ASSETS	$ 6,000	$ 4,000	$ 500	$ 4,500	$ 5,100
TRANSFERS FROM OTHER FUNDS	4,000	3,000	1,200	4,200	4,300
Grand Total	$437,000	$397,000	$36,000	$433,000	$431,000

Figure 9

A GOVERNMENTAL UNIT
Budget Summary
General Budget—1956

Estimated Resources		Estimated Expenditures	
General Fund			
Taxes............................	$288,000	Personal Services................	$219,000
Other Revenues...................	143,000	Other Current Expenses...........	63,600
		Capital Outlays..................	109,400
		Retirement of Debt..............	34,000
		Excess of Resources over Expenditures...	5,000
Total General Fund............	$431,000	Total General Fund............	$431,000
Special Revenue Fund			
Taxes............................	$100,000	Personal Services................	$ 75,000
Other Revenues...................	25,000	Other Current Expenses...........	30,000
		Capital Outlays..................	20,000
Total Special Revenue Fund...	$125,000	Total Special Revenue Fund...	$125,000
Total General Budget.........	$556,000	Total General Budget.........	$556,000

The chief executive pays careful attention also to the revenue estimates. Whereas no single operating department head knows the relationship between total estimated expenditures and total estimated revenues, the chief executive has these data. If estimated expenditures exceed estimated revenues, reductions in the amount requested should be made, or the governmental unit will incur a deficit. However, it should not be assumed that a good chief executive will make arbitrary adjustments at some fixed percentage. For example, if estimated expenditures exceed estimated revenues by 10 per cent, he will not automatically reduce each department's expenditures by this percentage but will consider each department's request individually. Whether a department's requests will be reduced, and the amount of the reduction, will depend on the extent to which the services are indispensable and the likely effect on the general community welfare of a reduction in them.

Presentation of the budget. After the chief executive has considered the requests of the various departments and taken action on them, he is in a position to present the budget document to the legislative body for consideration and adoption. The budget document consists of the following:

1. A budget message, in which the prinicpal budget items are explained, the governmental unit's experience during the past year and its financial status at the present time are outlined, and recommendations regarding the financial policy for the coming year are made.

2. A budget summary showing total estimated resources and expenditures by funds. Revenues are generally classified here by main sources, and expenditures by character and object (see Figure 9).

3. A schedule of actual and estimated revenues classified by source (Figure 8).

4. The departmental request forms with the column headed "Recommended by Chief Executive" filled in (see Figures 3-6).

5. Work programs (see Figure 7).

6. Schedules showing charges not applicable to any particular department, including such items as judgments and costs, interest on notes and bonds, maturing general serial bonds, contributions to sinking funds, contributions to pension funds, the governmental unit's share of special assessment costs, and estimated fund deficits.

7. Fund balance sheets showing estimated assets, liabilities, reserves, and surpluses or deficits as of the close of the current fiscal year.

8. A statement of actual and estimated cash receipts, disbursements, and balances (Figure 10). Note that this statement is prepared in addition to the revenue statement. The revenue statement shows merely the revenues estimated to be earned; some of these may not be collected during the year. On the other hand, the governmental unit will collect delinquent taxes and other receivables of the preceding years. Through a comparison of estimated total receipts with estimated total disburse-

Figure 10

A GOVERNMENTAL UNIT
General Fund
Statement of Actual and Estimated Cash Receipts, Disbursements, and Balances

	Actual 1954	Actual First Nine Months of 1955	Estimated Balance of 1955	Total Columns 2 and 3†	Estimated 1956
OPENING CASH BALANCE	$ 18,375	$ 10,340	$ 64,415	$ 10,340*	$ 36,200
RECEIPTS:					
General Property Taxes—Current and Delinquent	$287,000	$240,000	$ 49,300	$289,300	$290,600
Interest and Penalties on Taxes	1,300	925	275	1,200	1,150
Licenses and Permits	51,050	42,100	11,465	53,565	56,300
Fines, Forfeits, and Other Penalties	8,410	5,900	2,100	8,000	9,500
Revenues from Use of Money and Property	7,320	5,230	1,970	7,200	7,200
Revenues from Other Agencies	23,000	48,000	15,000	63,000	62,200
Charges for Current Services	7,775	5,225	1,800	7,025	6,800
Collections of Accounts Receivable	8,100	6,070	1,800	7,870	5,200
Sale of Fixed Assets	6,000	4,000	500	4,500	5,100
Transfers from Other Funds	4,000	3,000	1,200	4,200	4,300
Total Receipts	$403,955	$360,450	$ 85,410	$445,860	$448,350
Total Receipts and Balance	$422,330	$370,790	$149,825	$456,200*	$484,550
DISBURSEMENTS:					
Personal Services	$220,000	$165,000	$ 56,000	$221,000	$219,000
Contractual Services	7,800	5,000	3,000	8,000	8,165
Materials and Supplies	14,700	10,900	4,100	15,000	14,300
Other Charges	25,350	18,850	7,150	26,120	26,120
Capital Outlays	105,000	76,000	34,000	110,000	109,400
Retirement of Bonds	25,000	19,000	6,000	25,000	20,000
Retirement of Notes	8,000	7,825	2,175	10,000	14,000
Payment of Vouchers Payable	6,140	3,800	1,200	5,000	7,100
Total Disbursements	$411,990	$306,375	$113,625	$420,000	$418,085
CLOSING CASH BALANCE	$ 10,340	$ 64,415	$ 36,200	$ 36,200*	$ 66,465

† With exception of items starred.

33

ments, it is possible to determine whether short-term borrowing will be necessary. An additional statement, showing both actual and estimated receipts and disbursements by months, would also be helpful.

9. If short-term borrowing is contemplated, a schedule showing short-term borrowing transactions during the past two years and the current year and the proposed short-term borrowing for the coming year.

10. A statement showing bonded debt outstanding (see Figure 98).

11. Statements of tax collections (see Figures 84 and 85).

12. A draft for an appropriation ordinance (see Figure 11).

13. A draft for a tax levy ordinance (discussed in Chapter 15).

Consideration of the budget by the legislative body. The legislative body takes steps to adopt the budget after receiving the budget document. Frequently the budget document is first turned over to a special committee, which makes any investigations it deems necessary, calls on department heads to justify their requests and on the chief executive to explain his recommendations, and conducts public hearings on the proposed budget. The committee then makes its recommendations to the legislative body. Sometimes the legislative body, especially if it is small, will itself perform the duties necessary before the adoption of the budget.

Adoption of the budget. After completing the budget hearings and investigations, the legislative body proceeds to adopt the budget through the passage of an appropriation ordinance (or appropriation act, as it is known in the case of a state). Part of an appropriation ordinance is illustrated in Figure 11. Note that only a few objects of expenditure are shown. That is, although the budget document itself may specify in detail each object of expenditure, appropriations need not be made in so great detail. Detailed appropriations take away from the chief executive freedom of action and administrative discretion.

Providing revenues for financing the budget. The appropriation act or ordinance merely authorizes the expenditures. It is necessary, in addition, to provide the means of financing them. Some revenues (for example, profits on the sale of investments) will accrue to the governmental unit without any legal action on its part. Other revenues will come as a result of legal action taken in the past. Examples are licenses and fees, income taxes, sales taxes, and similar licenses and taxes, the rates for which continue until they are changed by the legislative body. A third type of revenue—for example, the general property tax—requires new legal action each year (every two years in most of the states levying property taxes). Accordingly, as soon as the legislative body has passed the appropriation ordinance or act, it proceeds to levy general property taxes (discussed in Chapter 15).

Execution of budget. After the appropriation ordinance or act is passed, steps are taken to control the budget properly. The appropriation ordinance or act does not specify the rate at which expenditures are to be made throughout the year. It is evident, however, that the flow of revenues and expenditures is not uniform. For example, expenditures for park maintenance are likely to be greater in summer than in winter. On the other hand, no expenditures for snow removal are incurred during the

Figure 11

CITY OF X

Appropriation Ordinance
An Ordinance Making Appropriations for the Fiscal Year Beginning January 1, 1956, and Ending December 31, 1956, in the Sum of Five Hundred Fifty-Six Thousand Dollars ($556,000) and Regulating the Payment of Money Out of the City Treasury.

BE IT ORDAINED by the Council of the City of X:

Sec. 1: That the amounts herein named, aggregating Five Hundred Fifty-Six Thousand Dollars ($556,000), or so much thereof as may be necessary, divided respectively as follows: (1) for the general fund Four Hundred Thirty-One Thousand Dollars ($431,000), and (2) for a special revenue fund One Hundred Twenty-Five Thousand Dollars ($125,000), are hereby appropriated, subject to the conditions hereinafter set forth in this ordinance, from current revenue for the use of the several departments of the city government, and for the purposes hereinafter mentioned for the fiscal year beginning January 1, 1956, and ending December 31, 1956, as follows:

GENERAL FUND

Departments and Code Numbers	Appropriations	
No. 1000—Council:		
A Personal Services	$ 7,000	
B Contractual Services	400	
C Materials and Supplies	300	
D Other Charges	300	
G Equipment	3,000	$11,000
No. 1100—Executive Department:		
A Personal Services	$10,000	
B Contractual Services	200	
C Materials and Supplies	200	
D Other Charges	100	
G Equipment	2,000	12,500
No. 1200—Courts:		
A Personal Services	$10,200	
B Contractual Services	300	
C Materials and Supplies	350	
D Other Charges	150	
G Equipment	2,100	13,100

summer months. Accordingly, it is necessary to adjust the expenditures for the various departments so that they will be made at the time they are needed and so that they may correspond as far as practicable to the flow of revenue.

Call for allotment schedules. The first step toward expenditure control is a call by the chief executive for departmental allotment schedules. Each department head at this time knows the maximum amount which his department may spend. His task now is to determine how much of the appropriation is to be spent during each month, quarter, or other period. His estimates are based on expenditure statistics for past periods and on his general knowledge of the rate and volume of activities carried on during various parts of the year. He also makes use of work programs. An example of a work program used to support a monthly allotment schedule is given in Figure 12.

The departmental allotment schedules, together with any additional data supporting the request for allotments, such as work programs, are submitted to the chief executive, who in the meantime has received statements from the budget officer showing estimated receipts by months, quarters, or other periods. Upon receipt of the departmental allotment schedules, the total allotments requested for each period during the year are tabulated and compared with the anticipated receipts. Adjustments are then made, as far as possible, to bring the expenditures within the actual resources available for the particular period. Work programs are helpful in this connection, and usually the chief executive will also confer with department heads if any adjustments in their allotments are necessary.

There is a fundamental distinction, from the standpoint of control, between an appropriation and an allotment. An appropriation is made by the legislative body and frequently can be changed by that body only. On the other hand, allotments are made by the chief executive and can be changed by him without any action of the legislative body. Changes are more likely to be made in allotments than in appropriations. Of course, if an appropriation is amended, a corresponding adjustment must be made in the allotment for the organization unit affected. Allotments will ordinarily not be changed by the chief executive without good reasons, since the continual adjustment of allotments is likely to upset the budget program.

If the budget is to be effectively controlled, organization units must stay within their appropriations and also within the amounts allotted to them for a particular period. Accordingly, as soon as the allotments are approved by the chief executive, they are certified to the finance officer (see Figure 13), who sets up the proper accounts for each unit so as to show both the amount appropriated and the allotments into which the appropriation is divided. It should be remembered, however, that many governmental units do not make allotments.

Recording the budget on the books. As soon as the appropriation ordinance is passed, an entry is made setting up estimated revenues and appropriations on the records. The entry is as shown on page 39.

Figure 12

A GOVERNMENTAL UNIT
Work Program—1956
by Months

Departmental Code: <u>4000</u>

Fund: <u>General</u>
Function: <u>Sanitation and Waste Remov</u>
Department: <u>Public Works</u>
Bureau: <u>Sanitation</u>
Submitted by: <u>M. A. Downs, Chief</u>
Date: <u>January 6, 1956</u>

Operation	Work Unit	TOTAL FOR YEAR			JANUARY		FEBRUARY		MARCH	
		No. of Units	Unit Cost	Total	No. of Units	Amount	No. of Units	Amount	No. of Units	Amount
Garbage Collection	Tons	170,000	$1.44	$244,800.00	14,175	$20,412.00	14,175	$20,412.00	14,175	$20,412.00
Incineration	Tons	182,000	1.19	216,580.00	15,150	18,028.50	15,150	18,028.50	15,150	18,028.50

37

Figure 13

Departmental Code: 2000

A GOVERNMENTAL UNIT
Allotment of Appropriation
1956

Fund: General
Function: Public Safety
Department: Police
Submitted by: A. Johnson, Chief
Date: January 6, 1956

Code No.	Classification	Total Appropriated	January	February	March	April	May
A	Personal Services	$26,000	$2,200	$2,150	$2,150	$2,175	$2,100
B	Contractual Services	3,200	275	265	260	260	270
C	Materials and Supplies	3,800	300	270	300	250	275
D	Other Charges	2,000	150	175	185	150	195

Estimated Revenues	$431,000	
Appropriations		$426,000
Unappropriated Surplus		5,000

To record estimated revenues and appropriations. Entries in subsidiary accounts:

DEBIT—ESTIMATED REVENUES

Taxes:

General Property Taxes (Less Allowance for Uncollectibles)	$288,000	
Interest and Penalties on Taxes (Less Allowance for Uncollectibles)	1,000	289,000

Licenses and Permits:

Motor Vehicle Licenses	$ 34,000	
Parking Meters	2,000	
Beer and Liquor Licenses	13,000	
Amusement Licenses	6,000	
Newsdealers' Licenses	1,300	56,300

Transfers from Other Funds		4,300
Grand Total		$431.000

	Total	Current Expenses	Capital Outlay
CREDIT—APPROPRIATIONS			
General Government:			
Council	$ 5,500	$ 4,000	$ 1,500
Executive Department	7,000	5,500	1,500
City Historian	2,300	2,000	300
Total General Government	$ 57,030	$ 48,000	$ 9,030
Interest	14,400	14,400	—
Total Current Expenses and Capital Outlays	$392,000	$282,600	$109,400
Retirement of Bonds	34,000		
Grand Total	$426,000		

The detail with which appropriation accounts are set up depends on the detail with which appropriations are made. For example, the above entry is based on the assumption that appropriations are made for two principal classes of expenditures, namely, current expenses and capital outlays. If appropriations are subdivided further, the subsidiary accounts are also subdivided. For example, if appropriations are made by main objects of current expenses and by major classes of capital outlays, the subsidiary accounts for appropriations exhibited above would be replaced by accounts showing details concerning each object of current expenses and each major type of capital outlay, as indicated below:

CREDIT—APPROPRIATIONS
General Government:
  Council:
    Current Expenses

Personal Services	$3,500		
Contractual Services	200		
Materials and Supplies	150		
Other Charges	150	$4,000	

    Capital Outlays

Equipment		1,500	$5,500

  Executive Department:
    Current Expenses

Personal Services	$5,000		
Contractual Services	200		
Materials and Supplies	200		
Other Charges	100	$5,500	

    Capital Outlays

Equipment		1,500	7,000

~~~~~~

  City Historian:
    Current Expenses

Personal Services	$1,900		
Materials and Supplies	75		
Other Charges	25	$2,000	

    Capital Outlays

Equipment		300	2,300

Total General Government	$ 57,030

~~~~~~

Interest	14,400
Retirement of Bonds	34,000
Grand Total	$426,000

Subsidiary accounts for revenues. Separate general ledger control accounts are established for actual and estimated revenues (that is, accounts entitled "Estimated Revenues" and "Revenues" are used). On the other hand, because of the large number of revenue accounts usually required, it is desirable, both from the standpoint of economy (fewer accounts are needed) and from the standpoint of ease of comparison of actual and estimated revenues, to record each estimated and actual revenue in the same subsidiary account. For example, the account for motor vehicle licenses would appear as illustrated in Figure 14. As the estimates are set up, they are recorded in the "Debit" and "Balance" columns of this account. Subsequently, as revenues are realized, the amount accrued or received is entered in the "Credit" column. At the end of the year, as the controlling account, Estimated Revenues, and the controlling account, Revenues, are closed out, the individual subsidiary accounts are debited if actual revenues for the particular source exceed the amount of estimated revenues, or credited if the amount of estimated revenues exceeds the amount of actual revenues. A debit balance in an individual revenue account always indicates an excess of estimated revenues over actual revenues, and a credit balance indicates an excess of actual over estimated revenues.

Figure 14

A GOVERNMENTAL UNIT Revenue Ledger					
		Account No.: <u>11</u> Class: <u>Licenses and Permits</u> Account Name: <u>Motor Vehicle Licenses</u>			
Date	Reference	Folio	Debit	Credit	Balance
1956 Jan. 3 10	Budget Estimate Licenses Issued	G. J. 1 C. R. 1	$34,000 —	— $34,500	$34,000 500*

* Red.

Subsidiary accounts for appropriations. Three separate accounts, namely, an Appropriations account, an Appropriation Expenditures account, and an Encumbrances account, are set up in the general ledger. On the other hand, in the subsidiary appropriation expenditure ledger (illustrated in Figure 15) the ledger sheet for each account shows not only the amount appropriated but also the expenditures and encumbrances charged to such appropriation. The reason for recording all of the information regarding an appropriation in one subsidiary account is that, since a large number of appropriation accounts are usually required, such an arrangement not only is more economical because it reduces the number of accounts needed but also results in better budgetary control since this arrangement makes it possible to tell at a glance the status of each appropriation.

It is assumed that separate appropriations are made for: (1) salaries and wages, (2) materials and supplies, (3) other current expenses, (4)

Figure 15

A GOVERNMENTAL UNIT
Appropriation Expenditure Ledger

Code No.: 2105-C
Function: Public Safety
Organization Unit: Department of Fire—
  Bureau of Fire Fighting
Activity: Fire Fighting
Character: Current Expenses
Object: Materials and Supplies
Year: 1956

Cumulative Allotments

Original		Revisions	
Jan. $350	July $2,300	Jan. —	July —
Feb. 700	Aug. 2,600	Feb. —	Aug. —
Mar. 1,000	Sept. 2,900	Mar. —	Sept. —
Apr. 1,400	Oct. 3,250	Apr. —	Oct. —
May 1,700	Nov. 3,550	May —	Nov. —
June 2,000	Dec. 3,800	June —	Dec. —

		ENCUMBRANCES				EXPENDITURES				
Date	Description	Order No.	Paid or Canceled	Issued	Balance	Voucher No.	Amount	Total Expenditures	Appropriations	Unencumbered Balance
1	2	3	4	5	6	7	8	9	10	11
1/3	Appropriation								$3,800	$3,800
1/5	Clothing	2	—	$200	$200	—	—	—	—	3,600
1/7	Lubricants	4	—	45	245	—	—	—	—	3,555
1/23	Clothing	2	$200	—	45	39	$205	$205	—	3,550
12/10	Clothing	20	—	300	300	—	—	3,000	—	500
12/31	Closing Entry					To Surplus	500	—	—	—

42

capital outlays, and (5) retirement of bonds. The account illustrated is assumed to cover materials and supplies—that is, item 2. As appropriations are made, they are entered in the "Appropriations" column and in the "Unencumbered Balance" column. At the top of the form, provision is made for filling in the cumulative allotments.

This form of account is invaluable to the finance officer in controlling appropriations. Regulations are set up providing that no purchase order or contract is valid unless it is approved by the finance officer. As the finance officer approves the order, he enters the amount of the encumbrance in columns 5 and 6 and reduces the balance in column 11 by a like amount. Subsequently, as the materials are received and the actual expenditures are determined, the encumbrances are canceled by entering the amount of the encumbrance in column 4 and reducing the balance in column 6. At the same time the actual expenditures are recorded by entering the amount of the expenditure in columns 8 and 9. Since the actual expenditure may be greater or smaller than the amount encumbered, it is necessary to adjust the last balance shown in column 11. By referring to the "Unencumbered Balance" column, the finance officer can see at a glance the unencumbered balance of the appropriation and therefore whether a sufficient balance is available for further encumbrance or expenditure. Again, by adding together the last figures in columns 6 and 9, and comparing the total with the cumulative allotment shown for the particular month involved, he can find the unencumbered balance of an allotment.

As we have already indicated, the above account is assumed to apply to materials and supplies. A separate account is set up for each appropriation for salaries and wages. Frequently, however, no encumbrances are set up for salaries and wages, because the number of employees and the amount of their pay will have been given in detail in the budget document, so that the exact expenditures for personal services are known. Where one appropriation is made for all current expenses of an organization unit (that is, no distinction is made in the appropriation ordinance between personal services and other current expenses), the amount of the estimated salaries and wages payable is frequently encumbered at the beginning of the year or the beginning of each allotment period. This procedure insures that a sufficient amount of the appropriation will be reserved to meet salaries and wages. In other words, expenses for personal services usually take precedence over other current expenses.

Accounting for changes in appropriations. Even though expenditures are carefully planned, changes in appropriations are often necessary. Some governmental units are prohibited by law from making such changes. Of course, even if appropriation amendments are permitted, they should not be made unless absolutely necessary; otherwise the budget plan will become unworkable. However, certain contingencies may arise requiring additional appropriations. Sometimes a lump sum contingent appropriation is made. A contingent reserve is thus provided from which transfers are made to departments for which the original appropriation is insufficient. Transfers from the contingent reserve may be made either pursuant to legislative authorization or upon the order of the chief executive depending on legal provisions. The entry, assuming a transfer of $8,000 has been authorized, is as follows:

Appropriations.............................. $8,000
   Appropriations.............................. $8,000
To record transfer of appropriations. Entries in subsidiary accounts: *Debit* Contingencies, $8,000. *Credit* Executive Department, $8,000.

Note that the Appropriations account carried in the general ledger is not affected; the only change is in the subsidiary accounts.

If no contingent reserve is provided, an additional appropriation creates a deficit or reduces any existing surplus, unless additional revenue is provided at the same time. The entry, if we assume that the additional appropriation will result in a decrease in unappropriated surplus, is as follows:

Unappropriated Surplus....................... $8,000
   Appropriations.............................. $8,000
To record additional appropriations. Subsidiary account: *Credit* Executive Department, $8,000.

If additional revenues are expected to cover the appropriation, the Estimated Revenues account instead of the Unappropriated Surplus account is debited.

Changes within a departmental or activity appropriation may also be necessary. For example, assume that the original appropriation for a department is subidivided as follows:

Personal Services.............	$15,000
Contractual Services..........	10,000
Materials and Supplies........	10,000
Equipment...................	15,000

Suppose that during the year it is found desirable to have some work done by the department's employees which was originally intended to be performed by contract and that this work is estimated to cost $5,000. In that case, assuming it is necessary to hire additional employees to do the work, the amount appropriated for the department for contractual services will have to be reduced by $5,000 and the amount appropriated for personal services will have to be increased by a corresponding amount. In some governmental units, the chief executive is given the power to make transfers between the various objects of an appropriation, whereas in other units, the legislative body alone is authorized to make such changes. The entry to record transfers between appropriations for different objects within the same organization unit is as follows:

Appropriations............................ $5,000	
Appropriations............................	$5,000

To record transfer of appropriations within Public Works Department. Entries in subsidiary accounts: *Debit* Contractual Services, $5,000. *Credit* Personal Services, $5,000.

As in the case of the next to the preceding entry, the Appropriations account carried in the general ledger remains unchanged; the subsidiary accounts alone are affected.

If transfers between appropriations involve different funds, the amount transferred must be treated as an expenditure of the fund from which transferred and as revenue of the fund benefiting from the transfer.

Budgetary statements. Most of the financial statements that are prepared for the general fund or special revenue funds aid in one way or another in controlling the budget. The two statements illustrated in Figures 16 and 17 are therefore merely examples of statements which are helpful for budgetary control. Others include (1) the balance sheet (Figure 20, page 55), (2) the statement of forecast of cash position (Figure 72, page 226), and (3) the statements of tax levies and tax collections (Figures 84 and 85, pages 254 and 255).

Special Budgets

A special budget is a budget for any fund other than the general fund and special revenue funds. Ordinarily no appropriations are required for payments out of sinking and trust and agency funds; consequently, these funds are not subject to formal budgetary control. Special budgets are therefore limited to (1) bond funds, (2) special assessment funds, (3) working capital funds, and (4) utility or other enterprise funds.

Bond funds. Authorizations for bond fund expenditures may be made at the time the general budget is adopted, for the following purposes: (1) for new bonds to be issued during the year, (2) for specifying definite projects to be constructed from a bond issue already authorized, and (3) to indicate the amount to be expended during the particular period from a single-project bond fund which is expected to be expended during more than one budget year. In all cases, the organization unit charged with carrying out the project to be financed by the bond fund will submit estimates of the proposed work and its cost. If new bonds are to be issued during the year, certain additional statements will have to be included in the budget document. These are (1) a statement of legal debt margin (see Figure 94, page 284), (2) statements showing debt service charges for all outstanding bond issues over their lives (see Figure 101, page 302), and (3) a statement showing debt service charges on all bond issues

Figure 16

A GOVERNMENTAL UNIT

General Fund

Comparative Statement of Monthly Receipts for Month Ending March 31, 1956, and Three Months Ending March 31, 1956

Sources of Receipts	Total Estimated 1956	MARCH			TOTAL TO DATE			
		Estimated	Actual	Over or Under* Estimate	Estimated	Actual	Over or Under* Estimate	Balance
General Property Taxes:								
Current and Delinquent..............	$290,600	$48,500	$46,990	$1,510*	$106,500	$103,435	$3,065*	$187,165
Interest and Penalties on Taxes......	1,150	100	90	10*	300	250	50*	900
Licenses and Permits................	56,300	4,800	7,000	2,200	15,000	18,000	3,000	38,300
Fines, Forfeits, and Other Penalties......	9,500	750	800	50	2,400	2,500	100	7,000
Revenues from Use of Money and Property...	7,200	610	580	30*	1,800	1,775	25*	5,425
Revenues from Other Agencies..........	62,200	5,200	5,300	100	17,000	18,000	1,000	44,200
Charges for Current Services..........	6,800	575	550	25*	1,600	1,550	50*	5,250
Collections of Accounts Receivable.........	5,200	440	450	10	1,300	1,375	75	3,825
Sale of Fixed Assets........	5,100	1,000	1,010	10	2,000	2,015	15	3,085
Transfers from Other Funds...........	4,300	500	500	—	1,500	1,550	50	2,750
Total Receipts................	$448,350	$62,475	$63,270	$ 795	$149,400	$150,450	$1,050	$297,900

46

Figure 17

A GOVERNMENTAL UNIT

General Fund

Statement of Actual Expenditures Compared with Appropriations for Month Ending March 31, 1956 and Three Months Ending March 31, 1956

Function and Organization Unit	Total Appropriations	MARCH			TOTAL TO DATE			Unexpended Balance	Encumbrances	Unencumbered Balance
		Estimated	Actual	Excess of Estimated over Actual, or Vice Versa*	Estimated	Actual	Excess of Estimated over Actual, or Vice Versa*			
CURRENT EXPENSES										
GENERAL GOVERNMENT:										
Council	$ 4,000	$ 350	$ 330	$ 20	$ 1,150	$ 1,150	—	$ 2,850	$ 50	$ 2,800
Executive Department	5,500	450	445	5	1,375	1,200	$ 175	4,300	100	4,200
Courts	5,500	500	500	—	1,600	1,700	100*	3,800	—	3,800
Board of Elections	2,000	175	275	100*	650	625	25	1,375	25	1,350
Department of Finance:										
Administration	$ 2,925	$ 240	$ 240	—	$ 725	$ 725	—	$ 2,200	$ 50	$ 2,150
Bureau of Accounts	3,575	300	250	50	800	750	50	2,825	—	2,825
Bureau of Treasury	3,500	280	230	50	850	750	100	2,750	50	2,700
Bureau of Purchases	3,050	350	325	25	1,000	1,000	—	2,050	50	2,000
Bureau of Assessments	3,250	275	275	—	800	775	25	2,475	25	2,450
Total Department of Finance	$ 16,300	$ 1,445	$ 1,320	$ 125	$ 4,175	$ 4,000	$ 175	$ 12,300	$175	$ 12,125
Department of Law	$ 4,000	$ 340	$ 300	$ 40*	$ 1,000	$ 1,100	$ 100*	$ 2,900	—	$ 2,900
City Clerk's Office	4,675	385	415	30*	1,150	1,150	—	3,525	—	3,525
Board of Zoning Appeals	1,525	125	125	—	390	370	20	1,155	$ 50	1,105
Civil Service Commission	2,500	200	175	25	650	625	25	1,875	25	1,850
City Historian	2,000	150	150	—	480	475	5	1,525	—	1,525
Total General Government	$ 48,000	$ 4,120	$ 4,035	$ 85	$ 12,620	$ 12,395	$ 225	$ 35,605	$425	$ 35,180
PUBLIC SAFETY:										
Department of Police:										
Bureau of Supervision	$ 5,000	$ 400	$ 350	$ 50	$ 1,250	$ 1,150	$ 100	$ 3,850	$100	$ 3,750
Bureau of Police Training	4,000	350	400	50*	1,100	1,050	50	2,950	50	2,900
Bureau of Identification Records	3,000	260	240	20	800	900	100*	2,100	—	2,100
RETIREMENT OF BONDS	$ 34,000	—	—	—	$ 12,000	$ 12,000	—	$ 22,000	—	$ 22,000
GRAND TOTAL	$426,000	$36,000	$34,900	$1,100	$108,000	$105,500	$2,500	$320,500	$700	$319,800

Figure 18

A GOVERNMENTAL UNIT
Budget Summary
1956

GENERAL BUDGET
General Fund

	Estimated Resources		Estimated Expenditures
Taxes	$288,000	Personal Services	$219,000
Total Special Revenue Fund	$125,000	Total Special Revenue Fund	$125,000
Total General Budget	$556,000	Total General Budget	$556,000

SPECIAL BUDGETS
Bond Funds

Unexpended Balances	$200,000	Construction Expenditures	$300,000
Sale of Bonds Authorized	100,000		
Total Bond Funds	$300,000	Total Bond Funds	$300,000

Working Capital Funds

Charges to Departments	$ 80,000	Current Expenses	$ 40,000
		Equipment	40,000
Total Working Capital Funds	$ 80,000	Total Working Capital Funds	$ 80,000

Utility or Other Enterprise Funds

Sale of Services	$200,000	Current Expenses	$175,000
Nonoperating Revenues	25,000	Capital Outlays	50,000
Total Utility or Other Enterprise Funds	$225,000	Total Utility or Other Enterprise Funds	$225,000

—that is, both those outstanding and those proposed to be issued. The entries necessary to record bond authorizations are discussed in Chapter 7.

Special assessment funds. Although new special assessment projects may be authorized at the time the general budget is prepared, usually authorizations for such projects will also be made throughout the year. Since special assessment authorizations are not limited to a particular period, no authorizations additional to the original one will be needed, unless expenditures exceed authorizations. The governmental unit will, however, make an appropriation for its share of the cost of special assessment improvements, but this appropriation will sometimes be made at the time the improvement is authorized, which may not be at the beginning of the year. The entries involved in the authorization of special assessment improvements are illustrated in Chapter 8.

Working capital funds. Ordinarily no appropriations are required for the expenditures financed from a working capital fund because appropriations are made by the legislative body for the departments for which the working capital fund renders services. Where, however, appropriations are required, the budget for the fund is prepared at the same time as the budget for the general fund. The entries necessary in recording the budgetary operations of working capital funds are given in Chapter 11.

Utility or other enterprise funds. Some governmental units do not require their utilities or other enterprises to present a budget. Others appropriate for their utilities or other enterprises in the same detail that they do for other departments, in which event the budgetary procedure is similar to that outlined above for general departments. Estimates are submitted to the chief executive, who, after making adjustments, transmits the estimates with his recommendations to the legislative body, which may in turn make changes before making appropriations. The budget for the utility or other enterprise fund is in that case embodied in the same document as the general budget and the appropriations are made at the same time as those for the general budget.

Modification of budget summary statement. The budget summary statement should show all of the expenditures which have been authorized at the beginning of the budget period and the resources estimated to become available for financing them. Consequently, the budget summary illustrated in Figure 10 would be expanded. In addition to the estimated expenditures of the general and special revenue funds and the resources available for financing them, the expenditures and resources of other funds would be included, as illustrated in Figure 18.

4

‹‹‹

THE GENERAL FUND BALANCE SHEET

THE GENERAL fund is established at the inception of a government and continues to exist throughout the government's life. To the extent, therefore, that the life of a government may be said to be perpetual, the same is true of this fund. Each year its resources are expended wholly or in part but are subsequently replenished.

In a newly organized government, the accounting for the fund begins as soon as the budget is adopted—that is, as soon as the appropriation act is passed. The entry, as we have seen, is

Estimated Revenues	$431,000	
Appropriations		$426,000
Unappropriated Surplus		5,000
To record appropriations and revenue estimates.		

Although the above entry has already been given in Chapter 3, it is repeated here in order that all transactions leading up to the preparation of the balance sheets illustrated later in this chapter may be reflected. *Moreover since this chapter deals with the balance sheet, only the principal accounts are shown in the above entry and in the subsequent entries.* The subsidiary accounts supporting the estimated revenues and appropriations accounts were discussed in Chapter 3, subsidiary accounts for actual revenues will be treated in Chapter 5, and subsidiary accounts for expenditures will be discussed in Chapter 6.

Operation of the general fund. The operation of the fund begins when revenue is accrued or received and expenditures are made. Taxes are the most important revenues of the general fund and usually the first to accrue. As they accrue, the following entry is made:

Taxes Receivable—Current	$300,000	
Allowance for Uncollectible Current Taxes		$ 12,000
Revenues		288,000
To record accrual of taxes.		

50

Note that an allowance is made for uncollectible taxes. As with accounts receivable of a business, a certain amount of taxes is estimated to remain uncollectible, and provision must be made for these taxes through an account against which they may be written off.

As other revenues accrue, the following entries are made:

Accounts Receivable..........................	$36,000	
Allowance for Uncollectible Accounts........		$ 1,000
Revenues...................................		35,000
To record accrual of miscellaneous revenues and the setting up of an allowance for estimated losses thereon.		

As already stated, to insure that appropriations will not be overexpended, provision is usually made for reducing the Appropriations account by the estimated amount of proposed expenditures through the use of Encumbrances accounts. As orders are placed, entries are made setting up encumbrances, with a resulting reduction in available appropriations. When the actual expenditure is determined, the entry setting up the encumbrances is reversed, and the appropriation is reduced by the actual amount of the expenditure.[1] Thus, if we assume that an order was placed for materials and equipment estimated to cost $30,000, the entry at the time the order was placed would be as follows:

Encumbrances..............................	$30,000	
Reserve for Encumbrances..................		$30,000
To record encumbering of appropriation.		

Assume, however, that subsequently, when the materials and equipment and the bill are received, it is found that the materials and equipment cost $29,900. The entries will in that case be as follows:

Reserve for Encumbrances...................	$30,000	
Encumbrances...........................		$30,000
To reverse entry encumbering the Appropriations account.		

Appropriation Expenditures..................	29,900	
Vouchers Payable.......................		29,900
To record expenditures.		

These entries accomplish two things. The appropriation against which the expenditures for materials and equipment are chargeable was first reduced by the estimated amount of the expenditure. Now, however, the exact amount of the expenditure is known; accordingly, the entry setting up the encumbrances is reversed. It is necessary also to record the actual liability incurred and to reduce the appropriation by the actual expenditure. The second entry accomplishes this.

In certain cases, to be discussed later in more detail, the appropriation is not encumbered first, but is reduced only at the time the expenditure is

---

[1] The detailed procedure for encumbering appropriations was outlined on page 43.

actually made. This is often true with payrolls. Thus, if the payroll at the end of a pay period was $40,000, the entry at the time the payroll was approved for payment would be as follows:

Appropriation Expenditures...................	$40,000	
Vouchers Payable.......................		$40,000
To record approval of payroll.		

Additional entries illustrating the operation of this fund follow.

Cash....................................	$195,000	
Taxes Receivable—Current...............		$180,000
Accounts Receivable....................		15,000
To record collection of taxes receivable and accounts receivable.		
Taxes Receivable—Delinquent.............	120,000	
Taxes Receivable—Current...............		120,000
To record taxes becoming delinquent.		
Allowance for Uncollectible Current Taxes....	12,000	
Allowance for Uncollectible Delinquent Taxes		12,000
To record setting up of allowance for estimated losses on delinquent taxes.		
Cash....................................	105,000	
Revenues...............................		105,000
To record receipt of miscellaneous revenues not previously accrued.		
Vouchers Payable.......................	40,000	
Cash....................................		40,000
To record payment of payroll voucher.		
Cash....................................	1,000	
Taxes Collected in Advance..............		1,000
To record collection of taxes in advance.		
Encumbrances...........................	20,000	
Reserve for Encumbrances................		20,000
To record reduction of appropriation by amount of estimated cost of purchase orders placed.		
Allowance for Uncollectible Delinquent Taxes	1,000	
Taxes Receivable—Delinquent............		1,000
To record writing off of certain delinquent taxes which have proved to be uncollectible.		
Appropriation Expenditures................	30,000	
Due to Working Capital Fund............		30,000
To record services rendered by working capital fund.		
Cash....................................	50,200	
Taxes Receivable—Delinquent............		50,000
Revenues...............................		200
To record collection of delinquent taxes and interest and penalties thereon.		
Interest and Penalties Receivable on Taxes...	550	
Allowance for Uncollectible Interest and Penalties....................................		50
Revenues...............................		500

To record interest and penalties accrued on delinquent taxes outstanding and to provide for estimated losses.

Appropriation Expenditures.................	$300,000	
Cash......................................		$300,000

To record appropriation expenditures for which no encumbrances have previously been set up.

Accounts of the general fund. The following is a trial balance of the accounts used in the illustrated journal entries:

Cash.....................................	$ 11,200	
Taxes Receivable—Delinquent..............	$ 69,000	
Allowance for Uncollectible Delinquent Taxes		$ 11,000
Interest and Penalties Receivable on Taxes...	550	
Allowance for Uncollectible Interest and Penalties....................................		50
Accounts Receivable......................	21,000	
Allowance for Uncollectible Accounts........		1,000
Estimated Revenues......................	431,000	
Vouchers Payable.........................		29,900
Due to Working Capital Fund..............		30,000
Taxes Collected in Advance.................		1,000
Appropriations...........................		426,000
Reserve for Encumbrances..................		20,000
Unappropriated Surplus....................		5,000
Revenues.................................		428,700
Encumbrances............................	20,000	
Appropriation Expenditures................	399,900	
	$952,650	$952,650

In order to illustrate the relationship between the various accounts, in Figure 19 the trial balance has been recast in the form of a balance sheet, which is assumed to have been prepared during the fiscal year.

Let us assume that no additional transactions have taken place between the preparation of the above balance sheet and the end of the year. At the end of a fiscal year, entries would be made closing out the budgetary accounts and revenue and expenditure accounts in order to determine how actual revenues compare with estimated revenues and how expenditures compare with appropriations, and also to determine whether revenues exceed expenditures or vice versa. In this case, the closing entries would be as follows:

Revenues.................................	$428,700	
Unappropriated Surplus....................	2,300	
Estimated Revenues....................		$431,000

To record closing out of actual and estimated revenues.

Appropriations...........................	426,000	
Appropriation Expenditures..............		399,900
Encumbrances........................		20,000
Unappropriated Surplus.................		6,100

To record closing out of appropriations, encumbrances, and appropriation expenditures.

Figure 19

A GOVERNMENTAL UNIT

General Fund

Balance Sheet
During Fiscal Year

ASSETS

Cash...		$11,200
Taxes Receivable—Delinquent..............	$ 69,000	
Less—Allowance for Uncollectible Delinquent Taxes.................................	11,000	58,000
Interest and Penalties Receivable on Taxes...	$ 550	
Less—Allowance for Uncollectible Interest and Penalties..............................	50	500
Accounts Receivable........................	$ 21,000	
Less—Allowance for Uncollectible Accounts...	1,000	20,000
Estimated Revenues........................	$431,000	
Less—Revenues...........................	428,700	2,300
		$92,000

LIABILITIES, APPROPRIATIONS, RESERVES, AND SURPLUS

Liabilities:			
Vouchers Payable........................		$ 29,900	
Due to Working Capital Fund............		30,000	
Taxes Collected in Advance..............		1,000	$60,900
Appropriations:			
Appropriations.........................		$426,000	
Less—Appropriation Expenditures	$399,900		
Encumbrances...........	20,000	419,900	6,100
Reserve for Encumbrances.........................			20,000
Unappropriated Surplus............................			5,000
			$92,000

Balance sheet at close of fiscal year. Assuming that the closing entries illustrated on the preceding page had been posted, we find that the balance sheet of the general fund would appear as shown in Figure 20.

Comments on the balance sheet. Although the balance sheet is for the most part self-explanatory, a few additional comments will help to give a clear picture of the characteristics of this financial statement. The comments will deal with (1) the exclusion of general fixed assets and general bonds from the general fund balance sheet, (2) the significance of the Unappropriated Surplus account, and (3) the nature of the Reserve for Encumbrances account.

Exclusion of fixed assets and bonds. Although some general fund expenditures represent outlays which should be capitalized, fixed assets are not included in the balance sheet of the general fund. For example, let us assume that, out of the total expenditures of $29,900 shown in the last entry on page 51, the sum of $2,000 was for equipment. In commercial accounting, this $2,000 would be shown in the general balance sheet as part of the assets. But not so in governmental accounting. Here, too, the expenditures are capitalized, but they are recorded in a separate group of accounts rather than as a part of the general fund (see page 201). Although bonds may be payable out of the general fund, and even

Figure 20

A GOVERNMENTAL UNIT

General Fund

Balance Sheet
at Close of Fiscal Year

ASSETS

Cash..		$11,200
Taxes Receivable—Delinquent..............	$69,000	
Less—Allowance for Uncollectible Delinquent Taxes................................	11,000	58,000
Interest and Penalties Receivable on Taxes...	$ 550	
Less—Allowance for Uncollectible Interest and Penalties.............................	50	500
Accounts Receivable......................	$21,000	
Less—Allowance for Uncollectible Accounts..	1,000	20,000
		$89,700

LIABILITIES, RESERVES, AND SURPLUS

Liabilities:		
Vouchers Payable......................	$29,900	
Due to Working Capital Fund............	30,000	
Taxes Collected in Advance..............	1,000	$60,900
Reserve for Encumbrances.........................		20,000
Unappropriated Surplus............................		8,800
		$89,700

if they have been issued to eliminate a deficit in the general fund, they are not recorded as a liability of the fund but in a separate group of accounts (see pages 205-207). The only bonds that are included are those which have matured and have become payable from the present resources of the fund.

Fixed assets are excluded from the general fund balance sheet because they do not represent resources out of which the government intends to meet its liabilities or by means of which it is enabled to earn revenues. These assets are acquired for the purpose of rendering service.

Bonds payable out of the general fund are not included as part of the liabilities of the fund because the resources of the fund in any one year are not held for the payment of all the bonds. The governmental unit's future taxing power will ultimately provide resources to pay them. When these bonds are about to mature, taxes are levied to provide revenue for their retirement. This revenue flows into the general fund, and the resulting assets are used to retire the maturing bonds. Accordingly, only matured bonds payable directly from the resources of this fund are considered liabilities of the fund.

Unappropriated surplus. The Unappropriated Surplus account represents the excess of the assets of the fund over its liabilities and reserves. A governmental body aims to create neither a surplus nor a deficit in the fund. Accordingly, if the fund shows a surplus, the legislative body is likely to use it in financing the budget for the succeeding year. To avoid the appropriation of surplus intended to be used for some special purpose, surplus reserves, such as the reserve for encumbrances, are set up. Certain assets are segregated for a particular use, and a corresponding portion of surplus representing these assets is set aside to indicate the segregation. For example, that portion of surplus represented by stocks of materials and supplies is frequently set aside in a Reserve for Inventories account, the entry being

Unappropriated Surplus....................	$10,000	
Reserve for Inventories..................		$10,000
To record setting up of a reserve for inventories.		

If the general fund has a deficit, the deficit should be exhibited on the balance sheet by a Deficit account shown in the same position as the Unappropriated Surplus account. Proper financial administration requires that the deficit be eliminated in the following fiscal year and that the necessary revenues for this purpose be provided in the budget.

The statement in Figure 21, analyzing changes in the Unappropriated Surplus account during a period, will help to illustrate further the nature of this account. The amounts are identical with those used in the illustrative entries.

Reserve for encumbrances. The reserve for encumbrances represents a reservation of a part of an appropriation against which expenditures are to be charged. The reserve, as previously indicated, is established by a debit to Encumbrances and a credit to Reserve for Encumbrances, this entry being reversed when the actual liability is determined. However, at the end of the year, the balance remaining in the Encumbrances account is frequently closed into unappropriated surplus, while the reserve for encumbrances is carried into the balance sheet.

At the beginning of the following year an entry is made to designate that the Reserve for Encumbrances has been carried forward from a preceding year, as follows:

Reserve for Encumbrances..................... $20,000
   Reserve for Encumbrances of Prior Years..... $20,000
To set up the Reserve for Encumbrances account
carried forward from the preceding year in a separate account so as to distinguish it from the
Reserve for Encumbrances account applicable to
the current year.

A GOVERNMENTAL UNIT

Figure 21

General Fund

**Analysis of Changes in Unappropriated Surplus
for Fiscal Year**

	Estimated	Actual	Actual Over* or Under
Unappropriated Surplus (Beginning of Period)	—	—	—
Add:			
Revenues.............................	$431,000	$428,700	$ 2,300
Total Balance and Additions...........	$431,000	$428,700	$ 2,300
Deduct:			
Appropriation Expenditures..............	$426,000	$399,900	$26,100
Reserve for Encumbrances...............	—	20,000	20,000*
Total Deductions.....................	$426,000	$419,900	$ 6,100
Unappropriated Surplus (End of Period)....	$ 5,000	$ 8,800	$ 3,800*

As expenditures chargeable against this reserve are incurred, they are
reflected in an Expenditures Chargeable Against Reserve for Encumbrances of Prior Years account. As an illustration let us refer back to the
entry which set up the reserve for encumbrances carried in the balance
sheet (see page 52). Assume that the invoices covered by this reserve
were received at the beginning of the *following fiscal year* and it was
found that the actual cost of the materials amounted to only $19,500.
The following entry would be made to record this transaction:

Expenditures Chargeable Against Reserve for
    Encumbrances of Prior Years............. $19,500
    Vouchers Payable........................ $19,500
To record expenditures and the resulting liability.

Note the distinction between expenditures chargeable against appropriations and those chargeable against the reserve for encumbrances. The
latter group of expenditures must be kept distinct from appropriation
expenditures because they do not again affect appropriations. At the end
of the year, they are closed out into the reserve for encumbrances, the
entry, in the case of the figures illustrated above, being as follows:

Reserve for Encumbrances of Prior Years...... $20,000
Expenditures Chargeable Against Reserve for
   Encumbrances of Prior Years............ $19,500
Unappropriated Surplus....................   500
To record closing out the reserve for encumbrances
and the expenditures chargeable thereto.

The statements previously illustrated were based on the assumption that the governmental unit was in its first year of operation and that there were no expenditures chargeable against the reserve for encumbrances. However, the statements would not have to be changed materially to take account of these expenditures. For example, the only change necessary in the general fund balance sheet prepared during the fiscal year (Figure 19) is to reduce the amount of the reserve for encumbrances by the amount of expenditures chargeable thereto, as follows:

Reserve for Encumbrances of Prior Years...... $20,000
Less—Expenditures Chargeable Against Reserve for
   Encumbrances of Prior Years.................   19,500 $500

Except for changes in amounts, the balance sheet prepared at the end of the fiscal year would appear in exactly the same form as the balance sheet illustrated in Figure 20. Even the statement analyzing the changes in unappropriated surplus would not have to be changed materially. The only change necessary is to show the increase in surplus resulting from an excess of the amount set aside in the reserve for encumbrances over the amount of expenditures chargeable thereto (see the first entry on this page), or the decrease in surplus resulting from an excess of expenditures chargeable to this reserve over the amount of the reserve.

On page 59 is an illustration of a statement analyzing the changes in unappropriated surplus based on the assumption that the reserve for encumbrances and the expenditures chargeable thereto are of the same amounts as those illustrated in the first entry on this page. Note also that the opening balance of unappropriated surplus in this statement ($8,800) corresponds to the closing balance of actual unappropriated surplus shown in Figure 21. The remaining amounts represent transactions which have taken place during the second year and have no relationship to the amounts shown in the preceding statements.

Some governmental units close out both the Encumbrances and Reserve for Encumbrances accounts at the end of the year. Under this procedure, the closing entry illustrated on page 53 would be changed to read as follows:

Appropriations............................ $426,000
Reserve for Encumbrances..................   20,000
Appropriation Expenditures.............. $399,900
Encumbrances...........................   20,000
Unappropriated Surplus.................   26,100
To record closing out of Appropriations, En-
cumbrances, Reserve for Encumbrances, and
Appropriation Expenditures accounts.

Note that the above entry differs from the closing entry illustrated on page 53 in that the reserve for encumbrances is closed out and the Unappropriated Surplus account is increased by the amount of the reserve. The balance sheet prepared at the close of the year would therefore not show any reserve for encumbrances.

Figure 22

A GOVERNMENTAL UNIT

General Fund

Analysis of Changes in Unappropriated Surplus for Second Fiscal Year

	Estimated	Actual	Actual Over* or Under
Unappropriated Surplus—Beginning of Second Year..................................	$ 8,800	$ 8,800	—
Add:			
Reserve for Encumbrances of Prior Years..	$ 20,000	$ 20,000	—
Revenues.............................	450,000	446,000	$ 4,000
Total Additions....................	$470,000	$466,000	$ 4,000
Total Balance and Additions.........	$478,800	$474,800	$ 4,000
Deduct:			
Appropriation Expenditures..............	$444,000	$418,000	$26,000
Expenditures Chargeable Against Reserve for Encumbrances of Prior Years.......	20,000	19,500	500
Reserve for Encumbrances..............	—	15,000	15,000*
Total Deductions...................	$464,000	$452,500	$11,500
Unappropriated Surplus—End of Second Year	$ 14,800	$ 22,300	$ 7,500*

No expenditures resulting from these encumbrances can in that case be incurred unless a similar appropriation has been provided for the current year. For example, if a purchase order had been placed for books for the law library and an appropriation had been made for the purchase of similar books in the current year's budget, the expenditure resulting from the purchase order could be charged against the similar appropriation for the current year. On the other hand, if no provision for such books had been made in the current budget, the purchase order would have to be cancelled. Ordinarily, governmental units which provide for the lapsing of encumbrances at the end of each year specify in the purchase order that they will not be responsible for goods delivered after the end of the year.

Some governmental units which do not close out the Reserve for Encumbrances account at the end of the year nevertheless do not permit expenditures to be charged against such reserve until it has been revalidated through legislative action. For example, assume the same conditions as in the example given on page 57, namely, that the reserve for encumbrances at the end of the year amounted to $20,000 and that the expenditures incurred against it at the beginning of the following year amounted to $19,500. This $19,500 could not, in that case, be charged against the reserve. Instead, a new authorization would have to be obtained from the legislative body, in the form of an ordinance at the beginning of the second year. The entry to record this authorization is as follows:[2]

Encumbrances..........................	$20,000	
Appropriations.........................		$20,000
To record appropriations by the legislative body for the encumbrances outstanding at the end of the year.		

Thereafter, the procedure is the same as for regular appropriations. For example, when the goods are received the following entries are made:

Reserve for Encumbrances..................	$20,000	
Encumbrances.........................		$20,000
To cancel encumbrances.		
Appropriations Expenditures................	19,500	
Vouchers Payable.......................		19,500
To record actual expenditures.		

[2] This entry is a short-cut. The steps necessary to give effect to this authorization and encumbrance are (1) closing out the Reserve for Encumbrances account into unappropriated surplus, (2) making appropriations out of unappropriated surplus, and (3) encumbering the appropriations. The entries (corresponding to the numbered items in the preceding sentence) are as follows:

(1) Reserve for Encumbrances..............	$20,000	
Unappropriated Surplus..............		$20,000
(2) Unappropriated Surplus................	20,000	
Appropriations.....................		20,000
(3) Encumbrances.......................	20,000	
Reserve for Encumbrances............		20,000

Since there are equal debits and credits to both the Unappropriated Surplus account and the Reserve for Encumbrances account, it is possible to eliminate them from the entries and to record the authorization and encumbering with one entry.

5

‹‹‹

GENERAL FUND REVENUES

THIS CHAPTER is concerned with the accounting procedure for the main sources of revenue of the general fund. These sources, as indicated before, are as follows: (1) taxes, (2) licenses and permits, (3) fines, forfeits, and other penalties, (4) revenues from use of money and property, (5) revenues from other agencies, (6) charges for current services, (7) sales, and compensation for loss, of fixed assets, and (8) transfers from other funds.

Taxes. For the purpose of the present discussion, it is advisable to divide tax revenues into two classes—general property taxes and other taxes. Because general property taxes are one of the main sources of revenue of local governments and because of the complicated procedure involved in accounting for them, they are discussed in a separate chapter. (See Chapter 15.)

On the other hand, general property taxes constitute no part or only a small part of the revenues of the states. Instead, states resort to other forms of taxation. A few of the taxes imposed by state governments are income taxes, sales taxes, inheritance taxes, gasoline taxes, taxes on tobacco and on alcoholic beverages, and chain store taxes. Although some of these taxes are also levied by local governments, most of them are important sources of state revenue alone. One of the chief characteristics of these revenues from an accounting standpoint is that they are usually self-assessable. That is, usually the taxpayer is not billed for the tax but instead submits a return in which he shows the total amount of tax due from him and the basis on which the tax was computed. This procedure is possible because, in contrast with the rate for general property taxes, the tax rate is fixed in advance; that is, it is not adjusted to the amount of revenue which the governmental unit may need each year. For example, sales tax rates or income tax rates are not likely to be changed at the beginning of the year so as to finance exactly the estimated expenditures of that year. And yet that is true with the general property tax; the tax rate is dependent on the amount of estimated expenditures for the coming year. As indicated below, this variation in tax levying procedure has an important bearing on the accounting procedure.

In the case of real estate taxes, the tax base—that is, the assessed value—is determined by the taxing unit's representative—the assessor. On the other hand, in the case of the taxes enumerated above, the returns on which the taxes are paid are prepared by the taxpayer. It is therefore necessary to determine whether the tax base (that is, the amount against which the rate is applied) has been properly reported. Similarly, it is important to determine whether the proper rates have been applied to the tax base to arrive at the total amount of the tax. The verification of the tax base is more important and involves more work than does the verification of the rates applied. For example, even if a governmental unit has a graduated income tax, it is relatively easy to determine whether the proper rates have been applied. The more difficult problem is to ascertain that all the income which should have been reported has been disclosed. Furthermore, investigation would not be limited to those taxpayers filing returns. The governmental unit must also make certain that all taxpayers who should pay taxes have filed returns and paid the proper amount.

The group of taxes named above is usually accounted for on a cash basis, because the return and the remittance are ordinarily made at the same time. There is thus no need to set up accruals, since the amount of the tax is not known before the return is filed. In some jurisdictions, income tax returns are filed at a certain time and the tax is paid in installments. In such a case, since the amount of the tax is known, the revenues are accrued as soon as the return is filed. Some taxes require the affixation of stamps to an article to indicate the fact that the tax has been paid. For example, liquor taxes and tobacco taxes are frequently paid through the purchase of stamps, which are affixed to bottles or packages. The stamps are sold to the manufacturer, dealer, or other party, who affixes them, and in such cases the taxes are considered as revenue as soon as the stamps are sold, as is also true where sales tax stamps are in use—that is, where the manufacturer, dealer, or other party must affix, cancel, or destroy stamps whenever a sales tax is paid.

Licenses and permits. The rates for licenses and permits are established through legislative action—that is, by the passage of an ordinance or statute. In contrast to the case of property taxes, however, completely new rates are not established each year. Instead, the legislative body usually makes adjustments in the rates for particular licenses from time to time as the need arises. Revenue from licenses and permits is not considered as such until it is received in cash, since the amount is not known until the licenses and permits are issued. Proper control over these revenues must insure not only that the revenues actually collected are properly handled but also that all the revenues which should be collected are collected. In other words, the governmental unit must see that all those who should have secured licenses or permits have done so. For example, if a license is required for the operation of a motor vehicle, the governmental unit must see that no vehicle is operated without one. Of course, the governmental unit must also see to it that the revenues acually collected are accounted for. This feature of control is accomplished in part through the use of controlled financial stationery. That is, licenses and permits are assigned series of numbers, and, when these documents are given to the employees who are to handle them, a record is made of the numbers on them. Thereafter, employees are required to account for the documents either by cash or by unused and spoiled documents.

Fines, forfeits, and other penalties. Revenues from these sources do not form an important part of a governmental unit's income. They are usually accounted for on a cash basis. It should be noted that penalties for the delinquent payment of taxes are to be distinguished from the penalties discussed in this section, since they are considered part of tax revenues. Similarly, penalties on account of the late payment of utility bills are considered utility operating revenues. Fines and other penalties included in this section are primarily those imposed by courts.

The money from forfeits is usually first accounted for in a trust fund. For example, assume that a person has been released on bail and that he has forfeited his bail. When bail is received, an entry is made in a trust fund debiting Cash or another asset and crediting the proper trust fund balance. Unless the law provides otherwise, when bail is forfeited, the money is transferred to the general fund. The entries to record the transfer in the trust fund and general fund, respectively, are as follows:

Bail Fund Balance...........................	$5,000	
Cash......................................		$5,000
To record reduction of trust fund balance through transfer of forfeited bail to general fund.		
Cash......................................	5,000	
Revenues.................................		5,000
To record receipt of money representing forfeited bail.		

Revenues from use of money and property. Revenues in the form of interest on bank deposits are diminishing in importance, because most banks are not allowed to pay interest on demand deposits. However, some governmental units still receive interest on time deposits. These revenues are recorded as of the year in which they are earned. Practice in regard to the recording of interest on investments varies between governmental units, and there is even a variation in the procedure for the different funds of the same governmental unit. Some governmental units record interest on investments as revenue as soon as it is earned; others do not record it as revenue until it is received in cash. The same difference in practice may be found between funds of one government. For example, a governmental unit may record interest on sinking fund investments as revenue as soon as it is earned, whereas in the general fund it may not record interest until it is actually collected.

Revenues from other agencies. These revenues consist primarily of state-collected, locally shared taxes and grants-in-aid. The difference between a state-collected, locally shared tax and a grant-in-aid is that the former is returned to the local unit on the basis of the amount collected whereas the latter is granted on the basis of need. This difference affects the accounting procedure of both the granting and receiving units. For example, assuming that a state is collecting taxes for its local units, these collections would be accounted for by the state in an agency fund in the manner described in Chapter 10, which deals with trust and agency funds. On the other hand, grants-in-aid constitute an expenditure and must be appropriated for. When the grant-in-aid is set up as a liability or is paid, the entry on the state's books is as follows:

Appropriation Expenditures.................	$390,000	
Due to Local Government (or Cash).......		$390,000

To record liability (or payment) of contribution to local governments, as follows:

Name of Unit	Total	PURPOSE FOR WHICH GRANT IS MADE		
		Education	Relief	Highways
County A.............	$ 90,000	$10,000	$ 50,000	$30,000
County B.............	135,000	15,000	70,000	50,000
County F.............	140,000	30,000	100,000	10,000
School District M.....	25,000	25,000	—	—
	$390,000	$80,000	$220,000	$90,000

The receiving unit would record both state-collected, locally shared taxes and grants-in-aid in a Revenues account. Due to the fact, however, that grants-in-aid are restricted to a special purpose, they must be accounted for in the Revenues account of a special revenue fund, whereas state-collected, locally shared taxes are usually not restricted and can therefore be accounted for in the Revenues account of the general fund. Continuing with the foregoing example, the entry to be made by the local unit for the amount of state-collected, locally shared taxes due from the state is as follows:

Due from State...........................	$40,000	
Revenues.................................		$40,000

To record notification by state of amount of state-collected, locally shared taxes due us. Entries in

subsidiary accounts: *Credit* Share of Income
Taxes, $25,000; Share of Gasoline Taxes, $15,000.

Similarly, the entry to record grants-in-aid due from the state is as
follows:

Due from State...........................	$40,000	
Revenues................................		$40,000
To record notification of grant made by state for schools.		

When the money is received, the entry is, in both cases, as follows:

Cash......................................	$40,000	
Due from State...........................		$40,000
To record receipt from state of share of state-collected, locally shared taxes (or grants-in-aid).		

Separate entries are, of course, made in each fund to which the receipts
apply.

The accounting procedure for grants-in-aid received from the Federal
government either by states or by local governments is the same as for
grants received by local governments from the state. Usually state
statutes provide specifically the manner in which such grants are to be
expended.

Charges for current services. These revenues consist of charges made
by various departments for services rendered by them. Although utility
or other enterprise fund revenues are also derived from the sale of
services to the public, they are usually, because of their importance,
treated separately. Again, special assessments for improvements can in
a certain sense be considered as revenues of the department which constructs the improvements financed from them, but they are, because of
their special nature, not so treated.

It is important to distinguish between revenues derived from licenses
and permits and departmental earnings. Only those revenues which result
directly from the activity of the department and are made for the purpose of recovering part of the expense of the department in rendering the
service are considered charges for current services. Some of these charges
may involve the issuance of permits, but the revenue should not be
classed as coming from permits but rather as charges for services.

Most of these revenues are not recorded until they are collected in cash.
All those revenues, however, which are not collected at the time the
service is rendered or immediately thereafter are recorded as soon as
the persons or governments served are billed. The following entries illustrate some of the transactions which result in revenues being recorded
as soon as they are earned:

Due from Other Governmental Units..........	$25,000	
Revenues................................		$25,000
To record earnings resulting from charges to other		

governmental units for patients quartered in hospital and for board of prisoners. Entries in subsidiary accounts: *Debit* each governmental unit. *Credit* Hospital Revenues, $10,000; Prison Revues, $15,000.

Accounts Receivable.........................	$25,000	
Revenues....................................		$25,000

To record street lighting, street sprinkling, and garbage collection charges made to property owners. Entries in subsidiary accounts: *Debit* each person for whom service was rendered. *Credit* Street Lighting Revenues, $5,000; Street Sprinkling Revenues, $10,000; Garbage Collection Revenues, $10,000.

The following entry, on the other hand, illustrates some of the transactions in which revenues are not considered as such until collected in cash:

Cash.......................................	$88,200	
Revenues...................................		$88,200

To record receipt of cash representing charges for current services. Entries in subsidiary accounts: *Credit*

Sale of Ordinances.........................	$ 1,200
Charges for Private Police Service...........	3,000
Charges for Fire Protection Service..........	54,000
Building Inspection Fees....................	5,000
Plumbing Inspection Fees...................	5,000
Boiler Inspection Fees......................	2,000
Inspection of Weights Fees.................	7,000
Fees for Transcribing Birth, Death, and Marriage Certificates........................	6,000
Fees for Inspection of Dairy Products........	5,000
	$88,200

Sales, and compensation for loss, of fixed assets. Although fixed assets financed from the general fund are not carried as part of the assets of such fund, the net proceeds from the sale, and compensation for loss, of these assets form part of the revenue of the general fund. Since fixed assets financed from special revenue funds, bond funds, and special assessment funds are not carried as part of these funds, the net proceeds from the sale, and compensation for loss, of these assets frequently flow into the general fund, where they are considered part of the revenues of the fund. On the other hand, proceeds from the sale, and compensation for loss, of fixed assets carried in working capital funds and utility or other enterprise funds would ordinarily be accounted for in those funds rather than in the general fund.

Transfers from other funds. These represent such items as the transfer of unappropriated surplus of bond funds or other funds which are being dissolved and transfers resulting from charges for services rendered by the general fund to other funds. Borrowings by the general fund from other funds do not belong in this classification because they do not increase general fund revenues; these receipts are offset by an increase in the liabilities of the borrowing fund. Similarly, the receipt of money by the general fund in the form of a repayment of an inter-fund loan should not be included in this classification because it does not result in revenue for the general fund. All it does is convert the receivable from the debtor fund into cash, with no effect on the net worth of the general fund.

Closing entries. Entries to record the closing out of the Estimated Revenues account and the Revenues account were illustrated in Chapter 4. The following entry shows not only how these two controlling accounts are closed out but also the effect of the entry on the subsidiary accounts. It should be remembered again that, although in the general ledger separate accounts are carried for estimated and actual revenues, in the subsidiary revenue ledger both the estimated and the actual revenues are recorded in one account (see Figure 14, page 41). The entry closing out revenues in both the general ledger and the subsidiary ledgers is as follows:

Revenues..................................	$428,700	
Unappropriated Surplus....................	2,300	
Estimated Revenues......................		$431,000

To record closing out of actual revenues into estimated revenues. Entries in subsidiary accounts:

	Debit (To close out excess of actual revenues over estimated revenues)	Credit (To close out deficiency of actual revenues over estimated revenues)
Interest and Penalties on Taxes		$ 300
Motor Vehicle Licenses........	$ 500	
Parking Meters..............	1,000	
Beer and Liquor Licenses......	1,000	
Amusement Licenses..........	500	
Newsdealers' Licenses.........	150	
Municipal Court Fines........	100	
Interest on Investments.......	200	
Rents......................	300	
Share of Income Taxes........		3,800
Share of Gasoline Taxes.......		2,700
Election Fee Revenues........	350	
Charges for Private Police Service...................	300	
Fees for Inspection of Dairy Products.................	100	
Net Proceeds from Sales of Fixed Assets..............	100	
Transfers from Other Funds...		$ 100
	$4,600	$6,900

SUMMARY

Deficiency of Actual Revenues over Estimated Revenues....................................	$6,900
Excess of Actual Revenues over Estimated Revenues	4,600
Net Deficiency.............................	$2,300

On the basis of all the subsidiary revenue accounts a statement is prepared showing estimated and actual revenues. Such a statement for the general fund is illustrated in Figure 23.

Figure 23

A GOVERNMENTAL UNIT

General Fund

Statement of Revenues—Estimated and Actual
for Fiscal Year

	Estimated Revenues	Actual Revenues	Excess or Deficiency*
TAXES:			
General Property Taxes (Less Allowance)	$288,000	$288,000	—
Interest and Penalties on Taxes (Less Allowance)......................	1,000	700	$ 300*
Total Taxes........................	$289,000	$288,700	$ 300*
LICENSES AND PERMITS:			
Motor Vehicle Licenses................	$ 24,600	$ 25,100	$ 500
Parking Meters.......................	2,000	3,000	1,000
Beer and Liquor Licenses..............	13,000	14,000	1,000
Amusement Licenses..................	6,000	6,500	500
Newsdealers' Licenses.................	1,300	1,450	150
Total Licenses and Permits.........	$ 46,900	$ 50,050	$3,150
FINES, FORFEITS, AND OTHER PENALTIES:			
Municipal Court Fines...............	$ 9,000	$ 9,100	$ 100
Forfeited Contractors' Deposits........	500	500	—
Total Fines, Forfeits, and Other Penalties.........................	$ 9,500	$ 9,600	$ 100
REVENUES FROM USE OF MONEY AND PROPERTY:			
Interest on Bank Deposits.............	$ 200	$ 200	—
Interest on Investments...............	2,000	2,200	$ 200
Rents................................	5,000	5,300	300
Total Revenues from Use of Money and Property...................	$ 7,200	$ 7,700	$ 500
REVENUES FROM OTHER AGENCIES:			
Share of Income Taxes................	$ 37,000	$ 33,200	$3,800*
Share of Gasoline Taxes...............	25,000	22,300	2,700*
Conscience Money....................	200	200	—
Total Revenues from Other Agencies..	$ 62,200	$ 55,700	$6,500*

CHARGES FOR CURRENT SERVICES:

Election Fee Revenues................	$ 1,000	$ 1,350	$ 350
Sale of Ordinances....................	1,000	1,000	—
Charges for Private Police Service......	4,000	4,300	300
Fees for Inspection of Dairy Products...	800	900	100
Total Charges for Current Services...	$ 6,800	$ 7,550	$ 750
NET PROCEEDS FROM SALES OF FIXED ASSETS...........................	$ 5,100	$ 5,200	$ 100
TRANSFERS FROM OTHER FUNDS.........	4,300	4,200	100*
Grand Total....................	$431,000	$428,700	$2,300*

The significance of comparing estimated and actual revenues can not be overemphasized. In the first place the comparison is valuable in the preparation of future estimates. Usually the finance officer will be called upon to explain why his estimates fell short of or exceeded actual revenues, and, if his errors are due to failure to take certain factors into account, he will take steps to remedy the situation in making future estimates. Secondly, the statement is likely to prevent the finance officer from purposely overestimating revenues, for, if he continues to overestimate the revenues over a period of years, it will become evident that he is doing so purposely. Such overestimates lead to the making of appropriations in excess of revenues, so that the governmental unit ends its operations with a deficit. In fact, some states consider these estimates so important that they forbid the making of revenue estimates in excess of the actual revenues of the preceding year.

Note that the total estimated revenues and actual revenues are carried to the Unappropriated Surplus account. The excess of estimated revenues over actual revenues is deducted from the balance of the Unappropriated Surplus account, or, if actual revenues exceed estimated revenues, the difference is added to the balance of the Unappropriated Surplus account. These facts become especially evident from examining the statement illustrated in Figure 21, page 56, which analyzes the changes in the Unappropriated Surplus account.

Revenue records. Since most of the revenues of a governmental unit are received in cash, a special book of original entry is not usually provided for recording accrued revenues. Instead, these revenues are recorded in the general journal. Revenues received in cash are, however, recorded in a cash receipts register. All the detailed revenue accounts are carried in a subsidiary ledger known as a revenue ledger. If necessary, more than one revenue ledger may be used.

6

<<<<<<<<<<<<<<<<<<<<<<<<<<<<<<<<<<<<<<<<<<<<<<<<<<<<<<<<<<<<<<

GENERAL FUND EXPENDITURES

EXPENDITURE data must be so recorded that they may be classified by function, by organization unit, by activity, by character, by object, or by combinations of two or more of these. The information for classifying expenditures under most of these groups is obtained when liabilities are first incurred or when payment is made. Since most liabilities are incurred and most payments are made for objects of expenditure (for example, wages are paid for personal services, contracts payable are incurred in connection with contractual services rendered, and accounts payable are incurred in connection with materials and supplies purchased), it will be best to center the discussion around objects of expenditure. That is, we shall discuss the procedure followed in securing expenditure data for objects of expenditure and shall indicate how the expenditure for each object is allocated to functions, organization units, and activities. The discussion is also applicable to capital outlays for construction, since these are composed of objects of expenditure—for example, labor and materials. However, the detailed procedure whereby the objects of expenditures are allocated to construction projects is deferred until Chapter 21.

The objects of expenditure to be discussed include (1) personal services, (2) contractual services, (3) materials and supplies, and (4) other charges.

Personal services. The steps in accounting for personal services are: (1) determining rates of pay, (2) ascertaining the amounts earned by employees, (3) recording payments made to employees, and (4) charging the resultant expenses to the proper appropriation and expense accounts.

Determining rates of pay. Rates of pay for public employees are generally determined by the legislative body, although sometimes this power is delegated to the chief executive or the civil service commission. If the

Figure 24

A GOVERNMENTAL
Payroll for Payroll

Department Public Welfare

Name, Class No., and Title	Salary Rate	Days 1 / 16	2 / 17	3 / 18
McNulty, George T70 Chief Probation Officer	$325.00	W	W	H

Signed _____ In Charge of Time Rolls

Approved _____ Appointing Officer

Symbols: W = Worked
V = Vacation
H = Nonworking day
SL = Sick leave, no deduction
O = Absence without leave, full deduction

UNIT
Register Period

Worked 14 / 29	15 / 30	31	Total Days	Gross Amount of Pay	Deductions For Pensions	Taxes	Bonds	Net Amount
SL	W	W	16	$162.50	$7.50	$11.90	$5.00	$138.10

Approved by Civil Service Commission

Signed _____ Secretary

Approved _____ Comptroller

rates are determined by the legislative body, they may be expressed in an appropriation ordinance, in an annual salary and wage ordinance, or in a continuing salary and wage ordinance. In general, the legislative body has the ultimate authority to fix rates of pay, subject to statutory and charter restrictions in the case of local governments and the state constitution in the case of state governments.

Determining amounts due employees. An employee's pay depends, of course, on two factors—his rate of pay and the amount of time he works. One requisite of payroll accounting, therefore, is the keeping of time records. Generally, governmental units do not employ time-recording devices, at least not for their office employees. Instead, they use time sheets. Each department head is held responsible for recording the attendance of the employees in his department. Some employee, who may also have other duties, is designated by the head of the department to keep attendance records. These records are submitted at the proper time to the general accounting department or to a special payroll division, where the payrolls are prepared.

A payroll register form is illustrated in Figure 24. Note that the form provides space for filling in the name of the employee, the salary rate, the time worked, the amount of pay, deductions, and the net amount due. In this case, it is assumed that the same form is used both for time-keeping purposes and for the preparation of the payroll. Some governmental units employ a separate form for each.

The names of employees, classes of position, and rates of pay are filled in by the accounting department. Many governmental units use addressograph plates for this purpose. As an employee is hired, the accounting department is notified and an addressograph plate is prepared showing the employee's name, his class of position, and any other information necessary for payroll purposes. The plates are kept under the control of the chief finance officer or the head of the payroll division, if such a division exists. They are used to imprint payroll sheets (and the time sheets as well if attendance and pay are reported on two separate sheets). When an employee leaves the employ of the governmental unit, the accounting department is notified and the plate is removed. Similarly, the accounting department is notified of changes in rates of pay, so that the new rates may be embossed on the proper plates. Finally, transfers of employees between departments are reported to the accounting department, so that plates can be kept in proper order.

The payroll sheets are run off at the beginning of the payroll period. Between the start and end of the payroll period, new employees may have been hired. The timekeeper is notified of these by the accounting department and adds their names on the payroll sheet. At the end of the payroll period, the payroll sheets are transmitted to the accounting department. Here the amount of pay due each employee and the deductions therefrom, such as for pensions and Federal income taxes, are calculated and recorded on the payroll sheets.

The payroll is not considered completed until it has been audited. Auditing of payrolls consists in verifying (1) that employees have been placed on the payroll by the appropriate authority, (2) that persons listed actually worked the time for which they are being paid, (3) that calculations are correct, (4) that classes of positions and rates of pay correspond with the provisions of the salary and wage ordinance or other documents designating rates of pay for employees, and (5) that, in the case of salaries and wages subject to appropriation, a sufficient amount is available to the credit of the appropriation to absorb the salary and wage expenses chargeable to it. This work may be performed by various departments. For example, the civil service commission may verify the classes of positions and rates of pay for civil service employees on the payroll. The budget officer may be required to ascertain that appropriations for particular departments have sufficient balances against which to charge the salary and wage expenses. On the other hand, all these functions may be entrusted to the governmental unit's finance officer.

The above discussion relates primarily to permanent employees hired on a salary basis. The payroll procedure for temporary employees is not materially different except that addressograph plates are not used. In this case, too, it is necessary to prove that employees have been placed on the payroll by the appropriate authority, that employees worked the time they are being paid for, that the payroll has been properly calculated, that rates of pay are as authorized, that the expenditures, if subject to appropriation, have been appropriated for, and that a sufficient amount is available to the credit of the appropriation against which the expenditures are to be charged.

Recording payments made to employees. After the payroll has been approved, checks are made out for the employees and, at the designated time, are distributed. Under a proper system of internal control, employees having to do with the preparation of time reports, payrolls, or checks are not permitted to distribute the checks to employees. At frequent intervals, endorsements on checks are verified by comparison with the signature cards on file in the accounting department. Some few governmental units pay employees in cash. In that case, a good system of internal control is even more important. If employees are paid in cash, they are required to sign for their pay.

Records are kept to show earnings of each employee, as well as deductions for pensions, Federal income tax withholdings, bonds, or other purposes. An essential part of payroll procedure is to account for the amounts withheld until they are turned over to the agency for which collected.

Charging personal service expenses to proper accounts. As soon as the payroll has been approved, an entry is made to record the authorization of the liability and to charge the proper accounts, as follows:

Appropriation Expenditures....................	$10,000	
Vouchers Payable..........................		$10,000
To record payroll for period May 1-15, 1956, chargeable as follows:		
Council...........................	$ 1,000	
Executive Department.............	2,000	
Courts..........................	2,000	
Board of Elections...............	200	
Etc..............................	4,800	
	$10,000	

The amounts shown in the explanation to the above entry would be posted to the "Expenditures" columns of the individual appropriation accounts in the appropriation ledger. These accounts are similar to the appropriation account illustrated in Figure 15, page 42.

As employees are paid, an entry is made debiting Vouchers Payable and crediting Cash. Frequently, a special payroll bank account is provided in which case one check is prepared for the amount of the entire payroll and is deposited to the credit of the account. The entry is made when the check for the total payroll is drawn. The payroll checks are charged against this bank account.

Contractual services. The accounting procedure for most contractual services is simple and requires little explanation. As contracts are awarded, an entry is made encumbering appropriations by the amount of the estimated contractual liability. Subsequently, when invoices are received, the entries setting up encumbrances are reversed and the actual expenditures are recorded. However, certain contractual services—for example, freight charges and utility bills—are of such small amounts or of such a nature that the appropriations for them are not previously encumbered.

Materials and supplies. The accounting procedure for materials and supplies may be divided into two parts: (1) accounting for *purchases,* and (2) accounting for the *use of materials and supplies purchased.*

Purchases. Purchasing procedure varies according to whether the materials are purchased directly by individual departments or through a central purchasing agency. It is possible to have all purchases made by a central purchasing agency without maintaining a central storeroom. Under this procedure, all purchases are made by the governmental unit's purchasing agent, but the materials are delivered directly to the departments. Throughout this chapter it is assumed that purchases are made through a central agency, even in those instances where central storerooms are not maintained. The purchasing procedure and the related accounting procedure may be said to consist of the following steps: (1) preparing purchase requisitions and placing them with the purchasing agent, (2) securing prices or bids, (3) placing orders, (4) receiving the materials, (5) receiving the invoice and approving the liability, and (6) paying the liability. All of these steps, except that relating to the payment of the liability, are discussed below.

Filing requisitions with purchasing agent. The first step in the purchasing procedure is the filing of a requisition with the purchasing agent, asking him to secure the desired materials or supplies. If the governmental unit has a central storeroom, a large number of purchase requisitions are likely to be initiated by storekeepers as soon as the amount on hand has reached a predetermined minimum. Where no central storeroom exists, requisitions are filed by the organization units needing materials. Even if a central storeroom is maintained, there are many occasions for departments to file requisitions for materials which cannot be economically carried in stock.

Securing bids. The law usually requires that all purchases over a certain amount, varying from $250 to $1,000 in different governmental units, be made by competitive bidding. When purchases are smaller, prices are requested by telephone or by mail. The purchasing agent sends out requests for bids as soon as he receives the requisitions. At a certain time, specified in the request, the bids are opened and the award is made to the lowest and best bidder. Normally the purchasing agent makes the award, but for purchases over a certain amount the approval of the chief executive and, in the case of local governments, sometimes also the legislative body may be required.

Placing orders. The next step is to place a purchase order, prepared by the purchasing agent, with the vendor selected. As already indicated, to insure proper budgetary control, provision is frequently made that no purchase order is valid unless approved by the finance officer. Accordingly, the finance officer is required to certify that a sufficient amount is available to the credit of the appropriation to which the purchase is chargeable. The finance officer will reduce the balance available to the credit of the appropriation before certifying the purchase order. The certified purchase order is then transmitted to the vendor. When materials are ordered for a central storeroom financed through a working capital fund, even though no appropriation is necessary for the expenditures made out of that fund, it is advisable to have a certification by the finance officer that funds are legally available for this expenditure.

Receiving the materials. The materials are received by the requisitioning departments or, if one is maintained, by the central storeroom. In either case, a receiving report is filled out indicating the kinds and quantities of materials received. The receiving report is used later to compare the quantities received with the quantities ordered. In case the materials apply to a contract for delivery over a period of time, the receiving report is used also as the basis for making an entry on the bidding form, the order form, or some special form reducing the quantities of materials remaining to be received on the contract.

Auditing invoices. Since most vendors allow a cash discount for the prompt payment of bills, governmental units find it desirable to audit invoices promptly to insure payment within the discount period. To facilitate the work of auditing invoices, some governmental units furnish the vendor with invoice blanks. The auditing of invoices consists in determining that (1) the purchase has been made as required by law, (2) each invoice is for materials or services actually received, (3) the quantities agree with the receiving report, (4) the unit prices are those indicated on the purchase order, and (5) extensions and footings are correct. Assurance that the materials are in accordance with specifications is the responsibility of the purchasing department and not of the accounting department. If the materials have been ordered directly for a department, the actual expenditure is compared with the amount encumbered. If the expenditure exceeds the amount encumbered, it is necessary to determine whether the unencumbered balance is sufficient to cover the excess. It is also necessary to see that bids were solicited, if required, and that the vendor was properly selected. After an invoice has been audited and the expenditures have been found to comply with all of these requirements, a voucher is prepared signifying the approval of the liability and designating the accounts to be charged. In small governmental units, vouchers frequently are approved by the legislative body.

Accounting for materials and supplies used. The above discussion discloses little difference between the accounting procedure for purchases made for a department directly and that for the purchase of materials for a central storeroom. The main difference is that a central storeroom is likely to be operated through a working capital fund and purchases may not therefore require appropriations. Consequently, it may not be necessary to set up encumbrances for the purchases and to cancel these encumbrances when the actual expenditure is determined. There is a considerable difference, however, in the accounting procedure for materials used by a department directly and for materials first placed in a central storeroom and subsequently withdrawn by departments.

Materials acquired for a department directly. Let us assume that materials are secured directly for a department's use and are chargeable to a particular appropriation. In that case, after the invoice has been approved, an entry is made canceling the encumbrances and charging an appropriation with the actual expenditure as follows:

Reserve for Encumbrances	$10,000	
Appropriation Expenditures	9,500	
Vouchers Payable		$ 9,500
Encumbrances		10,000

To record approval of invoice, cancellation of encumbrance, and reduction of appropriation by amount of actual expenditure. Subsidiary accounts:

Organization Unit	Encumbrances Canceled	Appropriation Expenditures Charged
Department of Public Works.........	$10,000	$9,500

The amounts shown in the explanation to the entry are posted to the "Encumbrances" and "Expenditures" columns of the individual appropriation accounts carried in the appropriation expenditure ledger (see Figure 15, page 42).

Each department should take a physical inventory of materials and supplies at the end of the fiscal year. Let us assume that departments do not keep perpetual inventory records, that this is the first time that departments have taken a physical inventory, and that the cost of materials on hand is ascertained to be $20,000. In that case, if the departments are all financed either from the general fund or from some special revenue fund, the following entry is made as soon as the value of materials on hand is determined:

Inventory of Materials and Supplies...........	$20,000	
Reserve for Inventories.....................		$20,000
To record inventories of materials and supplies on hand in following organization units:		
Department of Public Works................	$10,000	
Police Department........................	1,000	
Fire Department..........................	1,000	
Etc......................................	8,000	
	$20,000	

It should be noted that the credit is to a Reserve for Inventories account representing earmarked surplus and not to an Appropriation Expenditures account. A credit to the Appropriation Expenditures account would only be justified if the inventory were used to reduce expenditures. Such reduction would be accomplished by subtracting the inventory from the purchases for the period, thereby reflecting as an expenditure the cost of materials used rather than the cost of materials purchased. Such a procedure is not practicable, however, because, in the general and special revenue funds, appropriations are ordinarily made on the basis of the estimated cost of materials to be purchased during the year rather than on the basis of the amount to be used during such period. Otherwise agencies would find themselves without any inventories at the end of the year and might have to resort to emergency buying. Even in these cases, however, it is important for control purposes to set up an Inventory account. The credit is not made to the Unappropriated Surplus account because the same or possibly even a greater amount of inventory will probably

Figure 25
(a) Front.

A GOVERNMENTAL UNIT
Accounts Payable Voucher

No._____

Date_____

Payee	Requisition No._____
	Purchase Order No._____
_____	Terms_____
_____	Date Due_____
_____	

Invoice Date	Invoice Number	Description	Amount
		Cash Discount	
		Net	

Audited and Found O.K._____

Entry Authorized_____

Payment Authorized_____

Figure 25
(b) Reverse.

Accounts Payable Voucher				
Charge These Accounts				Summary
Code	Description	G. L.	S. L.	

Voucher No._____

Voucher Date_____

Due Date_____

Date Paid_____

Check No._____

Amount $_____

Discount   _____

Net $_____

PAYEE

_____

_____

_____

Journalized_____

Posted_____

_____

be required at all times, so that a portion of surplus is permanently appropriated for this purpose.

Materials acquired for a storeroom financed from a working capital fund. The accounting for these materials is described in Chapter 11, which deals with working capital funds.

Other charges. The data necessary to record other charges are obtained readily and do not require further discussion. Two types of charges—namely, depreciation and interest expenses—present accounting problems which are discussed in Chapters 16 and 17, respectively.

Fixed assets and retirement of debt. The foregoing discussion applies only to those expenditures which can be classified by object. It does not apply to fixed assets purchased (as distinguished from assets constructed by the governmental unit) or to the retirement of bonds. The acquisition of fixed assets is discussed in Chapter 16, and the retirement of bonds is discussed in Chapter 17. Throughout the remaining part of this chapter, however, the discussion will include all expenditures, including the two mentioned.

Thus far we have discussed the manner in which the data for recording expenditures are obtained and some of the entries used to record the expenditures. Let us now note the procedure followed in classifying and recording expenditures.

Classifying and recording expenditures. As already indicated, expenditures must be approved before they may be recorded. Approval is evidenced by a voucher, which is illustrated in Figure 25. The approved voucher is entered in a voucher register, illustrated in Figure 26. The information necessary for recording each transaction in the voucher register is obtained from the vouchers. At the time he audits invoices or payrolls, the audit clerk determines to which accounts and funds expenditures are chargeable. By using a prearranged code, he can designate the proper account readily.

Frequently, postings to the detailed appropriation accounts are made directly from the vouchers, especially if it is desirable to show more information in the account than can be obtained from the voucher register summary. This would be true, for example, of the voucher register here illustrated, which shows only the total charge against each fund.

Closing entries. Expenditures are recorded throughout the year. At the end of the year, closing entries are made and financial statements are prepared. The entry necessary to close out the controlling accounts for expenditures and encumbrances was given in Chapter 4. It is repeated on page 82, but subsidiary accounts have been added to show how *they* are affected by this entry.

Postings would, of course, be made to the individual appropriation accounts. That is, the amount shown opposite each account in the explanation to the entry would now be posted in the "Expenditures" column of

Figure 26

A GOVERNMENTAL UNIT
Voucher Register

Sheet No._____

Month of _____ 19___

Day	Details	Voucher No.	Payment		Amount	Code	Funds			
			Date	Check No.			General	Special Revenue	Bond	Working Capital

each appropriation account. The amount to be posted in each case is exactly equal to the amount of the unencumbered balance of each appropriation account. In other words, the unencumbered balance of each appropriation is closed out and transferred to unappropriated surplus.

		Appropriations	$426,000	
		Appropriation Expenditures		$399,900
		Encumbrances		20,000
		Unappropriated Surplus		6,100

To record closing out of appropriation expenditures, encumbrances, and unencumbered balances of appropriations. Entries (debits) in subsidiary accounts:

	Total	Current Expenses	Capital Outlays
General Government:			
Council	$ 300	$ 200	$ 100
Executive Department	300	300	
Courts	200	100	100
Department of Finance:			
Administration	100	100	
Bureau of Treasury	20		20
Bureau of Purchases	50	50	
Bureau of Assessments	100	100	
Department of Law	100		100
City Clerk's Office	155	100	55
Board of Zoning Appeals	175	50	125
Civil Service Commission	100		100
Public Safety:			
Department of Police:			
Bureau of Supervision	40	40	
Bureau of Identification Records	160	60	100
Bureau of Fire Fighting	500	500	
Board of Examiners—Plumbers	75		75
Board of Examiners—Electricians	25		25
Sanitation and Waste Removal	700	500	200
Health and Hospitals	1,900	1,900	
Public Welfare	50		50
Schools	200		200
Libraries	125		125
Recreation	175		175
Total	$6,100	$4,000	$2,100

For a more vivid illustration of the effect of the above entry on the individual appropriation accounts, the reader is referred to the last part of Figure 15, page 42, showing transactions at the close of the year. Note that the account shows encumbrances outstanding amounting to $300 and an unencumbered balance of $500. The latter amount is transferred to unappropriated surplus. The encumbered balances ($300 in the account under consideration) may be left in the old accounts (Figure 15), or transferred to new accounts (Figure 27). Regardless of whether encumbered balances are transferred to new accounts or retained in the old appropriation accounts, the accounts containing these balances must not be grouped with the new appropriation accounts but must be set up as a separate group supporting the Reserve for Encumbrances of Prior Years account in the general ledger.

Figure 27

A GOVERNMENTAL UNIT
Reserve for Encumbrances of Prior Years Account

Code No.: 2105-C   Activity: Fire Fighting

Function: Public Safety

Organization Unit: Department of Fire   Object: Materials and Supplies

Bureau of Fire Fighting   Year: 1956

Date	Explanation	Debit	Credit
Jan. 3	Transferred from Appropriation Account		$300.00
15	Expenditures	$280.00	

Statement of expenditures and encumbrances compared with appropriations. On the basis of the data contained in the individual appropriation accounts, a statement similar to that illustrated in Figure 28 is prepared for the general fund or special revenue funds comparing appropriations with the expenditures and encumbrances chargeable to them. To save space, organization units are shown only in some parts of the statement. In the remaining parts, the data are shown by functions. In actual practice, the data would be shown by organization units. If appropriations are made in detail for the activities carried on by an organization unit, the statement would be set up so as to show the information for each activity under each organization unit.

Such a statement is important because it shows for each department the appropriations, the expenditures and encumbrances chargeable to them, and the unencumbered balance of appropriations. The statement is somewhat similar to that illustrated in Figure 17, page 47. That statement, however, is prepared during the year, whereas the statement illustrated here is prepared only at the end of the year, after the accounts have been closed. The amount of detail in the statement depends on the detail with which the appropriations are made and the accounts are kept. For example, it is assumed that in making appropriations for the general fund, the legislative body distinguishes between current expenses, capital outlays, and retirement of bonds. Accordingly, the statement has been subdivided to show details for each class of expenditure.

On the other hand, it is assumed that appropriations are not detailed by objects of expenditures; therefore, no distinction is made between objects of expenditures in the statement. For example, the amounts in the "Appropriations" column on page 85 represent the total appropriated for each organization unit for all current expenses. If separate appropriations had been made and separate appropriation accounts had been kept by objects of expenditure, current expenses would be subdivided to show appropriations, expenditures, and encumbrances for the various objects of expense—for example, personal services, contractual services, materials and supplies, and other charges.

Since the totals from the statement are carried over to the statement analyzing the changes in the Unappropriated Surplus account (Figure 21, page 56), the present statement supports that statement.

A separate statement may be prepared for the Expenditures Chargeable Against the Reserve for Encumbrances of Prior Years account, or the statement illustrated in Figure 28 may be expanded to show this information. If the latter procedure is followed, the headings would read as follows:

A GOVERNMENTAL UNIT

General Fund

Statement of Expenditures and Encumbrances—Compared with Authorizations
for Fiscal Period

	AUTHORIZATIONS						
Function and Organization Unit	Appropriations (After Revisions)	Reserve for Encumbrances of Prior Years	Total	Expenditures	Unexpended Balance	Encumbrances	Unencumbered Balance

Detailed expenditure statements. The statement illustrated in Figure 28 is prepared primarily for the purpose of controlling appropriations and for reporting financial operations to the legislative body and the public. Expenditure data are, however, collected also for the purpose of financial administration, as, for example, the preparation of the budget. Even if appropriations are not detailed by objects of expenditure, it is nevertheless important in preparing the budget to know the amount expended for each object. Again, appropriations may have been made for large organization units, whereas in planning expenditures it may be necessary to have data for the subunits forming a part of the main organization unit. Accordingly, in addition to the statement just referred to, more detailed statements of expenditures are frequently prepared. Figure 29 illustrates a detailed expenditure statement. To save space, only three organization units are shown. It should be noted that no distinction is made on this statement between expenditures chargeable against the Appropriations account and those chargeable against the Reserve for Encumbrances of Prior Years account. If it is desired to show the data for more than one year, the statement may follow the arrangement illustrated in Figure 28,

General Fund

Statement of Expenditures and Encumbrances Compared with Appropriations
for Fiscal Year

Function and Organization Unit	Appropriations (After Revisions)	Expenditures	Unexpended Balance	Encumbrances	Unencumbered Balance
CURRENT EXPENSES					
General Government:					
Council..........	$ 4,000	$ 3,800	$ 200	—	$ 200
Executive Department....	5,500	5,000	500	$ 200	300
City Historian........	2,000	2,000	—	—	—
Total General Government....	$ 48,000	$ 46,000	$ 2,000	$ 1,000	$1,000
Public Safety........	$ 67,000	$ 64,100	2,900	$ 2,200	$ 700
Highways...........	21,000	18,000	3,000	3,000	—
Sanitation and Waste Removal....	19,000	16,000	3,000	2,500	500
Health and Hospitals......	18,700	13,800	4,900	3,100	1,800
Public Welfare........	13,200	12,000	1,200	1,200	—
Schools............	71,800	69,800	2,000	2,000	—
Libraries...........	3,200	3,200	—	—	—
Recreation..........	6,300	5,300	1,000	1,000	—
Interest............	14,400	14,400	—	—	—
Total Current Expenses....	$282,600	$262,600	$20,000	$16,000	$4,000
CAPITAL OUTLAYS					
General Government:					
Council..........	$ 1,500	$ 1,300	$ 200	$ 100	—
Executive Department....	1,500	1,500	—	—	$ 100
City Historian........	300	200	100	100	—
Total General Government....	$ 9,030	$ 8,030	$ 1,000	$ 400	$ 600
Public Safety........	$ 23,470	$ 21,270	$ 2,200	$ 1,550	$ 650
Highways...........	10,300	10,300	—	100	200
Sanitation and Waste Removal....	11,000	10,700	300	800	100
Health and Hospitals......	28,500	27,600	900	—	50
Public Welfare........	5,100	5,000	100	300	200
Schools............	12,000	11,500	500	300	50
Libraries...........	3,500	3,000	500	375	125
Recreation..........	6,500	5,900	600	425	175
Total Capital Outlays......	$109,400	$103,300	$ 6,100	$ 4,000	$2,100
Retirement of Bonds........	$ 34,000	$ 34,000	—	—	—
Grand Total...........	$426,000	$399,900	$26,100	$20,000	$6,100

85

Figure 29

A GOVERNMENTAL UNIT

General Fund

Statement of Expenditures, Classified by Function, Organization Unit, Character, and Object for Fiscal Year

Function and Organization Unit	Grand Total	Total Current Expenses	CURRENT EXPENSES				Total Capital Outlays	CAPITAL OUTLAYS		
			Personal Services	Contractual Services	Materials & Supplies	Fixed Charges		Land	Structures and Improvements	Equipment
General Government:										
Council	$ 5,100	$ 3,800	$ 3,500	$ 100	$ 150	$ 50	$ 1,300	—	—	$ 1,300
Executive Department	6,500	5,000	4,750	100	100	50	1,500	—	—	1,500
City Historian	2,200	2,000	1,900	—	75	25	200	—	—	200
Total General Government	$ 54,030	$ 46,000	$ 42,750	$ 975	$ 1,525	$ 750	$ 8,030	—	—	$ 8,030
Public Safety	$ 85,370	$ 64,100	$ 58,050	$1,900	$ 2,850	$ 1,300	$ 21,270	—	$ 6,000	$15,270
Highways	28,300	18,000	15,000	1,000	1,800	200	10,300	—	9,000	1,300
Sanitation and Waste Removal	26,700	16,000	13,500	700	1,500	300	10,700	—	8,700	2,000
Health and Hospitals	41,400	13,800	12,000	300	1,300	200	27,600	$5,000	12,000	10,600
Public Welfare	17,000	12,000	4,000	100	200	7,700	5,000	—	—	5,000
Schools	81,300	69,800	63,000	2,000	3,800	1,000	11,500	—	—	11,500
Libraries	6,200	3,200	2,500	100	100	500	3,000	—	—	3,000
Recreation	11,200	5,300	5,000	100	100	100	5,900	2,000	1,500	2,400
Interest	14,400	14,400	—			14,400	—	—	—	—
Total Current Expenses and Capital Outlays	$365,900	$262,600	$215,800	$7,175	$13,175	$26,450	$103,300	$7,000	$37,200	$59,100
Retirement of Bonds	34,000									
Grand Total	$399,900									

with the objects shown under each organization unit and the years shown horizontally. A variation of this arrangement is to show current expenses and capital outlays for each organization unit together. An example of such an arrangement is shown on the preceding page.

7

<<<<<<<<<<<<<<<<<<<<<<<<<<<<<<<<<<<<<<<<<<<<<<<<<<<<<<<<<<<<<<<

BOND FUNDS

Bond FUNDS are established to account for bond sale proceeds. A government may issue bonds for various purposes: for the construction of improvements, for funding deficits, for refunding previous bond issues, and for providing working capital funds. With the exception of special assessment or utility bonds which are discussed later, all bond proceeds should be handled through bond funds. Note particularly that bond funds are used only to handle the proceeds from the sale of general bonds. They have nothing whatever to do with bond retirements; retirements are handled through other funds.

Establishment of fund. Bonds must usually be authorized by the legislative body and must frequently also be approved by the voters. Local-government bonds may be authorized by the state legislature or the local government's own legislative body, or both. As soon as bonds are authorized, an entry is made to indicate the authorization and the potential asset thereby created. The entry is as follows:

Bonds Authorized—Unissued.............. $100,000
    Appropriations[1]........................ $100,000
To record authorization of bonds.

The next step is the sale of the bonds, the entry to record this transaction being

Cash..................................... $100,000
    Bonds Authorized—Unissued............ $100,000
To record sale of bonds.

The assumption in the present instance is that the bonds are sold at par. If they are sold at a premium or a discount, additional problems arise, but these will be discussed later.

---

[1] The Appropriations account was formerly known as the Reserve for Authorized Expenditures account.

Operation of fund. A bond fund continues to operate until all of the proceeds derived from the sale of the bonds are expended. The expenditure of proceeds from bonds issued for the purpose of financing a deficit, for providing working capital funds, or for refunding bonds is simple, involving merely a transfer of bond fund cash to some other fund. Thus, proceeds from the sale of bonds issued to provide working capital funds are, upon their receipt, transferred to the appropriate working capital fund. Proceeds from the sale of bonds issued to fund a deficit in the general fund are transferred to that fund. Finally, proceeds from the sale of refunding bonds are transferred to the fund which will finance the retirement of the bonds being refunded. The entry in the bond fund is in each instance as follows:

Appropriations.......................... $100,000
Cash.................................... $100,000
To record transfer of cash to another fund.

In the case of bonds issued to finance the acquisition or construction of permanent improvements, however, the money is not transferred to another fund but payments are made directly from the bond fund. If the improvement is purchased complete instead of being constructed, accounting for the fund is as simple as in the three instances mentioned above. On the other hand, if the fund finances the construction of improvements, proceeds are expended gradually as construction proceeds. The problem then is to see not only that the money is expended for proper fund purposes, but also that work is performed efficiently, that materials are properly handled, and that payrolls are in order. The latter three problems are not peculiar to the bond fund alone and are therefore discussed in Chapter 21. Only transactions peculiar to the bond fund are described here.

Transactions and entries—first fiscal year. The following transactions will be helpful in visualizing the accounting procedure for bond funds. Each of the transactions is illustrated by a journal entry.

Transactions

1. Bonds to the amount of $200,000 for the building of a bridge were authorized.
2. One half of the issue was sold at par.
3. The cost of handling and printing bonds was $500, which was paid.
4. The bridge is to be constructed partly by a contractor and partly by city labor. A contract has been entered into with White & Company for the construction of certain parts of the bridge, the estimated cost being $150,000.
5. Orders for materials, amounting to $5,000, were placed.
6. The payroll for the month amounted to $5,000 and was paid.
7. A bill for $60,000 was received from White & Company for part of the work.
8. Materials and a bill for same were received; the bill was for $4,800.
9. Payment of $60,000 was made to White & Company.
10. An order estimated to cost $6,000 was placed.

Entries

1. Bonds Authorized—Unissued.............	$200,000	
Appropriations......................		$200,000
To record authorization to issue bonds for construction of bridge.		
2. Cash................................	100,000	
Bonds Authorized—Unissued...........		100,000
To record sale of bonds.		
3. Appropriation Expenditures..............	500	
Cash................................		500
To record payment for handling and printing bonds.		
4. Encumbrances.........................	150,000	
Reserve for Encumbrances.............		150,000
To record encumbrances on account of contract entered into with White & Company for constructing certain parts of bridge.		
5. Encumbrances.........................	5,000	
Reserve for Encumbrances.............		5,000
To record encumbrances on account of materials ordered.		
6. Appropriation Expenditures..............	5,000	
Cash................................		5,000
To record payment of payroll.		
7. (a) Reserve for Encumbrances............	60,000	
Encumbrances....................		60,000
To reverse in part entry setting up reserve.		
(b) Appropriation Expenditures..........	60,000	
Contracts Payable.................		60,000
To record amount due White & Company on contract.		
8. (a) Reserve for Encumbrances............	5,000	
Encumbrances....................		5,000
To reverse entry setting up encumbrances.		
(b) Appropriation Expenditures..........	4,800	
Vouchers Payable.................		4,800
To record authorization for payment of bill.		
9. Contracts Payable......................	60,000	
Cash................................		60,000
To record payment to White & Company.		
10. Encumbrances.........................	6,000	
Reserve for Encumbrances.............		6,000
To record placing of order for materials.		

Let us assume that these were the only transactions occurring during the year. At the close of the year, the trial balance of the bond fund would appear as follows:

Cash...	$ 34,500	
Bonds Authorized—Unissued.................	100,000	
Appropriation Expenditures.................	70,300	
Encumbrances............................	96,000	
Vouchers Payable........................		$ 4,800
Reserve for Encumbrances.................		96,000
Appropriations...........................		200,000
	$300,800	$300,800

Closing entry—project uncompleted. The time element does not play so important a part in bond fund accounting as it does in general fund accounting. General fund appropriations of a local government are valid only for a fiscal year. It is therefore necessary in their case to close out the Appropriations account at the end of the year. On the other hand, authorizations to spend bond money are usually not limited as to time; that is, the appropriation continues until the project is completed. Accordingly, expenditures resulting from orders placed or contracts entered into during one fiscal year can be charged against the Appropriations account during the succeeding fiscal year. Therefore no entry is made closing out the Encumbrances account into the Appropriations account; instead of making such entry, both the Encumbrances and the Reserve for Encumbrances accounts are carried over into the next fiscal year.

Expenditures may or may not be closed out into the Appropriations account at the close of each fiscal year. If they are not closed out, it is desirable to identify the expenditures of each year. If they are closed out, the entry is:

Appropriations...........................	$70,300	
Appropriation Expenditures..............		$70,300
To record closing out of expenditures.		

Balance sheet—close of fiscal year. After the closing entry has been posted, the bond fund balance sheet will appear as follows:

Figure 30

A GOVERNMENTAL UNIT

Bond Fund

Balance Sheet
at Close of Fiscal Year

ASSETS

Cash...	$ 34,500
Bonds Authorized—Unissued.......................	100,000
	$134,500

LIABILITIES, RESERVES, AND APPROPRIATIONS

Vouchers Payable....................................		$ 4,800
Reserve for Encumbrances..........................		96,000
Appropriations (Unexpended Balance).......	$129,700	
Less—Encumbrances......................	96,000	33,700
		$134,500

As indicated previously, expenditures on uncompleted projects may or may not be capitalized at the close of each fiscal year. If capitalized, they are carried as work in progress, together with other fixed assets, in a separate group of accounts.[2]

Transactions and entries—second fiscal year. To complete the illustration, let us assume that the project was continued into the next fiscal year and that the transactions and the corresponding entries were as follows:

Transactions

1. The second half of the bond issue was sold at par.

2. The materials ordered (see transaction 10 on page 90) were received; and an invoice for $6,200 was received.

3. White & Company completed its part of the work; its bill was $90,000.

4. Total additional payments for labor, $30,000, were made.

5. White & Company's bill was paid, except for 5 per cent of the total contract, which was retained pending inspection and final approval of the completed project.

6. All other outstanding bills were paid.

Entries

1. Cash...................................	$100,000	
Bonds Authorized—Unissued..........		$100,000
To record sale of bonds at par.		
2. (a) Reserve for Encumbrances..........	6,000	
Encumbrances...................		6,000
To reverse entry setting up encumbrances on account of order placed at close of preceding fiscal year. Materials and invoice received.		
(b) Appropriation Expenditures.........	6,200	
Vouchers Payable................		6,200
To record expenditures on account of materials purchased.		
3. (a) Reserve for Encumbrances............	90,000	
Encumbrances...................		90,000
To reverse entry setting up encumbrances on contract with White & Company.		
(b) Appropriation Expenditures..........	90,000	
Contracts Payable.................		90,000
To record amount due White & Company on contract.		

[2] See pages 201-204.

4. Appropriation Expenditures. $30,000
    Cash. $30,000
    To record payments for labor.

5. Contracts Payable. 90,000
    Contracts Payable—Retained Percentage 7,500
    Cash. 82,500
    To record retention of 5 per cent of total
    contract, pending inspection and approval of
    project; to record payment of remainder of
    contract.

6. Vouchers Payable. 11,000
    Cash. 11,000
    To record payment of outstanding bills.

Closing entry—project completed. As soon as the project is completed, even if it is before the close of the fiscal year, an entry is made closing expenditures into the Appropriations account and transferring the balance into an Unappropriated Surplus account. The entry is as follows:

Appropriations. $129,700
    Appropriation Expenditures. $126,200
    Unappropriated Surplus. 3,500
    To record closing out of expenditures.

Balance sheet—project completed. After the above entry is posted, the balance sheet will read as follows:

Figure 31

A GOVERNMENTAL UNIT

Bond Fund

Balance Sheet
During, or at Close of, Fiscal Year

ASSETS

Cash. $11,000

LIABILITIES AND SURPLUS

Contracts Payable—Retained Percentage. . . . . $ 7,500
Unappropriated Surplus. 3,500

                                                         $11,000

Note that the resulting fixed assets are not set up in the bond fund even when the project is completed but are shown as part of the general fixed assets group of accounts. Again, bonds payable are not shown in the bond fund balance sheet but are carried as part of a group of general bonded debt and interest accounts. This procedure follows the principle previously stated—namely, that the bond fund is used only to account for bond sale proceeds. As soon as the project is completed, the bond fund has accomplished its purpose and ceases to exist. For example, from the above balance sheet it is evident that, were it not for the surplus in the fund, the fund would cease to exist as soon as the project was approved and the retained percentage on the contract was paid.

Disposing of surplus or deficit. From the foregoing example it is apparent that any existing unappropriated surplus must be disposed of before the bond fund is completely dissolved. Frequently, the legislative body specifies what shall be done with such surplus. In the absence of legislative restrictions, however, the surplus is usually transferred to the fund which will pay off the bonds. The reason is that the surplus arose because expenditures had been overestimated, with the result that a larger amount of bonds was sold than was necessary.

Suppose, on the other hand, that the fund has a deficit. Theoretically, it should not be possible for the fund to have a deficit, since the reserve for encumbrances should prevent the incurrence of a liability in excess of the authorized amount. The reserve is, however, merely an estimate, and the actual expenditure may prove to be greater than the estimate. In that event, the resulting deficit must be disposed of before the bond fund is dissolved. If the deficit is a small amount, it will usually be made up by a transfer of money from the general fund.

To illustrate how a deficit arises and how it is disposed of, let us assume that in the above case, owing to unforeseen circumstances, the materials ordered cost $13,200 instead of $6,200 and that the bill remained unpaid. The closing entry when the project was completed would in that event be as follows:

Appropriations.............................	$129,700	
Unappropriated Surplus....................	3,500	
Appropriation Expenditures...............		$133,200
To record closing out expenditures.		

The bond fund balance sheet would in this case read as follows:

Figure 32

A GOVERNMENTAL UNIT
Bond Fund
Balance Sheet
During, or at Close of, Fiscal Year

ASSETS

Cash...	$4,000

LIABILITIES AND DEFICIT

Contracts Payable—Retained Percentage................	$7,500
Unappropriated Surplus (Deficit).......................	3,500*
	$4,000

* Red

The deficit is eliminated simply through debiting Cash (upon its receipt from the general fund) and crediting the Unappropriated Surplus account. The following entries indicate the steps in eliminating the deficit and dissolving the fund:

Cash....................................	$3,500	
Unappropriated Surplus..................		$3,500
To record receipt of money from general fund to make up deficit in bond fund.		

Contracts Payable—Retained Percentage.....	7,500	
Cash....................................		7,500
To record payment of liabilities.		

Frequently, it becomes evident even before the work is completed that the project must be expanded. In such cases, approval of additional expenditures must come from those who authorized the issuance of the bonds in the first instance, and the procedure followed is the same as that for the original bonds.

Analysis of changes in Appropriations account. The Appropriations account is one of the most important bond fund accounts. A statement similar to the one shown in Figure 33, analyzing the changes in the account, should be prepared at the close of each fiscal year.

Figure 33

A GOVERNMENTAL UNIT

Bond Fund

Statement of Expenditures Compared with Appropriations for Fiscal Years

Appropriations.......................................		$200,000
Less—Appropriation Expenditures:		
Of This Year...........................	$126,200	
Of Prior Years.........................	70,300	
Total Appropriation Expenditures.................		196,500
Unexpended Balance...............................		$ 3,500
Less—Transfers to Unappropriated Surplus.............		3,500
		—

Sale of bonds at a premium or a discount. In order to simplify the discussion, we have assumed thus far that the bonds were sold at par. They are ordinarily sold, however, at either a premium or a discount. If the bonds are sold at a premium, the amount of premium received is first recorded in the bond fund. Since the premium, as indicated subsequently, represents an adjustment of the interest rate, the amount so received should be transferred to the fund which will pay the interest. In the case of general bonds, this will ordinarily be the general fund. For example, let us assume that the bonds referred to on page 89 were sold at a premium of $1,000. The entry to record this transaction in the bond fund will be as follows:

Cash....................................	$101,000	
Bonds Authorized—Unissued.............		$100,000
Unamortized Premiums on Bonds.........		1,000
To record sale of bonds at a premium.		

Subsequently, an entry would be made transferring the cash representing the premiums to the fund from which interest on these bonds is paid (ordinarily the general fund or a special revenue fund), the entry being:

Unamortized Premiums on Bonds...........	$1,000	
Cash...................................		$1,000
To record the transfer of premiums to general fund.		

If we assume, on the other hand, that these bonds had been sold at a discount, the entry to record the sale of such bonds is as follows:

Cash....................................	$99,000	
Unamortized Discounts on Bonds............	1,000	
Bonds Authorized—Unissued.............		$100,000
To record sale of bonds at a discount.		

Since these discounts represent an adjustment of the interest rate, cash corresponding to the amount of the discount theoretically should be transferred from the fund which will pay the interest (ordinarily either the general fund or a special revenue fund), and the discount should be amortized in that fund. For example, if interest on these bonds is to be paid from the general fund, $1,000 should be transferred from the general fund to the bond fund and used for financing construction. In the general fund, the discount would either be amortized over a number of years or charged as an interest expense of the year in which the transfer was made. In actual practice, however, because of legal complications, the discount is seldom made up by a transfer from the fund paying the interest on the bonds. Instead, the discounts are charged against the Appropriations account, the entry being

Appropriations............................	$1,000	
Unamortized Discounts on Bonds..........		$1,000
To record closing out of discount into the Appropriations account.		

The amount of cash available for construction is reduced by the amount of the discount, and the fund may thus have a deficit, which sometimes is made up by a transfer of cash from some other fund but not necessarily from the fund paying the interest on the bonds. Again, the amount transferred would not be charged as an interest expense in the fund from which the transfer was made but rather as a contribution.

If discounts are amortized, a question arises as to whether or not that part of the discount which is amortized during the construction period may be capitalized—that is, whether it may be included as part of the cost of construction. Since a discount represents an adjustment of the interest rate, the answer will depend on whether or not interest during construction is capitalized. That is, if interest paid during the construction period is capitalized, the discount should also be capitalized; if not, the discount should not be capitalized. Interest during the construction period on general bonds should not be capitalized, primarily for the reason that the government is not being deprived of money which it could use for revenue-producing purposes, and the related discount should therefore not be capitalized.

Financing several projects from one bond fund. Sometimes a bond issue is voted which does not specify the improvements which the bonds are to finance. For example, voters may be asked to approve a bond issue for "general improvements." In such cases, the designation of the specific improvements is left to the legislative body. The accounting procedure for such a bond fund is the same as that for a bond fund established for a specific project. The only difference is that it is necessary to account for each project separately. This can be accomplished by setting up separate accounts for each project. If many projects are financed out of the same bond fund, subsidiary accounts may be set up for each project, but controlling accounts for the bond fund must be carried in the general ledger. It is important to have a record of the amount appropriated for each particular project and the expenditures and encumbrances charged thereto. Whenever the actual cost of a project exceeds its estimated cost, an additional appropriation is made by the legislative body to cover the difference. The additional authorization results in lesser amounts becoming available for other contemplated projects; conversely, if expenditures are smaller than estimated, a greater amount of money will be available.

Surpluses or deficits in this fund, after all the projects financed from it have been completed, are disposed of in the same manner as those of single-project funds.

The statement analyzing the changes in the Appropriations account must be subdivided so as to show the information for each project separately. The following is an example of a heading for such a statement:

A GOVERNMENTAL UNIT

General Improvements Bond Fund

Statement of Expenditures and Encumbrances Compared with Appropriations
for Fiscal Years

Total	Project "A"	Project "B"	Project "C"	Projects Not Yet Determined

The data for this statement are similar to those illustrated in Figure 33.

Grouping bond funds. Thus far individual bond funds have been considered. However, a state or local government may have several bond funds. The accounting procedure is the same as for one bond fund, since each fund constitutes an independent entity. A separate balance sheet must be prepared for each fund, but the funds may be arranged in columnar form. The assets, liabilities, reserves, and surplus of each fund may be combined on this statement, but in no case must the totals be shown without the details applicable to each fund being exhibited or without reference being made to a statement showing these details. A statement of this kind prepared for a group of bond funds is illustrated in Figure 34.

As is indicated in this statement, a distinction is frequently made on the balance sheet between completed projects and uncompleted projects. Sometimes separate subtotals are shown for each group. The distinction between completed and uncompleted projects is especially important in connection with the analysis of the changes in the Appropriations account. For uncompleted projects it is important to compute the unexpended and unencumbered balances of the Appropriations account whereas for completed projects it is important to determine whether operations have resulted in a surplus or a deficit. Then, too, the total expenditures as shown by this statement for completed projects represent the amount to be set up in the fixed assets accounts.

Figure 34

A GOVERNMENTAL UNIT

Bond Funds

Balance Sheet
During, or at Close of, Fiscal Year

	Total	COMPLETED PROJECT Hospital Bond Fund	UNCOMPLETED PROJECTS Bridge "A" Bond Fund	Bridge "B" Bond Fund
ASSETS				
Cash.........................	$101,000	$11,000	$90,000	—
Bonds Authorized—Unissued.....	200,000	—	—	$200,000
	$301,000	$11,000	$90,000	$200,000
LIABILITIES, RESERVES, AND SURPLUS				
Liabilities:				
Vouchers Payable.............	$ 10,000	—	$10,000	—
Contracts Payable............	20,000	—	20,000	—
Contracts Payable—Retained Percentage.................	10,000	$10,000	—	—
	$ 40,000	$10,000	$30,000	—
Reserve for Encumbrances........	$ 50,000	—	$50,000	—
Appropriations (Unexpended Balance).....................	$260,000	—	$60,000	$200,000
Less—Encumbrances............	50,000	—	50,000	—
Unencumbered Balance.........	$210,000	—	$10,000	$200,000
Unappropriated Surplus..........	$ 1,000	$ 1,000	—	—
	$301,000	$11,000	$90,000	$200,000

If a government has numerous bond funds (that is, more than six or seven), the assets, liabilities, appropriations, reserves, and surplus may be shown in combined form on the balance sheet. Details would in that event be exhibited in a subsidiary schedule, and reference would be made in the balance sheet to this schedule. The schedule would be identical with the balance sheet exhibited above. In other words, because the exhibition of too many bond funds in the main statement might be confusing, the data for individual funds are presented in a subsidiary schedule, the totals of which agree with the figures in the balance sheet.

The statement analyzing the changes in the Appropriations account of a group of funds is not unlike a combined bond funds balance sheet. In other words, such a statement would be identical with that shown in the analysis of the appropriation for a single bond fund, except that it would contain a separate column for each fund. Specifically, the statement, in the case of the funds illustrated in the combined balance sheet, would be headed as follows:

A GOVERNMENTAL UNIT
Bond Funds
Statement of Expenditures and Encumbrances Compared with Appropriations for Fiscal Years

Total	COMPLETED PROJECT Hospital Bond Fund	UNCOMPLETED PROJECTS Bridge "A" Bond Fund	Bridge "B" Bond Fund

As in the case of the combined balance sheet, if the government has numerous bond funds, a separate statement would be prepared, supported by a subsidiary schedule exhibiting the same information as the principal statement, except that figures would be shown for each fund. The headings and columns of the schedule would be similar to those illustrated immediately above.

A bond fund for several projects would be shown in the combined bond funds balance sheet in the same manner as any other bond fund but reference would be made to a subsidiary statement which will give the details for each project separately. The following headings illustrate how this bond fund would be handled in the combined bond funds balance sheet. The funds are the same as those used in previous illustrations, except that another fund, which is assumed to finance several projects, has been added.

The figures in the "Total" column of Schedule A would be entered in the "General Improvements Bond Fund" column of the preceding statement.

The total expenditures, encumbrances, and so forth, for all projects financed by the fund should be shown on the statement analyzing the

A GOVERNMENTAL UNIT

Bond Funds

Balance Sheet
During, or at Close of, Fiscal Year

Total	COMPLETED PROJECT Hospital Bond Fund	UNCOMPLETED PROJECTS Bridge "A" Bond Fund	Bridge "B" Bond Fund	General Improvements Bond Fund (For detail see Schedule A)

Schedule A

A GOVERNMENTAL UNIT

General Improvements Bond Fund

Balance Sheet
During, or at Close of, Fiscal Year

Total	Project "M"	Project "N"	Project "O"	Projects Not Yet Determined

changes in the Appropriations account of the fund. As in the case of the combined bond funds balance sheet, reference should be made to a subsidiary statement which will give the details for each project separately. The balance sheet headings illustrated immediately above apply equally to the statements analyzing the changes in the Appropriations account.

Summary. The bond fund is used merely to account for proceeds from the sale of bonds. It is not used to retire bonds; consequently, the liability created by the issue of the bonds is not carried in the bond fund but in a separate group of accounts. Similarly, fixed assets representing capitalized bond fund expenditures are not shown in the bond fund. Authorizations to spend bond money, unlike appropriations out of the general fund, are not limited to a single fiscal year, but continue until the authorized projects are completed.

8

<<<<<<<<<<<<<<<<<<<<<<<<<<<<<<<<<<<<<<<<<<<<<<<<<<<<<<<<<<<

SPECIAL ASSESSMENT FUNDS

SPECIAL ASSESSMENT funds are established to account for the financing of services or improvements from special charges levied against the properties or persons benefited. Examples of services sometimes financed from special assessments are street cleaning and street lighting; examples of construction projects so financed are sewers, pavements, and street widening. This chapter will deal with the latter for two reasons: (1) special assessment funds are used to finance construction projects more often than services, and (2) accounting procedures for such projects are more complicated than for services.

Special assessments accounting procedure is complicated by the fact that property owners are usually permitted to pay their assessments over a number of years. In the meantime, construction expenditures must be financed from other sources. Sometimes a working capital fund is established to finance construction projects. Fund capital is secured through a special tax levy, through the issuance of bonds, or through a transfer from the general fund. Construction expenditures are met out of this fund, which is subsequently reimbursed from special assessment collections. The money is used again to finance later projects.

More frequently, however, special assessment projects are financed through bond issues. Either general-special assessment bonds or special-special assessment bonds are issued. A general-special assessment bond is one that becomes a charge against the full faith and credit of the governmental unit if assessment collections are inadequate to meet maturing interest or principal payments. A special-special assessment bond is one which is not a charge against the governmental unit as a whole but only against the assessment money collected, or against the properties benefited. The government's responsibility in the case of special-special assessment bonds is merely to enforce collections and to handle proceeds properly.

Usually serial bonds are issued, with maturity dates arranged so that part of the issue may be retired as soon as a special assessment installment is collected. Frequently, too, bonds are made payable from particular installment collections. In that case, bonds can be paid only from the collections of the installment to which they apply and no other. Bonds are sometimes made liens against specific pieces of property. Each bond, in that case, is payable only from the assessments levied against the particular piece of property with which it is identified.

Authorization of project. The first step in special assessment construction procedure is the authorization of the project. Projects are authorized by the legislative body or special district commissioners after due notice and hearings. Contracts are usually made after the project is authorized, although in a few cases proposals may be received in advance. The authorization is based on estimates submitted by contractors or, if the project is to be constructed by the government's own labor forces, on engineers' estimates. A sufficient amount must be authorized to cover not only the actual construction cost but also supervisory expenses, cost of surveys, and engineering and collection expenses.

The entry to record the authorization of a project is as follows:

Improvements Authorized.................	$500,000	
Appropriations[1].......................		$500,000
To record authorization of special assessment project.		

Authorization and sale of bonds. If construction is to be financed through the sale of bonds, the next step is the authorization to issue bonds. In contrast with the procedure in the bond fund, no entry is made in the special assessment fund to show bond authorizations. The reasons are as follows: (1) In the bond fund, the entry indicates not only the authorization to issue bonds but also the authorization to incur expenditures. In the special assessment fund, as shown above, the authorization to incur expenditures is recorded by a separate entry. (2) General bonds (that is, bonds handled through the bond fund) are not paid from taxes levied at the time the bonds are issued, and it is therefore necessary to record the authorization so as to indicate the authority to levy taxes for the repayment of the bonds. But special assessments for the purpose of retiring bonds are frequently levied before the bonds are issued. (3) Without the authorization to collect special assessments the authorization to issue bonds would be meaningless because with no provision for paying these bonds no one would buy them. Authorizations to issue special assess-

---

[1] The Appropriations account was formerly known as the Reserve for Authorized Expenditures account.

ment bonds need not therefore be recorded formally in the books, and no bond entries need be made until the bonds are sold.

If we assume that bonds to the amount of $350,000 are sold at a premium of $1,000, the entry is as follows:

Cash for Construction....................	$350,000	
Cash for Interest Payments...............	1,000	
Premiums on Bonds....................		$ 1,000
Bonds Payable.........................		350,000
To record sale of bonds at a premium.		

In the above entry, a distinction is made between cash to be used for construction purposes and cash available for the payment of interest. The special assessment fund accounts not only for the expenditure of bond proceeds for construction purposes but also for the payment of bonds and interest. Since the proceeds from the sale of bonds are to be used for financing construction, the cash received from the sale is specifically earmarked for this purpose. On the other hand, premiums on bonds represent an interest adjustment and should therefore be used only for making interest payments.

If the bonds had been sold at a discount, the entry would be as follows:

Cash for Construction....................	$349,000	
Discounts on Bonds......................	1,000	
Bonds Payable.........................		$350,000
To record sale of bonds at a discount.		

Since discounts on bonds also represent an interest adjustment, the Cash for Construction account should theoretically be increased by $1,000 through a transfer from the Cash for Interest Payments account. However, money for interest payments will not be received until assessments are levied, at which time property owners are charged interest on assessments receivable. And even after the interest is received, the money will be used for the payment of interest on bonds. Only the excess of the amount received over the amount paid could be transferred to cash for construction. Again, in many instances interest is not received until construction is completed. In practice, therefore, cash for construction is seldom replenished, and only the amount actually received for the bonds, when sold at a discount, is made available for construction.[2]

Sale of notes. An interval of time may elapse between the authorization of the bond issue and the sale of the bonds. Certain formalities may delay the sale of the bonds, or the delay may arise because of unfavorable market conditions. On the other hand, contractors have to be paid as the work progresses. If the sale of the bonds must be delayed, it may be preferable to issue short-term notes. Sometimes such notes are issued even though bonds can be sold immediately after construction is begun.

---

[2] The disposition of premiums and discounts is described on page 96.

This is done if short-term notes can be sold at a lower rate of interest than the bonds, the purpose being to save interest. Again, the issuance of notes may make it possible to delay the authorization and sale of bonds until after the project is completed and the exact cost of construction is determined. The advantage of this procedure is that the exact amount of bonds that must be issued is known.

The entry to record the sale of notes is as follows:

Cash for Construction......................	$340,000	
Notes Payable...........................		$340,000
To record sale of construction notes.		

If construction is financed primarily through the sale of notes, the notes may be sold from time to time throughout the construction period.

When the bonds are sold and the notes and interest are paid, the following entries are made:

Cash for Payment of Notes and Interest......	$350,000	
Bonds Payable...........................		$350,000
To record sale of bonds.		
Interest Expenses..........................	10,000	
Notes Payable............................	340,000	
Cash for Payment of Notes and Interest....		350,000
To record payment of notes and interest.		

Levying and collecting assessments. The levy of assessments is the next step in special assessment financing. Assessments are levied in some cases when the project is completed and in others as soon as construction is authorized. A brief description of assessment procedure will be of help in understanding special assessment accounting.

Assessments are levied on the basis of benefit. The benefited area is designated as the *benefit district*. Districts are numbered and are usually referred to by number. The area of a benefit district varies with the size and nature of the project and the methods of assessing. For example, the widening of a long street will involve a greater benefit area than the widening of a short street. It does not necessarily follow that only the abutting properties are included in the district, but, on the contrary, the district may embrace properties several streets removed from the improvement. In other words, the benefit district and the properties assessed consist of all the parcels which are deemed to be benefited by the improvement, regardless of how far they may be from it.

The governmental unit as a whole may receive some benefit from an improvement and may therefore bear part of the cost. The governmental unit's share will vary, for the reason that property owners are not expected to pay more than the amount of benefit accruing to their properties. If the total estimated assessments based on presumed benefits are smaller than the cost of the improvement, the government will make up the difference, but, if these estimated assessments are equal to the estimated cost of the improvement, the government may assume no part of the cost. The methods of determining total benefits as well as the distribution of cost between the benefited properties and the government at large are governed by many arbitrary rules.

The governmental unit may also share in the cost of special assessment improvements in the capacity of a property owner. For example, a police station, a fire station, or other government property may be located within the benefit district. Obviously it would be unfair to exempt this property from assessments and spread the cost over the privately owned property. The governmental unit, in the same manner as any property owner, must pay. Assessments on properties owned by governments independent of the governmental unit constructing the project (for example, assessments on state or county property located in a city) cannot ordinarily be levied unless statutes authorize such assessments.

The entry to record the levy of assessments and the governmental unit's share of the cost of the project is as follows:

Assessments Receivable—Current..........	$ 50,000	
Assessments Receivable—Deferred..........	350,000	
Governmental Unit's Share of Cost..........	100,000	
Improvements Authorized...............		$500,000
To record levy of assessments and government's share of cost.		

Special assessments and interest receivable may be recorded either on a special assessment roll, or on individual special assessment records. A special assessment roll is a record showing the assessments levied against each piece of property, payments received thereon, and related information. A form for a special assessment roll is illustrated in Figure 35. Note that only one line is provided for each property. By the use of insert sheets the form may be used where many installments are permitted. Some governments find it more practicable to use individual special assessment records similar to the one illustrated in Figure 36. Sometimes the same record is used to show both ad valorem taxes and special assessments receivable from each particular piece of property.

In spite of the fact that some of the assessments may prove to be uncollectible, no allowance for uncollectible assessments is set up, for the following reasons: The government is acting in a trust capacity; that is, its duty is to see that the assessments are collected and properly disbursed. The trust character of special assessment funds is especially evident in those instances where bonds are a lien against specific properties. As already indicated, the government may use only the proceeds from the assessments of particular pieces of property for the payment of such bonds. The payment of bonds may be further restricted to specific installments from particular pieces of property. Even if general-special assessment bonds are issued, an allowance for uncollectible assessments is im-

A GOVERNMENTAL UNIT
Special Assessment Roll

Name of Property Owner	Legal Description of Property	Total Assessment	Payments					
			Date	Principal	Interest	Date	Principal	Interest

Figure 35

A GOVERNMENTAL UNIT
Individual Special Assessment Record

Name of Owner _____ Date Assessed _____

Legal Description _____

Total Assessment _____ Interest Rate _____ No. of Installments _____

Installment No.	Principal	Interest	Additional Interest		Payments						Remarks
			Date	Amount	Date	Principal	Interest	Date	Principal	Interest	

Figure 36

practical. If such an allowance is to be made, assessments against all the benefited properties must be increased. But these properties are not supposed to be assessed for more than the amount of benefit. If the bonds are general-special assessment bonds, any deficiencies resulting from uncollectible assessments must be made up by the governmental unit.

The governmental unit may finance its share of the cost in various ways. If the amount is large, it may issue general bonds for this purpose. The bond proceeds in that case are handled first through the bond fund and from there are transferred to the special assessment fund.

If the government's share of the assessment cost is small, it may be financed from a special tax levy or through an appropriation from the general fund. Even if the government's part of the cost is large, it may be met through an appropriation or special tax levy. But in that case the government may pay its share in installments. Whether the government will finance its share through a bond issue or tax levy will depend on existing circumstances. For example, if the government is subject to a tax limit and is close to that limit, it is more likely to issue bonds. On the other hand, if it has limited bonding power, it may resort to taxation.

The entry to record the collection of current assessment installments is as follows:

Cash for Construction......................	$45,000	
Assessments Receivable—Current.........		$45,000
To record collection of current assessments.		

Similarly, the receipt of cash to cover the government's share of the cost is recorded as follows:

Cash for Construction......................	$50,000	
Governmental Unit's Share of Cost........		$50,000
To record transfer of money to cover governmental unit's share of cost.		

The entry would be the same if the government were to pay its share over a number of years, except that the Governmental Unit's Share of Cost account would be divided into two parts to indicate, respectively, the amount due currently and the amount deferred.

Note that the Cash for Construction account was debited in both of the above entries. It is assumed that the first installments, as well as the government's contribution, are to be used for the payment of construction costs. This is true only if assessments are levied as soon as construction is authorized. In such cases, the first installment and the government's contribution are collected soon after work is begun and can be used to finance part of the construction costs. If, however, assessments are not levied until construction is completed, Cash for Bond Payments is debited, since the proceeds will be used for the retirement of bonds.

When deferred assessments become due, they are transferred to the Assessments Receivable—Current account. The entry is

Assessments Receivable—Current............	$40,000	
Assessments Receivable—Deferred.........		$40,000
To record assessments becoming currently receivable.		

Delinquent assessments are set up separately. The entry is

Assessments Receivable—Delinquent.........	$5,000	
Assessments Receivable—Current.........		$5,000
To record delinquent assessments representing first installments.		

If delinquent assessments are not paid, the government may secure a lien against the property, and it may have the property sold to satisfy the lien. The accounting procedure involved is described on pages 120-122.

Accounting for interest. Since bonds are issued and interest costs arise because property owners are permitted to pay by installments, the owners are expected to bear the interest cost. The interest rate on assessments may be made a little higher than that which the government pays, for the following reasons: To save interest costs, some property owners may choose to pay the full amount of the assessment. If the government has issued callable bonds, it will reduce interest expenses by calling them in and redeeming them. If, however, the bonds are not callable and cannot be purchased in the open market, the government will continue to pay the full amount of interest, although its interest income will be reduced. Theoretically, the government should refuse to receive the full amount. But in actual practice the governmental unit sometimes finds it desirable to receive full payments if the interest losses will be small. Sometimes, too, statutes erroneously provide for the abatement of interest to property owners making full payment. Finally, the government cannot start collecting interest until assessments are levied. Usually, the assessments are made big enough to cover interest expenses up to the time of the first interest collections. If, however, no interest charges are included as part of the cost to be recovered from assessments, the interest rate charged must be sufficient to compensate for earlier losses. As interest on assessments becomes receivable, it is set up through the following entry:

Interest Receivable......................	$17,500	
Interest Revenues......................		$17,500
To record interest receivable on all of the unpaid installments.		

When interest on bonds becomes due, an entry is made setting up interest expenses and the resulting liability. The entry is as follows:

Interest Expenses..........................	$15,750	
Interest Payable........................		$15,750
To record interest due on bonds.		

The following entries illustrate the recording of interest receipts and payments:

```
Cash for Interest Payments.................   $17,000
     Interest Receivable......................            $17,000
To record receipt of interest.

Interest Payable..........................    15,750
     Cash for Interest Payments..............             15,750
To record payment of interest.
```

Accounting for construction expenditures. Special assessment projects, as indicated before, may be constructed either by contract or by the government's own labor forces. In either case, the accounting procedure is the same as for construction financed from general bonds. For the sake of simplicity, let us assume that the project is constructed by contract. As the contract is awarded, an entry is made setting up the Encumbrances and the Reserve for Encumbrances accounts. If we assume that the contract was for $440,000, the following entry would be made at the time the contract was awarded:

```
Encumbrances...........................   $440,000
     Reserve for Encumbrances................            $440,000
To record awarding of contract.
```

The contractor submits bills from time to time as the work progresses. As bills are received, the following entries are made:

```
Reserve for Encumbrances.................   $100,000
     Encumbrances........................            $100,000
To record cancellation of encumbrances by
amount of actual liability.

Appropriation Expenditures.................   100,000
     Contracts Payable......................            100,000
To record liability on account of contract.
```

When the bill is paid, an entry is made debiting Contracts Payable and crediting Cash for Construction.

Even if the work is performed by contract, the government itself will be incurring other expenditures chargeable to the project—for example, the cost of drawing up plans and specifications. If they are paid for directly out of the special assessment fund, these expenditures are recorded by a debit to Appropriation Expenditures and a credit to Cash for Construction. If the expenditures are first paid out of another fund, the liability to that fund is set up as soon as it is determined. When the money is finally paid, the liability account is debited and Cash for Construction is credited.

It may be necessary, in the case of many improvements, to condemn property. The procedure for condemning property is discussed in Chapter 17. The cost of the condemned property is part of construction expenditures, and the entry to record the transaction is as follows:

```
Appropriation Expenditures................   $40,000
     Judgments Payable.....................            $40,000
To record condemnation awards made.
```

As judgments are paid, the entry is

Judgments Payable........................	$40,000	
Cash for Construction.....................		$40,000
To record payment of judgments.		

Most of the condemnation awards are made for properties located in the benefit district. Even so, both the assessments receivable and the judgments payable are set up on the books. Sometimes, however, statutes provide for offsetting judgments payable against assessments receivable. In that event, too, both the assessments receivable and the judgments payable are recorded. An entry is made, at the time of the offset, debiting Judgments Payable and crediting Assessments Receivable—Current. If the amount awarded is greater than the assessment, the difference represents the balance of the judgment to be paid by the governmental unit. If the amount awarded is smaller than the amount assessed, the difference continues to be carried as an assessment receivable.

Interest on notes and any other interest expenses which are not expected to be recovered from interest on assessments should be considered as part of the cost of constructing the project. An Interest Expenses account might be debited at the time the expense is incurred. Subsequently, the account would be credited and the Appropriation Expenditures account debited. An alternative procedure is to debit the Appropriation Expenditures account directly as soon as the expense is incurred.

Trial balance before closing entries. On the basis of the entries illustrated previously (with the exception of the second entry shown on page 103 and the three entries shown on page 104), the trial balance of a special assessment fund, before closing entries, would appear as follows:

Cash for Construction...................	$ 405,000	
Cash for Interest Payments..............	2,250	
Assessments Receivable—Current........	40,000	
Assessments Receivable—Delinquent.....	5,000	
Assessments Receivable—Deferred........	310,000	
Governmental Unit's Share of Cost.......	50,000	
Interest Receivable.....................	500	
Interest Expenses......................	15,750	
Appropriation Expenditures.............	140,000	
Encumbrances.........................	340,000	
Contracts Payable.....................		$ 100,000
Bonds Payable........................		350,000
Premiums on Bonds....................		1,000
Interest Revenues.....................		17,500
Reserve for Encumbrances..............		340,000
Appropriations.......................		500,000
	$1,308,500	$1,308,500

Closing entries at end of fiscal year. At the end of each year, an entry is made closing out the Interest Revenues and the Interest Expenses accounts. The entry, if revenues exceed expenses, is as follows:

Interest Revenues........................	$17,500	
Interest Expenses.......................		$15,750
Unappropriated Surplus—Interest........		1,750
To record closing out of interest accounts.		

If interest expenses exceed revenues, the deficiency is charged to the Unappropriated Surplus—Interest account. The accounting procedure involved in the disposal of surpluses and deficits will be considered later.

Premiums and discounts on special assessment bonds ordinarily are not amortized and are closed out at the end of the fiscal year. Premiums are closed out through the following entry:

Premiums on Bonds.......................	$1,000	
Unappropriated Surplus—Interest........		$1,000
To record closing out premiums into unappropriated surplus.		

Since discounts reduce the cash available for construction, they are, if not amortized, usually closed out by debiting the Appropriations account and crediting the Discounts on Bonds account for the amount of the discount. If, however, the fund has a credit balance in the Unappropriated Surplus—Interest account, bond discount equal to such balance should be charged against the Unappropriated Surplus—Interest account. A corresponding transfer must, of course, be made from cash for interest payments to cash for construction.

The Appropriation Expenditures account may be closed out at the end of each fiscal year, or it may be closed out only at the time construction is completed. As indicated later, the procedure will depend on whether special assessment expenditures are capitalized at the close of the year or not until completion. If expenditures are closed out at the end of the fiscal year, the entry is as follows:

Appropriations...........................	$140,000	
Appropriation Expenditures...............		$140,000
To record closing out of expenditures for construction at the end of the fiscal year.		

A corresponding entry would be made in the general fixed assets group of accounts setting up the cost of work in progress (see Chapter 13).

Balance sheet for uncompleted project. After the above closing entries were posted, the special assessment fund balance sheet would appear as illustrated in Figure 37.

Figure 37

A GOVERNMENTAL UNIT

Special Assessment Fund

Balance Sheet
at Close of Fiscal Year

ASSETS

Cash:		
For Construction...	$405,000	
For Interest Payments...................................	2,250	$407,250
Assessments Receivable:		
Current..	$ 40,000	
Delinquent (Note: $5,000 is to be used to finance construction)	5,000	
Deferred..	310,000	355,000
Governmental Unit's Share of Cost.....................................		50,000
Interest Receivable..		500
		$812,750

LIABILITIES, RESERVES, APPROPRIATIONS, AND SURPLUS

Liabilities:			
Contracts Payable.......................................		$100,000	
Bonds Payable..		350,000	$450,000
Reserve for Encumbrances...............................		$340,000	
Appropriations (Unexpended Balance)..............	$360,000		
Less—Encumbrances............................	340,000	20,000	360,000
Unappropriated Surplus—Interest.....................................			2,750
			$812,750

Since the project is incomplete, it is not possible to tell whether actual construction costs exceeded or fell short of estimates. On the other hand, interest revenues and expenses are allocated to each year separately. Accordingly, even at the end of the first fiscal year, the fund will have either an interest surplus or an interest deficit, depending on whether interest revenues exceeded expenses or vice versa, because interest revenues seldom equal interest expenses.

Transactions and entries during second year. Let us assume that construction of the project was completed during the second year. The following list of transactions and entries illustrates the operation of the fund during this year:

Transactions

1. Deferred assessments to the amount of $40,000 became due.
2. Interest amounting to $17,500 became receivable.
3. Delinquent assessments of $4,000 were collected.
4. The remaining part of the governmental unit's share of the cost of the improvement was transferred.

5. Contracts payable of $100,000 were paid.

6. Current assessments of $75,000 were collected.

7. Interest of $16,500 was collected.

8. Interest of $15,750 was paid.

9. Supervisory expenses of engineers, amounting to $5,000, were paid.

10. The project was completed and a bill was received from the contractor for the remaining part of the cost of the contract ($340,000).

11. Bonds to the amount of $70,000 were retired.

12. Current assessments receivable of $5,000 became delinquent.

13. The amount due on the contract was paid except for $44,000, which was retained pending final approval of the project.

Entries

1. Assessments Receivable—Current......... $ 40,000
     Assessments Receivable—Deferred...... $ 40,000
     To record the setting up of deferred installments which have become due.

2. Interest Receivable.....................   17,500
     Interest Revenues....................   17,500
     To record interest receivable.

3. Cash for Construction..................   4,000
     Assessments Receivable—Delinquent....   4,000
     To record collection of delinquent assessments representing first installments.

4. Cash for Construction..................   50,000
     Governmental Unit's Share of Cost......   50,000
     To record transfer of remaining part of amount due from governmental unit.

5. Contracts Payable.....................   100,000
     Cash for Construction................   100,000
     To record payment of part of contract.

6. Cash for Bond Payments................   75,000
     Assessments Receivable—Current.......   75,000
     To record collection of current assessments receivable.

7. Cash for Interest Payments..............   16,500
     Interest Receivable...................   16,500
     To record interest collections.

8. Interest Expenses.....................   15,750
     Cash for Interest Payments...........   15,750
     To record payment of interest.

9. Appropriation Expenditures..............   5,000
     Cash for Construction................   5,000
     To record payment of supervisory expenses.

10. (a) Reserve for Encumbrances...........   340,000
        Encumbrances...................   340,000
     To record cancellation of encumbrances.

    (b) Appropriation Expenditures..........   340,000
        Contracts Payable................   340,000
     To record construction expenditures and corresponding liability to contractors.

11. Bonds Payable........................   70,000
     Cash for Bond Payments..............   70,000
     To record retirement of bonds.

12. Assessments Receivable—Delinquent...... $5,000
    Assessments Receivable—Current....... $5,000
    To record setting up delinquent assessments
    separately.

13. Contracts Payable...................... 340,000
    Contracts Payable—Retained Percentage 44,000
    Cash for Construction................. 296,000
    To record retention of part of amount due on
    contract and payment of remaining part.

Closing entries for completed project. Entries are made at the end of the fiscal year closing out the Interest Revenues, the Interest Expenses, and the Appropriation Expenditures accounts. These entries are as follows:

Interest Revenues........................ $ 17,500
    Interest Expenses...................... $ 15,750
    Unappropriated Surplus—Interest........ 1,750
    To record closing out of interest revenues and
    expenses and addition to surplus.

Appropriations........................... 360,000
    Appropriation Expenditures.............. 345,000
    Unappropriated Surplus—Construction..... 15,000
    To record closing out of Appropriation Expendi-
    tures account into the Appropriations account;
    to record, also, addition to surplus.

Balance sheet for completed project. After the above closing entries are posted, the balance sheet of the special assessment fund will read as indicated in Figure 38.

Figure 38

A GOVERNMENTAL UNIT

Special Assessment Fund

Balance Sheet
at Close of Fiscal Year

ASSETS

Cash:
  For Construction........................ $ 58,000
  For Bond Payments...................... 5,000
  For Interest Payments.................. 3,000 $ 66,000

Assessments Receivable:
  Delinquent (Note: $1,000 is to be used to
    finance construction).................. $ 6,000
  Deferred............................... 270,000   276,000

Interest Receivable................................. 1,500

$343,500

LIABILITIES AND SURPLUS

Liabilities:

Contracts Payable—Retained Percentage...	$ 44,000	
Bonds Payable........................	280,000	$324,000

Unappropriated Surplus:

Construction...........................	$ 15,000	
Interest...............................	4,500	19,500
		$343,500

Alternative form of balance sheet. If special assessment projects are financed from the sale of special assessment bonds, the special assessment fund really consists of three funds: (1) a bond fund which accounts for the proceeds from the sale of the bonds used to finance construction, (2) a special revenue fund which accounts for the special assessments used to retire the bonds, and (3) a special revenue fund which accounts for interest collected from special assessment payers and used to pay interest on the bonds. This fact is evident from the foregoing entries and from the balance sheets illustrated in Figures 37 and 38. It can be demonstrated further by rearranging the balance sheet carried in Figure 38, in the manner illustrated in Figure 39.

Figure 39

A GOVERNMENTAL UNIT

Special Assessment Fund

Balance Sheet
(Alternative Form)
at Close of Fiscal Year

	FUND FOR		
ASSETS	Construction	Payment of Bonds	Payment of Interest
Cash.................................	$58,000	$ 5,000	$3,000
Assessments Receivable:			
Delinquent.........................	1,000	5,000	
Deferred...........................		270,000	
Interest Receivable....................			1,500
	$59,000	$280,000	$4,500
LIABILITIES AND SURPLUS			
Liabilities:			
Contracts Payable—Retained Percentage	$44,000		
Bonds Payable......................		$280,000	
Unappropriated Surplus................	15,000		$4,500
	$59,000	$280,000	$4,500

Subsidiary schedule of installments receivable and bonds payable. If bonds are identified with and are made payable from particular installments, a subsidiary schedule, similar to the one illustrated in Figure 40, must be prepared. This schedule shows for each installment the amount of cash and other assets which will ultimately be used in paying bonds and interest, the amount of bonds and interest payable, and the surplus or deficit. The schedule supports the accounts illustrated in the last two columns of the above balance sheet.

Figure 40

A GOVERNMENTAL UNIT

Special Assessment Fund

Schedule of Installments to be Applied
to Payment of Bonds and Interest

Date

			YEARS		
		19—	19—	19—	19—
			INSTALLMENT NO.		
	Total	2	3	4	5
ASSETS					
Cash for Bond Payments...	$ 5,000	$ 5,000			
Cash for Interest Payments	3,000	3,000			
Assessments Receivable:					
Delinquent............	5,000	5,000			
Deferred..............	270,000		$90,000	$90,000	$90,000
Interest Receivable.......	1,500	1,500			
	$284,500	$14,500	$90,000	$90,000	$90,000
LIABILITIES AND SURPLUS					
Bonds Payable..........	$280,000	$10,000	$90,000	$90,000	$90,000
Unappropriated Surplus—					
Interest............	4,500	4,500			
	$284,500	$14,500	$90,000	$90,000	$90,000

Note that the delinquent assessments of $1,000 are not shown here. It will be remembered that it was assumed that the first installment was used to finance construction. The $1,000 is the amount of delinquent assessments applicable to that installment. That is, when the $1,000 is collected, it will be used not for the retirement of bonds but for meeting construction expenditures, and therefore it is not shown in the above schedule.

Analysis of changes in appropriations. A statement analyzing the Appropriations account should be prepared at the end of each fiscal year and at the time the project is completed. Figure 41 is an illustration of such a statement. The amounts used are based on the journal entries given previously.

Figure 41

A GOVERNMENTAL UNIT

Special Assessment Fund

Statement of Expenditures Compared with Appropriations
for Fiscal Years

Appropriations...............................		$500,000
Less—Appropriation Expenditures:		
Of This Year...................	$345,000	
Of Prior Years.................	140,000	485,000
Unexpended Balance................................		$15,000
Less—Transfers to Unappropriated Surplus.............		15,000
		—

It should be noted that the statement is similar to the one analyzing the Appropriations account in the bond fund (Figure 33).

Capitalizing expenditures. Since special assessment projects are, to a great extent, financed by private property owners, the question arises as to whether the government should capitalize the entire cost of the project or only that portion of the cost which it has financed. It would seem that, since the government financed only part of the project, it should not capitalize the complete cost. But the improvement cannot be considered the property of assessment payers; they are not at liberty to do as they please with it. Again, the government is responsible for the maintenance and repair of the improvement. For all practical purposes, therefore, the improvement can be considered as belonging to the governmental unit. Accordingly, the entire cost should be capitalized by the governmental unit, but the capitalization should be so recorded that it will be possible to distinguish the portion of the project financed by the governmental unit from that financed by the private owners.

Disposing of surpluses. After the project is completed, the fund may have two kinds of surplus. First, a surplus may result from an excess of interest revenues over interest expenses. Second, the fund may have a surplus arising from an excess of estimated expenditures over actual expenditures. The former type of surplus will hereafter be referred to as an interest surplus, and the latter will be designated as a construction surplus. The procedure for disposing of interest and construction surpluses is discussed below.

Theoretically, an interest surplus should be disposed of through reducing the interest rate on assessments. It is more practical, however, to leave the surplus intact until all bonds and interest are paid. In that manner, if, during any year, interest expenses exceed interest revenues, the deficit is charged against the accumulated surplus. Surplus remaining after all bonds and interest are paid may be rebated to the assessed property owners, transferred to other assessment districts, or placed in the general fund.

The disposal of construction surplus varies with assessment procedure. If the levy is made *after* the project is completed, there can be no surplus, since the assessment will be made large enough to recover only the actual cost of construction. If assessments are levied *before* the project is completed, and they are payable in one installment, rebates are granted in the form of cash or a reduction of the unpaid assessments. When assessments are paid in installments, reductions are spread over the remaining installments. Statutes may, however, in this case, prohibit the making of reductions in assessments until all bonds are paid, so that, in the event assessments become uncollectible, the surplus may be applied to the retirement of the bonds.

Disposing of deficits. Instead of two surpluses a fund may have two deficits—an *interest deficit* and a *construction deficit*. Again, it may have a surplus and a deficit—a construction surplus and an interest deficit, or vice versa. This section deals with the disposition of interest and construction deficits.

Interest deficits for any one year are disposed of by charging them against accumulated interest surplus. If there is no accumulated interest surplus, it may be necessary to raise interest rates. Sometimes, however, if legally feasible, construction surplus is used to make up interest deficits. Although this method penalizes those who have paid their assessments in full, it has the advantage of eliminating the ill feeling and litigation which are likely to accompany a rise in the interest rate. In many instances, those assessment owners who have paid in full are the very ones responsible for the decline in interest earnings. That is, if bonds cannot be retired as soon as collections are made from those paying in full, the government will continue to pay the same amount of interest on the outstanding bonds, although its interest earnings will probably be reduced (unless the money can be invested at a yield commensurate with the interest paid on the bonds).

Construction deficits arise only if assessments are levied *before* the completion of the project, since, if assessments are levied *after* the project is completed, the total cost is known, and the assessments plus the governmental unit's share of the cost are made large enough to cover the full cost. Usually the deficit is made up through the levy of supplemental assessments. If the assessments are payable in installments, the latter are adjusted to reflect the supplemental levy, or a separate supplementary roll may be made. Generally, interest surpluses are not applied to the extinguishment of construction deficits.

A third type of deficit—that arising as a result of delinquent assessments—will be discussed in the section beginning on page 120.

Transactions and entries illustrating disposal of surpluses or deficits.

The following transactions and entries illustrate the accounting procedure involved in disposing of construction and interest surpluses and deficits.

Transactions

1. Construction surplus amounted to $62,000. Rebates were made in cash as follows: to property owners, $10,000; to the governmental unit, $2,000. A reduction of $50,000 was made in assessments. Cash representing construction surplus to the amount of $50,000 was used to retire bonds.

2. Construction surplus was $10,000 and was applied toward wiping out an interest deficit of a corresponding amount.

3. A construction deficit of $100,000 was wiped out through supplemental assessments of $90,000, together with a supplemental contribution by the governmental unit of $10,000.

Entries

1. (a) Unappropriated Surplus—Construction......	$62,000	
Cash for Construction..................		$ 12,000
Assessments Receivable—Deferred........		50,000
To record making of cash rebates and the reduction in assessments.		
(b) Bonds Payable..........................	50,000	
Cash for Construction..................		50,000
To record use of cash representing construction surplus for the retirement of bonds.		
2. Unappropriated Surplus—Construction..........	10,000	
Cash for Interest Payments...................	10,000	
Unappropriated Surplus—Interest............		10,000
Cash for Construction......................		10,000
To record application of construction surplus to wiping out of interest deficit.		
3. Assessments Receivable—Supplemental.........	90,000	
Governmental Unit's Share of Cost—Supplemental	10,000	
Unappropriated Surplus—Construction.......		100,000
To record levy of supplemental special assessments to wipe out deficit.		

Groups of special assessment funds. A governmental unit may have many special assessment projects. In that case, it must establish a separate fund for each project. In presenting balance sheets or other statements of these funds, it is important to retain the identity of each fund. The following is an illustration of the heading for a combined special assessment fund balance sheet:

A GOVERNMENTAL UNIT
Special Assessment Funds
Balance Sheet
Date

	COMPLETED PROJECTS		UNCOMPLETED PROJECTS	
Total	No. 59	No. 60	No. 61	No. 62

It is desirable, as in the case of bond funds, to group special assessment projects in accordance with whether they represent completed projects or uncompleted projects.

If the governmental unit has many special assessment projects, it should prepare a combined balance sheet in which all assets, liabilities, reserves, and surpluses are combined. In such a case, a subsidiary schedule, showing the amount of assets, liabilities, reserves, and surplus applicable to each fund, must be prepared. The schedule heading would be similar to the one illustrated above for a combined columnar balance sheet. In other words, as in the case of bond funds, the combined balance sheet becomes a subsidiary schedule, and figures in the "Total" column of the schedule must correspond with the amounts shown in the main balance sheet.

The statement analyzing the changes in the Appropriations account for a group of special assessment funds is similar to the statement analyzing this account for a group of bond funds. The reader is therefore referred, for a further discussion, to Chapter 7.

Accounting for delinquent special assessments. We have already discussed the accounting procedure for assessments receivable up to the time they become delinquent. In this section, we shall discuss the procedure relating to the collection of delinquent special assessments.

Special assessments are usually made, by statute, a lien against the property against which they are levied, and, at the expiration of a certain time, the property may be sold and the proceeds used to satisfy the lien. The entry to record the sale of property for unpaid special assessments is as follows:

Cash for Bond Payments...................	$10,000	
Cash for Interest Payments................	150	
Cash for Other Payments..................	200	
Assessments Receivable—Delinquent.........		$2,000
Assessments Receivable—Deferred...........		8,000
Interest Receivable.......................		150
Cost of Holding Sale......................		200

To record sale of property for nonpayment of special assessments.

Note that the proceeds may be applied to satisfy not only the assessments receivable, but also the interest receivable up to the date of sale and the cost of holding the sale. Of course, specific authorization by statute is required for the use of the proceeds to cover interest and the cost of holding the sale.

The excess of the amount realized from the sale of the property over the amount of special assessments, interest, and the cost of holding the sale is held in a trust and agency fund for the benefit of the property owner until claimed by him. The transaction is recorded in that fund by debiting Cash and crediting the Property Owner's Trust Fund Balance account. If, on the other hand, the proceeds are not sufficient to cover special assessments, interest, and the cost of the sale, the property owner would ordinarily not be called upon to make up the difference.

The proceeds realized by the governmental unit from the sale of property for delinquent assessments may be used for various purposes. If general-special assessment bonds have been issued, the governmental unit may have paid the bonds and interest as they fell due with money borrowed from other funds. The proceeds would then be used to pay off the loans. If special-special assessment bonds are used, neither bonds due nor the interest on bonds will have been paid, and the proceeds will be used to retire the bonds and pay the interest. Unless bonds are callable, the governmental unit will not be able to retire all of the bonds at one time. Instead, bonds and interest will have to be paid as they fall due, so that the governmental unit will be faced with the problem of investing the money.

If the amount realized from the sale of the property is insufficient to cover the principal of the bonds and the interest, and the property owner cannot be called upon to make up the difference, the procedure followed depends on whether special-special assessment or general-special assessment bonds were issued. If special-special assessment bonds were issued, the bondholder will bear the loss. On the other hand, if general-special assessment bonds were issued, the deficiency will be made up by the governmental unit. Frequently, if the property cannot be sold for a sufficient amount to meet bonds and interest, the governmental unit bids it in. The entry to record this transaction is as follows:

Assessment Sale Certificates..................	$10,350	
Assessments Receivable—Delinquent..........		$2,000
Assessments Receivable—Deferred............		8,000
Interest Receivable.........................		150
Cost of Holding Sale.......................		200
To record bidding in of property for assessments.		

If the governmental unit bids in the property, payments on bonds and interest falling due are met, pending the disposition of the property, through loans from the general fund or through other loans.

The property owner is given the right to redeem his property within a certain period of time. If the property has been sold, the owner can redeem it by paying the purchase price plus interest and costs. If, however, the purchase price was not sufficient to pay the assessments, the property owner must also pay the remaining unpaid assessments.

If the property is purchased by a private buyer, the redemption is handled in a trust fund. On the other hand, if the property is bid in by the governmental unit, the transaction is handled in the special assessment fund. For example, if the property was bid in by a municipality and a loan was made to finance maturing bonds and interest and to meet the cost of holding the sale, the entry to record the redemption of the property is as follows:

Cash for Payment of Loans......................	$5,350	
Cash for Bond Payments........................	5,000	
Cash for Interest Payments.....................	50	
Assessment Sale Certificates..................		$10,350
Interest Revenues............................		50
To record redemption of property bid in by governmental unit.		

It should be noted that the Interest Revenues account consists of accrued interest from the time the property was bid in until the time of redemption. Interest prior to the date of bidding in the property is included in the Assessment Sale Certificates accounts.

If the property is not redeemed within the required period of time, the purchaser acquires a clear title. If the property was bid in by the governmental unit, the latter gets title. No entries are necessary to record this fact, the next entry being made when the property is sold by the governmental unit and the proceeds are used to pay the bonds and interest. Since the entry would be similar to the one described immediately above, it will not be illustrated here.

If the governmental unit intends to keep the property, an entry must be made in the special assessment fund to close out the Assessment Sale Certificates account. This will result in a deficit in the fund, unless general-special assessment bonds have been issued. If this type of bond is involved, it is necessary to transfer from the general fund to the special assessment fund an amount of money equal to the balance in the Assessment Sale Certificates account for the particular property. The entry to record the receipt of the cash by the special assessment fund is as follows:

Cash for Bond Payments.......................	$10,000	
Cash for Interest Payments....................	150	
Cash for Other Payments......................	200	
Assessment Sale Certificates.................		$10,350
To record transfer of cash from the general fund equal to the balance in the Assessment Sale Certificates account as a result of the bidding in of the delinquent property by this municipality.		

If money has already been advanced as a loan from the general fund to the special assessment fund, the loan will be cancelled and only the difference between the loan and the amount of the assessment sale certificate will be transferred from the general fund. If we assume that $5,350 has been borrowed from the general fund, the entry to record the cancellation of the loan and the receipt of money to cover bond payments yet to be made is as follows:

Cash for Bond Payments.......................	$5,000	
Due to General Fund..........................	5,350	
Assessment Sale Certificates.................		$10,350

To record cancellation of liability to general fund
and receipt of money from that fund for payment
of bonds.

It is assumed that the entire amount of special assessment bonds outstanding is to be paid at one time. If bonds are to be retired in installments, two procedures might be followed: One procedure is to transfer
at one time cash equivalent to the full amount of the assessment sale
certificate, as was assumed in the above entry. In that case, special assessment cash is invested, and the earnings on investments are used to pay
interest on bonds. The other procedure is to transfer each year an amount
sufficient only to retire that part of the bonds and interest falling due
during that year which the special assessment fund is unable to pay because of the transfer of the property.

Two additional facts should be noted about special assessments: The
first is that the law may provide for penalties on delinquent special assessments. These are accounted for in the same manner as interest on
delinquent special assessments. In fact, an examination of the interest
rates which governmental units are sometimes permitted to charge will
reveal that these interest charges also include penalties, although they are
referred to as *interest*. Sometimes the term *interest and penalties* is used.

The second fact to be noted is that the same property will be subject
to ad valorem real estate taxes and that these taxes are a lien against such
property. Sometimes a single lien is secured against the property to cover
both ad valorem taxes and special assessments. The proceeds from the
sale of the property are in that event used to satisfy both liens. For
example, the Illinois Supreme Court[3] has held that liens of general taxes
and local improvement special assessments are on a parity, with no
priority of one over the other.

Summary. It is evident that special assessment accounting may be simple or complicated. Complications usually arise because of installment
payments and because the special assessment fund possesses the characteristics of a trust fund. Officials have little discretion in the management
of such funds; the law outlines every step to be followed. And one must
be as careful in complying with the prescribed procedure as in following
out the provisions of a trust indenture. The accounting system must be
made sufficiently broad to cover all accounting transactions in as great
detail as is necessary, even if such procedure results in a large volume of
accounting work.

---

[3] People v. The Taylorville Sanitary District et al., 371 Ill. 280 (1939), 20 N. E.
(2d) 576.

9

<<<<<<<<<<<<<<<<<<<<<<<<<<<<<<<<<<<<<<<<<<<<<<<<<<<<<<<<<<<<<<<<<

SINKING FUNDS

A SINKING fund is established to accumulate resources for the retirement of term bonds. The fund is not to be used for the payment of interest. The interest on both term and serial bonds, as well as the principal of serial bonds, should be paid through the general fund or a special revenue fund.

One of the distinguishing characteristics of a sinking fund is the gradual accumulation of resources and their use in retiring bonds at maturity. If the annual contributions were the only characteristic of a sinking fund, the accounting procedure would be quite simple. The procedure is complicated by the fact that the contributions are invested and earn interest. In calculating the amounts which should be added periodically to the fund, therefore, it is necessary to take account of the earnings. Furthermore, these earnings are reinvested and continue to earn interest, so that compound interest must be taken into consideration in determining periodic contributions.

The following is an illustration of the method of determining required periodic contributions and earnings. Assume that a fund is to be accumulated for the retirement of bonds of $1,000,000, that the fund is to receive 20 contributions, and that each contribution except the last one will earn 4 per cent annual interest from the beginning of the year in which it is made until the end of the 19th year of the life of the fund. Reference to a sinking fund table will show that it is necessary to contribute $33,582 annually for 20 years in order to accumulate sufficient resources to retire the bonds at maturity. But, as is evident from Table 1, the total contributions make up only two thirds of the required resources ($671,633); the remainder ($328,367) represents interest earnings. Table 1 shows further that although the rate of return (4 per cent) is assumed to be the same throughout the life of the fund, the amount of return on the accumulated contributions in the fund increases from year to year. This is due not only to the increase in the cumulative amount of investments at the end of each year but also to the compounding of earnings. For example, if earnings were not compounded, the income of the fund at the end of the second year would be $2,686 ($1,343 + $1,343); instead it is $2,740, the difference, $54, being interest earnings of 4 per cent on the interest collected during the first year ($1,343 × 4 per cent = $54).

TABLE 1

SCHEDULE OF SINKING FUND REQUIREMENTS
(Assumed earnings rate of 4 per cent)

Contribution Year	Required Annual Contribution	Required Fund Income	Amount Required to Be Accumulated in Fund
1	$ 33,582	$ 1,343	$ 34,925
2	33,582	2,740	71,247
3	33,582	4,193	109,022
4	33,582	5,704	148,308
5	33,582	7,276	189,166
6	33,582	8,910	231,658
7	33,582	10,610	275,850
8	33,582	12,377	321,809
9	33,582	14,216	369,607
10	33,582	16,128	419,317
11	33,582	18,116	471,015
12	33,582	20,184	524,781
13	33,582	22,335	580,698
14	33,582	24,571	638,851
15	33,582	26,897	699,330
16	33,582	29,316	762,228
17	33,582	31,832	827,642
18	33,582	34,449	895,673
19	33,582	37,170	966,425
20	33,575*	—	1,000,000
	$671,633	$328,367	$1,000,000

* Owing to the omission of cents, an adjustment of $7 is necessary to bring the fund to $1,000,000.

Operation of sinking fund. When the earnings of the fund have been estimated and annual contributions have been determined, the accounting for the fund can begin. An entry is made at the beginning of each year setting up the required contribution and the required earnings and crediting a reserve account with a corresponding amount. For example, at the beginning of the first year, the entries, if we assume the amounts shown for that year in Table 1, would be as follows:

Required Installment Contribution............	$33,582	
Required Earnings...........................	1,343	
Reserve for Retirement of Sinking Fund Bonds		$34,925

To record setting up of sinking fund requirements for first year.

Sinking fund contributions may be made from another fund, such as the general fund or a special revenue fund, or they may be derived from a sinking fund tax levy. The accounting procedure involved in those cases where the sinking fund receives contributions from other funds is described later in this chapter. Here it is assumed that special taxes are levied for sinking fund purposes. In such a case it is necessary not only to record taxes receivable, but to go through all the steps involved in tax accounting procedure: to differentiate between current and delinquent taxes, to provide allowances for uncollectible taxes, to charge against these allowances taxes written off as uncollectible, and to credit the proper accounts for tax collections. The entries involved have been illustrated in Chapter 4; accordingly, only a few are given here.

Taxes Receivable—Current...................	$35,582	
Allowance for Uncollectible Current Taxes....		$ 2,000
Contribution Revenues.....................		33,582
To record accrual of taxes and setting up of allowance for estimated losses on taxes receivable.		
Cash.......................................	21,350	
Taxes Receivable—Current.................		21,350
To record collection of taxes.		
Taxes Receivable—Delinquent................	14,232	
Allowance for Uncollectible Current Taxes......	2,000	
Taxes Receivable—Current.................		14,232
Allowance for Uncollectible Delinquent Taxes		2,000
To record setting up of delinquent taxes and the provision for estimated losses thereon.		
Cash.......................................	6,030	
Taxes Receivable—Delinquent..............		5,800
Contribution Revenues.....................		230
To record collection of delinquent taxes and interest and penalties thereon.		
Interest and Penalties Receivable on Taxes.....	66	
Allowance for Uncollectible Interest and Penalties...................................		6
Contribution Revenues.....................		60
To record interest and penalties accrued on delinquent taxes and to set up allowances for estimated losses.		

Contributions are invested as soon as possible after their receipt, so that they may begin to earn interest immediately. Usually the money is invested in governmental securities, including not only the governmental unit's own securities but frequently also the very bonds to be retired. Securities are usually acquired at either a premium or a discount, and the purchase price includes interest which has accrued from the last interest payment date to the time of purchase. These factors are described and illustrated later in the chapter. In the present case, if we assume that no premiums, discounts, or accrued interest are involved, the entry to record the purchase of investments will be as follows:

```
Investments.................................  $25,000
    Cash.....................................             $25,000
    To record purchase of investments at par.
```

Subsequently, when interest is received (or becomes receivable), the following entry is made:

```
Cash (or Interest Receivable on Investments)...  $1,500
    Earnings..................................             $1,500
    To record receipt (or accrual) of interest on invest-
    ments.
```

Trial balance before closing entries. The trial balance of the sinking fund based on the entries illustrated above would be as follows:

```
Cash.......................................  $ 3,880
Taxes Receivable—Delinquent................    8,432
Allowance for Uncollectible Delinquent Taxes...           $ 2,000
Investments................................   25,000
Interest and Penalties Receivable on Taxes.....       66
Allowance for Uncollectible Interest and Penalties              6
Required Installment Contribution............   33,582
Required Earnings..........................    1,343
Contribution Revenues......................             33,872
Earnings...................................              1,500
Reserve for Retirement of Sinking Fund Bonds...          34,925
                                             _____   _____
                                             $72,303    $72,303
```

Closing entries. At the end of the fiscal year, or at any time immediately preceding the retirement of bonds, the accounts showing requirements and actual contributions and earnings are closed out, and it is determined whether revenues correspond to requirements. The entries are as follows:

```
Contribution Revenues......................  $33,872
    Required Installment Contribution..........             $33,582
    Unappropriated Surplus....................                 290
    To record closing out of accounts showing required
    and actual contributions.

Earnings...................................    1,500
    Required Earnings.........................               1,343
    Unappropriated Surplus....................                 157
    To record closing out of accounts showing required
    and actual earnings.
```

Balance sheet after closing entries. After the closing entries had been posted, the sinking fund balance sheet would appear as shown on page 128.

The Reserve for Retirement of Sinking Fund Bonds account indicates the amount of contributions and earnings which the fund should have accumulated at a particular time. For example, at the end of any year, the amount to the credit of the reserve should be equal to the sum shown for the particular year in the "Amount Required to Be Accumulated in Fund" column of Table 1. Thus, at the end of the first year, according to the table, the balance of the reserve should be $34,925; that is, the fund, at the end of the first year, should have accumulated $34,925. In the above illustration the fund had actually accumulated $35,372. The difference, $447, as is evident from the foregoing entries, represents the excess of actual contributions over required installment contributions plus the excess of actual earnings over required earnings.

Recalculation of reserve for retirement of sinking fund bonds. If contributions or earnings either exceed or fall short of requirements, it may be necessary to revise the schedule of requirements. Usually contributions to the fund correspond to requirements, and variations arise because of

Figure 42

A GOVERNMENTAL UNIT

Sinking Fund

Balance Sheet
at Close of Fiscal Year

ASSETS

Cash...		$ 3,880
Taxes Receivable—Delinquent..................	$8,432	
Less—Allowance for Uncollectible Delinquent Taxes...................................	2,000	6,432
Interest and Penalties Receivable on Taxes......	$ 66	
Less—Allowance for Uncollectible Interest and Penalties...................................	6	60
Investments................................		25,000
		$35,372

RESERVES AND SURPLUS

Reserve for Retirement of Sinking Fund Bonds..........	$34,925
Unappropriated Surplus.............................	447
	$35,372

a rise or fall in earnings. If the fluctuations in earnings are temporary, no adjustment is necessary, the assumption being that in the long run surpluses and deficits will cancel out. If, on the other hand, the change in the earnings represents a long-term trend rather than a mere temporary condition, it is necessary to revise the schedule of requirements.

Assuming that the schedule is to be revised because of an increase in the rate of interest, two factors must be taken into account, namely, the amount of the surplus and estimated future earnings. The investments representing the surplus of the fund will continue to earn money from the present time until the bonds are retired. The earnings of the fund would thus be greater than estimated even if the interest rate declined thereafter and became the same as originally estimated. The assumption is, however, that the rate will continue to be greater than originally estimated and will still further increase interest earnings. For example, assume that a fund which is to be built up over a period of 20 years has been in existence now for 10 years and has, at the end of the tenth year, accumulated a surplus of $10,000. In the first place, the total amount of contributions over the remaining 10 years must be reduced by $10,000, the amount of the surplus. Secondly, the investments representing the surplus will continue to earn interest over the remaining 10 years, and the total amount of contributions over that period must be reduced by these earnings. Finally, the earnings on the investments of the fund will be further increased as a result of the increased interest rate which is assumed to continue over the life of the sinking fund. Consequently, the remaining contributions must also be reduced by the amount of these expected increased earnings. With these factors known, the required new contributions can be readily determined and the new schedule can be set up. The Unappropriated Surplus account would be closed out into the Reserve for Retirement of Sinking Fund Bonds account by debiting the former account and crediting the latter.

If, on the other hand, the adjustment is necessary because of a decrease in the rate of interest, it is essential to take into account not only the reduced rate of interest but also the necessity of eliminating the deficit. Thus, if the fund referred to above had at the end of the tenth year a deficit of $10,000 instead of a surplus, it would be necessary to increase contributions to make up this deficit. Since the deficit arose because of a reduction in the interest rate, the fund will have smaller earnings than had been anticipated. This loss in earnings must be made up by increased contributions. Once the revised schedule has been completed, an entry is made debiting the Reserve for Retirement of Sinking Fund Bonds account and crediting the Unappropriated Surplus account.

Another factor which frequently makes necessary an adjustment in the schedule of requirements is the calling in of bonds prior to their date of maturity. Frequently, too, a government may purchase the sinking fund bonds in the open market. If such bonds are cancelled upon their acquisition, no interest will be received, and earnings will therefore not come up to expectations. This is one of the reasons why such bonds should be held alive in the sinking fund.

Finally, the payment of sinking fund administration expenses out of the sinking fund frequently necessitates an adjustment in the schedule of requirements. The best practice is to pay administration expenses out of some other fund. The required contributions and earnings can be calculated accurately only if the exact amount to be paid out of the fund and the date of payment are definitely known at the time the schedule is compiled.

Retirement of bonds. The accounting procedure for the retirement of bonds through the sinking fund is quite simple. As soon as bonds mature, the following entry is made:

Reserve for Retirement of Sinking Fund Bonds $2,000,000
   Matured Bonds Payable................ $2,000,000
   To record matured sinking fund bonds.

It will be noted that bonds payable are not recorded as a liability of the sinking fund until they mature. Until that time, they are carried in the general bonded debt and interest group of accounts. The entry for removing the Bonds Payable account from this group of accounts will be indicated later.

It is assumed that payments out of the sinking fund do not require an appropriation. Since the fund is established solely for the retirement of bonds, and since contribution payments are made into it pursuant to appropriation, an appropriation for payments out of the fund is not usually necessary. If, however, an appropriation is required, the above entry does not apply. Instead, an entry is made at the time the appropriation ordinance is passed debiting the Reserve for Retirement of Sinking Fund Bonds account and crediting an Appropriations account. When the bonds become due, an entry is made debiting the Appropriations account and crediting the Matured Bonds Payable account.

Balance sheet at maturity. After the bonds have matured, the balance sheet of the fund will appear as follows:

Figure 43

A GOVERNMENTAL UNIT

Sinking Fund

Balance Sheet

Date

ASSETS

Cash...		$1,955,540
Taxes Receivable—Delinquent..............	$55,000	
Less—Allowance for Uncollectible Delinquent Taxes...............................	11,000	44,000
Interest and Penalties Receivable on Taxes...	$ 510	
Less—Allowance for Uncollectible Interest and Penalties...............................	50	460
		$2,000,000

LIABILITIES

Matured Bonds Payable...........................	$2,000,000

Two problems present themselves. The first problem relates to the liquidation of delinquent taxes. Even though the taxes may ultimately be collected, cash is required for the payment of the bonds. If the government has many sinking funds, and if the law permits, part of the cash available in other sinking funds may be used. When delinquent taxes are collected, the appropriate sinking fund is replenished. Frequently, the general fund lends money to the sinking fund for this purpose, or it takes over the taxes itself and advances the necessary money to the sinking fund. If the law prohibits advances or loans from such funds, short-term borrowing may be necessary.

The second problem is the disposition of surpluses and deficits. In the above case, it was assumed the fund had the exact amount of cash and other assets to retire the bonds. Suppose, however, that the fund had more assets than were needed to retire the bonds; that is, it had a surplus. In that case, if the law permits, the surplus would be transferred to another sinking fund, especially if the latter's contributions or earnings are short of requirements. Sometimes, however, the surplus is transferred to the general fund. Similarly, if the fund had a deficit, the latter might be made up by transfers from the general fund, by an additional tax levy, or by transfers of surpluses of other sinking funds. Normally the surplus or deficit of a sinking fund will be small, for the simple reason that adjustments will have been made from time to time throughout the life of the fund. Deficits are sometimes particularly large, however, because of neglect to make contributions at proper intervals or because of failure to compute actuarial requirements properly. A special tax may have to be levied in such instances, or, if the deficit is too large, the bonds may have to be refunded, and there may even be a default.

Let us assume that a loan has been secured from the general fund. The entry at the time the money is received will be as follows:

Cash...	$10,000	
Due to General Fund......................		$10,000
To record loan from general fund.		

The disposal of surplus is recorded by a debit to Unappropriated Surplus and a credit to Cash. The Unappropriated Surplus account is, of course, not transferred to another fund until the delinquent taxes are collected and the loss on uncollectible taxes is definitely determined. A deficit is eliminated from the accounts by a debit to Cash and a credit to the Unappropriated Surplus account.

Bonds may be paid either through the governmental unit's treasury department, through a fiscal agent, or through both. The accounting procedure for recording the payment of matured bonds will be discussed in Chapter 17.

Sinking fund investments. The securities which a governmental unit may purchase are usually prescribed by statute or charter and are frequently limited to federal, state, and municipal securities. As far as practicable, sinking fund cash should be invested in the bonds for the retirement of which the sinking fund was created, for, even if these bonds do not offer as great a return as other securities, they have the advantage of being the safest investment. As indicated before, once these bonds are acquired, they should not be canceled. If they are, the fact that they no longer bear interest not only necessitates the recomputation of the annual contributions, but also reduces the earnings of the fund. In general, nothing seems to be gained by cancellation except preventing the resale of the bonds, which is not customary but which is sometimes desirable.

Only in two instances is it advisable to cancel reacquired bonds: (1) if all the bonds of a particular issue to be retired through a sinking fund are held by the governmental unit which issued them, or (2) if there is a surplus in the fund. In the latter case, however, only an amount equal to the accumulated surplus should be canceled. Some statutes or charters erroneously provide that all reacquired sinking fund bonds must be canceled.

The securities in which sinking fund cash is invested should bear an earlier maturity date than the bonds to be retired. Otherwise the governmental unit may be forced to sell investments at a loss. As a general rule, securities should be held until maturity. However, where there is a possibility not only of making a substantial profit on the sale of the investments but also of acquiring other investments of comparative safety at a price which will not wipe out the profit made on the sale of the first securities, it may be advisable to sell.

Securities should be safeguarded so that there will be no possibility of theft or mishandling. Only responsible officials should have access to them, and two or more officials should be present when the securities are handled. Whenever possible, the securities should be registered.

Records of investments. Detailed records should be kept of investments. Figure 44 illustrates a register of bond investments. Data as to accrued interest, amortization of premiums and discounts, and other details necessary for the proper accounting for investments are secured from this register. If the governmental unit has many different types of investments, a detailed subsidiary ledger, similar to the one illustrated in Figure 45, should be provided. The purpose of this ledger is to classify the information for each class of like bonds; that is, a separate sheet would be provided for each bond issue in which money is invested. More information would be shown on this sheet than on the register of bond investments, and the data would be classified by bond issues.

Interest on investments. As already indicated, a distinction must be made between accrued interest purchased and actual interest earnings. For example, assume that securities to the amount of $100,000, bearing interest at 4 per cent payable June 1 and December 1, were acquired on March 1 at par. The governmental unit acquiring the securities will ordinarily pay for them not $100,000 but $101,000. The additional $1,000 represents accrued interest purchased. On the first of June the governmental unit will receive interest of $2,000 (4 per cent of $100,000 for half

Figure 44

A GOVERNMENTAL UNIT
Register of Bond Investments

Purchase Date	Description	Bond Numbers	Amount Paid				Maturity Date	Nominal Interest Rate	Effective Interest Rate	Interest Dates	Amount of Interest Due Each Period	Date of Sale or Redemption
			Par Value	Premium or Discount	Accrued Interest	Total Amount Paid						

Figure 45

A GOVERNMENTAL UNIT
Investment Ledger

Maturity Date _____ Interest Dates _____

Description _____
Date Purchased _____ Price: Par _____ Premium or Discount _____ Where Payable _____ Accrued Interest Purchased _____
Interest Rate _____ Amount Each Period _____
If Registered—How? _____
Date Sold or Redeemed _____ Sale Price: Par _____ Premium or Discount _____ Accrued Interest Received _____

INTEREST EARNINGS

Date Received	Nominal Income	Amortized Premium or Discount*	Net Income	Unamortized Premium or Discount*	Date Received	Nominal Income	Amortized Premium or Discount*	Net Income	Unamortized Premium or Discount*

a year). But, of this amount, only $1,000 will represent interest revenues; the remaining $1,000 will represent a return of accrued interest purchased. The entries involved are illustrated on pages 143-144.

Amortization of premiums and discounts on investments. We have already indicated that it is necessary to take account of premiums and discounts in recording the interest revenues of a sinking fund. The same principles are involved in the amortization of premiums and discounts both on investments and on original issues of bonds sold. Since governmental units amortize premiums and discounts on investments more frequently than on bonds sold, we shall discuss amortization in connection with interest revenues. This discussion shows how the same principles may be applied to the amortization of premiums and discounts on original issues of bonds sold.

The same interest rate may be secured by buying at a premium securities which bear a high interest coupon rate or buying at a discount securities paying a low coupon rate of interest. Assume that investors are willing to accept 3.5 per cent interest on a particular security. In that case, if the security bears interest coupons of 3.5 per cent, investors will be able to buy the security at par. Suppose, however, that the security bears interest of 4 per cent—that is, ½ of 1 per cent higher than called for by market conditions. In that case, if the security is to be retired in 20 years, the investing governmental unit will pay a premium of $71.50 on each $1,000 bond it acquires.[1] Conversely, if the security bears only 3 per cent interest, it will be obtainable at a discount, the purchaser paying only $928.50 for each $1,000 bond.

The simplest procedure would be to have the rate of interest that is indicated on the security correspond to the market interest rate, so that the securities could be bought at par. This is, however, seldom possible, since market conditions change continually. To get the real, or effective,[2] rate of interest, therefore (as distinguished from the rate stated in the bond), the stated rate[3] must be adjusted by amortizing premiums or discounts as the case may be. The procedure whereby the balance of the unamortized bond premium account is gradually reduced is known as

---

[1] The amount of premium or discount to be paid can be determined readily by referring to bond tables. Some of the published bond tables available are the following: Johnson, David C.; Stone, Caleb; Cross, Milton C.; and Kircher, Edward A., *Yields of Bonds and Stocks.* New York: Prentice-Hall, Inc., 1938. Sprague, Charles E., *Extended Bond Tables.* New York: The Ronald Press Company, 1915. Bartholomew, James R., *Equitable Trust Company of New York Rapid Bond Tables.* New York: Published by the author with permission of the Equitable Trust Company of New York, 1917. *Standard Tables of Bond Values.* Boston: Financial Publishing Company, 1928.

[2] The effective interest rate is the actual rate received, premiums and discounts being taken into account.

[3] The rate stated on the bond and on the coupons attached to it is also referred to as the *coupon rate* and as the *nominal rate.*

amortization, and that whereby the balance of the discount account is reduced is known as *accumulation.* The term amortization is frequently made to cover both premiums and discounts, however, and therefore, in order to simplify the discussion, this usage will be followed here.

Some of the more common methods of amortization are (1) the straight-line method, (2) the interest method, and (3) the bonds outstanding method.

Straight-line method of amortization. The straight-line method of amortizing premiums or discounts is the simplest. Under it, the total amount of premium or discount is divided by the total number of interest-paying periods in order to arrive either at the amount by which the balance of the Unamortized Premiums on Investments account is to be reduced each period and revenues are to be correspondingly decreased, or at the amount by which the balance of the Unamortized Discounts on Investments account is to be reduced and interest revenues are to be correspondingly increased. This method results in showing equal annual interest revenues, whereas, theoretically, interest revenues should decrease each year in the case of bonds acquired at a premium and should increase in the case of bonds purchased at a discount. In the first instance, the investing governmental unit is receiving part of the premium each year, thereby reducing the amount of its investment. In the second instance, the borrowing governmental unit is postponing the payment of part of the interest until maturity, and, as the maturity date approaches, the investing governmental unit's equity increases.

Interest method. The interest method is more scientific than the straight-line method in that it takes account of the factors mentioned in the preceding paragraph. The effective interest rate, which is usually determined by the use of bond tables, is multiplied by the par value of bonds outstanding plus unamortized premium, or less unamortized discount, in order to give the amount of effective interest for an interest-paying period. This amount is then deducted from the nominal interest for the period, in the case of a premium, and the remainder is the amount of premium to be amortized during the period. In the case of a discount, on the other hand, the nominal interest for a period is deducted from the effective interest and the remainder represents the amount of discount to be amortized during the period.

The following is an illustration of the procedure used in arriving at the amount of bond premium to be amortized under this method. Assume that $100,000-par-value bonds, running over a period of 5 years and bearing a nominal interest rate of 3 per cent payable semiannually, were bought on March 1, 1950, to yield 2.8 per cent interest per year. By reference to a bond table, it will be found that $100,930 would have had to be paid for these securities. The effective interest for the first half year, is, therefore, $1,413.02 [($100,930 × 2.8 per cent)/2], whereas the amount of

TABLE 2

AMORTIZATION OF BOND PREMIUMS UNDER THE INTEREST METHOD[4]

1 Interest Payment Date	2 Interest Received (Figures in Column 6 Multiplied by 1.5%)	3 Effective Interest (Figures in Column 7 Multiplied by 1.4%)	4 Premium to Be Amortized (Column 2 Minus Column 3)	5 Un-amortized Premium (Column 5 Minus Column 4)	6 Par Value of Investments	7 Book Value (Column 5 Plus Column 6)
March 1, 1950	—	—	—	$930.00	$100,000.00	$100,930.00
Sept. 1, 1950	$ 1,500.00	$ 1,413.02	$ 86.98	843.02	100,000.00	100,843.02
March 1, 1951	1,500.00	1,411.80	88.20	754.82	100,000.00	100,754.82
Sept. 1, 1951	1,500.00	1,410.57	89.43	665.39	100,000.00	100,665.39
March 1, 1952	1,500.00	1,409.32	90.68	574.71	100,000.00	100,574.71
Sept. 1, 1952	1,500.00	1,408.05	91.95	482.76	100,000.00	100,482.76
March 1, 1953	1,500.00	1,406.76	93.24	389.52	100,000.00	100,389.52
Sept. 1, 1953	1,500.00	1,405.45	94.55	294.97	100,000.00	100,294.97
March 1, 1954	1,500.00	1,404.13	95.87	199.10	100,000.00	100,199.10
Sept. 1, 1954	1,500.00	1,402.79	97.21	101.89	100,000.00	100,101.89
March 1, 1955	1,500.00	1,398.11*	101.89*	—	100,000.00	100,000.00
Total.........	$15,000.00	$14,070.00	$930.00	—	$100,000.00	

* Adjustment of $3.32 necessary, because of carrying yields to two decimal places only.

[4] If the bonds had been purchased on April 1, 1950 (see example on page 140), the first two lines of the table would be as follows:

April 1, 1950..........	—	—	—	$915.50	$100,000.00	$100,915.50
Sept. 1, 1950..........	$ 1,250.00	$ 1,177.52	$ 72.48	43.02	100,000.00	100,843.02

The rest of the table, beginning with March 1, 1951, would remain unchanged.

TABLE 3

AMORTIZATION OF BOND DISCOUNTS UNDER THE INTEREST METHOD[5]

1	2	3	4	5	6	7
Interest Payment Date	Interest Received (Figures in Column 6 Multiplied by 1.5%)	Effective Interest (Figures in Column 7 Multiplied by 1.6%)	Discount to Be Amortized (Column 3 Minus Column 2)	Un-amortized Discount (Column 5 Minus Column 4)	Par Value of Investments	Book Value (Column 6 Minus Column 5)
March 1, 1950				$920.00	$100,000.00	$ 99,080.00
Sept. 1, 1950	$ 1,500.00	$ 1,585.28	$ 85.28	834.72	100,000.00	99,165.28
March 1, 1951	1,500.00	1,586.64	86.64	748.08	100,000.00	99,251.92
Sept. 1, 1951	1,500.00	1,588.03	88.03	660.05	100,000.00	99,339.95
March 1, 1952	1,500.00	1,589.44	89.44	570.61	100,000.00	99,429.39
Sept. 1, 1952	1,500.00	1,590.87	90.87	479.74	100,000.00	99,520.26
March 1, 1953	1,500.00	1,592.32	92.32	387.42	100,000.00	99,612.58
Sept. 1, 1953	1,500.00	1,593.80	93.80	293.62	100,000.00	99,706.38
March 1, 1954	1,500.00	1,595.30	95.30	198.32	100,000.00	99,801.68
Sept. 1, 1954	1,500.00	1,596.83	96.83	101.49	100,000.00	99,898.51
March 1, 1955	1,500.00	1,601.49*	101.49*	—	100,000.00	100,000.00
Total	$15,000.00	$15,920.00	$920.00	—	$100,000.00	$100,000.00

* Adjustment of $3.11 necessary, because of carrying yields to two decimal places only.

[5] If the bonds had been purchased on April 1, 1950 (see example on page 140), the first two lines of the table would be as follows:

April 1, 1950	—	—	—	$905.79	$100,000.00	$ 99,094.21
Sept. 1, 1950	$ 1,500.00	$ 1,321.07	$ 71.07	834.72	100,000.00	99,165.28

The rest of the table, beginning with March 1, 1951, would remain unchanged.

interest which will actually be received is $1,500 [($100,000 × 3 per cent)/2]. The difference between the amount of nominal interest (that is, interest actually received) and the amount of effective interest, or $86.98, represents the amount by which the premium for the first half year is to be amortized. Table 2 illustrates the amortization of premiums under the interest method on the basis of the assumptions made above.

The procedure for amortizing bond discounts is the same as for premiums. For example, assume that the bonds used in the above illustration are bought to yield 3.2 per cent interest per year. A bond table shows that only $99,080 will be paid for these bonds, that is, they will be purchased at a discount of $920. Therefore, the effective amount of interest for the first half year is $1,585,28 [($99,080 × 3.2 per cent)/2], while the nominal interest is $1,500 [($100,000 × 3 per cent)/2], the difference, $85.28, representing the amount by which the balance of the Unamortized Discounts on Investments account must be reduced. Table 3 illustrates the amortization of bond discount on the basis of these assumptions.

It was assumed above that the bonds all mature at one time. The interest method may be applied to serial bonds by treating each maturity as though it were a separate issue.

Bonds outstanding method. The bonds outstanding method is a modification of the straight-line method and is used in the amortization of premiums or discounts on serial bonds, for which the straight-line method is not applicable. Under this method, the amount of bonds that will be outstanding at the beginning of each half year is determined, and these amounts are totaled. Each amount is then divided by the total in order to arrive at the percentage of premium or discount to be amortized each half year. Applying the percentages to the total amount of premium or discount gives the amount of premium or discount to be amortized.

As an illustration, assume that $60,000-par-value bonds, bearing a nominal interest rate of 4 per cent payable semi-annually and maturing at the rate of $10,000 each year, were bought for $62,000—that is, at a premium of $2,000. The amount to be amortized each year is indicated in Table 4.

Thus, the percentage to be applied on the first interest date is 14.3 per cent, which is arrived at by dividing $60,000 by $420,000. Since the total bond premium is $2,000, the amount to be amortized on the first interest date is found by taking 14.3 per cent of $2,000. The amount to be amortized on the first interest date of the second year is obtained by applying the percentage shown in the third column for that year—namely, 11.9 per cent—to $2,000. The percentage and amount to be amortized on each of the succeeding interest dates of each year are similarly derived. The same procedure is followed in the calculation of the amount of discount to be amortized.

Entries. The entry to record interest revenues and the amortization of

TABLE 4

AMORTIZATION OF PREMIUMS UNDER THE
BONDS OUTSTANDING METHOD

Half Year	Amount Outstanding	Percentage of Premium to Be Amortized	Amount of Premium to Be Amortized
1	$ 60,000	14.3	$ 286.00
2	60,000	14.3	286.00
3	50,000	11.9	238.00
4	50,000	11.9	238.00
5	40,000	9.5	190.00
6	40,000	9.5	190.00
7	30,000	7.1	142.00
8	30,000	7.1	142.00
9	20,000	4.8	96.00
10	20,000	4.8	96.00
11	10,000	2.4	48.00
12	10,000	2.4	48.00
	$420,000	100.0	$2,000.00

premiums, in the case of the figures illustrated in Table 2 for September 1, 1950, is as follows:

Interest Receivable......................	$1,500.00	
Earnings.............................		$1,413.02
Unamortized Premiums on Investments...		86.98
To record interest revenues and reduction of same by amount of premium amortized.		

On the other hand, the entry to record interest revenues and the amortization of discounts, if the figures illustrated in Table 3 for September 1, 1950, are used, is as follows:

Interest Receivable......................	$1,500.00	
Unamortized Discounts on Investments.....	85.28	
Earnings.............................		$1,585.28
To record interest revenues and increase of same by amount of discount amortized.		

If we assume the figures illustrated in Tables 2 and 3, the Investments account would appear as follows on September 1, 1950:

Investments.....................................		$200,000.00
Unamortized Premiums on Investments.....	$843.02	
Less—Unamortized Discounts on Investments	834.72	8.30
		$200,008.30

Purchases between interest dates. Under the interest method of amortization, if securities are purchased between interest-paying dates at a premium, the carrying value of the investment can be determined by starting out with the price that would have been paid had the securities been purchased at the last preceding interest date and adjusting for elapsed time. For example, if we assume that the investments referred to in the preceding illustration were purchased on April 1, 1950 instead of on March 1, 1950, the computation and apportionment of the price would be made as follows:

Price on a 2.8% basis if purchased on March 1, 1950 (per bond table)...	$100,930.00
Add—Interest at yield rate (2.8%) for March:	
$100,930 × 2.8% × 1/12....................................	235.50
Total cost..	$101,165.50
Deduct—Portion of cost chargeable to accrued interest receivable:	
$100,000 × 3% × 1/12....................................	250.00
Carrying value, April 1, 1950...............................	$100,915.50

The amount of premium to be amortized at the interest date following the date of purchase is computed by deducting the carrying value of the investment on that date from the carrying value at the date of purchase. Continuing with the foregoing illustration, the amount of premium to be amortized between April 1, 1950 and September 1, 1950 is $72.48, computed as follows:

Carrying value at date of purchase, April 1, 1950............	$100,915.50
Carrying value on September 1, 1950 (see Table 2)..........	100,843.02
Amount of premium to be amortized, April 1-September 1, 1950 $	72.48

In the foregoing examples it was assumed that the securities were purchased at the beginning of the month. If they are purchased during the month, the same procedure applies except that it is necessary to use the number of days instead of one-twelfth of a year. For example, if the securities had been purchased on March 10, 1950, instead of on March 1, 1950, the interest at the assumed yield rate of 2.8% would be $70.65, computed as follows:

$$\$100,930 \times 2.8\% \times 9/360 = \$70.65.$$

What was said about premiums on investments applies equally to discounts on investments. The only difference is that in arriving at the amount of discount to be amortized, the price at the date of purchase is deducted from the carrying value at the next interest date to determine the amount to be amortized. To illustrate, if we assume that the securities referred to previously as having been purchased at a discount were acquired on April 1, 1950 instead of March 1, 1950, the computation and apportionment of the price would be made as follows:

Price on a 3.2% basis if purchased on March 1, 1950
(per bond table)............................... $99,080.00
Add—Interest at yield rate (3.2%) for March:
$99,080 × 3.2% × 1/12......................... 264.21

Total cost................................... $99,344.21

Deduct—Portion of cost chargeable to accrued interest
receivable:
$100,000 × 3% × 1/12......................... 250.00

Carrying value, April 1, 1950...................... $99,094.21

Continuing with the foregoing illustration, the amount of discount to be amortized between April 1, 1950 and September 1, 1950 is $71.07, computed as follows:

Carrying value, September 1, 1950 (see Table 3)....... $99,165.28
Carrying value, April 1, 1950...................... 99,094.21

Amount of discount to be amortized................. $ 71.07

If the straight-line method is used, the purchase of investments between interest dates at a premium or a discount presents no problem, since the premiums or discounts can be readily pro-rated equally over the number of months or days that the securities are expected to be held.

Accounting for the sale of investments. In accounting for the sale of investments, it is necessary to determine the profit or loss on them. Profit or loss is represented by the difference between the book value of the investment and the selling price. The book value is the par value of the securities plus unamortized premiums and less unamortized discounts. Another point to remember is that if investments are sold between interest dates, part of the proceeds represents accrued interest sold (to the purchaser, this amount represents accrued interest purchased). Unless this interest is segregated, profits on the sale of investments are overstated and losses on such sales are understated. The entry involved in recording the sale investments and accrued interest is given on page 144.

Statement of investments. A subsidiary statement should be prepared showing details concerning sinking fund investments. The column headings of such a statement should read as follows:

Description	Date Acquired	Interest Rate	Maturity Date	Par Value	Unamortized Premiums or Discounts	Book Value	Accrued Interest Purchased	Market Value

Single sinking fund for several bond issues. The law sometimes permits the establishment of one sinking fund for several bond issues. In that case, the procedure is the same as for a single-issue sinking fund. That is, the amount of required contributions and the amount of required earnings are determined for each bond issue, and a Reserve for Retirement of Sinking Fund Bonds account is established for each issue. However, as contributions and earnings are received, no attempt is made to allocate them to any particular bond issue. All contributions are credited, instead, to the Contribution Revenues account and all earnings to the Earnings account. Similarly, no attempt is made to allocate to individual issues any surplus or deficit. The excess of total contributions and earnings over requirements is recorded in the Unappropriated Surplus account. If the total actual contributions and earnings for any year fall short of requirements, the difference is charged against any existing surplus, and, if none exists, the difference is shown as a deficit. The Reserve for Retirement of Sinking Fund Bonds accounts are the only accounts that are identified by individual bond issues. If many bond issues are involved, a single Reserve for Retirement of Sinking Fund Bonds account is established for all the bonds. This reserve is supported by individual Reserve for Retirement of Sinking Fund Bonds accounts for each bond issue in a subsidiary ledger.

The trial balance illustrated below indicates, as of the beginning of a fiscal year, the nature of a sinking fund established for the purpose of retiring each of several bond issues. It is assumed in the present illustration that some of the sinking fund investments have been acquired at a premium and others at a discount, and that these premiums and discounts are being amortized. It is also assumed that the sinking fund receives its contributions from the general fund rather than by levying its own taxes.

Cash..	$ 10,500	
Investments...............................	268,000	
Unamortized Premiums on Investments......	2,000	
Unamortized Discounts on Investments......		$ 1,300
Interest Receivable on Investments..........	4,000	
Accrued Interest on Investments Purchased..	225	
Reserve for Retirement of Sinking Fund Bonds:		
Bridge Bonds...........................		94,100
City Hall Bonds.........................		75,580
Hospital Bonds..........................		112,720
Unappropriated Surplus...................		1,025
	$284,725	$284,725

The transactions and entries shown below illustrate the procedure in handling a sinking fund established to retire several bond issues.

Transactions

1. Required contributions and earnings for the year are as follows:

Bonds	Contributions	Earnings	Total Required
(a) Bridge..............	$ 6,900	$3,000	$ 9,900
(b) City Hall...........	5,220	2,400	7,620
(c) Hospital............	8,480	3,600	12,080
	$20,600	$9,000	$29,600

2. The contribution of $20,600 became receivable from the general fund.
3. The general fund paid over the $20,600.
4. Interest in the amount of $8,900 was collected. Of this amount $4,000 represents interest previously set up as receivable and $225 accrued interest on investments purchased.
5. In connection with the collection of the interest on the investments, premiums on some investments in the amount of $200 and discounts on other investments in the amount of $250 are to be amortized.
6. Investments with a par value of $25,000 were acquired at a premium of $500; the accrued interest purchased amounted to $175.
7. Investments with a par value of $10,000 were sold for $9,900 plus accrued interest of $130; unamortized discount applicable to these investments amounted to $45.
8. Interest accrued on investments at the end of the year amounted to $4,600, exclusive of $175 of accrued interest purchased.
9. Closing entries were made at the end of the fiscal year.

Entries

1. Required Installment Contribution.............. $20,600
   Required Earnings............................ 9,000
   Reserve for Retirement of Sinking Fund Bonds:
   Bridge Bonds............................. $ 9,900
   City Hall Bonds.......................... 7,620
   Hospital Bonds........................... 12,080

To record contributions and requirements for the year as follows:

Bonds	Contributions	Earnings	Total Required
Bridge....................	$ 6,900	$3,000	$ 9,900
City Hall.................	5,220	2,400	7,620
Hospital..................	8,480	3,600	12,080
	$20,600	$9,000	$29,600

2. Due from General Fund...................... $20,600
   Contribution Revenues..................... $20,600
   To record contribution receivable from general fund.

3. Cash....................................... 20,600
   Due from General Fund.................... 20,600
   To record receipt of sinking fund contribution from general fund.

4. Cash....................................... 8,900
   Interest Receivable on Investments.......... 4,000
   Accrued Interest on Investments Purchased.... 225
   Earnings.................................. 4,675
   To record collection of interest receivable on investments, accrued interest on investments purchased, and interest earned during the current year.

5. Unamortized Discounts on Investments.......... 250
   Unamortized Premiums on Investments........ 200
   Earnings.................................. 50
   To record amortization of premiums and discounts on investments and to credit the excess of amor-

tized discounts over amortized premiums to the
Earnings account.

6. Investments.................................. $25,000
   Unamortized Premiums on Investments..........   500
   Accrued Interest on Investments Purchased......   175
      Cash....................................... $25,675
   To record purchase of investments at a premium;
   to record also purchase of accrued interest.

7. Cash..   10,030
   Unamortized Discounts on Investments..........   45
      Investments................................   10,000
      Earnings...................................   75
   To record sale of investments at a loss of $55 com-
   puted as follows:
      Par value of investments............ $10,000
      Less—Unamortized discounts........   45

      Book value...................... $ 9,955
      Sold for.........................   9,900

      Net loss.......................... $ 55

   To record also interest earnings of $130 and to re-
   flect the difference between the interest earnings
   and the loss on the sale of the investments as a
   net credit of $75 to the Earnings account.

8. Interest Receivable on Investments.............   4,775
      Earnings...................................   4,600
      Accrued Interest on Investments Purchased....   175
   To record interest on investments becoming re-
   ceivable at the end of the year including accrued
   interest on investments purchased.

9. (a) Contribution Revenues.....................   20,600
      Required Installment Contribution........   20,600
   To record closing out of accounts showing ac-
   tual revenues and requirements.

   (b) Earnings.................................   9,400
      Required Earnings......................   9,000
      Unappropriated Surplus.................   400
   To record closing out of Earnings account into
   account showing required earnings.

Balance sheet for consolidated sinking fund. In Figure 46 is an illustration of a balance sheet for a sinking fund established to retire several
bond issues. The statement is based on the above opening trial balance
and the subsequent entries.

Note that the assets are *not* identified with particular bond issues. And
the only indication that the fund has been set up for the retirement of
three bond issues is the subdivision of the Reserve for Retirement of Sinking Fund Bonds account. However, even this subdivision is significant
only for the purpose of recomputing requirements or retiring a particular
bond issue. For example, it is evident that bond issues will not all be re-

tired simultaneously. Suppose, therefore, that one issue has matured and is to be retired. In that case, it is necessary to know how much of the reserve must be closed out. Further, if the fund has a deficit, it may be desirable to know how much of the deficit is applicable to the retiring issue. This information may be of particular significance if the deficit arose because of some peculiar circumstances and is expected to be can-

Figure 46

A GOVERNMENTAL UNIT
Consolidated Sinking Fund
Balance Sheet
at Close of Fiscal Year

ASSETS

Cash...			$ 24,355
Investments..		$283,000	
Unamortized Premiums on Investments...............	$2,300		
Less—Unamortized Discounts on Investments.........	1,005	1,295	284,295
Interest Receivable on Investments.....................			4,775
			$313,425

RESERVES AND SURPLUS

Reserve for Retirement of Sinking Fund Bonds:		
Bridge Bonds..	$104,000	
City Hall Bonds..	83,200	
Hospital Bonds..	124,800	$312,000
Unappropriated Surplus................................		1,425
		$313,425

celed ultimately through increased earnings. Since the particular issue will be retired, there will be no opportunity to make up its share of the deficit, and a special contribution is required.

The procedure in recording bonds retired is the same as for a single-issue sinking fund. As bonds mature, the Reserve for Retirement of Sinking Fund Bonds account is debited and the Matured Bonds Payable account is credited (if we assume that no appropriation is required for the retirement of sinking fund bonds). One advantage in accounting for various issues through a single fund is that at the maturity of any one issue all the assets of the fund need not be liquidated, since contributions and earnings received on other issues can be applied to this purpose.

Accounting for groups of sinking funds. Let us assume that the government has several bond issues but that the law does not permit the consolidation of the sinking funds for all bond issues in one fund. In that case, a separate fund is established for each issue. The procedure is the same for the establishment of one fund, except for pooled investments.

Even though each fund is accounted for separately, it may be desirable to pool the money of the various funds for investment purposes. In that case, the problem becomes one of maintaining a proper record of each sinking fund's contribution to the pool. Earnings and losses on investments are allocated among the various funds on the basis of their contributions. Since it is assumed above that the law requires separate sinking funds, a separate balance sheet must be prepared for each fund. Prior to the preparation of balance sheets, the equity of each fund in the pooled investments is determined.

If there are a few funds, they may be presented in a combined balance sheet arranged in columnar form, as follows:

A GOVERNMENTAL UNIT
Sinking Fund
Balance Sheet
Date

	Total	County Bridge Bonds	County Home Bonds	County Building Bonds

If numerous sinking funds exist, only the figures in the "Total" column need be shown in the main balance sheet. But a subsidiary schedule, giving the details for each fund, must be prepared. This schedule is set up in the same manner as the sinking fund heading illustrated above. In other words, if the government has a few sinking funds, the details for each sinking fund can be shown in the main statement; if the government has many funds, the same statement becomes a subsidiary schedule, and only the totals are shown in the main statement. It should be remembered, however, that a subsidiary schedule must be prepared in order that the details for each fund may be readily obtained and that proper reference must be made to the schedule in the principal statement.

Accounting for utility or other enterprise sinking funds. The accounting principles and procedures thus far discussed apply to sinking funds established for the retirement of general bonds. Sinking funds established to retire utility or other enterprise bonds require additional accounting. This procedure is described in Chapter 12, which deals with utility or other enterprise funds.

10

<<<<<<<<<<<<<<<<<<<<<<<<<<<<<<<<<<<<<<<<<<<<<<<<<<<<<<<<<<<<<<<

TRUST AND AGENCY FUNDS

A TRUST FUND is established to account for assets received and held by the government in the capacity of trustee or custodian. Trust funds may be classified as *expendable* and *nonexpendable*. As the name implies, expendable trust funds are those whose entire resources may be expended. Pension funds and special deposits are examples of expendable trust funds. Pension fund expenditures take the form of pension payments to beneficiaries; expenditures out of deposit funds are in the form of refunds to the depositors. In contrast to expendable trust funds are nonexpendable funds, which must be held intact. A loan fund whose principal must be kept intact represents a good example of a nonexpendable trust fund. Such a fund is usually established by the bequest of a sum of money or other property to be used in making loans for specified purposes. Since loans are expected to be repaid, the fund is not expended when the loans are made. In the absence of bad loans, the fund becomes more or less permanent, cash being replaced by accounts or notes receivable.

Trust funds may also be classified as *public* and *private*. A public trust fund is one whose principal, earnings, or both must be used for a public purpose. An example is a pension fund. A private trust fund is one which will ordinarily revert to private individuals or will be used for private purposes. Guarantee deposits are an example of a private trust fund. The accounting procedure will not, however, be determined by whether the fund is public or private but rather by whether it is expendable or nonexpendable.

An agency fund is established to account for assets received and held by a government in its capacity as agent for individuals or other governmental units. The similarity between an agency fund and an expendable trust fund is such that agency funds may be included with trust funds for accounting purposes. In fact, the chief difference between an agency fund and an expendable trust fund is that the latter is usually held for a longer period of time and may thus require additional accounting. For example, trust funds are frequently invested, and the accounting system must provide for the proper recording of investments and earnings thereon.

There are so many types of trust and agency transactions that it would be impracticable to discuss the accounting treatment of all of them. Accordingly, we shall attempt to illustrate only a few types of funds, but the principles thus brought out can be applied to all trust and agency funds.

Expendable trust funds. Two examples of expendable trust funds are illustrated below, namely, a guarantee-deposits fund and a pension fund.

Guarantee deposits fund. Most governments require deposits for some purpose. For example, contractors may be required to leave deposits with the government as a guarantee of the performance of their contracts. These deposits must be accounted for so that they may be returned to the depositors.

The accounting procedure is simple. As deposits are received, Cash is debited and a Deposits Fund Balance account is credited. Subsequently, as deposits are refunded, these entries are reversed. The balance sheet of such a fund would, therefore, consist of a few accounts, as indicated by the statement shown below.

Figure 47

A GOVERNMENTAL UNIT
Deposits Fund
Balance Sheet
at Close of Fiscal Year

ASSETS

Cash..................................	$ 3,370
Investments...........................	15,000
	$18,370

BALANCE

Deposits Fund Balance..................	$18,370

Utility deposits require a more complicated procedure, because they are more numerous and because the utility frequently agrees to pay interest on deposits. The accounting procedure for utility deposits is described in Chapter 12.

Pension fund. The discussion will be concerned with a pension fund which is limited to two types of activities: (1) the accumulation of resources for the benefit of both active and retired employees and (2) the payment of benefits to retired employees. Actually, a pension fund may be established for additional purposes such as the payment of death benefits to survivors of participants, payment of annuities to employees' beneficiaries, and sickness and accident payments. Each of these purposes requires a separate fund. A separate fund is also needed to account for the expenses of administering the various types of pension and other benefit funds. The accounting for these funds will not, however, be discussed here because the principles involved can be ascertained from the discussion of the pension retirement benefit funds as well as from the description of the accounting procedure for some of the other expendable funds.

Retirement benefit funds operate on the same principle as sinking funds. In both cases it is necessary to make actuarial computations in order to determine the rate at which the fund is to be accumulated. In both instances it is assumed that the contributions will be invested and that the interest earnings will be compounded. Both call for an estimated rate of return on the investment and an estimate of the length of time over which the investments are expected to be held. As in the case of the sinking fund, it is necessary to indicate in the accounts and financial statements whether or not the retirement benefit fund meets actuarial requirements and to reflect them by means of a Reserve account. In the case of both types of funds, too, it is essential to indicate in an Unappropriated Surplus account the excess of assets in the fund over the amount required to be in the fund, and to indicate in a Deficit account (or by a debit balance in the Unappropriated Surplus account) the deficiency of fund assets compared with requirements. Finally, in both the sinking fund and the retirement benefit fund, it is essential that the required contributions and earnings be recorded in budgetary accounts at the beginning of the year.

The following transactions and entries indicate more specifically how a pension fund set up to pay retirement benefits operates. It is assumed that the fund is financed from three sources, namely, deductions from employees' salaries, contributions by the employing governmental unit, and earnings on invested contributions. Although such a fund would not ordinarily make benefit payments until several years after it was established, in this case, in order to make the discussion complete, provision has been made for such payments. If these entries are posted to the accounts indicated by each entry, the resulting account balances will be found to agree with those shown in the balance sheet illustrated in Figure 48. The transactions are given first, followed by the entries, which have been keyed to the transactions.

Transactions

1. Required employees' contributions, $15,000; required contributions from governmental unit, $15,000; required earnings, $600.

2. The required contributions, divided equally between deductions from employees' salaries and the governmental unit's contribution, became receivable from other funds as follows: general fund, $27,000 and special assessment fund, $3,000.

3. The general fund and the special assessment fund paid the amounts due from them.

4. Securities with a par value of $20,000 were acquired for $20,300, exclusive of accrued interest purchased, for which an additional $50 was paid.

5. Securities with a par value of $8,000 were acquired at a discount of $100. They were acquired at an interest date so that no accrued interest had to be purchased.

6. Semi-annual interest payments on investments received, $400, of which $50 represents accrued interest purchased.

7. Premiums on investments in the amount of $30 and discounts on investments in the amount of $10 were amortized.

8. At the end of the year, interest in the amount of $375 became receivable.

9. Premiums on investments in the amount of $25 and discounts on investments in the amount of $15 were amortized.

10. Pensions in the amount of $120 became payable.

11. Pensions payable in the amount of $90 were paid.

12. Closing entries were prepared.

Entries

1. Required Contributions—Employees. $15,000
    Required Contributions—Governmental Unit. . . .   15,000
    Required Earnings.   600
        Pension Fund Reserve. $30,600
    To record required contributions and required earnings.

2. Due from General Fund.   27,000
    Due from Special Assessment Fund.   3,000
        Contributions—Governmental Unit.   15,000
        Contributions—Employees.   15,000
    To record amounts due from general fund and special assessment fund for contributions representing deductions from employees' salaries and the governmental unit's share.

3. Cash.   30,000
        Due from General Fund.   27,000
        Due from Special Assessment Fund.   3,000
    To record collection of amounts due from general fund and special assessment fund.

4. Investments.   20,000
    Unamortized Premiums on Investments.   300
    Accrued Interest on Investments Purchased.   50
        Cash.   20,350
    To record purchase of investments at a premium as well as accrued interest on investments purchased.

5. Investments.   8,000
        Unamortized Discounts on Investments.   100
        Cash.   7,900
    To record purchase of investments at a discount.

6. Cash.   400
        Accrued Interest on Investments Purchased. . .   50
        Earnings.   350
    To record receipt of semi-annual interest on investments.

7. Unamortized Discounts on Investments......... $10
   Earnings................................... 20
      Unamortized Premiums on Investments....... $30
      To record amortization of premiums and discounts
      on investments.

8. Interest Receivable on Investments............ 375
      Earnings...................................   375
      To record interest receivable on investments.

9. Unamortized Discounts on Investments......... 15
   Earnings................................... 10
      Unamortized Premiums on Investments.......   25
      To record amortization of premiums and discounts
      on investments.

10. Pension Expenditures......................... 120
      Pensions Payable.........................   120
      To record pensions payable.

11. Pensions Payable............................ 90
      Cash....................................   90
      To record payment of pensions payable.

12. (a) Pension Fund Reserve.................... 120
      Pension Expenditures...................   120
      To close out pension expenditures.

   (b) Contributions—Employees................. 15,000
      Contributions—Governmental Unit......... 15,000
      Required Contributions—Employees......   15,000
      Required Contributions—Governmental Unit   15,000
      To close out actual and required contributions.

   (c) Earnings................................ 695
      Required Earnings......................   600
      Unappropriated Surplus.................   95
      To close out actual and required earnings.

Balance sheet. A balance sheet for a pension fund based on the foregoing entries is illustrated in Figure 48. Note that, as in the case of a sinking fund balance sheet, the reserve indicates the amount which should be
in the fund at the balance sheet date on the basis of actuarial computations. In this particular case, the net assets exceed the reserve by $95 and
this amount is therefore reflected in the balance sheet as unappropriated
surplus.

Nonexpendable trust funds. There are two types of nonexpendable trust
funds: those in which neither the principal nor the earnings of the fund
may be expended, and those whose earnings may be expended but whose
principal must be kept intact. A loan fund is an example of the former
type of fund; examples of the latter type are some common forms of endowment funds. The accounting procedure for nonexpendable funds does
not differ materially from that for expendable trust funds.

Loan funds. The transactions and corresponding entries on page 152
illustrate the operation of a loan fund.

Figure 48

A GOVERNMENTAL UNIT
Pension Fund
Balance Sheet
at Close of Fiscal Year

ASSETS

Cash..			$ 2,060
Investments...		$28,000	
Unamortized Premiums on Investments..................	$245		
Less—Unamortized Discounts on Investments............	75	170	28,170
Interest Receivable on Investments.....................................			375
			$30,605

LIABILITIES, RESERVES, AND SURPLUS

Pensions Payable..	$ 30
Pension Fund Reserve...	30,480
Unappropriated Surplus..	95
	$30,605

Transactions

1. A cash donation of $100,000 was received for the purpose of establishing a loan fund.
2. Loans amounting to $60,000 were made.
3. A loan of $1,000 was repaid with interest of $20.
4. Earnings were closed out.

Entries

1. Cash...................................	$100,000	
Loan Fund Balance..................		$100,000
To record receipt of cash and establishment of loan fund.		
2. Loans Receivable......................	60,000	
Cash............................		60,000
To record loans made.		
3. Cash.................................	1,020	
Loans Receivable....................		1,000
Earnings............................		20
To record repayment of loan with interest.		
4. Earnings..............................	20	
Loan Fund Balance..................		20
To record closing out of earnings and increase in loan fund balance.		

A loan fund balance sheet built up from the above entries would read as follows:

Figure 49

A GOVERNMENTAL UNIT

Loan Fund

Balance Sheet
at Close of Fiscal Year

ASSETS

Cash...	$ 41,020
Loans Receivable...............................	59,000
	$100,020

BALANCE

Loan Fund Balance..............................	$100,020

No surplus account is shown in the above statement, even though the fund has been increased by earnings of $20. These earnings are added to the capital of the fund and increase the amount of money available for loans.

A question arises as to what would happen if the cost of administration were payable out of the fund. In that case the fund would cease to be a nonexpendable fund, since administration expenses would reduce its balance. Provision may sometimes be made, however, for meeting administration expenses out of earnings. In that case, we have another type of trust fund, one whose principal must be kept intact but whose earnings may be expended. This type of fund is discussed in detail below. Although theoretically the fund is nonexpendable, in actual practice the fund balance may be reduced through bad loans.

Endowment funds. Some trust transactions require the use of both expendable and nonexpendable funds. This is true with certain endowments. An individual may donate money, or other property, with a view to having the income therefrom used to finance certain activities. Since the donor intended the principal to be held intact and the income alone expended, two funds are necessary: (1) a nonexpendable trust fund to account for the principal, and (2) an expendable fund to account for the earnings.

The following list of transactions and entries illustrates the operation of this fund:

Transactions

1. Cash in the amount of $210,000 was received for the establishment of a fund whose income is to be used in granting scholarships.

2. Investments with a par value of $200,000 were purchased at a premium of $3,000; accrued interest purchased amounted to $400.

3. A check in the amount of $3,000 was received in payment of six months' interest.

4. Premiums in the amount of $125 were amortized.

5. Securities with a par value of $1,000 to which unamortized premiums in the amount of $14 were applicable were sold for $1,005, plus accrued interest of $10.

6. Securities with a par value of $2,000 to which $28 in unamortized premiums were applicable were sold for $2,050, plus accrued interest of $25.

7. Interest receivable in the amount of $2,600 was recorded.

8. Premiums in the amount of $120 were amortized.

9. The total earnings to-date were recorded as a liability of the endowment principal fund to the endowment earnings fund.

10. The endowment principal fund paid $2,500 to the endowment earnings fund.

11. A scholarship grant in the amount of $2,000 was made by the endowment earnings fund. (Note: This is an outright grant, not a loan.)

Entries

1. ENTRY IN ENDOWMENT PRINCIPAL FUND:

Cash....................................	$210,000	
Endowment Principal Fund Balance........		$210,000

To record receipt of cash for establishment of endowment fund.

2. ENTRY IN ENDOWMENT PRINCIPAL FUND:

Investments.............................	200,000	
Unamortized Premiums on Investments.......	3,000	
Accrued Interest on Investments Purchased...	400	
Cash...............................		203,400

To record purchase of investments at a premium; to record also accrued interest on investments purchased.

3. ENTRY IN ENDOWMENT PRINCIPAL FUND:

Cash...................................	3,000	
Accrued Interest on Investments Purchased..		400
Earnings................................		2,600

To record collection of interest.

4. ENTRY IN ENDOWMENT PRINCIPAL FUND:

Earnings................................	125	
Unamortized Premiums on Investments.....		125

To record amortization of premiums on investments.

5. ENTRY IN ENDOWMENT PRINCIPAL FUND:

Cash...................................	1,015	
Endowment Principal Fund Balance..........	9	
Investments............................		1,000
Unamortized Premiums on Investments.....		14
Earnings................................		10

To record sale of investments at a loss of $9; to record also interest income of $10.

6. ENTRY IN ENDOWMENT PRINCIPAL FUND:

Cash...................................	2,075	
Investments............................		2,000
Unamortized Premiums on Investments.....		28
Endowment Principal Fund Balance........		22
Earnings................................		25

To record sale of investments at a profit of $22; to record also interest income of $25.

7. ENTRY IN ENDOWMENT PRINCIPAL FUND:
Interest Receivable on Investments.......... $2,600
    Earnings............................... $2,600
To record interest accrued on investments.

8. ENTRY IN ENDOWMENT PRINCIPAL FUND:
Earnings..................................   120
    Unamortized Premiums on Investments.....   120
To record amortization of premiums on investments.

9. (a) ENTRY IN ENDOWMENT PRINCIPAL FUND:
Earnings..............................   4,990
    Due to Endowment Earnings Fund.....   4,990
To record liability by endowment principal fund to endowment earnings fund for earnings to-date.

(b) ENTRY IN ENDOWMENT EARNINGS FUND:
Due from Endowment Principal Fund....   4,990
    Endowment Earnings Fund Balance....   4,990
To record amount due from endowment principal fund for earnings to-date.

10. (a) ENTRY IN ENDOWMENT PRINCIPAL FUND:
Due to Endowment Earnings Fund.......   2,500
    Cash...............................   2,500
To record payment of part of total amount due to endowment earnings fund.

(b) ENTRY IN ENDOWMENT EARNINGS FUND:
Cash..................................   2,500
    Due from Endowment Principal Fund...   2,500
To record receipt of part of total amount due from endowment principal fund.

11. ENTRY IN ENDOWMENT EARNINGS FUND:
Endowment Earnings Fund Balance..........   2,000
    Cash...............................   2,000
To record payment of scholarship.

If the preceding entries are posted to the accounts designated in each entry, the account balances will go to make up the endowment fund balance sheets illustrated in Figures 50 and 51.

If endowments are in the form of fixed properties, the latter constitute the principal fund, and the net income therefrom is transferred to an expendable fund. It is important, in such cases, to account carefully for the income and expenses of the principal fund, so that the net income may be properly computed. Depreciation must also be considered. Whether depreciation is charged as an expense or not will depend on the provisions of the grant. If the grant contemplates the replacement of worn-out property, depreciation must be charged and a reserve for replacements must be provided. On the other hand, if the property is not to be replaced, de-

Figure 50

A GOVERNMENTAL UNIT

Endowment Principal Fund

Balance Sheet
at Close of Fiscal Year

ASSETS

Cash..		$ 10,190
Investments...................................	$197,000	
Unamortized Premiums on Investments..........	2,713	199,713
Interest Receivable on Investments.......................		2,600
		$212,503

LIABILITIES AND BALANCE

Due to Endowment Earnings Fund........................	$ 2,490
Endowment Principal Fund Balance.......................	210,013
	$212,503

Figure 51

A GOVERNMENTAL UNIT

Endowment Earnings Fund

Balance Sheet
at Close of Fiscal Year

ASSETS

Cash..	$ 500
Due from Endowment Principal Fund.....................	2,490
	$ 2,990

BALANCE

Endowment Earnings Fund Balance.......................	$ 2,990

preciation need not be charged as an expense. Both the revenues and the expenses connected with administering the property—for example, rents, repairs, decorating expenses, and janitor's wages—would be accounted for in the principal fund. The net earnings would, however, be transferred to the earnings fund and expended for the purpose designated—for example, granting scholarships.

Agency funds. The following entries illustrate the operation of an agency fund. It is assumed that the fund is established by a governmental unit to account for the taxes which it collects for other units. As indicated on page 50, when a governmental unit levies a tax, it debits the Taxes Receivable—Current account and credits the Allowance for Uncollectible Current Taxes account and the Revenues account. If the tax is to be collected by another unit, the levying government certifies the amount to be placed on the tax roll. After the agency collecting the taxes has placed them on the roll, it records the transaction by the following entry:

Taxes Receivable for Other Units.............	$500,000	
Taxes Fund Balance......................		$500,000
To record 1955 taxes placed on the tax roll for other units as follows:		
For State.......................	$ 50,000	
For Cities.......................	300,000	
(List each city)		
For Schools.....................	150,000	
(List each school district)		
Total.......................	$500,000	

Separate subsidiary accounts are established to show the balance to the credit of each governmental unit on account of the taxes placed on the tax roll for it. Each account is further subdivided to show the amount of real property taxes and personal property taxes for each year's levy.

It is highly important to establish control accounts applicable to each governmental unit for each year's levy and to account for tax collections in such a manner that they can be identified with the particular year's levy to which they apply. The unit for which the taxes are collected must be informed of the amount collected from each levy if it is to credit the proper funds with the proceeds. Furthermore, under certain circumstances the collecting agency will not know the amount to be transmitted to each unit unless it can allocate the proceeds to the proper year of levy. For example, assume that a city collects not only its own taxes but also those of a school district, park district, and sanitary district which are co-terminus with it, and that each taxpayer's bill covers the taxes for all of these units. Assume further that for two years each unit has certified to the city the amount of its levy as follows:

	1955		1954	
Unit	Amount Levied	Percentage of Total	Amount Levied	Percentage of Total
City A[1]...................	$100,000	25.0	$ 91,200	24.0
School District B.........	200,000	50.0	188,100	49.5
Park District X..........	50,000	12.5	49,400	13.0
Sanitary District Y.......	50,000	12.5	51,300	13.5
	$400,000	100.0	$380,000	100.0

City A would receive 25 per cent of all collections of the 1955 levy. On the other hand, it would receive 24 per cent of all the tax collections of the

[1] Although these taxes are the taxes of the collecting governmental unit, they are treated in the same manner as if they were being collected for it by another unit, in order to simplify the accounting procedure.

1954 levy. For example, if total tax collections for a period of time were $100,000, of which $50,000 was from the 1955 levy and $50,000 was from the 1954 levy, City *A* would receive $12,500 from the 1955 levy and only $12,000 from the 1954 levy, even though the total collections for the period from the two levies were the same ($50,000). If, therefore, the collecting unit is to know the amount of each collection belonging to each levying unit, it must be able to identify these collections by year of levy. Interest and penalties are similarly identified, the same percentages being used for them as for the taxes to which they apply. Frequently, interest and penalties are not accrued by the collecting unit but are recorded only when they are actually collected. If they are accrued, the entry is a debit to Interest and Penalties Receivable on Taxes for Other Units and a credit to Taxes Fund Balance.

If we assume that interest and penalties are not accrued, the entry to record on the books of the collecting unit the collection of taxes and interest and penalties is as follows:

Cash....................................	$315,000	
Taxes Receivable for Other Units..........		$300,000
Taxes Fund Balance.....................		15,000

To record cash collected for the various units as follows:

			Levy of 1954	
Unit	Total	Levy of 1955	Taxes	Interest and Penalties
City A.....................	$ 77,850	$ 56,250	$18,000	$ 3,600
School District B...........	157,050	112,500	37,125	7,425
Park District X..............	39,825	28,125	9,750	1,950
Sanitary District Y..........	40,275	28,125	10,125	2,025
	$315,000	$225,000	$75,000	$15,000

If the taxes are paid over immediately after collection, the only additional entry is made when the money is paid over to the proper units and is as follows:

Taxes Fund Balance......................	$315,000	
Cash.................................		$315,000

To record paying over of amounts due to other units for taxes and interest and penalties collected for them, as follows: [The details for year of levy and amount would be the same as those shown in the explanation to the foregoing entry.]

As we have already seen, the unit for which the taxes are collected, upon receipt of the money, debits the Cash accounts of the proper funds and credits the proper Taxes Receivable accounts and the Interest and Penalties Receivable on Taxes accounts (if it does not accrue interest and penalties, the credit would be to a revenue account).

It must be remembered that, in addition to crediting tax collections to the proper units and to the proper levy, the collecting unit also credits individual taxpayers' accounts. The information for crediting each governmental unit with the proper amount of the collection from each levy and the data necessary for posting to the individual account of each taxpayer are obtained from the tax bills.

Of course, placing the tax on the roll, crediting the amounts to the proper accounts, and handling the collections involves considerable expense, and the collecting unit usually charges the other units for these services. Such charges are legitimate financial expenses, and appropriations are made for them in the budget. Usually the collecting unit, instead of billing the individual governmental units for such services and then proceeding to collect the amounts billed, retains a certain percentage of the collections as payment for its services. The entry to record this transaction in the agency fund is

Taxes Fund Balance..........................	$1,500	
Cash.......................................		$1,500
To record paying over to general fund collection fees charged other units and deducted from collections transmitted to them.		

The corresponding entry in the general fund to record this transaction is as follows:

Cash.......................................	$1,500	
Revenues..................................		$1,500
To record revenues from fees charged for placing taxes on roll and collecting taxes for other units.		

Each governmental unit that has received the services makes an entry similar to the following:

Cash..	$77,350	
Appropriation Expenditures....................	500	
Taxes Receivable—Current.................		$56,250
Taxes Receivable—Delinquent..............		18,000
Interest and Penalties Receivable on Taxes...		3,600
To record receipt of tax collections from collecting unit and to charge as appropriation expenditures the amount of collection fees paid. Subsidiary accounts: *Debit* Tax Collection Expenses, $500. *Credit*		

Levy of	Total	Taxes	Interest and Penalties
1955....................	$56,250	$56,250	
1954....................	21,600	18,000	$3,600
	$77,850	$74,250	$3,600

Figure 52

A GOVERNMENTAL UNIT

Agency Fund

Balance Sheet
at Close of Fiscal Year

ASSETS

Taxes Receivable for Other Units...................... $200,000

BALANCE

Taxes Fund Balance................................. $200,000

An entry similar to the foregoing is made in each fund affected. If, however, the collection fees are all paid out of the general fund, they are all charged to the Appropriation Expenditures account in that fund.

In Figure 52 above is an illustration of an agency fund balance sheet based on those foregoing entries which apply to the agency fund, except the first entry on the preceding page.

Combined statements for trust and agency funds. If numerous trust

Figure 53

A GOVERNMENTAL UNIT

Trust and Agency Funds

Balance Sheet
at Close of Fiscal Year

| | Total all Funds | EXPENDABLE FUNDS | | | | NONEXPENDABLE FUNDS | |
		Deposits Fund	Pension Fund	Endowment Earnings Fund	Agency Fund	Endowment Principal Fund	Loan Fund
ASSETS							
Cash...............	$ 57,140	$ 3,370	$ 2,060	$ 500		$ 10,190	$ 41,020
Loans Receivable......	59,000						59,000
Investments..........	$240,000	$15,000	$28,000			$197,000	
Unamortized Premiums .	2,958		245			2,713	
Total.............	$242,958	$15,000	$28,245			$199,713	
Less: Unamortized Discounts..............	75		75				
Total Investments..	$242,883	$15,000	$28,170			$199,713	
Interest Receivable on Investments.........	2,975		375			2,600	
Due from Endowment Principal Fund......	2,490			$2,490			
Taxes Receivable for Other Units (Specify Each Unit)..........	200,000				$200,000		
	$564,488	$18,370	$30,605	$2,990	$200,000	$212,503	$100,020
LIABILITIES, RESERVES, BALANCES, AND SURPLUS							
Liabilities:							
Pensions Payable....	$ 30		$ 30				
Due to Endowment Earnings Fund....	2,490					$ 2,490	
	$ 2,520		$ 30			$ 2,490	
Reserves.............	30,480		30,480				
Fund Balances........	531,393	$18,370		$2,990	$200,000	210,013	$100,020
Unappropriated Surplus..	95		95				
	$564,488	$18,370	$30,605	$2,990	$200,000	$212,503	$100,020

and agency funds exist, a combined balance sheet may be presented in columnar form as in the statement illustrated in Figure 53, or the principal statement might be limited to showing the data in the "Total" column. In that case, the statement in Figure 53 would serve as a subsidiary schedule, and reference would be made to it in the main statement.

Summary. The aim in trust fund accounting is to insure that the money is handled in accordance with the terms of the trust agreement. The accounting procedure for agency funds must insure that the collections will be properly handled and will be turned over promptly to the party for whom they are collected. Since these two objectives involve similar accounting procedures, the two types of funds have been treated together.

11

<<<<<<<<<<<<<<<<<<<<<<<<<<<<<<<<<<<<<<<<<<<<<<<<<<<<<<<<

WORKING CAPITAL FUNDS

A WORKING capital fund is established to finance internal service activities rendered to a government's own departments. This fund should be distinguished from a utility or other enterprise fund, which finances services rendered for compensation to the general public. The operation of prison industries, such as license-plate factories established in state penal institutions, cement plants, asphalt plants, central garages, central storerooms, and central printing plants are activities financed from working capital funds. Although working capital funds may be found in all governments, they are more likely to exist in states, counties, and municipalities. Again, they are more likely to be found in large governmental units.

A working capital fund should be accounted for on the same basis as a private business. The accounting system must make possible a comparison of income and expenses in order to determine whether income was equal to, fell short of, or exceeded expenses.

Ordinarily it is not necessary to prepare a budget for the activities financed by the working capital fund, since each department will have prepared estimates for its part of such activities. Although it may be desirable to combine all of these estimates and arrive at the total expenditures estimated to be financed by the fund, usually no appropriations are necessary for these expenditures.

Some municipalities, however, do not permit the spending of money from a working capital fund without an appropriation. Where this is the case, it is necessary to record not only those transactions which affect the actual operations of the working capital fund (that is, those transactions which affect the actual revenues, expenditures, assets, liabilities, reserves, and surplus) but also those which affect appropriations. In order to simplify the discussion, however, we shall first assume that appropriations are not made for the working capital fund and shall, therefore, illustrate only the proprietary operations—that is, those which affect the proprietary as distinct from the budgetary accounts of the working capital fund. Subsequently, we shall indicate the modifications in accounting procedure which are necessary to record appropriations.

Accounting for Proprietary Operations

A working capital fund is established by setting aside a certain sum of money for the fund's use. This money may be obtained by appropriation from the general fund, through the sale of bonds, and in some cases through capital advances from other governments. The fund continues to operate as long as the activity it finances is carried on. As the expenditures involved in carrying out these activities are incurred, the cash of the fund is reduced; but it is subsequently replenished by cash received for services.

Establishment of fund. The first step in the establishment of the fund is the receipt of capital. The entry to record this transaction is a debit to Cash and a credit to a Capital account. The next step is to secure the fixed assets with which the fund is to carry on its operations. Let us assume that the fund has reached the point where these assets have already been obtained and have been set up on the records. A balance sheet of the working capital fund would at this point, if we assume the figures shown, appear as illustrated in Figure 54.

Figure 54

A GOVERNMENTAL UNIT
Working Capital Fund
Balance Sheet
Date

ASSETS

Current Assets:		
Cash..		$ 75,000
Fixed Assets:		
Land..................................	$10,000	
Structures and Improvements..............	40,000	
Machinery...............................	10,000	60,000
		$135,000

CAPITAL

Capital...	$135,000

Operation of working capital fund. In studying the operations of the working capital fund, it is important to remember that the fund is intended to be self-supporting; that is, the accounting procedure must insure that the capital of the fund remains intact. Of course, it may be desirable to increase or decrease the capital of the fund. For example, activities may increase to such an extent as to make desirable an increase in capital, or they may decrease sufficiently to justify a decrease in capital. These are problems of financial administration and need not concern us particularly here. From an accounting standpoint it is important that capital increases or decreases should be reflected in the records.

In order to illustrate clearly the operation of a working capital fund, let us assume that the fund for which a balance sheet is presented in Figure 54 was established to finance the operation of a central automotive equipment bureau. Automotive equipment consists of automobiles, trucks, tractors, and similar equipment. The bureau may own the equipment, or it may merely service the equipment purchased by the various departments. Throughout the following discussion it is assumed that the bureau owns the automotive equipment, but we shall indicate subsequently the modifications in accounting procedure necessary to make the discussion applicable to the operations of central equipment bureaus which merely service the equipment.

Transactions and entries. The procedure in accounting for the operations of a central equipment bureau may be summarized as follows: The quantity of services rendered for various departments is recorded; that is, the hours or miles each piece of equipment serves each job or each department. A record is also kept of the cost of operating each piece of equipment. Subsequently, departments are billed for an amount sufficient to recover the full cost of rendering the service. The following transactions and entries illustrate more specifically how a central equipment bureau operates:

Transactions

1. Purchased equipment for $40,000.
2. Materials and supplies purchased for $10,000.
3. Salaries and wages paid, $19,000, distributed as follows:

Direct Labor	$9,000
Indirect Labor	3,000
Superintendent's Salary	3,500
Office Salaries	3,500

4. Heat, light, and power paid, $2,000.
5. Depreciation:

Structures and Improvements	$2,400
Machinery	1,200
Equipment	8,000

6. Total billings to departments for services rendered, $42,800, of which $30,000 is chargeable to the general fund and $12,800 is chargeable to the utility or other enterprise fund.
7. Vouchers payable to the amount of $42,500 paid.
8. Office expenses paid, $200.
9. Materials and supplies issued during period, $7,000.
10. Accrued salaries and wages, $1,000, distributed as follows:

Direct Labor............................	$ 500
Indirect Labor.........................	150
Superintendent's Salary.................	175
Office Salaries........................	175

Entries

1. Equipment.............................. $40,000
   Vouchers Payable.................... $40,000
   To record purchase of equipment.

2. Inventory of Materials and Supplies........ 10,000
   Vouchers Payable.................... 10,000
   To record purchase of materials and supplies.

3. Direct Labor........................... 9,000
   Indirect Labor......................... 3,000
   Superintendent's Salary.................. 3,500
   Office Salaries......................... 3,500
   Cash................................. 19,000
   To record expenses for salaries and wages.

4. Heat, Light, and Power.................. 2,000
   Cash................................. 2,000
   To record heat, light, and power expense.

5. Depreciation—Structures and Improvements 2,400
   Depreciation—Machinery................ 1,200
   Depreciation—Equipment................ 8,000
   Allowance for Depreciation—Structures
   and Improvements.................. 2,400
   Allowance for Depreciation—Machinery.. 1,200
   Allowance for Depreciation—Equipment.. 8,000
   To record depreciation expenses.

6. Due from General Fund.................. 30,000
   Due from Utility or Other Enterprise Fund.. 12,800
   Billings for Services................... 42,800
   To record billings to departments.

7. Vouchers Payable....................... 42,500
   Cash................................. 42,500
   To record payment of vouchers payable.

8. Office Expenses......................... 200
   Cash................................. 200
   To record miscellaneous office expenses.

9. Cost of Materials and Supplies Used....... 7,000
   Inventory of Materials and Supplies...... 7,000
   To record cost of materials and supplies used.

10. Direct Labor........................... 500
    Indirect Labor......................... 150
    Superintendent's Salary.................. 175
    Office Salaries......................... 175
    Accrued Salaries and Wages............ 1,000
    To record accrued salaries and wages.

Trial balance before closing entries. After these entries have been posted, the trial balance of the accounts of the working capital fund will appear as follows:

Cash..	$ 11,300	
Due from General Fund.....................	30,000	
Due from Utility or Other Enterprise Fund...	12,800	
Inventory of Materials and Supplies.........	3,000	
Land..	10,000	
Structures and Improvements...............	40,000	
Allowance for Depreciation—Buildings.......		$ 2,400
Machinery.................................	10,000	
Allowance for Depreciation—Machinery......		1,200
Equipment.................................	40,000	
Allowance for Depreciation—Equipment.....		8,000
Vouchers Payable..........................		7,500
Accrued Salaries and Wages................		1,000
Capital....................................		135,000
Billings for Services........................		42,800
Cost of Materials and Supplies Used.........	7,000	
Direct Labor..............................	9,500	
Indirect Labor............................	3,150	
Superintendent's Salary....................	3,675	
Depreciation—Structures and Improvements..	2,400	
Depreciation—Machinery..................	1,200	
Depreciation—Equipment..................	8,000	
Heat, Light, and Power....................	2,000	
Office Salaries............................	3,675	
Office Expenses...........................	200	
	$197,900	$197,900

Closing entries. Closing entries are made to arrive at the profit or loss for the period and to close the books. The following are the closing entries on the basis of the transactions illustrated above:

Direct Cost...............................	$ 24,500	
Cost of Materials and Supplies Used.......		$ 7,000
Direct Labor...........................		9,500
Depreciation—Equipment................		8,000
To record direct cost.		
Cost of Services Rendered..................	40,800	
Direct Cost............................		24,500
Indirect Labor.........................		3,150
Superintendent's Salary..................		3,675
Depreciation—Structures and Improvements		2,400
Depreciation—Machinery................		1,200
Heat, Light, and Power.................		2,000
Office Salaries.........................		3,675
Office Expenses........................		200
To record total cost of services rendered.		
Billings for Services.......................	42,800	
Cost of Services Rendered................		40,800
Net Income............................		2,000
To arrive at net income.		
Net Income...............................	2,000	
Unappropriated Surplus.................		2,000
To record transfer of net income to unappropriated surplus.		

Balance sheet after closing entries. The balance sheet, after closing entries, will be as follows:

Figure 55

A GOVERNMENTAL UNIT
Working Capital Fund
Balance Sheet
at Close of Fiscal Year

ASSETS

Current Assets:

Cash....................................	$11,300	
Due from General Fund....................	30,000	
Due from Utility or Other Enterprise Fund..	12,800	
Inventory of Materials and Supplies........	3,000	$ 57,100

Fixed Assets:

Land....................................		$10,000	
Structures and Improvements.....	$40,000		
Less—Allowance for Depreciation..	2,400	37,600	
Machinery......................	$10,000		
Less—Allowance for Depreciation..	1,200	8,800	
Equipment......................	$40,000		
Less—Allowance for Depreciation..	8,000	32,000	88,400
			$145,500

LIABILITIES, CAPITAL, AND SURPLUS

Liabilities:

Vouchers—Payable.......................	$ 7,500	
Accrued Salaries and Wages..............	1,000	$ 8,500
Capital...		135,000
Unappropriated Surplus............................		2,000
		$145,500

The fixed assets employed in carrying out the operations of the working capital fund are included in its balance sheet. These assets are responsible for the accrual of revenues to the fund in the same manner as inventories. Their existence is essential to the operation of the enterprise. Consequently, the cost of these assets must be recovered through depreciation charges. Since departments are billed for overhead charges, including depreciation, part of the money received from departments represents depreciation charges. The money representing depreciation charges may be set up in a separate fund to insure its availability to replace assets, or it may be made part of the working capital fund's general cash and used for various purposes, pending the replacement of the assets. In the present case, it is assumed that no segregation is made.

The accounting procedure involved in making the segregation is discussed in Chapter 16.

Bonds sold for working capital fund purposes are not shown in the working capital fund balance sheet, unless the resources of the fund are used to pay off these bonds. Usually, however, such bonds will be paid out of general taxation or sources such as utility earnings (in the case of working capital funds furnishing services to a utility department). However, if a working capital fund is dissolved, some of its assets may be used to retire bonds still outstanding.

Income and expense statement. The income and expense statement of a working capital fund is similar to an industrial or commercial income and expense statement. This similarity is evident from the statement presented below, which is based on the entries previously illustrated.

Figure 56

A GOVERNMENTAL UNIT
Working Capital Fund
Income and Expense Statement
for Period

Billings for Services		$42,800
Less—Direct Costs:		
Materials and Supplies	$7,000	
Direct Labor	9,500	
Depreciation—Equipment	8,000	24,500
Gross Profit		$18,300
Less—Other Costs:		
Indirect Labor	$3,150	
Superintendent's Salary	3,675	
Depreciation—Structures and Improvements	2,400	
Depreciation—Machinery	1,200	
Heat, Light, and Power	2,000	
Office Salaries	3,675	
Office Expenses	200	16,300
Net Income		$ 2,000

As intimated before, the above procedure applies to those cases where a central equipment bureau owns the equipment. However, the procedure would not be materially different if the equipment was owned by the individual departments. In fact, the only difference is that billings to departments would be reduced by the amount of the depreciation charges. Depreciation may be computed in such an event, but the computation would be made merely for statistical purposes to determine the total cost, including depreciation, of operating each piece of equipment. In other words, depreciation of equipment would not be included as part of the expenses of operating the central equipment bureau, nor would depreciation charges be included in the income and expense statement. The cost of the new equipment would be recorded as an appropriation expenditure and charged against the appropriation of the particular organization unit for which the equipment was purchased.

Even if the fixed assets are owned by the various departments, they should be carried as part of the working capital fund and valued at their cost to the original department donating them. In the first place, these assets are used in carrying on the activities of the fund. Secondly, the reporting of such assets as part of the fund is essential if the proper officials are to be held responsible for their custody. Thirdly, for replacement purposes it is necessary to be able to identify the assets with the fund. Finally, the identification of assets is necessary also for the purpose of preparing depreciation data. No allowance for depreciation need be provided, but a notation should be made opposite each fixed asset account to indicate the cumulative amount of depreciation. This amount would be based on the depreciation charges calculated for statistical purposes.

Relationship between billings for services and net income. Whether a working capital fund operates at a profit, at a loss, or on a break-even basis will depend on the amount charged departments. Charges to departments may be made sufficiently high to result in a profit, they may be made so low that a loss results, or they may be sufficient merely to keep the capital intact—that is, to recover only the actual cost. Usually charges should be made large enough to recover only actual costs, because the fund is established to render a service and not to make a profit.

Frequently, however, the equipment bureau will operate at a profit or a loss, even though the charges are intended to cover only the cost of operating the equipment. The reason will become apparent after we examine the procedure followed in charging departments for services. This procedure may be described briefly as follows: A record is kept of the number of miles or the number of hours each piece of equipment works for each department. The amount to be charged is arrived at by multiplying the rental rate for the piece of equipment by the number of miles it covers or the number of hours it is used. A separate rental rate is established for each piece of equipment, based on the estimated cost of operation. The procedure for arriving at the cost is described in Chapter 21.

Were it possible to base the rental rates on actual cost determined at the close of a fiscal year, the working capital fund would seldom end its operations with either a profit or a loss. However, a predetermined rental rate is generally used for the following reasons: Some expenses are not determinable until the end of the month, whereas it may be desirable to bill departments before that time so that they may know how much expense to charge to jobs and activities at any time. Furthermore, charges based on actual monthly costs are likely to spread the burden unequally among departments. For example, assume that extensive repairs had been made on a truck in June. If the actual cost incurred in that month were charged to the departments which used the equipment in June, they would be charged with the cost of the repairs, whereas departments which used the equipment in several previous or succeeding months would escape these charges. Furthermore, even if one department used the equipment throughout the entire year, charges based on actual cost would, in the above case, result in an unequal distribution of the burden among jobs and activities carried on by the particular department as between June and other months.

As already indicated, rental rates may be expressed in terms of miles or hours. For passenger automobiles, the rates usually are expressed in terms of miles, whereas for trucks, tractors, and similar equipment the rate is expressed in terms of hours. The rates are estimated as follows: At the beginning of each year the miles or hours which the equipment will work during the year are estimated. The cost of operating the particular piece of equipment is also forecast. The rate per mile or hour is then arrived at by dividing the total estimated cost by the estimated number of miles or hours of use. For example, assume that it is expected that during the year a certain automobile will cost $600 to operate and will cover 12,000 miles. The rental charge would in that case be $.05 per mile, and each department using the automobile would be charged at that rate.

The fact that a predetermined rental rate is based on estimates has some disadvantages. If estimates are correct, the amount of earned rentals for each piece of equipment should closely approximate the cost of operating the piece of equipment. In practice, however, because of an overestimate or an underestimate of cost or of the amount of miles or hours run, the amount of earned rentals will be greater or smaller than actual cost. Theoretically, both the charges arising out of the excess of cost over rentals and the credit arising out of the excess of rentals over cost should be allocated among the various departments. It may, however, be impossible or impracticable to correct the previous charges, and the working capital fund will therefore end its operations with a profit or a loss. If the operations of the fund have resulted in a profit, the customary procedure is to lower the rates for the following period, so that the profit may be absorbed through the loss which will result from the lower rate. If, on the other hand, operations result in losses, these may be made up through raising the rates for the succeeding period. If profits are small, they are frequently retained in the fund to absorb losses.

Central stores bureau. Another example of accounting for working capital fund transactions is to be found in a central stores bureau. Such a bureau is established for the purpose of purchasing and storing materials for eventual distribution to departments. To simplify the discussion, it is assumed no appropriations are required for the bureau's expenditures.

The first step in the accounting process occurs here when the invoice is approved for payment. At that time, an entry is made to record the expenditure and to set up the liability. The entry is as follows:

Inventory of Materials and Supplies............	$20,000	
Vouchers Payable.........................		$20,000
To record the purchase of materials and supplies.		

Note that the debit is not made to a Purchases account but directly to an Inventory of Materials and Supplies account. The reason is that, where a central storeroom is in operation, perpetual inventory records should be kept.

The procedure in recording on the perpetual inventory cards the materials and supplies received is as follows: A separate card similar to that illustrated in Figure 57 is set up for each item carried in stock. The receipt of materials is entered on these cards. Some governmental units enter only the quantity received, whereas others enter also the total cost and the unit price. Freight charges are a part of the cost of the materials. The unit price, therefore, may be said to consist of the purchase price plus transportation expenses divided by the number of units purchased. Frequently, however, even if the unit price is entered on the stock card, the total cost of the materials received or on hand is not shown on the card.

Materials purchased for central storerooms are not charged against appropriations until they are actually withdrawn by departments. The procedure in withdrawing materials and charging appropriations is as follows: When a department needs materials, it fills out a stores requisition. This requisition is made out at least in duplicate and is presented to the storekeeper. The storekeeper hands over the amounts called for on the requisition and has the employee receiving the materials sign one copy of the requisition. This copy is retained by the storekeeper as evidence that the materials have been withdrawn and is also used as the basis of posting to the proper stock cards the amount of units withdrawn to reduce the amount shown by the card to be on hand. Subsequently, individual items on the requisition are priced and the total cost of materials withdrawn on the particular requisition is computed. Sometimes requisitions are priced before they are filled, in order to see that the cost of materials requisitioned does not exceed the amount available to the credit of the appropriation, but this procedure is not always practicable.

Requisitions are priced by multiplying the number of units withdrawn by the unit price. However, different units may have been acquired at

Figure 57

A GOVERNMENTAL UNIT
Stock Record

Location _____ Description _____ Article _____

Maximum _____ Minimum _____

No.	Vendor	No.	Vendor	No.	Vendor
1		4		7	
2		5		8	
3		6		9	

RECEIVED					ISSUED				ISSUED			
Date	Vendor Number	Quantity	Cost	Unit Price	Date	Requisition Number	Quantity Issued	Balance on Hand	Date	Requisition Number	Quantity Issued	Balance on Hand
1	2	3	4	5	6	7	8	9	10	11	12	13

172

different prices. For example, let us assume that receipts, unit costs, and withdrawals of a certain type of material were as follows:

Date Received	Number of Units Received	Cost per Unit	Units Withdrawn	Number of Units on Hand
Jan. 20	1,000	$1.00	—	1,000
Jan. 28	500	1.05	—	1,500
Feb. 15	2,500	1.06	—	4,000
Feb. 25	—	—	2,500	1,500

It would usually be found impracticable to determine from which shipment the 2,500 units withdrawn were taken. One of the simplest methods of pricing requisitions is to assume that the materials first received were those first used. The above requisition would, under this assumption, be priced as follows:

Number of Units Withdrawn	Cost per Unit	Cost of Materials Withdrawn
1,000	$1.00	$1,000
500	1.05	525
1,000	1.06	1,060
2,500		$2,585

Governmental units also use other methods of pricing requisitions. For example, an equally common method in larger governmental units is to compute a new average unit cost every time a shipment of materials is received. The first-in, first-out method of pricing materials is therefore presented merely as an example.

As we have indicated, the unit price includes the purchase price plus transportation expenses. If the working capital fund is to be kept intact, it is necessary also to recover overhead costs, such as the salary of the purchasing agent, wages of storekeepers, and amounts expended for heat, light, and power. Usually these expenses are allocated to each requisition as a predetermined percentage of the cost of the materials withdrawn. The percentage is determined by dividing the estimated total stores expenses by the total estimated cost of materials to be issued. To illustrate the procedure, assume that total stores expenses for the forthcoming year are estimated to be $20,000 and that the cost of the materials which will be withdrawn during the same period is estimated to be $500,000. In that case, the overhead rate applicable to materials issued is 4 per cent ($20,000 ÷ $500,000), and the amount of overhead to be charged to the requisition illustrated above is $103.40 (4 per cent of $2,585).

As soon as the requisition is priced, information is available for the purpose of billing the department withdrawing the materials. The entry to record the billing is as follows:

Due from General Fund...................... $2,688.40
    Sales of Materials to Departments............ $2,688.40
To record issuance of materials and supplies to
Department of Public Works on Requisition 1405.

Note that the general fund is billed for both the cost of the materials and a portion of the estimated overhead expenses ($2,585 + $103.40). At the time the materials are withdrawn, an entry is made to record the direct cost of the materials issued, the entry being

Cost of Materials Issued........................... $2,585
    Inventory of Materials and Supplies.............. $2,585
To record cost of materials issued to Department of
Public Works on Requisition 1405.

Entries to record actual overhead expenses in the working capital fund are made at the time the expenses are incurred and not at the time materials are issued. For example, at the time that storekeepers' salaries are approved for payment the following entry is made:

Operating Expenses............................... $1,000
    Vouchers Payable................................ $1,000
To record storekeepers' salaries. Subsidiary account:
Debit Salaries and Wages, $1,000.

At the end of the year, if overhead rates have been correctly estimated, the exact amount of overhead will have been recovered. Otherwise, the working capital fund will have either underabsorbed or overabsorbed overhead.

Under the system of accounting for materials described here, the inventory of materials on hand can be ascertained from the records at any time. To insure that the materials as shown by the records are actually on hand, a physical inventory is taken at least annually. Usually the actual amount of materials on hand as revealed by a physical count will be smaller than the amount shown by the records. The variation may be due to such factors as shrinkage, breakage, theft, or improper recording. In any event, the records must be adjusted to correspond with the actual physical count by making entries on each perpetual inventory card affected. The Inventory of Materials and Supplies account in the general ledger must also be adjusted. The procedure is as follows: The units of each type of material not accounted for (that is, the difference between the number of units shown by the records and the number revealed by the actual count) are priced in the same manner as materials issued on requisitions. These amounts are then totaled to arrive at the cost of materials not accounted for by requisitions, and an entry is subsequently made in the general ledger reducing or increasing the inventory valuation carried. If it is assumed that the amounts according to physical count are less than the amounts shown on the records, the entry is as follows:

```
Inventory Losses............................    $2,000
    Inventory of Materials and Supplies..........              $2,000
    To record inventory losses as revealed by actual
    physical count.
```

Inventory losses represent one of the costs which the working capital fund must recover if the capital of the fund is to be kept intact. Consequently, the Inventory Losses account is considered one of the overhead costs, in the same manner, for example, as storekeepers' salaries. And, in estimating the overhead expenses of the central storeroom for the purpose of establishing the overhead rate to be applied to requisitions, inventory losses are taken into account. In other words, departments must be charged a sufficient amount to recover (1) the actual cost of the materials withdrawn, (2) overhead expenses, and (3) losses on inventories.

A balance sheet like the one illustrated in Figure 55 and an income and expense statement similar to the one illustrated in Figure 56 are prepared at the end of the year or at more frequent intervals. The income and expense statement shows the sales to departments, the direct cost of the materials issued, and overhead expenses (including inventory losses). The procedure in disposing of net income or net losses resulting from overabsorbed or underabsorbed overhead expenses is the same as for a central equipment bureau financed from a working capital fund.

Thus far we have discussed the entries to be made in the working capital fund. Corresponding entries are, of course, made for the departments receiving the particular materials. In the case of a public works department whose activities are financed from the general fund, the entry is as follows:

```
Appropriation Expenditures...................   $2,688.40
    Due to Working Capital Fund...............               $2,688.40
    To record receipt of materials by the Department
    of Public Works and its liability to working capital
    fund. Subsidiary account: Debit Department of
    Public Works, $2,688.40.
```

Materials withdrawn by departments from a central storeroom and on hand at the close of the year should be treated the same as materials on hand at the close of the year which have been acquired by direct purchase.

Sometimes a storeroom system for a single department is financed from a working capital fund. Materials and supplies in that case are accounted for in the same manner as those handled through a central storeroom established for all departments.

Dissolution of working capital fund. When the services financed by a working capital fund are no longer needed, or when some preferable method of financing them is found, the fund is dissolved. The net current assets of a dissolved fund are usually transferred to the funds from which the capital was originally secured. However, as stated before, if capital was secured through the issuance of bonds, the net current assets are not transferred to the bond fund but to the fund which will retire the bonds.

Fixed assets are usually transferred to the department or departments which have contributed the capital or to other departments which can use them best. Unless transferred to one of the governmental unit's utilities or other enterprises, the assets are recorded with the general fixed assets of the government. If transferred to a utility or other enterprise, they are set up as part of the enterprise fund. Proceeds from the sale of such assets are handled in the same manner as other current assets.

Accounting for Budgetary Operations

Thus far we have assumed that no appropriations to spend money were made by the legislative body of the governmental unit for working capital funds. In this section, we shall point out the modifications in accounting procedure necessary to record appropriations. In other words, the accounting procedure thus far outlined is also applicable in its entirety to working capital funds which are subject to appropriations, but these funds require additional accounting.

Accounting for appropriations. If an activity financed from a working capital fund is to be operated as a self-supporting enterprise, appropriation accounts and the expenditures chargeable to them must be kept separate and distinct from the proprietary accounts, for many of the transactions affecting appropriations do not affect the profit or loss of the working capital fund and vice versa. For example, expenditures for fixed assets do not affect profits or losses but they are charges against appropriations. On the other hand, depreciation expenses reduce profits, but usually no appropriation is made for them and they therefore do not affect appropriations.

It is also evident from the above that there is no relationship between the estimated revenues of a working capital fund and the appropriations made for it. Thus, as we have seen, appropriations are frequently made for some expenditures which are not chargeable against revenues (for example, the acquisition of fixed assets), and no appropriations are made for some expenses chargeable to revenues (for example, depreciation expenses). Accordingly, appropriations are not offset by estimated revenues but by an account indicating budgetary requirements. For example, if we assume the figures illustrated, the entry setting up appropriations for a working capital fund is as follows:

Budget Requirements......................	$80,000	
Appropriations..........................		$80,000
To record appropriations.		

Since revenue estimates are not ordinarily subject to legal limitation or control, they need not be formally recorded. A memorandum account showing such estimates should, however, be kept.

Charging expenditures and encumbrances to appropriations. The following transactions and entries illustrate how appropriations are recorded and controlled. These transactions are similar to the ones given on page 164. It is thus possible to note readily what additional entries are necessary to record and to control appropriations.

Transactions

1. Equipment estimated to cost $40,500 was ordered.
2. The equipment was received; the actual cost was $40,000.
3. Materials and supplies estimated to cost $9,700 were ordered.
4. The materials and supplies were received; the actual cost was $10,000.
5. Salaries and wages paid, $19,000.
6. Heat, light, and power paid, $2,000.
7. Office expenses paid, $200.
8. A purchase order was placed for materials estimated to cost $5,000.
9. Accrued salaries and wages, $1,000.

Entries

1. Encumbrances............................ $40,500
      Reserve for Encumbrances............... $40,500
   To record placing order for equipment.

2. (a) Reserve for Encumbrances............. 40,500
        Encumbrances.....................   40,500
   To reverse entries setting up encumbrances.

   (b) Appropriation Expenditures........... 40,000
        Budget Requirements................   40,000
   To record reduction of budget requirements and appropriations on account of equipment purchased.

3. Encumbrances........................... 9,700
      Reserve for Encumbrances...............   9,700
   To record order placed for materials and supplies.

4. (a) Reserve for Encumbrances............. 9,700
        Encumbrances.....................   9,700
   To reverse entry setting up encumbrances.

   (b) Appropriation Expenditures........... 10,000
        Budget Requirements................   10,000
   To record reduction of budget requirements and appropriations on account of purchase of materials and supplies.

5. Appropriation Expenditures................ 19,000
      Budget Requirements..................   19,000
   To record reduction of budget requirements and appropriations on account of salaries and wages paid.

6. Appropriation Expenditures................ $2,000
    Budget Requirements................... $2,000
    To record reduction of budget requirements
    and appropriations on account of heat, light,
    and power expenses paid.

7. Appropriation Expenditures................   200
    Budget Requirements...................   200
    To record reduction of budget requirements
    and appropriations by amount of office expenses
    paid.

8. Encumbrances...........................   5,000
    Reserve for Encumbrances..............   5,000
    To record purchase order placed for materials
    and supplies.

9. Appropriation Expenditures................   1,000
    Budget Requirements...................   1,000
    To record reduction of budget requirements
    and appropriations by amount of accrued sal-
    aries and wages.

The foregoing entries are based on the assumption that appropriations are charged as soon as expenditures are incurred, regardless of when they are paid, but that no adjustments are made for appropriation expenditures applicable to more than one year. For example, it is assumed that no adjustment is made in the budgetary accounts for materials purchased during the year which have remained on hand at the close of the year. Again, it is assumed that depreciation is not charged to appropriations. These assumptions are in accordance with conditions existing in many governmental units but not in all. For example, some governmental units record their budgetary operations on a cash basis; that is, they do not record revenues until the money has been collected, and they do not record expenditures as charges against appropriations until the money is paid out. (However, they encumber appropriations as soon as an order is placed.) In determining whether and when an expenditure is chargeable against an appropriation, therefore, it is necessary to know the basis of accounting followed and to have some knowledge of the budgetary procedure of the particular governmental unit.

Trial balance before closing entries. Assuming the foregoing entries had been posted, the trial balance would be as follows:

Budget Requirements........................	$ 7,800	
Appropriation Expenditures..................	72,200	
Encumbrances..............................	5,000	
Reserve for Encumbrances...................		$ 5,000
Appropriations.............................		80,000
	$85,000	$85,000

Closing entries for the budgetary group. The closing entries are made for the purpose of determining to what extent appropriation expenditures exceed or are under appropriations and to close out the budgetary ac-counts. However, if encumbrances are outstanding at the close of the fiscal year, a sufficient balance to cover these encumbrances must be retained in the Budget Requirements account. The entries are as follows:

Appropriations...............................	$80,000	
Appropriation Expenditures.................		$72,200
Encumbrances.............................		5,000
Unappropriated Budget Surplus.............		2,800

To close out appropriations, appropriation ex-penditures, and encumbrances and to determine the excess of appropriations over expenditures and encumbrances or vice versa.

Unappropriated Budget Surplus..............	2,800	
Budget Requirements.....................		2,800

To close out account showing unappropriated budget surplus and part of account showing budget requirements.

Balance sheet. The balance sheet of the budgetary group of accounts after closing entries are posted contains only accounts to show budget requirements for encumbrances outstanding at the close of the fiscal year. If we assume the closing entries illustrated, the statement would appear as shown in Figure 58.

Figure 58

A GOVERNMENTAL UNIT

Working Capital Fund

Balance Sheet—Budgetary Group
at Close of Fiscal Year

Budget Requirements..................	$5,000
Reserve for Encumbrances.............	$5,000

As the actual amount of the expenditure is determined during the fol-lowing year, an entry is made debiting the Reserve for Encumbrances account and crediting the Budget Requirements account by the amount of the encumbrances (in this case, $5,000).

Summary. The accounting procedure for a working capital fund is similar in most respects to that of a business enterprise carrying on like activities. As in business, it is important to determine whether the enter-prise is being operated at a profit or a loss or whether it is breaking even. Frequently appropriations are not made for the working capital fund and the accounting is limited to proprietary operations. If, however, appropriations are made, it is also necessary to provide a self-balancing group of budgetary accounts.

12

<<<<<<<<<<<<<<<<<<<<<<<<<<<<<<<<<<<<<<<<<<<<<<<<<<<<<<<<<<<<<<

UTILITY OR OTHER ENTERPRISE FUNDS

UTILITY OR other enterprise funds are established to account for the financing of self-supporting enterprises which render services primarily to the public. These funds must be distinguished from working capital funds, which are established to finance services rendered to other departments of the governmental unit. Electric plants, water plants, gas plants, and sewer systems are examples of utilities while public markets, parking facilities, public housing, and municipal airports are examples of other enterprises. Although the accounting procedure may vary with each enterprise, the same principles apply to all of them. In all cases, the fund must be accounted for in the same manner as a commercial enterprise. That is, the financial operations of the fund must be so recorded that it is possible to determine whether the utility or other enterprise is being operated at a profit or a loss.

The present chapter deals for the most part with the accounting procedure and financial statements of utilities. Part of it is, however, devoted to a brief discussion of accounting for other enterprises and contains illustrations of the financial statements to be prepared for them.

Appropriations for utility or other enterprise funds. Before proceeding to a discussion of the accounting for utilities and other enterprises, we should like to point out the fact that, since sound financial administration requires that these entities be self-supporting, it is not desirable to control their expenditures rigidly by means of appropriations. For example, an increase in expenditures may be highly desirable if it is due to an increase in the number of customers, because ordinarily an increase in customers means a reduction in unit costs. If, however, these expenditures are controlled by means of inflexible appropriations, the necessary expansion of activities may be delayed.

In spite of the undesirability of the practice, many governmental units continue to make appropriations for utilities or other enterprises in the same manner as for other departments. Where this is true, it is necessary, as in the case of working capital funds, to record not only those transactions which affect the actual operations of the utility or other enterprise (that is, those transactions which affect the actual revenues, expenditures, assets, liabilities, reserves, and surplus) but also those which affect appropriations. In order to simplify the discussion, we shall assume that appropriations are not made for the utility or other enterprise. The modifications in accounting which are necessary to record appropriations for self-supported enterprises are outlined in Chapter 11 (pages 176-179). These modifications apply alike to working capital funds, utility funds, and other enterprise funds.

Accounting for Utilities

Establishment of fund and acquisition of plant. The acquisition of a utility may be financed by the sale of bonds to be retired from utility earnings, by contributions from a governmental unit, and by contributions from prospective customers. If we assume that the acquisition of a utility plant is financed through a contribution from the operating governmental unit, the entry to record the receipt of the contribution and the establishment of the fund is as follows:

Cash...................................	$400,000	
Governmental Unit's Contribution.........		$400,000
To record governmental unit's contribution for acquisition of utility.		

The next step is the acquisition of the plant. To simplify the discussion, let us assume further that a private water plant, already operating, is acquired. The entries to record the acquisition are as follows:

Land.....................................	$200,000	
Structures and Improvements...............	500,000	
Equipment...............................	150,000	
Accounts Receivable.......................	62,000	
Inventory of Materials and Supplies.........	10,000	
Allowance for Depreciation—Structures and Improvements.......................		$ 80,000
Allowance for Depreciation—Equipment....		40,000
Allowance for Uncollectible Accounts.......		12,000
Bonds Payable..........................		500,000
Vouchers Payable.......................		10,000
ABC Water Works Company.............		280,000
To record the acquisition of the assets and liabilities of the ABC Water Works Company.		

ABC Water Works Company...............	280,000	
Cash.................................		280,000
To record payment to ABC Water Works Company.		

Operation of fund. The following transactions and entries illustrate the operation of the utility fund. However, the procedure in accounting for (1) the receipt and expenditure of bond proceeds, (2) utility sinking funds, and (3) customers' deposits requires special attention and is not illustrated in this section but is discussed separately later. To simplify the discussion, all revenues, with the exception of interest revenues, are assumed to be credited to an Operating Revenues account, and all expenses, with the exception of depreciation, taxes, and interest, are assumed to be charged to an Operating Expenses account. The detailed revenue and expense accounts are listed and discussed later in the chapter.

Transactions

1. Total salaries and wages paid, $127,200.
2. Materials costing $59,000 were received.
3. Revenues billed during the year, $300,000.
4. Equipment costing $50,500 was purchased.
5. Telephone and telegraph paid, $500.
6. The allowance for estimated losses on accounts receivable was found to be overstated by $7,000.
7. Fire insurance paid in advance, $1,000 (2-year policy).
8. Collections on accounts receivable, $290,000.
9. Bill received from working capital fund for services rendered, $12,800.
10. Bonds paid, $50,000.
11. Interest paid, $20,000.
12. Interest received, $1,000.
13. Taxes paid, $10,500.
14. Vouchers payable to the amount of $70,000 paid.
15. Necessary adjusting entries were made as follows:

(a) Accrued salaries and wages	$6,000
(b) Accrued interest payable	2,000
(c) Accrued interest receivable	200
(d) Taxes accrued	7,500
(e) Prepaid insurance	600
(f) Closing inventory	30,000
(g) Estimated losses on accounts receivable	1,500
(h) Depreciation:	
Structures and improvements	20,000
Equipment	16,000

Entries

1. Operating Expenses	$127,200	
Cash		$127,200
To record payment of salaries and wages.		
2. Inventory of Materials and Supplies	59,000	
Vouchers Payable		59,000
To record purchase of materials.		
3. Accounts Receivable	300,000	
Operating Revenues		300,000
To record operating revenues.		

4. Equipment.................................. $50,500
    Vouchers Payable........................ $50,500
    To record purchase of equipment.

5. Operating Expenses........................ 500
    Cash....................................   500
 . To record telephone and telegraph expenses.

6. Allowance for Uncollectible Accounts......... 7,000
    Unappropriated Surplus..................   7,000
    To record adjustment of allowance for esti-
    mated losses on accounts receivable.

7. Operating Expenses........................ 1,000
    Cash....................................   1,000
    To record insurance expenses.

8. Cash..................................... 290,000
    Accounts Receivable.....................   290,000
    To record collection of accounts receivable.

9. Operating Expenses........................ 12,800
    Due to Working Capital Fund.............   12,800
    To record cost of services rendered by working
    capital fund.

10. Bonds Payable............................ 50,000
    Cash....................................   50,000
    To record retirement of part of issue of serial
    bonds.

11. Interest Expenses.......................... 20,000
    Cash....................................   20,000
    To record payment of interest.

12. Cash..................................... 1,000
    Interest Revenues.......................   1,000
    To record receipt of interest revenues.

13. Taxes.................................... 10,500
    Cash....................................   10,500
    To record payment of taxes.

14. Vouchers Payable.......................... 70,000
    Cash....................................   70,000
    To record payment of vouchers.

15. (a) Operating Expenses..................... 6,000
        Accrued Salaries and Wages...........   6,000
        To record salaries and wages accrued.

   (b) Interest Expenses..................... 2,000
        Interest Payable.....................   2,000
        To record accrued interest payable.

   (c) Interest Receivable.................... 200
        Interest Revenues....................   200
        To record accrued interest receivable.

   (d) Taxes................................. 7,500
        Accrued Taxes.......................   7,500
        To record accrued taxes.

(e) Prepaid Insurance......................	$600	
Operating Expenses....................		$600
To record setting up of amount of unexpired insurance.		
(f) Operating Expenses......................	39,000	
Inventory of Materials and Supplies....		39.000
To record operating expenses in connection with materials used during year.		
(g) Operating Expenses......................	1,500	
Allowance for Uncollectible Accounts...		1,500
To record estimated losses on accounts receivable.		
(h) Depreciation............................	36,000	
Allowance for Depreciation—Structures and Improvements.................		20,000
Allowance for Depreciation—Equipment		16,000
To record depreciation for fiscal year.		

Accounting for construction financed through the sale of bonds. The accounting procedure to be followed in accounting for construction financed through the sale of bonds is not unlike the procedure for accounting for private construction. However, if the construction and the bonds to be issued to finance it require authorization by the governmental unit, it is necessary to account not only for the receipt and expenditure of the bond proceeds but also for the authorizations. The accounting procedure for the authorizations and charges thereto are the same as those outlined for general bonds in Chapter 10. In addition, the entries following the list of transactions below must be made. Of course, if no authorization by the governmental unit is required, these would be the only entries needed and the entries relating to authorizations could be dispensed with.

Transactions

1. Bonds to the amount of $200,000 were sold at a premium of $2,000.
2. A contract was entered into with Smith & Company for the construction of part of the project at a cost of $100,000.
3. Materials costing $41,000 were purchased by the utility.
4. The bill for materials was paid.
5. A bill for $30,000 was received from Smith & Company.
6. Smith & Company was paid.
7. The utility paid $56,000, representing the cost of labor and supervisory expenses.
8. Smith & Company conmpleted its part of the project and submitted its bill for $70,000.
9. Smith & Company was paid in full except for $10,000, which was retained pending the final approval of the project.
10. The completed project was found to be satisfactory and was set up on the records as a fixed asset.
11. Smith & Company was paid the final amount due it.
12. The remaining bond cash was transferred to the sinking fund.

Entries

```
1. Bond Cash.............................. $200,000
   Cash...................................    2,000
      Unamortized Premiums on Bonds..........           $  2,000
      Bonds Payable..........................            200,000
   To record sale of bonds at a premium.
```

The subsequent treatment of the premium will depend on whether or not premiums are amortized. If they are, the amount of interest expense will be reduced each period by the amount of premium amortized. If the bonds had been sold at a discount, the entry would be a debit to Bond Cash for $198,000, a debit to Unamortized Discounts on Bonds for $2,000, and a credit to Bonds Payable for $200,000. Since discounts represent an adjustment of the interest rate, bond cash should theoretically be replenished for the amount of the discount; after all, bond cash is to be used only for construction and not for the payment of interest. Because of legal complications, this procedure is not always possible. Even if bond cash is not increased by the amount of the discount, the latter is not charged as a construction cost. Discounts, like premiums, may or may not be amortized. If they are amortized, that part of the discount applicable to the construction period may, as indicated below, be capitalized.

```
2. No entry necessary here to record making of
   contract.

3. Work in Progress......................... $ 41,000
      Vouchers Payable........................           $ 41,000
   To record cost of construction materials.

4. Vouchers Payable.........................   41,000
      Bond Cash...............................             41,000
   To record payment of bill for materials.

5. Work in Progress.........................   30,000
      Contracts Payable.......................             30,000
   To record receipt of bill from Smith & Company
   for part of cost of contract.

6. Contracts Payable........................   30,000
      Bond Cash...............................             30,000
   To record payment of amount due on contract.

7. Work in Progress.........................   56,000
      Bond Cash...............................             56,000
   To record cost of labor and supervisory ex-
   penses.

8. Work in Progress.........................   70,000
      Contracts Payable.......................             70,000
   To record receipt of bill from Smith & Company
   to cover remaining cost of contract.

9. Contracts Payable........................   70,000
      Bond Cash...............................             60,000
      Contracts Payable—Retained Percentage...             10,000
```

To record payment of amount due on contract and retention of part of amount due pending final approval of project.

10. Structures and Improvements................ $197,000

    Work in Progress......................... $197,000

    To close out Work in Progress account and to set up cost of completed structures and improvements.

11. Contracts Payable—Retained Percentage..... 10,000

    Bond Cash.............................. 10,000

    To record final payment to contractor.

12. (a) Sinking Fund Cash..................... 3,000

    Bond Cash.......................... 3,000

    To record transfer of unused bond proceeds to sinking fund.

    (b) Unappropriated Surplus[1]............... 3,000

    Reserve for Retirement of Sinking Fund Bonds............................. 3,000

    To reserve part of unappropriated surplus on account of transfer of cash to sinking fund.

As in commercial accounting, interest expenses during the construction period on money borrowed to finance the construction should be capitalized. And, even if the governmental unit does not borrow any money for construction, it may capitalize the interest it would have had to pay if it had borrowed money for this purpose. The reason is that, until the project is completed and is in a position to earn revenue, the utility is being deprived of the use of the money for revenue-producing purposes.

In capitalizing interest, it is necessary to take account of unamortized premiums and discounts. For example, let us assume that interest expenses in the amount of $4,500 are chargeable to construction which extended over the full year, and that the amount of premium to be amortized during the construction year is $100. The entry to record interest expenses and the amortization of premiums is as follows:

Interest Expenses............................ $4,400

Unamortized Premiums on Bonds.............. 100

    Interest Payable............................ $4,500

    To record interest expenses and reduction of same by amount of premium amortized.

Subsequently an entry would be made capitalizing interest expenses as follows:

Structures and Improvements.................. $4,400

    Interest Expenses........................... $4,400

    To record charging interest expenses to construction.

---

[1] The reason for this entry is given on page 188.

Utility sinking fund. As indicated before, the term *fund* is used in a different sense in governmental accounting than in commercial accounting. In this section, the term will be used in its commercial accounting sense to denote segregated assets. That is, as in commercial accounting, the term *sinking fund* will be used to designate a group of assets set aside for the purpose of retiring bonds. The distinguishing characteristic of the term *fund* when used in this sense is that there need not be (although there may be) any specific account or accounts on the liability side of the balance sheet offsetting the fund account or accounts. It would be better to use some term other than *sinking fund* in the present case were it not for the fact that the term is commonly used in commercial accounting in the sense which it is here intended to convey.

Sinking funds, whether governmental or commercial, operate on the same principle. Contributions are calculated on an actuarial basis and are added periodically to the fund. The money thus segregated is invested, and income from the investments is added to the fund.

No entry is made in a utility sinking fund until the cash representing the contribution has actually been segregated. The entry to record the contribution is as follows:

Sinking Fund Cash[2]..........................	$3,716	
Cash......................................		$3,716
To record contribution to sinking fund.		

At the same time another entry must be made segregating unappropriated surplus, as follows:

Unappropriated Surplus.......................	$3,716	
Reserve for Retirement of Sinking Fund Bonds..		$3,716
To record segregation of surplus representing the contribution to the sinking fund.		

---

[2] Since only a few sinking fund accounts are involved in this case, it is assumed that no sinking fund control accounts are used. If a control account were set up for the assets of the sinking fund, an account designated Sinking Fund would have been debited and postings would have been made to a subsidiary account, Sinking Fund Cash. The entry would on the basis of this assumption read as follows:

Sinking Fund..............................	$3,716	
Cash......................................		$3,716
To record contribution to sinking fund. Subsidiary account: *Debit* Sinking Fund Cash, $3,716.		

Again, the first entry on page 189 would read as follows:

Sinking Fund..............................	$6,600	
Sinking Fund..............................		$6,600
To record investment of sinking fund cash. Subsidiary accounts: *Debit* Sinking Fund Investments, $6,600; *Credit* Sinking Fund Cash, $6,600.		

Note that the accounts shown in the entries in this footnote as subsidiary accounts (for example, Sinking Fund Cash and Sinking Fund Investments) are shown in the entries illustrated in the text as general ledger accounts, the assumption being that no controlling sinking fund accounts are set up.

The reasons for the segregation of surplus are as follows: The segregation of cash results in a reduction in the utility's working capital. If the utility were to transfer each year to the general fund cash equivalent to the full amount of unappropriated surplus, the working capital position of the utility would continue to get weaker each year. For example, assume that a utility has net current assets (that is, current assets less current liabilities) of $200,000 and no surplus and that it is required to make contributions of $25,000 each year to a sinking fund. Let us assume further that the utility makes a profit of $30,000, which results in a surplus of $30,000 and in total current net assets of $230,000. Assume further that the utility transfers all of its profits to the general fund. In this case, therefore, the utility would make a transfer of $30,000, which would leave the working capital at $200,000. But the utility is now required to segregate cash of $25,000, thereby reducing its net current assets to $175,000. To prevent the unintentional transfer of surplus representing sinking fund assets (in this case $25,000), an entry is made segregating this surplus.

It should be noted that the Reserve for Retirement of Sinking Fund Bonds account is not of the same nature as the similarly named account carried in the general sinking fund (discussed in Chapter 9). In that fund, the reserve represented actuarial requirements, whereas here it ordinarily represents the amount of assets in the sinking fund. The fund may have more assets than called for by actuarial requirements, in which case the credit balance of the reserve would also be greater than called for. For example, if, on the basis of actuarial requirements, the fund should have accumulated assets of $100,000 but actually has assets of $120,000, the reserve would show a balance of $120,000. It is important to know, however, whether the fund is up to requirements. This can be accomplished by preparing a table similar to that illustrated in Chapter 9, and examining the fund at frequent intervals to see that it has accumulated the required amount of assets. A notation should be made opposite the Reserve for Retirement of Sinking Fund Bonds account on the balance sheet as to what the actuarial requirements of the fund are (see caption "Reserves" in Figure 59), so that it is possible to tell at a glance whether or not the fund is up to them.

No accounts need be provided to show required contributions and required earnings. Since these accounts are budgetary accounts, they cannot be combined with the proprietary accounts. Unlike appropriations, these accounts do not represent authorization of expenditures and therefore need not be formally recorded. The preparation of the table referred to above and the inclusion of a reference to the actuarial requirements in the balance sheet are sufficient.

The next step in the operation of the fund is the investment of sinking fund cash. If cash to the amount of $6,600 is invested and no accrued interest, premiums, or discounts are involved, the transaction is recorded as follows:

Sinking Fund Investments.....................	$6,600	
Sinking Fund Cash..........................		$6,600
To record investment of sinking fund cash.		

As interest on sinking fund investments accrues or is received, the following entry is made:

Sinking Fund Cash..........................	$150	
Sinking Fund Interest Receivable...............	150	
Sinking Fund Revenues......................		$300
To record sinking fund revenues.		

As will be indicated subsequently, sinking fund revenues are included as part of the income of the utility fund. After the net income has been transferred to surplus, an entry is made debiting Unappropriated Surplus and crediting the Reserve for Retirement of Sinking Fund Bonds for the amount of sinking fund earnings (in this case, $300).

Utility deposits. The utility frequently requires from its customers deposits on which it pays interest. The following transactions and entries illustrate the procedure in recording the deposits, earnings thereon, and interest paid to depositors:

Transactions

1. Deposits of $11,000 were received.
2. Deposits to the amount of $10,000 were invested (assume that no premiums, discounts, or accrued interest purchases are involved).
3. Interest accrued on investments but not received, $200.
4. Interest accrued on deposits but not paid, $150.

Entries

1. Customers' Deposits—Cash................	$11,000	
Customers' Deposits Payable.............		$11,000
To record receipt of customers' deposits.		
2. Customers' Deposits—Investments..........	10,000	
Customers' Deposits—Cash..............		10,000
To record investment of customers' deposits.		
3. Customers' Deposits—Interest Receivable....	200	
Customers' Deposits—Interest Revenues...		200
To record interest revenues.		
4. Customers' Deposits—Interest Expenses.....	150	
Customers' Deposits—Interest Payable....		150
To record interest expenses.		

Trial balance before closing entries. The following is a trial balance of the proprietary accounts of the utility fund before closing entries have been made and is based on all of the journal entries illustrated thus far in this chapter:

Land..	$ 200,000	
Structures and Improvements............	701,400	
Allowance for Depreciation—Structures and Improvements.....................		$ 100,000
Equipment.............................	200,500	
Allowance for Depreciation—Equipment..		56,000
Cash.................................	130,084	
Accounts Receivable....................	72,000	
Allowance for Uncollectible Accounts.....		6,500
Inventory of Materials and Supplies......	30,000	
Prepaid Insurance......................	600	
Interest Receivable.....................	200	
Sinking Fund Cash.....................	266	
Sinking Fund Investments...............	6,600	
Sinking Fund Interest Receivable........	150	
Customers' Deposits—Cash..............	1,000	
Customers' Deposits—Investments.......	10,000	
Customers' Deposits—Interest Receivable	200	
Bonds Payable.........................		650,000
Customers' Deposits Payable............		11,000
Vouchers Payable......................		49,500
Due to Working Capital Fund...........		12,800
Accrued Salaries and Wages.............		6,000
Accrued Taxes.........................		7,500
Interest Payable.......................		6,500
Customers' Deposits—Interest Payable...		150
Unamortized Premiums on Bonds........		1,900
Reserve for Retirement of Sinking Fund Bonds.............................		6,716
Governmental Unit's Contribution........		400,000
Unappropriated Surplus.................		284
Operating Revenues....................		300,000
Operating Expenses....................	187,400	
Depreciation..........................	36,000	
Taxes.................................	18,000	
Interest Revenues......................		1,200
Interest Expenses.....................	22,000	
Sinking Fund Revenues.................		300
Customers' Deposits—Interest Revenues..		200
Customers' Deposits—Interest Expenses..	150	
	$1,616,550	$1,616,550

Closing entries. The following are illustrative closing entries based on the accounts carried in the foregoing trial balance:

Operating Revenues.......................	$300,000	
Operating Expenses.....................		$187,400
Depreciation...........................		36,000
Taxes.................................		18,000
Operating Income......................		58,600

To record closing out of operating revenues, operating expenses, depreciation, and taxes.

Operating Income........................	58,600	
Interest Revenues........................	1,200	
Sinking Fund Revenues...................	300	
Customers' Deposits—Interest Revenues.....	200	

Interest Expenses......................		$22,000
Customers' Deposits—Interest Expenses....		150
Net Income...........................		38,150
To record closing out of operating income, non-operating income, and nonoperating expenses.		
Net Income............................	$38,150	
Unappropriated Surplus.................		38,150
To record closing out of net income into unappropriated surplus.		
Unappropriated Surplus...................	300	
Reserve for Retirement of Sinking Fund Bonds		300
To record segregation of earnings on sinking fund investments.		

Financial statements. The balance sheet, income and expense statement, and statement analyzing the changes in unappropriated surplus which are illustrated on pages 192 and 193 are based on the trial balance and the closing entries given above.

Comments on balance sheet. Note that the balance sheet exhibited is similar to that of a commercial enterprise. Like the balance sheet of a business enterprise, this statement contains both fixed assets and bonds payable. The statement follows the arrangement recommended by the National Association of Railroad and Utilities Commissioners. Under this arrangement, fixed assets precede current assets and bonds payable precede current liabilities.

Most of the accounts carried in the utility fund balance sheet do not require comment. The only one which requires any particular mention is the Governmental Unit's Contribution account.

Governmental unit's contribution. The Governmental Unit's Contribution account shows the amount invested in the utility by the operating governmental unit. As already indicated, the account is credited with the amount expended by the governmental unit in acquiring the utility. Similarly, the account is credited with any subsequent contributions made by the governmental unit to the utility. For example, the governmental unit may transfer money from the general fund to the utility fund to make up a deficit in the latter.

On the other hand, the Governmental Unit's Contribution account would be reduced by amounts transferred each year from the utility fund to the general fund. For example, the governmental unit may require its utility to transfer all, or a portion, of utility profits each year. Such transfers reduce the governmental unit's contribution to its utility.

A distinction in accounting procedure should, however, be made between transfers of profits to the general fund or the making up of utility deficits from the general fund and transfers which represent payments for services. The governmental unit should charge the utility with a proper amount of taxes and with the cost of services rendered for it. On the other hand,

Figure 59

A GOVERNMENTAL UNIT

Utility Fund

Balance Sheet
at Close of Fiscal Year

ASSETS

Fixed Assets:

Land..................................		$200,000	
Structures and Improvements..................	$701,400		
Less—Allowance for Depreciation..............	100,000	601,400	
Equipment....................................	$200,500		
Less—Allowance for Depreciation..............	56,000	144,500	$ 945,900

Current and Accrued Assets:

Cash..		$130,084	
Accounts Receivable..........................	$ 72,000		
Less—Allowance for Uncollectible Accounts......	6,500	65,500	
Inventory of Materials and Supplies......................		30,000	
Prepaid Insurance......................................		600	
Interest Receivable....................................		200	226,384

Sinking Fund:

Cash..	$ 266	
Investments.......................................	6,600	
Interest Receivable................................	150	7,016

Customers' Deposits:

Cash..	$ 1,000	
Investments.......................................	10,000	
Interest Receivable................................	200	11,200

	$1,190,500

LIABILITIES, DEFERRED CREDITS, RESERVES, CONTRIBUTIONS, AND SURPLUS

Liabilities:

Bonds Payable..			$ 650,000
Customers' Deposits Payable....................................			11,000
Current and Accrued Liabilities:			
Vouchers Payable....................................		$ 49,500	
Due to Working Capital Fund.........................		12,800	
Accrued Salaries and Wages..........................		6,000	
Accrued Taxes......................................		7,500	
Interest Payable....................................		6,500	
Customers' Deposits—Interest Payable.................		150	82,450

	$ 743,450

Deferred Credits:

Unamortized Premiums on Bonds................................	1,900

Reserves:

Reserve for Retirement of Sinking Fund Bonds (Actuarial Requirement, $6,966)...	7,016

Contributions and Surplus:

Governmental Unit's Contribution........................	$400,000	
Unappropriated Surplus................................	38,134	438,134

Figure 60

A GOVERNMENTAL UNIT

Utility Fund

Income and Expense Statement
for Fiscal Year

Operating Revenues			$300,000
Less—Operating Revenue Deductions:			
Operating Expenses		$187,400	
Depreciation		36,000	
Taxes		18,000	241,400
Utility Operating Income			$ 58,600
Other Income:			
Customers' Deposits—Interest Revenues	$200		
Less—Customers' Deposits—Interest Expenses	150	$ 50	
Interest Revenues		1,200	
Sinking Fund Revenues		300	1,550
			$ 60,150
Other Deductions:			
Interest Expenses			22,000
Net Income Transferred to Surplus			$ 38,150

Figure 61

A GOVERNMENTAL UNIT

Utility Fund

Analysis of Changes in Unappropriated Surplus
for Fiscal Year

Unappropriated Surplus—Beginning of Year		—
Add:		
Receipts on Accounts Receivable Charged Off	$ 7,000	
Net Income for Year	38,150	$45,150
Deduct:		
Contributions to Sinking Fund	$ 6,716	
Transfer of Earnings on Sinking Fund Investments	300	7,016
Unappropriated Surplus—End of Year		$38,134

the utility should charge the governmental unit for services. Such transactions should not be handled through the Governmental Unit's Contribution account but through revenue and expense accounts. For example, if the governmental unit charges the utility with taxes, the entry to record the transaction in the utility fund is as follows:

Taxes	$10,000	
Due to General Fund		$10,000
To record liability for general property taxes.		

On the other hand, if the utility charges the governmental unit for services rendered by it, the entry in the utility fund is as follows:

Due from General Fund......................	$40,000	
Operating Revenues.......................		$40,000
To record revenue from water supplied to the		
operating governmental unit.		

If the above transactions had not been charged to expense accounts or credited to revenue accounts, there would have been an understatement of both revenues and expenditures.

Briefly, the Governmental Unit's Contribution account is used to record only those transactions which constitute a contribution by the governmental unit to the utility or vice versa. The account is not used to record changes or credits which are subject to current settlement.

Comments on income and expense statement. It should be noted that the income and expense statement is divided into four main sections: (1) operating revenues, (2) operating revenue deductions, (3) other income, and (4) other deductions. Each of these items is discussed immediately below.

Operating revenues. Utility operating revenues are those derived directly from the operations of the utility and consist primarily of revenues obtained from the sale of services. In order to show details concerning operating revenues, it is customary to prepare, in addition to the income and expense statement, a detailed statement of revenues similar to the one illustrated in Figure 62. The total revenues shown in such a schedule must, of course, agree with the amount shown for operating revenues in the income and expense statement.

Operating revenue deductions. Operating revenue deductions, as the income and expense statement illustrated in Figure 60 shows, consist of (1) operating expenses, (2) depreciation, and (3) taxes. Although depreciation and taxes are ordinarily considered operating expenses, the National Association of Railroad and Utilities Commissioners has recommended that they be shown separately from operating expenses in the income and expense statement. Further details concerning operating expenses and taxes are given immediately below while details regarding depreciation, because the latter is directly related to accounting for fixed assets, are deferred until Chapter 16.

Operating expenses. Operating expenses of utilities are classified by functions and activities. An example of such a classification will be found in the detailed statement of operating expenses illustrated in Figure 63. Since this schedule supports the operating expense account in the income and expense statement illustrated in Figure 60, the total expenses shown in it must agree with the balance of the operating expenses account in the income and expense statement.

Figure 62

A GOVERNMENTAL UNIT

Electric Fund

Detailed Statement of Operating Revenues
for Fiscal Year

Electric Service Revenues:

Residential Sales	$125,000	
Commercial Sales	85,000	
Industrial Sales	50,000	
Public Street Lighting	10,500	
Sales to Water Plant	25,000	
Total Electric Service Revenues		$295,500

Other Electric Revenues:

Rent from Electric Property	$ 3,000	
Customers' Penalties	500	
Miscellaneous Revenues	1,000	
Total Other Electric Revenues		4,500
Total Operating Revenues		$300,000

Taxes. Governmental utilities may have to pay some or all of the following taxes: (1) special assessments, (2) general property taxes, and (3) sales taxes. The special assessments referred to here are those paid by the governmental utility as an owner of property in the special assessment district. Such taxes are not, however, expenses; they are capital expenditures, and the amount of the assessment should therefore be added to the value of the land.

General property taxes may be classified into two groups—those which constitute capital outlays and those which are to be treated as current expenses. Ordinarily, general property taxes are considered as current expenses. The only exception is taxes which are paid on property during the construction period, those taxes being considered as a part of the cost of construction.

A governmental utility may pay two types of sales taxes—taxes on sales to customers and taxes on materials purchased by the utility. The treatment of the first type of sales tax will vary somewhat according to whether or not the customer is billed for it. If the sales tax is not to be passed on to the customer, it is considered an operating revenue deduction. The entry, as far as controlling accounts are concerned, is, therefore, as follows:

Taxes	$5,000	
Taxes Accrued		$5,000

To record expenses in the form of taxes and to set up liability therefor.

Figure 63

A GOVERNMENTAL UNIT

Electric Fund

**Detailed Statement of Operating Expenses
for Fiscal Year**

PRODUCTION EXPENSES:
 Electric Generating—

Supervision...	$ 3,000	
Station Labor..	15,000	
Fuel...	54,000	
Water...	4,000	
Supplies and Expenses.................................	8,400	$ 84,400

 Maintenance of Plant and Equipment—

Supervision...	$ 2,000	
Maintenance of Structures and Improvements..............	8,000	
Maintenance of Boiler Plant Equipment...................	10,000	
Maintenance of Generating and Electric Plant Equipment...	10,000	30,000

Power Purchased...		2,000
Total Production Expenses...................................		$116,400

DISTRIBUTION EXPENSES:

Supervision...	$ 2,500	
Services on Consumers' Premises..........................	4,500	
Street Lighting and Signal System........................	4,000	
Overhead System..	18,200	
Maintenance and Servicing of Mobile Equipment.............	3,000	
Utility Storeroom Expenses...............................	4,000	
Total Distribution Expenses..................................		36,200

ACCOUNTING AND COLLECTION EXPENSES:

Customers' Contracts and Orders..........................	$ 2,500	
Meter Reading..	3,500	
Collecting Offices.......................................	1,000	
Delinquent Accounts—Collection Expense...................	2,000	
Customers' Billing and Accounting........................	4,000	
Provision for Doubtful Accounts..........................	1,800	
Total Accounting and Collection Expense......................		14,800

SALES PROMOTION EXPENSES.....................................		1,000

ADMINISTRATIVE AND GENERAL EXPENSES:

Salaries of Executives...................................	$ 8,000	
Other General Office Salaries............................	3,500	
General Office Supplies and Expenses.....................	400	
Insurance..	2,000	
Employees' Welfare Expenses..............................	1,500	
Pension Fund Contributions...............................	2,800	
Miscellaneous General Expenses...........................	800	
Total Administrative and General Expenses.....................		19,000

TOTAL OPERATING EXPENSES..		$187,400

Even where the customer is billed for the tax, the amount of taxes billed is not included as part of the revenue of the utility. The amount due from each customer for taxes is included with the other accounts receivable, and the equal liability for taxes is recorded. The entry, as far as the controlling accounts are concerned, is as follows:

Accounts Receivable............................	$5,000	
Taxes Accrued................................		$5,000
To record billing customers for sales taxes.		

Sales taxes on materials purchased by governmental utilities are recorded as part of the cost of the materials, and no separate account is ordinarily provided for them. The Taxes account appearing in an income and expense statement ordinarily consists of general property taxes and of sales taxes which cannot be shifted to customers. It should be remembered, however, that the discussion of these taxes does not imply that governmental utilities pay all or any one of them. Some governmental utilities pay no taxes, whereas others pay most of the taxes discussed above.

Other income. Other income consists of the net interest income on the investment of customers' deposits, interest on other investments, interest on bank deposits, and net sinking fund revenues. These items are self-explanatory.

Other deductions. These deductions consist primarily of interest expenses and the amortization of utility plant acquisition adjustments. Interest expenses do not call for further discussion whereas the amortization of utility plant acquisition adjustments does because it is peculiar to utility accounting.

Utility plant acquisition adjustments usually arise out of the fact that the governmental unit pays more for the plant than called for by its physical value. The physical value of the plant may be (1) its original cost plus additions and minus depreciation and other deductions, (2) its appraised value at the date of acquisition, or (3) its value computed on some other basis.[3] For example, assume that the net book value of the fixed assets of a private plant (that is, the value as shown by the books, less accumulated depreciation) is $1,000,000, that an appraisal is made and the value of the property is determined to be $1,000,000, and that the utility has current assets to the amount of $100,000 and liabilities of $250,000. The net book value of the utility's assets is in that case $850,000. Next let us assume that the plant is sold to a govern-

---

[3] Thus, governmental utilities subject to regulation by a state public service commission are frequently required to record the property acquired at its cost to the first owner who devoted it to the public service plus cost of additions and less retirements and accrued depreciation. The utility is in that event required to record in the Utility Plant Acquisition Adjustments account the difference beween this value and the amount actually paid.

mental unit. If the governmental unit pays more than $850,000, it must record the excess in the Utility Plant Acquisition Adjustments account. For example, if the governmental unit pays $950,000, the Utility Plant Acquisition Adjustments account should be debited for $100,000. The transaction is recorded as follows:

Land	$200,000	
Structures and Improvements	700,000	
Equipment	250,000	
Accounts Receivable	103,000	
Utility Plant Acquisition Adjustments	100,000	
Allowance for Depreciation—Structures and Improvements		$100,000
Allowance for Depreciation—Equipment		50,000
Allowance for Uncollectible Accounts		3,000
Vouchers Payable		50,000
Bonds Payable		200,000
Cash		950,000

To record acquisition of plant of *XYZ* Company.

The Utility Plant Acquisition Adjustments account, although shown on the asset side of the balance sheet, is not a tangible asset. Even if it is justifiable for a private utility to capitalize the excess of the amount paid over the net book value and to show the resulting figure as "goodwill" or "going concern" value, it is improper for a governmental utility to do so, for there are other intangible assets which a governmental unit might better capitalize—for example, its taxing power. Accordingly, the excess is set up as a deferred charge and is prorated over a period of time, so that the revenues of any one year may not be charged with the entire amount. The entry to record the amortization of the adjustments is as follows:

Amortization of Utility Plant Acquisition Adjustments	$5,000	
Allowance for Amortization of Utility Plant Acquisition Adjustments		$5,000

To record amortization of utility plant acquisition adjustments.

It should be noted that the Allowance for Amortization of Utility Plant Acquisition Adjustments account is a valuation account and must be shown as a deduction from the Utility Plant Acquisition Adjustments account in the balance sheet. For example, if we assume that the two preceding entries are posted, the Utility Plant Acquisition Adjustments account and the related allowance would be shown in the balance sheet as follows:

Utility Plant Acquisition Adjustments	$100,000
Less—Allowance for Amortization of Utility Plant Acquisition Adjustments	5,000
	$ 95,000

When the entire account is written off, an entry is made debiting the Allowance for Amortization of Utility Plant Acquisition Adjustments account for $100,000 and crediting the Utility Plant Acquisition Adjustments account for a corresponding amount.

Clearing accounts. Thus far we have assumed that all expenses can be readily identified and charged to the appropriate accounts. Certain expenditures, however, are incurred under circumstances that prevent their being charged to the proper accounts at the time they are incurred. These charges are first recorded in clearing accounts and are transferred from these accounts to the expense accounts. Since this subject is related to cost accounting, its discussion is deferred until Chapter 21.

Accounting for Other Enterprises

As indicated earlier, examples of enterprises other than utilities are public markets, parking facilities, public housing, and municipal airports.

Figure 64

A GOVERNMENTAL UNIT
Other Enterprise Fund—Public Market Fund
Balance Sheet
at Close of Fiscal Year

ASSETS

Current Assets:			
Cash..		$ 20,000	
Accounts Receivable.........................	$ 4,000		
Less—Allowance for Uncollectible Accounts.......	200	3,800	$ 23,800
Fixed Assets:			
Land..		$350,000	
Structures and Improvements..................	$425,000		
Less—Allowance for Depreciation...............	40,000	385,000	
Machinery and Equipment.....................	$ 50,000		
Less—Allowance for Depreciation...............	10,800	39,200	774,200
			$798,000

LIABILITIES, CONTRIBUTIONS, AND SURPLUS

Liabilities:			
Current Liabilities—			
Vouchers Payable................................		$ 9,800	
Interest Payable................................		1,300	$ 11,100
Bonds Payable.......................................			648,000
			$659,100
Contributions and Surplus:			
Governmental Unit's Contribution......................		$100,000	
Unappropriated Surplus...............................		38,900	138,900
			$798,000

The same accounting principles apply to these enterprises as to utilities and the same type of balance sheet and income and expense statement apply to both. The similarity of the financial statements of utilities to those of other enterprises becomes evident when one compares the balance sheet and the income and expense statement illustrated in Figures 64 and 65, respectively, with those illustrated in Figures 59 and 60. It should be noted, however, that enterprises other than utilities usually have fewer kinds of assets, liabilities, revenues, and expenditures. They therefore call for fewer accounts and for simpler statements than utilities.

Figure 65

A GOVERNMENTAL UNIT

Other Enterprise Fund—Public Market Fund

Income and Expense Statement
for Fiscal Year

Operating Revenues:		
Rentals of Stalls	$100,000	
Market Fees	16,000	
Parking Fees	5,000	$121,000
Operating Expenses:		
Salaries and Wages	$ 48,000	
Light, Power, and Steam Service	4,500	
Maintenance and Repairs	7,200	
Insurance	2,300	
Social Security Taxes	700	
Uncollectible Accounts	50	
Depreciation	15,000	
Other Expenses	1,000	
Total Operating Expenses		78,750
Operating Income		$ 42,250
Other Income:		
Interest Income		200
		$ 42,450
Other Deductions:		
Interest on Bonds		8,500
Net Income Transferred to Surplus		$ 33,950

13

<<<<<<<<<<<<<<<<<<<<<<<<<<<<<<<<<<<<<<<<<<<<<<<<<<<<<<<<<<<<

GENERAL FIXED ASSETS. GENERAL BONDED DEBT AND INTEREST. INTER-FUND RELATIONSHIPS

THE DISCUSSION of governmental fund accounting procedure is concluded in this chapter. The first part of the chapter deals with the accounting procedure for general fixed assets and explains the relationship between them and the funds from which they are financed. The second part is concerned with the accounting procedure for a government's general bonded debt and interest, and points out the relationship of the indebtedness to the general fund, the bond fund, and the sinking fund. The third part is devoted to a discussion of inter-fund relationships.

General Fixed Assets

For the purpose of this chapter general fixed assets may be defined as those assets which are not a part of any fund. In other words, the general fixed assets of a municipality consist of all of its fixed assets other than those carried in the working capital fund and utility or other enterprise funds and other than the fixed assets carried as investments of trust funds. The importance of recording fixed assets on the books should not be overlooked or minimized, for in that manner alone can proper control be exercised over them. Yet there are many governments which keep no records of such assets. General fixed assets should be set up in a separate self-balancing group of accounts.[1] The following trial balance illustrates the control accounts making up this group:

---
[1] See pages 54-55.

Land................................	$1,000,000	
Structures and Improvements...........	2,000,000	
Equipment...........................	490,000	
Investment in Fixed Assets from:		
Current Revenues...................		$ 690,000
Bonds............................		2,314,000
Special Assessments.................		386,000
Governmental Unit's Share of Cost of		
Assessment Improvements...........		100,000
	$3,490,000	$3,490,000

Methods of financing. In previous chapters we stated that general fixed assets may be financed from three sources: (1) from current revenues, such as taxes, (2) from general bonds, and (3) from special assessments. The entries to record the capital expenditures in each fund have already been given. However, in order to illustrate more clearly the relationship between these funds and the general fixed assets accounts, some of the fund entries will be repeated, and the corresponding entry in the general fixed assets group of accounts will be indicated.

Assets financed from current revenues. Let us assume that, out of the appropriation expenditures of $399,900, shown on page 53, $103,300 represented expenditures for fixed assets. The entry in the general fund at the time the expenditure was made would be

Appropriation Expenditures.................	$103,300	
Vouchers Payable......................		$103,300
To record purchase of equipment.		

At the same time an entry would be made in the general fixed assets group of accounts as follows:

Land.......................................	$ 7,000	
Structures and Improvements..............	37,200	
Equipment...............................	59,100	
Investment in Fixed Assets from Current		
Revenues...........................		$103,300
To record cost of fixed assets financed from		
current revenues.		

Assets financed from bonds. As indicated previously, construction expenditures may be closed out at the end of each year or they may not be closed out until construction is completed. If we assume that expenditures are closed out at the end of each year, the entry in the bond fund (as illustrated on page 91) is as follows:

Appropriations...........................	$70,300	
Appropriation Expenditures..............		$70,300
To record closing out of construction expenditures.		

The corresponding entry in the fixed assets group of accounts is

| Construction Work in Progress............... | $70,300 | |
| Investment in Fixed Assets from Bonds.... | | $70,300 |

To record construction work in progress financed
from bonds.

When the project is completed, the entry in the bond fund (page 93) is
as follows:

Appropriations...........................	$129,700	
Appropriation Expenditures..............		$126,200
Unappropriated Surplus.................		3,500

To close out construction expenditures and to
record surplus resulting from the excess of the
amount authorized over the amount expended.

In the general fixed assets group of accounts, the entry is

Structures and Improvements...............	$196,500	
Construction Work in Progress...........		$ 70,300
Investment in Fixed Assets from Bonds....		126,200

To record cost of completed project financed
from bonds and to close out accounts showing
cost of construction work in progress.

Assets financed from special assessments. If construction expenditures
are closed out at the end of each year, even though the project is uncompleted, the entry in the special assessment fund, as previously illustrated (page 111), is as follows:

| Appropriations........................... | $140,000 | |
| Appropriation Expenditures.............. | | $140,000 |

To record closing out of construction expenditures financed from special assessments.

The corresponding entry in the general fixed assets group of accounts is

Construction Work in Progress...............	$140,000	
Investment in Fixed Assets from Special As-		
sessments...........................		$140,000

To record work in progress financed from special
assessments.

When the project is completed, the entry in the special assessment fund,
as indicated before (page 114), is as follows:

Appropriations...........................	$360,000	
Appropriation Expenditures..............		$345,000
Unappropriated Surplus—Construction.....		15,000

To record completion of project and to close out
balance in the Appropriations account.

The entry in the fixed assets group of accounts is

Structures and Improvements...............	$485,000	
Construction Work in Progress...........		$140,000
Investment in Fixed Assets from Special As-		
sessments...........................		245,000
Investment in Fixed Assets from Govern-		
mental Unit's Share of Cost of Assessment		
Improvements.......................		100,000

To record fixed assets financed from special
assessments and governmental unit's share of
cost.

As indicated in Chapter 8, a record should be made of the amount contributed by the governmental unit and by property owners to finance the cost of the project. No such distinction is usually made, however, in the general fixed assets group of accounts until the project is completed, the Investment in Fixed Assets account being subdivided enough to show merely the combined investment of the governmental unit and the property owners in construction work in progress.

Gifts. Thus far we have treated those fixed assets which are first recorded as expenditures of some fund—for example, the general fund, the bond fund, and the special assessment fund. A governmental unit may, however, acquire fixed assets as a gift. In that case, an entry is made only in the general fixed assets group of accounts. This entry is as follows:

Structures and Improvements...............	$40,000	
Investment in Fixed Assets from Gifts.....		$40,000
To record value of donated fixed assets.		

Fixed assets acquired as a gift should be appraised and should be carried on the records at their appraised value.

Balance sheet. The following is a balance sheet of the general fixed assets group of accounts based on the foregoing trial balance and journal entries. It will be noted that the Investment in Fixed Assets account has been subdivided to show the sources from which the assets are financed.

Figure 66

A GOVERNMENTAL UNIT

General Fixed Assets

Balance Sheet
at Close of Fiscal Year

Land...	$1,007,000
Structures and Improvements......................	2,758,700
Equipment.......................................	549,100
	$4,314,800

Investment in Fixed Assets from:	
Current Revenues..............................	$ 793,300
Bonds...	2,510,500
Special Assessments...........................	771,000
Governmental Unit's Share of Cost of Assessment Improvements................................	200,000
Gifts...	40,000
	$4,314,800

General Bonded Debt and Interest

For the purpose of this chapter, the general bonded debt may be defined as all the outstanding bonds of the governmental unit with the exception of utility and special assessment bonds. General bonded debt and the interest payable thereon in future years are not shown as part of any fund but are recorded in a separate group of accounts.[2] The liability account is offset by an account which shows the amount available for the retirement of bonds and the amounts to be provided for both the retirement of bonds and the payment of interest in future years. Interest payable during the current year would not be shown here but would be reflected, instead, in the general fund or a special revenue fund. The amount available would consist of current cash or other assets of the sinking fund, while the amount to be provided would represent future tax levies or future sinking fund contributions and earnings thereon. The following is an illustration of a balance sheet for a group of general bonded debt and interest accounts:

Figure 67

A GOVERNMENTAL UNIT
General Bonded Debt and Interest
Balance Sheet
at Beginning of Fiscal Year

Amount Available for Retirement of Bonds...........	$2,282,900
Amount to Be Provided for Retirement of Bonds......	767,100
Amount to Be Provided for Payment of Interest.......	400,000
	$3,450,000
Bonds Payable...................................	$3,050,000
Interest Payable in Future Years...................	400,000
	$3,450,000

Entries during year. The entries to record the receipt of the proceeds from the sale of bonds and the retirement of the bonds have already been illustrated. They will, however, be repeated in part at this point in order to show the relationship between the bond funds and the funds from which the bonds are retired, on the one hand, and the general bonded debt accounts, on the other.

When the bonds are sold, the entry in the bond fund (as illustrated on page 90) is as follows:

Cash....................................	$100,000	
Bonds Authorized—Unissued.............		$100,000
To record sale of bonds.		

[2] See pages 54-56.

At the same time the following entry is made in the general bonded debt and interest group of accounts:

Amount to Be Provided for Retirement of Bonds	$100,000	
Amount to Be Provided for Payment of Interest	50,000	
Bonds Payable..........................		$100,000
Interest Payable in Future Years..........		50,000
To record liability for bonds and interest payable in future years.		

The combined entries in the sinking fund to close out actual and required revenues (page 144) are as follows:

Contribution Revenues.....................	$20,600	
Earnings.................................	9,400	
Required Installment Contribution........		$20,600
Required Earnings.......................		9,000
Unappropriated Surplus..................		400
To record closing out accounts showing required and actual contribution and earnings.		

The corresponding entry in the general bonded debt group of accounts is

Amount Available for Retirement of Bonds...	$30,000	
Amount to Be Provided for Retirement of Bonds.................................		$30,000
To record additions made to sinking fund.		

When bonds mature, the entry in the sinking fund (page 130) is

Reserve for Retirement of Sinking Fund Bonds................................	$2,000,000	
Matured Bonds Payable..............		$2,000,000
To set up matured bonds as a liability of the sinking fund.		

The entry in the general bonded debt group of accounts is

Bonds Payable.........................	$2,000,000	
Amount Available for Retirement of Bonds		$2,000,000
To remove bond liability.		

If serial bonds have been issued, a certain amount of the bonds will be retired annually and will be appropriated for in the budget. As these bonds mature, they are charged against the appropriation, and the liability is recorded in the general fund or a special revenue fund. The entry is as follows:

Appropriation Expenditures...................	$50,000	
Matured Bonds Payable.....................		$50,000
To set up matured bonds as a liability and to charge appropriations with amount of such matured bonds.		

The entry to remove the liability from the general bonded debt group of accounts is

Bonds Payable............................. $50,000
 Amount to Be Provided for Retirement of Bonds $50,000
 To reduce bond liability by amount of bonds
 which have matured.

The National Committee on Governmental Accounting has recommended that interest on all general bonds, regardless of whether they are serial bonds or sinking fund bonds, should be paid from the general fund or a special revenue fund. Such payment, however, is not made until the bonds mature. When the budget for the general fund or the special revenue fund, as the case may be, is adopted, there is included, along with the other appropriations for expenditures out of the particular fund, an appropriation for the payment of interest on general bonds. When the interest becomes payable, the entry made in the general fund or the special revenue fund is

Appropriation Expenditures................. $25,000
 Matured Interest Payable................. $25,000
 To record matured interest as a liability and to
 charge appropriations with the amount of such
 matured interest payable.

The corresponding entry in the general bonded debt and interest group of accounts is

Interest Payable in Future Years.............. $25,000
 Amount to Be Provided for Payment of Interest $25,000
 To reduce the amount to be provided for interest
 in future years as well as the liability for interest
 payable in future years by the amount of interest recorded as a liability in the general fund (or
 in a special revenue fund).

It is necessary to reduce the liabilities for general bonded debt and interest and the offsetting debit-balance accounts for two reasons. In the first place, matured bonds and interest are shown at maturity as liabilities of certain funds. To continue to show them in the general bonded debt and interest statements would be to reflect the same liability twice. In the second place, it is no longer necessary to provide for the retirement of serial bonds or the payment of interest on all general bonds since the fund in which the matured bonds and interest are carried has provided the resources for their retirement.

Balance sheet. After the above entries have been posted to the accounts listed in Figure 67, the balance sheet of the general bonded debt and interest group of accounts will appear as shown in Figure 68.

Inter-Fund Relationships

Transactions and entries. Thus far in this chapter we have indicated how the transactions in certain funds affect general fixed assets as well

Figure 68

A GOVERNMENTAL UNIT

General Bonded Debt and Interest

Balance Sheet
at Close of Fiscal Year

Amount Available for Retirement of Bonds...........	$ 312,900
Amount to Be Provided for Retirement of Bonds......	787,100
Amount to Be Provided for Payment of Interest.......	425,000
	$1,525,000
Bonds Payable....................................	$1,100,000
Interest Payable in Future Years...................	425,000
	$1,525,000

as general bonded debt and interest thereon. The following entries illustrate how certain transactions in one fund affect another fund or funds:

Transactions Originating in the General Fund

1. Money was advanced by the general fund to the working capital fund for the purpose of providing capital for that fund.

ENTRY IN GENERAL FUND:
Appropriation Expenditures.....................	$ 50,000	
Cash.......................................		$ 50,000

To record capital advance to working capital fund.

ENTRY IN WORKING CAPITAL FUND:
Cash.......................................	50,000	
Capital...................................		50,000

To record receipt of capital from general fund.

2. A loan was made by the general fund to the sinking fund.

ENTRY IN GENERAL FUND:
Due from Sinking Fund.......................	$ 40,000	
Cash.......................................		$ 40,000

To record loan made to sinking fund.

ENTRY IN SINKING FUND:
Cash.......................................	40,000	
Due to General Fund.......................		40,000

To record loan from general fund.

3. A contribution was made by the general fund to the sinking fund.

ENTRY IN GENERAL FUND:
Appropriation Expenditures.....................	$ 50,000	
Cash.......................................		$ 50,000

To record payment of contribution to sinking fund.

ENTRY IN SINKING FUND:
Cash.......................................	50,000	
Contribution Revenues.....		50,000

To record receipt of contribution from general fund.

ENTRY IN GENERAL BONDED DEBT AND INTEREST
GROUP OF ACCOUNTS:

Amount Available for Retirement of Bonds........	$50,000	
Amount to Be Provided for Retirement of Bonds		$50,000

To decrease amount to be provided and to increase
the amount available for the retirement of bonds.

4. The governmental unit is required to pay part of the cost of special assessment improvements.

ENTRY IN GENERAL FUND:

Appropriation Expenditures.....................	$100,000	
Due to Special Assessment Fund..............		$100,000

To record governmental unit's liability for contribution toward construction of special assessment improvements.

ENTRY IN SPECIAL ASSESSMENT FUND:

Due from General Fund......................	100,000	
Governmental Unit's Share of Cost............		100,000

To record amount due from general fund for governmental unit's share of cost of project.

5. Services were performed by the general fund for the special assessment fund.

ENTRY IN GENERAL FUND:

Due from Special Assessment Fund..............	$ 10,000	
Appropriation Expenditures..................		$ 10,000

To record reduction of appropriation expenditures by cost of services rendered on special assessment projects.

ENTRY IN SPECIAL ASSESSMENT FUND:

Appropriation Expenditures.....................	$ 10,000	
Due to General Fund.......................		$ 10,000

To record cost of services performed by general fund.

6. A contribution was made by the general fund to a pension (trust) fund.

ENTRY IN GENERAL FUND:

Appropriation Expenditures....................	$ 10,000	
Cash.......................................		$ 10,000

To record contributions on account of employees' pensions.

ENTRY IN PENSION (TRUST) FUND:

Cash.......................................	10,000	
Contributions—Governmental Unit............		10,000

To record receipt of contribution from general fund on account of employees' pensions.

Transactions Originating in Bond Fund

1. Premiums on bonds were transferred to the general fund.

ENTRY IN BOND FUND:

Unamortized Premiums on Bonds..............	$ 1,000	
Cash.......................................		$ 1,000

To record transfer of premiums to the general fund.

ENTRY IN GENERAL FUND:

Cash.......................................	1,000	
Revenues...................................		1,000

To record receipt of cash representing premiums on bonds.

2. Proceeds from the sale of bonds issued were transferred out of the bond fund to finance
   (a) the governmental unit's share of special assessment improvement costs
   (b) the governmental unit's contribution toward the establishment of a working capital fund
   (c) a deficit in the general fund
   (d) the acquisition of a utility or other enterprise (the bonds to be repaid from taxes).

ENTRY IN BOND FUND:
Appropriations................................. $100,000
   Cash... $100,000
To record transfer of proceeds out of bond fund.

(a) ENTRY IN SPECIAL ASSESSMENT FUND:
    Cash for Construction...................... 100,000
       Governmental Unit's Share of Cost.........   100,000
To record receipt of cash representing governmental unit's share of cost.

(b) ENTRY IN WORKING CAPITAL FUND:
    Cash...................................... 100,000
       Capital.................................   100,000
To record receipt of capital from sale of bonds.

(c) ENTRY IN GENERAL FUND:
    Cash...................................... 100,000
       Revenues..............................   100,000
To record receipt of proceeds from the sale of bonds issued to fund a deficit.

(d) ENTRY IN UTILITY OR OTHER ENTERPRISE FUND:
    Cash...................................... 100,000
       Governmental Unit's Contribution........   100,000
To record receipt of proceeds from the sale of bonds issued to finance the acquisition of a utility or other enterprise. Bonds are to be repaid from taxes.

3. Services were rendered by the bond fund for the general fund.

ENTRY IN BOND FUND:
Due from General Fund....................... $ 5,000
   Appropriation Expenditures.................. $ 5,000
To record reduction of construction expenditures by cost of services rendered for general fund.

ENTRY IN GENERAL FUND:
Appropriation Expenditures................... 5,000
   Due to Bond Fund..........................   5,000
To record amount due to bond fund on account of services rendered.

4. Bond fund surplus was transferred to the general fund (or to a sinking fund).

ENTRY IN BOND FUND:
Unappropriated Surplus....................... $ 4,000
   Cash...................................... $ 4,000
To record transfer of unappropriated surplus out of bond fund to general fund (or sinking fund).

ENTRY IN GENERAL FUND (OR SINKING FUND):
Cash....................................... $4,000
    Revenues (or Contribution Revenues)......... $4,000
To record receipt of bond fund surplus.

ENTRY IN GENERAL BONDED DEBT AND INTEREST
    GROUP OF ACCOUNTS (if previous entry is in sink-
    ing fund):
Amount Available for Retirement of Bonds....... 4,000
    Amount to Be Provided for Retirement of Bonds 4,000
To record receipt of bond fund surplus by sinking
fund and corresponding increase in amount available
for retirement of sinking fund bonds.

Transactions Originating in Working Capital Fund

1. Services were rendered to departments whose activities are financed from the following funds:
    (a) General fund
    (b) Special assessment fund
    (c) Utility or other enterprise fund

ENTRY IN WORKING CAPITAL FUND:
Due from General Fund........................ $ 15,000
Due from Special Assessment Fund............. 10,000
Due from Utility or Other Enterprise Fund....... 8,000
    Billings for Services.......................... $ 33,000
To record amounts due from other funds for services
rendered to departments financed from them.

(a) ENTRY IN GENERAL FUND:
    Appropriation Expenditures................. 15,000
        Due to Working Capital Fund............. 15,000
To record cost of services rendered by working
capital fund.

(b) ENTRY IN SPECIAL ASSESSMENT FUND:
    Appropriation Expenditures................. 10,000
        Due to Working Capital Fund............. 10,000
To record cost of services rendered by working
capital fund.

(c) ENTRY IN UTILITY OR OTHER ENTERPRISE FUND:
    Operating Expenses....................... 8,000
        Due to Working Capital Fund............. 8,000
To record cost of services rendered by working
capital fund.

Columnar form of combined fund balance sheet. Although each fund constitutes an independent entity, it is desirable to bring together the financial data in summary form in one place. This can be accomplished best by preparing, in addition to the individual balance sheets, a combined balance sheet in columnar form, as illustrated in Figure 69. This balance sheet is composed of some of the balance sheets illustrated throughout the previous chapters.

Since each fund is an independent entity, the "Total" column of a combined balance sheet is misleading unless the figures in it are analyzed in the light of the data presented in the individual statements. For that

Figure 69

A GOVERNMENTAL UNIT
All Funds
Combined Balance Sheet
at Close of Fiscal Year

ASSETS AND OTHER DEBITS	Total	General Fund (Figure 20)	Bond Funds (Figure 34)	Special Assessment Fund (Figure 37)	Sinking Fund (Figure 42)	Trust and Agency Funds (Figure 53)	Working Capital Fund (Figure 55)	Utility Fund (Figure 59)	Other Enterprise Fund (Figure 64)	General Fixed Assets (Figure 66)	General Bonded Debt and Interest (Figure 68)
Assets:											
Assets—Other than Fixed											
Cash	$ 334,604	$11,200	$101,000		$ 3,880	$ 57,140	$ 11,300	$ 130,084	$ 20,000		
Cash for Construction	405,000			$405,000							
Cash for Interest Payments	2,250			2,250							
Total Cash	$ 741,854	$11,200	$101,000	$407,250	$ 3,880	$ 57,140	$ 11,300	$ 130,084	$ 20,000		
Taxes Receivable—Delinquent	$ 77,432	$69,000			$ 8,432						
Less: Allowance for Uncollectible Delinquent Taxes	13,000	11,000			2,000						
Total Taxes Receivable	$ 64,432	$58,000			$ 6,432						
Interest and Penalties Receivable on Taxes	$ 616	$ 550			$ 66						
Less: Allowance for Uncollectible Interest and Penalties	56	50			6						
Total Interest and Penalties	$ 560	$ 500			$ 60						
Assessments Receivable:											
Current	$ 40,000			$ 40,000							
Delinquent	5,000			5,000							
Deferred	310,000			310,000							
Total Assessments Receivable	$ 355,000			$355,000							
Accounts Receivable	$ 97,000	$21,000						$ 72,000	$ 4,000		
Less: Allowance for Uncollectible Accounts	7,700	1,000						6,500	200		
Total Accounts Receivable	$ 89,300	$20,000						$ 65,500	$ 3,800		

Governmental Unit's Share of Cost	$ 50,000			$ 50,000						
Loans Receivable	59,000					$ 59,000				
Due from General Fund	30,000						$ 30,000			
Due from Utility or Other Enterprise Fund	12,800						12,800			
Due from Endowment Principal Fund	2,490					2,490				
Inventory of Materials and Supplies	33,000						3,000	$ 30,000		
Prepaid Insurance	600							600		
Interest Receivable	3,675			500		2,975		200		
Taxes Receivable for Other Units	200,000					200,000				
Investments	$ 265,000				$25,000	$240,000				
Unamortized Premiums (Net of Discounts)	2,883					2,883				
Total Investments	$ 267,883				$25,000	$242,883				
Sinking Fund:										
Cash	$ 266							266		
Investments	6,600							6,600		
Interest Receivable	150							150		
Total Sinking Fund	$ 7,016							$ 7,016		
Customers' Deposits:										
Cash	$ 1,000							$ 1,000		
Investments	10,000							10,000		
Interest Receivable	200							200		
Total Customers' Deposits	$ 11,200							$ 11,200		
Total Assets—Other than Fixed	$1,928,810	$89,700	$101,000	$812,750	$35,372	$564,488	$ 57,100	$ 244,600	$ 23,800	
Fixed Assets										
Land	$1,567,000						$ 10,000	$ 200,000	$350,000	$1,007,000
Structures and Improvements	3,925,100						40,000	701,400	425,000	2,758,700
Less: Allowance for Depreciation	142,400						2,400	100,000	40,000	
Total Structures and Improvements	$3,782,700						$ 37,600	$ 601,400	$385,000	$2,758,700
Machinery and Equipment	$ 849,600						$ 50,000	$ 200,500	$ 50,000	$ 549,100
Less: Allowance for Depreciation	76,000						9,200	56,000	10,800	
Total Machinery and Equipment	$ 773,600						$ 40,800	$ 144,500	$ 39,200	$ 549,100
Total Fixed Assets	$6,123,300						$ 88,400	$ 945,900	$774,200	$4,314,800
TOTAL ASSETS	$8,052,110	$89,700	$101,000	$812,750	$35,372	$564,488	$145,500	$1,190,500	$798,000	$4,314,800

Figure 69 (*Cont.*)

	Total	General Fund (Figure 20)	Bond Funds (Figure 34)	Special Assessment Fund (Figure 37)	Sinking Fund (Figure 42)	Trust and Agency Funds (Figure 53)	Working Capital Fund (Figure 55)	Utility Fund (Figure 59)	Other Enterprise Fund (Figure 64)	General Fixed Assets (Figure 66)	General Bonded Debt and Interest (Figure 68)
OTHER DEBTS:											
Amount Available for Retirement of Bonds	$ 312,900										$ 312,900
Amount to Be Provided for Retirement of Bonds	787,100										787,100
Amount to Be Provided for Payment of Interest	425,000										425,000
Bonds Authorized—Unissued	200,000		$200,000								
TOTAL OTHER DEBTS	$1,725,000		$200,000								$1,525,000
GRAND TOTAL	$9,777,110	$89,700	$301,000	$812,750	$35,372	$564,488	$145,500	$1,190,500	$798,000	$4,314,800	$1,525,000
LIABILITIES, OTHER CREDITS, AND SURPLUS											
LIABILITIES:											
Liabilities—Other than Long-Term											
Vouchers Payable	$ 106,700	$29,900	$ 10,000					$ 49,500	$ 9,800		
Taxes Collected in Advance	1,000	1,000									
Accrued Salaries and Wages	7,000						$ 7,500	6,000			
Accrued Taxes	7,500							7,500			
Contracts Payable	120,000		20,000	$100,000							
Contracts Payable—Retained Percentage	10,000		10,000				1,000				
Pensions Payable	30					$ 30					
Due to Working Capital Fund	42,800	30,000						12,800			
Due to Endowment Earnings Fund	2,490					2,490					
Customers' Deposits Payable	11,000							11,000			
Customers' Deposits—Interest Payable	150							150			
Other Interest Payable	7,800							6,500	1,300		
Total Liabilities—Other than Long-Term	$ 316,470	$60,900	$ 40,000	$100,000		$ 2,520	$ 8,500	$ 93,450	$ 11,100		
Long-Term Liabilities											
Bonds Payable	$2,748,000			$350,000				$650,000	$648,000		$1,100,000
Interest Payable in Future Years	425,000										425,000
Total Long-Term Liabilities	$3,173,000			$350,000				$650,000	$648,000		$1,525,000
TOTAL LIABILITIES	$3,489,470	$60,900	$ 40,000	$450,000		$ 2,520	$ 8,500	$743,450	$659,100		$1,525,000

214

OTHER CREDITS:

	Total										
Unamortized Premiums on Bonds	$ 1,900							$ 1,900			
Net Balance of Appropriations	230,000		$210,000	$ 20,000							
Fund Balances	531,393					$531,393					
Reserve for Encumbrances	410,000	$20,000	50,000	340,000							
Reserve for Retirement of Sinking Fund Bonds	41,941				34,925			7,016			
Pension Fund Reserve	30,480					30,480					
Governmental Unit's Contribution	500,000							400,000	$100,000		
Capital	135,000						$135,000				
TOTAL OTHER CREDITS	**$1,880,714**	$20,000	$260,000	$360,000	$34,925	$561,873	$135,000	$408,916	$100,000		

SURPLUS:

	Total										
Investment in Fixed Assets	$4,314,800									$4,314,800	
Unappropriated Surplus	89,376	$ 8,800	$ 1,000		$ 447	$ 95	$ 2,000	$ 38,134	$ 38,900		
Unappropriated Surplus—Interest	2,750			$ 2,750							
TOTAL SURPLUS	**$4,406,926**	$ 8,800	$ 1,000	$ 2,750	$ 447	$ 95	$ 2,000	$ 38,134	$ 38,900	$4,314,800	
GRAND TOTAL	**$9,777,110**	$89,700	$301,000	$812,750	$35,372	$564,488	$145,500	$1,190,500	$798,000	$4,314,800	$1,525,000

reason, no combined balance sheet should be presented showing totals of all assets, liabilities, reserves, and surplus, unless the amount applicable to each fund is shown in the same statement. The presentation of the totals for all types of asset, liability, reserve, and surplus accounts in one statement and the details as to the amount applicable to each fund in a subsidiary schedule is not recommended.

Some of the columns in the combined balance sheet are applicable to groups of funds. For example, as indicated at the head of the column, the figures for the bond funds are those of the totals of the group of bond funds illustrated in Figure 34, page 98. To get further details regarding individual bond funds, one would have to refer to this schedule. The same facts apply to the trust and agency funds; the figures shown in the column are for the entire group of trust and agency funds. These figures correspond with those shown in the "Total" column in Figure 53.

Sectional form of combined fund balance sheet. An alternative form of combined balance sheet is one in which a separate section is provided for each fund or group of related funds (see Figure 110, page 334). Such a balance sheet does not show the total of each kind of asset (for example, the total of taxes receivable or total investments) applicable to all funds, nor the total of each kind of liability, reserve, and surplus applicable to such funds. Again, in the sectional form of combined fund balance sheet it is not possible, without making a special compilation, to compare the accounts of one fund with those of another fund or funds or to note the relative importance of the same accounts in different funds. Finally, it is not possible to obtain a bird's-eye view of the financial condition of the governmental unit from a cursory examination of a sectional combined fund balance sheet. For these reasons, the columnar form of combined fund balance sheet is to be preferred over the sectional form.

Inter-fund borrowing. Inter-fund receivables and payables may arise from two sources: (1) from charges for services performed by one fund for another, and (2) from inter-fund loans. No question arises as to the authority for one fund to perform services for another, provided that such services are within the scope of the activities financed from the fund. It is not certain, however, whether, in the absence of express authorization to do so, loans may be made by one fund to another. Some court decisions have held that, unless specially authorized, such loans constitute a diversion of funds. On the other hand, in an important case[3] decided in 1908 and relied on in later decisions, it was held that a temporary loan of money by the general fund to a special fund did not constitute a diversion of funds. Upon examining the circumstances surrounding that case, however, two rules can be laid down. In the first place, the lending and borrowing funds must both be under the control of the same body. Secondly, it must be evident that the borrowing fund will be able to repay the loan.

---

[3] Griffin v. Tacoma, 49 Washington 524 (1908), 95 Pac. 1107.

As a personal loan of magnitude is not ordinarily made to an individual who is insolvent, so a city should not transfer its general-fund moneys as temporary loans to other funds that have not assured and certain sources of income, the collection of which is under the control of the city itself.[4]

Offsetting inter-fund receivables and payables. Sometimes inter-fund receivables are offset against inter-fund payables in the combined balance sheet, on the theory that these assets and liabilities both belong to the same governmental unit. This procedure is incorrect, because each fund is an independent fiscal entity. The error is best illustrated by the following example. Assume that the inter-fund receivables and payables shown below are carried on the asset and liability sides, respectively, of a combined balance sheet.

	General Fund	Bond Fund	Special Assessment Fund	Elimination
ASSET SIDE				
Due from General Fund...........		$20,000	$40,000	(a) $60,000
LIABILITY SIDE				
Due to Bond Fund................	$20,000			(a) 20,000
Due to Special Assessment Fund....	40,000			(a) 40,000

According to this theory, the amounts shown as receivables in the bond fund and the special assessment fund would be canceled against the liability to these two funds by the general fund. But the legislative body has no authority to cancel any asset of the special assessment fund. Similarly, if the bonds have been authorized by a vote of the people, the legislative body has no right to cancel any receivable of the bond fund.

General summary of fund accounting. The outstanding characteristic of governmental accounting is the use of funds. The details of fund accounting are apparent from the discussion of the individual funds. At this point, therefore, we shall only summarize some of the main principles which evolve from the discussion of the detailed accounting procedure for each fund.

In the first place, it is apparent that a fund is an independent fiscal entity and must be accounted for as such. The accounting system must be so devised that the assets, liabilities, reserves, surplus, revenues, and expenditures can be identified with the particular fund to which they apply. It follows that each fund must have a self-balancing group of accounts. A fund need not necessarily consist of cash only; it may even have fixed assets. Neither does it follow that cash segregated for certain purposes constitutes a fund (as is true in the case of funds established under commercial accounting procedures).

In some cases, assets are shown in one fund, but the liabilities incurred in their acquisition are shown in another fund. For example, special as-

---
[4] *Ibid.*

sessment improvements are shown in the general fixed assets group of accounts, whereas special assessment bonds payable are shown as a liability of the special assessment fund. Again, although the bond fund receives the proceeds from the sale of the bonds, the liability is not shown in that fund.

The second important fact is that a governmental unit may have many funds of the same type. That is, it may have many bond funds, sinking funds, and so forth. Each of these groups of funds has been referred to as a related group of funds. The accounting procedure is the same for all the related funds of a group—that is, for all general bond funds, sinking funds, and so forth.

The third fact to note is the variation in the accounting procedure for the several funds with respect to (1) accruing similar items, (2) combining budgetary and proprietary accounts, and (3) excluding certain assets and liabilities. The accrual basis of accounting is followed more consistently in utility, other enterprise, and working capital funds than in any other funds. Since it is essential when working with these funds to arrive at the profit or loss figure for a period, it is important to take into account all the revenues and expenses properly allocable to a period. Revenues are recorded as soon as they become receivable, and expenses are recorded as soon as they are incurred. Furthermore, depreciation expenses are recorded periodically. In the other funds, the degree of accrual varies. Some transactions are recorded on an accrual basis, whereas others are not. For example, accrued interest receivable on investments and bank deposits is usually not recorded in the general fund because it is an insignificant item compared with the other assets of this fund. Accrued interest payable on general bonds is usually not recorded because the appropriation for it will not be made until the beginning of the following fiscal year. If the interest were recorded, therefore, the expenditure would have to be charged against this year's appropriations, whereas actually it is chargeable to the appropriations for the following year.

Budgetary and proprietary accounts are carried in one group in all funds except utility, other enterprise, and working capital funds. If no appropriations are made for working capital, utility, or other enterprise funds, budgetary accounts need not be used except as memoranda accounts. Frequently, however, appropriations are made for these funds. In that case, the budgetary accounts are made a formal part of the accounting system, but they are not combined with the proprietary accounts. In other words, they constitute a complete self-balancing group. However, only those budgetary operations which are affected by legal provisions are included as part of the accounting system. All other budgetary operations are recorded in budget memoranda accounts. For example, estimated revenues need not be formally recorded.

From the discussion in an earlier part of this section, it appears that identical types of assets and liabilities may be included in some funds and excluded from others. For example, fixed assets and bonds payable are included in a utility or other enterprise fund but not in the general fund. Special assessment bonds payable are shown as a liability of the special assessment fund, but the special assessment improvements are not shown as assets of this fund.

14

<<<<<<<<<<<<<<<<<<<<<<<<<<<<<<<<<<<<<<<<<<<<<<<<<<<<<<<<<<<<<<

CASH

THE ACCOUNTING procedure for cash consists in seeing that (1) receipts reach the treasury, (2) disbursements are made only pursuant to legal authorization, (3) both receipts and disbursements are accurately recorded, and (4) cash on hand is accounted for.

Accounting for cash receipts. Cash is one of the assets most likely to be misappropriated; special care must therefore be taken to insure that it will be handled properly. The mishandling of cash can be prevented by (1) providing that employees handling cash should not have access to the accounting records, (2) using pre-numbered financial stationery, and (3) providing for the prompt deposit of all cash receipts to the credit of the governmental unit. The last two provisions apply both to the receipts of the treasury office and to departmental collections. Not all cash receipts come to the treasury directly; some originate in departments. Departmental collections should either be transmitted to the treasury office or be deposited promptly in the bank to the credit of the governmental unit. In the latter case, the depository issues two deposit tickets, one of which is kept by the depositing department and the other transmitted to the treasurer's office.

In some places, an official may collect taxes and hold the money temporarily as a debtor of the governmental unit instead of depositing it to the credit of the government. For example, a tax collector is sometimes not required to turn the cash over immediately upon collection but does so only at stated intervals. In the meantime, he deposits the money to the credit of his own personal account, and when the time for settlement comes, he draws a check on this account for the amount to be turned over. However, this procedure is to be condemned. All money collected by an official should be deposited at once to the credit of the governmental unit.

Recording cash receipts. The account to be credited with cash receipts will depend on whether revenue or nonrevenue receipts are involved. Revenue receipts result in an increase in fund revenue, and they must therefore be credited to revenue accounts. Non-revenue receipts, on the other hand, either decrease assets other than cash or increase liabilities and certain reserves. The proper asset, liability, or reserve account must therefore be credited for the amount of cash received.

Collections are evidenced by documents, and the information necessary for debiting the Cash account of the proper fund and crediting the asset, liability, reserve, revenue, or surplus account of that fund is obtained from these documents. For example, tax receipts are evidenced by tax bills. That is, every time a tax is paid, the collecting unit must retain one part of the tax bill, so that it may have the necessary data for (1) debiting the Cash accounts of the various funds, (2) crediting the taxes receivable control accounts of each fund, and (3) crediting individual taxpayers' accounts. Again, license collections are evidenced by carbon copies of the licenses issued. Since licenses are usually not set up as receivables (that is, they are not recorded as revenue until they are collected in cash), the carbon copies of each license are used as the basis for (1) debiting the Cash account of the particular fund to which license revenues apply, (2) crediting the Revenues control account of that fund, and (3) crediting the individual Licenses accounts in the revenue ledger for the particular fund.

The procedure in recording cash receipts is as follows: Documents are grouped for the purpose of securing control totals. For example, receipt documents are first grouped for the purpose of classifying collections for each fund by main sources—taxes, licenses, permits, accounts receivable, and so forth. Thus, to arrive at the total amount of license collections, it is necessary to group all the license documents together. Another grouping is made for the purpose of determining the total amount of cash applicable to each fund. As a result of these groupings, the amounts necessary for the purpose of crediting the proper control accounts for each fund in the general ledger (that is, the Taxes Receivable account of each fund, the Accounts Receivable account, the Revenues account, and so forth) are secured. A still further grouping of documents is required to arrive at the amount to be posted to the subsidiary accounts. For example, to arrive at the total amount to be posted to the Motor Vehicle License account in the revenue ledger, it is necessary to group all duplicates of motor vehicle license documents.

The above procedure is subject to modification. Procedures vary, in the first place, because of variation in the duties of the accounting department and of the treasurer's office in accounting for receipts. Frequently, if the accounting department and the treasurer's office are under the control of two independent officials, the treasurer is concerned only with classifying the documents so that he can arrive at the amount of cash applicable to each fund. As soon as he obtains these data, he turns the documents over to the accounting department.

On the other hand, if the treasury office and the accounting department are both under the supervision of one official, such as a director of finance, the grouping of the receipt documents by main sources of receipts (for example, taxes, and accounts receivable) is frequently made by the treasurer. On the basis of these groupings, the treasurer prepares a daily cash report, a copy of which, together with the grouped documents on which the report is based, is turned over to the accounting department. The report is checked here against the grouped documents and is used as a basis for making postings to the revenue and receipts register (Figure 70). Where the treasurer reports collections only by fund, receipts are classified only by fund totals in his daily report. A detailed cash report is in that case prepared by the accounting department and is similarly used for making postings to the revenue and receipts register.

Another modification in cash accounting procedure is brought about by the fact that some of the money may be collected by departments instead of by the treasurer. In that event, departments are frequently required to group documents by fund and source. In many governmental units, departments are not permitted to deposit their collections with the treasurer until they secure a pay-in warrant from the accounting officer. The accounting officer will not approve the warrant until the department has grouped the documents by fund and source and has indicated on the warrant the amount of cash collections applicable to each fund and source. Usually the report is prepared in triplicate, and all three copies, together with the grouped documents, are presented for approval to the accounting officer, who signs the three copies and retains one of them, along with the accompanying documents. The other two copies are turned over to the department, which then proceeds to deposit the money with the treasurer. The treasurer in turn signs the two remaining copies and returns one copy to the department as evidence that the money has been received by him.

The accounting officer's copies of treasury pay-in warrants are checked against the documents for the purpose of verifying that the documents have been properly grouped. The warrants are then used as the basis for an entry in the revenue and receipts register. In the treasurer's office, on the other hand, the warrants are used as the basis for preparing the treasurer's daily report of collections. In this case, collections would be classified only by funds in the treasurer's daily report.

A third modification is introduced by the fact that certain departments may keep some of the detailed accounts. For example, the water department may keep the individual accounts of water customers. In that case, the cashier's stubs are not turned over to the treasurer or to the accounting department but are retained by the department and used in posting to the

Figure 70

A GOVERNMENTAL UNIT

Revenue and Receipts Register

Month of _____

Day	Total for Day	GENERAL FUND								SPECIAL REVENUE	
		TAXES						OTHER RECEIPTS		TAXES	
		REAL ESTATE		PERSONAL PROPERTY		Interest & Penalties on Taxes	Motor Vehicle Licenses	Rents	Name of Account	Amount	REAL ESTATE	
		Year	Amount	Year	Amount						Year	Amount

Figure 71

A GOVERNMENTAL UNIT

Check Register

Month of _____

Day	Check No.	Name	FUNDS				
			General			Special Revenue	Working Capital
			Bank A	Bank B	Bank C	Bank A	Bank B

individual accounts receivable. The department, however, submits a summary of the revenues collected, and this summary is used as the basis for crediting the accounts receivable controlling account and any other controlling accounts of the proper funds.

A final modification in cash accounting procedure results from the use of various types of mechanical accounting and tabulating equipment. Where mechanical equipment is employed, the number of groupings is reduced, since many of the desired totals can be secured from one cash register, bookkeeping machine summary, or punched card tabulation.

Recording collections. As we have already indicated, postings to the revenue and receipts register are made from the daily summaries of collections, as prepared by the various departments which collect money, by the treasurer, or by the accounting department. The revenue and receipts register illustrated in Figure 70 is based on the assumption that the governmental unit has only a few sources of receipts. If a governmental unit had many sources, and if a separate column were provided for each source, the register would obviously become too complicated. In that event, subregisters would be established for certain of the accounts. For example, one subregister might be established for licenses and permits, another for revenues from the use of money and property, and so on. Postings to the individual revenue accounts would in that event be made at the end of each month.

Sometimes a separate sheet is set up for each revenue account, to which postings are made daily. Each sheet is totaled at the end of the month, and each total is posted to another sheet. This sheet is similar to the one from which the postings are made except that it shows only the total receipts from the particular source for each month rather than for each day. For example, a separate sheet might be established for marriage licenses, to which receipts from this source would be posted daily. At the end of the month, the total amount of marriage license receipts, as indicated by this sheet, would be added, and the total would be posted to another sheet, which showed marriage license receipts by month only. In this manner, the total amount of receipts for the month and to date, from the particular source, are readily available in summary form.

Receipts are sometimes not entered in any register but are posted directly from the daily reports of cash collections to the accounts. In some cases no daily postings are made. Instead, the daily cash collection reports are summarized at the end of each month into a journal entry which is posted to the accounts. It must be remembered that the detailed accounts, such as each taxpayer's account, are usually credited from the documents themselves and not from any register.

Accounting for cash disbursements. As indicated previously, when an expenditure is approved, a voucher is issued signifying the approval of the liability. Frequently, the voucher and the check are prepared at the same time. Vouchers are prepared in duplicate, and they are so designed that the original can be used as a check and the duplicate can be used as the basis for an entry in the voucher register and as evidence of the approval of the claim. The original of the voucher document becomes a check when it is signed by the treasurer.

An alternative disbursement procedure is to use a voucher, a warrant, and a check. The difference between a voucher and a warrant is that a voucher designates the approval of the claim and serves as the basis for charging the proper expenditure and other accounts, whereas a warrant is an order by the accounting officer on the treasurer to pay the amounts specified. The treasurer in turn issues a check to cover the warrant. Sometimes, however, no additional checks are issued, the warrant becoming a check when it is signed by the treasurer and when the bank account is designated thereon.

Disbursements are recorded in a check register, a form for which is illustrated in Figure 71, page 223. On examining Figure 26, page 81, it will be noted that the voucher register can be converted into a check register by providing space for inserting the name of the bank. If a special payroll bank account has been established, the payroll sheets can be converted into a check register by putting in the check numbers opposite the names on these sheets. If no special payroll account is set up, the same procedure may be followed, but it is necessary also to record in the check register the total amount of checks issued.

Cash statements. Cash statements can be classified into two groups: (1) those prepared during the year primarily for the purpose of budgetary administration, and (2) other cash statements. The first group includes statements comparing actual with estimated receipts, statements forecasting the cash position of a governmental unit, and statements of tax collections. Other cash statements are those showing receipts, disbursements, and cash balances of special assessment funds and trust and agency funds. Each of these statements is discussed below.

1. *Comparative statement of monthly receipts.* This statement is prepared at the end of each month usually for those funds for which appropriations are required—that is, for the general fund and for special revenue funds. The statement is illustrated in Figure 16, page 45.

2. *Statement of forecast of cash position* (Figure 72). The cash position of the governmental unit must be estimated carefully each month. On the basis of the statement of forecast of cash position, a governmental unit is in a position to determine whether or not sufficient money will be available to finance the expenditures for the following month.

3. *Statement of tax levies and tax collections.* This statement is illustrated in Figure 84, page 254. It shows tax collections both for the current month and from the beginning of the year to date and supplements in part the comparative statement of monthly receipts. Whereas the latter shows

Figure 72

A GOVERNMENTAL UNIT

Statement of Forecast of Cash Position
for Month

	Total All Funds	FUNDS			
		General	Special Revenue	Bond	Sinking
Cash on Hand—Beginning of Month.................	$200,000	$ 50,000	$10,000	$10,000	$60,000
Estimated Receipts.........	300,000	100,000	20,000	40,000	—
Total................	$500,000	$150,000	$30,000	$50,000	$60,000
Estimated Disbursements....	450,000	160,000	20,000	40,000	55,000
Estimated Cash Balance—End of Month.........	$ 50,000	$ 10,000*	$10,000	$10,000	$ 5,000
Estimated Loans Necessary..	12,000	12,000	—	—	—
Estimated Cash Balance (After Loans)..........	$ 62,000	$ 2,000	$10,000	$10,000	$ 5,000

* Red.

merely the total amount of taxes collected, this statement shows the amount collected from each year's levy. It should be noted, however, that, whereas the statement comparing actual and estimated receipts shows the data separately for each fund, no fund distinction is made in this statement. The reason is that the statement is supposed to show primarily the trend of collections of the entire tax roll.

4. *Statement of cash receipts, disbursements, and balances—special assessment funds* (Figure 73). It is especially important to prepare a statement analyzing the cash receipts, disbursements, and balances of special assessment funds, because these funds have cash available for three purposes: for construction, for bond payments, and for interest payments. Such a statement gives some evidence that the distinction between the various kinds of cash is being recognized by officials.

5. *Statement of cash receipts, disbursements, and balances—trust and agency funds* (Figure 74). This statement should be prepared because cash transactions are the predominant types of transactions taking place in trust and agency funds.

6. *Statement of cash receipts, disbursements, and balances—all funds* (Figure 75). This is a summary statement showing the cash receipts, disbursements, and balances for each fund and indicating in summary form the changes which have taken place in the Cash account of each fund or group of related funds. It should be noted that both the cash receipts and disbursements include inter-fund transactions, the assumption being that inter-fund balances are settled by check, in the same manner as other liabilities. If inter-fund settlements are made through both journal entries

Figure 73

A GOVERNMENTAL UNIT

Special Assessment Funds

Statement of Cash Receipts, Disbursements, and Balances
for Fiscal Year

	Total	DISTRICT No. 1	DISTRICT No. 2	DISTRICT No. 3
Cash Balance—Beginning of Year:				
For Construction...............	$110,000	$10,000	$20,000	$ 25,000
For Bond Payments..............	60,000	5,000	10,000	15,000
For Interest Payments...........	18,000	2,000	3,000	4,000
Total........................	$188,000	$17,000	$33,000	$ 44,000
Receipts:				
Current Special Assessments—For Construction...................	$ 52,000	$ 5,000	$ 8,000	$ 13,000
Current Special Assessments—For Bonds.......................	70,000	5,000	10,000	20,000
Delinquent Special Assessments—For Construction..................	16,000	2,000	2,000	4,000
Governmental Unit's Share of Cost...	34,000	3,000	4,000	10,000
Interest.........................	36,000	3,000	5,000	10,000
Proceeds from Sale of Bonds........	100,000	—	—	50,000
Total Receipts..................	$308,000	$18,000	$29,000	$107,000
Total........................	$496,000	$35,000	$62,000	$151,000
Disbursements:				
Capital Outlays..................	$180,000	$15,000	$30,000	$ 45,000
Bonds Redeemed.................	60,000	5,000	10,000	15,000
Interest.........................	18,000	2,000	3,000	4,000
Total Disbursements...........	$258,000	$22,000	$43,000	$ 64,000
Cash Balance—End of Year:				
For Construction.................	$132,000	$ 5,000	$ 4,000	$ 57,000
For Bond Payments..............	70,000	5,000	10.000	20,000
For Interest Payments...........	36,000	3,000	5,000	10,000
Total........................	$238,000	$13,000	$19,000	$ 87,000

and cash payments, only that part actually received or paid in cash should be included among the receipts and disbursements. Note also that the bank accounts in which the cash of each fund is held are shown.

The foregoing are not the only cash receipts and disbursements statements which may be needed, for circumstances may indicate that the Cash accounts of other funds call for similar analysis. Again, these statements may be prepared not only at the end of a month or a year but also at other times. For example, cash statements may be needed in the preparation of the budget. For an illustration of a statement used in budget preparation, see Figure 10, page 33.

Figure 74

A GOVERNMENTAL UNIT

Trust and Agency Funds

Statement of Cash Receipts, Disbursements, and Balances for Fiscal Year

	Total All Funds	EXPENDABLE FUNDS				NONEXPENDABLE FUNDS	
		Deposits Fund	Pension Fund	Endowment Earnings Fund	Agency Fund	Endowment Principal Fund	Loan Fund
Cash Balance—Beginning of Year	$76,000	$20,000	$5,000	$1,000	$25,000	$10,000	$15,000
Receipts:							
Deposits	$25,000	$25,000					
Taxes for Other Units (Itemize)	50,000				$50,000		
Contributions	15,000		$15,000				
Gifts	60,000					$60,000	
Sale of Investments	15,000	15,000					
Loans Repaid	20,000						$20,000
Transfer from Endowment Principal	50,000			$50,000			
Total Receipts	$235,000	$40,000	$15,000	$50,000	$50,000	$60,000	$20,000
Total Receipts and Balance	$311,000	$60,000	$20,000	$51,000	$75,000	$70,000	$35,000
Disbursements:							
Taxes Paid to Other Units (Itemize)	$70,000				$70,000		
Deposits Refunded	50,000	$50,000					
Pensions Paid	1,000		$1,000				
Band Concerts	41,000			$41,000			
Loans Made	30,000						$30,000
Transfer to Endowment Earnings	50,000					$50,000	
Investments Purchased	32,000		17,000			15,000	
Total Disbursements	$274,000	$50,000	$18,000	$41,000	$70,000	$65,000	$30,000
Cash Balance—End of Year	$37,000	$10,000	$2,000	$10,000	$5,000	$5,000	$5,000

Figure 75

A GOVERNMENTAL UNIT

All Funds

Summary Statement of Cash Receipts, Disbursements, and Balances for Fiscal Year

Fund	Cash Balance—Beginning of Year	Receipts Regular	Receipts Inter-Fund	Disbursements Regular	Disbursements Inter-Fund	Cash Balance—End of Year	Banks A	Banks B	Banks C
General	$180,000	$300,000	$15,000	$390,000	$90,000	$15,000	$10,000	$5,000	—
Special Revenue	40,000	50,000	—	70,000	5,000	15,000	—	—	$15,000
Bond	60,000	40,000	10,000	50,000	10,000	50,000	20,000	10,000	20,000
Sinking	100,000	150,000	—	200,000	—	50,000	20,000	30,000	—
Working Capital	45,000	5,000	100,000	130,000	—	20,000	3,000	—	17,000
Special Assessment	55,000	150,000	10,000	180,000	20,000	15,000	5,000	10,000	—
Trust and Agency	25,000	50,000	—	55,000	—	20,000	10,000	—	10,000
Utility or Other Enterprise	50,000	200,000	10,000	200,000	20,000	40,000	40,000	—	—
Total	$555,000	$945,000	$145,000	$1,275,000	$145,000	$225,000	$108,000	$55,000	$62,000

Funds and bank accounts. Solely from an accounting standpoint, there is no need for a separate bank account for each fund, the mere segregation of cash by funds on the books being sufficient. An independent fund may be said to exist even if no separate bank account is provided for it. Nevertheless, if a governmental unit does not have many funds, it should establish a separate bank account for each fund or group of related funds. The use of one bank account for all funds frequently leads to hidden interfund borrowing; that is, cash really applicable to one fund is used to meet the expenditures of another fund. Hidden borrowing is especially likely to be resorted to if statutes prohibit inter-fund loans.

As an illustration, suppose the balance sheet of the general fund and a special revenue fund was as follows:

A GOVERNMENTAL UNIT
General Fund and Special Revenue Fund
Balance Sheet
Date

	General Fund	Special Revenue Fund
ASSETS		
Cash.....................................	$100,000	$40,000
Taxes Receivable (Net)..................	200,000	50,000
	$300,000	$90,000
LIABILITIES AND SURPLUS		
Vouchers Payable.......................	$200,000	$60,000
Unappropriated Surplus...................	100,000	30,000
	$300,000	$90,000

Suppose, further, that the only transaction which occurred during the particular period was the issuance of checks amounting to $50,000, all of which was payable out of the special revenue fund. After this transaction had been made effective, the balance sheet would appear as follows:

A GOVERNMENTAL UNIT
General Fund and Special Revenue Fund
Balance Sheet
Date

	General Fund	Special Revenue Fund
ASSETS		
Cash.....................................	$100,000	—
Taxes Receivable (Net)..................	200,000	$50,000
	$300,000	$50,000

LIABILITIES AND SURPLUS

Cash Overdraft...........................	—	$10,000
Vouchers Payable.......................	$200,000	10,000
Unappropriated Surplus..................	100,000	30,000
	$300,000	$50,000

Note that the above transaction results in the use of $10,000 belonging to the general fund. In effect, the special revenue fund borrowed $10,000 from the general fund, and the transaction should have been recorded in the same manner as an inter-fund borrowing transaction; that is, an entry should have been made in the general fund debiting Due from Special Revenue Fund and crediting Cash, and an entry should have been made in the special revenue fund debiting Cash and crediting Due to General Fund. Furthermore, on the balance sheet an asset account, Due from Special Revenue Fund, should have been shown for the general fund, and a liability account, Due to General Fund, should have been shown for the special revenue fund. Instead, one gathers from the above statement that the governmental unit owes the bank $10,000. The necessity for showing inter-fund borrowings is especially important if statutes prohibit such loans. Where one bank account is used, it is relatively easy to evade the law intentionally or unintentionally. If separate bank accounts are used, no checks will be drawn on any fund unless there is sufficient money to the credit of the fund because the bank would refuse to honor checks in excess of the balance in the bank account.

In addition to the factors discussed above, there are also others that must be taken into account in determining the number of bank accounts to be used. If the governmental unit has many funds, the establishment of separate bank accounts is likely to hinder the effective administration of cash. For example, some governmental units have hundreds of trust funds, and others have separate tax levy funds for each department. To use a separate bank account for each of these funds would mean complicating the accounting procedure considerably.

In the light of the above factors and of the experience encountered in recent times, it would seem that the proper procedure would be somewhat as follows: If the accounting system is such that the amount of cash applicable to each fund cannot readily be determined, a separate bank account should be established for each fund. In all other cases, separate bank accounts should be established for each *type* of fund; that is, a separate bank account might be established for the general fund, for all bond funds, for all sinking funds, and so forth.

Inter-fund settlements. Either as a result of inter-fund borrowing or as a result of the performance by one fund of services for another, a fund may have money coming from another fund and may in turn owe money to the same fund or to other funds. Many governmental units settle inter-fund transactions at the end of each month. Others make settlements at more or less frequent intervals. The procedure in making inter-fund settlements depends on whether or not a separate bank account is provided for each of the funds involved. If separate bank accounts are provided for each fund, inter-fund settlements are made by check; otherwise they are made through a journal entry. In either case, the settlement should be authorized in the same manner as other charges.

Choosing the depository. Usually the law provides that depositories be chosen by the legislative body of the governmental unit. The statutes also prescribe the conditions under which money is to be deposited. For example, the law may specify that before a governmental unit may deposit its funds in a bank, the capital stock and surplus of the institution must equal a certain minimum amount or must be a certain number of times the average amount of the unit's deposits. Banks are frequently required to furnish security for public deposits, thereby enabling governmental units to avoid losses.

Accounting for petty cash and change funds. Petty cash is accounted for in the same manner as the petty cash of private businesses. The only additional point to remember is that such cash is not available for appropriation. Similarly, funds established for the purpose of making change must not be considered as available for appropriation.

Reconciliations. Statements must be prepared at the end of each month or, in the case of large governmental units, at more frequent intervals to reconcile the cash balance as shown by the bank statement with the cash balance carried on the books of the treasurer and on the books of the comptroller. The procedure is the same as for a private business.

The extent of the reconciliation required between the Cash account as shown on the treasurer's records and on the bank statement will depend on the method of recording disbursements on the treasurer's books. If the treasurer records checks as disbursements as soon as they are issued, checks outstanding must be taken into account. If, on the other hand, the treasurer, contrary to sound financial administration, does not record checks as disbursements until they have cleared through the bank, then the only item to be taken into account in making the reconciliation is cash on hand for deposit.

The extent of reconciliation between the balance of the Cash account shown on the comptroller's books and that shown on the bank statement will vary. If the Cash account on the comptroller's books is reduced as soon as warrants are issued, it is necessary to take into account, in addition to outstanding checks, warrants issued by the comptroller for which the treasurer has not yet issued checks. Otherwise, only outstanding checks need to be taken into account.

Summary. The accounting procedure for cash must be so devised that the possibility of misappropriation is reduced to a minimum. One of the prerequisites is a proper system of internal control under which provision is made for (1) the prompt deposit of cash, (2) the identification of cash with the fund to which it applies, (3) its disbursement for authorized purposes only, and (4) the proper recording of disbursements.

15

<<<<<<<<<<<<<<<<<<<<<<<<<<<<<<<<<<<<<<<<<<<<<<<<<<<<<<<<<<<<<<<<

GENERAL PROPERTY TAXES

GENERAL PROPERTY taxes are ad valorem taxes levied in proportion to the assessed valuation of real or personal property. The procedure in the administration of general property taxes is as follows: (1) The assessed valuation of each piece of real property and of the taxable personal property of each taxpayer is determined; (2) the legislative body levies the total amount of taxes which it needs but not in excess of the amount permitted by law; (3) the tax levy is distributed among taxpayers on the basis of the assessed value of property owned by them; (4) taxpayers are billed; (5) tax collections are credited to taxpayers' accounts; (6) tax collections are enforced by the imposition of penalties and the sale of property for taxes. Each of these steps in general property tax administration is discussed below.

Assessment of property. By assessment of property is meant the valuing of property for purposes of taxation. The assessment of property for local taxes is usually performed by an official known as an assessor, who may be either elected or appointed. The assessed value of each piece of real property or of the personal property of each personal property owner is recorded on a sheet known as an assessment roll. Each sheet contains the assessed value of several pieces of property or the assessed values of the personal property of several owners. In the case of real property, however, for each piece of property a separate continuing property record, on which the assessed valuation for that piece alone is shown, is frequently provided. As we shall indicate subsequently, the assessment roll may be converted into a tax roll. Thus, for example, the first five columns of Figure 76 may be said to constitute an assessment roll. After the assessments have been made, they are reviewed by a board which hears protests and makes adjustments.

The total assessed value of real estate in a governmental unit is deter-

Figure 76

A GOVERNMENTAL UNIT
Combined Assessment Roll and Tax Roll of Real Property

Year _____

Taxpayer's Name and General Description of Property	Block and Lot No.	Value of Real Estate	Value of Improvements	Total Assessed Valuation	Composite Tax Rate	Total Tax	Bill No.	PAYMENTS			Liens
								Date Paid	Amount of Tax	Penalties	

mined by adding the assessed values of the individual pieces of property; the total assessed value of personal property is determined by adding the assessed values of the personal property of the individual owners. But it must be remembered that several governmental units may levy taxes on the same real and personal property. Thus, the state, county, city, and school district within whose jurisdiction the property is located may each tax the property. A saving in time and effort is therefore effected if one unit does the assessing. The total assessed value of any governmental unit is, in that event, determined by adding the individual assessed values of the real property situated within its jurisdiction and the assessed values of the personal property of personal property owners located within the jurisdiction. For example, assume that the assessment is made by a county and that within this county are located cities, villages, and independent school districts. To get the assessed value for city tax purposes, it is necessary merely to add the individual assessed values of the real property and the personal property located within the city. Similarly, to get the assessed value for school purposes, it is necessary merely to add the individual assessed values of the property located within the school district.

Levying the tax. Taxes are levied through the passage of a tax levy act or ordinance. Local taxes are levied annually, usually at the time the appropriation act or ordinance is passed. State property taxes may be levied biennially, but a separate amount is specified for each year.

Tax levies are made in one or two lump sums in some governmental units, whereas in others the levies are very detailed. The extent to which levies are made in detail depends on legal provisions. Frequently, statutes and even charters specify that certain taxes are to be levied for particular purposes. In that event, the legislative body must indicate specifically the amount levied for each purpose. In fact, tax levy ordinances are sometimes so detailed that they are confused with appropriation ordinances. Of course, the distinction between the two must be kept in mind. The appropriation ordinance merely authorizes the expenditure of money, whereas the tax levy ordinance provides the means for financing expenditures.

The effect of detailed tax levies is to create special revenue funds. For example, if a special levy is made for parks, it is necessary to create a special revenue fund for parks, so as to insure that the taxes collected are not used for any other purposes. It must be understood, however, that the mere levy of a tax may not enable a governmental unit to spend the money since the expenditure of money requires an appropriation. For example, under such circumstances, if a governmental unit levied a tax for parks but made no appropriation for park purposes, tax collections would be placed in a special revenue fund and not expended.

Determining the tax rate. The tax rate is determined by dividing the amount of taxes levied by the assessed valuation. Thus, if a governmental unit has an assessed valuation of $10,000,000 and its total tax levy is $250,000, the tax rate for the governmental unit is 25 mills per dollar of assessed value ($250,000 ÷ $10,000,000). The total tax rate consists of the tax rate for general purposes and special tax rates, if any, for particular purposes. For exmple, if we assume that, out of the total levy of $250,000, $150,000 was for general purposes, $10,000 was for park purposes, $50,000 was for schools, and $40,000 was for debt service, the tax rates would be as follows:

Purpose	Rate (In Mills per Dollar of Assessed Value)
General	15
Parks	1
Schools	5
Debt Service	4
	25

Maximum tax rates are frequently prescribed for governmental units by constitutions, statutes, or charters. Some laws go further and provide a maximum aggregate tax rate for all the governmental units levying taxes on property within a jurisdiction. For example, in one state the total tax levy of all the local units occupying a particular area must not exceed 40 mills per dollar of assessed value, divided as follows: county, 10 mills; city, 15 mills; schools, 10 mills; state, 2 mills; and road district, 3 mills. Taxes to meet the payment of bonds and interest are, however, exempted from this limitation. The tax limit may be exceeded only upon approval by a three-fifths majority of those voting on the proposition.

Before arriving at the amount to be levied, the legislative body will want to know what tax rate will result from the levy. If it appears that the total levy will produce a rate higher than the maximum permitted by law, the levy will be made only sufficiently high to produce a rate not greater than the maximum specified by statute. Sometimes the statutes authorize the maximum tax levy in dollars and cents instead of fixing a tax rate. For example, the law may provide that the maximum tax rate of a particular governmental unit shall be such as will produce $100,000. Such a levy is known as a "pegged levy," since the levying authority is guaranteed a definite sum and is not concerned with the resulting tax rate.

Determining the amount due from each taxpayer. The amount of taxes due from each taxpayer is arrived at by multiplying the assessed value of his property by the tax rate. For example, if a taxpayer owns real estate with an assessed value of $10,000 and the city tax rate is 25 mills per dollar of assessed value, his city tax will be $250 ($10,000 × .025).

Setting up taxes receivable and billing taxpayers. As soon as the amount due from each taxpayer is determined, it is entered on the tax roll. A tax roll is a record showing the amount of taxes levied against each piece of real property and against each owner of personal property. As already indicated, in some cases the assessment roll is made to serve as a tax roll by the addition of space for filling in the amount of taxes levied and any other information relating to the levy and collection of taxes. In others, assessment rolls and tax rolls are prepared separately. Figure 76 illustrates a combined assessment roll and tax roll of real property.

Note that provision is made on this tax roll for recording not only the amount of taxes levied but also tax collections. In other words, the tax roll may be thought of as a subsidiary ledger supporting the taxes receivable controlling accounts in the general ledger. If interest and penalties on delinquent taxes are accrued at the end of each year, provision is made for showing the accruals.

Because of tax delinquencies and because taxpayers are frequently permitted to pay taxes in installments, individual property tax cards similar to that illustrated in Figure 77 are sometimes used. In that case, the tax roll shows only the amount of taxes levied on each property; it does not show the amount of taxes collected, the latter data being shown on the individual property tax cards. In general, these cards show considerably more information than the tax roll. They provide a continuous tax history of each piece of property, for, in contrast with the tax roll, no new card is made out for each tax levy. Instead, the card shows assessed values, taxes levied, and collections of taxes, interest, and penalties from the time the record was set up until the present. These cards are analogous to the accounts receivable of a commercial enterprise, which show for each customer the beginning balance, the amount billed, the amount received, the balance outstanding, and other related information.

Properties are grouped by districts both on the assessment roll and on the tax roll. That is, even if several pieces of property are owned by the same individual, they are not listed together but are grouped with the properties of the particular district in which they are located. Separate tax bills are usually prepared for each piece of property, for the reason that real estate taxes are frequently taxes on the property and not on the owner. Real property owners will also own personal property. They are frequently billed separately for such taxes; that is, the real property and personal property taxes are shown on separate bills.

Collection of a government's taxes by another unit. We have assumed thus far that each governmental unit collects its own taxes. Frequently, one governmental unit acts as collecting agent for other units. In that case, each governmental unit certifies its tax levy to the collecting unit, which in turn bills the taxpayers. Some tax bills show separately the amounts levied on the particular property by each of the governmental units, whereas others show merely the total amount due and indicate the tax rate for each of the units for which taxes are being collected. These taxes are handled by the collecting unit in an agency fund. The accounting procedure involved is therefore discussed in Chapter 10, which deals with trust and agency funds.

Enforcing the collection of taxes. Tax bills may be payable in install-

Figure 77

A GOVERNMENTAL UNIT
Real Estate Tax Ledger

Property No._____

Ward_____ Lot_____ County Lot_____ Block_____ Acres_____

Subdivision_____ Description_____

House No._____ Street_____

Address_____

Assessed to	Year	Ref.	Assessed Valuation	Composite Tax Rate	Amount of Tax	Paid or Canceled			Balance of Tax
						Date	Taxes	Int. & P'lty	

239

ments or in a single payment. After a certain date, usually prescribed by statute, unpaid taxes become delinquent, whereupon they are subject to interest and penalties. Some governmental units accrue the interest and penalties at the end of each fiscal year, whereas others do not record them as revenue until they are collected.

Statutes usually provide that taxes and interest and penalties become a lien against property without any action on the part of the governmental unit. At the expiration of a certain period of time, the governmental unit has the right to sell the property in order to satisfy its lien. Any excess of the amount received from the sale of the property over the amount of taxes, interest, penalties, and cost of holding the sale is turned over to the property owner. On the other hand, as in the case of special assessments, if the proceeds from the sale of the property are insufficient to cover the amount due, the property owner may or may not be called upon to make up the difference, depending on the legal provisions of the state.

The property owner is given the privilege of redeeming the property within a certain period of time. If the property was purchased by a private party, it can be redeemed by payment to the buyer of the purchase price plus interest. If it was bid in by the governmental unit, the property can be redeemed by payment of the taxes, interest, penalties, and other charges. If the property is not redeemed by a certain date, the private purchaser or governmental unit, as the case may be, secures title.

Personal property taxes are frequently a lien not only on the property taxed but also on any other property owned by the taxpayer. In fact, sometimes statutes provide that such taxes shall be a lien against the real estate of the personal property owner. In that case, the procedure in selling the property for taxes and for its redemption is the same as for property on which there is a lien for unpaid real estate taxes. Of course, any personal property owned by the taxpayer (with the exception of a certain amount exempted by statute from sale for taxes) is subject to sale to satisfy unpaid personal property taxes.

In discussing the accounting procedure for delinquent taxes and the sale for taxes and redemption of the property, we have assumed that only one governmental unit is involved. Actually, all of the governmental units which levy taxes on the particular piece of property have liens on it, and proceeds from its sale must be shared by these units. If each government were left to enforce its own lien and sell the property for taxes, not only would the cost of sale be greatly increased but such a procedure would also result in considerable confusion. Accordingly, even where each government collects its own taxes, provision is usually, although not always, made for transferring delinquent tax rolls to one governmental unit. Sometimes current taxes are collected by one governmental unit for all the other governments, but, as soon as the taxes become delinquent, they are turned over for collection to another unit. For example, a city may be empowered to collect not only its own current taxes but also state, county, and school taxes. When the taxes become delinquent, however, the city may be required to turn over the delinquent tax rolls to the county. This unit attempts to collect the delinquent taxes and goes through all the steps necessary to enforce the lien. That is, it holds tax sales, and, if necessary, bids in the property. Unless otherwise provided by statute, each unit receives from the collecting unit its proportionate share of tax collections. Sometimes, however, the statutes provide that collections from delinquent taxes shall be turned over first to certain units until their levy is fully satisfied. The remainder is distributed among the other governmental units in proportion to their levies.

Recording taxes on the books. The entries to record the levy and collection of taxes have already been mentioned in connection with the discussion of fund accounting procedure. Further details will be given in this chapter.

When taxes are levied, the entry, in each fund, as we have previously indicated, is a debit to Taxes Receivable—Current and a credit to Allowance for Uncollectible Current Taxes and to Revenues. Later, when the taxes became delinquent, an entry is made debiting Taxes Receivable—Delinquent as well as Allowance for Uncollectible Current Taxes, and crediting Taxes Receivable—Current as well as Allowance for Uncollectible Delinquent Taxes. An additional fact to remember in this connection is that separate Taxes Receivable accounts are set up for real property taxes and personal property taxes. Delinquent taxes are recorded in such a manner that the amount applicable to each individual year can be readily determined.

For example, if full details regarding delinquent taxes were to be shown on the balance sheet, the Taxes Receivable account would appear as follows:

Real Property Taxes Receivable—Delinquent:
Levy of 1954	$30,000	
1953	20,000	
1952	10,000	
1951	5,000	
1950 and prior	3,000	$68,000
Less—Allowance for Uncollectible Delinquent Taxes	10,000	$58,000

Personal Property Taxes Receivable—Delinquent:
Levy of 1954	$20,000	
1953	15,000	
1952	10,000	
1951	4,000	
1950 and prior	5,000	$54,000
Less—Allowance for Uncollectible Delinquent Taxes	15,000	39,000
Total Taxes Receivable—Delinquent		$97,000

As taxes are collected, the entry made in each fund is as follows:

```
Cash......................................  $100,000
    Taxes Receivable—Current................            $80,000
    Taxes Receivable—Delinquent.............            20,000
    To record collection of current and delinquent
    taxes, as follows:
```

Year of Levy	Amount
1955 (Current)...................	$ 80,000
1954...........................	10,000
1953...........................	5.000
1952...........................	3,000
1951...........................	1,000
1950...........................	500
1949...........................	500
	$100,000

It is important to be able to identify each year's levy, so that the proper Taxes Receivable accounts may be credited and the proceeds of tax collections may be allocated to the proper fund, for the proportion of the total tax levy made for each purpose may vary from year to year. For example, assume that the tax levy is $100,000 both for this year and for last year but that the levies are divided as follows:

Purpose	This Year Amount Levied	This Year Percentage of Total	Last Year Amount Levied	Last Year Percentage of Total
General...........	$ 46,700	46.7	$ 40,000	40.0
Parks.............	13,300	13.3	13,300	13.3
Schools...........	26,700	26.7	33,400	33.4
Sinking Fund......	13,300	13.3	13,300	13.3
	$100,000	100.0	$100,000	100.0

The part of the proceeds of this year's tax levy that is to be placed in the general fund is found by multiplying the amount collected from the levy by 46.7 per cent. Thus, if $90,000 is collected, $42,030 is placed to the credit of the general fund ($90,000 × 46.7 per cent). On the other hand, the amount of collections from last year's levy that is to be placed to the credit of the general fund is obtained by multiplying the collections from that levy by 40 per cent. For example, if collections amount to $10,000, the sum of $4,000 ($10,000 × 40 per cent) is placed to the credit of the general fund. Collections from the other levies are allocated to the proper funds in the same manner. It is evident, therefore, that tax collections cannot be applied to the proper funds unless the amount collected from each levy is known.

We have indicated above the necessity of keeping a separate control account for each year's levy. It is similarly important to divide a large governmental unit into taxing districts and to establish a controlling account for each district. Frequently, these districts are further divided into subdistricts, with a separate subcontrol account for each. These accounts facilitate the proper control of taxes receivable and help in proving the accuracy of the work. For example, in a large governmental unit even a single tax district will contain thousands of taxpayers, for each of whom an account must be established. Therefore, if the total of the balances of the individual accounts for a district were found to be in disagreement with the district control account, it might be necessary to check thousands of accounts. By introducing subdistrict control accounts, the number of accounts which must be checked in the event of error is reduced considerably, since subdistrict control accounts control a much smaller number of accounts than the district control accounts.

The accounting procedure thus far outlined is also applicable to governmental units which do not collect their own taxes. The collecting unit, in that event, transmits a report indicating the amount collected from each year's levy of real property taxes and of personal property taxes. The receiving unit, on the basis of this report, distributes the proceeds among the various funds and credits the proper control accounts. In fact, the accounting procedure for a governmental unit which collects its own taxes differs from that of one which does not, only in that the latter does not prepare a tax roll and may not keep a record of the amounts paid or owed by the individual taxpayers, the latter records being kept for it by the collecting governmental unit.

Recording discounts on taxes. A few governmental units allow discounts on taxes paid before a certain date. These discounts should be considered as revenue deductions; that is, the tax revenues should be credited only for the net amount of the tax, and an Allowance for Estimated Discounts account should be provided. For example, if the tax levy was $300,000, on which it is estimated that discounts of $2,000 will be taken, the entry to record the levy of the tax and the allowance for discounts is as follows:

Taxes Receivable—Current.................	$300,000	
Allowance for Uncollectible Current Taxes..		$ 9,000
Allowance for Discounts on Taxes.........		2,000
Revenues.................................		289,000
To record levy of taxes and provision of allowances for estimated losses as well as for estimated discounts to be taken.		

As taxes are collected and discounts are taken, the discounts are charged against the allowance. For example, if tax collections amounted to $150,000 and discounts to the amount of $1,500 had been taken, the entry to record the transaction would be as follows:

Cash......................................	$150,000	
Allowance for Discounts on Taxes...........	1,500	
Taxes Receivable—Current...............		$151,500

To record collection of taxes and allowance of discounts thereon.

As the discount period is passed, the following entry is made:

Allowance for Discounts on Taxes...........	$500	
Revenues................................		$500

To record increase in revenues by amount of estimated discounts which were not taken.

Some governmental units are not permitted to give discounts unless an appropriation is made for them. In that case it is necessary to increase revenues by the amount of the discount and to make an appropriation for the discount on the expenditure side of the budget. For example, in the case of the figures used in the foregoing illustrations, the entry to record the levy of taxes would be as follows:

Taxes Receivable—Current.................	$300,000	
Allowance for Uncollectible Current Taxes..		$ 9,000
Revenues................................		291,000

To record levy of taxes and provision for estimated losses.

The entry to record the collection of taxes and the taking of the discount would, with the figures used in the first entry on this page, be as follows:

Cash......................................	$150,000	
Appropriation Expenditures.................	1,500	
Taxes Receivable—Current..............		$151,500

To record collection of taxes and allowance of discount.

The Appropriation Expenditures account is treated in the same manner as any other expenditure account. This method is not desirable, since it has the effect of overstating both the revenues and the expenditures and requires greater legal formality than the first method. It should be used only in cases where legal provisions make it impossible to employ the first method.

Recording interest and penalties on taxes. As we have said before, some governmental units accrue interest and penalties on delinquent taxes, whereas others do not record them as revenue until they are collected. If interest and penalties are accrued, they are added to the tax roll. The entry to record the accrual of interest and penalties is as follows:

Interest and Penalties Receivable on Taxes...	$15,000	
Allowance for Uncollectible Interest and Penalties................................		$ 1,000
Revenues................................		14,000

To record revenues from interest and penalties on delinquent taxes and to provide allowance for amount of such revenues which it is estimated will never be collected, as follows:

Subsidiary Account	Levy of	Amount
Interest and Penalties.....	1954	$2,000
Interest and Penalties.....	1953	1,900
Etc.		

It will be noted that it is essential to identify the revenues from interest and penalties with the particular tax levy to which they apply.

If interest and penalties are not accrued but are recorded as revenues only at the time the cash is received, the entry to record revenues from this source is as follows:

Cash....................................... $10,000

    Revenues............................... $10,000

To record receipt of interest and penalties on delinquent taxes, as follows:

Subsidiary Account	Levy of	Amount
Interest and Penalties.....	1954	$3,000
Interest and Penalties.....	1953	4,000
Etc.		

Accounting for tax sales. When the property is sold for taxes, the following entry is made:

Cash....................................... $29,000

    Taxes Receivable—Delinquent............ $25,000

    Interest and Penalties Receivable on Taxes.. 3,000

    Cost of Holding Tax Sale................ 1,000

To record sale of properties for taxes, as follows:

Levy of	Taxes	Interest and Penalties	Total
1953........	$10,000	$1,000	$11,000
1952........	15,000	2,000	17,000
	$25,000	$3,000	$28,000

A similar entry is made for each fund to which the taxes apply. Each taxpayer's account is, of course, credited with the amount of the tax collected and, if interest and penalties are accrued, also with the amount of interest and penalties collected.

If the proceeds from the sale of the property are in excess of the amount of taxes, interest, penalties, and other charges, the cash representing the excess is placed in a trust fund for the property owner. The following entry is made in the trust fund to record this transaction:

Cash....................................... $1,000

    Property Owners' Trust Fund Balance...... $1,000

To record receipt of cash representing excess of sales price over amount of taxes, interest, and other charges, such cash to be held in trust for property owners and eventually to be paid over to them.

On the other hand, if the cash received from the sale of the property is not sufficient to cover delinquent taxes, interest, and penalties, and if taxes are a lien only against the property, the difference is charged to the allowance for estimated losses. The entry to record this transaction is as follows:

Cash.....................................	$10,000	
Allowance for Uncollectible Delinquent Taxes	2,000	
Allowance for Uncollectible Interest and Penalties...............................	100	
Taxes Receivable—Delinquent............		$12,000
Interest and Penalties Receivable on Taxes..		100
To record sale of property for taxes and to charge difference between cash received and amount of taxes and interest and penalties to allowances for estimated losses.		

If the property owner decides to redeem property sold to another private party, the governmental unit may act for him. The transaction is handled through a trust fund, and the entries are as follows:

Cash.....................................	$12,000	
Property Owners' Trust Fund Balance.....		$12,000
To record receipt of cash for purpose of redeeming property sold for taxes.		
Property Owners' Trust Fund Balance.......	12,000	
Cash.....................................		12,000
To record payment of money to purchaser of property.		

If the governmental unit bids in properties, the entry to record the transaction is as follows:

Tax Sale Certificates......................	$30,500	
Taxes Receivable—Delinquent............		$29,800
Interest and Penalties Receivable on Taxes..		500
Cost of Holding Tax Sale................		200
To record acquisition of properties at tax sale for nonpayment of taxes.		

At the same time an entry is made to provide an allowance for estimated losses on tax sale certificates, as follows:

Allowance for Uncollectible Delinquent Taxes..	$2,000	
Allowance for Uncollectible Interest and Penalties...............................	50	
Allowance for Uncollectible Tax Sale Certificates...................................		$2,050
To record allowance for estimated losses on tax sale certificates.		

As properties are redeemed, an entry is made debiting Cash and crediting Tax Sale Certificates. If properties are not redeemed, and the governmental unit decides to use some of the unredeemed properties for its own purposes—for example, for playgrounds—the Tax Sale Certificates accounts are removed from the funds in which they are carried through the following entry:

Appropriation Expenditures.................	$1,000	
Allowance for Uncollectible Tax Sale Certificates	700	
Tax Sale Certificates....................		$1,700
To record removal of tax sale property as asset of fund.		

Note that the allowance for Uncollectible Tax Sale Certificates account is not charged for the full amount of the tax certificates removed. It is charged only with the difference between the salable value of the tax sale certificates and the value carried on the books. For example, in the entry illustrated above it is assuming that tax sale certificates with a book value of $1,700 can be sold for only $1,000. Consequently, the allowance is reduced by $700 (book value, $1,700, minus market value, $1,000), the remaining $1,000 being charged against the Appropriation Expenditures account.

Since the property will be part of the governmental unit's fixed assets, it is necessary to record it in the general fixed assets group of accounts. The entry to record this transaction is as follows:

Land....................................	$300	
Structures and Improvements..............	700	
Investment in Fixed Assets from Current Revenues...........................		$1,000
To record property acquired at tax sale and not redeemed.		

It should be noted that these fixed assets are capitalized at the market value of the tax sale certificates outstanding against them (in this case, $1,000). The apportionment between land and buildings is usually made on some arbitrary basis.

Several governmental units may have liens on the same piece of property. The accounting procedure for the sale of the property is the same as that for property sold to satisfy the lien of only one governmental unit. The proceeds from the sale of the property are distributed among the various units to satisfy their liens, and any remaining cash is turned over to the property owner. Each governmental unit makes an entry on its records debiting Cash and crediting Taxes Receivable—Delinquent, Interest and Penalties Receivable on Taxes, and Cost of Holding Tax Sale. If the proceeds are not sufficient to cover all the liens, each governmental unit receives a proportionate share of the money realized, unless statutes specify another basis of distribution. Each governmental unit charges to allowances for estimated losses the differences between amounts due and amounts received.

If a governmental unit bids in property on which other governmental units have tax liens, it cannot dispose of it without the consent of the others. Sometimes, if the property is income producing, the governmental unit will operate it and distribute the net income from operations among the governmental units holding liens. Again, sometimes the tax-delinquent properties bid in will be distributed among the various governmental units.

Accounting for nonrevenue taxes. Thus far we have considered the accounting procedure for taxes which form part of the revenues of the governmental unit. The governmental unit may, however, collect taxes which do not form a part of its revenues. Examples are taxes collected in advance, which do not become revenues until later, and taxes collected for other units. The accounting procedure for taxes collected for other units is described in Chapter 10, which deals with trust and agency funds, while the procedure for taxes collected in advance is described immediately below.

Accounting for taxes collected in advance. Sometimes a taxpayer will pay his taxes before being billed or even before the tax has been levied. Such tax collections are not revenue. They may be recorded either in the general fund or in a trust fund, the entry in either case being as follows:

Cash...	$2,500	
Taxes Collected in Advance....................		$2,500
To record collection of taxes on 1956 roll.		

These tax collections represent a deferred credit to revenues, and the Taxes Collected in Advance account is therefore shown as a deferred credit on the liability side of the balance sheet. The entries made subsequently, when the taxes are levied and the Taxes Receivable accounts are set up, depend on where the transaction is originally recorded. If the cash from the advanced tax collections was recorded in a trust fund, an entry must be made transferring the money out of that fund to the proper funds. This entry is as follows:

Taxes Collected in Advance.....................	$2,500	
Cash..		$2,500
To record paying over to each fund of proper amount		
of taxes belonging to it.		

The corresponding entry in each of the funds receiving the cash is

Cash...	$1,000	
Taxes Receivable—Current....................		$1,000
To record receipt of cash from trust fund represent-		
ing share of taxes collected in advance applicable to		
this fund.		

If, on the other hand, the taxes collected in advance are recorded in the general fund, and the taxes are also applicable to other funds, the entry after the Taxes Receivable accounts are set up is as follows:

Taxes Collected in Advance.....................	$2,500	
Taxes Receivable—Current..................		$1,000
Cash.......................................		1,500

To record application of taxes collected in advance
to reduce taxes receivable of general fund and to
record transfer of cash to other funds on account
of advanced tax collections applicable to them.

In each of the other funds affected, an entry is made debiting Cash and crediting Taxes Receivable—Current.

If the amount of taxes collected in advance exceeds the amount levied, the excess is either refunded or continues to be carried as a deferred credit until the next levy is made. If, on the other hand, the amount collected is less than the amount levied, the taxpayer is billed for the difference.

General property tax statements. Property tax statements are prepared for the purpose of showing further details about property taxes. These statements may be divided into two classes: (1) those which are directly tied in with the financial statements of the current period, and (2) those which show data also for a number of other periods. As already indicated, statements of the former type are usually referred to as *subsidiary financial statements*, whereas those in the latter group are usually known as *statistical statements*. The statements illustrated here are as follows: (1) statement of changes in taxes receivable, (2) detailed statement of taxes receivable, (3) statement of changes in tax sale certificates, (4) detailed statement of tax sale certificates, (5) statement of assessed value and estimated true value of all taxable property, (6) statement of tax rates and tax levies, (7) statement of tax levies and tax collections (during the year), and (8) statement of tax levies and tax collections (at end of year). The first four statements are subsidiary financial statements, and the last four are statistical statements. Each of these statements is discussed in detail below.

Statement of changes in taxes receivable (Figure 78). This statement shows the changes which have taken place in the Taxes Receivable accounts during a particular period of time. It shows the amount of taxes levied, collections, and the balance of current taxes receivable. Then follows the beginning balance of delinquent taxes, from which are deducted cancellations and collections, to arrive at the closing balance of delinquent taxes receivable. The statement also shows the combined total of current and delinquent taxes receivable.

Detailed statement of taxes receivable (Figure 79). This statement shows more details about taxes receivable than can be obtained from the Taxes Receivable account in the balance sheet. For example, the Taxes Receivable—Delinquent account is shown as only one account in the balance sheet, whereas in this statement delinquent taxes are subdivided by years. The statement is also subdivided so as to show the data for

Figure 78

CITY OF SAGINAW

Statement of Changes in Taxes Receivable[1]
for Fiscal Year Ended June 30, 1952

	General Fund	Debt Retirement Fund	Total
Tax Levy 1951–52:			
Real Estate...................	$1,187,589.36	$360,473.82	$1,548,063.18
Personal Property..............	400,028.28	121,422.21	521,450.49
	$1,587,617.64	$481,896.03	$2,069,513.67
Collections During the Year........	1,558,655.76	473,105.04	2,031,760.80
Total Current Taxes Receivable	$ 28,961.88	$ 8,790.99	$ 37,752.87
Delinquent Taxes Receivable at July 1, 1951...................	$ 43,924.43	$ 5,084.96	$ 49,009.39
Cancellations....................	164.49	30.66	195.15
	$ 43,759.94	$ 5,054.30	$ 48,814.24
Collections During the Year........	29,603.05	3,428.94	33,031.99
Total Delinquent Taxes Receivable	$ 14,156.89	$ 1,625.36	$ 15,782.25
Total Taxes Receivable........	$ 43,118.77	$ 10,416.35	$ 53,535.12

real property taxes and personal property taxes separately. In addition, the statement brings together in one place all data concerning taxes receivable.

Statement of changes in tax sale certificates (Figure 80). This statement is similar to the statement showing changes in taxes receivable.

Detailed statement of tax sale certificates (Figure 81). This statement shows detailed information concerning tax sale certificates. Note that the cost of conducting the tax sale is included in the amount of the certificate and that certificates are apportioned among the various funds.

Statement of assessed value and estimated true value of all taxable property (Figure 82). This statement is self-explanatory; we shall therefore point out only the significance of including the estimated true value. There is a tendency for assessors to underassess property, and, since the amount of taxes which can be raised will usually depend on the assessed valuation, it is important to know the relationship between assessed value and true value. Furthermore, a fall or rise in the tax rate must be judged in the light of the assessed valuation, for a fall in the tax rate may have been compensated for by a rise in the ratio of assessed value to true value. Finally, unless the ratio of assessed value to true value is known,

---

[1] Adapted from the *Annual Report of the Department of Finance of Saginaw, Michigan, for Fiscal Year Ending June 30, 1952*, p. 48.

Figure 79

CITY OF SAGINAW

Detailed Statement of Taxes Receivable by Funds[2]

June 30, 1952

	General Fund	Debt Retirement Fund	Total
Real estate taxes (see note):			
1951	$27,464.33	$ 8,336.35	$35,800.68
1950	11,709.83	1,240.81	12,950.64
1949	663.52	90.31	753.83
1948	12.48	3.52	16.00
1947	.53	.16	.69
	$39,850.69	$ 9,671.15	$49,521.84
Personal property taxes:			
1951	$ 1,497.55	$ 454.64	$ 1,952.19
Prior to 1951	1,770.53	290.56	2,061.09
	$ 3,268.08	$ 745.20	$ 4,013.28
	$43,118.77	$10,416.35	$53,535.12

Note: Unpaid real estate taxes have been adjusted to reflect the cancellation of all taxes on properties acquired by the State of Michigan pursuant to Act 155, Public Acts of 1937, and the City's share of proceeds from the sale of such properties by the State Land Office Board has been recorded as revenue of the period in which it was received.

Figure 80

A GOVERNMENTAL UNIT

Statement of Changes in Tax Sale Certificates for Fiscal Year

Tax Sale Certificates—Beginning of Year		$ 78,000
Add:		
Tax Liens Acquired—		
Transfers from Taxes Receivable	$20,000	
Interest, Penalties, and Costs on Taxes Transferred	3,000	23,000
Total		$101,000
Deduct:		
Payments Received	$22,000	
Tax Sale Certificates Canceled or Abated	3,000	
Property Transferred to General Fixed Assets	5,000	30,000
Tax Sale Certificates—End of Year		$ 71,000

[2] Adapted from the *Annual Report of the Department of Finance of Saginaw, Michigan, for Fiscal Year Ending June 30, 1952,* p. 48.

Figure 81

A GOVERNMENTAL UNIT

Detailed Statement of Tax Sale Certificates
at Close of Fiscal Year

	Amount of Tax	Interest & Penalties Accrued to Date of Sale	Costs of Sale	Total Amount of Certificate	Less Allowance for Uncollectibles	Net Amount of Certificate
Taxes of:						
1954	$18,700	$2,800	$ 500	$22,000	$ 3,500	$18,500
1953	12,800	1,800	400	15,000	2,500	12,500
1952	8,500	1,300	200	10,000	1,500	8,500
1951	6,800	1,000	200	8,000	1,000	7,000
1950 and Prior Years	13,600	2,000	400	16,000	1,500	14,500
Total	$60,400	$8,900	$1,700	$71,000	$10,000	$61,000
Made up as Follows:						
General Fund	$42,280	$6,230	$1,190	$49,700	$ 7,000	$42,700
A Special Revenue Fund	12,080	1,780	340	14,200	2,000	12,200
Sinking Funds	6,040	890	170	7,100	1,000	6,100
Total (as above)	$60,400	$8,900	$1,700	$71,000	$10,000	$61,000

Figure 82

MONTGOMERY COUNTY, MARYLAND

Statement of Assessed Value and Estimated True Value of
All Taxable Property[3]
for Fiscal Years Ended June 30, 1943-1952

Fiscal Year Ended	REAL PROPERTY		BUSINESS PERSONAL PROPERTY OF INDIVIDUALS		Ratio of Total Assessed Value to Total True Value
	Assessed Value	Estimated True Value	Assessed Value	Estimated True Value	
1943	$146,299,475	$243,832,450	$3,752,450	$ 4,690,563	63.96%
1944	151,539,900	275,527,090	3,759,740	4,699,675	59.44
1945	154,391,530	308,783,060	3,974,145	4,967,681	54.44
1946	155,148,470	344,774,377	4,210,460	5,263,075	49.31
1947	157,078,515	392,696,287	6,821,000	8,526,250	44.59
1948	180,644,545	516,127,271	5,054,390	6,317,988	38.26
1949	212,592,760	607,407,885	5,888,790	7,360,988	38.06
1950	288,675,620	721,689,050	7,525,890	9,407,363	42.90
1951	310,124,850	775,312,125	7,826,000	9,782,500	43.00
1952	367,466,280	816,591,733	9,055,810	11,319,763	48.07

Figure 83

CITY OF SAGINAW

Statements of Tax Rates and Tax Levies[4]
for Fiscal Years Ended June 30, 1944-1953

TAX RATES PER $1,000 ASSESSED VALUATION

Fiscal Year*	County	City	School	Total
1944	$3.400	$ 8.710	$ 5.670	$17.780
1945	3.400	8.610	5.670	17.680
1946	3.331	8.455	5.882	17.668
1947	3.638	8.286	6.339	18.263
1948	4.201	8.127	6.303	18.631
1949	5.280	6.909	6.327	18.516
1950	5.203	12.444	7.784	25.431
1951	5.383	12.076	8.641	26.100
1952	5.405	14.348	13.638	33.391
1953	6.005	14.435	13.200	33.640

TAX LEVIES

Fiscal Year*	County	City	School	Total
1944	$364,663.36	$ 934,135.22	$ 608,099.49	$1,906,898.07
1945	371,006.52	939,470.30	618,675.50	1,929,152.32
1946	384,596.06	976,212.69	679,134.49	2,039,943.24
1947	428,447.30	975,836.41	746,539.59	2,150,823.30
1948	514,711.10	995,770.92	772,282.90	2,282,764.92
1949	672,414.95	879,873.40	805,754.66	2,358,043.01
1950	691,208.99	1,653,165.55	1,034,091.41	3,378,465.95
1951	742,057.76	1,664,785.88	1,191,240.19	3,598,083.83
1952	779,595.97	2,069,513.67	1,967,105.46	4,816,215.10
1953	907,613.93**	2,181,759.70	1,995,088.06	5,084,461.69

* Fiscal Year for County of Saginaw begins January 1.
** Levy made but not spread at date of this report.

[3] Adapted from the *Annual Financial Report of Montgomery County, Maryland, for the Fiscal Year Ended June 30, 1952*, p. 92.
[4] Adapted from the *Annual Report of the Department of Finance of Saginaw, Michigan, for Fiscal Year Ending June 30, 1952*, p. 63.

Figure 84

A GOVERNMENTAL UNIT

Statement of Tax Levies and Tax Collections

January 1 to May 30, 1955

Year	Total Tax Levy for Year	Uncollected at Beginning of This Year	Amount Collected This Month	Amount Collected from Beginning of This Year to Date	Amount Uncollected at This Date	RATIO OF Column 3 to Column 2	RATIO OF Column 5 to Column 3	RATIO OF Column 6 to Column 2
1	2	3	4	5	6	7	8	9
1946	$500,000	$ 30,500	$ 1,567	$ 5,093	$25,407	6.1%	16.7%	5.1%
1947	450,000	35,750	1,789	6,613	29,137	7.9	18.5	6.5
1948	425,000	45,475	2,140	9,868	35,607	10.7	21.7	8.4
1949	400,000	53,600	2,560	13,024	40,576	13.4	24.3	10.1
1950	430,000	68,370	3,429	19,553	48,817	15.9	28.6	11.4
1951	460,000	87,860	5,223	29,257	58,603	19.1	33.3	12.7
1952	500,000	108,500	9,342	45,244	63,256	21.7	41.7	12.7
1953	505,000	123,725	10,355	53,820	69,905	24.5	43.5	13.8
1954	504,000	140,350	11,960	66,385	73,965	27.8	47.3	14.7
1955	505,000	150,420	13,197	75,360	75,060	29.8	50.1	14.9

Figure 85

CITY OF PONTIAC, MICHIGAN

Statement of Tax Levies and Tax Collections[5]
for Fiscal Years Ended December 31, 1943-1952

Fiscal Year	Total Tax Levy	Collection of Current Tax During Fiscal Year	Percent of Levy Collected During Fiscal Year	Collection of Prior Years' Tax During Fiscal Year	Ratio of Total Tax Collections to Current Tax Levy	Accumulated Delinquent Taxes	Ratio of Accumulated Delinquency to Levy for Current Fiscal Year
1943	$ 968,272.39	$ 907,425.56	93.72%	$123,848.04	106.51%	$906,663.03	93.64%
1944	1,010,645.42	971,920.03	96.17	142,637.23	110.28	784,208.39	77.59
1945	1,191,804.64	1,143,627.14	95.96	129,178.09	106.80	704,632.34	59.12
1946	1,448,564.77	1,236,549.27	85.36	62,753.82	89.70	866,224.39	59.80
1947	1,142,031.25	1,083,620.06	94.89	209,227.51	113.21	715,408.06	62.64
1948	1,795,957.20	1,724,324.85	96.01	76,292.69	100.26	710,747.72	39.57
1949	1,834,000.00	1,776,282.50	96.85	181,532.79	106.75	586,932.43	32.00
1950	2,024,917.37	1,970,344.95	97.30	103,248.39	102.40	483,684.04	23.89
1951	2,139,289.42	2,074,995.16	96.99	39,322.79	101.84	498,933.67	23.32
1952	2,269,247.30	2,205,869.69	97.21	79,855.11	100.73	483,372.82	21.30

[5] Adapted from the *Financial Report of the Director of Finance, City of Pontiac, Michigan, for the Fiscal Year Ended December 31, 1952,* p. 82.

comparable tax rates for different governmental units cannot be compiled.

Statement of tax rates and tax levies (Figure 83). This statement shows the tax rates and tax levies not only for one governmental unit but for all the governmental units which levy taxes on property in a particular jurisdiction.

Statements of tax levies and tax collections (Figures 84 and 85). One of the most important facts to know about taxes receivable is the success with which taxes are being collected. Even though a governmental unit has wide taxing power, it will suffer financial embarrassment unless it is able to collect the taxes it levies. The statements illustrated in Figures 84 and 85 both furnish information regarding tax levies and collections. The main difference between them is that the first is prepared during the year and shows collections from the beginning of the year to the date of the preparation of the statement and for the current month, whereas the second is prepared at the end of the fiscal year and shows information regarding the success with which each year's levy has been collected, collections of delinquent taxes during each fiscal period, and accumulated delinquent taxes.

16

<<<<<<<<<<<<<<<<<<<<<<<<<<<<<<<<<<<<<<<<<<<<<<<<<<<<<<<<<<<<<<<<<<

FIXED ASSETS

THIS CHAPTER is divided into three parts. The first part deals with the accounting procedure applicable to all fixed assets. The second part deals with the accounting procedure for general fixed assets; that is, those fixed assets which are not included in working capital and utility or other enterprise funds. Assets carried in working capital and utility or other enterprise funds are discussed in the third part.

All Fixed Assets

Classifying fixed assets. Fixed assets may be classified into three principal groups: (1) land, (2) structures and improvements, and (3) equipment.

Land. The cost of land includes the amount paid for the land itself, costs incidental to the acquisition of land, and expenses incurred in preparing the land for use. Costs incidental to the acquisition of land are legal expenses for perfection of title, fees to brokers, and so forth. The expenses of preparing land for use include, among others, the cost of demolishing buildings (less salvage value), the cost of relocating structures, and expenses connected with clearing land. As stated previously, governmental units may pay special assessments on their properties located in special assessment districts. Since special assessment improvements are presumed to benefit the properties assessed, the amount of special assessments paid by the governmental unit as an owner of property should be added to the cost of the land.

If the governmental unit acquired the land through purchase, provision for such purchase will have been made in the regular budget or in some special budget.

Structures and improvements. Structures and improvements include all buildings and fixtures which are permanently attached to and made a part of buildings and which cannot be removed without cutting into the walls, ceilings, or floors, or without in some way impairing the buildings; bridges; pavements; and all other nonmovable fixed assets. Structures and improvements, exclusive of those obtained through tax foreclosures or gifts, may be obtained through (1) purchase, (2) construction by contract, and (3) construction by the governmental unit's own labor forces. Frequently, two or more methods are used in the acquisition of a single asset. For example, the governmental unit may have part of a bridge constructed by contract and part by its own labor forces. For the purpose of the present discussion, however, it will be helpful if each of the methods of acquiring structures and improvements is discussed separately.

1. Purchasing structures and improvements. Few governmental structures and improvements are acquired by purchase. However, if they are, it is important to record as part of their cost not only the purchase price but also all expenses incidental to their acquisition. Among these are legal expenses, brokers' fees, cost of engineering tests to determine the condition of structures, other similar expenses, and cost of repairing secondhand assets before placing them in use. It will be noted that some of these expenses are also allocable to the land. For example, if both land and buildings are purchased, brokers' fees apply to both, and it is necessary to allocate to each a proportionate share of the cost.

The purchasing procedure for the acquisition of such assets is simple. Purchases of fixed assets usually require special authorization of the legislative body. The authorization may be made at the beginning of the year, when the general budget is adopted, or, if the purchase is financed through the sale of bonds, sometime during the year.

2. Construction by contract. The cost of structures and improvements built by contract can be readily determined, since it is made up primarily of the amount charged by the contractor. However, cognizance must be taken of all other costs incidental to the construction of the project, such as the cost of preliminary engineering surveys, supervision expenses, and other overhead expenses.

3. Construction by governmental unit. The procedure in recording the cost of assets constructed by the governmental unit's own labor forces is discussed in Chapter 21.

Equipment. The third class of fixed assets is equipment. Equipment consists of fixed assets other than land and structures and improvements. Examples are trucks, automobiles, desks, typewriters, and bookcases. Since equipment is movable, it must be accounted for with particular care. If the governmental unit constructs part of its equipment instead of buying it complete, overhead expenses should be considered as part of the cost. If equipment is purchased, the cost includes the purchase price, transportation expenses, and expenses incurred in installing the equipment.

Tools which have a relatively small value (less than $10) are usually accounted for in the same manner as materials and supplies. A perpetual inventory record is kept, supported by an actual physical count.

Valuing assets acquired through foreclosure or gifts. We have already indicated the basis of valuing property acquired through foreclosure proceedings on account of the nonpayment of taxes or special assessments. Briefly, the value of such assets should be either (1) the amount of taxes or special assessments due, interest and penalties, and the cost of foreclosing the property, or (2) the appraised value of the property, whichever is lower. As we have pointed out before, property obtained as a gift should be appraised at the time it is acquired and should be recorded at its appraised value.

Establishing property records. After the cost or other value of a fixed asset has been determined, it is recorded on an individual property record. A separate record is established for each unit of property, by which is meant any item which can be readily identified and accounted for by itself. These records of individual properties constitute the subsidiary accounts which support the general fixed assets accounts in the general ledger.

Land records. A separate record should be established for each piece of land, each structure and improvement, and each piece of equipment. A property record form for land is illustrated in Figure 86. Note that provision is made on this record for showing the legal description of the land, its location, its use, the authority for acquiring it, the method of financing its acquisition, and similar information. Note also the references to the general ledger control account and to the accounting documents approving the expenditure.

Records for structures and improvements. A property record form for structures and improvements is illustrated in Figure 87. This form is similar to the form illustrated in Figure 86, with the exceptions that it does not show the legal description of the property and that provision is made for recording deductions resulting from retirements. Note also that reference is made to construction work orders. With the aid of this reference, it is possible to substantiate the original cost of each structure and improvement and the cost of additions or replacements made after the property was acquired.

Equipment records. An individual property record form for equipment —in this case, office furniture—is illustrated in Figure 88. Different kinds of property records may be needed for different types of equipment. For example, the form illustrated in Figure 88 would not be suitable for automotive equipment. Records for this type of equipment must show, in addition to the information carried on the card here illustrated, data as to depreciation, number of miles covered annually, total annual cost of operation, and annual rentals earned. Postings to such a record would

Figure 86

A GOVERNMENTAL UNIT
Land Ledger

Department_____

_____

Legal Description_____

_____

_____

_____

_____

_____

_____

_____

Location_____

_____

Size_____

Purpose for Which Obtained_____

_____

Present Use_____

_____

_____

General Ledger Control
Date_____Amount_____
Date_____Revised Amount_____

Plat Book
Plat Book Page No._____
Property No._____ _____

Legal Authorization
Date_____Ordinance No._____
Date_____Ordinance No._____

Deed
Revision Clause? Yes_____No_____
If yes, give deed conditions_____

_____

_____

_____

Grantor_____
Type of Deed_____Date_____
Recorded_____Vol._____Page_____
No._____
Copy on File with_____

For Land Purchased
Date_____ Amount_____ Voucher No._____
Date_____ Amount_____ Voucher No._____
Date_____ Amount_____ Voucher No._____
Date_____ Amount_____ Gen. Jour. Page_____

For Land Otherwise Acquired
Date_____Amount_____Reference_____
Explanation_____

Method of Financing
Method	Amount
Bonds	_____
Current Revenues	_____
Gifts, Bequests	_____

Disposition Made
Date_____
How Disposed of_____
Price_____
Receipt Document_____
Other References_____

A GOVERNMENTAL UNIT
Structures and Improvements Ledger

Number_____

Department_____

Location_____

_____

Purpose for Which Obtained_____

_____

Present Use_____

_____

Estimated Life_____

_____

_____

Method of Financing

	Original Amount	Additions or Deductions*
Current Revenues	——	——
Gifts	——	——
Special Assessments:		
Govt. Share	——	——
Property Owners'		
Share	——	——
Bonds	——	——

Disposition Made_____

_____

_____

Date_____

Salvage Proceeds_____ G. J. or
               C. R.* Page____

Cost of Dismantling_____

Retirement Order No._____

Authorization
Date_____Ordinance No._____
Date_____Ordinance No._____

General Ledger Control
Date_____Amount_____
Date_____Revised Amount_____
Date_____Revised Amount_____

For Assets Constructed
Date Completed_____
Cost_____
Work Order No._____

For Assets Purchased
Date_____ Cost_____
Voucher No._____

For Donated Assets
Date_____
Amount_____
Reference_____
Explanation_____
_____
_____

Additions
Date_____ Cost_____
Work Order No._____
Date_____ Cost_____
Work Order No._____

Deductions
Date_____ Amount_____
References_____

Figure 88

```
┌─────────────────────────────────────────────────────────────────────┐
│                      A GOVERNMENTAL UNIT                              │
│                        Equipment Ledger                              │
│                                              Item No._____  │
│   Description_____ │
│   _____ │
│                                                                       │
│   Department_____  Division_____  │
│   Serial No._____  Make_____ Model_____  │
│   Date Received_____  Purchase Order No._____ Estimated Life_│
└─────────────────────────────────────────────────────────────────────┘
```

Cost _____ Vo. No._____	Additions
Freight_____ Vo. No._____	Date_____ Amount_____
_____ Vo. No._____	Reference_____
Total Original Cost_____	
Date_____ Revised Cost_____	Date_____ Amount_____
Date_____ Revised Cost_____	Reference_____

Method of Financing			Deductions
	Original Amount	Additions or Deductions*	Date_____ Amount_____
Current Revenues____.__		_____	Reference_ _____
Gifts	_____	_____	
_____	_____	_____	Disposition_____

| Remarks_____ | Date_____ Amount_____ |
| _____ | Reference_____ |

be made at the end of each year from the individual equipment property records illustrated in Figure 119, page 358.

Classifying individual property records. As we have seen, general fixed assets are set up in a separate group of accounts in the general ledger, where they are divided into three main classes—land, structures and improvements, and equipment. The totals of the balances carried on the individual property records must agree with the totals of the values shown for general fixed assets accounts in the general ledger. That is, the total of the balances shown on the property records for land must equal the balance shown for the Land account in the general ledger; the total of the balances shown for structures and improvements must equal the balance shown for the Structures and Improvements account in the general ledger; and the total of the balances carried on the individual equipment records must equal the balance shown for the Equipment account in the general ledger.

It should be noted, however, that the cards are not arranged in three main groups with one group covering land, another structures and improvements, and a third equipment. Rather, they are grouped by departments, and under each department the cards are arranged in three subgroups, one for land, another for structures and improvements, and still another for equipment. Structures and improvements are still further subdivided by classes of property—for example, buildings, sidewalks, and bridges. Equipment, too, is subdivided into a number of classes: automotive equipment, office machinery, office equipment, and so forth. Each of these types of equipment may be subdivided still further. For example, office equipment may be subdivided as follows: bookcases, books, carpets, chairs, coat trees, desk lamps, desks, drafting tables, electric fans, filing equipment, linoleum, lockers, map cases, mimeograph equipment, safes, telephone switchboards, time clocks, visible index equipment, water coolers, and so forth. All the cards falling within a particular subclass are grouped together. For example, all cards for office equipment used by a particular organization unit would be placed in one group. In that manner, it is possible to arrive readily at the total value of office equipment used by the department. Similarly, all cards for other classes of equipment are grouped together. Subcontrol accounts may or may not be established for various subclasses of equipment, depending on the number of items included under each subclass. For example, if a department has many items of office equipment, it may establish a subcontrol account entitled "Office Equipment," which would be supported by the cards set up for the individual items of office equipment.

If a department is composed of several subdivisions, or if its property is located in various places, separate control accounts are established for each subdivision or location. For example, if a municipality has several fire stations, each of which is located in a different part of the city, separate control accounts would be established for the fixed assets at each fire station. Thus, the cards for the property in station A would be arranged as follows:

Station *A*
>Land
>Structures and Improvements
>Fire-Fighting Equipment
>>Aerial-Ladder Trucks[1]
>>Chemical Engines
>>Combination Fire Trucks
>>Fire Extinguishers
>>Fire Hose
>>Ladders

---

[1] A separate card is prepared for each piece of equipment listed under each of the groups. For example, if station *A* had more than one aerial-ladder truck, a separate card would be provided for each.

> Pumpers
> Squad Wagons
> Household Equipment
> Beds
> Chairs
> Stove
> Etc.

To arrive at the total value of the fixed assets used by the fire department, it is necessary to add the amounts shown for land, structures and improvements, and equipment for each fire station and for the fire department headquarters, as illustrated below:

Station	Total	Land	Structures & Improvements	Equip-ment
Headquarters................	$ 30,000	—	—	$ 30,000
Station *A*..................	60,000	$10,000	$ 20,000	30,000
Station *B*..................	100,000	20,000	40,000	40,000
Station *C*..................	145,000	30,000	55,000	60,000
Station *D*..................	25,000	5,000	10,000	10,000
Total Fire Department.......	$360,000	$65,000	$125,000	$170,000

Additions to fixed assets. Before the cost of additions to fixed assets is recorded, it should be determined that the expenditure has actually bettered the asset. In general, expenditures for work performed on fixed assets should be analyzed to determine what part of the expenditure has resulted in bettering the asset and what part has merely restored the asset to its former condition. The part that has bettered the asset should be capitalized and added to the original cost or other value of the asset, whereas the other part should be treated as a current expense. No hard or fast rules can be laid down as to what constitutes a repair or a betterment. In general, if the life of the asset is prolonged or the asset is made more useful, the expenditure may be said to have resulted in a betterment.

Additions to fixed assets are not classified according to whether they are structures or equipment until they are completed. For example, if an addition to a fire station was made during the year but was uncompleted at the end of the year, the entry to record the cost of the addition in the fixed asset group of accounts is

Work in Progress...........................	$ 50,000	
Investment in Fixed Assets from Current Revenues..............................		$50,000
To record cost of uncompleted addition to fire station at December 31.		

When the addition is finally completed, the following entry is made:

Structures and Improvements................. $120,000		
Work in Progress.........................	$50,000	
Investment in Fixed Assets from Current Revenues..............................	70,000	

To record completion of addition to fire station.

No entry would be made on the individual property records for fire department property until the building was completed. At that time, the total cost of the addition would be entered in the individual property record for the particular fire station.

Transfer of fixed assets. Fixed assets should not be transferred from one location to another, or from one use to another, without formal written authorization by the proper authority. Unless transfers are formally authorized, fixed assets cannot be properly controlled. An order authorizing the transfer of fixed assets is illustrated in Figure 89.

The transfer of fixed assets between departments financed from the same fund does not necessarily affect the general ledger accounts. However, a new property card must be prepared. Transfers between departments financed from different funds affect both the general accounts and the individual property records. For example, if equipment was transferred from the water department to the fire, police, and public works departments, the entry to record this transaction, if we assume that the three departments receiving the equipment are financed from the general fund, is as follows:

ENTRY IN UTILITY FUND:

Unappropriated Surplus (or Governmental Unit's Contribution)... $10,000
Allowance for Depreciation—Equipment.............. 20,000
Equipment..................................... $30,000

To record transfer of equipment to other departments, as follows:

Department	Cost of Equipment	Accumulated Depreciation	Net Value
Police...............	$ 5,000	$ 3,000	$ 2,000
Fire.................	10,000	6,500	3,500
Public Works.........	15,000	10,500	4,500
	$30,000	$20,000	$10,000

ENTRY IN GENERAL FIXED ASSETS GROUP OF ACCOUNTS:

Equipment..................................... $10,000
Investment in Fixed Assets from Gifts........... $10,000

To record transfer of equipment by water utility to following departments:

Police Department..................	$ 2,000
Fire Department...................	3,500
Public Works Department..........	4,500
	$10,000

Figure 89

A GOVERNMENTAL UNIT
Asset Transfer Order

Number _____   Date _____

Transferred from _____ Department _____

Received by _____ Department _____

IDENTIFICATION		Date of Purchase	Description	Cost	Accumulated Depreciation[2]	Net Value[2]	ACCOUNT		AMOUNT
Inventory or Property No.	Mfg's. No.						Name	No.	Debit or Credit*

Requested by _____   Received by _____   Date _____

Approved _____   Charge Accepted _____   Dept. Head _____

Approved _____   Noted on Property Record _____   Property Clerk _____

Remarks _____

[2] For transfers from self-supporting enterprises.

A separate property record is, of course, established for this equipment in each department.

Inventory of fixed assets. A physical inventory of equipment should be taken at the end of each year. If assets are properly recorded when they are acquired, and if retirements are accurately recorded, the inventory as disclosed by physical inspection should equal the amounts shown by the records. All variations between the two should be investigated.

An interesting problem arises with respect to taking an inventory of property for the first time. For example, assume that a governmental unit has not kept a record of its physical assets and that the officials decide to keep such a record. Obviously, the first step would be to take an inventory. As a result of the inventory, information should be available as to (1) the name of each asset, (2) identification marks, such as the manufacturer's number, (3) the location of the asset, (4) its estimated life, and (5) other data necessary to set up an individual property record for each asset. One of the difficult tasks in this connection is to arrive at the value at which to record the assets. If invoices and other documents bearing on the cost of the asset are available, these can be used. If such documents are not available, it is necessary to appraise the assets as of the date of the inventory and to record them at the appraised value.

If, as a result of taking the inventory, it is discovered that articles are missing, an investigation should be made. At the same time the general fixed assets accounts must be reduced by the book value of the missing fixed assets, and the individual property accounts for the particular assets in the property ledger must be canceled.

Asset retirements and replacements. Assets should be retired only by a retirement order, which should show as charges the cost of the asset and the cost of its dismantling and removal, and should show as a credit the amount received as insurance or as proceeds from the sale of salvage. A form for a retirement order is illustrated in Figure 90. Note that provision is made, in the case of assets of self-supporting enterprises, for showing as a credit on the retirement order the amount of the accumulated depreciation.

To account properly for fixed asset retirements, it is essential to distinguish between units of property and minor items. A unit of property is any item of property which can be identified and accounted for separately. Minor items, on the other hand, are the parts which go to make up a property unit. For example, a truck is a unit for retirement purposes, whereas tires are minor items.

When a unit of property is retired, an entry must be made reducing the property accounts by the book value of the unit. The entry removing the value of the property from the books must be made even for property which is replaced. The replacement is reflected in the records in the same

Figure 90

A GOVERNMENTAL UNIT
Asset Retirement Order

Number _____ Retired from _____ Department _____ Date _____

| IDENTIFICATION | | Date of Purchase | Description | Cost (Including Additions) | Accumulated Depreciation³ | Salvage Value | Cost of Dismantling | Date | Voucher No. or Receipt No. | ACCOUNT | | Amount | |
Property No.	Mfg's. No.									Name	No.	Debit or Credit*	

Remarks _____

Requested by _____
Approved _____
Approved _____
Noted on Property Record _____

³ For retirement of assets of self-supporting enterprises.

268

manner as any other newly acquired asset, while the cost of the asset which it replaces is removed from the accounts.

The procedure in recording the retirement and replacement of minor items is somewhat different from that followed in recording the retirement of units of property. If a minor item of property is retired and is not replaced, the unit of property of which the minor item is a part is reduced by the amount of the book value of the minor item. If, however, the book value of the minor item of property will be accounted for in the book value of the unit of property when the latter is retired, the property account need not be reduced by the amount of the minor item.

If minor items of property are retired and replaced, the cost of replacement is considered a current expense and not an addition to the property. However, if the replacement of the minor item results in a betterment, the expenditure for replacements must be analyzed to determine the portion attributable to replacements and the portion attributable to betterments. The former is considered an expense, whereas the latter is added to the cost of the unit.

General Fixed Assets

Thus far the discussion was concerned with the accounting for all fixed assets. This part deals with the accounting procedure peculiar to general fixed assets. To simplify the discussion, with one exception, only controlling accounts are used in the entries illustrated throughout the remainder of this chapter.

Depreciation not computed. One of the features of accounting for general fixed assets is that depreciation need not be computed on them. As the National Committee on Governmental Accounting points out, no useful purpose is accomplished by computing depreciation on assets of this sort for the following reasons:

Depreciation charges represent the cost expirations of fixed assets. In commercial accounting these expirations must be reflected in the accounts because they must be related to the revenues which the fixed assets produced, in order to ascertain the amount of net profit or loss for a fiscal period. On the other hand, except in the case of utilities or other self-supporting enterprises, a municipality is not concerned with profits or losses. Moreover, since general fixed assets are not presumed to produce tax or other general revenues, charging current operations with depreciation has the effect of reducing revenues by costs to which they did not give rise in violation of the principle of matching costs with their relevant revenues. Finally, unless cash can be set aside out of current revenues, depreciation charges cannot be included in the budget. If cash is therefore not set aside (and depreciation thus not included in the budget and in the appropriation ordinance) but depreciation is included in the financial statements of the annual report, there will not only be no agreement between the results shown in the budget and those reflected in the annual report, but the annual report is likely to show expenditures in excess of appropriations and thereby create the impression that the law has been violated.[4]

Asset retirements. The entries to be made to record the acquisition of fixed assets were given in Chapter 13. The entries to record retirements are more complicated because in accounting for fixed asset retirements, it is important to take into account not only the book value of the asset but also the cost of retirement and the proceeds received from the sale of salvage. For example, assume that a fire station was torn down, that the book value of the building was $60,000, that the cost of tearing it down was $1,000, and that $5,000 was realized from the sale of salvage. The entries to record these transactions are as shown below.

ENTRY IN GENERAL FIXED ASSETS GROUP OF ACCOUNTS:

Investment in Fixed Assets from Current Revenues..	$60,000	
Structures and Improvements..................		$60,000
To record retirement of fire station.		

ENTRIES IN GENERAL FUND:

Appropriation Expenditures......................	1,000	
Cash..		1,000
To record cost of dismantling building, such cost to be reimbursed from sale of salvage.		
Cash..	5,000	
Appropriation Expenditures....................		1,000
Revenues....................................		4,000
To record sale of salvage and reimbursement for cost of dismantling fire station.		

On the other hand, if the cost of dismantling was $2,000, and if only $1.000 had been realized from the sale of salvage, the entries would be as follows:

Appropriation Expenditures......................	$ 2,000	
Cash..		$ 2,000
To record cost of dismantling building, such cost to be reimbursed from sale of salvage.		
Cash..	1,000	
Appropriation Expenditures....................		1,000
To record sale of salvage and to reduce the dismantling cost by the amount of cash realized from the sale of salvage.		

It will be noted that only $1,000 of the dismantling cost was recovered. The remaining $1,000 would be charged as an expense.

Sale of general fixed assets. Two entries are necessary to record the sale of general fixed assets—one in the fund receiving the proceeds and another in the general fixed assets group of accounts. Thus, if a fire truck with a book value of $10,000 is sold for $2,000, the following entries are made:

---

[4] National Committee on Governmental Accounting, *Municipal Accounting and Auditing* (Chicago: The Committee, 1951), p. 127.

ENTRY IN GENERAL FUND:

Cash..............................	$ 2,000	
Revenues...........................		$2,000
To record sale of fire truck.		

ENTRY IN GENERAL FIXED ASSETS GROUP OF ACCOUNTS:

Investment in Fixed Assets from Current Revenues..	10,000	
Equipment....................................		10,000
To record sale of fire truck with book value of $10,000.		

Note that, although only $2,000 was realized from the sale of the truck, the full book value—namely, $10,000—must be written off. Of course, the individual property record for the particular truck would be canceled.

If the above truck is traded in on a new truck costing $12,000, and an allowance of $3,000 is made on the old truck, the transaction is recorded as follows:

ENTRY IN GENERAL FUND:

Appropriation Expenditures......................	$ 9,000	
Cash...		$ 9,000
To record purchase of fire truck costing $12,000, which was reduced by trade-in allowance of $3,000.		

ENTRIES IN GENERAL FIXED ASSETS GROUP OF ACCOUNTS:

Investment in Fixed Assets from Current Revenues..	10,000	
Equipment....................................		10,000
To record sale (trade-in) of old fire truck with book value of $10,000.		
Equipment....................................	12,000	
Investment in Fixed Assets from Current Revenues		12,000
To record purchase of fire truck at a cost of $9,000 plus trade-in allowance on old fire truck of $3,000.		

Thus far we have assumed that the assets were sold to private persons. Sometimes one fund sells property to another fund. Let us assume, for example, that a utility or other enterprise fund sells equipment to the public works department, which is financed from the general fund. The following entries would be made:

ENTRY IN UTILITY OR OTHER ENTERPRISE FUND:

Due from General Fund.........................	$15,000	
Allowance for Depreciation—Equipment...........	1,000	
Equipment...................................		$16,000
To record sale of equipment to department of public works at net book value.		

ENTRY IN GENERAL FUND:

Appropriation Expenditures......................	15,000	
Due to Utility or Other Enterprise Fund.........		15,000
To record purchase of equipment from utility or other enterprise fund for department of public works and liability owing to that fund.		

ENTRY IN GENERAL FIXED ASSETS GROUP OF ACCOUNTS:

Equipment....................................	15,000	
Investment in Fixed Assets from Current Revenues		15,000
To record purchase of equipment for public works department.		

It should be noted that the equipment is recorded at its depreciated value —that is, at gross book value less the allowance for depreciation ($16,000 − $1,000). Although general fixed assets are not depreciated on the records, the allowance for depreciation is deducted because the public works department purchased the asset at its depreciated value. The asset is also recorded on the individual property record at its depreciated value.

Property damaged or destroyed. Expenditures for repairs necessary to restore damaged property to its former condition are charged to the Appropriation Expenditures account in the fund from which the cost of repairs is financed and are classified as current expenses. If the expenditures not only restore the asset to its former condition but also result in bettering it, the excess of the total amount expended over the amount required to restore the asset to its former condition is capitalized in the general fixed assets group of accounts.

As an illustration, let us assume that an asset is damaged and that $40,000 is spent for its repair and $10,000 for its betterment. If the expenditures are financed out of the general fund, the entries are as follows:

ENTRY IN GENERAL FUND:
Appropriation Expenditures....................... $50,000
  Cash.. $50,000
To record expenditures for repairs to damaged police station, of which $10,000 are due to betterments.
Subsidiary accounts:

Organization Unit	Current Expenses	Capital Outlays
Department of Police........	$40,000	$10,000

ENTRY IN GENERAL FIXED ASSETS GROUP OF ACCOUNTS:
Structures and Improvements.................... $10,000
  Investment in Fixed Assets from Current Revenues $10,000
To record improvement of police station.

An entry is made on the individual property record for the particular police station to indicate the increase of $10,000 in the book value of the station.

Let us assume further that the total book value of the police station is $100,000, that the station is destroyed by fire, and that the governmental unit collects insurance of $90,000. The following entries would be made in the general fixed assets group of accounts and in the general fund, respectively, to record these transactions:

ENTRY IN GENERAL FIXED ASSETS GROUP OF ACCOUNTS:
Investment in Fixed Assets from Current Revenues $100,000
  Structures and Improvements................. $100,000
To record destruction of police station by fire.

Entry in General Fund:

Cash for Replacements......................	$90,000	
Reserve for Restoring Police Station...........		$90,000

To record collection of insurance, which is to be used in restoring police station destroyed by fire.

It should be noted that the reserve for restoring the police station is a surplus reserve. The reason the reserve was credited instead of the Revenues account is to make certain that the cash received from the insurance company is not appropriated for other than replacement purposes. Of course, if the governmental unit does not intend to restore the property, the proceeds are credited to the Revenues account. Likewise, if, because of a decline in construction costs, the total cost of reconstructing the property is less than the amount of insurance proceeds received, the balance of the proceeds is credited to the Revenues account.

Statements of general fixed assets. A statement analyzing the changes in general fixed assets accounts, similar to that illustrated in Figure 91, is needed to account for the additions to general fixed assets and the disposal of the assets. Note particularly that the additions to fixed assets shown in this statement correspond to the totals of expenditures of the particular funds from which they were financed. Work in progress set up in prior years but completed during the current year is deducted in the "Work in Progress" column of the statement, since it can now be classified as either structures and improvements or as equipment.

Another statement needed is that illustrated in Figure 92. Although a statement showing general fixed assets classified by main classes of property was illustrated in Figure 66, page 204, that statement showed merely the total of each kind of property. It is important to show also the assets allocated to each department; only in that manner can effective control be exercised. Attention is again called to the fact that no account is taken of depreciation, the assets being shown in this statement at cost or appraised value at the time of their acquisition.

Fixed Assets of Self-Supporting Enterprises

Accounting for depreciation. Depreciation may be defined as expiration in the service life of fixed assets, other than wasting assets, due to wear and tear through use and lapse of time, obsolescence, inadequacy, or other physical or functional cause. Although depreciation on general fixed assets need not be recognized in general fund appropriation accounting, it should be computed on assets of self-supporting enterprises. Depreciation accounting is a means of charging each year's revenues with their proper share of the cost of retiring fixed property. Unless each year's revenues are charged with a proper share of depreciation expense, the profit or loss will be overstated in some years and understated in others.

Figure 91

A GOVERNMENTAL UNIT

Statement of Changes in General Fixed Assets
for Fiscal Year

	Total	Land	Structures & Improvements	Equipment	Work in Progress
Balance of General Fixed Assets—Beginning of Year..	$3,710,300	$1,000,000	$2,000,000	$500,000	$210,300
Add:					
Expenditures from:					
General Fund..............	$ 103,300	$ 7,000	$ 37,200	$ 59,100	—
Bond Funds:					
This Year.............	126,200	—	126,200	—	—
Prior Years...........	70,300	—	70,300	—	—
Special Assessment Funds:					
This Year.............	345,000	—	345,000	—	—
Prior Years...........	140,000	—	140,000	—	—
Gifts.....................	40,000	—	40,000	—	—
Total Additions........	$ 824,800	$ 7,000	$ 758,700	$ 59,100	—
Total.............	$4,535,100	$1,007,000	$2,758,700	$559,100	$210,300
Deduct:					
Fixed Assets Sold or Otherwise Disposed of........	$ 10,000	—	—	$ 10,000	—
Work in Progress of Prior Years Completed.......	210,300	—	—	—	$210,300
Total Deductions..........	$ 220,300	—	—	$ 10,000	$210,300
Balance of General Fixed Assets—End of Year.......	$4,314,800	$1,007,000	$2,758,700	$549,100	—

Figure 92

A GOVERNMENTAL UNIT

Statement of General Fixed Assets

Classified by Function and Organization Unit at Close of Fiscal Year

Function and Organization Unit	Total	Land	Structures & Improvements	Equipment
General Government:				
Council	$ 20,000	—	—	$ 20,000
Executive Department	13,080	—	—	13,080
Courts	100,148	$ 22,437	$ 72,700	5,011
Department of Law	$ 15,000	—	—	$ 15,000
City Clerk's Office	20,000	—	—	20,000
Board of Zoning Appeals	2,000	—	—	2,000
Civil Service Commission	7,000	—	—	7,000
City Hall	241,672	$ 65,000	$ 167,600	9,072
Total General Government	$ 451,800	$ 88,437	$ 245,200	$118,163
Public Safety	1,022,580	182,000	671,710	168,870
Highways	673,625	25,000	588,625	60,000
Sanitation and Waste Removal	643,710	200,000	393,710	50,000
Health and Hospitals	519,330	150,500	309,830	59,000
Public Welfare	51,375	20,000	28,375	3,000
Schools	667,435	211,063	401,372	55,000
Libraries	90,380	45,000	35,313	10,067
Recreation	194,565	85,000	84,565	25,000
Grand Total	$4,314,800	$1,007,000	$2,758,700	$549,100

One of the important problems in depreciation accounting is therefore to establish appropriate depreciation rates.

Determining periodic depreciation charges. There are many methods of computing depreciation rates, but no method will allocate depreciation charges perfectly, for only an approximation to actual conditions can be hoped for under any of them. However, the charges are made as equitable as possible, so that the revenues of any one year may not be unduly burdened and those of another year bear too light a burden. The most common methods employed by governmental units are (1) the straight-line method and (2) the work-unit method. The straight-line method is the one most commonly used for depreciating all fixed assets except automotive equipment, which is usually depreciated on the basis of work units. The straight-line method is relatively simple. The amount to be depreciated is found by deducting the estimated net salvage value from the book value. Dividing this amount by the number of years the asset is estimated to last gives the amount to be depreciated each year.

As an illustration, assume the following facts:

ASSET—BUILDING

Cost..	$21,000
Estimated Net Salvage Value...........................	1,000
Amount to Be Depreciated.............................	$20,000

Estimated Life, 10 Years.
Annual Rate of Depreciation, 10 per cent ($\frac{1}{10}$).
Amount to Be Depreciated Annually, $2,000 (10 per cent of $20,000).

The following table shows the depreciation charges under the straight-line method in the case of the assumptions just made:

TABLE 5

DEPRECIATION CHARGES UNDER STRAIGHT–LINE METHOD

End of Year	Amount of Depreciation to Be Charged	Depreciation Reserve	Net Value of Asset
1	$2,000	$ 2,000	$19,000
2	2,000	4,000	17,000
3	2,000	6,000	15,000
4	2,000	8,000	13,000
5	2,000	10,000	11,000
6	2,000	12,000	9,000
7	2,000	14,000	7,000
8	2,000	16,000	5,000
9	2,000	18,000	3,000
10	2,000	20,000	1,000*

* Salvage value.

The work-unit method is explained in connection with the discussion of the accounting procedure for equipment (see Chapter 21).

Sometimes a combination of the straight-line and work-unit methods is used; that is, the annual depreciation rate for the asset is determined on a straight-line basis, but monthly depreciation charges are determined on the basis of work units. For example, assume that the annual amount of depreciation on a particular truck is found to be $2,000 on the basis of straight-line depreciation. It is estimated, however, that the truck will work 2,000 hours during the year. The estimated depreciation rate per hour will in that case be $1.00. If the truck worked 150 hours during the month of May, $150 is charged as depreciation on the truck for that month. Of course, if the actual number of hours worked during the year is in excess of or short of the number estimated, actual annual depreciation charges will be more or less than $2,000, and an adjustment will be necessary to reduce the annual total to $2,000 or to bring it up to $2,000.

Recording depreciation. After the amount of depreciation to be charged is determined, the following entry is made to record depreciation expenses:

```
Depreciation—Equipment......................    $2,000
    Allowance for Depreciation—Equipment.......            $2,000
To record depreciation of equipment.
```

Re-examining the allowance for depreciation. The allowance for depreciation may be built up too rapidly or too slowly. In the first instance, the asset would be fully depreciated on the books before its useful life is ended, whereas in the second case an undepreciated value will be carried on the books even after the asset can no longer be used. Since such a situation necessitates adjustments and has the effect of understating or overstating past years' profits, the allowance for depreciation must be re-examined at regular intervals to see whether or not the depreciation rates are overstated or understated because of errors in estimating the lives of the assets. This procedure is particularly important if a composite rate of depreciation is used. It is beyond the scope of this book to discuss the manner in which a composite rate is determined, but it may be said that in general a composite rate is an average depreciation rate applied to all, or to a group of, the fixed assets of the enterprise.

If, upon examination, the allowance is found to be inadequate or more than adequate, adjustments must be made. If the allowance is inadequate, the Unappropriated Surplus account is charged with past inadequate depreciation expenses, and future depreciation rates are raised. If the allowance is more than adequate, the Unappropriated Surplus account is credited, and future depreciation rates are lowered.

Retirement of assets. The accounting procedure for the retirement of fixed assets that are being depreciated is similar to the procedure followed in accounting for the retirement of general fixed assets. The only difference between the two is that in accounting for the retirement of assets that are being depreciated cognizance must be taken of the depreciation allowance.

If the net amount to be received from the sale of salvage (that is, proceeds from the sale of salvage less cost of dismantling the asset) and the life of the asset were estimated correctly, the amount to the credit of the allowance for depreciation plus the net amount received from the sale of salvage will exactly equal the book value of the asset to be retired. The entry to record the receipt of the net proceeds from the sale of salvage and the retirement of the asset is as follows:

Cash..	$ 1,000	
Allowance for Depreciation—Equipment.......	29,000	
Equipment................................		$30,000
To record retirement of equipment and sale of salvage.		

If, however, either the net proceeds from the sale of salvage or the life of the asset have not been estimated correctly, the salvage proceeds plus the allowance will be greater or smaller than the book value of the asset to be retired. The entry to record the retirement of the asset and the receipt of the net proceeds (if there is a loss) is as follows:

Cash..	$ 1,000	
Allowance for Depreciation—Equipment.......	28,000	
Loss on Equipment Retired...................	1,000	
Equipment................................		$30,000
To record sale of salvage and retirement of equipment.		

If the life of the asset or the net amount to be received from the sale of salvage had been underestimated, a profit would have been realized.

Replacements. It is not essential to depreciation accounting that a fund for replacing fixed assets be established. The establishment of a fund means that cash must be set aside for the replacement of the assets. If the governmental unit can, however, use the cash to better advantage for other purposes, it will not make any segregation but, when the asset is completely depreciated, will use any cash of the particular fund (working capital fund, utility fund, or other enterprise fund) which is not otherwise appropriated to finance the replacement of the assets. No special accounting procedure is required to account for such replacements.

However, if a governmental unit does set up a fund for the replacement of assets, the unit must account not only for the replacement of the assets but also for the replacement fund itself. Since it is important to distinguish between accounting for the replacement fund and accounting for its use in replacing retired assets, the two phases of accounting for replacements are discussed separately.

Accounting for replacement fund. A replacement fund is ordinarily built up in the same manner as a sinking fund. Periodic contributions are made to the fund, and the cash contributed is invested, the earnings being added to the fund. Therefore, the total contributions to the fund are smaller than the amount necessary to replace the assets, the difference being made up through the earnings of the fund. For example, if the total cost of replacing an asset is estimated to be $20,000, and if it is contemplated that the fund will earn $2,000 during its existence, only $18,000 will have to be contributed. The following are the steps involved in accounting for replacement funds and the related entries to be made.

The first step is the making of the contribution to the fund, the entry to record this transaction being

Replacement Fund Cash....................	$1,000	
Cash.....................................		$1,000
To record setting up replacement fund.		

No entry is made to segregate surplus, because the fund is accumulated out of depreciation charges, and these charges are made against operating revenues. The allowance for depreciation thus measures the amount of current assets acquired from the depreciation charged to customers as part of the utility rates. By charging depreciation as an expense, assets representing the depreciation allowance will not unknowingly be transferred to the general fund, because the net income has already been reduced by the amount of depreciation charges.

If replacement fund cash is not invested, no other types of entries are needed; that is, the entry to be made each year would be similar to the one illustrated above. If, however, the money is invested, it is necessary to record not only the purchase of investments but also the earnings on them. The entry to record the purchase of investments, if no premiums, discounts, or accrued interest are involved, is as follows:

Replacement Fund Investments..............	$5,000	
Replacement Fund Cash..................		$5,000
To record purchase of investments.		

Earnings are recorded by the following entry:

Replacement Fund Cash.....................	$100	
Replacement Fund Revenues..............		$100
To record earnings on replacement fund investments.		

Replacement fund revenues are considered as part of the general earnings of the utility or other enterprise and are closed out into net income.

Making replacements out of the fund. The replacement fund is not affected until an asset is replaced (that is, it is not affected by the retirement of the asset). Let us assume that the replacement fund contains the exact amount of cash required to replace the asset. The entry will in that case be

Equipment................................	$29,000	
Replacement Fund Cash..................		$29,000
To record replacement of equipment.		

Figure 93

A GOVERNMENTAL UNIT
Utility Fund
Statement of Fixed Assets
at Close of Fiscal Year

PRODUCTION:

Land and Land Rights.............................	$ 130,000	
Structures and Improvements.........................	443,500	
Boiler Plant Equipment.............................	1,155,200	
Engines and Engine Driven Generators................	26,000	
Turbo-Generator Units..............................	1,522,000	
Accessory Electric Equipment........................	307,000	
Miscellaneous Power Plant Equipment.................	16,000	
Total Production...................................		$ 3,599,700

TRANSMISSION:

Land and Land Rights..............................	$ 20,000	
Poles and Fixtures.................................	48,000	
Overhead Conductors and Devices....................	67,000	
Total Transmission.................................		135,000

DISTRIBUTION:

Land and Land Rights..............................	$ 87,500	
Structures and Improvements.........................	117,000	
Station Equipment.................................	950,200	
Poles, Towers and Fixtures..........................	269,300	
Overhead Conductors and Devices....................	459,000	
Underground Conduit...............................	1,660,000	
Underground Conductors and Devices..................	1,187,200	
Line Transformers..................................	602,000	
Services..	502,000	
Meters...	439,000	
Street Lighting Systems............................	446,000	
Total Distribution.................................		6,719,200

GENERAL:

Land and Land Rights..............................	$ 77,000	
Structures and Improvements........................	289,100	
Office Furniture and Equipment......................	68,200	
Transportation Equipment...........................	169,300	
Stores Equipment..................................	16,000	
Shop Equipment...................................	23,000	
Laboratory Equipment..............................	16,000	
Communication Equipment...........................	36,400	
General Equipment.................................	21,000	
Total General.....................................		716,000
Grand Total......................................		$11,169,900

Again, let us assume that the replacement cost of the asset is $29,000, that its original cost was $32,000, and that the replacement fund had accumulated assets of $32,000. The entry to record the replacement of the asset is as follows:

```
Equipment................................... $29,000
    Replacement Fund Cash...................          $29,000
    To record replacement of equipment.
```

The replacement fund would have an excess in cash of $3,000, which would be returned to free cash.

On the other hand, if the asset cost $34,000 to replace, the entry to record the replacement would be

```
Equipment................................... $34,000
    Replacement Fund Cash...................          $32,000
    Cash....................................            2,000
    To record replacement of equipment.
```

There is only one instance in which the retirement (as contrasted with the replacement) of an asset may affect the replacement fund—namely, if, in estimating the amount to be accumulated in the fund, it is assumed that the net proceeds to be realized from the sale of salvage will be placed in the replacement fund. In that event, when the asset is retired, the entry, in the case of the figures used in the first entry on page 278, will be as follows:

```
Replacement Fund Cash..................... $ 1,000
Allowance for Depreciation—Equipment.......  29,000
    Equipment.............................          $30,000
    To record retirement of equipment.
```

Statement of fixed assets—electric utility. In Figure 93 there is illustrated a statement of the fixed assets of an electric utility. Note that the assets are grouped by functions and are classified under each function as land, structures and improvements, and equipment. The classification used in this statement has been adapted from the classification of accounts prescribed by the Federal Power Commission for electric utilities, including municipal utilities.

17

<<<<<<<<<<<<<<<<<<<<<<<<<<<<<<<<<<<<<<<<<<<<<<<<<<<<<<

LIABILITIES

THIS CHAPTER is divided into two parts, the first part dealing with liabilities other than bonds and the second part dealing with bonds. Before proceeding to a discussion of the accounting for each of these groups of liabilities, let us note some of the legal limitations which apply to all indebtedness.

The broadest limitation on indebtedness is the requirement that liabilities may be incurred only for a governmental purpose. The next broadest limitation pertains to the amount of indebtedness which a governmental unit may incur. The reasons for debt limitation are as follows: The power to incur indebtedness is in itself not primarily significant; the primary factor is the ability of the governmental unit to raise revenue by taxation for the payment of interest and the retirement of debt. Once indebtedness payable from taxation is legally incurred, the governmental unit can be forced by court action to levy a tax to pay the principal and interest. If, therefore, no limitation were placed on the amount of indebtedness, tax limitation would be ineffective, for governmental units could finance current expenditures through the incurrence of indebtedness which would subsequently have to be paid out of taxes.

The limitation on debt is usually expressed as a percentage of the assessed valuation. For example, the indebtedness of many governmental units is restricted to 5 per cent of their assessed value. Under such a limitation, a governmental unit having an assessed value of $100,000,000 may not incur indebtedness in excess of $5,000,000 (5 per cent of $100,-000,000).

Because debt limitations are based on assessed values, the restriction will fluctuate with changes in values. Thus, a rise in the assessed valuation of taxable property will increase the debt margin. By "debt margin" is meant the amount by which the debt limit exceeds the amount of existing indebtedness which is subject to the debt limit. For example, if a governmental unit that may legally incur indebtedness up to $5,000,000 already has $4,000,000 of bonds outstanding, its debt margin is $1,000,000. If its assessed value should double but the rate of limitation remain the same, the maximum amount of indebtedness which it might incur would be $10,000,000, and its debt margin would be $6,000,000. On the other hand, a lowering of the assessed value would result in a reduced debt margin.

The same assessed valuation is used for both tax and debt limitation purposes. In the case of local governments, it is the assessed value for local tax purposes that is used also for debt limitation purposes. For example, let us assume that the true value of the taxable property of a municipality is $10,000,000, that for local tax purposes the assessed value is $5,000,000 (50 per cent of true value), and that for state tax purposes the assessed value is $7,500,000 (75 per cent of true value). The assessed value to be used in determining the debt limit for the local government is $5,000,000. It is evident, therefore, that a low ratio of assessed value to true value has the effect of restricting not only the taxing power but also the borrowing power of a governmental unit.

Finally, it must be remembered that, if governmental units overlap, each has its own separate assessed valuation for debt limitation purposes, in the same manner that each has an assessed valuation for tax purposes. For example, let us assume that the assessed valuation of a municipality is $1,000,000, that an independent park district occupies the same territory as the municipality, and that the debt limit is 5 per cent for each unit. In that case, the municipality and the park district could each legally incur indebtedness up to $5,000,000.

Debt limitations may be imposed by constitutions, statutes, or charters. Sometimes restrictions are imposed by both constitutions and statutes or by all three. For example, the state constitution may provide that governmental units shall not incur indebtedness in excess of 5 per cent of the assessed value of taxable property. Statutes, on the other hand, may provide further that the rate of indebtedness for all governmental units or certain governmental units shall not exceed 4 per cent. Then the charter of a particular governmental unit may still further restrict the amount of indebtedness to 3 per cent of the unit's assessed valuation.

Since one of the main reasons for imposing restrictions on borrowing is to prevent an increase in taxation, indebtedness not payable from taxation is frequently exempted from the debt limit. For example, utility or other enterprise debts and debts payable from special assessments may be exempted from the debt limit, especially if the utility or other enterprise bonds are payable solely from earnings and if special assessment bonds are payable solely from special assessment collections. If the governmental unit guarantees that general funds will be used to meet utility or other enterprise bonds in the event that utility or other enterprise revenues are insufficient, then these bonds are sometimes included within the limitation. In many cases, one debt limit is set up for indebtedness repayable from taxation, and another is provided for indebtedness not primarily repayable from taxation.

Finally, it should be remembered that the debt limit is usually imposed on net indebtedness. Thus, in computing the legal debt margin, sinking fund assets may be deducted from the bonds to which they apply, only the net bonded debt being charged against the limitation. Similarly, some courts have held that cash on hand may be deducted from any liabilities, whether they are bonds or other indebtedness. The legal debt margin is computed in a statement of legal debt margin, an example of which is given in Figure 94.

Figure 94

CITY OF DALLAS, TEXAS
Statement of Legal Debt Margin[1]
September 30, 1952

Assessed Value...		$862,957,550
Constitutional Debt Limit (14.485% of Assessed Value)..		$125,000,000
Total Bonded Debt...................................	$91,916,500	
Less:		
Water Revenue Bonded Debt............ $6,918,000		
General Revenue Bonded Debt.......... 210,000	7,128,000	
Total Amount of Debt Applicable to Debt Limit..................		84,788,500
Legal Debt Margin...		$ 40,211,500

Liabilities Other Than Bonds

The nature of many of the liabilities is evident from the discussion of fund accounting procedure and the balance sheets illustrated in connection with it. Some of the liabilities, however, require further explanation. These are (1) vouchers payable, (2) warrants payable, (3) tax anticipation notes, (4) bond anticipation notes, (5) judgments payable, and (6) accrued liabilities.

Vouchers payable. We have already indicated that the approval of the expenditure and the resulting liability may be evidenced by a voucher. Vouchers payable are open-account liabilities and are of the same nature as other accounts payable, the only distinction between the two being that a voucher contains formal written evidence of the approval of the liability. The entries to record the approval of the expenditure and the resulting liability have been illustrated previously.

---

[1] Adapted from *Annual Financial Statement, City of Dallas, Texas for Fiscal Year Ended September 30, 1952,* p. 99.

Warrants payable. As indicated before, when the liability has been approved, a warrant may be issued to the claimant, who presents it to the treasurer for payment. Ordinarily, as warrants are issued, the proper fund Cash account is reduced in the general ledger, the entry being a debit to Vouchers Payable and a credit to Cash. If, however, the governmental unit has no cash with which to pay the liability, provision is frequently made for registering the warrants. The procedure in that case is as follows: At the time warrants are issued, the accounting officer knows whether or not the money is available for their payment. Consequently, if there is no probability of warrants being paid immediately, the Cash account is not reduced by the amount of warrants issued. Instead, the following entry is made:

Vouchers Payable	$15,000	
Warrants Payable		$15,000
To record issuance of warrants.		

When the warrant is presented to the treasurer, he registers it. The law usually provides that registered warrants shall bear interest. As funds become available, the treasurer calls in the warrants in the order of their registration and pays both the warrants and accrued interest. The entry to record the payment of the warrants and the interest on them is as follows:

Appropriation Expenditures	$ 100	
Warrants Payable	10,000	
Cash		$10,100
To record payment of warrants.		

It should be remembered that a governmental unit ordinarily cannot pay interest on warrants unless it is specifically authorized to do so by statute, although, because of differences in the degree of home rule enjoyed by local governments, some variations are likely to be found. Some states prohibit local governments from issuing warrants unless cash is available for their payment. Governmental units operating under such a restriction are frequently on a cash basis; that is, they do not incur an expenditure unless cash for the payment of the resulting liability is available at the time the expenditure is made and the liability is incurred.

Tax anticipation notes. Tax anticipation notes are issued by governmental units pending the collection of taxes. If a governmental unit does not collect its taxes until after the beginning of the fiscal year, it may have to borrow. One method of borrowing is to issue tax anticipation notes, which may be made payable solely from the collections of a particular levy or from all tax collections. As taxes are collected, the proceeds are used to retire the notes. If tax anticipation notes are payable solely from the tax levy of a particular year, the statutes usually provide that the total amount of notes issued shall not exceed a certain percentage of the tax levy. For example, if the tax levy for 1955 is $100,000, a governmental unit would usually not be permitted to issue tax anticipation notes for more than about $80,000, or 80 per cent of the tax levy for that year.

A maximum limit on tax anticipation borrowing is usually fixed for several reasons: In the first place, at least part of the expenditures will be financed from collections during the year. Secondly, the full amount of the levy may never be collected, or part of the taxes may not be collected for several years, thus making a portion of the tax anticipation notes long-term securities.

The entry to record the sale of tax anticipation notes is as follows:

Cash..	$80,000	
Tax Anticipation Notes—1955..............		$80,000
To record sale of tax anticipation notes applicable to 1955 levy.		

Tax anticipation notes bear interest, the maximum interest rate usually being specified by statute or charter. If these notes are payable from the tax levy of a specific year, they bear no maturity date. That is, the governmental unit will not retire them until the taxes against which they are issued are collected. In many cases, the governmental unit is not permitted to retire these notes from any revenues other than the tax collections to which they apply. In that case, as taxes are collected, the cash applicable to the payment of the notes must be segregated. The entry to record the collection of taxes and the segregation of cash is as follows:

Cash for Tax Anticipation Notes—1955........	$48,000	
Taxes Receivable—Current.................		$48,000
To record collection of part of 1955 levy and segregation of cash to be used in the payment of tax anticipation notes applicable thereto.		

Subsequently, as tax anticipation notes are retired, the following entry is made:

Tax Anticipation Notes—1955................	$48,000	
Cash for Tax Anticipation Notes—1955......		$48,000
To record retirement of tax anticipation notes.		

Since the notes will ordinarily run for less than a year and will be issued in the early part of the fiscal year, the interest on them is not accrued. Interest is usually paid at the time the notes are redeemed, the entry to record the transaction being

Appropriation Expenditures..................	$1,000	
Cash.......................................		$1,000
To record payment of interest on tax anticipation notes applicable to 1955 levy.		

Bond anticipation notes. In discussing the accounting procedure for special assessments, we indicated that sometimes notes are issued pending the levy of assessments and the issuance of bonds. In a similar manner, pending the sale of bonds, the governmental unit may issue notes to finance the construction of general improvements. As the bonds are sold, the proceeds are used to retire the notes. The advantages of issuing notes in anticipation of the sale of any type of bonds—special assessment, general improvement, or utility or other enterprise—are as follows: (1) If the project is constructed over a period of time, the notes can be sold from time to time as the need for money arises, thereby making it unnecessary to pay interest on funds not used and obviating the necessity of investing idle bond cash (the rate of interest earned on the idle funds will frequently be lower than the rate that will be paid by the governmental unit on its bonds). (2) The issuance of bonds for general improvements which are delayed or abandoned is prevented.

The entry to record the sale of bond anticipation notes is

Cash[2]..................................... $50,000
    Bond Anticipation Notes................... $50,000
    To record sale of bond anticipation notes.

When the bonds are sold, an entry is made debiting Cash for Bond Anticipation Notes and crediting Bonds Authorized—Unissued (in the case of general bonds) or Bonds Payable (in the case of special assessment bonds, utility bonds, or other enterprise bonds). As the notes are retired, an entry is made debiting Bond Anticipation Notes and crediting Cash for Bond Anticipation Notes.

The entries to record the payment of interest on bond anticipation notes are the same as for the payment of interest on the particular type of bonds which the notes anticipate—namely, general, special assessment, or utility or other enterprise bonds.

Judgments payable. We have already outlined in Chapter 8 the accounting procedure for those judgment liabilities which arise from condemnation of land for special assessment construction purposes.[3] The same procedure is applicable to judgments rendered in connection with the condemnation of property for the construction of projects financed from a bond fund or a utility or other enterprise fund. To clarify the exact nature of these liabilities, however, we shall explain briefly how judgment liabilities arise.

Most governmental units enjoy the power of eminent domain. This power enables a governmental unit to obtain property needed for public use, or to injure or destroy any property if such destruction or injury is incidental to the construction of a public improvement or any other public use. However, the governmental unit must pay for the damage. If the property owner and the governmental unit agree as to the amount

[2] In the special assessment fund and the utility or other enterprise fund the debit would be to Cash for Construction.
[3] See pages 109-110.

of compensation, the power of eminent domain obviously need not be exercised. Suppose, however, the owner refuses to accept the price offered or refuses to sell the property for any price. In that case, the governmental unit may take steps to take over the property.

The procedure is as follows: The governmental unit brings suit to condemn the particular property. The court then holds a public hearing, at which expert testimony is offered by the property owner and by the governmental unit as to the value of the property. On the basis of the testimony, the court decides the amount to be paid to the owner. If the case is tried before a jury, the jury decides the amount to be paid to the property owner. As soon as the verdict is rendered, the court enters a judgment against the governmental unit for the amount to be paid.

Since it is assumed that the property has been condemned in connection with a construction project, the full amount of the judgment is chargeable as a construction cost.

Judgments may also be rendered against a governmental unit for purposes other than the condemnation of property. All municipal corporations may be sued, and even quasi-municipal corporations may be authorized by statute to sue and to be sued.[4] For example, a city may be sued for injuries sustained on account of a broken sidewalk, for injury or damage caused by municipal vehicles, and so forth. As soon as a verdict is rendered by the court against the governmental unit (if no appeal is taken), the resulting liability must be recorded on the books. The type of judgment here referred to is usually that payable out of the general fund and subject to appropriation in the same manner as any other expenditures payable out of that fund. These judgments are fixed charges, like bond retirements and interest payments, and must be provided for in the budget in the same manner as other fixed charges. The entry to record the expenditure and liability is as follows:

Appropriation Expenditures.................. $15,000
Judgments Payable....................... $15,000
To record liability on account of judgments rendered.

Creditors may secure judgments against the governmental unit for unpaid bills. Such judgments frequently arise because the governmental unit disputes the amount of the bill. For example, let us assume that creditors claim $10,000 is due them, but the governmental unit acknowledges a liability of only $8,000. If the creditors secure a judgment for $10,000, and the governmental unit has recorded that part of the liability which it had acknowledged, the entry to be made at the time the judgment is rendered is as follows:

---

[4] States, as well as the Federal government, may be sued only with their consent, except that one state may sue another.

Appropriation Expenditures.................. $2,000
Vouchers Payable.......................... 8,000
   Judgments Payable...................... $10,000
To record judgments rendered.

Accrued liabilities. In discussing the accounting procedure for short-term liabilities, we gave no consideration to accrued liabilities. Accrued liabilities are those which are not payable at the time the statement is prepared. For example, assume that employees are paid on the tenth of the month and that a balance sheet is prepared showing the financial position of a utility or other enterprise fund as of December 31. If all the expenses of operating the utility or other enterprise are to be taken into account, it is necessary to record the salaries and wages due from December 10 to December 31, even though employees are not entitled to their pay until January 10. The liability for the salaries and wages of the period from December 10 to December 31 is known as an accrued liability.

As already indicated, no uniform practice is followed with respect to recording accrued liabilities. One fact is certain: Governmental units accrue fewer liabilities than private businesses. Variations can, however, be found between governmental units and between various funds within each unit. There is no question that the recording of accrued liabilities is essential if the true financial condition and true financial operations of self-supporting enterprises are to be shown. However, in the case of the general fund, as stated before, the recording of some accruals may frequently be impractical.

Bonds

A bond is a written promise to pay a specified sum of money at a certain date, with interest at a fixed rate payable periodically. The difference between a note and a bond is that the latter requires greater legal formality and usually runs for a longer period of time. The length of time varies, but ordinarily bonds are not issued for a period longer than thirty years except for certain public service enterprises. Before proceeding to examine the accounting procedure for bonds, it is important to distinguish between various types of bonds, because in certain respects the procedure will vary with the type of bond.

Classification of bonds. Bonds may be classified in many ways, among them the following: (1) the purpose for which issued, (2) the source from which debt service charges will be paid, (3) the nature of the security behind the bond, (4) the procedure in paying bonds and interest, and (5) the method of retirement. Each of these classifications is discussed immediately below.

Purpose. In the discussion of fund accounting, we indicated that bonds may be issued (1) for the purpose of financing the construction of general or special assessment improvements, (2) for the purpose of providing capital for a working capital fund, (3) for financing the acquisition of a utility or other enterprise, (4) for funding a deficit, and (5) for refunding purposes. The general characteristics of each type of bond have already been discussed, but a few additional details will be given here. Where bonds are issued to finance an improvement, statutes frequently require that they should not be outstanding for a longer period than the estimated life of the improvement. Bonds issued to finance a deficit are usually made to run for a shorter period than those issued to finance a permanent improvement. Neither funding nor refunding bonds in reality represent new liabilities; these bonds merely substitute one group of creditors for another group.

Sources of financing debt service charges. The sources of financing debt service charges will vary with the purpose for which the bonds were issued. Generally debt service charges are financed from taxation, from other general revenues, from special assessments, from utility or other enterprise earnings, or from a combination of any of these sources. Usually bonds are classified according to the source from which they are primarily payable, even though the governmental unit may also use other sources of revenue in financing them. On this basis governmental bonds may be classified into three groups: (1) general obligation bonds, payable primarily from general taxes or other revenues of the general fund or a special revenue fund, (2) special assessment bonds, payable primarily from special assessments, and (3) revenue bonds, payable from the earnings of self-supporting enterprises.

Nature of security. The resources provided for paying debt service charges indicate partially the nature of the security behind the bonds. For example, the security behind general obligation bonds is the taxing power of the governmental unit; the security behind special assessment bonds are special assessment collections; and the security behind revenue bonds are the revenues of the enterprise. However, as already pointed out, although bonds may be payable from special assessments, they may also carry a guarantee that, if sufficient assessments are not collected, the governmental unit will levy a general tax for their payment. Special assessment bonds can thus be classified further into special-special assessment bonds, which are payable only from special assessments, and general-special assessment bonds, which are payable primarily from assessments but also, in case of necessity, from general taxes or other general revenues.

Revenue bonds are payable solely from the revenues or the property of an enterprise. Security may be provided in the form of a mortgage, which, in case of default, the bondholders may foreclose to satisfy their debt. In actual practice, however, few if any governmental utility or other enterprise properties have been sold to satisfy mortgages. If utility or other enterprise property is mortgaged, provision is frequently made for the appointment of a receiver in case of failure to pay interest or principal. Even this procedure has not been entirely satisfactory, because the governmental unit will, in the event of the appointment of a receiver, consider the property privately owned and will proceed to tax it. The best additional security, even in the case of bonds payable from revenues, is the pledge of the governmental unit's general credit for the payment of the bonds—that is, the governmental unit's pledge to levy taxes or to provide other general revenue sources from which to pay the bonds, in the event that the revenues of the enterprise are insufficient for this purpose. Bonds issued by self-supporting enterprises may thus be classified into (1) general revenue bonds, or bonds for which only the revenues of the enterprise have been pledged as security for payment, (2) revenue mortgage bonds, or bonds for which the property of the enterprise, in addition to its earnings, has been pledged, and (3) general obligation utility or other enterprise bonds, that is, bonds for which both the revenues of the enterprise and the general credit of the governmental unit have been pledged. Usually revenue mortgage bonds are not general obligation bonds; that is, if the revenues and the property are pledged as security for the payment of the bonds, the general credit of the governmental unit is not pledged in addition.

Procedure in paying interest and principal. Bonds may be classified as coupon or registered or a combination of the two. Coupon bonds are those to which coupons are attached, each coupon representing the amount of interest payable at each interest payment date. Interest on these bonds is paid to the person presenting the proper coupon; and the principal is payable to the person who presents the bond. A registered bond, on the other hand, is one which has been registered in the name of the owner by the governmental unit. Payment is made only to the registered owner, and, in case a registered bond is sold, the change in ownership must be recorded on the records of the issuing governmental unit.

Bonds may be registered as to interest or principal or both. If bonds are registered as to interest or as to principal and interest, no coupons are necessary. If, however, the bonds are registered as to principal only, coupons are attached to them, interest in that case being paid to the person presenting the coupon and the principal being paid to the registered owner.

Method of retirement. An entire issue of bonds may be paid off at one time, or the debt may be reduced in approximately equal amounts each year. Bonds retired under the first method are usually referred to as term bonds; those retired under the second method are called serial bonds.

Term bonds are usually retired from a sinking fund. Serial bonds are retired regularly throughout the life of an issue. Usually, approximately equal amounts of bonds are paid off each year, but this is not always true. Frequently greater amounts of bonds are retired in the earlier part of the life of the bonds or in the later part of their life, depending on the extent to which other issues are being retired concurrently and upon other contemplated bond issues. Sometimes, too, the retirement of serial bonds is not begun the first year after their issuance. Instead, the first installment of bonds to be retired is deferred for a few years. In general, the aim is to equalize the entire annual debt burden of the governmental unit or have it gradually decrease. The important feature about serial bonds is that the retirement is gradual and continuous, with some bonds paid off each year.

Steps in the accounting procedure for bonds. Having discussed the various types of bonds, we are now in a position to take up the accounting procedure. This procedure may be illustrated best by outlining the steps involved from the time the bonds are authorized until they are paid. The transactions take place in the following order: (1) The issuance of bonds is authorized. (2) The bonds are sold. (3) Debt service charges are met. These transactions and the related accounting procedures are discussed below.

Authorization of bonds. We have already indicated that, before bonds may be issued, they must be authorized by the legislative body and that in the case of local units the authorization may have to be made not only by the legislative body of the governmental unit but by the state legislature as well. In addition, the approval of the voters or taxpayers may be required. The authorization for the issuance of state bonds and for the issuance of local bonds, if they require statutory authorization, are contained in the state constitution and statutes. Usually, however, even if statutes authorize the local governmental unit to issue bonds, the authorization of the local governmental unit's legislative body is also required.

If bond issues must be approved by the voters, the proposal to issue bonds is submitted in the same manner as other proposals and is voted upon at either a general or a special election (more frequently the former). In some cases, the approval of a bare majority of the voters is necessary; in others, the approval of two thirds of the voters must be secured. In some jurisdictions, only property owners are permitted to vote on bond issues. Whenever a vote of the people is required, the bond issue is not considered authorized until the approval is secured. The entries to record the authorization of bonds were discussed in Chapter 7 and will therefore not be illustrated here.

Sale of bonds. After the bonds have been authorized, steps are taken to sell them. Municipal bonds are usually sold on the basis of competitive bidding, the bonds being awarded to the highest responsible bidder. Frequently, bonds are not printed until they have been sold, the purchaser being given a temporary bond certificate or a receipt pending the delivery of the bonds. Purchasers will usually not buy the bonds without an attorney's opinion signifying that the bonds have been issued in strict accordance with statutory requirements.

Recording sale of bonds. As soon as bonds have been sold, entries should be made in the proper records to show the receipt of the proceeds and to indicate the liability. The required entries were illustrated in Chapters 7, 8, and 12. At this point, therefore, we shall only mention some of the records involved. The entries are made in the cash receipts register and are posted to the proper general ledger accounts of the particular fund affected. However, if a governmental unit has many bond issues outstanding, a subsidiary bonds payable ledger, which supports the Bonds Payable account in the general ledger, is established. A separate sheet is provided for each bond issue. This ledger sheet, like the ordinary ledger sheet, shows debits, credits, and balances. Sometimes, if bonds run for a period of less than about 15 years, the reverse side of the sheet is used to record interest which has become due. In that case, the sheets constitute both a bonds payable ledger and an interest payable ledger. The heading of each account in this ledger shows, among other things, the name of the bond and carries a reference both to the bond and interest record discussed below and to the proper bonds payable or interest payable control account. The account shows on one side the amount of bonds paid and outstanding and on the reverse side the amount of interest paid and payable.

As soon as the bonds are sold, it is important to calculate and to record (1) the amount of interest due semiannually, (2) the amount of principal due each year for serial bonds, and (3) the required annual contributions to sinking funds for sinking fund bonds. These required debt service charges are set up in a special record, commonly referred to as a bond and interest record, similar to the one which is illustrated in Figure 95.

If bonds are registered as to either principal or interest, an additional book is required for showing details concerning the bonds. This record is illustrated in Figure 96. Sometimes this book is dispensed with by making out a separate bond and interest record for each issue of bonds held by each registered bond owner. Each record bears the name and address of the bond owner.

Meeting debt service charges. The next step is to account for debt service charges. The entry to record interest expenses will depend on whether the interest is payable from the general fund or from another fund. If interest is payable from the general fund, the following entry is made when it becomes due (or is paid):

Figure 95

A GOVERNMENTAL UNIT
Bond and Interest Record

Title _____

Kind of Bonds and Maturities _____ Purpose _____

Amount of Issue _____

Date of Bonds _____

Interest Dates _____

Authorized by _____ Date of Sale _____ Interest Rates _____

Legality Approved by _____ Effective Interest Rate _____ Purchaser _____

Denomination of Bonds _____

Discount _____ Accrued Interest _____

Date of Delivery _____ Sale Price _____ Premium _____ Where Payable _____

Are Any Bonds of This Issue Registered? _____

Date of Maturity	Interest Due			Principal Due*		Principal and Interest Due Each Date
	Coupon No.	Bonds Numbered	Amount	Bonds Numbered	Amount	

* In the case of sinking funds, a column entitled "Sinking Fund Contribution" would be substituted for these two columns.

294

Appropriation Expenditures.....................	$2,000	
Matured Interest Payable (or Cash)...........		$2,000
To record interest expenses.		

The proper expenditure account would also be debited in the appropriation expenditure ledger. On the other hand, if interest is payable from a utility or other enterprise fund, the entry is a debit to Interest Expenses and a credit to Interest Payable or Cash, and, if from a special assessment fund, the entry is a debit to Interest Expenses and a credit to Interest Payable or Cash for Interest Payments.

Figure 96

A GOVERNMENTAL UNIT
Registered Bond Record

Purpose and Title of Issue————————————————Date of Issue————

Interest Rate————————————Payable on————————————————

Principal Payable at————————————————————————————

Item No.	Date	Bond No.	Name Registered in or Transferred to	Address	Amount	Maturity Date	Amount of Interest Each Period

In accounting for interest expenses, cognizance must be taken of premiums and discounts on bonds. The principles governing the amortization of premiums and discounts on investments, which were discussed in Chapter 9, are fully applicable to the amortization of premiums and discounts on bonds. Frequently, however, premiums and discounts on bonds are amortized only in a utility or other enterprise fund. The entry to record the amortization of premium in that fund has already been given (Chapter 12, page 186). The amortization of discount is recorded by the following entry:

Interest Expenses..............................	$2,100	
Unamortized Discounts on Bonds.............		$ 100
Interest Payable...............................		2,000
To record interest liability.		

The disposition of premiums and discounts that are not amortized was discussed in Chapters 7, 8, and 12.

Another fact which must be taken into account in recording interest expenses is the sale of accrued interest. If the bonds are sold during an interest period—that is, on any date other than one on which interest is due—the governmental unit in reality sells part of the accrued interest, since the purchaser will receive interest for a full half year, although he will have held the bond for a shorter period of time. The principles are the same as those discussed in connection with the acquisition of bond investments between interest payment dates, except that in this case the governmental unit is the borrower rather than the investor. The procedure is to set up the accrued interest sold as a liability and to reduce the amount of interest expense by the amount of the accrued interest sold.

To illustrate, if general bonds to the amount of $100,000, bearing interest of 3 per cent and dated February 1, are sold on March 1 for par plus accrued interest, the entry to record this transaction in the bond fund is as follows:

Cash..	$100,250	
Bonds Authorized—Unissued.............		$100,000
Accrued Interest Sold....................		250
To record sale of bonds.		

Subsequently the following entry is made in the bond fund to transfer out the cash representing the accrued interest:

Accrued Interest Sold.....................	$250	
Cash......................................		$250
To record transfer of cash representing accrued interest to the general fund.		

The corresponding entry in the general fund is as follows:

Cash......................................	$250	
Matured Interest Payable................		$250
To record transfer of cash representing accrued interest sold.		

As interest becomes due, an entry is made charging as an expenditure only that part of the interest which has not been sold, the entry being

Appropriation Expenditures.................	$1,250	
Matured Interest Payable................		$1,250
To record interest liability.		

When the interest is paid, an entry is made debiting Matured Interest Payable for $1,500 and crediting Cash for a corresponding amount. Although the above entries are applicable only to general bonds, the same principle applies also to both special assessment bonds and utility or other enterprise bonds. Note also that the accrued interest on bonds sold is adjusted on the first interest date, while premiums and discounts are amortized at each interest date.

Immediately after the bonds are sold, officials determine the part of the proceeds represented by bond principal, by premiums, and by accrued interest sold. The first step is to deduct from the total proceeds the amount representing accrued interest sold. The remainder can then be apportioned between bond principal and premiums. It should be noted that accrued interest must be identified and accounted for separately even if bonds are sold at a discount. Of course, the amount of accrued interest sold can be readily determined, since it is the interest which has accrued from the last interest date to the date of the sale or, if the bonds are sold within the first interest payment period, from the date shown on the bond to the date of the sale.

Recording matured bonds payable and their payment. The entries to record matured bonds payable in both the sinking fund and the general fund were discussed in Chapters 9 and 13. Matured sinking fund bonds, as already indicated, may be carried in the sinking fund or transferred to the general fund. If the liability and the cash available for its retirement are transferred to the general fund, the entry in the latter fund is:

Cash for Payment of Matured Sinking Fund Bonds $100,000
 Matured Bonds Payable...................... $100,000
To record transfer to general fund of liability on
account of matured sinking fund bonds, as well as
transfer of cash for payment of the liability.

The payment of the matured bonds is, of course, recorded by a debit to the Matured Bonds Payable account and a credit to the Cash for Payment of Matured Sinking Fund Bonds account.

Paying matured bonds and interest through fiscal agent. The governmental unit usually pays matured bonds and interest through a fiscal agent or through both its own treasury office and a fiscal agent. The procedure is as follows: A short time preceding the date on which bonds and interest become due, the money is transmitted to the fiscal agent, the entry to record this transaction being

Cash with Fiscal Agents........................ $70,000
 Cash....................................... $70,000
To record transmission of cash to fiscal agents for
payment of matured bonds and interest payable.

At periodic intervals the fiscal agent is required to submit reports of bonds and interest paid. A form for such a report is illustrated in Figure 97. Note that provision is made for showing the amount of bonds paid of each issue and the interest coupons paid. The fiscal agent also turns in the redeemed interest coupons and bonds.

The first step is to verify that the report agrees with the bonds and coupons turned in. If it does, an entry is made in the general records reducing the liability and the Cash with Fiscal Agents accounts, as follows:

Matured Interest Payable...................... $ 20,000
Matured Bonds Payable........................   100,000
    Cash with Fiscal Agents...................... $120,000
To record payment of bonds and interest by fiscal
agent as per report dated_____.

A similar procedure is followed with respect to bonds and coupons paid by the governmental unit's treasurer. The bonds and coupons are sorted and a report similar to that illustrated in Figure 97 is prepared, both the report and paid bonds and coupons being turned over by the treasurer to the accounting department. Here the report is verified, and, if bonds and coupons have not already been canceled, they are canceled at this time.

Figure 97

A GOVERNMENTAL UNIT					
Report from Fiscal Agent					
Date_____					

Title of Issue	BONDS PAID		COUPONS PAID		Total Paid
	Quantity*	Amount	Quantity*	Amount	

* If the fiscal agent is required to itemize bonds and coupons by numbers, the word *Numbers* should be substituted for *Quantity*.

Canceled bonds and coupons should be filed in such a manner that they can be readily audited. Bonds are filed by issue and number, and coupons are filed by issue, bond number, and coupon number. Under no circumstances should either bonds or coupons be destroyed before the governmental unit's books have been audited by independent auditors and the amount reported as paid has been verified by canceled coupons and bonds. Usually governmental units keep the canceled bonds and coupons on file for a 2- or 3-year period, after which time they destroy them by cremation. The cremation must be witnessed by some responsible officials. A statement is prepared showing the title of the issues and the bond and coupon numbers. This statement is checked and signed by the officials witnessing the cremation and is filed permanently.

Subsidiary debt statements. Information as to the amount of indebtedness outstanding is, of course, shown in the appropriate fund balance sheet. The exceptions, as we have seen, are general bonds payable and interest payable on bonds in future years, which are shown in a separate statement. Further details than those shown in the above statements may, however, be required about the bonded debt. For this purpose subsidiary debt statements are prepared. These statements may be divided into two groups: (1) subsidiary financial statements, and (2) statistical statements.

Financial statements. Subsidiary financial statements for bonds are those supporting the Bonds Payable accounts of each fund and of the general bonded debt and interest group of accounts in the general ledger. The statement illustrated in Figure 98, showing bonds payable, is an example of a detailed financial statement. Note that each issue is listed in this statement and that details such as rate of interest, date of issue, date of maturity, amount authorized, amount issued, and amount outstanding are shown for each bond issue. Since each issue is listed in this statement, it is convenient to show the actuarial requirements and the actual accumulations in the sinking fund for each sinking fund bond issue. Through such an arrangement, it is possible to note not only how the sinking fund for each bond issue compares with requirements but also the relationship between each bond issue outstanding and the sinking fund accumulated for its retirement. If interest is accrued on the records, the amount of accrued interest payable on each bond issue may also be shown. The data for this statement are secured from the bond and interest record (Figure 95) and from the bond and interest payable ledger.

Statistical statements. Statistical debt statements do not refer to any particular account in the balance sheet. They may show data for a number of years rather than for any one particular year; they may include data which are not part of the formal records; and they may not show the data by funds. Among the more important statistical debt statements are the following: (1) statement showing ratios of net general bonded debt to assessed value and net bonded debt per capita, (2) statement of direct and overlapping debt, and (3) statements of debt service requirements and sinking fund bond maturities. In addition, there is the statement of legal debt margin, which has already been discussed.

Ratio of net general bonded debt to assessed value and net bonded debt per capita (Figure 99). Since debt limitation is based on the ratio of indebtedness to assessed value of taxable property and particularly because the assessed valuation is the basis for raising the revenue from which general bonds will be paid, it is desirable to show the ratio of net general bonded debt to assessed value. Note that the statement is concerned only with the general bonded debt—that is, that part of the bonded indebtedness of the governmental unit which is payable from taxes. If general-special assessment and general utility or other enterprise bonds are issued, it is advisable to show two groups of ratios: (1) the ratio of net

Figure 98

A GOVERNMENTAL UNIT

Statement of Bonds Payable

General Bonds, Special Assessment Bonds, and Utility or Other Enterprise Bonds

December 31, 1955

Description	Rate of Interest	Date of Issue	Maturity	Bonds Authorized	Issued	Outstanding	Sinking Fund Required	Actual	Excess or Deficiency*
GENERAL BONDS									
Sinking Fund Bonds:									
Hospital Bonds...................	3%	1943	1967	$ 315,000	$ 315,000	$ 315,000	$124,800	$125,160	$360
City Hall Bonds..................	3¼	1944	1968	230,000	230,000	230,000	83,200	83,440	240
Bridge Bonds....................	3	1945	1969	255,000	255,000	255,000	104,000	104,300	300
				$ 800,000	$ 800,000	$ 800,000	$312,000	$312,900	$900
Serial Bonds:									
Sewer...........	4	1953	$25,000 annually	$ 350,000	$ 350,000	$ 300,000			
Total General Bonds (Figure 68)......				$1,150,000	$1,150,000	$1,100,000			
SPECIAL ASSESSMENT BONDS									
Special Assessment Project #8.......	5	1955	1964 callable	$ 350,000	$ 350,000	$ 350,000			
Total Special Assessment Bonds (Figure 37)......				$ 350,000	$ 350,000	$ 350,000			
UTILITY OR OTHER ENTERPRISE BONDS									
Sinking Fund Bonds:									
Sinking Fund Bonds...............	3¼	1955	1972	$ 200,000	$ 200,000	$ 200,000	$ 6,966	$ 7,016	$ 50
Total Sinking Fund Bonds...........				$ 200,000	$ 200,000	$ 200,000	$ 6,966	$ 7,016	$ 50
Serial Bonds:									
Series A......................	3½	1941	$25,000 annually	$ 500,000	$ 500,000	$ 150,000			
Series B......................	4½	1948	$25,000 annually	500,000	500,000	300,000			
Total Serial Bonds............				$1,000,000	$1,000,000	$ 450,000			
Total Utility or Other Enterprise Bonds (Figure 59)......				$1,200,000	$1,200,000	$ 650,000			
Total Bonds Payable (Figure 69)......				$2,700,000	$2,700,000	$2,100,000			

Figure 99

MONTGOMERY COUNTY, MARYLAND
Ratio of General Bonded Debt to Assessed Value and Bonded Debt per Capita[5]

1943-1952

Fiscal Year Ended	Estimated Population	Assessed Value—End of Period	Bonded Debt*	Ratio of Bonded Debt to Assessed Value	Bonded Debt Per Capita
1943.........	107,000	$183,058,496	$10,365,050	5.66%	$ 96.87
1944.........	110,000	186,245,518	9,926,000	5.33	90.24
1945.........	115,000	186,279,153	9,725,000	5.22	84.57
1946.........	120,000	192,065,691	11,683,000	6.08	97.36
1947.........	130,000	207,730,761	13,828,500	6.66	106.35
1948.........	135,000	244,602,138	16,015,000	6.55	118.63
1949.........	145,000	326,759,272	18,266,250	5.59	125.97
1950.........	164,401	352,353,988	20,682,400	5.87	125.80
1951.........	175,000	417,833,528	28,615,550	6.85	163.52
1952.........	185,000	496,727,312	34,849,700	7.02	188.38

* All bonds mature serially. There are no sinking funds.

general bonded debt to assessed value, and (2) the ratio of the total of net general bonded debt, general-special assessment bonded debt, and net general utility or other enterprise bonded debt to assessed value.

The statement also shows the changes in per capita bonded debt for a number of years. Increases in per capita debt may be due to a decrease in population, an increase in bonded debt, or a more rapid increase in debt

Figure 100

CITY OF DALLAS, TEXAS
Statement of Direct and Overlapping Debt [6]

September 30, 1952

	Gross Debt Less Sinking Fund*	Percentage of Debt Applicable to City of Dallas	City of Dallas Share of Debt
City of Dallas.....................	$81,151,567	100%	$ 81,151,567
Dallas Independent School District...	24,765,032	96%	23,774,431
County of Dallas.................	20,452,478	85%	17,384,606
Total Direct and Overlapping Debt			$122,310,604

* Only the cash and investments of the Sinking Fund are considered as deductions from gross debt.

---

[5] Adapted from the *Annual Financial Report of Montgomery County, Maryland, for the Fiscal Year Ended June 30, 1952*, Table XII.

[6] Adapted from *Annual Financial Statement, City of Dallas, Texas for Fiscal Year Ended September 30, 1952*, p. 102.

than in population. Similarly, decreases can be traced to variations either in the bonded debt itself or in population. This statement is therefore important not only because it shows details concerning per capita bonded debt but also because the reason for the variation can be ascertained from it.

Statement of direct and overlapping debt (Figure 100). From an economic standpoint, it is important to know not only the indebtedness of the governmental unit under consideration but also the indebtedness of all other jurisdictions occupying the same territory. For example, it is important to know not only the debt of a municipality but also the propor-

Figure 101

CITY OF PONTIAC, MICHIGAN
General Bonds
Debt Service Requirements Until Maturity[7]
December 31, 1952

Fiscal Year	Serial Bonds	Interest on Bonds	Total Bonds and Interest
1953...................	$ 205,000	$ 42,078.75	$ 247,078.75
1954...................	369,000	35,203.75	404,203.75
1955...................	365,000	27,066.25	392,066.25
1956...................	143,000	20,897.50	163,897.50
1957...................	170,000	16,366.25	186,366.25
1958...................	95,000	12,585.00	107,585.00
1959...................	128,000	9,257.50	137,257.50
1960...................	127,000	5,368.75	132,368.75
1961...................	70,000	2,476.25	72,476.25
1962...................	45,000	945.00	45,945.00
1963...................	17,000	191.25	17,191.25
	$1,734,000	$172,436.25	$1,906,436.25

tion of the general debt of the county, of independent school districts, and so forth, that will have to be paid by city taxpayers. Figure 100 illustrates a statement of direct and overlapping debt as it applies to the City of Dallas. Note that the overlapping debt of the State of Texas is not included, since statements of direct and overlapping debt are usually limited to the debt of local overlapping governments alone.

Statement of debt service requirements (Figure 101). This statement shows the required debt service charges on bonded debt on the basis of bonds outstanding at the date the statement is prepared. A separate statement should be prepared for each class of bonds—that is, for general bonds, for special assessment bonds, for utility bonds, and for other enter-

---

[7] Adapted from the *Financial Report of the City of Pontiac, Michigan for Fiscal Year Ended December 31, 1952*, p. 64.

prise bonds. Figure 101 shows the debt service requirements for general bonds. Note particularly that the statement shows required future charges rather than past charges. The statement is important in the preparation of the budget and in the formulation of a governmental unit's debt policy.

18

<<<<<<<<<<<<<<<<<<<<<<<<<<<<<<<<<<<<<<<<<<<<<<<<<<<<<<<<<<

AUDITING AND FINANCIAL REPORTING

THIS CHAPTER deals with auditing and the resulting audit report, with the annual financial report prepared by the finance officer of a governmental unit, with the use of the audit report as a report of the finance officer, and with the monthly report to be issued by the finance officer. The chapter is therefore divided into the five following parts: Auditing Standards and Procedures, the Audit Report, the Annual Financial Report, the Combined Financial and Audit Report, and the Monthly Financial Report.

Auditing Standards and Procedures

It is beyond the scope of this book to discuss the detailed audit procedures involved in auditing a governmental unit. The discussion will therefore be limited to some of the highlights of governmental auditing with emphasis on those standards and procedures which are peculiar to governmental auditing as distinguished from commercial auditing.

Standards and procedures distinguished. Auditing procedures deal with what is to be done whereas auditing standards relate to the quality of the work performed. An example of an auditing standard is the requirement that the auditor be well qualified to do the particular work. In the case of governmental auditing, it is essential that the auditor be qualified by both training and experience to make an audit of a governmental unit; the fact that an auditor is qualified to audit a private business does not automatically qualify him to audit a governmental unit. One of the factors which is likely to detract from the quality of the work is the awarding of audits on a competitive bid basis. Accordingly, the National Committee on Governmental Accounting, the American Institute of Accountants, and many state societies of certified public accountants have registered their disapproval of awarding audits of governmental bodies on a competitive bid basis.

Classifications of audits. Audits may be classified, first of all, according to whether they are pre-audits or post-audits. A pre-audit is an examination made of a transaction or transactions before they have taken place, or after they have taken place but before they have been recorded. Pre-audits are made by the staff of a governmental agency. Examples of pre-audits are (1) the checking of carbon copies of tax bills, license forms, and other documents to see, among other things, that they are properly classified and coded for entry in the records, (2) the checking of purchase orders to see that there is a sufficient balance for them in the designated appropriation, and (3) the checking of invoices for legality, propriety, receipt of goods, and for the other requirements described in connection with the discussion of invoice audit procedure on page 76. Post-audits, on the other hand, are made after the transactions to be audited have taken place and have been recorded. This chapter deals with post-audits.

The National Committee on Governmental Accounting classifies post-audits according to whether they are (1) general or special audits and (2) complete or limited audits. It defines a general audit as "one which embraces all financial transactions and records and which is made regularly at the close of an accounting period, usually a year. A special audit, on the other hand, is one which is limited to some particular phase of a governmental unit's activities as for example the examination of a sinking fund, or an audit which covers all of the governmental unit's activities for a shorter or longer period of time than the usual audit period."[1]

The Committee points out that both general and special audits may in turn be classified as complete or limited. In a complete audit all transactions, books, documents, and other supporting data are examined. In a limited audit, only selected items are examined, on the assumption that the selected transactions are representative of the entire group from which selected, and therefore, if no errors are found in them, the unchecked items in the group are assumed to be correct.

Most governmental audits are general, that is, they cover a year, and limited, that is, they involve the examination of only selected items. In this chapter, therefore, it is also assumed that a limited general audit is involved and that the audit report is the result of this type of audit.

Classification of auditors. Post-audits are usually performed by independent auditors, that is, by persons who are independent of the administrative organization of the unit audited. There are three groups of independent auditors: (1) the independent auditor who is an official of the governmental unit, (2) the state audit agency, and (3) the independent private auditor. Most states and a few municipalities have an independent

---

[1] National Committee on Governmental Accounting, *Municipal Accounting and Auditing* (Chicago: The Committee, 1951), p. 187.

auditor either elected by the people or appointed by the legislative body. In such cases, the auditor is usually responsible directly to the legislative body or to the people; he is not responsible to the chief executive. Sometimes this auditor is vested with the powers of pre-audit; that is, no claim can be paid until it has been approved by him. In that case, of course, the pre-audit constitutes an independent audit, and no post-audit is necessary, because the auditor would be reviewing his own work. Such an arrangement is undesirable because administrative auditing is thereby weakened or entirely eliminated.

State audit agencies have been established in some states with the power to audit the books of local governmental units either with or without the request of the units. These audit agencies do not necessarily audit any of the state's books. In some states—Wisconsin, for example—local governmental units have a choice of having their books audited either by the state audit agency or by independent private accountants. Most local governmental audits are made by independent private accountants, although in some states local units must be audited by a state agency.

The audit standards and procedures described here apply with modifications to all of these classes of auditors. An example of one modification is the requirement that the auditor familiarize himself with the organization of the governmental unit which he is going to audit. Naturally, an independent auditor on the staff of the governmental unit would be familiar with the organization. Again, the question of competitive bidding is not involved in the case of this type of auditor.

Purpose of audit. An audit of a governmental unit is intended to establish fidelity and compliance with legal provisions as well as to call attention, where appropriate, to the need for greater efficiency. While efficiency is always considered, emphasis is on fidelity and compliance with legal provisions.

Preliminary steps. Before starting to audit a governmental unit, the auditor must take some of the same preliminary steps which he would take if he were performing a commercial audit. For example, he must familiarize himself with the nature of the organization he is going to audit, must look into its system of internal control, and must ascertain the basis of accounting being followed. In addition, the auditor must make sure that he knows the similarities and differences between governmental and commercial accounting. He must remember particularly that governmental units are subject to a great many legal restrictions which affect their accounting and reporting procedures. He must give special attention to the legal provisions governing taxes, licenses, and other revenues which the municipality is authorized to raise, and to the purposes for which they may be spent. He must also carefully study legal provisions relating to funds and to the adoption and execution of the budget. The foregoing, as well as other related legal provisions, can be ascertained by reading the appropriate sections of the state statutes, municipal charter, and municipal ordinances.

But the auditor must not only be familiar with legal provisions; he must also know what are the accepted principles of governmental accounting. These principles have been described throughout the preceding chapters and are summarized in Appendix I. They will not, therefore, be discussed further.

In making his examination, the auditor must satisfy himself that each transaction audited (1) complies with legal requirements and (2) is recorded in accordance with sound governmental accounting principles. It must be remembered, however, that legal provisions take precedence over sound accounting principles or good financial administration. That this fact is sometimes forgotten by the auditor is evident from the following case. A city treasurer was criticized by the auditors for not depositing all of the city's receipts daily in the bank when, as a matter of fact, legal provisions made it impossible for him to do so. The auditors should have criticized the law which made this practice necessary rather than the city treasurer, who after all could do nothing more than comply with the provisions of the law.

On the other hand, officials sometimes do the right thing from the standpoint of sound accounting and financial administration but must nevertheless be criticized because their procedures are not in accord with legal provisions. For example, in one state the statutes provide that no state agency shall establish a revolving fund in excess of $500. In spite of such a provision, one agency had established a revolving fund of $60,000. This was good procedure from the standpoint of sound financial administration because the particular operation could be performed most effectively through the use of a revolving fund of $60,000. The agency was, however, rightfully criticized for disregarding the law.

Another fact which the auditor must ascertain before he starts to make the audit is exactly what agencies or funds he is going to cover. Thus, if the municipality has a utility, he must ascertain definitely before he makes, an estimate of the cost of the audit or of the time required to perform it whether or not he is expected to include the utility. The problem of determining which agencies are going to be covered by a particular audit arises especially in the case of such governmental units as counties which have numerous independent or quasi-independent boards and commissions.

Audit procedure. Having carried out the preliminary steps, the auditor can now proceed to the actual audit work. The procedures involved are in a great many respects similar to those employed in a commercial audit. Only those phases of the audit procedure which are peculiar to governmental agencies will, therefore, be mentioned and only those which are most significant will be more fully described. The discussion will deal with revenues, expenditures, assets, liabilities, other credits, and surplus.

Revenues. Since the general property tax is still one of the most important revenue sources of local governments, it always requires the attention of the auditor. For example, the auditor must determine whether the particular governmental unit is getting all the revenues from this source to which it is entitled. This involves, among other things, obtaining from the assessor a confirmation of the assessed value, examining the tax levy ordinance to verify the accuracy of the total tax levy, and recomputing the tax rate by dividing the tax levy by the assessed value. Reference must also be made to the statutes or the charter to determine that the tax rate does not exceed the maximum permitted by law.

Naturally, the auditor must not only determine that the proper amount of taxes was levied but also that all the taxes which have been collected have been turned into the treasury. Since this part of the procedure is similar to that involved in verifying cash receipts in a commercial audit, it will not be discussed. One fact to be noted in this connection, however, is the importance of circularizing taxpayers. Experience has shown that failure to circularize taxpayers can prove to be very costly. For instance, some defalcations which have resulted in the payment of damages by the auditor and in embarrassing publicity could have been avoided had taxpayers been circularized.

The auditor must ascertain the nature of the legal provisions governing interest and penalties on delinquent taxes and see to it that all of the interest and penalties which should have been collected were actually collected. He must also see whether adequate provision was made for uncollectible taxes. He must familiarize himself with legal provisions concerning tax refunds and the write-off of uncollectible taxes and must see to it that such write-offs or refunds are in accordance with these legal provisions and are properly approved.

The auditor should insist that licenses be pre-numbered by the printer. If this is done, some check of the accuracy of reported license revenues can be obtained through accounting for used and unused license forms. For example, the number of licenses issued multiplied by the rate should indicate the amount that should have been received from this source. Frequently, however, it is necessary to take into account duplicates, half-rates for licenses issued after the middle of the year, and similar other factors. But this method is helpful as a general guide. Another check (which may not always be practicable) is provided by comparing selected business establishments which are supposed to be licensed with the number of licenses which have been issued for such businesses. In one case, the classified telephone directory listed 15 dancing schools but the city records showed that only 5 dancing school licenses had been issued.

Other important revenue sources in many local government units are taxes shared with the state and grants by the federal and state governments. These revenues can be readily verified by communicating with the granting governmental unit.

In general, a comparison of estimated with actual revenues should be helpful in determining whether the governmental unit has received all the revenues to which it is entitled. For example, other things being equal, revenues which fall short of the amount estimated call for more attention than those which are equal to or exceed estimates.

Finally, the auditor must see that taxes and other revenues are allocated to the proper funds. In this connection it is important to see that revenues are properly classified by source because the source of revenue frequently determines the fund into which it is to flow.

Expenditures. Since municipal expenditures must be authorized in the budget, the first step in auditing expenditures is to determine whether they have been properly authorized by the legislative body. As we have seen, such authorizations are made by means of an appropriation ordinance and the resulting authorized amounts of expenditures are known as appropriations. It is the auditor's duty to see, among other things, that expenditures were charged to the proper appropriations and that expenditures did not exceed the related appropriations. If an encumbrance system is employed (and the auditor should recommend that it be adopted if it is not in use), he must determine that all encumbrances have been recorded and that no appropriation has been over-encumbered.

Ordinarily, payrolls of civil service employees must be approved by the civil service commission. The auditor must ascertain whether such approval has been obtained. He should verify pension deductions with the particular pension board to which they are supposed to have been transmitted. The payment of bonds and interest is best verified by examining the canceled bonds and coupons. The auditor should impress upon governmental officials the importance of filing these documents in such a way as to facilitate their audit.

Assets. For the most part, the same procedure should be followed in the examination of the assets of a governmental unit as is followed in the verification of assets of a business. Several differences should, however, be noted. Governmental units are frequently required to maintain a separate bank account for each fund, and the auditor must determine whether this legal provision has been complied with. Again, banks are frequently required to furnish the governmental unit collateral as security for the government's deposits. The auditor must determine not only that such collateral has been furnished but also that it is the kind specified by law and that it is adequate.

The kinds of securities in which the governmental unit may invest are frequently specified by law and the auditor must determine, among other things, whether legal provisions have been followed. He must also see that any necessary amortization procedures have been properly applied to premiums and discounts on investments.

Except for inventories of working capital funds, inventory control is frequently lacking. The auditor should recommend a perpetual inventory system wherever such a system appears to be practical, and should point out the need for supplementing it with a physical inventory at least once each year. If a perpetual inventory system is not practical, it is particularly important to see that a good system of internal control in the handling of important inventory items is established.

With respect to general fixed assets, two extreme situations are frequently found to exist. At one extreme are the cases where no records of fixed assets are kept. The auditor should recommend that such records be established. At the other extreme are cases where the governmental unit depreciates its general fixed assets. The auditor should recommend against taking depreciation on general fixed assets because the use which can be made of these data does not warrant the additional accounting expense.

Liabilities. The audit of a government's liabilities involves generally the same procedures as the audit of the liabilities of a private business. There are exceptions, however. Two examples of such exceptions are tax anticipation notes and taxes collected for other units. Some local governments issue tax anticipation notes. These notes are usually payable from a particular tax levy and may not exceed a certain percentage of the tax levy. It is the auditor's duty to see that the total amount of notes issued against a particular tax levy does not exceed the maximum permitted by law, and that the proceeds from a particular levy have been applied to the notes issued against that levy and no other. In many states, one governmental unit collects taxes for other units. In such a case, the liability of the governmental unit being audited for these tax collections can be verified by communicating with the units for which the taxes are being collected.

Finally, the auditor will frequently find that encumbrances are being treated as liabilities. In such a case, he should explain to the governmental officials that an encumbrance creates a contingent and not an actual liability. He should point out that actual liability is created only when the governmental unit receives the materials or services. He should see that proper adjustments are made.

Other credits. As indicated previously, the caption "other credits" covers accounts which normally have credit balances but which are neither liabilities nor surpluses. Examples are appropriations; fund balances of trust and agency funds; the capital of a working capital or utility or other enterprise fund; reserves for encumbrances; reserves for retirement of sinking fund bonds; and reserves for pension fund retirements. Most of these accounts will have been verified as a result of the auditing procedures described previously. The auditor must pay particular attention, however, to the Reserve for Retirement of Sinking Fund Bonds account.

We stated in Chapter 9 that in the case of sinking funds, the Reserve for Retirement of Sinking Fund Bonds account should indicate what the actual requirements of the sinking fund are at the balance sheet date. The auditor must determine whether the balance in such reserve does represent the actuarial requirements of the fund. In other words, the balance in the reserve should show the amount which on the basis of actuarial computations should be in the fund at the balance sheet date. If the assets in the fund are greater than the balance in the reserve, the difference represents a surplus; if smaller, the difference represents a deficit. Frequently, it will be found that no such distinction is made by the governmental unit and that the Reserve for Retirement of Sinking Fund Bonds account is made to equal the amount of assets in the fund without regard to actuarial requirements. The auditor should be particularly on guard if he finds that the sinking fund has neither a surplus nor a deficit. What was said about the Reserve for Retirement of Sinking Fund Bonds account applies equally to the Reserve for Pension Fund Retirements account carried in a pension fund.

Surplus. In determining whether unappropriated surplus is being properly presented or computed, the auditor must remember that the surplus of each fund must be considered separately. He must further remember that it is wrong to present a balance sheet in which the general fixed assets are shown on the assets side, the bonded debt on the credit side, and the difference between such assets and liabilities designated as surplus. The general fixed assets and the general bonds should each be set up in a separate group of accounts. General fixed assets should be offset on the credit side by an account indicating the governmental unit's equity in such assets; general bonds payable plus the interest thereon payable in future years should be offset on the assets side by accounts indicating the amount available and the amount to be raised from future taxation for the retirement of these bonds and the payment of the interest thereon.

The Audit Report

An audit report is prepared in order to indicate the scope of the audit, to point out weaknesses in the organization or procedures and make suggestions for their improvement, and to certify that the financial statements included in the report are in agreement with the records and fairly present the financial condition and financial operations of the various funds of the governmental unit. The audit report should contain (1) a letter of transmittal and (2) financial statements. Each of these is discussed separately below.

Letter of transmittal. The letter of transmittal should be similar to one included in an audit report of a private business. In it the auditor should discuss such matters as the scope and limitations of the audit, should present a summary of audit findings, and should make recommendations for desirable changes. The letter should contain an opinion worded along the lines of an opinion given in a commercial audit but modified to indicate that the financial statements comply with generally accepted principles of *governmental* accounting. An example of an audit certificate suitable for a governmental unit is illustrated in Figure 102.

Figure 102

Auditor's Certificate

To the City Council
City of *X*
Gentlemen:

We have examined the balance sheets of the various funds of the City of *X* as of December 31, 1955, and the related statements of revenues, expenditures, and surplus for the year then ended. Our examination was made in accordance with generally accepted auditing standards, and accordingly included such tests of the accounting records and such other auditing procedures as we considered necessary in the circumstances.

In our opinion, the accompanying balance sheets and related statements of revenues, expenditures, and surplus present fairly the financial position of the various funds of the City of *X*, on December 31, 1955, and the results of their operations for the year then ended, in conformity with generally accepted governmental accounting principles applied on a basis consistent with that of the preceding year.

February 15, 1956
_____

Certified Public Accountants

Financial statements. The following is an outline of the financial statements to be included in an audit report. The outline is based primarily on the statements illustrated throughout this book. Of course, an actual report may have a greater or smaller number of statements than are listed here, depending on the number of funds, the magnitude of transactions, and the importance of analyzing the changes taking place in particular accounts during the year.

FINANCIAL STATEMENTS OF AUDIT REPORT

Section A. General Fund

It should be noted that the report consists of two kinds of statements: (1) principal statements and (2) subsidiary statements. Subsidiary statements are those which support an account or group of accounts in another statement. Such support may consist of giving further details about the account or of showing the changes which have taken place in the account between two dates. All statements which are not subsidiary statements are classified as principal statements. Usually principal statements are prepared from those accounts which are carried in the general ledger.

Arrangement of financial statements. Since one of the distinguishing characteristics of governmental accounting is the use of funds, the statements should be classified by funds. In other words, the statements pertaining to each fund should be grouped in a separate section. For example, both the principal and subsidiary statements of the general fund should be grouped in one section and those of the bond fund in another section. If a subsidiary statement is applicable to an account carried in more than one fund and if the information to be shown for the account is practically the same in all funds to which the account applies, the statement may be grouped with all the others pertaining to that account. Thus, for example, the statement of bonds payable which supports the Bonds Payable account in the special assessment fund, in the utility or other enterprise fund, and in the general bonded debt and interest group of accounts is not broken up into three individual statements. Instead, one statement is prepared for the Bonds Payable accounts in the three funds. In that way, this statement not only shows details regarding the bonds of each of these funds but also supports the Bonds Payable account in the combined fund balance sheet illustrated in Figure 69.

The arrangement of the statements within each section presents no difficult problem. The balance sheet should be the first statement in each fund and should be followed by the other principal statements, the subsidiary statements coming last. Subsidiary statements themselves may be arranged in the order in which the accounts which they support are arranged in the balance sheet or other principal statements. Exceptions to this rule are, however, quite common. Thus, because of its importance, the statement analyzing the changes in the Appropriations account is frequently shown before the statement of cash receipts, disbursements, and balances, even though the Cash account precedes the Appropriations account in the balance sheet.

The order in which the funds should be shown is another problem. There is no general rule as to what this order should be except that the section containing the statements for the general fund is usually shown first, because that fund is the most important fund, and the section containing the combined balance sheet and related subsidiary statements is the last, because it pertains to all funds.

The Annual Financial Report

The annual financial report is prepared by the finance officer of a governmental unit to show its financial condition and financial operations. It should consist of (1) a letter of transmittal, (2) financial statements, and (3) statistical tables. Each of these is discussed immediately below.

Letter of transmittal. In his letter of transmittal, the finance officer should discuss such topics as the basis of accounting followed and the funds employed, and he should comment on the most significant changes in the financial condition of the governmental unit which have taken place during the year, on its financial condition at the end of the year, and on prospects for the coming year.

Financial statements. The financial statements should be identical in form and arrangement with those included in an audit report. These statements were described in the preceding part of this chapter.

Statistical tables. The National Committee on Governmental Accounting makes the following distinction between financial statements and statistical tables.

> Financial statements are prepared directly from the accounts, ordinarily contain no other data except those taken directly from the accounts, and usually cover a period of one or two fiscal years. On the other hand, statistical tables may cover several fiscal years and may consist entirely or in part of data not contained in the accounting records. Examples of such non-accounting data are assessed values and tax rates. The purpose of financial statements is, among other things, to show that legal provisions have been complied with and that all funds have been properly accounted for. Statistical tables, on the other hand, show non-financial data and financial trends. For example, they show past trends of assessed values, tax rates, revenues, and expenditures and they indicate, on the other hand, the debt service charges to be met each year over a period of years in the future.[2]

Arrangement of statistical tables. The statistical tables should be arranged in four groups dealing respectively with (1) assessed values and property taxes, (2) revenues and expenditures, (3) bonded debt, and (4) miscellaneous statistical facts, such, for example, as the salaries and surety bonds of principal officials. The following is an outline of the statistical tables to be included in an annual financial report based primarily on the tables illustrated in this book.

STATISTICAL TABLES IN ANNUAL FINANCIAL REPORT

Figure

SECTION A. ASSESSED VALUES AND PROPERTY TAXES

1. Statement of Assessed Value and Estimated True Value of All Taxable Property.. 82
2. Statement of Tax Rates and Tax Levies............................... 83
3. Statement of Tax Levies and Tax Collections......................... 85

SECTION B. REVENUES AND EXPENDITURES

1. Revenues—Other Than Property Taxes and Special Assessments for the Last Ten Fiscal Years.. (3)

[2] National Committee on Governmental Accounting, *Municipal Accounting and Auditing* (Chicago: The Committee, 1951), pp. 15-16.

[3] The following is a columnar heading for this table:

Fiscal Year	Taxes (Other Than Property Taxes)	Licenses and Permits	Fines, Forfeits, and Penalties	Revenue from Use of Money and Property	Revenue from Other Agencies	Charges for Current Services	Profits or Losses of Utilities or Other Enterprises	Other Revenues
1947								
1948								
1956								

SECTION C. BONDED DEBT

SECTION D. MISCELLANEOUS

Again it must be remembered that an actual financial report may show a greater or a smaller number of statements under each section than are listed here. Furthermore, there may be additional sections, as would be the case if a governmental unit also prepared other types of statistical tables. For example, statistical tables showing unit costs might be included, in which case a "Unit Costs" section would be added.

Combined Financial and Audit Report

We have thus far spoken of two types of reports: (1) the audit report issued by an independent auditor and (2) the annual financial report issued by the governmental unit's finance officer. There is great similarity between the two types of reports. Accordingly, it is possible to incorporate in the annual financial report the data contained in the audit report, or vice versa, and to issue only one report.

The combination might be effected in several ways. One would be for the governmental unit's finance officer to prepare the report and for the auditor to render an opinion with respect to the financial statements included therein. In that case, the finance officer's report would differ from the annual financial report described in one respect only. It would contain the auditor's letter of transmittal outlining the scope and limitations of the audit, together with his formal opinion.

An alternative procedure is for the finance officer to incorporate the auditor's report as part of his report. That is, the financial part of the finance officer's report would consist of the financial statements prepared

---

[4] The following is a columnar heading for this table:

Fiscal Year	General Government	Public Safety	Highways	Sanitation and Waste Removal	Health and Hospitals	Public Welfare	Schools	Libraries	Recreation
1947									
1948									
1956									

[5] The following is a columnar heading for this table:

Official Title	Salary	Amount of Surety Bond
Members of City Council (List each member)		
Mayor		
City Manager		
Etc.		

and certified to by the auditor. The report would in all other respects be similar to the annual financial report discussed above. In other words, the report would consist of a letter of transmittal prepared by the finance officer, a financial part containing the financial statements prepared by the auditor and adopted by the finance officer, and a statistical part containing the statistical tables prepared by the finance officer. If this procedure is followed, a separate audit report is prepared primarily for the legislative body and administrative officials. It is usually not published but is made a matter of public record.

The advantages of issuing only one annual report are so self-evident that they require little comment. Briefly, they are (1) economy, and (2) the avoidance of confusion, which might arise if two different reports were issued. Confusion is especially likely to result if the auditor makes adjustments which are not taken into account in the finance officer's report, or vice versa. The disadvantages are that the audit is usually made sometime after the close of the fiscal year, and, by the time the report is published, important changes in the financial condition and financial operations may have taken place. The remedy lies in having the books audited promptly at the close of the fiscal year and in having the audit report prepared immediately thereafter.

The Monthly Financial Report

The monthly financial report is prepared primarily for the use of the legislative body and administrators but may also have a limited circulation among the public, especially among groups particularly interested in the governmental unit's financial operations. The general principles outlined above in connection with the preparation of the annual financial report apply also to the monthly financial report, but the latter contains fewer statements and shows the financial operations for a month instead of a full year. However, some of the operating statements included in the monthly financial report show the financial operations not only for the particular month but also for the period extending from the beginning of the year to the date of the report.

On the next page is an outline of the contents of a monthly financial report. Some of the statements referred to in this outline have already been included in the list of statements making up the annual financial report. The reason is that the form of these statements is the same regardless of whether they cover a full year or only part of a year. For example, the balance sheet illustrated in Figure 55, page 167, has the same form whether it is prepared at the close of any month during the year or at the close of the year. It should also be noted that, as in the case of the annual financial report, a monthly report issued by any one governmental unit may have a greater or smaller number of statements than are listed here.

Several facts should be noted carefully in regard to the outline of contents. In the first place, the letter of transmittal is usually much briefer than the one carried in the annual financial report. Second, many of the financial statements included in the annual financial report are not included in the monthly financial report. For example, the statement analyzing the changes in the Unappropriated Surplus account of the general fund is not included; neither is the statement analyzing the changes in the Appropriations account in the bond fund or special assessment fund ordinarily included. Similarly, fewer statistical tables are shown. On the other hand, the monthly financial report contains some statements which are not included in the annual financial report. An example is the statement illustrated in Figure 72, page 226, which forecasts the cash position of the governmental unit.

CONTENTS OF MONTHLY FINANCIAL REPORT

19

<<<<<<<<<<<<<<<<<<<<<<<<<<<<<<<<<<<<<<<<<<<<<<<<<<<<<<<

ACCOUNTING FOR HOSPITALS

This chapter and the chapter which follows discuss the accounting procedures for institutions. The present chapter deals with the accounting procedures for hospitals, the next with college and university accounting. The principles of governmental accounting discussed thus far in this book apply also to institutions. For example, if institutions are government-owned, they are subject to the same restrictions as any other governmental organization. But even if privately owned, institutions have at least one common characteristic with government: they have to use fund accounting. They must employ this method of accounting because they obtain some of their income and property through gifts, which frequently carry with them restrictions. Through the use of funds, they are able to show that they have complied with these restrictions.

Although many institutional funds are similar to governmental funds, some of them are sufficiently different to justify discussing institutional accounting separately. Moreover, since there are differences in the types of funds employed by hospitals on the one hand and colleges and universities on the other, the accounting for each of these two types of institutions is discussed. Before proceeding with the description of the accounting procedures for these institutions, we would like to point out that hospitals, colleges and universities, and other types of institutions adopt a budget and are subject to budgetary control. Since, however, the operation of a budget system is described in detail in other parts of the book, it will not be discussed here.

Funds. Let us assume that the hospital under consideration is a non-profit institution financed from fees charged to patients and from donations. The following discussion is based on the principles of accounting recommended by the American Hospital Association. The Association recommends the accrual basis and the following kinds of funds: (1) gen-

320

eral fund, (2) temporary funds, (3) endowment funds, and (4) plant funds.

General fund. This fund is used to account for all of the transactions of a hospital not accounted for in any other fund. Agency transactions (such, for example, as receiving cash and holding it in safekeeping for patients) are also handled through the general fund. The liabilities resulting from agency transactions are reflected in a special account carried in the liability section of the general fund balance sheet.

Temporary funds. These are used to account for assets expendable for specific operating purposes. If donations are made for plant acquisitions, they should not be considered as temporary funds but should be accounted for in plant funds.

Endowment funds. These are used to account for donated cash or other assets the principal of which is to be kept intact and only the income from which may be expended. The income of endowment funds (1) may first be accounted for in the endowment fund and then transferred to the fund that is going to spend it, or (2) may be accounted for immediately in the spending fund. The spending fund would be either the general fund (if no spending restrictions are attached) or a temporary fund (if restrictions are attached). The circumstances under which the income must be first accounted for in the endowment fund are discussed later.

Plant funds. In these funds are accounted (1) the cash and investments intended to finance the acquisition or construction of fixed assets and (2) the fixed assets used by the hospital in carrying on its operations. Plant funds should not be used to account for fixed assets held as investments of endowments; such assets should be carried in an endowment fund.

Each of the foregoing types of funds should have a separate group of self-balancing accounts consisting of assets, liabilities, reserves, balances, and surplus, so as to make possible the preparation of fund balance sheets. Accounts must also be provided to show the necessary details concerning the revenues and expenses of the general fund. Each of the other funds has so few types of revenues and expenses that the credits and charges may be made directly to the Fund Balance account. In the discussion which follows, the operation of each of the foregoing types of funds is illustrated by giving typical transactions for the particular fund, the related entries, and the resulting balance sheet. In the case of the general fund, the resulting income and expense statement is also given.

Transactions and entries of the general fund. The following transactions are assumed to have taken place in the general fund during the year and the following entries are assumed to have been made to reflect them.

Transactions

1. Bills to patients at standard rates: routine services, $800,000; special services, $1,000,000. Deductions from gross revenue (exclusive of allowances for uncollectible accounts): contract service allowances, $18,000; clinics, $2,000.

2. Accounts receivable estimated to be uncollectible, $15,000.

3. General contributions in the amount of $100,000 were received.

4. Collections of accounts receivable, $1,600,000.

5. Net income from cafeteria, $25,000, which was turned over by the cafeteria in cash.

6. Materials and supplies (including food) purchased on account during the year, $250,000.

7. Materials and supplies used, $230,000, distributed among the different departments as follows:

Administrative and general	$ 5,000
Dietary	175,000
Household and property	20,000
Professional care of patients	25,000
Out-patient and emergency	5,000

8. Accounts payable paid, $182,000.

9. Salaries and wages paid during the year, $1,500,000, which are chargeable as follows:

Administrative and general	$185,000
Dietary	75,000
Household and property	300,000
Professional care of patients	900,000
Out-patient and emergency	40,000

10. Salaries and wages accrued at the end of the year are chargeable as follows:

Administrative and general	$ 7,000
Dietary	3,300
Household and property	11,900
Professional care of patients	37,000
Out-patient and emergency	1,800

11. Administrative and general expenses other than for salaries and materials and supplies amounted to $4,000 and were paid in cash.

12. Interest on mortgages amounted to $7,000, of which $5,000 was paid in cash.

13. Money collected as agent for special nurses for services rendered by them, $2,000.

14. Money received from patients for safekeeping, $500.

15. Of the total collected for special nurses, $1,850 was paid to them; the remainder has not yet been claimed.

16. Of the total amount held in safekeeping for patients, $400 was returned to those discharged from the hospital.

17. Depreciation on buildings, $20,000; on furniture and equipment, $30,000.

18. $20,000 cash, the amount of the charges for depreciation of equipment, was transferred to the improvements and replacements fund.

19. Of the total cost of materials and supplies charged to household and property, $5,000 was for equipment.

20. Of the salaries charged to professional care of patients, $2,000 represents salaries payable out of a temporary fund.

21. Closing entries were made at the end of the year.

Entries

1. Accounts Receivable.................... $1,780,000
   Contract Service Allowances............ 18,000
   Clinics................................ 2,000
      Revenue from Routine Services......... $ 800,000
      Revenue from Special Services......... 1,000,000
   To record billings for services.

2. Uncollectible Accounts................. 15,000
      Allowance for Uncollectible Accounts.... 15,000
   To record estimated uncollectible accounts.

3. Cash................................... 100,000
      General Contributions................. 100,000
   To record receipt of general contributions.

4. Cash................................... 1,600,000
      Accounts Receivable.................. 1,600,000
   To record collection of accounts receivable.

5. Cash................................... 25,000
      Income from Cafeteria................. 25,000
   To record income from cafeteria.

6. Inventory of Materials and Supplies....... 250,000
      Accounts Payable..................... 250,000
   To record purchase of materials and supplies.

7. Administrative and General............. 5,000
   Dietary................................ 175,000
   Household and Property................. 20,000
   Professional Care of Patients............. 25,000
   Out-Patient and Emergency............. 5,000
      Inventory of Materials and Supplies..... 230,000
   To record materials and supplies charged to
   various functions.

8. Accounts Payable....................... 182,000
      Cash............................... 182,000
   To record payment of accounts payable.

9. Administrative and General............. 185,000
   Dietary................................ 75,000
   Household and Property................. 300,000
   Professional Care of Patients............. 900,000
   Out-Patient and Emergency............. 40,000
      Cash............................... 1,500,000
   To record payment of salaries and wages.

10. Administrative and General............. 7,000
    Dietary................................ 3,300
    Household and Property................. 11,900
    Professional Care of Patients............ 37,000
    Out-Patient and Emergency............. 1,800
       Accrued Salaries and Wages........... 61,000
    To record accrued salaries and wages.

11. Administrative and General............. 4,000
       Cash............................... 4,000
    To record payment of general and adminis-
    trative expenses other than for salaries and
    materials and supplies.

12. Interest Expense...................... $7,000
    Cash.................................. $5,000
    Interest Payable..................... 2,000
To record interest on mortgage. (Mortgage carried as a liability in investment in plant fund.)

13. Cash................................. 2,000
    Due to Special Nurses................ 2,000
To record collection of fees as agent for special nurses.

14. Cash................................. 500
    Safekeeping Deposits Payable......... 500
To record receipt of money from patients for safekeeping.

15. Due to Special Nurses.................. 1,850
    Cash................................. 1,850
To record paying of part of fees collected by the hospital as agent for special nurses.

16. Safekeeping Deposits Payable........... 400
    Cash................................. 400
To record return of part of safekeeping deposits to patients.

17. Depreciation.......................... 50,000
    Unappropriated Surplus............... 50,000
To record depreciation on buildings and furniture and equipment.

18. Unappropriated Surplus................. 20,000
    Cash................................. 20,000
To record transfer of cash equal to depreciation charges on equipment to improvements and replacements fund.

19. Due from Improvements and Replacements Fund............................. 5,000
    Household and Property............... 5,000
To reduce expenses charged in error to household and property.

20. Due from Temporary Fund.............. 2,000
    Transfers of Income from Temporary Fund 2,000
To record reimbursement due from temporary fund for expenses.

21. (a) Revenue from Routine Services....... 800,000
    Revenue from Special Services........ 1,000,000
    General Contributions................ 100,000
    Income from Cafeteria................ 25,000
    Transfers of Income from Temporary Funds........................... 2,000
    Uncollectible Accounts.............. 15,000
    Contract Service Allowances......... 18,000
    Clinics............................. 2,000
    Administrative and General.......... 201,000
    Dietary............................. 253,300
    Household and Property.............. 326,900
    Professional Care of Patients....... 962,000

Out-Patient and Emergency........		$46,800
Interest Expense.................		7,000
Depreciation.....................		50,000
Net Income or Loss...............		45,000
To close out revenues and expenses and to arrive at net income or loss.		

21. (b) Net Income or Loss................	$45,000	
Unappropriated Surplus............		45,000
To close out net income.		

Comments on transactions and entries. An examination of the foregoing transactions will reveal that they are divided into four groups dealing, respectively, with (1) revenues, (2) expenditures, (3) agency transactions, and (4) transactions affecting more than one fund. It is assumed that billings are made at standard rates and that allowances (such as those made to families of physicians, to hospital plan groups, and to government agencies) are reflected as deductions from gross income. It is also assumed that a perpetual inventory system is in use, and that an inventory account is charged with purchases and credited with the cost of materials and supplies used. Agency transactions have to do with such matters as safekeeping deposits and monies collected for special nurses.

Depreciation is an example of a transaction which affects several funds. As transaction and entry no. 17 show, in the general fund, depreciation is charged to a Depreciation Expense account and credited to an Unappropriated Surplus account. The credit cannot be to an Allowance for Depreciation account because the fixed assets are not carried in the general fund. The credit to the Allowance account must therefore be in the investment in plant fund. Cash equal to the depreciation charges may or may not be transferred from the general fund to the improvements and replacements fund, depending on the method of financing adopted for the replacement of assets. If cash is transferred, entries similar to entry no. 18 above and entry no. 8 in the improvements and replacements fund should be prepared.

The acquisition of fixed assets under certain circumstances is another example of a transaction affecting several funds. To illustrate, fixed assets should be financed from an improvements and replacements fund. Suppose, however, the purchase of fixed assets has erroneously been charged as an expenditure of the general fund. In that case, as transaction and entry no. 19 show, a receivable from the improvements and replacements fund must be recorded in the general fund. (See also entry no. 3 in the improvements and replacements fund.) If, however, the reason for financing the equipment from the general fund is lack of money in the improvements and replacements fund, the transaction would be reflected in the general fund by debiting the Unappropriated Surplus account and crediting Cash.

A third example of an inter-fund transaction is given in entry no. 20

which involves not only the general fund but also the temporary funds. It is assumed that the salary is chargeable to an activity normally carried on by a hospital. Accordingly, the cost of the particular activity is reflected among the operating expenses of the general fund. On the other hand, it is necessary to show also the related revenues. This is accomplished by entry no. 20. (See also entry no. 2 in the temporary fund.) If the salary had not represented a normal hospital expense it would have been handled directly in the temporary fund by debiting the Temporary Fund Balance account and crediting the Cash account of that fund.

Balance sheet of the general fund. A balance sheet of the general fund based on the foregoing transactions and entries is illustrated in Figure 103. Four facts should be noted particularly about this balance sheet. The

Figure 103

A HOSPITAL

General Fund

Balance Sheet
at Close of Fiscal Year

ASSETS

Cash..		$ 14,250
Accounts Receivable...........................	$180,000	
Less—Allowance for Uncollectible Accounts.......	15,000	165,000
Due from Improvements and Replacements Fund		5,000
Due from Temporary Fund.....................		2,000
Inventory of Materials and Supplies.............		20,000
		$206,250

LIABILITIES AND SURPLUS

Liabilities:		
Accounts Payable...........................	$ 68,000	
Accrued Salaries and Wages.................	61,000	
Interest Payable...........................	2,000	
Due to Special Nurses........................	150	
Safekeeping Deposits Payable.................	100	$131,250
Unappropriated Surplus......................		75,000
		$206,250

first is that the balance sheet is limited to current assets and liabilities; it does not include fixed assets or bonds payable. The second is that the balance sheet reflects accrued salaries and wages and accrued interest payable and is to that extent on a more strict accrual basis than the balance sheet of a governmental unit. The third is that amounts received by the hospital as agent are reflected as a liability. The fourth is that, while the difference between assets and liabilities has been designated in this balance sheet as unappropriated surplus, it is frequently also referred to as the general fund balance.

Income and expense statement of the general fund. An income and expense statement in summary form is presented in Figure 104. This statement should be supported by schedules showing details concerning both revenues and expenses. For example, the account for revenues from special services would be supported by a schedule similar to the one illustrated in Figure 105. Again, the expenditure accounts appearing in this summary

Figure 104

A HOSPITAL

General Fund

Income and Expense Statement
for Fiscal Year

Operating Revenues:		
Routine Services............................	$ 800,000	
Special Services [Figure 105]...............	1,000,000	$1,800,000
Less—Deductions from Revenue:		
Contract Service Allowances...............	$ 18,000	
Clinics..................................	2,000	
Uncollectible Accounts....................	15,000	35,000
Gross Operating Revenues.........................		$1,765,000
Operating Expenses:		
Administrative and General................	$ 201,000	
Dietary..................................	253,300	
Household and Property...................	326,900	
Professional Care of Patients [Figure 106]...	962,000	
Out-Patient and Emergency...............	46,800	
Depreciation.............................	50,000	1,840,000
Net Operating Deficit.............................		$ 75,000
Non-Operating Income and Expense:		
Net Income from Cafeteria................	$ 25,000	
Less—Interest Expenses...................	7,000	18,000
Net Loss from Hospital Activities..................		$ 57,000
Contributions:		
General Contributions....................	$ 100,000	
Transfer from Temporary Fund............	2,000	102,000
Net Income..		$ 45,000

statement would be supported by schedules showing details concerning them. An example of such a schedule is presented in Figure 106. In actual practice, objects of expenditure (salaries, materials and supplies, and so on) would be shown under each class of expenditures in the schedule. They have been omitted in order to save space.

Temporary funds. The following are examples of transactions handled in temporary funds and the entries made to record them. A balance sheet of temporary funds based on these transactions and entries is illustrated

Figure 105

A HOSPITAL

General Fund

Detailed Statement of Revenues from Special Services
for Fiscal Year

Operating Rooms...................	$ 120,000
Delivery and Pending Rooms.......	43,400
Anesthesia.......................	77,000
X-Ray Services...................	181,000
Fluoroscopy......................	600
Radium Rental....................	1,100
Laboratory Services..............	190,000
Blood Bank Services..............	33,000
Drugs...........................	188,000
Dressings and Treatments..........	21,000
Oxygen..........................	46,500
Intravenous Solutions..............	39,400
Emergency.......................	59,000
	$1,000,000

Figure 106

A HOSPITAL

General Fund

Details of Expenses for Professional Service
for Fiscal Year

Medical and Surgical...............	$460,000
Operating Rooms..................	100,000
Delivery and Pending Rooms.........	37,000
Nursery..........................	53,000
Central Supply....................	40,000
Medical Records and Library.........	26,000
X-Ray............................	80,000
Laboratory.......................	75,500
Pharmacy........................	90,500
	$962,000

in Figure 107. It should be noted that in this case a separate Temporary Fund Balance account has been provided for each fund because only two funds are involved. If many temporary funds are used, a single control account should be provided for all temporary fund balances, and the control account should, in turn, be supported by detailed accounts.

Transactions

1. A check for $10,000 was received from a donor to help pay part of the salary of a special physician.

2. At the end of the year, the general fund submitted a bill for $2,000 to the temporary fund for the latter's share of the physician's salary which the general fund had paid. [See also entry no. 20 in the general fund.]

3. Interest earned on investments carried in endowment fund X created for the purpose of financing special recreational programs for patients amounted to

$5,000. Of this amount $4,000 was collected in cash. [*Note:* The income is in this case accounted for directly in the spending fund.]

4. The sum of $3,500 was paid for special recreational programs.

5. The improvements and replacements fund was erroneously charged with expenditures of $300. These expenditures should have been charged to temporary fund *B* set up to finance special recreational programs. [See also entry no. 2 in the plant funds.]

Entries

1. Cash.................................... $10,000
        Temporary Fund *A* Balance.............. | | $10,000
   To record receipt of cash for purpose of paying part of salary of physician.

2. Temporary Fund *A* Balance................ 2,000
        Due to General Fund.................... | | 2,000
   To record amount due to general fund for part of physician's salary.

3. Cash...................................... 4,000
   Interest Receivable....................... 1,000
        Temporary Fund *B* Balance............. | | 5,000
   To record interest on investments carried in endowment fund *X* to be used for the purpose of providing special recreational programs.

4. Temporary Fund *B* Balance................ 3,500
        Cash................................... | | 3,500
   To record payments for special recreational programs.

5. Temporary Fund *B* Balance................ 300
        Due to Improvements and Replacements Fund............................... | | 300
   To correct error. Improvements and replacements fund was erroneously charged with expenditures chargeable to temporary fund set up to finance special recreational programs.

Endowment funds. The following are some examples of transactions handled in the endowment funds and the entries used to record them. It is assumed that some of these endowments are the ones the income of which has been reflected as income of temporary funds. In order to simplify the discussion, it is further assumed that securities have been purchased at par and that the income of these endowment funds flows directly to the temporary funds without having first to be accounted for in the endowment funds. Finally, transactions and entries nos. 3 and 5 illustrate the fact that the gains and losses on the sale of securities affect the principal of an endowment fund and not its income. A balance sheet based on these transactions and entries is illustrated in Figure 108.

Transactions

1. A donation of $100,000 was received for the purpose of establishing an endowment fund, the income of which was to be used to provide special recreation programs for patients.

Figure 107

A HOSPITAL
Temporary Funds
Balance Sheet
at Close of Fiscal Year

ASSETS

Cash	$10,500
Interest Receivable	1,000
	$11,500

LIABILITIES AND BALANCES

Liabilities:

Due to General Fund	$2,000	
Due to Improvements and Replacements Fund	300	$ 2,300

Balances:

Fund *A*	$8,000	
Fund *B*	1,200	9,200
		$11,500

Figure 108

A HOSPITAL
Endowment Funds
Balance Sheet
at Close of Fiscal Year

ASSETS

Cash	$ 7,700
Investments	242,000
	$249,700

BALANCES

Fund Balances:

Fund *X*	$ 99,500
Fund *Y*	150,200
	$249,700

2. The money was invested in bonds which were acquired at par.

3. Securities of this fund with a par value of $5,000 were sold for $4,500.

4. Another donor gave stocks which had a market value at the time they were donated of $150,000. The income from these securities is not restricted to any special purpose.

5. Securities of this fund with a book value of $3,000 were sold at a gain of $200.

Entries

1. Cash	$100,00C	
Endowment Fund *X* Balance		$100,000

To record receipt of cash for the purpose of establishing an endowment, the income from which is to be used to provide special recreation programs for patients.

2. Investments........................... $100,000

    Cash................................. $100,000

    To record purchase of investments at par.

3. Endowment Fund *X* Balance............   500

    Cash................................. 4,500

        Investments..........................   5,000

    To record sale of investments at a loss and to charge the endowment fund with such loss.

4. Investments........................... 150,000

        Endowment Fund *Y* Balance..........   150,000

    To record receipt of donation in the form of securities the income from which is not restricted to any special purpose.

5. Cash................................. 3,200

        Investments..........................   3,000

        Endowment Fund *Y* Balance...........   200

    To record gain on sale of investments and to credit endowment fund with such gain.

Plant funds. There are two types of plant funds. One type consists of a self-balancing group of accounts which shows the hospital's investment in plant (hereafter referred to as the "investment in plant" fund); the other consists of cash or other assets intended to be used to finance additions and improvements to, or replacements of, plant and equipment (hereafter referred to as the "improvements and replacements" fund). Due to the fact that certain transactions affect both funds, these two types of funds will be treated together. A balance sheet for these funds based on the transactions and entries which follow is illustrated in Figure 109.

Transactions

1. The following amounts were spent in constructing and equipping a hospital: land, $100,000; building, $1,100,000; equipment, $450,000. The acquisition of these assets was financed by cash contributions of $1,450,000 and a mortgage of $200,000.

2. The plant funds were charged erroneously with expenditures of $300 for equipment; these expenditures should have been charged to temporary fund *B*. [See also entry no. 5, in the temporary fund.]

3. Expenditures of $5,000 for equipment chargeable to the plant funds were charged erroneously as household and property expenses in the general fund. [See also entry no. 19, in the general fund.]

4. Cash in the amount of $4,000 and stock with a market value of $10,000 were donated for the purpose of financing improvements.

5. Dividends of $400 were received on this stock.

6. Additional equipment was obtained for cash at a cost of $3,000.

7. Depreciation on buildings amounted to $20,000 and on furniture and equipment to $30,000. [See also entry no. 17 in the general fund.]

8. $20,000 in cash, an amount equivalent to the amount of depreciation on equipment, was transferred from the general fund to the improvements and replacements fund. [See also entry no. 18, in the general fund.]

Entries

1. ENTRY IN INVESTMENT IN PLANT FUND
   Land... $ 100,000
   Building... 1,100,000
   Equipment.. 450,000
      Mortgage Payable................................. $ 200,000
      Investment in Plant..............................   1,450,000
   To record investment in plant.

2. (a) ENTRY IN IMPROVEMENTS AND REPLACEMENTS FUND
      Due from Temporary Fund....................... 300
         Improvements and Replacements Fund Balance   300
      To record amount due from temporary fund on account
      of expenditure chargeable to that fund.

2. (b) ENTRY IN INVESTMENT IN PLANT FUND
      Investment in Plant............................... 300
         Equipment.....................................   300
      To remove from Equipment account expenditure
      chargeable to temporary fund.

3. (a) ENTRY IN IMPROVEMENTS AND REPLACEMENTS FUND
      Improvements and Replacements Fund Balance...... 5,000
         Due to General Fund...........................   5,000
      To record liability to general fund on account of equip-
      ment paid for by it.

3. (b) ENTRY IN INVESTMENT IN PLANT FUND
      Equipment.. 5,000
         Investment in Plant...........................   5,000
      To record cost of equipment.

4. ENTRY IN IMPROVEMENTS AND REPLACEMENTS FUND
   Cash... 4,000
   Investments.. 10,000
      Improvements and Replacements Fund Balance.......   14,000
   To record donation of cash and investments for the purpose
   of making improvements and replacements.

5. ENTRY IN IMPROVEMENTS AND REPLACEMENTS FUND
   Cash... 400
      Improvements and Replacements Fund Balance.......   400
   To record receipt of dividends.

6. (a) ENTRY IN IMPROVEMENTS AND REPLACEMENTS FUND
      Improvements and Replacements Fund Balance...... 3,000
         Cash..   3,000
      To record purchase of equipment.

   (b) ENTRY IN INVESTMENT IN PLANT FUND
      Equipment.. 3,000
         Investment in Plant...........................   3,000
      To set up equipment on the records and to increase
      investment in plant with cost of such equipment.

7. ENTRY IN INVESTMENT IN PLANT FUND
   Investment in Plant.................................. 50,000
      Allowance for Depreciation—Buildings...............   20,000
      Allowance for Depreciation—Equipment..............   30,000
   To record depreciation.

Figure 109

A HOSPITAL
Plant Funds
Balance Sheet
at Close of Fiscal Year

ASSETS			LIABILITIES AND BALANCES		
Improvements and Replacements Fund			*Improvements and Replacements Fund*		
Cash		$ 21,400	Due to General Fund		$ 5,000
Due from Temporary Fund		300	Fund Balance		26,700
Investments		10,000			
Total		$ 31,700	Total		$ 31,700
Investment in Plant Fund			*Investment in Plant Fund*		
Land		$ 100,000	Mortgage Payable		$ 200,000
Buildings	$1,100,000		Investment in Plant		1,407,700
Less—Allowance for Depreciation	20,000	1,080,000			
Equipment	$ 457,700				
Less—Allowance for Depreciation	30,000	427,700			
Total		1,607,700	Total		1,607,700
Total Plant Funds		$1,639,400	Total Plant Funds		$1,639,400

Figure 110

A HOSPITAL

All Funds

Combined Balance Sheet
at Close of Fiscal Year

ASSETS

General Fund
Cash		$ 14,250
Inventory of Materials and Supplies	20,000	
Total General Fund		$ 206,250

Temporary Funds
Cash	$ 10,500	
Interest Receivable	1,000	
Total Temporary Funds		11,500

Endowment Funds
Cash	$ 7,700	
Investments	242,000	
Total Endowment Funds		249,700

Plant Funds
Improvements and Replacements Fund
Cash	$ 21,400		
Due from Temporary Fund	300		
Investments	10,000	$ 31,700	
Investment in Plant Fund			
Land	$100,000		
		1,607,700	
Less—Allowance for Depreciation	30,000	1,607,700	
Total Plant Funds			1,639,400
Grand Total			$2,106,850

LIABILITIES

General Fund
Accounts Payable		$ 68,000
Unappropriated Surplus	75,000	
Total General Fund		$ 206,250

Temporary Funds
Due to General Fund		$ 2,000
Balances		9,200
Total Temporary Funds		11,500

Endowment Funds
Balances:
Fund X	$ 99,500	
Fund Y	150,200	
Total Endowment Funds		249,700

Plant Funds
Improvements and Replacements Fund
Due to General Fund	$ 5,000	
Balance	26,700	$ 31,700
Investment in Plant Fund		
Mortgage Payable	$ 200,000	
Investment in Plant	1,407,700	1,607,700
Total Plant Funds		1,639,400
Grand Total		$2,106,850

8. Entry in Improvements and Replacements Fund
    Cash.. 20,000
        Improvements and Replacements Fund Balance.......   20,000
    To record transfer of cash from general fund equivalent to
    depreciation charges on equipment.

Combined balance sheet—all funds. Two types of combined balance sheets may be prepared. One is a combined balance sheet for related funds. For example, a combined balance sheet similar to the one illustrated in Figure 109 might be provided for plant funds, that is for the improvements and replacements fund and the investment in plant fund. Another type of combined balance sheet is one covering all funds. This balance sheet may be either in columnar or sectional form. In the columnar balance sheet a separate column is provided for each fund or group of related funds. An example of such a balance sheet is given in Figure 69, page 212. In the sectional form of combined balance sheet a separate section is provided for each fund or group of related funds. An example of such a balance sheet is given in Figure 110. This combined balance sheet consists of the individual fund balance sheets illustrated throughout this chapter except that, for the purpose of simplification, some of the accounts have been omitted.

As was indicated in Chapter 13, the columnar form of combined balance sheet of all funds is preferable to the sectional form because (1) it shows the total of each kind of asset (for example, cash or investments), liability, reserve, balance, and surplus, (2) it reflects the relative importance of each account in the different funds, and (3) it makes it possible for the reader to get a bird's-eye view of the financial condition of the organization unit at a glance. But whatever form of combined fund balance sheet is employed, the assets, liabilities, reserves, balance, and surplus of each fund or group of related funds must be identifiable. Under no circumstances should a combined balance sheet of all funds be prepared in which the items applicable to each fund or group of related funds cannot be identified.

20

<<<<<<<<<<<<<<<<<<<<<<<<<<<<<<<<<<<<<<<<<<<<<<<<<<<<<

ACCOUNTING FOR COLLEGES
AND UNIVERSITIES

COLLEGES AND UNIVERSITIES, like hospitals, use fund accounting. In fact, general funds, endowment funds, and plant funds are common to both. There are, however, also several differences between hospital and college and university accounting. For example, colleges and universities use, in addition to the foregoing funds, loan funds and annuity funds, but do not employ the so-called temporary funds encountered in hospital accounting. There are also differences between the classifications of revenue and expenditure accounts in these two types of institutions. In addition the National Committee for Standard Reports for Institutions of Higher Education, on whose recommendations this chapter is based, has recommended that no depreciation be computed on fixed assets used by colleges and universities to carry on operations except under certain circumstances, a recommendation which, as we have seen, is contrary to that of the American Hospital Association for hospitals. Finally, the National Committee has recommended modifications in the accrual basis of accounting. For example, according to the Committee, few institutions find it either necessary or desirable to report accrued interest receivable, or to allocate unexpired insurance premiums to subsequent periods. The American Hospital Association has, on the other hand, called for the full accrual basis for hospitals.

Funds. The National Committee on Standard Reports for Institutions of Higher Education has recommended the use of the following funds: (1) current funds, (2) loan funds, (3) endowment and other non-expendable funds, (4) annuity funds, (5) plant funds, and (6) agency funds. Current funds account for assets available for general or restricted current operations. Loan funds account for loans to students. Endowment and other non-expendable funds are used to account for assets the income of which may be expended, whereas the principal may not. Annuity funds handle those assets the income from which must be used to pay annuities. "Plant funds" is the collective name for three types of funds, namely, (1) funds used to show the net investment in plant, (2) funds which show the assets available to replace, add to, or otherwise improve the plant, and (3) funds which reflect the assets available to retire indebtedness incurred in connection with the acquisition of the plant. Agency funds are those held by the institution in the capacity of agent or trustee. Each of these funds is described in greater detail below and typical transactions and entries are given to illustrate its operations.

Current funds. Current funds are divisible into two groups, namely, general and restricted. However, in those cases where it is not practicable to make such a separation, the Committee permits the use of only one fund, provided that the general and restricted balances are shown separately.

General current funds may be divided into two separately balanced groups of accounts—one for general funds and the other for auxiliary enterprises. Auxiliary enterprises are those operated primarily for service to students and staff and intended to be self-supporting, such as residence halls, dining halls, student hospitals, student unions, and bookstores. This subdivision is particularly desirable if there are mortgages or other forms of indebtedness outstanding against fixed assets used to carry on the operations of auxiliary enterprises. In the present case, it is assumed that two current funds are used (a general current fund and a restricted current fund) and that the operations of auxiliary enterprises are accounted for as part of the general current fund.

Transactions and entries of the general current fund. The following are some typical transactions of this fund and the entries made to reflect them. It should be noted that transactions nos. 10, 11, and 12 require entries not only in the general current fund but in the plant funds as well.

Transactions

1. Educational and general revenues earned during the year amounted to $2,600,000, of which $2,550,000 has been collected.
2. It is estimated that $2,000 of the accounts receivable will never be collected.
3. Other revenues collected include $700,000 from auxiliary enterprises.
4. Total purchases for the year amounted to $600,000, of which $560,000 has been paid.
5. Materials used during the year amounted to $550,000 of which $250,000 is chargeable to educational and general activities and $300,000 to auxiliary enterprises.
6. Salaries and wages paid amounted to $2,200,000 of which $1,920,000 is chargeable to educational and general activities and $280,000 to auxiliary enterprises.

7. Legal fees, insurance expenses, interest on money borrowed for plant additions, and telephone and telegraph expenses, all chargeable to the educational and general activities, amounted to $100,000 and had all been paid by the end of the year.

8. Other expenses chargeable to auxiliary enterprises and paid for in cash, $10,000.

9. Student aid granted, $20,000.

10. Current funds in the amount of $25,000 were used to pay an installment of the mortgage note carried as a liability in the investment in plant fund.

11. The general current fund transferred $30,000 to the improvements and replacements fund for the purpose of financing additions to the plant.

12. The general current fund also spent $10,000 for other plant additions.

13. In accordance with a resolution of the board of trustees of the university, the general current fund transferred $100,000 to the endowment funds group for the purpose of establishing a fund which is to function as an endowment.

14. Closing entries were prepared.

Entries

1. Cash................................... $2,550,000
      Accounts Receivable.................... 50,000
         Educational and General Revenues..... $2,600,000
      To record educational revenues earned.

2. Educational and General Expenses........ 2,000
      Allowance for Uncollectible Accounts....   2,000
      To record provision for uncollectible accounts.

3. Cash................................... 700,000
      Revenues of Auxiliary Enterprises......   700,000
      To record revenues of auxiliary enterprises.

4. Inventory of Materials and Supplies....... 600,000
      Cash...............................   560,000
      Accounts Payable....................   40,000
      To record purchases of materials and supplies.

5. Educational and General Expenses........ 250,000
      Expenses of Auxiliary Enterprises......... 300,000
         Inventory of Materials and Supplies.....   550,000
      To record cost of materials and supplies used.

6. Educational and General Expenses........ 1,920,000
      Expenses of Auxiliary Enterprises......... 280,000
         Cash.............................   2,200,000
      To record salaries and wages paid.

7. Educational and General Expenses........ 100,000
      Cash.............................   100,000
      To record legal expenses, insurance expenses, interest on money borrowed for plant additions, and telephone and telegraph expenses.

8. Expenses of Auxiliary Enterprises......... 10,000
      Cash.............................   10,000
      To record expenses of auxiliary enterprises other than those for materials and supplies or for salaries.

9. Student Aid Grants	20,000	
Cash		20,000
To record student aid granted.		

10. Unappropriated Surplus	25,000	
Cash		25,000
To record payment of mortgage note carried as a liability in investment in plant fund.		

11. Unappropriated Surplus	30,000	
Cash		30,000
To record transfers to plant fund for purpose of making additions to plant.		

12. Unappropriated Surplus	10,000	
Cash		10,000
To record cost of plant additions financed from general current fund.		

13. Unappropriated Surplus	100,000	
Cash		100,000
To transfer cash to endowment funds group for the purpose of establishing a fund which is to function as an endowment.		

14. (a) Educational and General Revenues	2,600,000	
Revenues of Auxiliary Enterprises	700,000	
Educational and General Expenses		2,272,000
Expenses of Auxiliary Enterprises		590,000
Student Aid Grants		20,000
Net Income or Loss		418,000
To close out revenues and expenditures.		

14. (b) Net Income or Loss	418,000	
Unappropriated Surplus		418,000
To close out net income to unappropriated surplus.		

Balance sheet of the general current fund. A balance sheet of the general current fund is exhibited in Figure 111. This balance sheet is based on the transactions and entries illustrated in the preceding sections.

Figure 111

A UNIVERSITY

General Current Fund

Balance Sheet
at Close of Fiscal Year

ASSETS

Cash		$195,000
Accounts Receivable	$50,000	
Less—Allowance for Uncollectible Accounts	2,000	48,000
Inventory of Materials and Supplies		50,000
		$293,000

Accounts Payable...................................	$ 40,000
Unappropriated Surplus.............................	253,000
	$293,000

Statement of unappropriated surplus—general current fund. A statement analyzing the changes in unappropriated surplus of the general current fund is illustrated in Figure 112. The excess of revenues over expenditures shown in this statement is obtained from the income and expense statement illustrated in Figure 114.

Figure 112

A UNIVERSITY

General Current Fund

Statement Analyzing Changes in Unappropriated Surplus
for Fiscal Year

Unappropriated Surplus, Beginning of Year...........		—
Add:		
Excess of Revenues over Expenditures [Figure 114]....		$418,000
		$418,000
Deduct:		
Mortgage Notes Paid....................	$ 25,000	
Transfers to Plant Fund.................	30,000	
Plant Additions........................	10,000	
Transfers to Endowment Funds..........	100,000	165,000
Unappropriated Surplus, End of Year................		$253,000

Transactions and entries of restricted current fund. The following are typical transactions of this fund and the entries made to record them. It should be noted that while depreciation should not be taken on the fixed assets used by the university in carrying on its operations, it should, on the other hand, be computed for fixed assets held as endowments. This is done in transactions and entries nos. 3 and 4. The subject is discussed further on page 348 in connection with the description of endowment funds.

Transactions

1. Income received in cash as follows: endowments, $100,000; gifts and grants, $200,000; auxiliary enterprises, $170,000; student aid, $35,000.
2. Expenditures were incurred as follows:

Educational and general.............	$285,000
Auxiliary enterprises.................	120,000
Student aid.......................	35,000

These expenditures were all paid in cash except for several invoices totalling $4,000, which have not yet been paid.

3. Depreciation charges on auxiliary plant carried as an endowment, $20,000. [See also entry no. 9 in endowment funds.]

4. Cash in the amount of $20,000 representing these depreciation charges was transferred from this fund to the endowment fund. [See also entry no. 9 in endowment funds.]

5. Closing entries were made at the end of the year.

Entries

1. Cash............................... $505,000
   Educational and General Revenues...... $300,000
   Revenues of Auxiliary Enterprises....... 170,000
   Student Aid Revenues................. 35,000
   To record revenues earned.

2. Educational and General Expenses........ 285,000
   Expenses of Auxiliary Enterprises......... 120,000
   Student Aid Grants.................... 35,000
   Cash............................... 436,000
   Accounts Payable.................... 4,000
   To record expenditures.

3. Expenses of Auxiliary Enterprises......... 20,000
   Due to Endowment Principal Fund *E*... 20,000
   To record amount due to endowment fund
   on account of annual depreciation charge on
   enterprise plant, carried as an investment
   in the endowment fund.

4. Due to Endowment Principal Fund *E*..... 20,000
   Cash............................... 20,000
   To record payment of amount due to endow-
   ment fund *E*.

5. (a) Educational and General Revenues.... 300,000
   Revenues of Auxiliary Enterprises..... 170,000
   Student Aid Revenues.............. 35,000
   Educational and General Expenses... 285,000
   Expenses of Auxiliary Enterprises.... 140,000
   Student Aid Grants............... 35,000
   Gain or Loss..................... 45,000
   To close out revenues and expenditures.

5. (b) Gain or Loss........................ 45,000
   Restricted Current Fund Balance.... 45,000
   To close out net gain to fund balance.

Balance sheet of the restricted current fund. A balance sheet for a restricted fund is exhibited in Figure 113. This statement is based on the transactions and entries illustrated in the preceding section.

Income and expense statement—current funds. An income and expense statement based on the transactions and entries illustrated thus far in this chapter and covering both general current funds and restricted current funds is given in Figure 114. The statement shows at a glance the total revenues received from each source and the total amount spent for each major activity, irrespective of whether they apply to the general current fund or to the restricted current funds, as well as the amount

Figure 113

A UNIVERSITY

Restricted Current Fund

Balance Sheet
at Close of Fiscal Year

ASSETS

Cash...................... $49,000

LIABILITIES AND BALANCES

Accounts Payable............ $ 4,000
Fund Balance............... 45,000

$49,000

applicable to each fund. At no time should a combined income and expense statement be prepared for current funds without showing separately the amounts applicable to the general and restricted current funds.

To save space, detailed revenues and expenses were not used in the journal entries and are not given in the statement. In order, however, to illustrate the nature of the revenues and expenditures, some of the more common ones are listed without showing dollar amounts for them. The statement would be supported by schedules showing more details regarding both the revenues and expenditures. For example, a separate income and expense statement should be prepared for each auxiliary enterprise. Again, details concerning operating expenses would be shown for each department and for each object under each department.

Loan funds. These funds are used to account for loans. Usually loans are made to students, but they may also be made to faculty and staff. If only the income of a fund may be loaned, the principal should be grouped with the endowment funds and the income should be included with the loan funds. In the present case, it is assumed that the loan fund was established to lend money to students at no interest and that income on fund investments is to be added to the principal of the fund. A balance sheet for loan funds based on the transactions and entries which follow is illustrated in Figure 115.

Transactions

1. A donation of $100,000 was received for the purpose of making loans to students.

2. Loans in the amount of $50,000 were made.

3. The sum of $25,000 was invested in bonds. The bonds were purchased at par but there was accrued interest of $100 on them at the time of purchase.

4. A check in the amount of $500 to cover six-months' interest was received.

5. A student died and it was decided to write off his loan of $500 as uncollectible.

A UNIVERSITY

Figure 114

Current Funds

Summary of Current Income and Expenditure
for Fiscal Year

	Total	General Current Funds	Restricted Current Funds
Educational and General:			
Income			
Student Fees..........................	xx	xx	—
Endowment Income....................	xx	xx	xx
Gifts and Grants.....................	xx	xx	xx
Sales and Services of Educational Departments.........................	xx	xx	—
Organized Activities Relating to Educational Departments.................	xx	xx	—
Other Sources........................	xx	xx	—
Total Income....................	$2,900,000	$2,600,000	$300,000
Less—Expenditures			
General Administration...............	xx	xx	xx
General Expenses.....................	xx	xx	—
Instruction and Departmental Research	xx	xx	xx
Organized Activities Relating to Educational Departments.................	xx	xx	—
Organized Research...................	xx	xx	xx
Extension and Public Services.........	xx	xx	—
Libraries............................	xx	xx	—
Operation and Maintenance of Physical Plant............................	xx	xx	xx
Total Expenditures...............	$2,557,000	$2,272,000	$285,000
Excess of Income Over Expenditures....	$ 343,000	$ 328,000	$ 15,000
Auxiliary Enterprises:			
Income...............................	$ 870,000	$ 700,000	$170,000
Less—Expenditures....................	730,000	590,000	140,000
Excess of Income over Expenditures....	$ 140,000	$ 110,000	$ 30,000
Student Aid:			
Income...............................	$ 35,000	$ —	$ 35,000
Less—Expenditures....................	55,000	20,000	35,000
Excess of Expenditures over Income....	$ 20,000*	$ 20,000*	—
Net Income......................	$ 463,000	$ 418,000	$ 45,000

* Red

Entries

1. Cash..................................	$100,000	
Loan Fund Balance...................		$100,000
To record donation received for the purpose of setting up loan fund.		
2. Loans Receivable......................	50,000	
Cash..............................		50,000
To record loans made.		
3. Investments...........................	25,000	
Accrued Interest on Investments Purchased	100	
Cash..............................		25,100
To record investments and accrued interest purchased.		
4. Cash..................................	500	
Accrued Interest on Investments Purchased		100
Loan Fund Balance...................		400
To record receipt of semiannual interest payment.		
5. Loan Fund Balance.....................	500	
Loans Receivable.....................		500
To write off loan as uncollectible.		

Figure 115

A UNIVERSITY

Loan Fund

Balance Sheet
at Close of Fiscal Year

ASSETS

Cash........................	$25,400
Loans Receivable............	49,500
Investments.................	25,000
	$99,900

BALANCES

Fund Balance................	$99,900

Endowment and other non-expendable funds. These funds are used to account for assets which themselves cannot be expended, although the income from them may be. They consist of cash or other assets donated by outsiders directly to the institution, or turned over to a trustee or trustees to be held for the benefit of the institution, as well as funds set aside by the board of trustees of the institution as endowments. The difference between endowments set aside by the board of trustees and the first two classes of endowments is that the board of trustees is at liberty to change any endowment fund created by itself into an expendable fund. The first two classes of funds, on the other hand, can never be expended without the donor's permission; only the income can be spent without such permission. The liability side of the balance sheet of endowment and other non-expendable funds should show separately the balances applicable to each of these three classes of funds. Funds from which annuities are to be paid may be included in this fund group unless they are of major importance, in which case they should be accounted for in a separate fund group.

Transactions and entries of endowment funds. The following transactions and entries illustrate the operation of endowment and other non-expendable funds:

Transactions

1. Cash in the amount of $2,000,000 was received during the year to establish three separate endowments, as follows:

Endowment A...................	$1,000,000
Endowment B...................	600,000
Endowment C...................	400,000

2. It was decided to invest this money in securities which were to be pooled for this purpose. The following securities were acquired at the prices indicated:

Preferred stocks..................	$ 500,000
Common stocks..................	1,000,000
Bonds:	
Par value......................	200,000
Premiums.....................	10,000
Bonds:	
Par value......................	250,000
Discounts.....................	5,000
Accrued interest on investments purchased......................	1,000

3. Actual income on these investments for the year, all received in cash, was as follows:

Dividends on preferred stocks.......	$20,000
Dividends on common stocks.......	60,000
Interest........................	9,000

4. Premiums on investments in the amount of $500 and discounts in the amount of $200 were amortized at the end of the year.

5. It was decided to allow 4 per cent interest to each fund on its principal and to make these credits at the end of each year. The interest at the end of the first year amounted to $78,000.

6. Common stock with a book value of $10,000 was sold for $10,500.

7. An individual donated common stock which had cost him $65,000 (hereafter referred to as endowment fund D). At the time of the donation the stock had a market value of $75,000. The income from these securities is available for general purposes.

8. An individual had a dormitory constructed and equipped and then turned it over to the university with the specification that the net income therefrom was to be used for certain purposes (hereafter referred to as endowment fund E). The total cost was $850,000 divided as follows:

Land......................	$100,000
Building...................	600,000
Equipment.................	150,000

9. Gross income from this enterprise (endowment fund E) for the current year was $170,000 and the total expenses amounted to $120,000, exclusive of depreciation of $20,000. The income and expenses were accounted for in a restricted current fund. The latter fund transferred to endowment fund E cash in the amount of $20,000, representing the depreciation charges for the current year. [See transaction no. 4 in the restricted current fund.]

10. The sum of $100,000 was received from the general current fund for the purpose of establishing an endowment in accordance with the resolution adopted by the university's board of trustees. [See transaction no. 13 in the general current fund.]

11. An individual set up a trust in the amount of $200,000, the income from which was to go to the university.

Entries

1. Cash... $2,000,000
   Endowment Fund A Balance....................... $1,000,000
   Endowment Fund B Balance....................... 600,000
   Endowment Fund C Balance....................... 400,000
   To record receipt of money for the purpose of establishing three endowments.

2. Preferred Stocks.................................. 500,000
   Common Stocks.................................... 1,000,000
   Bonds... 450,000
   Accrued Interest on Investments Purchased........... 1,000
   Unamortized Premiums on Investments............... 10,000
   Unamortized Discounts on Investments.............. 5,000
   Cash.. 1,956,000
   To record purchase of pooled investments.

3. Cash.. 89,000
   Reserve for Income on Pooled Investments.......... 88,000
   Accrued Interest on Investments Purchased......... 1,000
   To record income received as follows:

Dividends on preferred stock...........		$20,000
Dividends on common stock.............		60,000
Interest received................	$9,000	
Less—Interest purchased........	1,000	8,000
Total............................		$88,000

4. Unamortized Discounts on Investments............... 200
   Reserve for Income on Pooled Investments............. 300
   Unamortized Premiums on Investments............ 500
   To record amortization of premiums and discounts.

5. Reserve for Income on Pooled Investments............ 78,000
   Cash... 78,000
   To record payment of endowment income to restricted funds at rate of 4 per cent per year on book value of pooled investments. Amount to be credited to the income of each endowment fund computed as follows:

Fund	Fund Balance	Percentage of Total	Income Apportioned
A	$1,000,000	50%	$39,000
B	600,000	30	23,400
C	400,000	20	15,600
	$2,000,000	100%	$78,000

6. Cash.. 10,500
    Common Stock................................... 10,000
    Endowment Fund *A* Balance...................... 250
    Endowment Fund *B* Balance...................... 150
    Endowment Fund *C* Balance...................... 100
To record sale of common stock at a profit of $500 and the addition of the gain to the balance of each endowment fund as follows:

Fund	Fund Balance	Percentage of Total	Gain Apportioned
A	$1,000,000	50%	$250
B	600,000	30	150
C	400,000	20	100
	$2,000,000	100%	$500

7. Common Stocks................................. 75,000
    Endowment Fund *D* Balance...................... 75,000
To record donation of common stock with a market value of $75,000.

8. Land... 100,000
  Building... 600,000
  Equipment....................................... 150,000
    Endowment Fund *E* Balance...................... 850,000
To record establishment of dormitory as endowment, net income of which is restricted to certain purposes.

9. Cash... 20,000
    Allowance for Depreciation—Building.............. 6,000
    Allowance for Depreciation—Equipment............ 14,000
To record receipt of money from restricted current fund equivalent to depreciation charges on auxiliary enterprise. Money to be used to replace building and equipment when they become completely worn out.

10. Cash... 100,000
    Fund Functioning as Endowment—Balance.......... 100,000
To record receipt of money from general current fund for purpose of setting up a fund to function as an endowment fund in accordance with resolution adopted by the university's board of trustees.

11. Funds Held in Trust by Others...................... 200,000
    Funds Held in Trust by Others—Balance........... 200,000
To record setting up of trust by individual. Income from this trust is to be available to the university to spend as it sees fit.

Comments on transactions and entries. The following points should be noted with respect to the foregoing transactions and entries:

1. Three types of non-expendable funds were illustrated: (1) "pure" endowment funds exemplified by transactions and entries nos. 1-9, (2) funds being accounted for as endowments through action of the board of trustees of the university, illustrated by transaction and entry no. 10, and (3) funds turned over by a donor to a trustee or trustees with the stipulation that the income therefrom is to go to the university, exemplified by transaction and entry no. 11.

2. It is assumed that the investments of several endowment funds have been pooled and that premiums, discounts, and accrued interest purchases are involved.

3. In accounting for the income from pooled investments, two courses of action are possible. One is to allocate to each fund its share of the total income of the pool for the year. The other is to assume an arbitrary rate of return and to credit each participating fund with its share of the pool income determined on this basis. The latter procedure is desirable if it is necessary for the fund to have the same amount of income each year.

In the present case an arbitrary rate of return is assumed. It will be noted from entries and transactions nos. 3 and 5 that the amount earned exceeded the amount allocated to the various funds participating in the pool, resulting in a credit balance in the Reserve for Income on Pooled Investments account. If the actual earnings had fallen short of the allocated amount (which would not happen often because a conservative rate of return is usually assumed) a debit balance would have resulted, which would have been carried as a deferred charge until the income of the following year or years was sufficient to wipe out such balance.

4. In the present case both premiums and discounts on investments are amortized. Some universities, in an effort to be conservative, amortize premiums but not discounts.

5. Losses or gains on the sale of pooled investments may be treated in two ways: (1) Gains may be credited and losses charged to a Reserve for Gains or Losses on Pooled Investments account, which eventually is closed out into the principal of each participating fund. (2) Gains may be credited and losses charged to the principal of each participating fund. If there are frequent sales of pooled securities, the first method is desirable; if there are few sales, the second method should be employed. In the entries which follow the second method is used.

6. Transaction and entry no. 7 illustrate the fact that securities should be taken up at their market value at the date they were donated. It should be noted that if investments of funds which already have securities are to be pooled, such securities must be adjusted to market value as of the date the pool is started. Gains resulting from such adjustment should be credited to the principal of the particular fund and losses should be charged to such principal. This revaluation is made in order that each of the funds may start participation in the pool on an equal basis.

7. Transaction and entry no. 9 illustrate the fact that depreciation charges must be taken into account in computing the income of an endowment fund which has investments in the form of fixed assets, if the fund is to remain non-expendable. It illustrates further the fact that it is essential to transfer cash equal to depreciation charges from the income fund to the endowment fund. If prices are rising, such depreciation

charges and transfers may not provide sufficient resources to replace the fixed assets. But these charges will at least assure that the original cost is recovered. If the donor desires it, provision can, of course, be made for additional charges sufficient to replace the depreciated fixed assets. If these supplementary charges are made, the resulting credit would not be to an Allowance for Depreciation account but rather to a Reserve for Replacements account.

Balance sheet of endowment funds. A balance sheet of endowment funds is illustrated in Figure 116. This balance sheet is based on the immediately preceding transactions and entries.

Figure 116

A UNIVERSITY

Endowment Funds

Balance Sheet
at Close of Fiscal Year

ASSETS

Assets Other Than Fixed:

Cash		$ 185,500	
Investments:			
Preferred Stocks	$ 500,000		
Common Stocks	1,065,000		
Bonds	450,000		
	$2,015,000		
Unamortized Premium on Investments	9,500		
	$2,024,500		
Less—Unamortized Discount on Investments	4,800	2,019,700	
Funds Held in Trust by Others		200,000	$2,405,200
Fixed Assets:			
Land		$ 100,000	
Buildings	$ 600,000		
Less—Allowance for Depreciation	6,000	594,000	
Equipment	$ 150,000		
Less—Allowance for Depreciation	14,000	136,000	830,000
			$3,235,200

RESERVES AND BALANCES

Reserve for Income on Pooled Investments		$ 9,700
Fund Balances:		
Endowment Fund *A*	$1,000,250	
Endowment Fund *B*	600,150	
Endowment Fund *C*	400,100	
Endowment Fund *D*	75,000	
Endowment Fund *E*	850,000	
Fund Functioning as Endowment	100,000	
Funds Held in Trust by Others	200,000	3,225,500
		$3,235,200

Annuity funds. These funds are used to account for assets which belong to the institution, except that the institution is required to make annuity payments. For example, an individual may donate cash, securities, or other assets under an agreement that he is to get a fixed or variable amount as an annuity for life, but that after he dies the principal is to belong to the university. As stated above, if these funds are small in amount, they may be accounted for as part of the endowment and other non-expendable fund group. The transactions and entries for these funds are similar to those for the endowment funds. For example, a typical transaction would be the donation of cash or securities for the establishment of an annuity fund. The entry to record such a transaction is

Cash....................................	$ 10,000	
Investments.............................	100,000	
Annuity Funds Balance.................		$110,000
To record establishment of annuity fund.		

As income is received, the portions belonging to the annuitant and the institution, respectively, must be determined and an entry must be made to record the liability to each. For example, assuming that the income amounts to $4,000 and that $3,000 is due to the annuitant and the remainder is available for spending by the institution, the entry would be as follows:

Cash...	$4,000	
Due to Annuitant...........................		$3,000
Due to General Current Fund.................		1,000
To record receipt of income and resulting liability to annuitant and to general current fund.		

As these amounts are paid over, the entry is

Due to Annuitant............................	$3,000	
Due to General Current Fund.................	1,000	
Cash..		$4,000
To record payment of liabilities.		

From the standpoint of conservatism, it may be desirable to set aside part of the income in a reserve. The latter would be used to absorb any payments made to annuitants in excess of the income for a particular year. Otherwise, it is necessary to meet such excess payments out of the general current fund. The decision to establish such a reserve must be based on past experience. The need for this money by the general current fund would also be a factor in making this determination.

A balance sheet of an annuity fund is illustrated in Figure 117. This balance sheet is based on the transactions and entries described immediately above.

Plant funds. These funds are used to account for (1) cash or securities earmarked for the acquisition of fixed assets; (2) resources accumulated

Figure 117

A UNIVERSITY

Annuity Funds

Balance Sheet
at Close of Fiscal Year

ASSETS

Cash......................	$ 10,000
Investments...............	100,000
	$110,000

BALANCES

Fund Balance...............	$110,000

for the purpose of retiring indebtedness incurred in connection with the acquisition of fixed assets; (3) fixed assets used to carry on operations (as distinguished from fixed assets held as endowments) together with the liabilities outstanding against these assets, such as mortgages or bonds. A separate group of accounts is necessary to account for each of these three types of assets. The accounts relating to the first group will hereafter be referred to as the improvements and replacements fund group (also known as unexpended plant funds), those relating to the second as the retirement of indebtedness fund group, and those in the third as the investment in plant group. The accounting for each of these groups is described separately below. The results of the transactions and entries of each fund group are reflected in the balance sheet for that group illustrated in Figure 118.

Transactions and entries of improvements and replacements fund. Some typical transactions and the related entries for this fund are illustrated below. It should be noted that transaction and entry no. 3 affect not only this fund but also the investment in plant fund.

Transactions

1. A donation of preferred stocks in the amount of $20,000 was made by an individual for the purpose of financing additions to the plant.

2. Cash in the amount of $30,000 was transferred from the general current fund to this fund for the purpose of financing additions to the plant. [See also transaction no. 11 in the general current fund.]

3. Equipment costing $12,000 was purchased for cash. [See also transaction no. 4 in the investment in plant fund.]

Entries

1. Investments.................................	$20,000	
Improvements and Replacements Fund Balance		$20,000
To record investments donated for purpose of financing additions to plant.		
2. Cash.......................................	30,000	
Improvements and Replacements Fund Balance		30,000
To record receipt of cash from general current fund for purpose of financing additions to plant.		

3. Improvements and Replacements Fund Balance. .   12,000
   Cash.   12,000
   To record purchase of equipment.

Transactions and entries of retirement of indebtedness fund. The following are some typical transactions of this fund and the related entries. In this connection attention is called to the fact that transaction no. 2 affects not only this fund but also the investment in plant fund.

Transactions

1. A donation of $15,000 was made for the purpose of paying part of the mortgage installment falling due during the current year.
2. The money was used for this purpose. [See also transaction no. 5 in investment in plant fund.]
3. A donation of $25,000 was made for the purpose of paying the mortgage installment falling due next year.

Entries

1. Cash. $15,000
      Retirement of Indebtedness Fund Balance. $15,000
      To record receipt of money to pay part of mortgage
      installment falling due during the current year.

2. Retirement of Indebtedness Fund Balance.   15,000
      Cash.   15,000
      To record payment of part of mortgage installment.

3. Cash.   25,000
      Retirement of Indebtedness Fund Balance.   25,000
      To record receipt of money to pay part of mortgage
      installment falling due during the following year.

Transactions and entries of investment in plant fund. In studying the transactions and entries of this fund the following facts should be kept in mind:

1. It is assumed that the opening balances in the investment in plant fund were as follows:

	Debit Balances	Credit Balances
Land.	$ 300,000	
Buildings.	4,000,000	
Equipment.	1,000,000	
Mortgage Payable.		$ 400,000
Investment in Plant from Gifts.		4,600,000
Investment in Plant from Current Funds.		300,000

2. All of the transactions illustrated in this fund, except the last one, originated in some other fund.

Transactions Originating in:

1. GENERAL CURRENT FUND [see transaction no. 12 in that fund]: Equipment was purchased for $10,000.
2. ENDOWMENT FUND [see transaction no. 8 in that fund]: An individual

donated a fully-equipped dormitory which cost him $850,000 distributed as follows: land, $100,000; building, $600,000; equipment, $150,000.

3. RESTRICTED CURRENT FUND [see transaction no. 3 in that fund]: Depreciation on the dormitory building was computed to be $6,000, and on the dormitory equipment, $14,000.

4. IMPROVEMENTS AND REPLACEMENTS FUND [see transaction no. 3 in that fund]: Equipment costing $12,000 was purchased for cash.

5. RETIREMENT OF INDEBTEDNESS FUND [see transaction no. 2 in that fund]: Part of an installment mortgage note in the amount of $15,000 was retired.

6. INVESTMENT IN PLANT FUND: A piece of uninsured equipment financed from current revenues and costing $1,000 was destroyed by fire.

Entries

1. Equipment................................... $ 10,000
    Investment in Plant from Current Funds.... $ 10,000
    To record purchase of equipment out of the general current fund.

2. Land....................................... 100,000
   Building................................... 600,000
   Equipment.................................. 150,000
     Investment in Plant from Endowment Funds   850,000
   To record donation of dormitory.

3. Investment in Plant from Endowment Funds... 20,000
    Allowance for Depreciation—Buildings......   6,000
    Allowance for Depreciation—Equipment.....   14,000
   To record reduction in value of dormitory building and equipment due to depreciation.

4. Equipment................................... 12,000
    Investment in Plant from Current Funds....   12,000
   To record purchase of equipment out of improvements and replacements fund.

5. Mortgage Payable........................... 15,000
    Investment in Plant from Gifts............   15,000
   To record payment of part of mortgage payable from retirement of indebtedness fund.

6. Investment in Plant from Current Funds...... 1,000
    Equipment...............................   1,000
   To remove from this fund the cost of equipment destroyed.

Balance sheet for plant funds. A combined balance sheet for plant funds is illustrated in Figure 118. It should be noted that the fixed assets of endowment funds invested in institutional property are included in this balance sheet. These assets are offset on the credit side by the account Investment in Plant from Endowments. Although these fixed assets are shown as assets of the particular endowment fund to which they relate, they are also included in this balance sheet in order to show the total investment in plant. The allowances for depreciation shown in the statement apply only to the fixed assets held as endowments.

Combined balance sheet—all funds. A combined balance sheet of all

Figure 118

A UNIVERSITY
Plant Funds
Balance Sheet
at Close of Fiscal Year

ASSETS

Improvements and Replacements Fund

Cash..............................	$ 18,000	
Investments.......................	20,000	
Total.........................		$ 38,000

Retirement of Indebtedness Fund

Cash..............................	25,000

Investment in Plant Fund

Land..............................		$ 400,000
Buildings............	$4,600,000	
Less—Allowance for Depreciation.........	6,000	4,594,000
Equipment...........	$1,171,000	
Less—Allowance for Depreciation.........	14,000	1,157,000
Total.........................		6,151,000
Total Plant Funds.................		$6,214,000

LIABILITIES

Improvements and Replacements Fund

Fund Balance.....................	$ 38,000	
Total.........................		$ 38,000

Retirement of Indebtedness Fund

Fund Balance.....................	25,000

Investment in Plant Fund

Mortgage Payable.................		$ 385,000
Investment in Plant from:		
Endowments.........	$ 830,000	
Other Gifts.........	4,615,000	
Current Funds......	321,000	5,766,000
Total.........................		6,151,000
Total Plant Funds.................		$6,214,000

funds may be prepared either in columnar or sectional form. An example of a combined fund balance sheet in columnar form is illustrated in Figure 69, page 212, while an example of a sectional combined fund balance sheet is illustrated in Figure 110. The relative merits of the columnar and sectional balance sheets are discussed on page 216.

21

<<<<<<<<<<<<<<<<<<<<<<<<<<<<<<<<<<<<<<<<<<<<<<<<<<<<<<<<<<<<<<<<

COST ACCOUNTING

Cost accounting has been defined as that method of accounting which provides for the searching out and recording of all the elements of cost incurred in performing an activity, a job, *or* a unit of work. The purpose of cost accounting is to provide expenditure data to be used in (1) preparing the budget, (2) determining whether operations are being carried on efficiently, (3) determining whether to have certain work performed by the governmental unit's employees or by an outside contractor, and (4) arriving at the cost of fixed assets constructed.

In a certain sense, all systems which provide for expenditure accounting may be called cost accounting systems, since they make it possible to secure expenditure data for organization units and for the activities carried on by each organization unit. The main distinction between a general accounting system and a cost accounting system may be said to lie in the fact that under a cost accounting system *all* the elements which go to make up the cost of carrying on the activity are allocated to the activity, whereas under a general system of accounting certain elements of cost, such as overhead, are not likely to be allocated. For example, take the activity of garbage collection. At least part of the salary of the head of the bureau of sanitation should be allocated to this activity. Yet, under a general accounting system, the salary of this official is charged to a separate account (Supervision), and none of the activities carried on by the bureau of sanitation are charged with any part of it.

Another distinction between general accounting and cost accounting is that under a cost accounting system the data may be collected not only for activities but also for the operations making up a particular activity. For example, part of the activity of street cleaning consists of beat patrol work, broom gang work, and machine sweeping. A final distinction is that under a cost accounting system an attempt is made to correlate cost with the amount of work done.

It is beyond the scope of this book to go into the details of governmental cost accounting. The discussion will therefore be limited to five examples of cost accounting: (1) securing the cost of operating automotive equipment, (2) securing maintenance activity costs, (3) arriving at the cost of fixed assets constructed by the governmental unit, (4) cost accounting as applied to utilities and other enterprises, and (5) cost accounting applied to institutions.

Equipment Operation Costs

As already indicated, by automotive equipment is meant automobiles, trucks, tractors, and similar equipment. If the equipment is handled by a central equipment bureau, it is important to know the cost of operating each piece of equipment in order that (1) the central equipment bureau may recover the cost from the departments using the equipment, (2) each activity may be charged with a proper share of the cost, and (3) it may be determined which pieces of equipment are still operating efficiently enough to warrant their continued use and which pieces should be scrapped or otherwise disposed of. Even if the equipment is not operated by a central equipment bureau, it is important to know the cost of operating each piece of equipment because of the last two reasons.

It is assumed here that the equipment is operated by a central equipment bureau. However, only slight modifications are necessary in those cases where departments operate the equipment.

Securing direct costs. The expenses involved in operating each piece of equipment include the cost of gasoline, oil, and other supplies, materials and labor used in repairing and maintaining equipment, depreciation of equipment and garage, and general overhead.

The basic data for arriving at the cost of operating each piece of equipment are gathered on an individual equipment record similar to that illustrated in Figure 119. The record is prepared annually, but postings for each item of expense are made at the end of each month. The nature of the expenses listed in columns 2-5 is self-evident. Overhead includes all the expenses connected with operating the central equipment bureau which cannot be assigned directly to any one piece of equipment. These expenses include, among others, the salary of the superintendent of equipment, salaries of foremen, the use of small tools and of such supplies as grease, paint, and rags, and the cost of operating the garage office. These expenses are first compiled in separate expense accounts, and, at the end of each month, or year, they are distributed to all pieces of equipment on some established basis. One of the bases frequently used is the number of labor hours spent on each piece of equipment during the month. A labor hour is one hour of work by one employee. For example, if

Figure 119

A GOVERNMENTAL UNIT
Individual Equipment Record
for Year Ending _____ 19 ____

1. Equipment No._____ Serial No._____
2. Motor No._____
3. Make_____
4. Type_____
5. Capacity_____
6. Date Purchased_____
7. Original Cost_____ $_____
8. Value Start of This Year_____ $_____

9. Estimated Salvage Value_____ $_____
10. Remaining Depreciation_____ $_____
11. Estimated Depreciation This Year__ $_____
12. Estimated Hours or Miles This Year_____
13. Depreciation Rate per Hour_____ $_____
          per Mile_____
14. Rental {Date_____ Rate_____ per Mi. or Hr.
    Rates {Date_____ Rate_____ per Mi. or Hr.

Month	Gasoline		Oil			Tires and Supplies	Mainte- nance and Repairs	Overhead	Deprecia- tion	Total Cost	Miles Run	Hours Run	Cost per Mile or Hour	Miles per Gallon	Rentals Earned (Credits)
1	2		3			4	5	6	7	8	9	10	11	12	13
	Gals.	Amt.	Qts.	Amt.		Amt.	Amt.	Amt.	Amt.	Amt.			Amt.		Amt.

358

one mechanic works for four hours on an automobile, the job is said to have required four labor hours. Again, if four employees work an hour on one job, the job is similarly said to have required four labor hours.

Securing overhead costs. The procedure in distributing overhead expenses to each piece of equipment is as follows: The expenses shown in the individual overhead expense accounts are added to arrive at the total equipment overhead expenses for the month. This total is recorded on a form similar to that illustrated in Figure 120. The total number of labor hours is also recorded on this form. The total cost per labor hour is arrived at by dividing the total overhead expenses for the month by

Figure 120

A GOVERNMENTAL UNIT
Summary of Equipment
Overhead Expenses
for Month

Total Overhead Expenses
for Month_____
Total No. of Labor Hours_____
Rate per Labor Hour_____

Equipment No.	Labor Hours	Amount	Equipment No.	Labor Hours	Amount

the total number of labor hours. Provision is made for recording for each piece of equipment the number of labor hours worked on it. This information is obtained from reports not illustrated here. The amount of overhead chargeable to each piece of equipment is arrived at by multiplying the number of labor hours spent on it by the rate per labor hour, and each amount is posted to column 6 of the equipment record.

To illustrate, if the total overhead expenses amounted to $2,000 and a total of 2,000 labor hours was spent on repairing and maintaining equipment, the overhead expense rate would be $1.00 per labor hour. And, if we assume that 30 labor hours were spent on a particular piece of equipment, the overhead expense posted to the individual equipment record for the particular piece of equipment would be $30.

To arrive at the total cost of operating each piece of equipment, it is also necessary to take account of depreciation. One of the methods for depreciating equipment is the work-unit method. Under this method, the net value of each piece of equipment is arrived at. The net value is then divided by the total estimated number of work units for the life of the asset, and the charge to each activity is determined by multiplying the number of units of work put in on the activity by the rate per work unit. For example, assume that a truck was acquired at a cost of $2,400, that it is estimated to cover 40,000 miles, and that the estimated salvage value of the truck is $400. In that event, the depreciation rate per mile would be $.05 ($2,000 ÷ 40,000). If the truck covered 1,500 miles during the month of July, the depreciation to be posted to the individual equipment record for the particular truck for July is $75 (1,500 × $.05).

The last column in the individual equipment record refers to rentals earned. Since these rentals were discussed in Chapter 11, they will not be considered here.

Statements of equipment costs. As indicated before, one of the purposes of securing equipment costs is to measure the efficiency of each piece of equipment. Accordingly, a statement is prepared at the end of each month and each year showing the total cost of operating the piece of equipment, the number of miles or hours operated, and the cost per mile or hour. These unit costs serve as an index of the efficiency of equipment operations. This statement contains the same columns as the individual equipment record form illustrated in Figure 119 except that an "Equipment No." column is substituted for the first column in the record.

Maintenance Activity Costs

Costs of carrying on maintenance activities have a special significance if the relationship between the amount of work done and the cost of doing the particular work can be determined. Such a relationship can be readily established for those activities which are susceptible of unit cost measurement. For example, if a record is kept of the number of miles of streets cleaned and if all the costs applicable to cleaning streets are also compiled, it is possible to arrive at the cost of cleaning a mile of street. The assumption throughout this section is that the costs are being assembled for activities susceptible of unit cost measurement.

Unit cost measures. The following are examples of the activities susceptible of unit cost measurement and the units of measurement employed:

BUREAU OF SANITATION

Operation or Account Title	Work Unit
WASTE COLLECTION:	
Loading and Hauling Nonburnables	Tons or Cubic Yards
Maintenance of Dumps	Tons or Cubic Yards
Loading and Hauling Burnables	Tons or Pounds
Dead Animals and Other Special Collection	Number and Kind

INCINERATOR OPERATION AND MAINTENANCE:

Charging...	Tons
Firing...	Tons
Removing Ashes.....................................	Tons or Pounds

STREET CLEANING:

Machine Sweeping (including removal of sweepings)........	Cleaning Mile
Beat Patrol (cleaning sections)..........................	Cleaning Mile

Compiling costs and units of work. If accurate unit costs are to be secured, both the cost of an activity and the number of units of work must be compiled. One method of compiling such information is through the use of work orders like the one illustrated in Figure 121. These work orders taken together constitute a work and cost ledger.

Note that provision is made for filling in the cost of labor, the cost of materials, the cost of equipment use, overhead costs, total cost of the job, number of units of work involved, and the cost per unit. The scope of this book does not permit a detailed outline of the procedure for compiling the various elements of cost, but the procedure will be discussed briefly.

Labor. A daily record is kept by the foreman or special timekeeper of the amount of work put in by each employee on each job. This form also provides space for filling in the number of units of work completed. The form is transmitted daily to the accounting department, where the hours are multiplied by the rate per hour to arrive at the cost of labor put in on the particular activity. This total is then posted to the work order. The amount of time worked is also entered on the payroll register and forms the basis for calculating the amount of pay due employees.

Materials and supplies. A daily report is prepared showing the amount of materials and supplies used in connection with each activity. The number of the requisition on which the materials were withdrawn is shown on this report. On the basis of the requisitions, the cost of materials used is determined by the accounting department and is entered on the work order in the work and cost ledger. It should be noted that reference is here to materials which can be definitely allocated to a particular job or activity, as, for example, materials used in repairing streets. If the materials are such that they cannot be allocated to a particular job or activity, they are considered part of overhead expenses.

Equipment use. We have indicated before how costs for equipment use are determined and that these costs are recovered by charging a rental fee per mile or hour of use. The foreman records the number of hours or the number of miles worked on each activity by each piece of equipment. When the report is turned in to the accounting department, total equipment use costs for the activity are determined by multiplying the number of miles or hours used by the proper rental rates. The amount is then posted to the work order. The procedure is not materially different if equipment is rented from a private trucking company. Usually the com-

Figure 121

A GOVERNMENTAL UNIT

Work Order

Control Account _____ No. _____ Job or Operation _____ Page No. _____

Unit Cost Standard _____ Per _____ For Fiscal Year _____ No. _____

_____ 19 _____

Date	FIELD LABOR		Req. No.	Quan.	MATERIALS			EQUIPMENT EXPENSE			Engineering and Overhead	Total Cost	Work Units	Unit Costs
	Hours	Amount			Description	Price	Amount	Hours	Amount				

pany charges a rental rate per hour or mile, and the cost of equipment use is determined by multiplying the number of miles or hours used for the particular activity by the rate per mile or hour.

Overhead. As already stated, certain expenses cannot be charged directly to individual activities and must therefore be allocated on some arbitrary basis. Some of these are the cost of supervision, heat, light, and power, and watchmen's wages. From a theoretical standpoint even a part of the cost of operating the general accounting office should be charged to each activity. But, since this is seldom practical, only the overhead of the department carrying on the activity is usually allocated.

One of two procedures may be followed. The first is to wait until the end of the month, when the total amount of overhead will have been determined, and then distribute actual overhead costs among jobs and operations on the basis of some factor common to all, such as the total cost of labor or the number of labor hours. For example, if we assume that total overhead expenses amounting to $50,000 are to be distributed among all the activities on the basis of labor costs and that the total labor cost for all such activities is $500,000, the rate to be applied to each activity is 10 per cent. Therefore, if the total cost of labor on activity *A* is $20,000, the amount of overhead to be applied to that activity is $2,000 ($20,000 × 10 per cent).

The second procedure is to use the factor just illustrated as a basis of apportioning overhead but to employ estimated, rather than actual, rates. Thus, at the beginning of the year the total amount of overhead chargeable to all activities and the cost of labor for all activities are estimated. The rate is arrived at by dividing the estimated total overhead cost by the estimated total labor cost. The amount of overhead applicable to each activity is in turn secured by multiplying the cost of the labor put in on the activity by the predetermined rate.

For example, if estimated overhead costs of $100,000 are to be distributed among activities for which the total labor cost is estimated to be $500,000, the overhead rate will be 20 per cent ($100,000 ÷ $500,000). The amount to be charged to an activity at any time would be arrived at by multiplying the total labor cost for the activity by the predetermined rate. Of course, if the overhead cost or total labor cost is either greater or smaller than the amount originally estimated, corresponding adjustments must be made at the end of the year by pro-rating the unapplied or overapplied overhead among the activities or by increasing or decreasing the rate for the following year.

After these overhead costs are determined, they, too, are posted to the work orders in the work and cost ledger. The total cost is then arrived at by adding the costs of labor, materials and supplies, equipment use, and overhead. As we have indicated before, provision is made for posting the total number of work units to the work order. By dividing the total cost by the number of work units, the cost per unit can be established.

Unit cost standards. It will be noted that provision is made on the work order for filling in the unit cost standard. A unit cost standard is defined as the minimum cost necessary to perform a unit of work. Unit cost standards are developed scientifically by studying the necessary operations or by noting the trend of unit costs over a period of time but eliminating from consideration those unit costs which are the result of abnormal operating conditions. By comparing actual unit costs with unit cost standards, it is possible to tell to what extent the actual unit costs depart from possible minimum costs.

Cost statements. On the basis of the data collected on the individual work orders, cost statements are prepared. These statements show the various operations connected with a particular activity, standard work units, the total cost of carrying on the activity, units of work done, unit cost, number of man hours, units per man hour, number of equipment hours, and units per equipment hour. Figure 122 illustrates part of a form for a cost statement.

Construction Costs

Cost accounting is used in construction work for two reasons: (1) to determine that the operations involved in constructing the project are being performed efficiently, and (2) to arrive at the total cost of a project. The following, for example, are some of the operations involved in the construction of sewers and the units of measure used to determine unit costs:

Operation	Unit of Measure
Earth Excavation—Hand	Cubic Yards
Earth Excavation—Machine	Cubic Yards
Rock Works	Cubic Yards
Sheeting and Bracing	Lineal Feet of Trench
Underdrain	Lineal Feet
Laying Pipe	Lineal Feet
Form Work	Lineal Feet
Placing Concrete	Lineal Feet or Cubic Yards
Backfilling	Cubic Yards
Surface Restoration	Square Yards

By comparing the unit cost of performing these operations with unit cost standards, it is possible to determine whether or not work is being carried on at the lowest possible cost.

Compiling costs and units of work. The data necessary for computing the cost of construction and unit costs are accumulated on a construction work order, a form for which is illustrated in Figure 123. Note that provision is made for recording both estimated and actual costs. The estimated cost of a project is determined before the project is approved. To increase the reliability of estimates, they are detailed by objects,

Figure 122

A GOVERNMENTAL UNIT
Work and Cost Statement
for Month

Department _____

Bureau _____

Operation	Standard Work Units	Total Cost	Units of Work Done	Unit Cost	No. of Man Hours	Units per Man Hour	No. of Equipment Hours	Units per Equipment Hour
STREET CLEANING								
1 White Wing	Cleaning Mi.							
2 Broom Gang	" "							
3 Machine Sweeping	" "							
4 Machine Flushing	" "							
5 Hose Flushing	" "							
6 Street Sprinkling	" "							
7 Sweepings Removed	Cu. Yds.							
8 Snow and Ice Removed	" "							
STREET REPAIRS								
11 Concrete Street Repairs	Sq. Yds.							
12 Brick Street Repairs	" "							
13 Asphalt Street Repairs	" "							
14 Macadam Surface Treatment	" "							
15 Plumbers' and Utility Cuts	" "							
16 Cold Patch Repairs	Tons							
17 Curb and Gutter	Lin. Feet							
22 Sidewalk Repairs	Sq. Ft.							
23 Sidewalk Construction	" "							

Figure 123
(a) Front.

A GOVERNMENTAL UNIT
Construction Work Order

No. _____

Date _____

To _____

You are directed to initiate and complete the work described below.

_____

_____

_____

ESTIMATES

Kind of Work	Mate-rials	Labor	Equip-ment	Over-head	Total	No. of Units	Unit Cost
Totals							

Approved

_____

Figure 123
(b) Reverse.

Construction Work Order

Work Order No._____   19____

ACCUMULATION OF COSTS   Work Completed

Kind of Work	Materials	Labor	Equipment	Overhead	Total Cost	Units	Actual Unit Cost	Total Estimated Cost	Excess or Deficiency* of Total Actual over Estimated Cost	Estimated Unit Cost	Excess or Deficiency* of Actual Unit Cost over Estimated Unit Cost
Totals											
Over or Under* Estimate											

367

separate expenditure estimates being made for materials, labor, equipment use, and overhead. Some construction activities cannot be expressed in terms of unit costs, and the columns showing number of units and the unit costs in those cases cannot therefore be filled in.

Estimated cost data are based on engineering forecasts. The kinds and quantities of materials to be used, the amount of labor, and the amount of equipment use are estimated by the governmental unit's engineering department. The quantities are priced on the basis of current quotations for materials, payroll and other labor reports, and reports of equipment use. Estimated overhead is applied either on the basis of labor hours or on the basis of the total cost of materials, labor, and equipment use. Of course, in pricing materials, labor, and equipment use, cognizance is also taken of probable price trends during the construction period.

Thus far we have discussed the procedure for accumulating the data on which estimated costs are based. The actual cost of materials, labor, and so forth must be recorded as the work progresses. Under a cost accounting system the procedure for recording construction costs is generally the same as that for recording maintenance costs. To make the discussion clearer, each element of cost will be considered separately.

Materials. Data for the cost of materials are secured from requisitions However, materials are frequently ordered directly for a particular job In that case, the cost of materials used is based on the purchase invoices and on invoices and interdepartmental bills for transportation and handling charges.

Labor. Data for the cost of labor on each project are obtained from daily labor reports similar to those discussed on page 361. These reports are used as a basis both for making postings to the construction work order and for preparing payrolls. Sometimes these reports are first summarized at certain intervals and the totals are posted to the work order.

Equipment use. Construction projects are charged with the cost of equipment use in the same manner as are maintenance jobs. A record is kept of the number of hours that each piece of equipment is used on the job, and the cost chargeable to the project is arrived at by multiplying the number of hours worked by the rate per hour. The cost of the use of hired private equipment is usually arrived at by multiplying the number of units by the agreed rate per unit—for example, the number of hours worked by the rate per hour or cubic yards of earth excavated by the rate per cubic yard.

Overhead. Overhead expenses consist of all expenses other than the cost of materials, labor, and equipment use. They include cost of workmen's compensation insurance and a portion of general and administrative expenses. If the actual amount of the overhead cost applicable to a particular project is determinable, it is allocated directly to the project. All other overhead is applied on some predetermined arbitrary basis, such as the cost of labor or the total cost of materials, labor, and equipment use. Sometimes an estimated overhead rate is applied. The procedure for arriving at this rate was given on page 363.

Entries. The entries necessary to record the cost of construction work in progress and the cost of the completed project have already been illustrated in Chapter 16. It should be remembered that the individual property records for assets constructed by the governmental unit are set up on the basis of the data contained in the construction work order.

Cost statements. Two types of cost statements are prepared monthly or at less frequent intervals on the basis of the data contained in the individual construction work orders. The first is a statement summarizing, for completed projects, the information contained in the construction work orders (Figure 123). The second is a statement showing the unit costs of construction operations carried on during the month or other period. A form for this statement is illustrated in Figure 124.

Cost Accounting as Applied to Utilities and Other Enterprises

The principles and procedures discussed in connection with cost accounting for a governmental unit's general activities are equally applicable to the activities carried on by a utility or other enterprise. However, some phases of cost accounting are peculiar to utilities and other enterprises. These include the use of clearing accounts, the allocation of joint expenses, and the use of cost units and cost statements which are different from those illustrated previously in this chapter. Each of these phases is discussed separately below.

Clearing accounts. Certain expenditures are incurred under circumstances that prevent their being charged to the proper accounts at the time they are incurred. Even if the expenses can be charged directly, they are sometimes recorded in a clearing account, in order that the *total* expenses may be computed before they are distributed among the various accounts. For example, it may be desirable not only to allocate shop expenses among the various activities for whose benefit the shop is operated but also to know what the *total* shop expenses for a particular period of time have been. The charges are, therefore, first recorded in clearing accounts and are transferred from these accounts to the expense accounts. The following are some of the expenditures for which clearing accounts are established: (1) stores, (2) transportation, and (3) shop.

Stores Expenses—Clearing. In discussing the accounting procedure for materials issued from a central storeroom, we indicated that charges to departments consist of two elements—the direct cost of the materials and overhead charges. All overhead charges may be accumulated in the

Figure 124

A GOVERNMENTAL UNIT
Report of Construction Operation Costs
for Period

Operation	Standard Work Units	Units of Work Done				Unit Cost				Total Cost				Production Ratios	
		Last Month	This Month	Last Year to Date	This Year to Date	Last Month	This Month	Last Year to Date	This Year to Date	Last Month	This Month	Last Year to Date	This Year to Date	Units per Labor Hour	Units per Equipment Hour
Underdrain Form Work Backfilling	Lin. Ft. " " Cu. Yds.														

Stores Expenses—Clearing account and then redistributed to the proper accounts on various bases. Since the subject has been treated in Chapter 11, the discussion will not be repeated here.

Transportation Expenses—Clearing. This account is charged with the cost of operating the utility's equipment. The procedure in charging expenses to individual pieces of equipment and to the Transportation Expenses—Clearing account is evident from the discussion in the first part of this chapter. The Transportation Expenses—Clearing account is reduced as charges are made to the various jobs and activities on which the equipment was used (see the second entry below).

Shop Expenses—Clearing. This clearing account is used to accumulate the cost of operating utility or other enterprise shops. At certain intervals, the account is cleared by charging the proper expenditure accounts and crediting the clearing account. Charges to jobs and activities may be made either on the basis of the actual cost of materials, labor, and overhead chargeable to each job or activity or on the basis of some predetermined rate. In general, the principles involved in allocating shop expenses are the same as those involved in charging transportation expenses.

Entries. When the expenses chargeable to a clearing account are first incurred, an entry is made charging the clearing account and crediting Cash or an appropriate liability account. The allocation of these expenses is accomplished by an entry which charges the various expense accounts involved and credits the clearing account. The following is an example of how this is accomplished in the case of the Transportation Expenses—Clearing account. The same procedure would, of course, be followed for the other clearing accounts.

At the time the expenditure chargeable to the clearing account is first incurred, an entry is made debiting the Transportation Expenses—Clearing account and crediting Cash or a liability account. For example, if the payroll for mechanics is $5,000, the transaction is recorded as follows:

Transportation Expenses—Clearing.............	$5,000	
Vouchers Payable.........................		$5,000
To record expenses for garage labor.		

Entries would also be made in the individual equipment records.

As the particular jobs and activities are charged, the following entry is made:

Operating Expenses............................	$7,000	
Construction Work in Progress.................	3,000	
Transportation Expenses—Clearing...........		$10,000
To record distribution of clearing expenses among jobs and activities, as follows:		

OPERATING EXPENSES:
  Transmission Expenses:
    Repairs to Transmission System................... $ 2,000
    Maintenance of Poles, Towers, Fixtures, and
      Conduits:
      Repairs to Poles, Towers, and Fixtures...... $2,000
      Repairs to Underground Conduits.......... 1,000   3,000

  Distribution Expenses:
    Repairs to Distribution Structures and Equip-
      ment................................ $1,000
    Repairs to Overhead Distribution Conductors   500
    Repairs to Underground Distribution Con-
      ductors................................   500   2,000

        Total Operating Expenses..................... $ 7,000

CONSTRUCTION WORK IN PROGRESS:

Work Order No.	Amount
11.....................................	$1,000
12.....................................	500
13.....................................	1,000
14.....................................	300
15.....................................	200

        Total Construction Work in Progress............. 3,000

        Grand Total................................. $10,000

Entries would also be made in the "Rentals Earned" column of each individual equipment record (Figure 119) showing the total amount of charges which have been applied to jobs and activities on account of work done by the equipment.

Activities and jobs are not charged until clearing accounts are cleared out. Accordingly, it is important to distribute the expenses carried in the account among the various jobs and activities to which they apply and to reduce the clearing account correspondingly. It is especially important to distribute the expenses carried in the clearing accounts before the close of the year, so that all the expenses applicable to the particular year may be included as part of the cost of operations of that year. A clearing account should have no balance at the end of the fiscal year, except where the expenses charged to the account are applicable in part to the succeeding year. These balances are shown among the deferred debits on the asset side of the balance sheet.

Allocation of joint expenses. Some governmental units operate electric and water utilities under joint management. In some cases both these utilities are financed from one fund, whereas in other cases separate funds are set up for each. To insure proper accounting for each utility, it is best that each be accounted for in a separate fund. It will be assumed throughout the following discussion that this method is used, although the same governmental unit operates both utilities.

The accounting procedure for each utility is the same as for utilities which are not operated jointly. The only point to note about jointly operated utilities is the importance of allocating joint costs equitably to each enterprise. An example of such joint costs is the salary of the superintendent where the same man is in charge of both the water and the electric plant. It is usually impractical to keep a record of the time devoted by the superintendent to each utility, and therefore his salary, and other expenses which cannot be definitely allocated to either utility, must be apportioned on an arbitrary basis. For example, administrative expenses incurred jointly by both utilities might be allocated on the basis of the amount of gross revenue earned by each.

Another accounting problem that arises when the two utilities are jointly operated is occasioned by the use by one utility of the services of another. For example, assume that the water plant furnishes water to the electric plant, and the electric plant furnishes electricity to the water plant. In such cases, each utility should bill the other at cost and should record as an expense the charges for services rendered by the other. On the other hand, the plant furnishing the service should record as a revenue the amount charged to the plant using the service. The accounting procedure must be so devised that the cost of rendering this service can be readily determined.

To illustrate, assume that the water utility supplies the electric utility with water at a cost of $10,000. The transaction is recorded in each fund as follows:

ENTRY IN WATER FUND:
Due from Electric Fund.................... $10,000
    Operating Revenues...................... $10,000
To record sale of water to electric utility.

ENTRY IN ELECTRIC FUND:
Operating Expenses....................... 10,000
    Due to Water Fund......................   10,000
To record purchase of water from water utility.

Postings would be made to the proper subsidiary operating revenue accounts and operating expense accounts.

Cost units and statements. On pages 374-375 is an example of cost units used by water utilities for both maintenance and construction purposes. On the basis of the data compiled on the work orders, statements are prepared monthly or quarterly to show unit costs for various maintenance and construction activities carried on by the utility. These statements are similar to the ones illustrated in Figures 122 and 124.

In addition to the monthly or quarterly cost statements, statistical statements based on the cost data are prepared at the close of the fiscal year. Examples of some of the statements prepared by water utilities and included in their annual financial reports are given in Figures 125-129. These statements show the following: (1) cost of pumping per million gallons, (2) cost of purification per million gallons, (3) cost of transmission and distribution per million gallons pumped, (4) operating revenues, operating revenue deductions, net operating revenues, and net income, and (5) cost per foot of main laid classified by size.

Type of Work	Units of Measurement
Maintenance of Mains:	
Opening Blowoffs and Flushing Mains	No. of
Thawing Main Pipes	No. of
Locating Main Pipe Leaks	No. Located
Inspecting, Cleaning, and Oiling Main Gates	No. of
Emergency Main Shut-Offs and Turn-Ons	No. of
Repairing Main Pipes	No. of Jobs
Lowering Mains	Lineal Feet
Repairing Main Gates	No. of Jobs
Resetting and Grading Main Gate Boxes	No. of Boxes
Maintenance of Hydrants:	
Inspecting Hydrants	No. of
Flushing Hydrants	No. of
Oiling and Packing Hydrants	No. of
Thawing, Pickling, and Pumping Hydrants	No. of
Painting Hydrants	No. of
Inspecting, Cleaning, and Oiling Hydrant Gates	No. of
Repairing Hydrants	No. of Jobs
Grading and Resetting Hydrant Gate Boxes	No. of
Maintenance of Services:	
Repacking and Tightening Service Meter Connections	No. of
Cleaning Services (Cellar work)	No. of
Thawing Services	No. Thawed
Shut-Offs and Turn-Ons	No. of
Cleaning Service for Stop Boxes	No. of
Repairing Services	No. of Jobs
Lowering Service Pipes	Lineal Feet
Resetting and Grading Service Boxes	No. of
Repairing and Lighting Trenches	No. of
Maintenance of Meters:	
Flushing or Inspecting Meters on Premises	No. of
Packing or Cleaning Ground Meter Boxes	No. of
Removing or Resetting Meters or Meter Interiors	No. of
Testing Meters	No. of
Repairing Meters	No. of
Fixing Meter Parts	No. of
Construction of Mains:	
Excavation	Lineal Feet
Laying Pipe	Lineal Feet
Backfilling	Lineal Feet
Hydrants	No. of
Connections	Lineal Feet

Hydrants:
Establishing New Hydrants on Existing Mains.............. No. of
Inserting Hydrant Gates............................... No. of
Replacing Hydrants.................................... No. of
Pumping.. Millions of Gallons
Filtering... Millions of Gallons
Transmission and Distribution........................... Millions of Gallons

Figure 125

A GOVERNMENTAL UNIT

Water Works

Cost of Pumping per Million Gallons
for Fiscal Years Ending
December 31, 1946-1955

Year	Millions of Gallons Pumped	Total Cost	Cost per Million Gallons
1946	5,972.42	$ 87,867.10	$14.71
1947	6,342.16	92,006.19	14.51
1948	6,095.93	79,154.90	12.98
1949	7,730.86	107,024.78	13.84
1950	8,756.26	107,897.18	12.32
1951	7,805.63	97,013.62	12.43
1952	7,365.49	90,220.88	12.25
1953	7,872.23	93,364.14	11.86
1954	7,308.91	90,301.12	12.35
1955	7,206.26	90,072.32	12.50

Figure 126

A GOVERNMENTAL UNIT

Water Works

Cost of Purification per Million Gallons
for Fiscal Years Ending
December 31, 1946-1955

Year	Millions of Gallons Purified	Total Cost	Cost per Million Gallons
1946	4,364.74	$33,306.06	$7.63
1947	5,123.26	43,083.82	8.41
1955	6,088.30	53,340.34	8.76

Figure 127

A GOVERNMENTAL UNIT

Water Works

Cost of Transmission and Distribution per Million Gallons Pumped
for Fiscal Years Ending
December 31, 1946-1955

Year	Millions of Gallons Pumped	Total Cost	Cost per Million Gallons
1946	5,972.42	$26,517.54	$4.44
1947	6,342.16	27,271.29	4.30
1955	7,206.26	30,266.29	4.20

Figure 128

A GOVERNMENTAL UNIT

Water Works

Operating Revenues, Operating Revenue Deductions,
Net Operating Revenues, and Net Income
for Fiscal Years Ending
December 31, 1946-1955

Year	Operating Revenues	Operating Revenue Deductions	Net Operating Revenues	Net Income
1946	$444,520	$369,220	$75,300	$65,000
1947	486,000	405,900	80,100	70,000
1955	503,000	426,700	76,300	65,000

Figure 129

A GOVERNMENTAL UNIT

Water Works

Cost per Foot of Main Laid Classified by Size[1]
for Fiscal Years Ending
December 31, 1946-1955

Year	2″ No. of Feet Laid	2″ Unit Cost	4″ No. of Feet Laid	4″ Unit Cost	24″ No. of Feet Laid	24″ Unit Cost
1946	700	$1.0136	16,150	$1.3484	—	—
1947	3,405	.593	19,711	1.2061	—	—
1948	—	—	54,720	1.1623	2,147	$9.1633
1949	2,920	.7351	22,529	1.1204	—	—
1950	2,380	.653	22,548	1.1733	—	—
1951	1,510	.6056	13,330	1.0669	7,434	9.7357
1952	—	—	12,910	1.0321	—	—
1953	—	—	5,812	.8940	—	—
1954	480	.7533	—	—	—	—
1955	502	.7044	1,461	1.0921	—	—

Cost Accounting Applied to Institutions

It is beyond the scope of this book to describe in detail the cost accounting procedure for institutions. In general, however, it may be said that most of the principles and procedures described throughout this chapter apply equally to institutions. Like utilities, however, institutions use special kinds of unit costs. The following are some examples of costs incurred in the operation of a hospital and the units into which they are divided to arrive at the unit cost. While costs per patient day (one patient for one day) are given here for a hospital as a whole, in actual practice the cost per patient day would also be computed for each of the major activities carried on by the hospital, such as nursing service and medical and surgical service.

---

[1] A separate table should be prepared for each kind of pipe.

Activity	Unit
Care and treatment of patients in hospital............	Patient-day
Care and treatment of patients in clinic..............	Visit
Cost of X-ray division............................	Exposure or treatment
Cost of surgery and anesthesia (part only)............	Operating man-minutes
Ambulance service................................	Per mile and per passenger
Bakery..	Pounds baked
Laundry...	Pounds of laundry
Electricity.......................................	Kilowatt hours
Steam...	1,000 pounds
Kitchen...	Meal

College and university costs are classified by divisions, departments, and other organization units, and unit costs are obtained for each one of these units, as well as for the various activities carried on by some of them. Unit costs are usually expressed in terms of credit-hours as well as in terms of the number of full-time students enrolled. Part-time student enrollments are converted into full-time student equivalents by dividing the total number of credit hours for part-time students for the year by the number of normal credit hours per student per year. In allocating the cost of using class rooms, lecture halls, laboratories, and other space, the square foot unit is frequently used. This unit is arrived at by multiplying the number of hours the space is used by a department during the week by the number of square feet of space involved.

APPENDICES

I

SUMMARY OF ACCOUNTING PRINCIPLES AND PROCEDURES RECOMMENDED BY THE NATIONAL COMMITTEE ON GOVERNMENTAL ACCOUNTING[1]

Principles

1. A municipal accounting system must make it possible (1) to show that legal provisions have been complied with and (2) to reflect the financial condition and financial operations of the municipality.

2. If legal and sound accounting provisions conflict, legal provisions must take precedence. It is, however, the finance officer's duty to seek changes in the law which will make such law in harmony with sound accounting principles.

3. The general accounting system should be on a double-entry basis with a general ledger in which all financial transactions are recorded in detail or in summary. Additional subsidiary records should be kept where necessary.

4. Every municipality should establish the funds called for either by law or by sound financial administration. It should be recognized, however, that funds introduce an element of inflexibility in the financial system. Accordingly, consistent with legal provisions and requirements of sound financial administration, as few funds as possible should be established.

5. Depending on the legal and financial requirements mentioned immediately above, the following types of funds are recognized: (1) General, (2) Special Revenue, (3) Working Capital, (4) Special Assessment, (5) Bond, (6) Sinking, (7) Trust and Agency, and (8) Utility or Other Enterprise. This classification of funds to the extent required should be followed in the budget document and in the municipality's financial reports.

---

[1] National Committee on Governmental Accounting, *Municipal Accounting and Auditing* (Chicago: The Committee, 1951), pp. 1-3.

6. A complete balancing group of accounts should be established for each fund. This group should include all of the accounts necessary to set forth the financial condition and financial operations of the fund and to reflect compliance with legal provisions.

7. A clear segregation should be made between the accounts relating to current assets and liabilities and those relating to fixed assets and liabilities. With the exception of Working Capital, Utility or Other Enterprise, or Trust Funds, fixed assets should not be carried in the same fund with the current assets but should be set up in a self-balancing group of accounts known as the General Fixed Assets Group of Accounts. Similarly, except in Special Assessment and Utility Funds, long-term liabilities should not be carried with the current liabilities of any fund but should be shown in a separate self-balancing group of accounts forming part of the General Bonded Debt and Interest group of accounts.

8. The fixed asset accounts should be maintained on the basis of original cost, or the estimated cost if the original cost is not available, or, in the case of gifts, the appraised value at the time received.

9. Depreciation on general municipal fixed assets should not be computed unless cash for replacements can legally be set aside. Depreciation on such assets may be computed for unit cost purposes even if cash for replacements cannot legally be set aside providing these depreciation charges are used for memorandum purposes only and are not reflected in the accounts.

10. The accounting system should provide for budgetary control for both revenues and expenditures, and the financial statements should reflect, among other things, budgetary information.

11. The use of the accrual basis in accounting for revenues and expenditures is recommended to the extent applicable. Revenues, partially offset by provisions for estimated losses, should be taken into consideration when earned, even though not received in cash. Expenditures should be recorded as soon as liabilities are incurred.

12. Revenue should be classified by fund and source; and expenditures by fund, function, department, activity, character, and by main classes of objects, in accordance with standard classifications. (See the Committee's publication *A Standard Classification of Municipal Accounts*.)

13. Cost accounting systems should be established wherever costs can be measured. Each cost accounting system should provide for the recording of all the elements of cost incurred to accomplish a purpose, to carry on an activity or operation, or to complete a unit of work or a specific job. Although depreciation on general municipal fixed assets may be omitted in the general accounts and reports, it should be considered in determining unit costs if a cost accounting system is used.

14. A common terminology and classification should be used consistently throughout the budget, the accounts, and the financial reports.

Standard Procedures

1. The accounts should be centralized under the direction of one officer. He should be responsible for keeping or supervising all accounts and for preparing and issuing all financial reports.

2. A budget should be prepared by every municipality even if not required by law because such budgets are essential to the proper management of its financial affairs. A distinction between the different funds must be made in such budget.

3. As soon as purchase orders or contracts are signed, the resulting obligations

should be recorded at once as encumbrances of the funds and appropriations affected.

Inventories of both consumable and permanent property should be kept in subsidiary records controlled by accounts in the general accounting system. Physical inventories of both consumable and permanent property should be taken at least annually and the accounts and records should be made to agree with such inventories.

5. The accounting for municipal business enterprises should follow the standard classifications employed by similar private enterprises. Each college, hospital, library, and other public institution should follow the standard classification for such institutions.

6. Financial reports should be prepared monthly or oftener, to show the current condition of the budgetary accounts and other information necessary to control operations. At least once each year a general financial report should be prepared and published.

7. There should be general uniformity in the financial reports of all municipalities of similar size and type.

8. A periodic audit by independent accountants is desirable.

II

<<<<<<<<<<<<<<<<<<<<<<<<<<<<<<<<<<<<<<<<<<<<<<<<<<<<<<<<<<<<<<<<<<<<<<<

GOVERNMENTAL ACCOUNTING TERMINOLOGY[1]

(The letters "q.v." in parentheses mean "which see.")

Abatement. Complete or partial cancellation of amounts levied or of charges made for services. See **Levy.**

Accounting period. A period at the end of which and for which financial statements are prepared. See also **Fiscal period.**

Activity. A specific line of work carried on by a governmental unit in order to perform its functions, for example, "food inspection" in connection with the function of "health conservation." See also **Function.**

Actuarial basis. A basis used in computing the amount of contributions to be made periodically to a fund so that the total contributions plus the compounded earnings thereon will equal the required payments to be made out of the fund. The factors taken into account in arriving at the amount of the contribution include the length of time over which each contribution is to be held and the rate of return compounded on such contribution over its life. A Sinking Fund is an example of a fund set up on an actuarial basis.

Allot. To divide an appropriation (q.v.) into amounts for certain periods or for specific purposes.

Allotment. The amount allotted for a certain period or purpose. See also **Allot.**

Allotment ledger. A subsidiary ledger which contains an account for each allotment (q.v.) showing the amount allotted, expenditures, encumbrances, the net balance, and other related information. See also **Appropriation ledger.**

Appropriation. An authorization granted by the legislative body to make expenditures and to incur obligations for specific purposes.

Note: An appropriation is usually limited in amount and as to the time when it may be expended. See, however, **Indeterminate appropriation.**

Appropriation balance. See **Unallotted balance of appropriation, Unencum-**

---

[1] Adapted with permission from National Committee on Governmental Accounting, *Municipal Accounting and Auditing* (Chicago: The Committee, 1951), pp. 221-250.

bered balance of appropriation or allotment and **Unexpended balance of appropriation or allotment**.

Appropriation expenditure. An expenditure chargeable to an appropriation.

Appropriation expenditure ledger. See **Appropriation ledger**.

Appropriation ledger. A subsidiary ledger containing an account with each appropriation. Each account usually shows the amount originally appropriated, transfers to or from the appropriation, amounts charged against the appropriation, the net balance, and other related information. If allotments are made and a separate ledger is maintained for them, each account in the appropriation ledger usually shows the amount appropriated, transfers to or from the appropriation, the amount allotted, and the unallotted balance. See also **Allotment ledger**.

Appropriation ordinance or resolution. An ordinance (q.v.) or resolution (q.v.) by means of which appropriations are given legal effect.

Note: It is the means by which the expenditure side of the budget (a.v.) is enacted into law.

Assess. To value property officially for the purpose of taxation.

Note: The term is also sometimes used to denote the levy of taxes, but such usage is not recommended since it fails to distinguish between the valuation process and the tax levy process.

Assessed valuation. A valuation set upon real estate or other property by a government as a basis for levying taxes.

Assessment. (1) The process of making the official valuation of property for the purpose of taxation. (2) The valuation placed upon property as a result of this process.

Note: "Assessment" is sometimes used to denote the amount of taxes levied but such usage is not recommended since it fails to distinguish between the valuing process and the tax levying process. The term is also used erroneously as a synonym for "special assessment" (q.v.).

Assessment roll. In the case of real property, the official list containing the legal description of each parcel of property and its assessed valuation. In the case of other property, the official list containing the name and address of each owner of such property and its assessed value.

Note: In the case of real property, too, the name and address of the last known property owner are frequently shown. These additional facts are usually given merely for convenience, however, and are not essential to make the assessment legal.

Authority bonds. Bonds payable from the revenues of a specific public authority (q.v.). Since such authorities usually have no revenue other than charges for services, their bonds are ordinarily revenue bonds (q.v.).

Note: Such bonds differ from other revenue bonds (q.v.) in that the protections offered the bondholder, in addition to the pledges written into the bond contract, are often partially embodied in the statute which creates the authority.

Bond anticipation notes. Short-term notes of a municipality sold in anticipation of bond issuance which are full faith and credit obligations of the governmental unit and are to be retired from the proceeds of the bonds to be issued. See also **Interim borrowing**.

Bond ordinance or resolution. An ordinance (q.v.) or resolution (q.v.) authorizing a bond issue.

Bond premium. The excess of the price at which a bond is acquired or sold, over its face value.

Note: The price does not include accrued interest at the date of acquisition or sale.

Bonded debt. That portion of indebtedness represented by outstanding bonds. Note: If there are Sinking Fund bonds, this term should be replaced by "gross bonded debt" (q.v.) and "net bonded debt" (q.v.).

Bonded indebtedness. See **Bonded debt.**

Bonds issued. Bonds sold.

Budget. A plan of financial operation embodying an estimate of proposed expenditures for a given period or purpose and the proposed means of financing them.
Note: The term "budget" is used in two senses in practice. Sometimes it designates the financial plan presented to the appropriating body for adoption and sometimes the plan finally approved by that body. It is usually necessary to specify whether the budget under consideration is preliminary and tentative or whether it has been approved by the appropriating body. The term is also sometimes confused with the budget document (q.v.).

Budget document. The instrument used by the budget-making authority to present a comprehensive financial program to the appropriating body. The budget document usually consists of three parts. The first part contains a message from the budget-making authority together with a summary of the proposed expenditures and the means of financing them. The second consists of schedules supporting the summary. These schedules show in detail the proposed expenditures and means of financing them together with information as to past years' actual revenues and expenditures and other data used in making the estimates. The third part is composed of drafts of the appropriation, revenue, and borrowing measures necessary to put the budget into effect.

Budget message. A general discussion of the proposed budget presented either in writing or sometimes both orally and in writing by the budget-making authority before the legislative body. The budget message should contain an explanation of the principal budget items, an outline of the governmental unit's experience during the past period and its financial status at the time of the message, and recommendations regarding the financial policy for the coming period.

Budgetary accounts. Those accounts necessary to reflect budget operations and condition, such as estimated revenues, appropriations, and encumbrances, as distinguished from proprietary accounts. See also **Proprietary accounts.**

Budgetary control. The control or management of a governmental unit or enterprise in accordance with an approved budget with a view of keeping expenditures within the limitations of available appropriations or revenues.

Capital budget. An improvement program and the methods of its financing. Note: The term is frequently limited to a long-term budget for improvements but is sometimes also used to designate that part of the current budget (q.v.) which deals with improvements. See also **Long-term budget.**

Capital expenditures. See **Capital outlays.**

Capital outlays. Expenditures which result in the acquisition of or additions to fixed assets.

Character. As applied to an expenditure classification, this term refers to certain important groups of expenditures which are distinguished on the basis of the periods they are presumed to benefit. The three chief classes are expenses, provisions for the retirement of debt, and capital outlays. Expenses are presumed to benefit primarily the current fiscal period (but see "Note" following definition of **Expenses**). Provisions for the retirement of debt involve expenditures on account of benefits received at least in part in prior fiscal periods although their benefits may extend to the present period and future periods. Capital outlays represent expenditures for durable assets the benefit of which applies both to this fiscal period and to some subsequent period or periods. See also **Activity, Expenses, Function,** and **Object.**

Collector's roll. See **Tax roll.**

Contingent fund. Assets or other resources set aside to provide for unforeseen expenditures, or for anticipated expenditures of uncertain amount.

> Note: The term should not be used to describe a reserve for contingencies. The latter is set aside out of the unappropriated surplus of a fund but does not constitute a separate fund. Similarly, an appropriation for contingencies is not a contingent fund since an appropriation is not a fund.

Continuing appropriation. An appropriation which, once established, is automatically renewed without further legislative action, period after period, until altered or revoked.

> Note: The term should not be confused with "indeterminate appropriation" (q.v.).

Current budget. (1) The budget prepared for the succeeding fiscal year, or in the case of some state governments, the budget prepared for the succeeding biennium. (2) The budget in force during the current fiscal year or biennium.

> Note: It is assumed that the budget is prepared and adopted before the beginning of the fiscal year or biennium to which it relates.

Current resources. Resources to which recourse can be had to meet current obligations and expenditures. Examples are current assets, estimated revenues of a particular period not yet realized, transfers from other funds authorized but not received, and, in case of certain funds, bonds authorized and unissued.

Current special assessments. (1) Special assessments levied and becoming due during the current fiscal period, from the date special assessment rolls are approved by the proper authority to the date on which a penalty for non-payment is attached. (2) Special assessments levied in a prior fiscal period but becoming due in the current fiscal period, from the time they become due to the date on which a penalty for non-payment is attached.

Current taxes. (1) Taxes levied and becoming due during the current fiscal period, from the time the amount of the tax levy is first established to the date on which a penalty for non-payment is attached. (2) Taxes levied in the preceding fiscal period but becoming due in the current fiscal period, from the time they become due until a penalty for non-payment is attached.

> Note: The term is also sometimes used to designate taxes levied for the current fiscal period but such usage is not recommended.

Current year's tax levy. Taxes levied for the current fiscal period.

Debt limit. The maximum amount of gross or net debt legally permitted.

Debt service requirement. The amount of money necessary periodically to pay the interest on the outstanding debt and the principal of maturing bonded debt not payable from a Sinking Fund and to provide a fund for the redemption of bonds payable from a Sinking Fund.

Deferred special assessments. Special assessments which have been levied but are not yet due.

Delinquent special assessments. Special assessments remaining unpaid on and after the date on which a penalty for non-payment is attached.

Delinquent taxes. Taxes remaining unpaid on and after the date on which a penalty for non-payment is attached. Even though the penalty may be subsequently waived and a portion of the taxes may be abated or cancelled, the unpaid balances continue to be delinquent taxes until abated, cancelled, or converted into tax liens.

Note: The term is sometimes limited to taxes levied for the fiscal period or periods preceding the current one but such usage is not recommended. See also **Current taxes, Current year's tax levy,** and **Prior years' tax levies.**

Direct debt. The debt which a governmental unit has incurred in its own name or assumed through the annexation of territory. See also **Overlapping debt.**

Encumbrances. Obligations in the form of purchase orders, contracts, or salary commitments which are chargeable to an appropriation and for which a part of the appropriation is reserved. They cease to be encumbrances when paid or when the actual liability is set up.

Endowment fund. A fund whose principal must be maintained inviolate but whose income may be expended.

Note: An endowment fund is usually a Trust Fund and is accounted for under that category.

Estimated revenue. If the accounts are kept on an accrual basis, this term designates the amount of revenue estimated to accrue during a given period regardless of whether or not it is all to be collected during the period; if the accounts are kept on a cash basis, the term designates the amount of revenues estimated to be collected during a given period. See also **Revenue** and **Revenue receipts.**

Estimated revenue receipts. A term used synonymously with "estimated revenue" (q.v.) by some governmental units reporting their revenues on a cash basis. See also **Revenue** and **Revenue receipts.**

Estimated uncollectible taxes. A provision out of tax revenues for that part which, it is estimated, will never be collected.

Expendable fund. A fund whose resources, including both principal and earnings, may be expended. See also **Non-expendable fund.**

Expenditure disbursements. A term sometimes used by governmental units operating on a cash basis as a synonym for expenditures (q.v.).

Expenditures. If the accounts are kept on the accrual basis this term designates total charges incurred, whether paid or unpaid, including expenses, provision for retirement of debt not reported as a liability of the fund from which retired, and capital outlays. If they are kept on the cash basis, the term covers only actual disbursements for these purposes.

Note: Encumbrances are not considered expenditures.

Expenses. Charges incurred, whether paid or unpaid, for operation, maintenance, and interest, and other charges which are presumed to benefit the current fiscal period.

Note: Legal provisions sometimes make it necessary to treat as expenses charges whose benefits extend over future periods. For example, purchases of materials and supplies which may be used over a period of more than one year and payments for insurance which is to be in force for a longer period than one year frequently must be charged in their entirety to the appropriation of the year in which they are incurred and classified as expenses of that year even though their benefits extend also to other periods.

Fiscal period. Any period at the end of which a governmental unit determines its financial condition and the results of its operations and closes its books.

Note: It is usually a year, though not necessarily a calendar year.

Force account method. The employment of the governmental unit's own working forces in the making and maintaining of improvements instead of letting out the work to contractors.

Note: This method also calls for the purchase of materials by the governmental unit and the possible use of its own equipment but the principal distinguishing characteristic of the force account method is the use of the unit's own working forces.

Full faith and credit. A pledge of the general taxing power for the payment of obligations.

Note: Bonds carrying such pledges are usually referred to as "general obligation bonds" (q.v.) or "full faith and credit bonds."

Function. A group of services aimed at accomplishing a certain purpose or end; for example, public safety. See also **Activity, Character** and **Object.**

Fund. A sum of money or other resources segregated for the purpose of carrying on specific activities or attaining certain objectives in accordance with special regulations, restrictions, or limitations and constituting an independent fiscal and accounting entity.

Note: A fund is both a sum of resources and an independent accounting entity. A self-balancing group of accounts must be provided for each fund to show the assets and other resources on the one hand and obligations, surplus, and other credits on the other. Accounts must also be set up to permit the identification of revenues and expenditures and receipts and disbursements with the fund to which they apply.

Although the General Fund is available for all legally authorized purposes the definition also applies to it, for the fund can be used for governmental purposes only and expenditures cannot be made from it without legal authorization. Moreover, frequently the General Fund cannot be used for those purposes for which special funds have been established.

Fund accounts. All accounts necessary to set forth the financial operations and financial condition of a fund.

Note: Sometimes the term is used to denote budgetary accounts as distinguished from proprietary accounts but such usage is not recommended.

Fund group. A group of related funds. See **Related funds.**

Fund surplus. See **Unappropriated surplus.**

Funded debt. Same as **Bonded debt,** which is the preferred term.

Funded deficit. A deficit eliminated through the sale of bonds issued for that purpose. See also **Funding bonds.**

Funding. The conversion of judgments and other floating debt into bonded debt (q.v.).

Funding bonds. Bonds issued to retire outstanding floating debt and to eliminate deficits.

General obligation bonds. Bonds for whose payment the full faith and credit of the issuing body are pledged. More commonly, but not necessarily, general obligation bonds are considered to be those payable from taxes and other general revenues. See also **Full faith and credit.**

General obligation special assessment bonds. See **Special assessment bonds.**

Governmental accounting. The preparation, reporting, and interpretation of accounts for governmental bodies.

Grant. A contribution by one governmental unit to another unit. The contribution is usually made to aid in the support of a specified function (for example, education) but sometimes also for general purposes.

Grants in aid. See **Grant.**

Gross bonded debt. The total amount of direct debt of a governmental unit represented by outstanding bonds before deduction of Sinking Fund assets. See also **Direct debt.**

Indeterminate appropriation. An appropriation which is not limited either to any definite period of time or to any definite amount, or to both time and amount. Note: A distinction must be made between an indeterminate appropriation and a continuing appropriation. In the first place, whereas a continuing appropriation is indefinite only as to time, an indeterminate appropriation may be indefinite as to both time and amount. In the second place, even indeterminate appropriations which are indefinite only as to time are to be distinguished from continuing appropriations in that such indeterminate appropriations may eventually lapse. For example, an appropriation to construct a building may be made to continue in effect until the building is constructed. Once the building is completed, however, the unexpended balance of the appropriation lapses. A continuing appropriation, on the other hand, may continue forever; it can only be abolished by specific action of the legislative body.

Inter-fund accounts. Accounts in which transactions between funds are reflected. See **Inter-fund transfers.**

Inter-fund loans. Loans made by one fund to another.

Inter-fund transfers. Amounts transferred from one fund to another.

Interim borrowing. The sale of short-term paper in anticipation of bond issuance. See also **Bond anticipation notes.**

Judgment. An amount to be paid or collected by a governmental unit as the result of a court decision, including a condemnation award in payment for private property taken for public use.

Judgment bonds. Bonds issued to fund judgments (q.v.). See also **Funding.**

Lapse. (Verb) As applied to appropriations, this term denotes the automatic termination of an appropriation.
Note: Except for indeterminate appropriations (q.v.), and continuing appropriations (q.v.), an appropriation is made for a certain period. At the end of this period, any unexpended or unencumbered balance thereof lapses, unless otherwise provided by law.

Legal opinion. (1) The opinion of an official authorized to render it, such as an attorney general or city attorney, as to legality. (2) In the case of municipal bonds, the opinion, usually of a specialized bond attorney, as to the legality of a bond issue. A preliminary legal opinion is made in advance of the original sale of the bonds; a final opinion, after the bonds have been issued and sold.

Levy. (Verb) To impose taxes or special assessments. (Noun) The total of taxes or special assessments imposed by a governmental unit.

Long-term budget. A budget prepared for a period longer than a fiscal year, or in the case of some state governments, the budget prepared for a period longer than a biennium.
Note: Ordinarily a long-term budget is prepared for improvements and covers a period of five or more years. See also **Capital budget.**

Lump sum appropriation. An appropriation made for a stated purpose, or for a named department, without specifying further the amounts that may be spent for specific activities or for particular objects of expenditure; for example, an appropriation for the police department which does not specify the amounts to be spent for uniform patrol, traffic control, etc., or for salaries and wages, materials and supplies, travel, etc.

Net bonded debt. Gross bonded debt (q.v.) less applicable cash or other assets.

Non-expendable fund. A fund the principal, and sometimes also the earnings, of which may not be expended. See also **Endowment fund.**

Non-expenditure disbursements. Disbursements which are not chargeable as expenditures; for example, a disbursement made for the purpose of paying off an account payable previously recorded on the books.

Object. As used in an expenditure classification, this term applies to the article purchased or the service obtained (as distinguished from the results obtained from expenditures); for example, personal services, contractual services, and materials and supplies. See also **Activity, Character,** and **Function.**

Objects of expenditure. See **Object.**

Obligations. Amounts which the governmental unit may be required legally to meet out of its resources. They include not only actual liabilities but also unliquidated encumbrances.

Ordinance. A by-law of a municipality, enacted by the council or governing body as a local law. If it is not in conflict with any higher form of law, it has, within the municipal limits, the binding force of a state law.

> Note: The difference between an ordinance and a resolution (q.v.) is that the latter requires less legal formality. Ordinarily the statutes or character will specify or imply which action must be by ordinance and all other action may be by resolution.

Overlapping debt. The proportionate share of the debts of local governmental units located wholly or in part within the limits of the reporting government which must be borne by property within such government.

> Note: Except for special assessment debt, the amount of debt of each unit applicable to the reporting unit is arrived at by (1) determining what percentage of the total assessed value of the overlapping jurisdiction lies within the limits of the reporting unit, and (2) applying this percentage to the total debt of the overlapping jurisdiction. Special assessment debt is allocated on the basis of the ratio of assessments receivable in each jurisdiction which will be used wholly or in part to pay off the debt to total assessments receivable which will be used wholly or in part for this purpose.

Pay-as-you-go basis. Basis upon which a governmental unit operates when it meets its expenditures (including those for improvements) from current revenues rather than by borrowing. A governmental unit which pays for some improvements from current revenues and others by borrowing is said to be on a "partial" or "modified" pay-as-you-go basis.

Prepayment of taxes. The deposit of money with a governmental unit on condition that the amount deposited is to be applied against the tax liability of a designated taxpayer after the taxes have been levied and such liability has been established.

Prior years' tax levies. Taxes levied for fiscal periods preceding the current one.

Proportionately shared state tax. See **Shared state tax.**

Proprietary accounts. Those accounts which show actual financial condition and operations such as actual assets, liabilities, reserves, surplus, revenues, and expenditures, as distinguished from budgetary accounts (q.v.).

Public authority. A public agency usually created to perform a single function which is financed from tolls or fees charged those using the facilities operated by the agency; for example, a bridge or tunnel authority.

Rebates. Abatements (q.v.) or refunds.

Receipts. The term indicates cash received, unless otherwise qualified.

Recoverable expenditure. An expenditure made for or on behalf of another governmental unit, fund, or department, or for a private individual, firm, or corporation, which will subsequently be recovered in cash or its equivalent.

Registered warrant. A warrant which is registered by the paying officer for future payment on account of present lack of funds and which is to be paid in the order of its registration. In some cases, such warrants are registered when issued; in others, when first presented to the paying officer by the holders. See **Warrant.**

Reimbursable expenditure. See **Recoverable expenditure.**

Reimbursement. Cash or other assets received as a repayment of the cost of work or services performed, or of other expenditures made for or on behalf of another governmental unit, or department, or for an individual, firm, or corporation.

Related funds. Funds of a similar character which are brought together for administrative and reporting purposes; for example, Sinking Funds.

Reserve. An account set up to indicate the segregation of surplus to meet contingent liabilities or other segregations of surplus.

Reserve for encumbrances. A reserve representing the segregation of surplus to provide for unliquidated encumbrances (q.v.). See **Reserve.**

Reserve for retirement of sinking fund bonds. A reserve (q.v.) which indicates the amount of cash and other resources which should have been accumulated at a certain date in order eventually to redeem bonds outstanding.

Note: In a Utility or Other Enterprise Fund, the reserve may equal the actual resources in the fund rather than the amount which should have been accumulated, since a Utility or Other Enterprise Fund is accounted for in the same manner as a like private enterprise. However, the amount which should have been accumulated should also be shown on the balance sheet either in parentheses following the reserve account or in a footnote.

Reserve for uncollectible taxes. See **Estimated uncollectible taxes.**

Resolution. A special or temporary order of a legislative body; an order of a legislative body requiring less legal formality than an ordinance.

Note: For a fuller discussion of the distinction between a resolution and an ordinance, see **Ordinance.**

Revenue. The increase in ownership equity during a designated period of time. If the accounts are kept on an accrual basis, this term designates additions to assets which do not increase any liability, nor represent the recovery of an expenditure, and the cancellation of liabilities without a corresponding increase in other liabilities or a decrease in assets. The same definition applies in its entirety to those cases where the accounts are kept on a cash basis except that the additions must be to cash only.

Revenue bonds. Bonds the principal of and interest on which are to be paid solely from earnings, usually those of a municipally owned utility or other public service enterprise the revenues and possibly the properties of which are pledged for this purpose.

Revenue receipts. A term used by some governmental units reporting their revenues on a cash basis synonymously with "revenue" (q.v.).

Self-supporting or self-liquidating debt. Debt obligations whose principal and interest are payable primarily or solely from the earnings of the municipal utility or enterprise for the construction or improvement of which they were originally issued.

Shared state tax. A specific state-imposed tax shared with local governments in proportion, or substantially in proportion, to the amount of tax collected or produced in each local unit. The tax may be collected either by the state in the first instance and shared with the localities or collected locally and shared with the state.

Sinking fund bonds. Bonds issued under an agreement which requires the governmental unit to set aside periodically, ordinarily out of its revenues, a sum which, with earnings thereon, will be sufficient to redeem the bonds at their stated date of maturity.

Note: Sinking Fund bonds are usually also term bonds.

Sinking fund requirements. The amount by which a Sinking Fund must be increased periodically through contributions and earnings so that the accumulation thereof will be sufficient to redeem Sinking Fund bonds as they mature.

Note: The amount required periodically should be calculated on an actuarial basis unless another basis is provided by law.

Sinking fund reserve. See **Reserve for retirement of sinking fund bonds.**

Special assessment. A compulsory levy made by a local government against certain properties to defray part or all of the cost of a specific improvement or service which is presumed to be of general benefit to the public and of special benefit to the owners of such properties.

Note: The term should not be used without a modifier (for example, "special assessments for improvements" or "special assessments for street sprinkling") unless the intention is to have it cover both improvements and services or unless the particular use is apparent from the context.

Special assessment bonds. Bonds payable from the proceeds of special assessments (q.v.). If the bonds are payable only from the collections of special assessments, they are known as "special-special assessment bonds." If, in addition to the assessments, the full faith and credit of the governmental unit is pledged, they are known as "general obligation special assessment bonds."

Special assessment liens. Claims which governmental units have upon properties until special assessments (q.v.) levied against them have been paid.

Note: The term is sometimes limited to those delinquent special assessments for the collection of which legal action has been taken through the filing of liens.

Special assessment roll. The official list showing the amount of special assessments (q.v.) levied against each property presumed to be benefited by an improvement or service.

Special district bonds. Bonds of a local taxing district which has been organized for a special purpose, such as road, sewer, fire, drainage, irrigation, and levee districts.

Special fund. Any fund which must be devoted to some special use in accordance with specific regulations and restrictions.

Note: The term applies to all funds other than the General Fund.

Special lien bonds. Special assessment bonds which are liens against particular pieces of property.

Special-special assessment bonds. See **Special assessment bonds.**

State-collected, locally shared tax. See **Shared state tax.**

Tax anticipation notes. Notes (sometimes called "warrants") issued in anticipation of collection of taxes, usually retirable only from tax collections, and frequently only from the proceeds of the tax levy whose collection they anticipate.

Tax anticipation warrants. See **Tax anticipation notes.**

Tax certificate. A certificate issued by a governmental unit as evidence of the conditional transfer of title to tax delinquent property from the original owner to the holder of the certificate. If the owner does not pay the amount of the tax arrearage and other charges required by law during the specified period of redemption, the holder can foreclose to obtain title. Also called in some jurisdictions "tax sale certificate" and "tax lien certificate." See also **Tax deed.**

Tax deed. A written instrument under seal by which title to property sold for taxes is transferred unconditionally to the purchaser. A tax deed is issued upon foreclosure of the tax lien (q.v.) obtained by the purchaser at the tax sale. The lien can not be foreclosed until the expiration of the period during which the owner may redeem his property through paying the delinquent taxes and other charges. See also **Tax certificate.**

Tax levy ordinance or resolution. An ordinance (q.v.) or resolution (q.v.) by means of which taxes are levied.

Tax liens. Claims which governmental units have upon properties until taxes levied against them have been paid.

> Note: The term is sometimes limited to those delinquent taxes for the collection of which legal action has been taken through the filing of liens.

Tax limit. The maximum rate or amount of general property tax which a local government may levy. The limit may apply to taxes raised for a particular purpose, or to taxes raised for all purposes, and may apply to a single government, to a class of governments, or to all governments operating in a particular area. Over-all tax limits usually restrict levies for all purposes and of all governments, state and local, having jurisdiction within a given area.

Tax notes. See **Tax anticipation notes.**

Tax rate. The amount of tax stated in terms of a unit of the tax base; for example, 25 mills per dollar of assessed valuation.

Tax roll. The official list showing the amount of taxes levied against each taxpayer or property.

> Note: Frequently the tax roll and assessment roll (q.v.) are combined but even in these cases the two can be distinguished.

Tax title notes. Obligations secured by pledges of the governmental unit's interest in certain tax liens or tax titles.

Taxes. Compulsory charges levied by a governmental unit for the purpose of financing services performed for the common benefit.

> Note: The term does not include specific charges made against particular persons or property for current or permanent benefits, as, for example, special assessments. Neither does the term include charges for privileges accruing only to those paying such charges, as, for example, licenses and permits.

Taxes collected in advance. Taxes collected before the tax levy has been made or before the liability of the taxpayer has been established.

Taxes levied for other governmental units. Taxes levied by the reporting government for other governmental units which when collected are to be paid over to these units.

Taxes receivable. The uncollected portion of taxes which a governmental unit has levied.

Unallotted balance of appropriation. An appropriation balance available for allotment (q.v.).

Unappropriated budget surplus. If the balance of unappropriated surplus at the close of the preceding year is not included in the budget, the term designates that portion of the current fiscal year's estimated revenues which has not been appropriated. If the balance is included, the term is synonymous with unappropriated surplus (q.v.).

Unappropriated surplus. That portion of the surplus of a given fund which is not segregated for specific purposes.

Unencumbered allotment. See **Unencumbered balance of appropriation or allotment.**

Unencumbered appropriation. See **Unencumbered balance of appropriation or allotment.**

Unencumbered balance of appropriation or allotment. That portion of an appropriation or allotment not yet expended or encumbered; the balance remaining after deducting from the appropriation or allotment the accumulated expenditures and outstanding encumbrances.

Unexpended appropriation. See **Unexpended balance of appropriation or allotment.**

Unexpended balance of appropriation or allotment. That portion of an appropriation or allotment which has not been expended; the balance remaining after deducting from the appropriation or allotment the accumulated expenditures.

Warrant. (1) An order drawn by the legislative body or an officer of a governmental unit upon its treasurer directing the latter to pay a specified amount to the person named or to the bearer. It may be payable upon demand, in which case it usually circulates the same as a bank check; or, it may be payable only out of certain revenues when and if received, in which case it does not circulate as freely. (2) An order for the treasurer to receive money. See also **Registered warrant.**

Warrants payable. The amount of warrants outstanding and unpaid.

Work program. A plan of the work proposed to be done during a particular period by a department or other agency. The work program is useful both in planning and in executing the budget since it provides a basis for making expenditure estimates. The program usually contains not only estimates of proposed work but also data concerning work done in preceding years on which the estimates are partly based.

III

‹‹‹

BIBLIOGRAPHY

Chapter 1. Principles and Standards of Governmental Accounting

1. "Financial Organization," *Municipal Finance*, November 1942, entire issue.
2. Frisbee, Ira N., "The Application of Governmental Accounting Principles to Practice," *Accounting Review*, March 1939, 14:27-33.
3. James, Robert M., "Three Major Concepts in Governmental Accounting Theory," *Accounting Review*, July 1950, 25:307-314.
4. Lowery, Joseph M., "The National Committee on Governmental Accounting," *Municipal Finance*, February 1951, 23:120-123.
5. Municipal Finance Officers Association, *County Finance and Accounting Standards*. Chicago: The Association, 1937. 35 pp.
6. ———, *Standard Practice in Municipal Accounting and Financial Procedure*. Chicago: The Association, 1943. 26 pp.
7. Nelson, Oscar S., "Trends and Problems in Governmental and Institutional Accounting," *Accounting Review*, April 1951, 26:179-184.
8. Tenner, Irving, "Recent Developments in Municipal Accounting," *Municipal Finance*, November 1951, 24:71-77.

Chapter 2. Classification of Accounts

1. Aten, Murl K., "Uniform Classification of Accounts," *Municipal Finance*, August 1950, 23:46-48.
2. Kilpatrick, Wylie, "Classification and Measurement of Public Expenditures," *Annals of the American Academy of Political and Social Science*, January 1936, 183:19-26.
3. Lorig, Arthur N., "Classification of Municipal Income and Expenditures," *Accounting Review*, June 1937, 12:163-173.
4. National Committee on Governmental Accounting, *A Standard Classification of Municipal Accounts*. Chicago: The Committee, 1953. 129 pp.
5. Public Administration Service, *Handbook of Financial Administration, Commonwealth of Kentucky*. Chicago: The Service, 1937, pp. 279-313.
6. ———, *Report on Financial Administration in the Michigan State Government*. Chicago: The Service, 1938, pp. 427-482.
7. Tenner, Irving, "Revised Classification of Accounts," *Municipal Finance*, February 1953, 25:106-110.

Chapter 3. Budgeting

1. Alex, Robert P., "Annual Budget Based on Unit Costs of Services Provided," *Public Management*, October 1949, 31:277-278.
2. Brighton, Gerald R., "Application of Cost Accounting to Budgeting," *Municipal Finance*, February 1950, 22:123-128.
3. "Budget Procedures," *Municipal Finance*, February 1941, entire issue.
4. Donaho, John A., "The Performance Budget," *Municipal Finance*, February 1950, 22:103-106.
5. ———, "Financial Planning for Governments," *Municipal Finance*, February 1949, entire issue.
6. Municipal Finance Officers Association, *County Finance and Accounting Standards*. Chicago: The Association, 1937, pp. 4-9.
7. ———, *Municipal Budget Procedure and Budgetary Accounting*. Chicago: The Association, 1942. 100 pp.
8. ———, *Standard Practice in Municipal Accounting and Financial Procedure*. Chicago: The Association, 1943, pp. 2-6.
9. Tenner, Irving, "Justifying Budgetary Requests," *Public Management*, October 1946, 28:297-299.
10. Uniform Accounting Committee, League of California Municipalities, *Budgeting for California Municipalities*. Los Angeles: The League, 1939. 107 pp.

Chapter 4. The General Fund Balance Sheet

1. Lowery, Joseph M., "Surplus in a Municipal Balance Sheet," *Municipal Finance*, February 1940, 12:22-25.
2. Municipal Finance Officers Association, *Accounting Manual for Texas Cities and Towns*. Chicago: The Association, 1938, pp. 54-62.
3. National Committee on Governmental Accounting, *Municipal Accounting and Auditing*. Chicago: The Committee, 1951, pp. 19-29.
4. Public Administration Service, *Report on Financial Administration in the Michigan State Government*. Chicago: The Service, 1938, pp. 33-34.
5. Rowland, Charles J., "Surplus in Municipal Balance Sheets," *Municipal Finance*, February 1945, 17:20-23.
6. Tenner, Irving, "Reserves in Municipal Balance Sheets," *Municipal Finance*, February 1945, 17:9-12.
7. Wasser, Max, "Terms 'Surplus' and 'Reserves' as Applied to Non-Profit Institutions," *New York Certified Public Accountant*, October 1952, 22:617-618.

Chapter 5. General Fund Revenues

1. Lorig, Arthur N., *Accounting Manual for Small Cities of the State of Washington*. Olympia: Division of Municipal Corporations of the Office of State Auditor, 1945, pp. 16-21.
2. Municipal Finance Officers Association, *Manual of Accounting and Financial Procedure in the Office of the Controller of the City and County of San Francisco, California*. Chicago: The Association, 1938, pp. 99-114.
3. National Committee on Governmental Accounting, *A Standard Classification of Municipal Accounts*. Chicago: The Committee, 1953, pp. 37-62.
4. New York City Comptroller, *Manual of Revenue Accounts; Finding List*. New York: The Comptroller, 1942. 40 pp.

5. Uniform Accounting Committee, League of California Municipalities, *Manual of Accounting Procedures for California Municipalities*. Los Angeles: The League, 1939, pp. 45-48.

Chapter 6.   General Fund Expenditures

1. Hunter, Joel, "Expenditure Accounting for Smaller Counties and Cities," *Journal of Accountancy*, July 1941, 72:17-21.
2. Larson, Philip E., "County Accounting and Travel Expense," *New Mexico Tax Bulletin*, July 1942, 21:109-111.
3. Lorig, Arthur N., *Accounting Manual for Small Cities of the State of Washington*. Olympia: Division of Municipal Corporations of the Office of State Auditor, 1945, pp. 48-72.
4. Municipal Finance Officers Association, *Accounting for Governmental Supplies*. Chicago: The Association, 1940. 60 pp.
5. ————, *Governmental Timekeeping and Payroll Procedure*. Chicago: The Association, 1940. 62 pp.
6. National Committee on Governmental Accounting, *A Standard Classification of Municipal Accounts*. Chicago: The Committee, 1953, pp. 63-116.
7. Sherman, William, "Suggested Procedure in Small Municipalities to Account for Payroll Deductions," *Minnesota Municipalities*, December 1942, 27:419-422.
8. Stone, Donald C., *The Management of Municipal Public Works*. Chicago: Public Administration Service, 1939, pp. 126-174.
9. Uniform Accounting Committee, League of California Municipalities, *Manual of Accounting Procedures for California Municipalities*. Los Angeles: The League, 1939, pp. 49-52.

Chapter 7.   Bond Funds

1. Borge, Michael, "General Obligation Municipal Bonds—Legal Aspects," *Municipal Finance*, May 1953, 25:144-148.
2. Dietrich, O. A., "Accounting for Serial Bond Issues," *Municipal Finance*, February 1948, 20:11-13.
3. Ellinwood, David M., "Preparing Municipal Bonds for Public Sale," *Municipal Finance*, August 1947, 20:56-60.
4. Municipal Finance Officers Association, *Accounting Manual for Texas Cities and Towns*. Chicago: The Association, 1938, pp. 70-75.
5. National Committee on Governmental Accounting, *Municipal Accounting and Auditing*. Chicago: The Committee, 1951, pp. 72-83.

Chapter 8.   Special Assessment Funds

1. Chatters, Carl H., and Albert M. Hillhouse, *Local Government Debt Administration*. New York: Prentice-Hall, Inc., 1939, pp. 187-240.
2. Johnson, William J., "Special Assessments," *Municipal Finance*, August 1947, 20:10-13.
3. Lindsay, John R., "Committee Report: Committee on Special Assessments," *Municipal Finance*, August 1940, 13:48-53.
4. Lorig, Arthur N., *Accounting Manual for Small Cities of the State of Washington*. Olympia: Division of Municipal Corporations of the Office of State Auditor, 1945, pp. 10-11, 92-96, and 140-148.

5. National Committee on Governmental Accounting, *Municipal Accounting and Auditing.* Chicago: The Committee, 1951, pp. 54-72.
6. Russell, Henry E., "Financing School Facilities," *Municipal Finance,* May 1953, 25:148-151.

Chapter 9. Sinking Funds

1. Chatters, Carl H., and Albert M. Hillhouse, *Local Government Debt Administration.* New York: Prentice-Hall, Inc., 1939, pp. 119-164.
2. Funk, Robert L., "Permissive Legislation Regarding Investment of Government Funds," *Municipal Finance,* February 1953, 25:111-119.
3. Hurless, Virgil H., "A Large City's Investment Practices," *Municipal Finance,* February 1953, 25:122-124.
4. Johns, Ralph S., "A Plan for Pooling the Investments of Endowment Funds," *Journal of Accountancy,* January 1939, 67:31-37. (Comments in subsequent two issues, February 1939, pp. 91-93; March 1939, pp. 166-170.)
5. Johnson, A. R., "Investment of Retirement Funds," *Municipal Finance,* February 1953, 25:125-129.
6. Lillywhite, Ray L., "Investment of Public Funds in Wisconsin," *Municipal Finance,* February 1953, 25:130-136.
7. Municipal Finance Officers Association, *Accounting Manual for Texas Cities and Towns.* Chicago: The Association, 1938, pp. 76-80.
8. National Committee on Governmental Accounting, *Municipal Accounting and Auditing.* Chicago: The Committee, 1951, pp. 84-94.

Chapter 10. Trust and Agency Funds

1. Meyers, Arthur C. Jr., *Criteria for Evaluating Retirement Systems for Public Employees.* Chicago: Municipal Finance Officers' Association, September, 1953. 8 pp.
2. Mucklow, Walter, *Cemetery Accounts.* New York: American Institute Publishing Company, 1935. 208 pp.
3. National Committee on Governmental Accounting, *Municipal Accounting and Auditing.* Chicago: The Committee, 1951, pp. 95-105.
4. "Retirement Systems," *Municipal Finance,* February 1944, entire issue.

Chapter 11. Working Capital Funds

1. Aho, Jarl W., "Effective Use of Working Capital Funds," *Municipal Finance,* November 1952, 25:95-97.
2. Lorig, Arthur N., *Accounting Manual for Small Cities of the State of Washington.* Olympia: Division of Municipal Corporations of the Office of State Auditor, 1945, pp. 9-10.
3. Municipal Finance Officers Association, *Accounting for Government-Owned Motor Equipment.* Chicago: The Association, 1940. 60 pp.
4. ———, *Accounting for Governmental Supplies.* Chicago: The Association, 1940. 60 pp.
5. National Committee on Governmental Accounting, *Municipal Accounting and Auditing.* Chicago: The Committee, 1951, pp. 42-53.
6. Stone, Donald C., *The Management of Municipal Public Works.* Chicago: Public Administration Service, 1939, pp. 101-110.

Chapter 12.   Utility or Other Enterprise Funds

1. Baker, Harold L., "Municipal Accounting Methods for Off-Street Parking Facilities," *Municipal Finance*, February 1948, 20:29-32.
2. Cooper, Nathan B., "Financial Control and Administration of Municipal Enterprises," *Municipal Finance*, November 1951, 24:92-97.
3. Federal Power Commission, *Uniform System of Accounts Prescribed for Public Utilities and Licensees*. Washington: Government Printing Office, 1937, pp. 12-36, 84-152.
4. ———, *Uniform System of Accounts Prescribed for Public Utilities and Licensees*, Appendix III, "Application of Uniform System of Accounts to Class C and Class D Public Utilities and Licensees." Washington: The Commission, 1938, pp. 6-9, 14-27.
5. Foster, J. Rhoads, and Bernard S. Rodey, Jr., *Public Utility Accounting*. New York: Prentice-Hall, Inc., 1951. 690 pp.
6. Municipal Finance Officers Association and American Water Works Association, *Manual of Water Works Accounting*. Chicago and New York: The Associations, 1938. 483 pp.
7. "Municipal Utility Accounting," *Municipal Finance*, August 1945, entire issue.
8. National Committee on Governmental Accounting, *Municipal Accounting and Auditing*. Chicago: The Committee, 1951, pp. 105-125.
9. New York State Public Service Commission, *Uniform System of Accounts for Municipal Electric Utilities*. Albany: The Commission, 1936, pp. 34-52, 91-155.
10. Public Service Commission of Kentucky, *Uniform System of Accounts for Municipal Water Utilities*. Frankfort: The Commission, 1936, pp. 28-41, 62-65.
11. "Revenue Bonds," *Municipal Finance*, May 1949, entire issue.
12. Tenner, Irving, *Financial Administration of Municipal Utilities*. Chicago: Public Administration Service, 1947. 152 pp.
13. ———, "Principles of Municipal Utility Accounting," *Municipal Finance*, February 1948, 20:25-29.

Chapter 13.   General Fixed Assets. General Bonded Debt and Interest. Inter-Fund Relationships

1. Appleby, H. G., "Accounting for Property and Equipment," *Municipal Finance*, August 1949, 22:42-45.
2. Gucfa, Sigmund J., and Douglas M. Lasher, "Real Estate Acquisition and Accounting," *Municipal Finance*, May 1950, 22:146-149.
3. James, Robert M., "Interrelationships in Governmental Accounting Theory," *The Accounting Review*, January 1951, 26:88-92.
4. Magraw, Daniel B., and Charles Redfield, "Budgeting for Fixed Assets," *Municipal Finance*, February 1949, 21:20-22.
5. Municipal Finance Officers Association, *Accounting for Public Property*. Chicago: The Association, 1939. 42 pp.
6. National Committee on Governmental Accounting, *Municipal Accounting and Auditing*. Chicago: The Committee, 1951, pp. 126-140.
7. Tobin, Benjamin J., "General Fixed Assets in Municipal Balance Sheets," *Municipal Finance*, February 1945, 17:16-19.

Chapter 14. Cash

1. Bittner, Frank, "Interest Earnings on Liquid Funds," *Municipal Finance*, November 1948, 21:28-32.
2. Faust, Martin L., *The Security of Public Deposits*. Chicago: Public Administration Service, 1936. 45 pp.
3. Municipal Finance Officers Association, *Accounting Manual for Missouri Cities and Towns*. Chicago: The Association, 1938, pp. 25-28.
4. —— and American Water Works Association, *Manual of Water Works Accounting*. Chicago and New York: The Associations, 1938, pp. 293-303.
5. "Municipal Treasury Management," *Municipal Finance*, February 1942, entire issue.
6. Olson, Gustav E., "Accounting for Parking Meters," *Municipal Finance*, May 1950, 22:150-154.

Chapter 15. General Property Taxes

1. "Advantages of Unit Tax Ledger Accepted in Counties of Arkansas," *American City*, July 1945, 60:93.
2. Crawford, K. Grant, "Prepayment Discounts and Penalties on Tax Delinquents," *Municipal Finance*, February 1947, 19:12-16.
3. Holt, Horace H., Jr., and Edwin W. Murray, "Accounting for Real Estate Taxes," *Municipal Finance*, November 1949, 22:56-60.
4. McQueen, D. D., "Municipal District Tax Accounting," *Municipal Finance*, May 1947, 19:23-27.
5. Ruston, C. E., "Delinquent Tax and Tax Sale Certificate Procedure," *Municipal Finance*, February 1947, 19:17-19.
6. Tobin, Benjamin J., "Accounting for Tax-Foreclosed Real Estate in the City of Detroit," *Municipal Finance*, February 1947, 19:20-24.
7. Whitley, W. Raymond, "New Tax Billing Procedure," *Municipal Finance*, November 1947, 20:23-26.

Chapter 16. Fixed Assets

1. Federal Power Commission, *Uniform System of Accounts Prescribed for Public Utilities and Licensees*. Washington: Government Printing Office, 1937, pp. 37-83.
2. ——, *Uniform System of Accounts Prescribed for Public Utilities and Licensees*, Appendix III, "Application of Uniform System of Accounts to Class C and Class D Public Utilities and Licensees." Washington: The Commission, 1938, pp. 10-12.
3. Gotaas, Harold B., "Physical Property Cards," *Journal of the American Water Works Association*, March 1939, 31:517-525.
4. ——, "Use of Property Ledgers in City Departments," *American City*, July 1939, 54:44-46, 72-73.
5. Municipal Finance Officers Association, *Accounting for Government-Owned Motor Equipment*. Chicago: The Association, 1940. 60 pp.
6. ——, *Accounting for Public Property*. Chicago: The Association, 1939. 42 pp.
7. —— and American Water Works Association, *Manual of Water Works*

Accounting. Chicago and New York: The Associations, 1938, pp. 217-226, 340-360.

8. National Association of Railroad and Utilities Commissioners, *List of Retirement Units for Electric Utilities.* New York: State Law Reporting Company, 1937. 24 pp.

9. ———, *Report of Special Committee on Depreciation: Depreciation Principles and Methods.* New York: State Law Reporting Company, 1938. 85 pp.

10. Tenner, Irving, "Depreciation Accounting for Municipal Property," *Public Management,* October 1942, 24:305-306.

11. ———, *Financial Administration of Municipal Utilities.* Chicago: Public Administration Service, 1947, pp. 110-123.

Chapter 17.   Liabilities

1. Chatters, Carl H., and Albert M. Hillhouse, *Local Government Debt Administration.* New York: Prentice-Hall, Inc., 1939, pp. 8-118, 165-186, 241-291.

2. Ellinwood, David M., "Preparing Municipal Bonds for Public Sale," *Municipal Finance,* August 1947, 20:56-60.

3. Hagerman, Earl E., "Programming Bond Issues," *Municipal Finance,* August 1948, 21:63-64.

4. "Revenue Bonds," *Municipal Finance,* May 1949, entire issue.

5. Seaholm, W. E., "Adoption of an Accounts Payable Fund Reduces Check-Writing by One-Third, Austin, Texas," *American City,* November 1945, 60:109.

6. Tenner, Irving, *Financial Administration of Municipal Utilities.* Chicago: Public Administration Service, 1947, pp. 45-60.

7. "The Finance Officer and Municipal Bonds," *Municipal Finance,* May 1953, entire issue.

Chapter 18.   Auditing and Financial Reporting

1. "Auditing Public Accounts," *Municipal Finance,* November 1941, entire issue.

2. "Financial Reports of Governments," *Municipal Finance,* May 1941, entire issue.

3. James, Robert M., "Some Aspects of a Governmental Audit," *The Accounting Review,* July 1951, 26:347-351.

4. Lafferty, George W., "Influences of Law on the Auditor in the Examination of Local Government Accounts," *Journal of Accountancy,* August 1950, 90:122-26.

5. Morey, Lloyd, "A Forward Look in Municipal Accounting," *Municipal Finance,* February 1948, 20:3-8.

6. ———, "Municipal Audits," *Illinois Certified Public Accountant,* December 1950, 13:33-39.

7. ———, "Toward a Common Language," *Municipal Finance,* February 1951, 23:104-109.

8. Municipal Finance Officers Association, and American Water Works Association, *Manual of Water Works Accounting.* Chicago and New York: The Associations, 1938, pp. 387-425.

9. National Committee on Governmental Accounting, *Municipal Accounting and Auditing.* Chicago: The Committee, 1951, pp. 185-220.

10. Tenner, Irving, "Accounting Services to Governmental Units," *Illinois Certified Public Accountant*, September 1951, 14:14-18.
11. ———, "Improving the Financial Report," *Municipal Finance*, February 1951, 23:109-113.
12. Tobin, Benjamin J., "Auditing the Welfare Department," *Municipal Finance*, May 1950, 22:154-160.

List of Reports. In addition to the references on reporting just cited, the following should prove helpful to an understanding of governmental reporting. These reports have received certificates of conformance from the Municipal Finance Officers Association as evidence of their complying with the recommendations of the National Committee on Governmental Accounting. Copies can ordinarily be secured by writing to the finance officer.

States and Territories

State of Michigan
State of Rhode Island
Territory of Hawaii

Cities

Barrington, Rhode Island
Beloit, Wisconsin
Berkeley, California
Dallas, Texas
Detroit, Michigan
Gainesville, Florida
Harrisonburg, Virginia
Honolulu, Hawaii
Kansas City, Missouri
New Haven, Connecticut
Oakland, California
Pontiac, Michigan
Richmond, Virginia
Saginaw, Michigan
San Diego, California
San Jose, California
Stockton, California
University City, Missouri

Counties

Jackson County, Missouri
Montgomery County, Maryland
San Diego County, California

Other Units

Buffalo Sewer Authority, Buffalo, New York
Chicago Park District, Chicago, Illinois
Knoxville Utilities Board, Knoxville, Tennessee

Chapter 19. Accounting for Hospitals

1. American Hospital Association, *Handbook on Accounting, Statistics and Business Office Procedures for Hospitals. Section 1: Uniform Hospital Statistics and Classifications of Accounts*. Chicago: The Association, 1950. 155 pp.

2. Dawson, William A., "The Ratio Control System for Hospitals," *Journal of Accountancy*, February 1940, 69:112-113.
3. Harris, Walter O., *Institutional Cost Accounting*. Chicago: Public Administration Service, 1944. 153 pp.
4. Martin, T. Leroy, *Hospital Accounting Principles and Practices*. Chicago: Physicians' Record Co., 1951. 230 pp.
5. Rorem, C. Rufus, "Hospital Accounting," in *How to Improve Accounting and Tax Service to American Business*. New York: American Institute of Accountants, 1950, pp. 145-156.
6. Roswell, Charles G., *Accounting, Statistics and Business Office Procedures for Hospitals*. New York: United Hospital Fund of New York, 1946. 287 pp.
7. Weiner, Julian S. H., "Inclusion of Depreciation of Hospital Plant and Equipment with Operating Costs," *New York Certified Public Accountant*, August 1951, 21:551-554.

Chapter 20.   Accounting for Colleges and Universities

1. Baldassare, Ernest W., "Reasons Why University Accounting Must Differ from Conventional Commercial Accounting," *Journal of Accountancy*, August 1949, 88:111-120.
2. Daines, Harvey C., "Theory and Procedure for Pooled Investments in Colleges and Universities," *Journal of Accountancy*, February 1940, 69:114-130.
3. Fields, Francis X., "Allocation of University Endowment Fund Income," *New York Certified Public Accountant*, October 1952, 22:614-616.
4. McGladrey, Ira B., "Something Is Wrong with College Financial Reports," *Journal of Accountancy*, August 1949, 88:103-110.
5. Morey, Lloyd, "Better Application of Recognized Principles Would Improve University Accounting," *Journal of Accountancy*, September 1950, 90:201-210.
6. National Committee on the Preparation of a Manual on College and University Business Administration, *College and University Business Administration*. Washington: American Council on Education, 1952. 217 pp.
7. Scheps, Clarence, *Accounting for Colleges and Universities*. Baton Rouge: Louisiana State University Press, 1949. 391 pp.
8. Sherer, Harvey, "Modern Trends in Financial Reporting for Colleges and Universities Are Revealed in a Study of Reporting Practices over Past 20 Years," *Journal of Accountancy*, September 1950, 90:211-212.
9. Withey, Howard A., "Budgetary Control for Colleges and Universities," *New York Certified Public Accountant*, August 1951, 21:542-547.

Chapter 21.   Cost Accounting

1. Baldwin, Emma V., and William E. Marcus, *A Study of Cost Accounting in Public Libraries*. New York: R. R. Bowker Co., 1941. 201 pp.
2. "Cost Accounting," *Municipal Finance*, February 1950, entire issue.
3. Cranch, E. T., "Public Works—Good Service at Low Cost," *Municipal Finance*, November 1948, 21:18-24.
4. Dreher, Richard G., "Cost Accounting—A Managerial Aid," *Public Management*, May 1952, 34:101-105.
5. Kimpel, H. M., "Cost Accounting for Municipalities," *Municipal Finance*, May 1944, 16:30-32.
6. Nelson, W. Porter, "How a Cost Accounting System Is Installed in a Govern-

mental Organization by Independent CPA's," *Journal of Accountancy*, October 1951, 92:456-460.

7. Riehl, E. P., "Potential Cost Accounting Applications," *Municipal Finance*, August 1948, 20:53-56.

8. Roberts, Samuel M., "Management Responsibility for Cost Accounting," *Municipal Finance*, February 1948, 20:14-18.

9. Sedgwick, R. M., "Cost Accounting for Water Utilities," *Journal of the American Water Works Association*, April 1942, 34:564-568.

10. Washburn, Earle L., "Institutional Unit Costs, *"New York Certified Public Accountant,* October 1952, 22:606-608.

List of Periodicals Cited

1. *Accounting Review* (quarterly). American Accounting Association, University of Illinois, Urbana, Illinois.

2. *American City* (monthly). American City Magazine Corporation, 470 Fourth Avenue, New York 16, New York.

3. *Illinois Certified Public Accountant* (quarterly). Illinois Society of Certified Public Accountants, 208 South LaSalle Street, Chicago 4, Illinois.

4. *Journal of Accountancy* (monthly). American Institute Publishing Company, Inc., 270 Madison Avenue, New York 16, New York.

5. *Journal of the American Water Works Association* (monthly). 22 East 40th Street, New York, New York.

6. *Municipal Finance* (quarterly). Municipal Finance Officers Association, 1313 East 60th Street, Chicago 37, Illinois.

7. *New York Certified Public Accountant* (monthly). New York Society of Certified Public Accountants, 677 Fifth Avenue, New York 22, New York.

8. *Public Management* (monthly). International City Managers' Association, 1313 East 60th Street, Chicago 37, Illinois.

IV

<<<<<<<<<<<<<<<<<<<<<<<<<<<<<<<<<<<<<<<<<<<<<<<<<<<

QUESTIONS AND PROBLEMS

Questions and Problems on Chapter 1

Questions

Question 1-1. Assume that a bond indenture requires that sinking fund income should be credited to a sinking fund reserve. Should such income be included in the profit and loss statement prepared for a business or should it be credited directly to the sinking fund reserve?

Question 1-2. The following are names of funds encountered in governmental reports and the purposes for which these funds have been set up. You are required to indicate the corresponding fund name recommended by the National Committee on Governmental Accounting.

1. School fund (to account for special taxes levied to finance the operation of schools).

2. Bond redemption fund (to account for taxes and other revenues to be used in retiring sinking fund bonds).

3. Capital fund (to account for the proceeds from the sale of bonds).

4. Park fund (to account for special taxes levied to finance the operation of parks).

5. Street improvement trust fund (to account for the expenditure of money raised by special assessments on property deemed to be benefitted by an improvement).

6. Inter-department printing shop fund (to account for revenues received from departments for printing done for them by the inter-department printing shop).

7. City printing shop fund (to account for revenues received from the public for printing services).

8. Money collected for the state fund (to account for money collected as agent for the state).

9. Operating fund (to account for revenues not handled through any other fund).

10. Electric fund (to account for revenues received from the sale of electricity to the public).

Question 1-3. It is said that one of the differences between government and business is that business expenditures create revenues, whereas governmental expenditures do not. Is this statement entirely true, or are there any governmental expenditures which create revenues?

Question 1-4. What is the difference, if any, between an income and expense statement prepared on a cash basis and a statement of receipts and disbursements?

Question 1-5. A governmental unit has a choice of adopting either a cash basis or a modified cash basis of accounting. Which method of accounting should it adopt and why?

Question 1-6. One of the standard procedures recommended by the National Committee on Governmental Accounting is that the accounts should be centralized under one official. Do you agree? Why?

Question 1-7. A municipality's financial activities are administered by three officials: a comptroller, a treasurer, and a purchasing agent. Allocate each of the following duties to the proper official:

    Keeping records of bank deposits
    Requesting bids
    Preparing financial statements
    Seeing that the government receives all revenues to which it is entitled
    Designating the methods of accounting to be followed
    Pre-auditing expenditures
    Making disbursements
    Supplying employees with forms necessary for filling in budget estimates
    Seeing that materials are tested
    Preparing receipts and disbursements statements
    Collecting interest on investments
    Placing orders for materials

Question 1-8. Cite at least two examples of procedures which may not be required by law but are nevertheless required by sound financial administration or accounting.

Problems

Problem 1-1. The following is a balance sheet prepared on a cash basis.

CITY OF X

General Fund

Balance Sheet
at Close of Fiscal Year

ASSETS

Cash..		$150,000
Taxes Receivable.........................	$300,000	
Less—Reserve for Uncollected Taxes.........	300,000	—
		$150,000

SURPLUS

Unappropriated Surplus............................	$150,000

Additional facts:

Estimated uncollectible taxes	$10,000
Accounts payable	65,000

Required:

Recast the foregoing balance sheet (a) on an accrual basis and (b) on a modified cash basis.

Problem 1-2. The following is an income and expense statement prepared by a municipality's bookkeeper:

CITY OF B

Working Capital Fund

Income and Expense Statement
for Fiscal Year Ended December 31, 1955

Sales to Departments......................	$85,000	
Borrowed from Other Funds.................	17,500	$102,500
Less—Cost of Operating:		
Materials.........................	$60,000	
Labor.............................	5,000	
Heat..............................	2,000	
Light and Power...................	2,000	
Superintendent's Salary............	3,000	
Purchase of Machinery..............	11,000	
Payment of Liability to Bond Fund...	15,000	
Total Cost of Operating...................		98,000
Net Profit.............................		$ 4,500

The following are additional facts concerning this statement:

1. The cost of materials shown in this statement is the total amount paid for materials during the year. An inventory of $20,000 was carried over from last year; $10,000 was paid for materials purchased during the preceding year; materials costing $30,000 were purchased during the year but have not yet been paid for; the closing inventory is $24,000.

2. The amounts shown for labor, heat, light and power, and superintendent's salary represent actual payments. Charges incurred last year but not paid until this year include the following: labor, $750; heat, $150; light and power, $300; superintendent's salary, $150. Charges incurred but not yet paid include the following: labor, $450; heat, $100; light and power, $225; superintendent's salary, $190.

3. The amount shown for sales represents actual receipts of cash from other funds; only $75,000 of the total collections is applicable to sales of this year; $45,000 is still due from other funds on account of sales made this year.

Required:

Prepare a correct income and expense statement of the working capital fund on a cash basis.

Problem 1-3. If we assume that the above income and expense statement was prepared on an accrual basis, is it accurate? If not, recast the statement so that it will show the financial operations on an accrual basis.

Problem 1-4. From the data in Problem 1-2, prepare an income and expense statement on a modified cash basis, assuming that the modified cash basis was also used during the preceding year.

Problem 1-5. The following is the trial balance at December 31, 1955 of a park refectory operated by the City of H:

Cash....................................	$ 2,150	
Inventory..............................	12,900	
Equipment.............................	16,850	
Allowance for Depreciation..............		$ 3,500
Accounts Payable.......................		200
Capital................................		10,000
Unappropriated Surplus.................		7,000
Sales..................................		97,000
Purchases.............................	42,000	
Personal Services.......................	40,000	
Laundry................................	500	
Equipment Repairs.....................	400	
Heat, Light, and Gas....................	2,100	
Telephone and Telegraph................	600	
Miscellaneous..........................	200	
	$117,700	$117,700

Adjustments:

    Depreciation, 10 per cent

    Closing inventory, $11,500

Required:

Prepare a balance sheet and an income and expense statement on an accrual basis.

Questions and Problems on Chapter 2

Questions

Question 2-1. Classify the follow'ng accounts according to whether they are (1) assets, (2) other debits, (3) offsets to assets or other debits, (4) liabilities, (5) other credits, (6) offsets to liabilities or other credits, or (7) surplus.

Land
Estimated Revenues
Due from Other Funds
Investments
Appropriations
Vouchers Payable
Pensions Payable
Allowance for Depreciation—Buildings
Revenues
Bonds Authorized—Unissued
Reserve for Retirement of Sinking Fund Bonds
Reserve for Inventories
Investment in General Fixed Assets
Interest Payable on Bonds in Future Years
Required Sinking Fund Contribution
Sinking Fund Contribution Revenues
Encumbrances
Reserve for Encumbrances
Reserve for Rebates
Taxes Collected in Advance
Allowance for Uncollectible Current Taxes

Question 2-2. For which of the following would you set up revenue accounts?
Revenues from Use of Money and Property:
    Interest on Bank Deposits
    Interest on Investments
    Rents and Concessions:
        Rents and Concessions from Clifton Park
        Rents and Concessions from Atlas Park
        Rents and Concessions from Beverly Park

Question 2-3. Designate the main sources of revenue (Taxes, Revenue from Use of Money and Property, and so forth) to which the following revenues apply:
Court Fines
Cigarette Tax Received from State
Interest on Investments
Park Board Concessions
Motor Vehicle Registration Fees Received from State
Rent from Market Stalls
Telephone Pay Stations
General Property Taxes
Sales Taxes

410

Plumbing Installation Permits
Conscience Money
Rent from Water-Front Land
Charges for Hospital Services
Rent from Public Buildings
City Railways Company Franchise
Taxi Meter Testing Fee
Scavengers' Licenses
Comfort Station Concessions
Sale of "No Parking" Signs
Interest on Bank Deposits
Gasoline Tax Received from State
Ticket Speculator's License
Income Taxes
Milk Hauler License
Subscriptions to City Publications
Liquor Tax Received from State
Donations for Venereal Clinic
Sales of Electrical Code
Library Fines
Donations from Community Chest
Building Permits

Question 2-4. Designate the functions to which the following activities apply:
Granting Aid to Libraries
Operating a Museum
Operating a Port
Retirement of Debt
Operating a Water Plant
Enacting Laws
Judicial Activities
Detecting Crime
Preventing Fires
Supervising Banks
Maintaining a Sewer System
Operating Hospitals
Payment of Old Age Assistance
Operating a Jail
Operating a Park
Payments for Pupils Attending Schools of Another Governmental Unit
Rendering Aid to Dependent Children
Activities of Parole Boards
Personnel Administration
Providing Pasteur Treatments
Operating a Hospital for the Blind
Operating a School
Operating an Old Soldiers' Home
Constructing and Maintaining Highways
Fighting Fires
Prosecuting Offenders
Administering Elections
Rendering Legal Advice to the Legislative Body
Training the National Guard

Payment of Interest
Inspecting Buildings
Keeping Accounts

Question 2-5. Distinguish between an expenditure and an expense.

Question 2-6. The following is a part of an expenditure statement. Set up account headings to designate the function, organization unit, and so forth, with which the accounts are identified (see page 20).

Public Safety:
Police Department:
Current Expenses:

Personal Services	$40,000		
Contractual Services	2,000		
Materials and Supplies	2,000	$44,000	

Capital Outlays:

Equipment		6,000	

Total Police Department			$50,000

Fire Department:
Current Expenses:

Personal Services	$30,000		
Contractual Services	2,000		
Materials and Supplies	1,500	$33,500	

Capital Outlays:

Equipment		6,500	

Total Fire Department			40,000

Total Public Safety			$90,000

Problems

Problem 2-1. From the following information, prepare a statement for the City of *A* for the year ended December 31, 1955, classifying expenditures by character, function, and object. (*Hint*—Divide the statement into three sections —a current expenses section, a capital outlays section, and a retirement of bonds section. Within each section arrange the expenses by function, showing under each function the objects going to make up the function.)

Rent of Equipment—Constructing Bridges	$ 3,500
Wages—Snow and Ice Removal	3,000
Salaries—Board of Elections	15,000
Compensation Insurance—Firemen	1,000
Postage—City Council	350
Wages—Street Repair	10,000
Rent of Equipment—Repair of Bridges	1,000
Purchase of Land—Police Department	15,000
Salaries—Policemen	40,000
Salaries—City Court Judges	10,000
Salary—Mayor	18,000
Purchase of Comptometers—Bureau of Accounts	1,000
Heat, Light, and Power—Police Department	1,000
Salaries—Councilmen	15,000
Telephone and Telegraph—City Council	300
Purchase of Desk—Council	175

Compensation Insurance—Policemen....................	1,000
Wages—Resurfacing Streets...........................	15,000
Postage—Bureau of Purchases........................	500
Wages—Constructing Bridges.........................	17,500
Salaries and Wages—Construction of New Fire Station...	7,500
Purchase of Police Cars.............................	10,000
Printing of Ballots.................................	1,000
Telephone and Telegraph—Fire........................	850
Interest on Bonds...................................	40,000
Salaries—Department of Highways (All chargeable to Maintenance)......................................	8,000
Purchase of Land—Fire Department...................	15,000
Wages—Constructing Streets.........................	30,000
Salaries—Firemen...................................	60,000
Rent of Equipment—Fire Department..................	750
Traveling Expenses—Mayor...........................	650
Salaries—Bureau of Accounts........................	7,500
Telephone and Telegraph—Police.....................	2,000
Contributions to Pension Funds......................	10,000
Repairs to Fire Department Buildings—By Contract.....	3,500
Retirement of Serial Bonds..........................	50,000
Purchase of Materials—Construction of Police Station....	5,000
Telephone and Telegraph—Bureau of Purchases.........	100
Purchase of Bookcases for City Court.................	500
Repair of Streets—By Contract.......................	5,000
Construction of Bridge—By Contract..................	2,000
Grants to Other Governmental Units..................	5,000
Heat, Light, and Power—Bureau of Purchases..........	500
Purchase of Law Books for City Court.................	1,000
Salaries—Civil Service Commissioners.................	12,000
Purchase of Materials—Construction of Fire Station......	10,000
Wages—Repair of Bridges............................	3,500
Heat, Light, and Power—Fire Department.............	2,500
Salaries—Bureau of Purchases........................	7,000

Problem 2-2. On the basis of the data in Problem 2-1, prepare a statement classifying expenditures by organization units.

Problem 2-3. Code the following expenditures, using the code symbols illustrated in the chapter:

1. Serial bonds were retired.
2. Interest on bonds was paid.
3. The city historian subscribed for periodicals.
4. Contributions were made to a sinking fund.
5. Office equipment was purchased for the city council.
6. The mayor was paid his salary.
7. Policemen were paid their salaries.
8. Rent was paid for office space occupied by the Health Department.
9. An automobile was purchased for the Police Department.
10. Firemen were paid.
11. An employee of the Civil Service Commission took a long distance trip. (Charge only the traveling expenses; disregard other expenses of the trip.)
12. Accountants submitted a bill for auditing the city's accounts.
13. A firm of reporters was hired to report a special court case and was paid in full.
14. Jurors were paid.
15. The law department paid wages to temporary employees.

Problem 2-4. Prepare a set of symbols to be used in coding revenue accounts. Use the main sources of revenue described in Chapter 2, and list three detailed municipal revenue sources under each of four of the main sources.

Problem 2-5. The following is part of an expenditure statement for a department of public welfare:

Rents—Lands and Buildings	$ 2,221.97
Electricity	485.86
Gas Fuel	27.90
Paints, Varnishes, and Painters' Supplies	173.53
Plaster, Lime, and Mortar Materials	5.02
Putty	2.54
Postage	122.82
Chalk and Crayons	.80
Motion Picture Supplies	45.10
Photographic Supplies	45.39
Repairing and Servicing Building Equipment	261.94
Repairing and Servicing Small Tools and Minor Equipment	68.87
Salaries, Continuing	32,367.49
Binding Records	3.00
Glass	12.05
Subscriptions—Newspapers and Periodicals	2.00
Blueprinting and Photostating	5.40
Telephone—Toll Service	14.96
Drugs, Medicines, and Chemicals (not otherwise classified)	94.04
Office Supplies	500.18
Fittings—Plumbing	.44
Washers and Valve Seats	.20
Salaries, Seasonal or Temporary	2,015.07
Insurance—Fidelity—Personal	5.00
Hardware	35.41
Freight and Express (not otherwise classified)	4.15
Artcraft and Handicraft Supplies	185.21
Baseball and Playground Ball Supplies	581.82
Basketball Supplies	166.11
Telephone—Installation and Changes	5.50
Gymnasium Supplies	116.13
Horseshoe Court Supplies	17.05
Traveling Expenses—Fare, Public Conveyance	230.00
Referees' Supplies	2.55
Supplies for Dramatic Presentation	107.88
Repairing and Servicing Office Machines and Appliances	3.00
Sash and Blind Cord	.78
Sheet Metal and Sheet Metal Products	.78
Repairing and Servicing Furniture and Furnishings	12.75
Poster Supplies	12.87
Books	5.05
Friction Tape	.20
Fuses and Fuse Blocks	.36
Telegrams	.94
Wages of Laborers	48.49
Rents—Equipment	1.47
Nails, Screws, and Bolts	20.23
Instructors	1,200.00
Sockets, Switches, and Plugs	9.29
Wire	4.41
Cloth	71.66

Telephone—Regular Service....................	345.41
Rope and Twine.............................	2.76
Soaps, Cleansers, and Disinfectants..............	77.95
Toilet Paper and Holders.....................	7.20
Repair Supplies for Boilers and Furnaces...........	1.86
Repair Supplies for Building Maintenance Equipment	6.12
Other Recreation Supplies......................	146.49
Traveling Expenses—Allowances for Personally Owned Automobiles...............................	615.00
Coal, Fuel.................................	711.43
Drinking Cups..............................	42.63
Other Athletic Game Supplies..................	76.51
Traveling Expenses—Meals and Lodging...........	19.10
Kerosene.................................	.69
Laundry Supplies, Miscellaneous.................	.99
Traveling Expenses—All Other..................	1.15

Required:

Prepare a statement classifying these expenditures by main objects (that is, Personal Services, Contractual Services, Materials and Supplies, and Other Charges).

Problem 2-6. The following is a statement of the general fund expenditures of the County of *P* for the fiscal year ended December 31, 1955:

Assessor...	$ 100,800
Bridges and Ferries..............................	322,500
Debt Fund.......................................	1,223,200
Hospital—Operation and Maintenance...............	276,000
Farm—Main Division.............................	121,900
Old Age Pensions.................................	524,200
Road Department.................................	372,000
County Clerk—Main Office.........................	107,800
Public Assistance.................................	183,300
Indigent Soldiers—Fund............................	60,000
Agricultural Extensions............................	3,500
Armory..	9,000
Sheriff—Civil Department..........................	43,100
Sheriff—Criminal Department......................	66,800
Sheriff—Election and Rental.......................	23,400
Sheriff—Identification Department..................	8,000
Sheriff—Jail.....................................	46,000
Sheriff—Kelly Butte..............................	45,300
Sheriff—Tax Department (Collection of Taxes)........	91,100
Frazer Detention Home—Operation and Maintenance	10,000
Free Dispensary Supplies..........................	8,500
Auditor..	21,900
Automobile Service...............................	2,500
Blind Assistance.................................	21,500
Board of County Commissioners (including Purchasing Agent)..	27,900
Insurance.......................................	4,500
Interest on Warrants..............................	25,000
Justice Court....................................	1,000
Lone Fir Cemetery...............................	6,300
Constable.......................................	29,900
Coroner..	14,600
Hospital Laundry—Operation and Maintenance.......	17,500
Indemnity—Livestock.............................	1,000
Indigent Soldiers—Disbursement....................	8,900

Board of Equalization.............................	1,400
Board of Health...................................	18,100
Child Welfare.....................................	103,000
Circuit Court.....................................	113,600
Pest Control......................................	1,000
Probate Court....................................	13,700
County Treasurer.................................	10,300
Court House—Operation and Maintenance...........	79,400
Court of Domestic Relations.......................	22,300
Public Health Association.........................	7,200
Registration and Election—County Clerk..............	82,400
Special Tax Foreclosure...........................	7,000
Superintendent of Schools.........................	8,600
Supervisor of Elections............................	3,400
Surveyor...	3,000
Tax Supervising and Conservation Commission........	8,600
Tubercular Pavilion...............................	21,600
Veterinary.......................................	3,100
District Attorney.................................	32,500
District Court....................................	32,700
Emergency Fund..................................	65,300
Farm—Farm Division..............................	33,400
Total.......................................	$4,500,500

Required:

Prepare a statement classifying these expenditures by function. (Place any items which you cannot classify by function in a Miscellaneous Expenditures group.)

Questions and Problems on Chapter 3

Questions

Question 3-1. Prepare a budget calendar based on the assumption that a budget is prepared for a small town, that it is prepared by the chief executive himself, and that the city council has no finance committee but that the entire council conducts the budget hearings and performs the other duties which a finance committee does in a larger city.

Question 3-2. What is meant by a performance budget?

Question 3-3. A municipality's budget is prepared on a cash basis. What basis of accounting would you recommend?

Question 3-4. Allotments may be made either by quarters or by months. Which allotment period do you think is better and why?

Question 3-5. Prepare a table of contents for a budget document, using the statements illustrated in the chapter.

Question 3-6. Are the terms "budget" and "budget document" synonymous? If not, what is the difference between them?

Question 3-7. In certain states, municipalities are required to pay property taxes of a fixed amount annually to the state. The municipalities in turn levy taxes for this purpose. Should an appropriation be made by the municipality to cover these payments?

Question 3-8. Distinguish between an appropriation and a special revenue fund.

Question 3-9. An ordinance provides that collections from the sale of dog licenses are "hereby appropriated for the maintenance of the dog pound." During the month of January, $5,000 was collected. Is another appropriation necessary to spend this money for the maintenance of the dog pound?

Question 3-10. (a) Why are both estimated and actual revenues reflected in the same *subsidiary* account whereas separate accounts are provided for estimated and actual revenues in the general ledger? (b) Why are appropriations, expenditures, and encumbrances shown in the same *subsidiary* account whereas separate appropriation, expenditure, and encumbrance accounts are carried in the general ledger?

Problems

Problem 3-1. The City of *G* has adopted the following budget for the fiscal year 1955:

Estimated Revenues, $790,000, consisting of the following:

Real Property Taxes	$390,000
Interest on Investments	2,000
Motor Vehicle Licenses and Fees	20,000
Portion of Sales Tax to Be Received from State	10,000
Interest on Bank Deposits	500
Grants-in-Aid to Be Received from State	5,000
Other Revenues	169,500
Court Fines	5,000
Personal Property Taxes	140,000

Income Taxes	25,000
Alcoholic Beverage Licenses	15,000
Interest and Penalties on Taxes	5,000
Building Permits	3,000

Appropriations, $787,000, consisting of the following:

Civil Service Commission	$ 5,000
Department of Police—Bureau of Uniformed Patrol	40,000
Department of Fire—Bureau of Fire Fighting	40,000
Court	20,000
Department of Police—Bureau of Supervision	20,000
Department of Police—Bureau of Communication System	20,000
Interest	40,000
Department of Fire—Bureau of Supervision	15,000
Board of Elections	5,000
Department of Law	25,000
Department of Fire—Bureau of Prevention	20,000
Retirement of Bonds	100,000
Department of Finance—Bureau of Administration	10,000
Department of Finance—Bureau of Purchases	6,000
City Clerk	10,000
Department of Finance—Bureau of Accounts	15,000
Mayor	15,000
Department of Finance—Bureau of Assessment	15,000
Department of Fire—Bureau of Training	10,000
Department of Police—Bureau of Criminal Investigation	20,000
Department of Police—Bureau of Police Training	8,000
Department of Finance—Bureau of Treasury	8,000
City Council	20,000
All Other Departments	300,000

Required:

a. Prepare a journal entry to record the adoption of the budget, showing both the general ledger accounts and all of the subsidiary accounts involved, the latter properly classified.

b. Post the general ledger accounts to "T" accounts.

c. Post the estimated revenues for Real Property Taxes, Court Fines, and Building Permits to revenue accounts similar to the account illustrated in Figure 14.

d. Post the appropriations for the Court, Department of Police—Bureau of Uniformed Patrol, and City Clerk to appropriation accounts similar to the account illustrated in Figure 15.

Problem 3-2. The following appropriations were made for 1955 by the City of *F*:

City Council	$ 15,000
Mayor	15,000
Courts	30,000
City Clerk	15,000
Department of Finance	30,000
Department of Police	75,000
Department of Fire	60,000
Department of Public Works	30,000
Interest	15,000
Retirement of Bonds	15,000
Reserve for Contingencies	30,000
	$330,000

The following transfers between appropriations were subsequently authorized:

Transferred from	Transferred to	Amount
City Council	City Clerk............................	$ 750
City Clerk	Mayor...............................	1,500
Department of Finance	Department of Public Works........	1,500
Department of Public Works	Courts..............................	1,000
	⎧ Department of Police..............	1,500
Reserve for Contingencies	⎪ Department of Fire................	2,200
	⎨ City Council......................	750
	⎩ Department of Public Works........	3,000

Estimated revenues are $350,000.

Required:

a. Prepare the journal entry necessary to record the adoption of the budget, showing both the general ledger and the subsidiary accounts.

b. Prepare the journal entry to record the transfers between appropriations, showing both the general ledger and the subsidiary ledger accounts involved.

c. Prepare a statement showing the appropriation balances after the transfers have been made effective.

Problem 3-3. From the following information prepare a departmental estimate of personal services (see Figure 3) for 1955 for the Finance Department of the City of X. Submission date: October 1, 1954.

Information as of January 1, 1954

Code	No.	Positions	Rate per Annum
1420-A1.1	1	Director of Finance....................	$7,500
1420-A1.2	1	Cashier...............................	3,900
1420-A1.3	2	Revenue Clerk........................	3,200
1420-A1.4	2	Parking Meter Collector................	2,820
1420-A1.5	1	License Clerk..........................	2,900
1420-A1.6	2	Machine Operator......................	2,800
1420-A1.7	1	Accountant............................	4,200

As of September 1, 1954, stenographer-clerk (A1.8) was added to the staff at a salary of $2,900.

The Director of Finance, Adam Smith, recommended that for 1955 all salaries be increased by 5 per cent.

The chief executive recommended that the staff be reduced by one parking meter collector, that Mr. Smith's salary be increased by $350, and that all other salaries be increased by 3 per cent.

The legislative body approved the recommended staff reduction and allowed a 4 per cent increase in all salaries, including the salary of the Director of Finance.

Problem 3-4. From the information below prepare a departmental estimate of current expenses—other than personal services (see Figure 4) for the Fire Department of the City of S. Submission date: October 15, 1955.

The following additional information is available: The expenditures for the first nine months of 1955 are estimated to be 75 per cent of the total expenditures for 1955. Fire Chief A. C. Carr proposed that the 1956 appropriations for his department be 105 per cent of the total 1955 expenditures, with the exception of account 2100-C41, for which he proposed that $2,000 be appropriated. City Manager Johnson made the recommendation that the amounts for 1956 appropriations be the same as the actual (for the first nine months) plus the estimated (for the remaining three months) expenditures for 1955, with the exceptions that only

$1,000 be appropriated for clothing, that accounts 2100-B26, C22, and C52 be decreased 7, 10, and 5 per cent, respectively, from the 1955 estimated and actual expenditures, and that accounts 2100-C61 and C62 be increased 10 per cent over the 1955 expenditures. The city council appropriated $1,000 for account 2100-B26, and for the remainder of the accounts it appropriated the amounts recommended by the city manager.

Actual Expenditures

Code		1953	1954	1955 (First Nine Months)
	CONTRACTUAL SERVICES:			
2100-B11	Transportation.............	$ 70	$ 84	$ 150
2100-B26	Hospital..................	230	1,396	750
2100-B31	Light and Power..........	6,138	5,090	3,876
2100-B43	Apparatus Repair.........	650	772	378
2100-B44	Automotive Repair........	11,578	13,878	8,436
	MATERIALS & SUPPLIES:			
2100-C11	Office....................	432	530	420
2100-C22	Coal.....................	15,066	11,742	9,750
2100-C41	Clothing..................	840	1,030	798
2100-C51	Mechanical...............	648	364	300
2100-C52	Automotive...............	4,070	4,534	3,306
2100-C61	Chemical.................	206	200	234
2100-C62	Medical..................	216	364	138
2100-C71	Books & Reports..........	30	36	24
	OTHER CHARGES:			
2100-D12	Insurance................	900	950	750
2100-D25	Pension Contribution......	12,274	12,286	9,240

Problem 3-5. On the basis of the data shown in the statement illustrated in Figure 98, prepare a schedule showing the amount which must be appropriated for interest on general bonds and the amount to be appropriated for the retirement of general serial bonds for 1955. (Assumed date of issue January 1.)

Problem 3-6. On October 1, 1954, you are given the following data concerning the City of N:

Work Unit		1953 No. of Units	1953 Unit Cost	Estimated 1954 No. of Units	Estimated 1954 Unit Cost	Estimated 1955 No. of Units	Estimated 1955 Unit Cost
Hauling Sweepings..	Cubic Yard	3,546	$ .87	3,721	$ .85	3,500	$ .84
White Wing.......	Cleaning Mile	8,041	2.60	9,236	2.90	9,000	2.90
Snow Removal:							
Plowing.........	Cleaning Mile	12,200	2.16	15,306	2.17	13,000	2.16
Loading and Hauling.......	Cubic Yard	60,742	1.11	83,140	1.09	75,000	1.10
Street Flushing....	Cleaning Mile	20,129	.84	22,439	.86	22,000	.86

Required:

a. Prepare a work program to be submitted on October 1 by J. P. Abner, Chief of the Division of Street Cleaning of the Department of Public Works.

b. Assuming that the estimates for 1955 were adopted by the legislative body, prepare a work program as of January 2, 1955, dividing the appropriations into four quarterly installments as follows:

	First Quarter	Second Quarter	Third Quarter	Fourth Quarter
Hauling Sweepings..........	15%	40%	30%	15%
White Wing...............	20	35	25	20
Snow Removal:				
Plowing.................	85	—	—	15
Loading and Hauling......	85	—	—	15
Street Flushing.............	—	40	40	20

Problem 3-7. You are asked as the City of *K*'s Director of Public Works, on January 5, 1956, to submit an allotment of the appropriation for your department for 1956 based on three-month periods. (1) Prepare such a schedule from the following data, using Figure 13 as a model and (2) submit the journal entry necessary to record the allotment for the first quarter.

	Personal Services	Contractual Services	Materials & Supplies	Other Charges	Capital Outlays
First Quarter.......	$7,500	$625	$400	$105	$2,300
Second Quarter.....	6,500	591	120	105	200
Third Quarter......	6,500	675	85	105	450
Fourth Quarter.....	7,500	610	240	105	300

Problem 3-8. From the following information, prepare a comparative statement of monthly receipts (see Figure 16):

CITY OF *J*

General Fund

Receipts	Total Estimated 1956	June 1956 Estimated	June 1956 Actual	January 1–June 30 Estimated	January 1–June 30 Actual
General Property Taxes.......	$750,000	$100,000	$87,312	$450,000	$444,726
Charges for Current Services..	35,000	2,800	3,200	19,500	21,437
Fines, Forfeits, and Other Penalties.....................	12,000	1,000	806	6,000	5,900
Interest and Penalties on Taxes	14,000	2,500	4,193	6,500	8,173
Licenses and Permits........	21,000	1,800	2,206	13,000	15,921
Revenues from Use of Money and Property..............	18,000	2,300	2,175	9,500	9,995
Revenues from Other Agencies	60,000	5,000	8,752	30,000	48,732
Collections from Accounts Receivable.................	10,000	900	757	5,300	5,200

Problem 3-9. From the following information, prepare a statement of actual and estimated revenues (see Figure 8) for the City of *Q*'s general fund. The percentages apply to the first column.

	Actual 1955	Actual First Nine Months of 1956	Estimated Remainder of 1956	Estimated 1957
General Property Taxes...	$601,202	94%	—	101%
Interest and Penalties—				
Delinquent Taxes......	13,450	84	—	110
Police Fines............	1,410	80	30%	112
Concessions............	1,750	42	21	50
Sewer Permits..........	2,500	75	25	105
Building Permit Fees.....	145	125	50	200

	Actual 1955	Actual First Nine Months of 1956	Estimated Remainder of 1956	Estimated 1957
Vendors' Licenses........	7,200	67	30	98
Share of State-Collected Franchise Taxes........	18,530	84	27	140
Fire Protection Service...	4,365	69	30	103
Rent of Public Properties	1,720	77	23	95

Problem 3-10. Make up a statement of actual expenditures compared with appropriations from the following information (see Figure 17). Percentages are to be applied to figures in the preceding columns (estimated expenditures).

CITY OF Q

General Fund

	Total 1956 Appropriations	June 1956 Estimated	June 1956 Actual	January 1-June 30, 1956 Estimated	January 1-June 30, 1956 Actual	Encumbrances
Election Expense....	$ 460	—	—	350	97%	—
Zoning Board........	175	25	80%	110	83	—
Reduction of Debt...	49,000	40,000	100	49,000	100	—
Public Library.......	7,000	600	93	4,200	95	$ 25
Collector's Office and Accounting....	9,000	800	106	4,900	103	5
Board of Health.....	1,400	120	101	840	99	10
Garbage Disposal....	12,000	1,100	99	6,000	98	22
Administration......	3,900	300	102	1,900	105	75
Police Protection.....	46,000	3,800	93	22,800	91	44
Legal Counsel.......	1,080	90	100	500	100	—
Parks and Plazas.....	7,500	600	128	3,700	130	25
Street Lighting......	14,300	800	91	7,100	94	13
Patriotic Celebrations	1,300	120	86	640	89	2
Interest on Debt.....	31,800	9,300	100	22,400	100	—
Municipal Building...	5,600	480	75	2,900	80	—
Streets—Repairs and Maintenance......	13,600	2,300	96	8,400	95	70
Sewers and Sewage Disposal..........	10,000	840	100	5,200	103	18
Recreation and Playgrounds..........	5,200	400	131	2,500	129	51
Poor Relief..........	546	45	112	275	115	—
Fire Protection......	23,500	2,000	115	11,700	112	421
Assessor's Office......	1,800	80	122	850	118	4

Questions and Problems on Chapter 4

Questions

Question 4-1. In your opinion, should revenues or expenditures applicable to a preceding year be credited directly to or charged directly against unappropriated surplus?

Question 4-2. (a) John Smith, a taxpayer, discovered that he had paid the same tax bill of $100 twice. He discovered the error before the end of the year, applied for a rebate, and was paid $100. How should the city reflect this rebate on its books? (b) Suppose he did not discover the error and was therefore not paid until the following year. How should the city reflect the rebate on its books?

Question 4-3. Included in a municipality's balance sheet were the following two accounts:

Taxes Receivable—Current....................	$ 5,000
Less—Allowance for Uncollectible Current Taxes	6,000
	$(1,000)

It was decided to reduce the Allowance for Uncollectible Current Taxes account by $1,000. Give the necessary entry or entries.

Question 4-4. The Ace Company rendered services on December 22, 1954, amounting to $150, but the invoice was not received until January 3, 1955. However, the appropriation accounts had been encumbered for $160 on December 21, 1954. Assuming the accrual basis is used, should the expenditure be reported in 1954 or 1955?

Question 4-5. In a certain municipality bonds in the amount of $10,000 and interest in the amount of $5,000 matured on May 1, 1955. Appropriations for these items were made on January 2, 1955. What entry should be made to record these current liabilities and when should it be made (that is, on January 2, 1955, or on May 1, 1955)?

Question 4-6. Referring to Figure 19, page 54, suppose that, after the balance sheet illustrated there was prepared but before the end of the year, additional revenues amounting to $5,000 were collected. Would the total assets be changed? Would the Unappropriated Surplus account be affected?

Question 4-7. Due to legal technicalities, the tax on a certain property will not be collected until 5 years from the date of the balance sheet, December 31, 1955. There is some certainty that it will be collected at that time. Disregarding penalties and interest, how should these taxes be handled in the balance sheet of December 31, 1955?

Question 4-8. The following is a balance sheet of the general fund of the County of X:

COUNTY OF *X*

General Fund

Balance Sheet

December 31, 1954

ASSETS

Cash..		$ 50,000
Taxes Receivable...	$200,000	
Less—Allowance for Uncollectible Taxes....................	30,000	170,000
Amount to Be Provided for Retirement of Funding Bonds..............		280,000
		$500,000

LIABILITIES AND SURPLUS

Liabilities:		
Funding Bonds of 1942 (that is, bonds issued to finance a deficit)	$280,000	
Accounts Payable.......................................	70,000	$350,000
Unappropriated Surplus..		150,000
		$500,000

The funding bonds (total issued, $1,000,000) were issued in 1942 to finance accumulated deficits. They have been retired at the rate of $60,000 each January. (*a*) Is the amount of surplus stated in this statement correct? (*b*) Does the statement show the true financial condition of the general fund? (*c*) If not, recast the balance sheet so as to show the true financial condition of this fund.

Question 4-9. It is claimed that the term *surplus* has no place in a general fund balance sheet because the term applies to accumulated profits, and a governmental unit is not established for the purpose of making profits. Is this claim correct?

Problems

Problem 4-1. The trial balance of the general fund of the City of *W* on January 1, 1955 was as follows:

Cash..	$15,000	
Taxes Receivable—Delinquent................	20,000	
Allowance for Uncollectible Delinquent Taxes...		$ 3,000
Interest and Penalties Receivable on Taxes.....	1,000	
Allowance for Uncollectible Interest and Penalties		75
Accounts Receivable........................	10,000	
Allowance for Uncollectible Accounts..........		1,000
Vouchers Payable...........................		20,500
Reserve for Encumbrances—Prior Years........		10,000
Unappropriated Surplus......................		11,425
	$46,000	$46,000

The following are transactions which took place during the year 1955:

1. Revenues were estimated at $110,000; appropriations of $108,000 were made.

2. An order placed at the end of the preceding year and estimated to cost $10,000 was received; the invoice indicated an actual cost of $9,500.

3. Taxes to the amount of $110,000 have accrued; an allowance of 5 per cent was made for possible losses.

4. Collections were made as follows:

Current taxes.........................	$90,000
Delinquent taxes.....................	10,000
Interest and penalties receivable on taxes	300
Accounts receivable..................	5,000

5. Taxes amounting to $20,000 have become delinquent; the allowance for uncollectible current taxes was transferred to the allowance for uncollectible delinquent taxes.

6. Delinquent taxes amounting to $2,000 were written off; interest and penalties receivable on taxes to the amount of $20 were also written off.

7. An order was placed for materials estimated to cost $20,000.

8. Delinquent taxes amounting to $200, which were written off in preceding years, were collected with interest and penalties of $35. (*Hint*—Credit Revenues.)

9. Payments were made as follows:

Vouchers payable....................	$15,500
Payrolls...........................	20,000

10. The materials ordered were received; a bill for $21,000 was also received.

11. An order was placed for an automobile for the police department; the estimated cost was $3,000.

12. Payrolls of $25,000 were paid.

13. The automobile ordered for the police department was received; the actual cost was $3,000.

14. Bonds to the amount of $10,000 have matured. (*Hint*—Charge Appropriation Expenditures.)

15. The matured bonds were paid.

16. Interest amounting to $5,000 was paid.

17. Interest of $600 accrued on delinquent taxes, and an allowance for uncollectible losses thereon of 5 per cent was provided.

18. An order was placed for materials estimated to cost $19,000.

Required:

a. Post the opening trial balance to "T" accounts.

b. Prepare journal entries.

c. Post to "T" accounts.

d. Prepare a balance sheet before closing entries.

e. Prepare closing entries.

f. Post to "T" accounts.

g. Prepare a balance sheet as of the close of the fiscal year (that is, after closing entries).

h. Prepare a statement analyzing the changes in the Unappropriated Surplus account.

Problem 4-2. The following is a trial balance of the general fund of the City of *D* as of December 31, 1955, after closing entries (interest and penalties on taxes are not accrued):

Cash...	$33,600	
Taxes Receivable—Delinquent................	25,400	
Allowance for Uncollectible Delinquent Taxes..		$ 5,900
Accounts Receivable........................	15,500	
Allowance for Uncollectible Accounts..........		2,500
Vouchers Payable............................		42,000
Reserve for Encumbrances....................		16,000
Unappropriated Surplus......................		8,100
	$74,500	$74,500

The following transactions took place during 1956:

1. The budget for the year was adopted. Revenues were estimated at $216,000; appropriations of $229,000 were made, including an appropriation of $16,000 for materials ordered in 1955, covered by the Reserve for Encumbrances.

2. The materials ordered in 1955 and set up as an encumbrance of that year for $16,000 were received; the actual cost was $15,000.

3. Delinquent taxes amounting to $2,800 were declared uncollectible and written off the books.

4. Taxes to the amount of $210,000 accrued; a 3 per cent allowance for estimated losses was provided.

5. Uniforms estimated to cost $15,000 were ordered.

6. Collections were made as follows:

Current taxes.....................	$182,000
Delinquent taxes.................	8,500
Interest and penalties on taxes.......	200
Accounts receivable...............	7,300

7. Interest of $3,000 was paid.

8. Payroll vouchers for $100,000 were approved.

9. The uniforms were received; the invoice was for $16,000.

10. Serial bonds to the amount of $35,000 matured.

11. Delinquent taxes to the amount of $350, written off in preceding years, were collected. (*Hint*—Credit Revenues.)

12. Current taxes became delinquent; the amount of estimated uncollectible current taxes was transferred to estimated uncollectible delinquent taxes.

13. The payroll vouchers were paid.

14. An order was placed for a snow plow estimated to cost $3,500.

15. Vouchers paid amounted to $60,000.

16. The snow plow was received; the invoice was for $3,800.

17. Matured serial bonds were retired.

18. Miscellaneous revenues of $5,000 were collected.

19. An order was placed for civil defense equipment at an estimated cost of $24,000.

Required:

a. Post the opening trial balance to "T" accounts.

b. Prepare journal entries.

c. Post to "T" accounts.

d. Prepare a balance sheet as of December 31, 1956, before closing entries.

e. Prepare closing entries.

f. Post closing entries to "T" accounts.

g. Prepare a balance sheet as of December 31, 1956, after closing entries.

h. Prepare a statement analyzing the changes in the Unappropriated Surplus account.

Problem 4-3. (Adapted from an American Institute of Accountants' examination.) From the following information concerning the operations of a municipal expendable revenue fund for the fiscal year ended April 30, 1954 prepare:

A. Entry or entries to close the books of the fund for the year ended April 30, 1954.

B. A balance sheet of the fund as of April 30, 1954.

C. A statement analyzing the changes in the Unappropriated Surplus account for the year ended April 30, 1954.

Information concerning the Expendable Fund, for the year ended April 30, 1954 is as follows:

1. Unappropriated surplus at May 1, 1953, consisted entirely of cash $ 2,350
2. Budget estimate of revenue   185,000
3. Budget appropriations   178,600
4. Tax levy $115,620, against which a reserve of $4,000 is set for estimated losses in collection.
5. Tax receipts, $112,246, with penalties of $310 in addition.
6. Receipts from temporary loans $20,000, all of which were repaid during period with interest of $300.
7. Balance of encumbrances unliquidated, April 30, 1954   3,250
8. Vouchers approved for expense   146,421
9. Vouchers approved for capital expenditures   21,000
10. Vouchers approved for payment of bonds falling due during the year, $5,000, and for interest on bonds, $2,000.
11. Miscellaneous revenue received   74,319
12. Rebate of current year's taxes collected in error   240
13. Warrants issued and payable on demand   169,400
14. Refund on an expense voucher on which an excess payment was made.

Problem 4-4. (Adapted from an American Institute of Accountants' examination.) From the April 30, 1954, trial balance of the general fund of the City of *W* and the transactions of the succeeding year stated below, prepare:

(a) Balance sheet of April 30, 1955.

(b) Statement analyzing the changes in the Unappropriated Surplus account for the year ended on that date.

(c) Work sheet.

Trial Balance—April 30, 1954

	Debits	Credits
Cash on Hand..	$ 910	
Cash in Banks...	54,670	
Petty Cash...	100	
Taxes Receivable—1952 Levy..............................	22,420	
Reserve for Taxes not Collected—1952 Levy..............		$ 22,420
Taxes Receivable—1953 Levy..............................	260,000	
Reserve for Taxes not Collected—1953 Levy..............		260,000
Taxes Receivable—1953 Levy, Pledged on Anticipation Notes	5,000	
Stores Inventory..	3,700	
Due from Water Fund.......................................	8,000	
Accounts Payable...		9,240
Tax-Anticipation Notes Payable..........................		5,000
Reserve for Encumbrances..................................		14,140
Special Reserve for Contingencies.........................		2,000
Unappropriated Surplus....................................		42,000
	$354,800	$354,800

(1) The estimated revenues for the year ended April 30, 1955, amounted to $405,000.

(2) The city's share of general property taxes from the 1954 tax levy amounted to $285,000. The accounting for tax revenues is on a cash basis, but a control account for each tax levy is set up.

(3) The operating budget was approved in the sum of $408,000.

(4) Revenues were collected in the sum of $392,450, as follows:

1952 Levy.................	$ 22,420
1953 Levy.................	233,580
1953 Levy (pledged)........	5,000
Miscellaneous Revenue......	131,450
	$392,450

(5) Tax-anticipation notes against the 1954 levy were issued and cash was received in the amount of $20,000. Receipts from tax-anticipation notes are entered as revenues, and an equivalent amount of taxes receivable is set up as an asset against the liability created by the notes.

(6) Purchase orders were issued for commodities in the sum of $138,610.

(7) Invoices received, approved, and vouchered amounted to $139,033, which included $5,310 purchases for store inventory.

(8) Tax-anticipation notes against the 1953 levy for $5,000 and interest thereon amounting to $7 were paid.

(9) Payrolls were vouchered and approved for payment in the amount of $246,500.

(10) Supplies were issued on stores vouchers from the central stores in the amount of $6,760, which included $1,500 stores issued to the water fund.

(11) Warrants were issued to cover interest $6,000 and principal of bonds $10,000.

(12) Warrants were issued in payment of approved vouchers in the amount of $383,643.

(13) The petty cash fund was increased $100.

(14) The general fund advanced $5,000 to the water fund.

(15) Total cash deposited in the banks amounted to $412,100.

(16) An analysis of the appropriation ledger showed that purchase orders encumbered amounted to $387 more than the corresponding purchase orders liquidated.

(17) The encumbrances as at April 30, 1955, amounted to $18,640.

(18) The City Council authorized the setting up of a reserve for stores for $10,000.

(19) The necessity for a special reserve for contingencies was terminated and this item closed to surplus.

(20) Taxes collected in prior years were refunded in the amount of $1,000.

Questions and Problems on Chapter 5

Questions

Question 5-1. (*a*) What is the difference between state-collected, locally shared taxes, and grants-in-aid? (*b*) A statute provides that 50 per cent of state motor vehicle license collections are to be distributed annually among the municipalities and counties (that is, county territory outside of municipalities) on the basis of the number of licenses issued to residents thereof during the year. Are such payments a distribution of state-collected, locally shared taxes, or grants-in-aid? (*c*) Would your answer be different if the statute had provided, in addition, that the money received by the municipalities and counties was to be employed only for road purposes?

Question 5-2. (*a*) What is the difference between revenues from charges for current services and license revenues? (*b*) A department charges $10, the approximate cost of inspection, for issuing a building permit. Would you classify this as revenues from permits or as charges for current services?

Question 5-3. Both tax rates and license rates are established by legislative action. Which rates (license or tax) are likely to remain in effect over a longer period of time?

Question 5-4. The comptroller of the City of *F* publishes a statement of actual revenues alone. His argument is that he purposely underestimates revenues so as to keep expenditures down. If he were to publish estimated and actual revenues, the underestimation would become evident, and he would be forced to report accurate estimates of revenue, with the result that expenditures would rise. Is the comptroller's argument justified?

Question 5-5. In the City of *L*, persons fined on account of traffic violations are permitted to work out these fines by performing such work as washing and greasing police cars or painting curbs and lines on pavements for the traffic department. Should these fines be accounted for in the records? If so, give the entry or entries, using assumed figures.

Problems

Problem 5-1. The following is a list of the revenue accounts in the general fund revenue ledger of the City of *P* at December 31, 1955:

Revenue Source	Estimated	Actual
Scavenger's License..	$ 500	$ 500
Sale of "No Parking" Signs..............................	300	300
Interest on Bank Deposits...............................	500	500
Real Estate Taxes (Net).................................	100,000	95,000
Personal Property Taxes (Net)..........................	58,000	50,000
Interest and Penalties on Taxes........................	5,000	5,500
Sales Taxes..	42,000	42,000
Plumbing Installation Permits...........................	5,000	4,800
Motor Vehicle Registration Fees Received from State......	17,000	15,500
Rent from Market Stalls.................................	2,000	2,100

Revenue Source	Estimated	Actual
Telephone Pay Stations................................	1,000	1,200
Ticket Speculator's License...........................	600	400
Milk Hauler's License.................................	1,000	1,200
Subscriptions to City Publications.......................	500	450
Alcoholic Beverage Licenses..........................	19,000	18,000
Sales of Electrical Code...............................	800	600
Library Fines..	1,000	1,100
Donations from Community Chest......................	5,000	5.000
Building Permits.....................................	3,000	3,100
Charges for Private Police Service......................	2,000	1,800
Sale of Fixed Assets..................................	1,000	500
Gasoline Tax Received from State......................	28,000	28,000
Conscience Money....................................	200	300
Court Fines...	5,000	4,200
Cigarette Tax Received from State......................	12,000	12,500
Interest on Investments...............................	300	300
Charges for Hospital Services..........................	5,000	5,500
Rent from Public Buildings............................	2,000	2,000
City Railways Company Franchise.......................	3,000	3,000
Taxi Meter Testing Fee...............................	500	600

Required:

a. Set up "T" accounts for the general ledger accounts and enter in them the total amount of estimated revenues and actual revenues, respectively; also set up a "T" account for unappropriated surplus.

b. Set up the following (subsidiary) revenue ledger accounts (see Figure 14, page 41) and post the amount of estimated and actual revenue thereto:

Real Estate Taxes
Court Fines
Building Permits

c. Prepare a journal entry to close out the estimated and actual revenues, showing both the general ledger and revenue ledger (that is, subsidiary) accounts.

d. Post the amounts shown in the closing entry to the general ledger accounts and to those subsidiary revenue accounts for which you have set up accounts.

e. Prepare a statement, properly arranged, comparing the estimated and actual revenues of the general fund of the City of P for the year ended December 31, 1955.

Problem 5-2. The following are the estimated revenues for the City of A at January 1, 1955:

Taxes...............................	$175,000
Interest and Penalties...............	2,000
Fines and Fees......................	700
Permits............................	300
Dog Tax............................	900
Rents..............................	500
Licenses...........................	3,500
Interest...........................	1,000

The city reports its transactions on a cash basis.
At the end of January, the following collections had been made:

Taxes...............................	$90,000
Interest and Penalties...............	1,000
Fines and Fees......................	50
Permits............................	140

Dog Tax.........................	800
Rents............................	45
Licenses........................	2,000

An unanticipated grant-in-aid of $5,000 was received from the state. Collections for the remaining eleven months were as follows:

Taxes............................	$70,000
Interest and Penalties..............	800
Fines and Fees....................	400
Permits...........................	30
Dog Tax..........................	70
Rents............................	455
Licenses..........................	300
Interest..........................	900

Required:

a. Prepare the entries necessary to record on the books the estimated revenues as well as revenue collections.

b. Post to "T" accounts and to subsidiary revenue accounts (see Figure 14).

c. Prepare closing entries.

d. Post to the "T" accounts and to the subsidiary revenue accounts.

e. Prepare a statement of estimated revenues compared with actual revenues for 1955.

Problem 5-3. From the following accounts taken from a municipality's report for the fiscal year ended June 30, 1954, prepare a statement of estimated revenue compared with actual.

	Estimated	Actual
Property Taxes—Current...........................	$1,126,000	$1,127,000
Permits..	5,200	5,850
Proceeds of Sales of Commodities and Services........	29,000	11,275
Gas and Weight Tax...............................	106,000	161,725
Rents...	3,500	3,200
Licenses...	35,000	65,900
Severance Tax....................................	200	190
Grants, Donations, and Contributions................	36,000	27,450
Interest, Dividends, and Premiums..................	22,000	54,800
Franchise Tax....................................	1,200	1,300
Fines, Penalties, and Forfeitures.....................	25,000	35,600
Miscellaneous Receipts............................	2,000	2,875
Dockage Fees....................................	25	350
Nuisance Tax.....................................	—	75
Fees...	10,000	14,800

Problem 5-4. The following is a list of the estimated and actual general fund revenues for the fiscal year ended June 30, 1955, for the State of Y:

	Estimated	Actual
Sales Tax...	$11,826,000	$11,701,526
Gasoline Inspection...............................	750,000	806,408
Beer Tax...	400,000	623,815
Oil Inspection....................................	100,000	106,028
Capital Issues....................................	5,000	12,671
Miscellaneous Taxes...............................	—	6,019
Railroad Dividends................................	210,000	210,000
Interest on Bank Deposits..........................	50,000	11,671
Sales Tax on Gasoline.............................	2,750,000	2,360,000

	Estimated	Actual
Miscellaneous Earnings	14,500	918
Poll Tax	—	3,823
Refund Imprest Cash—Revenue Department	—	25,000
State Property Tax (Schools)	175,000	153,744
Utilities Commission Fees	—	10
State Board of Elections	—	6,208
Inheritance Taxes	750,000	530,617
Licenses	3,500,000	3,496,866
Franchise Taxes	7,267,800	7,245,754
Insurance Department Fees	14,700	15,692
Income Taxes	7,690,000	8,088,119
Secretary of State	60,000	71,682
Governor's Office	15,000	18,551

Required:

Prepare a statement of estimated and actual revenues for the fiscal year ended June 30, 1955.

Problem 5-5. (Adapted from an American Institute of Accountants' examination.)

The treasurer of the Board of Education of the City of Q submitted the following statement of the school accounts as at September 1, 1953, the beginning of the fiscal year 1953-1954:

RESOURCES	Tuition Fund	Maintenance Fund	Building Fund
Cash on hand	$1,500	$ 500	$ 3,000
Taxes receivable	3,600	900	600
Buildings and land			200,000
School equipment			10,000
Total	$5,100	$1,400	$213,600

LIABILITIES			
Audited vouchers		$ 500	
Reserve for uncollected taxes	$2,160	540	$ 360
Current surplus	2,940	360	3,240
Capital surplus			210,000
Total	$5,100	$1,400	$213,600

In accordance with the state laws the accounts of the board must show budgetary estimates, resources, and outstanding liabilities, but the revenues must be recorded on a cash basis. The treasurer had estimated that 40 per cent of the balance of taxes receivable would be collected in 1953-1954, and had therefore set up 60 per cent of the amounts due as a reserve for uncollected taxes.

The following budget covering the fiscal year ended August 31, 1954, had been approved by the board:

APPROPRIATIONS:	Tuition Fund	Maintenance Fund	Building Fund
For teachers' salaries	$36,000		
For interest on tax anticipation warrants	1,380		
For fuel, supplies, janitor, etc.		$9,000	
For interest		345	
For new school equipment			$12,000
Total	$37,380	$9,345	$12,000

	Tuition Fund	Maintenance Fund	Building Fund
RESOURCES:			
Estimated tax collections:			
Prior levies—40% of balance.........	$ 1,440	$ 360	$ 240
1953-1954 levy.....................	34,440	8,985	8,760
	$35,880	$9,345	$ 9,000
Less—Audited vouchers, September 1, 1953		500	
	$35,880	$8,845	$ 9,000
Cash on hand, September 1, 1953.......	1,500	500	3,000
	$37,380	$9,345	$12,000

On November 15, 1953, the treasurer received notice from the county clerk that actual assessments for 1953-1954 amounted to:

Tuition.....................	$45,043
Maintenance................	11,367
Building....................	10,446

During the year the treasurer recorded the following receipts and disbursements:

	Tuition Fund	Maintenance Fund	Building Fund
RECEIPTS:			
Sale of tax anticipation warrants........	$24,000.00	$ 6,000.00	
Tax collections—prior levies............	1,480.00	320.00	$ 240.00
Tax collections—1953-1954 levy.........	36,230.96	9,492.44	9,051.40
	$61,710.96	$15,812.44	$ 9,291.40
DISBURSEMENTS:			
Tax anticipation warrants paid..........	$24,000.00	$ 6,000.00	
Interest on tax anticipation warrants....	1,380.00	345.00	
Teachers' salaries.....................	36,000.00		
Unpaid bills of September 1, 1953.......		500.00	
Fuel, supplies, janitor, etc.............		7,100.00	
On account of $12,000 school equipment installed............................			$11,400.00
	$61,380.00	$13,945.00	$11,400.00

On August 31, 1954, a bill was rendered to the board for $1,300 covering the repairs to the school building made in that month. The bill was approved but not paid until later in September, 1954.

It was estimated that of the taxes not collected at August 31, 1954, the following percentages would prove uncollectible:

80% of the taxes of prior levies
20% of the taxes of 1953-1954 levy

and adequate reserves are to be set up.

From the foregoing information prepare a columnar work sheet, showing for each fund the budgetary estimates, cash transactions, adjustments, and closing entries, as well as the resources, liabilities, reserves, and surpluses.

Questions and Problems on Chapter 6

Questions

Question 6-1. In a certain municipality the purchase of materials is charged against an appropriation set up for that purpose. Subsequently, as materials are withdrawn, their cost is charged to the appropriations of the departments by which they are withdrawn. What is wrong with this procedure, and what remedy would you propose?

Question 6-2. (*a*) Should the inventory of materials and supplies carried in the general fund of a governmental unit be recorded at cost, at cost or market, whichever is lower, or on some other basis? (*b*) Would your answer be different if the inventory was owned by a municipal water utility?

Question 6-3. On January 2, 1956, materials costing $100 were transferred from inventory to the Police Department. Give the journal entry or entries to be made.

Question 6-4. A governmental unit takes advantage of purchase discounts by paying its bills promptly. Should the full purchase price be recorded on the records with the discounts treated as revenue, or should the purchases be recorded at their net cost (that is, after deduction of discounts)?

Question 6-5. In your opinion, is it preferable to head up the statement as is done on page 84 rather than to prepare a separate statement for expenditures chargeable against the Reserve for Encumbrances? Give reasons for your answer.

Question 6-6. Referring to Question 3-7, what entry should be made when the municipality pays the money over to the state?

Question 6-7. It has been suggested that the amounts paid by the general fund to a pension fund for the city's share of pension fund contributions be charged to the departments in which the covered employees work. Do you agree? Explain.

Question 6-8. Suppose that bonds are issued to finance the construction of a city hall. Would it be desirable to allocate the interest on those bonds among the different departments using the city hall?

Question 6-9. In one municipality vouchers must be approved not only by the finance officer but also by the four members of the finance committee of the city council. In your opinion is the approval of the finance committee desirable? Give reasons.

Problems

Problem 6-1. The following is a list of the accounts in the general fund appropriation ledger of the City of *B* at December 31, 1955.

434

| Organization Unit | APPROPRIATIONS | | EXPENDITURES | | ENCUMBRANCES OUTSTANDING | |
	Current Expenses	Capital Outlays	Current Expenses	Capital Outlays	Current Expenses	Capital Outlays
Public Works Department (Sanitation and Waste Removal Function).........	$22,000	$ 7,500	$21,000	$ 6,700	—	$ 750
Public Works Department (Highways Function).........	20,000	30,000	19,000	28,000	$1,000	1,000
Civil Service Commission...............	7,500	—	6,700	—	750	—
Public Welfare Department.......	30,000	1,500	26,000	800	2,250	100
Court..............	7,500	—	6,700	—	—	—
Interest............	7,500	—	7,500	—	—	—
Council............	15,000	3,000	13,500	3,000	—	—
City Clerk's Office...	15,000	3,000	15,000	1,500	—	500
Department of Police	40,000	7,500	38,500	6,000	1,000	1,000
Mayor.............	20,000	1,500	18,000	500	1,500	750
Department of Finance..........	15,000	1,500	13,500	1,500	1,500	—
Department of Law..	15,000	—	9,000	—	—	—
Department of Fire..	30,000	7,500	19,000	4,000	750	750
Department of Health	20,000	6,000	19,000	5,000	500	500
Retirement of Bonds	15,000*	—	15,000*	—	—	—

* Not part of current expenses; shown in "Current Expenses" column to save space.

Required:

a. Set up "T" accounts for the general ledger accounts and enter in them the proper totals of appropriations, expenditures, encumbrances, and reserve for encumbrances, respectively; set up a "T" account for unappropriated surplus. *Hint*—Set up "T" accounts for appropriations (to include both current expenses and capital outlays), for appropriation expenditures, and so forth. You need not distinguish between current expenses, capital outlays, and retirement of debt in your *general ledger* accounts.

b. Set up the following (subsidiary) appropriation accounts (see Figure 15, page 42) and post appropriations, expenditures, and encumbrances to them:

City Clerk's Office—Current Expenses
Department of Fire—Capital Outlays
Department of Law—Current Expenses
Mayor—Capital Outlays
Public Works Department—Highways—Current Expenses
Public Welfare Department—Public Welfare—Current Expenses

c. Prepare a journal entry to close out appropriations, expenditures, and encumbrances, showing both the general ledger and appropriation ledger (subsidiary) accounts.

d. Post the amounts shown in the closing entry to the general ledger accounts and to those subsidiary accounts for which you have set up accounts.

e. Prepare a statement, properly arranged, comparing appropriations with expenditures and encumbrances of the general fund for 1955.

Problem 6-2. The following is a balance sheet of the School District of *Z* as of January 1, 1955:

SCHOOL DISTRICT OF Z

General Fund
Balance Sheet
January 1, 1955

ASSETS

Cash		$150,200
Taxes Receivable—Delinquent	$ 59,300	
Less: Allowance for Uncollectible Delinquent Taxes	3,000	56,300
Interest and Penalties Receivable on Taxes	$ 3,600	
Less: Allowance for Uncollectible Interest and Penalties	1,400	2,200
Accounts Receivable	$ 10,800	
Less: Allowance for Uncollectible Accounts	1,800	9,000
Due from Utility Fund		10,000
		$227,700

LIABILITIES AND SURPLUS

Liabilities:		
Vouchers Payable	$120,000	
Taxes Collected in Advance	3,300	
Due to Working Capital Fund	15,000	$138,300
Unappropriated Surplus		89,400
		$227,700

The following transactions took place during the year:

1. The school board adopted the following budget:

Appropriations:	
General Control	$ 42,000
Instructional Service	126,000
Operation of Plant	42,000
Maintenance of Plant	25,000
Auxiliary Agencies	25,000
Capital Outlays	70,000
Debt Service	30,000

Estimated Revenues:	
Taxes	275,000
Interest and Penalties on Taxes	2,000
Interest Earnings	2,000
Rents and Concessions	200
State Appropriation	20,000
Tuition	30,000
Sale of Supplies	2,300
Telephone Receipts	650

2. The school board levied a tax of $284,000. It was estimated that $9,000 of this levy would never be collected, and an allowance for this amount was set up.

3. Current tax collections amounted to $210,400.

4. New equipment estimated to cost $70,000 was ordered.

5. Materials had been ordered last year, but the Encumbrances and Reserve for Encumbrances accounts had been closed out at the end of the year. However, they were reappropriated this year (and included in the above appropriation), and the following amounts were encumbered:

Instructional service	$15,000
Operation of plant	7,000
Auxiliary agencies	4,500

6. Miscellaneous revenues were collected as follows:

Interest earnings	$ 1,000
Rents and concessions	140
Tuition	10,000
Sale of supplies	1,800
Telephone receipts	200

7. Current taxes receivable of $3,300 were applied against the taxes collected in advance.

8. Salaries and wages were paid as follows:

General control	$22,000
Instructional service	60,000
Operation of plant	8,000
Maintenance of plant	3,200
Auxiliary agencies	6,700

9. The actual costs of materials ordered last year were as follows:

Instructional service	$14,500
Operation of plant	7,700
Auxiliary agencies	4,350

Vouchers were approved for these expenditures.

10. Delinquent tax collections amounted to $13,490.

11. Materials and supplies were ordered, estimated to cost as follows:

General control	$ 7,500
Maintenance of plant	11,300
Auxiliary agencies	8,650

12. Uncollected current taxes were transferred with the allowance for uncollectible current taxes to delinquent accounts.

13. Vouchers in the amount of $106,500 were paid.

14. Taxes of $1,200 written off the books in previous years were collected without interest or penalties. (*Hint*—Credit Revenues.)

15. The equipment was received; the actual cost was $68,000.

16. Supplies were ordered at the following estimated costs:

Operation of plant	$13,000
Maintenance of plant	2,500
Auxiliary agencies	1,800

17. Supplies ordered in transaction 16 were received. Vouchers were approved for the actual cost as follows:

Operation of plant	$12,500
Maintenance of plant	3,000
Auxiliary agencies	1,700

18. Serial bonds in the amount of $25,000 were paid.

19. Miscellaneous collections of revenue were as follows:

Rents and concessions	$ 150
Tuition	13,240
Sale of supplies	1,250
Telephone receipts	169

20. The liability to the working capital fund was paid.

21. Supplies were ordered at the following estimated costs:

General control	$ 4,200
Instructional service	11,500
Maintenance of plant	5,000

22. Collections from interest and penalties receivable on taxes amounted to $800.

23. Interest on bonds accrued amounted to $5,000.

24. Materials and supplies ordered in transaction 11 were received with bills as follows:

General control	$ 7,000
Maintenance of plant	11,100
Auxiliary agencies	9,000

25. The state appropriation became due.

26. Delinquent taxes of $980 were written off.

27. The utility fund paid its liability to this fund.

28. Interest revenues in the amount of $700 accrued.

29. Interest and penalties of $2,607 accrued on taxes, but it was estimated that of this amount $500 would never be collected.

30. The following salaries and wages accrued:

General control	$ 3,500
Instructional service	29,500
Operation of plant	8,600
Maintenance of plant	1,000
Auxiliary agencies	3,400

Required:

a. Post the balance sheet accounts to "T" accounts.

b. Prepare all the entries necessary to record the transactions for the year.

c. Post to controlling accounts ("T" accounts) and to subsidiary revenue and appropriation accounts (see Figures 14 and 15, respectively).

d. Prepare all closing entries and post to controlling and subsidiary accounts.

e. Prepare a balance sheet as of December 31, 1955.

f. Prepare a statement analyzing the changes in the Unappropriated Surplus account.

g. Prepare a statement of estimated and actual revenues.

h. Prepare a statement of expenditures and encumbrances compared with appropriations.

Problem 6-3. On the basis of the data in the appropriation ledger on the opposite page, prepare a schedule classifying expenditures by character and main classes of objects.

CITY OF X
Appropriation Expenditure Ledger

Organization Unit: Department of Police
Year: 1955

Date	Description	Encumbrances — Order No.	Paid or Canceled	Issued	Balance	Voucher No.	Expenditures — Amount	Total Expenditures	Appropriations	Unencumbered Balance
1	2	3	4	5	6	7	8	9	10	11
1/4	Appropriation	—	—	—	—	—	—	—	$50,000	$50,000
	Insurance	—	—	—	—	20	$ 200	$ 200	—	49,800
	Expert Services	—	—	—	—	25	300	500	—	49,500
1/7	Office Supplies	10	—	$110	$110	—	—	500	—	49,390
	Land	—	—	—	110	32	1,000	1,500	—	48,390
1/10	Filing Cabinets	17	—	400	510	—	—	1,500	—	47,990
	Auto Repairs	—	—	—	510	40	200	1,700	—	47,790
1/14	Lubricants	42	—	50	560	—	—	1,700	—	47,740
1/16	Firearms	—	—	—	560	53	180	1,880	—	47,560
	Office Supplies	73	$110	—	450	57	120	2,000	—	47,550
1/20	Electricity	—	—	—	450	60	50	2,050	—	47,500
	Typewriters	35	—	250	700	—	—	2,050	—	47,250
1/22	Typewriters	35	250	—	450	72	250	2,300	—	47,250
	Gasoline	—	—	—	450	75	340	2,640	—	46,910
	Medical Services	—	—	—	450	79	60	2,700	—	46,850
1/24	Motorcycle Repairs	—	—	—	450	85	140	2,840	—	46,710
	Gas Masks	—	—	—	450	91	60	2,900	—	46,650
1/27	Surety Bond Premium	—	—	—	450	94	50	2,950	—	46,600
	Clothing	49	—	250	700	—	—	2,950	—	46,350
1/29	Lubricants	27	30	—	670	97	50	3,000	—	46,330
	Printing	—	—	—	670	106	125	3,125	—	46,205
	Filing Cabinets	17	400	—	270	111	475	3,600	—	46,130
1/31	Regular Salaries	—	—	—	270	133	1,480	5,080	—	44,650
	Water	—	—	—	270	135	20	5,100	—	44,630

Problem 6-4. The following is a balance sheet of the City of M as of January 1, 1956:

CITY OF M

General Fund

Balance Sheet

January 1, 1956

ASSETS

Cash..		$ 77,000
Taxes Receivable—Delinquent...................	$480,000	
Less: Allowance for Uncollectible Delinquent Taxes	41,000	439,000
Interest and Penalties Receivable on Taxes.......	$ 9,500	
Less: Allowance for Uncollectible Interest and Penalties...	720	8,780
Accounts Receivable...........................	$ 15,000	
Less: Allowance for Uncollectible Accounts.......	400	14,600
Due from Utility or Other Enterprise Fund...............		5,000
		$544,380

LIABILITIES, RESERVE, AND SURPLUS

Liabilities:		
Vouchers Payable...........................	$109,000	
Judgments Payable..........................	55,000	
Due to Special Assessment Fund..............	70,000	
Taxes Collected in Advance...................	12,000	$246,000
Reserve for Encumbrances—Prior Years*..................		31,000
Unappropriated Surplus.................................		267,380
		$544,380

* Reserve for Encumbrances includes supply orders for the following:

Fire Department.............	$13,500
City Jail...................	17,500

The following transactions took place during the year:
1. Appropriations and estimated revenues were as follows:

APPROPRIATIONS

Public Works Department............	$ 69,752
Interest on Bonds...................	10,450
Retirement of Bonds................	10,000
City Commission....................	3,500
City Manager......................	9,205
City Clerk.........................	5,600
Civil Service Board.................	1,800
Department of Health and Welfare....	21,235
City Jail...........................	19,200
Park Department...................	27,251
Election Board......................	5,366
City Court.........................	10,390
Attorney..........................	4,485

APPROPRIATIONS—Continued

Zoning Board......................	720
Auditor...........................	12,000
Treasurer.........................	11,093
Assessor..........................	10,494
Purchasing Agent..................	9,500
Fire Department...................	205,090
Police Department.................	210,160
	$657,291

ESTIMATED REVENUES

Property Taxes....................	$425,000
Interest and Penalties on Taxes.......	4,951
Licenses..........................	42,000
Franchises........................	50,000
Fines and Fees....................	26,340
Rents.............................	6,500
State Gas Tax.....................	80,500
Service Charges...................	22,000
	$657,291

2. The city commission levied a tax of $442,000, of which $18,000 is estimated never to be collected.

3. Current tax collections amounted to $345,000. Of this amount, $2,000 had been collected previously and is to be refunded to taxpayers.

4. Orders for supplies were placed as follows:

City Manager......................	$ 500
City Clerk........................	500
Civil Service Board................	300
Election Board....................	4,300
City Court........................	200
Attorney..........................	100
Zoning Board......................	400
Auditor...........................	650
Treasurer.........................	900
Assessor..........................	1,200
Department of Health and Welfare......	2,000

5. The foregoing supplies ordered were received, and vouchers were approved as follows:

City Manager......................	$ 510
City Clerk........................	507
Civil Service Board................	290
Election Board....................	4,325
City Court........................	195
Attorney..........................	90
Zoning Board......................	400
Auditor...........................	643
Treasurer.........................	950
Assessor..........................	1,240
Department of Health and Welfare......	2,000

6. Interest and penalties accrued on taxes amounted to $4,000. It was estimated that $150 of this amount would never be collected.

7. Interest paid on outstanding bonds amounted to $10,450, and bonds retired amounted to $10,000.

8. Taxes collected in advance totaled $1,850.

9. Miscellaneous revenues received and other collections were as follows:

Interest and Penalties Receivable on Taxes.....	$ 4,500
Licenses...................................	40,350
Franchises................................	45,000
Fines and Fees............................	20,436
Rents......................................	4,700
State Gas Tax.............................	85,000
Service Charges...........................	18,760
Accounts Receivable.......................	7,450
Delinquent Taxes..........................	151,000

10. Salaries and wages were paid during the year as follows:

City Commission...........................	$ 3,600
City Manager.............................	9,200
City Clerk.................................	5,500
Civil Service Board........................	900
Election Board............................	1,100
City Court................................	10,100
Attorney..................................	4,800
Auditor...................................	10,500
Treasurer.................................	9,600
Assessor..................................	9,000
Purchasing Agent..........................	8,500
Fire Department...........................	190,050
Police Department.........................	185,900
Department of Health and Welfare...........	18,800
City Jail..................................	8,880
Park Department..........................	5,060
Public Works Department...................	35,450

11. The supplies ordered last year were received. The actual cost of these supplies was as follows:

City Jail..................................	$17,490
Fire Department...........................	14,150

12. The judgments were paid in full.

13. The utility or other enterprise fund paid off its debt to the general fund.

14. An additional appropriation of $1,000 was made out of surplus to the city jail, and $2,000 was transferred from the police department's appropriation to the city jail.

15. Delinquent taxes of $1,500 were written off.

16. Delinquent taxes in the amount of $3,000 and interest and penalties of $50, written off as uncollectible last year, were received.

17. All uncollected current taxes were transferred with the allowance for uncollectible current taxes to delinquent accounts.

18. The following capital outlays were made and paid for:

Purchasing Agent.....................	$ 750
Fire Department......................	25,800
Police Department....................	33,300
City Jail............................	14,350
Park Department.....................	21,500
Public Works Department.............	35,300

19. The following supply orders were placed:

Civil Service Board	$200
Election Board	100
Treasurer	300
Public Works Department	500

Required:

a. Prepare a balance sheet as of December 31, 1956.

b. Prepare a statement analyzing the changes in the Unappropriated Surplus account.

c. Prepare a statement comparing estimated and actual revenues.

d. Prepare a statement comparing expenditures and encumbrances with appropriations.

Problem 6-5. (Adapted from an American Institute of Accountants' examination.) From the following information concerning the general accounts of the City of D, prepare:

1. A statement analyzing the changes in the Unappropriated Surplus account for the year 1954.

2. A balance-sheet of the general fund as of December 31, 1954.

3. A comparative statement of revenue and budget estimates for the year.

4. A statement of expenditures and encumbrances in comparison with the budget estimates.

5. Closing entries.

The trial balance of the general accounts of the City of D at the beginning of the new fiscal year, January 1, 1954, was as follows:

Cash	$37,452	
Taxes receivable—prior years	3,729	
Miscellaneous accounts receivable	1,868	
Tax liens	2,046	
Audited vouchers		$20,370
Reserve for encumbrances		8,010
Unappropriated surplus		16,715
	$45,095	$45,095

The transactions for 1954 are summarized below:

1. The budget was adopted for the 1954 fiscal year as follows:

EXPENDITURES

State and county taxes	$ 10,370
Addition to sinking fund	20,000
General administration	28,200
Protection of life and property	30,000
Protection of health	21,000
Streets and roads	40,000
Education	120,000
	$269,570

REVENUES

Licenses and permits	$ 6,250
Fines and penalties	6,715
Miscellaneous	11,580
Taxes	245,025
	$269,570

2. Appropriations were made to cover encumbrances outstanding at January 1, 1954, as follows:

General administration..............	$ 110
Protection of life and property........	2,450
Protection of health.................	750
Streets and roads...................	2,500
Education........................	2,200
	$8,010

3. Of the taxes receivable for prior years, $3,427 was collected. Tax liens were obtained against the remaining delinquent taxpayers.

4. All of the tax liens outstanding at the beginning of the year were sold for cash, and all the outstanding miscellaneous accounts receivable were collected.

5. The tax levy for 1954 was $245,025, of which $236,421 was collected in cash.

6. Contracts were let and open-market orders were placed in the estimated amount of $126,382, as follows:

General administration..............	$ 10,824
Protection of life and property........	15,933
Protection of health.................	8,422
Streets and roads...................	25,727
Education........................	65,476
	$126,382

7. Cash was received from licenses and permits totaling $5,276, and from fines and penalties totaling $6,956. Miscellaneous income aggregated $11,475, of which $9,375 was collected.

8. Claims presented and approved against outstanding contracts and open-market orders amounted to $125,955, as follows:

General administration..............	$ 10,853
Protection of life and property........	13,877
Protection of health.................	8,887
Streets and roads...................	28,951
Education........................	63,387
	$125,955

The claims are the same as the amounts originally estimated except for one streets-and-roads claim which exceeded the original estimate by $1,000.

9. Payroll vouchers amounting to $116,450, not covered by contracts and open-market orders, were approved as follows:

General administration..............	$ 16,621
Protection of life and property........	17,500
Protection of health.................	11,850
Streets and roads...................	13,479
Education........................	57,000
	$116,450

10. Vouchers were approved for payment of $20,000 appropriated to the sinking fund and of $10,370 for taxes due the state and county.

11. Cash payments made against audited vouchers amounted to $270,653, including those outstanding at January 1, 1954.

Problem 6-6. (Adapted from an American Institute of Accountants' examination.) From the following information, prepare a statement for the year 1954 showing operating budget appropriations, expenditures, and other commitments against the appropriations, as well as unencumbered balances, for the Town of *E*:

The following appropriations were included in the operating budget adopted:

Administrative expenses:	
Salaries	$ 3,600
Telephone	600
Stationery and supplies	1,800
Assessment and collection of taxes:	
Salaries	5,000
Telephone	100
Stationery and supplies	800
Police department:	
Salaries	25,000
Supplies	1,500
Radio maintenance	550
Operation expense and maintenance of squad cars	3,500
Telephone	200
Fire department:	
Salaries	15,000
Supplies	500
Operation expense and maintenance of equipment	1,200
Telephone	100
Street repairs and maintenance:	
Salaries and wages	5,550
Sand, gravel, stone, etc.	7,400
Interest on bonds	21,000
Payment of bonds	45,000
	$138,400

No provision was made in this budget for purchase of new equipment or for capital improvements.

Cash disbursements for all divisions of the accounts were recorded in the same cash disbursement book. A summary of the amounts so recorded for the year follows:

Name and Description		Total Payments	
Telephone Co.:			
Telephone service:			
Collector's office	$ 84		
Police department	167		
Fire department	85		
Treasurer's office	540	$	876

Payrolls:

Salaries of policemen......................	$24,500	
Salaries of firemen........................	14,800	
Salary of treasurer........................	2,500	
Salary of assistant to treasurer.............	1,100	
Salary of tax collector.....................	3,000	
Salary of assessor.........................	2,000	
Salary of superintendent of streets..........	2,000	
Wages of street employees.................	3,450	53,350

A.B.C. Stationery Co.:

Tax duplicates, tax cash books, etc..........	$ 300	
Treasurer's books, ledger sheets, etc.........	450	750

W & B Garage Co.:

Repairs to police cars.....................	$ 550	
Tires for police cars.......................	300	
Repairs to fire trucks.....................	450	1,300

Gulf Oil Corporation:

22,000 gallons of gasoline delivered to disbursing pump at police station at 10¢ per gallon. (All gasoline purchased is charged to police department. Periodic adjustments are made for gasoline used by other departments. During the year the fire department used 6,000 gallons.)	2,200

Penrod Printing Company:

Purchase orders, vouchers, checks, etc.......	$ 600	
Tax bills.................................	425	1,025

Colonial Outfitters:

Police uniforms and sundry supplies........	$ 900	
Firemen's uniforms and sundry supplies.....	300	1,200

Barrett Company:

30,000 gallons of tarvia at 10¢ per gallon....	3,000
(Of the above, 20,000 gallons were used in the repair of existing roads and the balance was used in the construction of new streets.)	

State Trust Co.:

For interest on coupon bonds..............	21,000

Consolidated Stone and Sand Co.:

600 tons crushed stone at $10 per ton........	6,000
(Of the above, 500 tons were used in the repair of existing roads and the balance was used in the construction of new streets.)	

American Fabric & Rubber Co.:

Repairs to fire line hose....................	150

Johnson Radio Company:

Incidental repairs to police radio system.....	450

State Trust Company:

For payment of bonds.....................	45,000

Johnson's Food Store:
    Food for prisoners.........................   300

DeCozen Motor Co.:
    Cars for Police Department................   3,750

RCA Mfg. Co.:
    Short-wave receivers and transmitters, includ-
    ing installation, per contract..............   1,250

                                    $141,601

The following commitments and accrued expenses remained unpaid at December 31, 1954:

Name and Description	Total Payments	
Payroll:		
Wages accrued—street department............		$ 95
Penrod Printing Company:		
Stationery and vouchers for treasurer's office...		250
(Not received until January 15, 1955.)		
Johnson Radio Company:		
Repairs to police radio.....................		85
Telephone Company:		
Telephone bill for December:		
Treasurer's office........................	$50	
Collector's office........................	14	
Police department........................	23	
Fire department........................	12	99
		$529

Questions and Problems on Chapter 7

Questions

Question 7-1. A municipality sold bonds and then finding that it would not need the money for several months invested it. Assuming that interest in the amount of $500 was received, give the entry to record this transaction.

Question 7-2. Referring to Question 7-1, assume that the bonds had originally been sold at a discount of $300 and give the entry to record the receipt of such interest.

Question 7-3. Referring to Question 7-1, assume that the appropriations amounted to $100,000, that the bonds were sold at par, but that it is now apparent the project will cost $100,500. Can the $500 be used to finance the additional expenditure without authorization from the legislative body?

Question 7-4. A bond fund had a deficit of $1,000, which arose because of the sale of bonds at a discount. The deficit was subsequently made up by a contribution from the general fund. Would you charge the amount transferred as an interest expense of the general fund or as a contribution expense of that fund?

Question 7-5. At the beginning of the year $100,000 of an issue of serial bonds was sold at a discount of $1,000. Subsequently there was a rise in the price of the bonds so that $200,000 of the same issue was sold several months later at a premium of $2,000. How should these premiums and discounts be recorded? Give entries.

Question 7-6. Assume the same facts as in Question 7-5, except that the bonds were sold at a discount of $2,000 and at a premium of $1,000, respectively. Give the necessary entries.

Question 7-7. Assume the same facts as in Question 7-5, except that the first sale was in one year and the second sale during the following year. Would the premiums and discounts be handled in the same way as those described in Question 7-5? If not, in what way should they be handled? Give entries.

Question 7-8. The following is a statement of expenditures and encumbrances compared with appropriations:

CITY OF K

Bond Fund

Statement of Expenditures and Encumbrances Compared with Appropriations

for Fiscal Year Ended June 30, 1955

Appropriations...................................		$100,000
Less—Appropriation Expenditures............	$99,000	
Discount on Bonds...................	1,000	100,000
Net Balance of Appropriations........................		—

At what amount would you capitalize the expenditures of this fund? Give reasons for your answer.

448

Problems

Problem 7-1. Part I. The following is a list of transactions which took place in the Village of *A* during 1955:

1. A bond issue of $120,000 was authorized for the construction of a library.
2. The bonds were sold at a premium of $900.
3. The cost of handling the bonds was $800, which was paid.
4. An order was placed for materials estimated to cost $65,000.
5. Salaries and wages amounting to $5,000 were paid.
6. The premium was transferred to the general fund.

Required:

a. Prepare all entries, exclusive of closing entries, to record the transactions for 1955.

b. Post to "T" accounts.

c. Prepare a balance sheet as of December 31, 1955.

Problem 7-1. Part II. The following transactions took place during 1956:

11. The materials were received; the actual cost was found to be $65,850.
12. Salaries and wages amounting to $40,100 were paid.
13. All bills outstanding were paid.
14. The project was completed. The surplus, if any, was to be transferred to the general fund.

Required:

a. Prepare all journal entries, including closing entries, to record the transactions for 1956.

b. Post to "T" accounts.

c. Prepare a statement analyzing the changes in the Appropriations account for the two years ended December 31, 1956.

Problem 7-2. Part I. The following transactions took place in the County of *M* during 1954:

1. A bond issue of $500,000 was authorized for the construction of a bridge.
2. One half of the bonds was sold; the sale was at par.
3. The cost of handling the bonds was $700, which was paid.
4. A contract was entered into with White & Company for the construction of the bridge at a cost of $420,000.
5. A bill for $175,000 was received from White & Company for work done on the bridge to date.
6. Salaries of state engineers amounting to $5,350 were paid.

Required:

a. Prepare journal entries. (Do not prepare closing entries.)

b. Post to "T" accounts.

c. Prepare a balance sheet as of December 31, 1954.

Problem 7-2. Part II. The following transactions took place during 1955:

11. The bill due White & Company was paid.
12. A bond issue of $400,000 was authorized for the purpose of constructing a garage.
13. Bonds (garage) to the amount of $200,000 were sold at par.
14. The cost of handling the bonds amounted to $2,500, which was paid.
15. Orders were placed for materials (garage project) estimated to cost $52,000.
16. A bill for $125,000 was received from White & Company for further work performed on the contract.

17. Salaries and wages paid amounted to $51,000; of this total $4,000 applies to the bridge project and the remainder to the garage project.

18. The materials ordered were received; the actual cost was $53,000.

19. An order was placed for materials (garage project) estimated to cost $100,000.

Required:

a. Prepare journal entries. (Do not prepare closing entries.)

b. Post to "T" accounts.

c. Prepare a combined balance sheet of all funds as of December 31, 1955.

d. Prepare a combined statement analyzing the changes in the Appropriations account for the two years ended December 31, 1955.

Problem 7-3. The trial balances of the general fund and the bond fund of the City of *W* as of January 1, 1955, are as follows:

GENERAL FUND

Cash...	$ 27,000	
Taxes Receivable—Current....................	57,000	
Allowance for Uncollectible Current Taxes......		$ 3,500
Taxes Receivable—Delinquent................	41,000	
Allowance for Uncollectible Delinquent Taxes...		11,000
Interest and Penalties Receivable on Taxes.....	4,200	
Allowance for Uncollectible Interest and Penalties		1,000
Accounts Receivable.........................	35,500	
Allowance for Uncollectible Accounts..........		3,000
Vouchers Payable............................		82,000
Contracts Payable...........................		48,000
Reserve for Encumbrances—Prior Years........		10,000
Unappropriated Surplus......................		6,200
Totals..................................	$164,700	$164,700

BOND FUND

Bonds Authorized—Unissued.................	$150,000	
Appropriations..............................		$150,000
	$150,000	$150,000

The following transactions took place in the two funds during the year:

1. The city council passed an appropriation ordinance. Revenues were estimated at $310,000, and appropriations amounted to $310,000.

2. Taxes to the amount of $250,000 were accrued, and a 2 per cent allowance for uncollectible current taxes was set up.

3. Bonds with a par value of $150,000 were sold at a premium of $2,000, the proceeds to be used for the construction of a municipal library.

4. The premium was transferred to the general fund.

5. The cost of printing the bonds and miscellaneous handling charges connected with their sale amounted to $300 and were paid.

6. The actual cost of the materials ordered in 1954 for the public works department and set up as an encumbrance of that year for $10,000 was $10,100.

7. A contract was let for the partial construction of the library. The Abner Contracting Company was awarded the contract on a bid of $95,000.

8. On February 1, orders were placed for materials for the following:

City Court..........................	$ 2,400
Board of Elections..................	1,800
Department of Finance..............	1,300
Library Construction................	10,200
	$15,700

9. The materials ordered on February 1 were received. Actual bills were as follows:

City Court..........................	$ 2,300
Board of Elections..................	1,900
Department of Finance..............	1,400
Library Construction................	10,000
	$15,600

10. Current taxes of $49,000 became delinquent, and $2,000 of the allowance for uncollectible current taxes was transferred to the allowance for uncollectible delinquent taxes.

11. Payroll vouchers were approved for the following:

General City.......................	$72,000
Library Construction................	11,000

12. A bill was received from the Abner Contracting Company for $15,000.

13. Collections were made as follows:

Current taxes......................	$230,000
Delinquent taxes....................	5,500
Interest and penalties receivable on taxes	520
Accounts receivable.................	29,000
Miscellaneous revenues not previously accrued.........................	72,000

14. The approved payroll vouchers were paid.

15. Judgments incurred in connection with the construction of the library totaled $7,500.

16. Materials were ordered by the city for library construction at an estimated cost of $12,500.

17. The Abner Contracting Company was paid.

18. Interest and penalties accrued on delinquent taxes amounted to $4,200; a provision of 2.5 per cent for estimated uncollectible interest and penalties on delinquent taxes was made.

19. Vouchers for bills for materials ordered on February 1 were paid.

20. Delinquent taxes of 1952 to the amount of $300, written off as uncollectible in 1954, were collected. (*Hint*—Credit Revenues.)

21. A bill was received from the Abner Contracting Company for $40,000.

22. The judgments were paid.

23. The city council certified $2,200 of delinquent taxes to be uncollectible, and they were written off.

24. The Abner Contracting Company was paid.

25. Current taxes collected amounted to $15,000.

26. Vouchers payable of $82,000 carried in the general fund were paid.

27. Deferred serial bonds to the amount of $40,000 matured.

28. The payroll for library construction work to the amount of $7,000 was approved and paid.

29. The matured serial bonds were retired.

30. Interest paid on bonded debt amounted to $8,000.

31. The materials ordered for the library at an estimated cost of $12,500 were received; the invoice was for $13,000.

32. The Abner Contracting Company submitted a bill covering the remaining cost of the contract.

33. Orders were placed for materials for general departments at an estimated cost of $100,000.

34. A payroll for general departments amounting to $57,000 was paid.

35. The materials ordered for the general departments were received, together with a bill for $105,000.

36. Taxes collected in advance amounted to $500.

37. Materials were ordered for the fire department at an estimated cost of $3,000.

38. Contracts payable in the general fund to the amount of $48,000 were paid.

39. The Abner Contracting Company was paid, but 5 per cent of the contract was held pending the final approval of the project.

40. The surplus in the bond fund was transferred to the general fund.

Required:

a. Post the above trial balances to "T" accounts.

b. Prepare journal entries.

c. Post to "T" accounts.

d. Prepare closing entries.

e. Post the closing entries to the "T" accounts.

f. Prepare a balance sheet for each fund as of December 31, 1955.

g. Prepare a statement analyzing the changes in the Unappropriated Surplus account of the general fund.

h. Prepare a statement analyzing the changes in the Appropriations account of the bond fund.

Problem 7-4. (Adapted from an American Institute of Accountants' examination.) From the following data prepare a columnar work schedule, showing the financial transactions of the City of Y in 1954 together with general-fund and bond-fund balance sheets at the close of that year:

1. Balance sheet—January 1, 1954:

ASSETS

Cash..............................	$ 2,000
Taxes receivable—arrears...........	15,000
	$ 17,000

LIABILITIES

Reserve for uncollectible taxes—arrears	$ 10,000
Accounts payable...................	3,000
Unappropriated surplus..............	4,000
	$ 17,000

2. Budget for the year 1954:

Estimated revenues:

Taxes receivable—1954 levy	$225,000
Court fines	10,000
Licenses	6,000
Permits	10,000
Interest and penalties	8,000
	$259,000

Current appropriations:

General government	$ 68,000
Police department	61,000
Fire department	12,000
Highway department	44,000
Sanitation department	39,000
Retirement of serial bonds	15,000
Interest on bonds	17,000
Interest on tax notes	3,000
	$259,000

3. The amount of taxes levied for the year 1954 is $236,250, which includes a 5% allowance for uncollectible accounts.

4. Receipts and disbursements in 1954:

Receipts:

Current taxes		$223,000
Taxes in arrears		6,000
Tax anticipation notes		90,000
Other revenues		
Court fines	$10,600	
Licenses	6,100	
Permits	9,800	
Interest and penalties	8,400	34,900
		$353,900

Disbursements:

Sundry appropriations		
General government	$67,000	
Police department	59,250	
Fire department	10,750	
Highway department	42,000	
Sanitation department	40,000	
Retirement of serial bonds	15,000	
Interest on bonds	17,000	
Interest on tax notes	2,700	$253,700
Tax anticipation notes		90,000
Accounts payable		3,000
		$346,700

5. Bills unpaid at December 31, 1954, amounted to $2,600.

6. The uncollected taxes originating prior to January 1, 1954, should be fully reserved for.

7. Other transactions in 1954:

(a) The construction of a new municipal center was authorized at an estimated cost of $100,000.

(b) 4½% serial bonds in the principal amount of $100,000 were authorized and issued at par.

(c) Contracts were let for construction of the municipal center, aggregating $95,000.

(d) $60,000 was paid on these contracts.

(e) On December 31, 1954, $80,000 construction work was completed.

Questions and Problems on Chapter 8

Questions

Question 8-1. An illustration is given in the text of a special assessment fund which consists of three funds. Under what circumstances would a special assessment fund consist of four funds?

Question 8-2. Suppose that it is decided to use interest on assessments to make up a discount on bonds in the amount of $1,000. Give the entries to record (a) the receipt of the interest and (b) its use in eliminating the discount.

Question 8-3. What is meant by "callable" bonds?

Question 8-4. What is the difference between a special assessment and a reimbursement?

Question 8-5. Would it be advisable to prepare a statement comparing revenues and expenditures of a special assessment fund for any given year?

Question 8-6. Property A has been assessed $5,000 and granted a condemnation award of $5,000. Should the assessment and judgment be recorded on the books or should they both be ignored, since they offset each other? Explain.

Question 8-7. What is meant by "making assessments liens against property"?

Problems

Problem 8-1. Edward Lawrence's property, designated as Lot No. 7 in Block 8, was assessed $1,500 on January 15, 1954. The assessments are payable in ten equal installments beginning with 1954, and the interest rate is 3½ per cent. On January 25, 1954, Mr. Lawrence paid the first installment. On January 15, 1955, he paid the second installment, together with interest on the nine deferred installments; on January 15, 1956, he paid the third installment, together with interest on the eight deferred installments.

Required:

Set up an individual special assessment record (Figure 36, page 106) and record the above transactions.

Problem 8-2. The following transactions took place during 1955 in the City of A:

1. The construction of pavements estimated to cost $150,000 and to be financed from special assessments was authorized.

2. Pending the collection of assessments, construction was financed through the sale of notes for $90,000.

3. A contract was entered into with Acher & Wallace for the construction of the pavements at a cost of $140,000.

4. Assessments to the amount of $120,000 were levied; the municipality agreed to contribute $30,000 as its share of the cost of financing the project.

5. A bill was received from Acher & Wallace for $50,000.

6. Supervisory engineering expenses amounting to $5,000 were paid.

7. Acher & Wallace was paid.

8. All assessments and the city's contribution were collected.

9. A bill was received from Acher & Wallace for the remaining amount due on the contract.

455

10. Notes payable outstanding and interest of $3,000 were paid.

11. The project was completed.

12. Acher & Wallace was paid in full, except for $10,000 which was retained pending the final inspection and approval of the project.

Required:

a. Prepare journal entries, including closing entries.

b. Post to "T" accounts.

c. Prepare a balance sheet as of December 31, 1955.

d. Prepare a statement analyzing the changes in the Appropriations account.

Problem 8-3. Part I. The following is a list of transactions which took place in the City of N during 1955:

1. The city commission authorized the paving of certain streets at an estimated cost of $200,000, the work to be performed by the city's own labor forces.

2. The project is to be financed in the following manner:

City's share........................	$ 50,000
1955 installment....................	15,000
Deferred assessments (nine installments)	135,000
	$200,000

3. Special-special assessment bonds were sold at par in the amount of $135,000. These bonds will be paid from the deferred assessments.

4. Assessments were levied.

5. The city paid over its share of the estimated cost.

6. Assessments to the amount of $13,000 were collected.

7. Materials estimated to cost $92,000 were ordered.

8. The Tact Company was paid $3,000 in surveying fees.

9. The materials ordered were received. The actual cost was $92,500, and the invoice was approved for payment.

10. A bill for $4,500 was received from the Petri Construction Company covering the rental charges for equipment hired by the city and was approved for payment.

11. Payrolls paid during the year amounted to $67,000.

12. Judgments for $10,000 on account of condemnation of property were awarded and paid.

13. Interest on bonds to the amount of $3,000 became due.

14. Vouchers payable amounting to $94,000 were paid.

15. Uncollected current assessments became delinquent.

16. Interest accrued on deferred assessments amounted to $3,500.

Required:

a. Prepare all journal entries, exclusive of closing entries.

b. Post to "T" accounts.

c. Prepare a balance sheet as of December 31, 1955.

d. Prepare a schedule showing the assets, liabilities, and so forth, applicable to each bond installment.

Problem 8-3. Part II. Transactions taking place in 1956 were as follows:

20. Another special assessment installment became due.

21. Collections were made as follows:

1955 installments....................	$ 1,200
Current installments.................	10,500
Interest collected...................	2,300

22. Interest due on bonds was paid.

23. Uncollected current assessments became delinquent.

24. Payrolls amounted to $5,000 and were paid.

25. Interest on bonds to the amount of $4,000 became due.

26. Interest on assessments to the amount of $4,500 accrued.

27. The cost of selling properties for unpaid special assessments was $65, which was paid out of construction cash.

28. Property A, on which no assessments had been paid, was sold. Total unpaid special assessments on this parcel of property amounted to $1,200, accumulated interest was $70, and the cost of selling the property was $20. The property was sold for $1,500.

29. Properties E and L, on which no assessments had been paid, were offered for sale, but, the price not being satisfactory, the governmental unit bid them in. Unpaid assessments, interest, and cost of holding the sale of these properties were as follows:

Property	Unpaid Assessments	Interest	Cost of Holding Sale
E	$2,000	$180	$35
L	2,200	135	30

30. Property E was redeemed by the owner, who paid, in addition to all other interest and charges due, interest of $40.

31. Bonds to the amount of $15,000 were called in and retired, and interest of $500 due thereon was paid.

32. Property L was taken over by the city and is to be used for recreation purposes. The city paid the full amount of the assessment certificate out of the general fund.

Required:

a. Prepare all journal entries, including closing entries.

b. Post to "T" accounts.

c. Prepare a balance sheet as of December 31, 1956.

d. Prepare a statement analyzing the changes in the Appropriations account for the two years ended December 31, 1956.

Problem 8-4. Part I. The following transactions took place in the City of F during 1954:

1. The legislative body authorized the widening of a street at an estimated cost of $450,000.

2. Bonds to the amount of $300,000 were authorized and were sold at a discount of $1,300.

3. The city agreed to contribute $120,000 as its share of the estimated cost; the remainder was assessed against property owners. The assessments were made payable in installments, and particular series of bonds were to be paid from particular installments and no others. Assessment installments and bonds retirable therefrom were as follows:

No.	Due Date	Amount of Installment	Amount of Bonds to Be Retired
1	1954	$30,000	—
2	1955	33,000	$33,000
3	1956	33,000	33,000
4	1957	33,000	33,000
5	1958	33,000	33,000
6	1959	33,000	33,000
7	1960	33,000	33,000
8	1961	33,000	33,000
9	1962	33,000	33,000
10	1963	36,000	36,000

4. A contract was entered into with the Fame Construction Company for the construction of the project at a cost of $360,000.

5. Supervisory engineering expenses amounting to $10,000 were paid.

6. The city's contribution was received in full and assessments to the amount of $27,000 were also received.

7. The remainder of the first installment became delinquent.

8. Judgments to the amount of $120,000 were awarded for property condemned.

9. A bill for $100,000 was received from the Fame Construction Company.

10. Payments were made as follows:

Judgments payable..................	$120,000
Fame Construction Company.........	100,000

11 and 12. Interest of $8,200 became receivable; of this amount $7,500 was collected.

13 and 14. Interest of $6,100 became payable; of this amount $4,000 was paid.

Required:

a. Prepare all entries, including closing entries.

b. Post to "T" accounts.

c. Prepare a balance sheet as of December 31, 1954.

Problem 8-4. Part II. The transactions taking place in 1955 were as follows:

20. Delinquent assessments to the amount of $1,500 were collected.

21. A bill was received from the Fame Construction Company for the remaining amount due on the contract.

22. Interest payable outstanding at the close of the last fiscal year was paid.

23 and 24. Interest of $9,000 became receivable during this year; interest receivable collected amounted to $8,900.

25. Current assessments receivable were set up.

26 and 27. Interest of $7,100 became payable; of this amount $3,550 was paid.

28 and 29. Current assessments amounting to $32,000 were collected; the remaining part of the second installment became delinquent.

30. The Fame Construction Company was paid the full amount of the contract, except for $50,000 which was retained pending the final approval of the project.

31. Collections (transaction 28) were applied to the payment of bonds.

Required:

a. Prepare all entries, including closing entries.

b. Post to "T" accounts.

c. Prepare a balance sheet as of December 31, 1955.

d. Prepare a subsidiary schedule supporting the balance sheet as of December 31, 1955, and showing the assets, liabilities, and so on, applicable to each bond installment.

e. Prepare a statement analyzing the changes in the Appropriations account for the fiscal years ended December 31, 1954 and 1955.

Problem 8-4. Part III. The transactions taking place in 1956 were as follows:

40. Interest payable outstanding at the close of 1955 was paid.

41. The city agreed to contribute $10,000 for the purpose of eliminating the deficit.

42. The remaining part of the deficit was to be eliminated through the levy of supplemental assessments. Supplemental assessments were subsequently levied and were made payable in three equal annual installments.

43. Notes to cover the last two annual installments of the supplemental assessments were issued and sold.

44. Current assessments receivable were set up.

45. Assessments (not supplemental) were collected as follows:

From 1st installment.................	$ 750
From 2nd installment...............	750
From 3rd installment...............	32,250

46. The proceeds, in so far as applicable, were used to retire bonds.

47. The uncollected portion of the third installment was set up as delinquent.

48 and 49. Interest on assessments to the amount of $7,900 became receivable during this year; interest receivable collected amounted to $7,750.

50 and 51. Interest on bonds to the amount of $6,240 became payable; of this amount $3,120 was paid.

52. The first installment of the supplemental assessment was collected in full, except for $800, which is to be set up as delinquent.

53. The city paid over its contribution.

54 and 55. Interest on supplemental assessments to the amount of $464 was collected; $16 was set up as receivable but was not collected.

56. The project was found to be satisfactory, and the Fame Construction Company was paid the amount due it. The additional cash necessary for this purpose was borrowed from the general fund.

57. Interest on notes to the amount of $360 was paid.

Required:

a. Prepare journal entries, including closing entries.

b. Post to "T" accounts.

c. Prepare a balance sheet as of December 31, 1956.

d. At what amount should the improvement be capitalized? Give reasons for your answer.

Problem 8-5. Part I. The following is a trial balance of the special assessment fund of the City of *V* as of January 1, 1948:

Assessments Receivable—Deferred.........	$450,000	
City's Share of Cost....................	80,000	
Bonds Payable.........................		$530,000
	$530,000	$530,000

Special assessments were levied after all construction had been completed. Installments and bond maturities are as follows:

No.	Year	Installments	City's Share of Installments	Bonds Maturing
1	1948	$ 45,000	$ 8,000	$ 53,000
2	1949	45,000	8,000	53,000
3	1950	45,000	8,000	53,000
4	1951	45,000	8,000	53,000
5	1952	45,000	8,000	53,000
6	1953	45,000	8,000	53,000
7	1954	45,000	8,000	53,000
8	1955	45,000	8,000	53,000
9	1956	45,000	8,000	53,000
10	1957	45,000	8,000	53,000
		$450,000	$80,000	$530,000

The following transactions took place during 1948:
1. The first installment became current.
2. Interest on assessments accrued amounted to $13,500.
3. Collections of current assessments amounted to $44,000.
4. The general fund paid the city's 1948 installment.
5. Collections of interest amounted to $13,400.
6. Bonds in the amount of $52,000 were retired.
7. Interest paid on bonds amounted to $13,000.
8. Uncollected current assessments became delinquent.

Required:
A. Prepare journal entries, including closing entries.
B. Post to "T" accounts.
C. Prepare a balance sheet as of December 31, 1948.

Problem 8-5. Part II. The following transactions took place during 1949:
20. The 1949 installment became current.
21. Accrued interest to the amount of $24,300 became receivable.
22. Cash collections for this fund were as follows:

1949 installment.....................	$44,000
Interest on deferred assessments.......	21,000
City's installment....................	8,000

23. Payments were made as follows:

Bonds.............................	$52,000
Interest...........................	21,000

24. The uncollected portion of the 1949 installment was placed in the delinquent account.

Required:
a. Prepare journal entries, including closing entries.
b. Post to "T" accounts.
c. Prepare a balance sheet as of December 31, 1949.

Problem 8-5. Part III. The following transactions took place during the years 1950 to 1955, inclusive:
30. The installments for 1950-1955 became current.
31. Interest becoming receivable on assessments during this period amounted to $84,550.
32. Collections during this period were as follows:

Current assessments.................	$252,000
Interest on assessments..............	82,000
City's installments..................	48,000
Delinquent assessments..............	2,000

33. Payments were made as follows during these six years:

Bonds.............................	$300,000
Interest...........................	78,000

34. The uncollected current assessments became delinquent.
35. Cash for interest payments to the amount of $75 was used to pay the county for the cost of holding the sale of delinquent properties.
36. At the end of 1955, the properties listed below, on which the last two (1954 and 1955) installments had not been paid, were put up for sale. Property L was sold to a private person for $2,745, and properties M and N were bid in by this fund.

	Unpaid Assessments	Accrued Interest	Cost of Sale	Total
L..............	$2,500	$220	$25	$2,745
M.............	3,000	260	25	3,285
N.............	2,300	210	25	2,535

Required:

a. Prepare journal entries, including closing entries.

b. Post to "T" accounts.

c. Prepare a balance sheet as of December 31, 1955.

Problem 8-5. Part IV. The following transactions took place during 1956:

40. The installment for this year became current.

41. Interest accrued on assessments amounted to $3,000.

42. Collections for this fund during the year were as follows:

1956 installment.....................	$42,000
Delinquent assessments...............	10,000
Interest on assessments..............	5,200
City's installment...................	8,000

43. Bonds retired this year amounted to $59,000.

44. Interest expenses on bonds paid amounted to $6,200.

45. Property B was redeemed by the owner, who was charged additional interest of $15.

46. The uncollected portion of the 1956 installment became delinquent.

Required:

a. Prepare journal entries, including closing entries.

b. Post to "T" accounts.

c. Prepare a balance sheet as of December 31, 1956.

Problem 8-5. Part V. The following transactions took place during 1957:

50. The final installment became current.

51. Interest receivable on assessments amounted to $2,400.

52. Property N was transferred to the general fixed assets of the city, and the general fund reimbursed this fund for the amount of the special assessment sale certificate.

53. Collections from assessments were as follows:

1957 installment.....................	$43,050
City's installment...................	8,000

54. Cash for interest payments of $35 was used to pay the county for holding a delinquent assessment sale.

55. Property P, with a total unpaid assessment of $1,300, plus $200 interest and $35 for cost of sale, was sold for $1,600.

56. All delinquent installments were collected.

57. All interest receivable was collected.

58. The remaining bonds were retired.

59. Interest paid on bonds amounted to $1,600.

60. The surplus was rebated.

Required:

a. Prepare journal entries, including closing entries.

b. Post to "T" accounts.

Problem 8-6. (Adapted from an American Institute of Accountants' examination.)

The City of P voted a bond issue for the purpose of constructing a modern sewer system in a section of the city. The cost is to be borne 10% by general revenues of the city and 90% by assessment against the property in the area of the improvement.

You are to prepare a balance-sheet of the fund as of the close of the fiscal year of the city, December 31, 1954.

The following transactions are to be considered:

February 1, 1954—The city engineer submits to city council an estimate of the cost of the project, showing a total of $445,000. The council approves the estimate and project, subject to voter approval of the necessary bond issue.

April 1, 1954—A ten year 4% bond issue of $460,000 was approved by the voters of the city, the proceeds to be used for the project.

April 10, 1954—A contract for $15,000 covering preliminary planning was entered into by the trustees who are carrying out the project.

April 15, 1954—The assessment roll is certified on the basis of $415,000 due in ten equal annual installments starting with May 1, 1955. Interest at 4% per annum from May 1, 1954 is to be paid on each installment due date, based on the total assessment outstanding.

April 30, 1954—The preliminary plans are completed and an invoice of $13,700 is received from the contractor in full payment. The trustees borrow $25,000 from the general fund of the city to pay this and other costs. The invoice was paid on May 5, 1954.

May 20, 1954—A contract for construction was entered into at a price of $420,000 subject to some possible future adjustments.

June 1, 1954—$200,000 of the authorized bonds were sold at 101. The entire issue is to be dated June 1, 1954, with interest payable December 1 and June 1 each year. The bonds mature at the rate of $46,000 per year, starting June 1, 1955.

July 31, 1954—A partial payment of $26,100 was made to the contractor, which amount was 90% of the amount due based on percentage of completion. The loan from the general fund was repaid.

November 1, 1954—The remaining bonds were sold at 98 and accrued interest.

August 1, 1954 to December 31, 1954—Payments to the contractor amounted to $284,400; 10% of the amount due having been withheld pending completion. $4,210 of costs in connection with administering the construction project were paid during the period. The bond interest was paid at due date. The city paid $2,300 on its part of the cost of the project.

Questions and Problems on Chapter 9

Questions

Question 9-1. A sinking fund was established for the purpose of retiring Dorchester Street Bridge bonds, which do not mature until 1969. In 1954, the sinking fund included among its investments $40,000 of Dorchester Street Bridge bonds. Should these bonds be canceled, or should they be held alive until 1969?

Question 9-2. In choosing investments for a sinking fund would you select those selling at a premium or at a discount?

Question 9-3. Give the entries to record the following: (a) the sale of general sinking fund investments with a par value of $100,000 at a profit of $2,000; (b) the sale of general sinking fund investments with a par value of $95,000 at a loss of $1,500.

Question 9-4. (a) General sinking fund securities have risen in value. Should the appreciation in value be recorded on the books? (b) Would your answer be different if the securities had declined in value?

Question 9-5. If the investments referred to in the preceding question are owned by a governmental utility, should an appreciation in value be recorded on the books? Should a decline in value be recorded?

Question 9-6. A fund was established for the retirement of bonds of $100,000 maturing at the end of ten years. Annual contributions of $10,000 are to be made, but all earnings on the contributions are to be transferred to the general fund. Is this fund a sinking fund in the sense in which the term is used in the present chapter? Give reasons for your answer.

Question 9-7. A certain municipality provides that its sinking fund is to be built up from various licenses and fines. The revenues from these sources have been as follows: 1952, $5,000; 1953, $3,000; 1954, $8,000. Can you see what is wrong with such a provision?

Question 9-8. Matured sinking fund bonds may be shown as a liability of either the sinking fund or the general fund. Point out the arguments for showing these bonds as a liability of (a) the sinking fund, and (b) the general fund.

Problems

Problem 9-1. Set up a schedule showing the required sinking fund contributions and required earnings if it is assumed that a $100,000 bond issue is to be retired in ten years and contributions are to earn 3 per cent interest compounded annually. (*Hint*—Required annual contributions, $8,723.)

Problem 9-2. In 1952 Central City issued bonds amounting to $100,000 and maturing in five years.

At the same time a sinking fund was established through an appropriation from the general fund. Subsequently, the general fund paid over the amount due to the sinking fund. The money was immediately invested (assume that no premiums, discounts, or accrued interest purchases are involved).

The procedure described in the preceding paragraph was repeated in 1953, 1954, 1955, and 1956, except that the contribution received in 1956 was not invested and except that there was no income in 1956.

463

The investments all matured in 1956 and were liquidated.

In 1956, the matured bonds were set up in the sinking fund, and cash for their retirement was transmitted to fiscal agents.

Contributions at all times equaled requirements.

A comparison of sinking fund earnings with requirements showed the following:

Year	Excess of Earnings over Requirements	Deficiency of Earnings over Requirements
1952.............	$300	
1953.............		$500
1954.............	400	
1955.............	200	

Surplus was transferred to the general fund.

Required:

a. Prepare a schedule showing required contributions and earnings. (Assume that sinking fund investments will earn 3 per cent per year. According to sinking fund tables, the required annual contribution on the basis of this rate of interest is $18,835.94.)

b. Prepare journal entries, including closing entries, to be made each year.

c. Prepare a balance sheet as of December 31 of each year.

Problem 9-3. On July 1, 1954, the City of A purchased bonds with a par value of $200,000 at a premium of $4,280 plus accrued interest. The bonds are to run for five years and bear a nominal interest rate of 4½ per cent, payable semiannually on April 1 and October 1. Bond tables show that bonds purchased on this basis would require the payment of a premium of $5,400 as of April 1, and would yield 3.9%.

Required:

a. Prepare an entry to record the purchase of the bonds.

b. Prepare a table similar to Table 2, showing the amortization of premiums over the life of the investments.

c. Prepare the entries to be made when interest is received on (1) October 1, 1954, (2) October 1, 1956, and (3) April 1, 1957.

Problem 9-4. Assume that the City of A sold the investments on June 1, 1957, for $201,750, and give the entry to record this transaction.

Problem 9-5. On July 1, 1954, the City of R purchased bonds with a par value of $200,000 at a discount of $4,200 plus accrued interest. The bonds are to run for five years and bear a nominal interest rate of 4½ per cent, payable semiannually on April 1 and October 1. Bond tables show that bonds purchased on this basis would be acquired at a discount of $5,240 as of April 1 and would yield 5.1%.

Required:

a. Prepare an entry to record the purchase of the bonds.

b. Prepare a table similar to Table 3, showing the amortization of discounts over the life of the investments.

c. Prepare the entries to be made when interest is received on (1) October 1, 1954, (2) October 1, 1956, and (3) April 1, 1957.

Problem 9-6. Assume that the City of R sold the investments on June 1, 1957, for $203,620, and give the entries to record this transaction.

Problem 9-7. A municipality purchased investments with a par value of $90,000 at a premium of $3,000. The bonds are to run for ten years, with $9,000 maturing each year and interest to be paid semiannually. Set up a table showing the amount of premium to be amortized at each interest payment date on the basis of the bonds outstanding method (see Table 4).

Problem 9-8. A municipality purchased investments with a par value of $200,000, and a discount of $2,000. The bonds are to run for ten years, with $20,000 maturing each year and interest to be paid semiannually. Set up a table showing the amount of discount to be amortized at each interest payment date on the basis of the bonds outstanding method (see Table 4).

Problem 9-9. The City of *B*, pursuant to state law, consolidated all of its sinking funds into one fund, the balance sheet for which was as follows:

CITY OF *B*

Consolidated Sinking Fund

Balance Sheet

December 31, 1954

ASSETS

Cash...		$150,000
Taxes Receivable—Delinquent..............	$ 90,000	
Less—Allowance for Uncollectible Delinquent Taxes................................	10,000	80,000
Investments............................	$276,000	
Less—Discounts on Investments...........	1,000	275,000
		$505,000

RESERVES AND SURPLUS

Reserve for Retirement of Sinking Fund Bonds:		
School Bonds..........................	$250,000	
Library Bonds.........................	175,000	
Recreation Bonds......................	75,000	$500,000
Unappropriated Surplus......................		5,000
		$505,000

The state supreme court subsequently held the law authorizing consolidated sinking funds unconstitutional.

Required:

Recast the above balance sheet so as to comply with the court decision (that is, show the financial condition of *each* fund).

Problem 9-10. From the following data prepare a statement comparing sinking fund contributions and earnings for 1955 with requirements of that year.

Required contribution for current year, $20,000
Required earnings, $30,000
Actual contribution, $20,000
Interest earned, $29,000
Amortization of discounts, $550
Amortization of premiums, $2,300

Questions and Problems on Chapter 10

Questions

Question 10-1. Taxes for the Sanitary District of R are collected by the county of C. The county clerk maintains the records of the individual taxpayers and enters in them the amount due from each taxpayer. For rendering this service, the clerk is permitted to add to each taxpayer's bill 2 cents for each governmental unit. For example, if a taxpayer is charged with taxes for the county, city, and sanitary district, 6 cents is added to his bill. Taxes are collected by the county treasurer, who is allowed a fee of 2 per cent of the amount collected. Before transmitting the proceeds of any collections to a governmental unit, the treasurer deducts the county clerk's fee and his own fee. (*a*) Should the county clerk's fee be included as part of the sanitary district's tax levy? If not, should such fee be recorded at all on the sanitary district's books? (*b*) Should the treasurer's fees be included as part of the tax levy of the sanitary district? How would you treat such fees on the sanitary district's books?

Question 10-2. In one state, cities collect their own current taxes, but delinquent taxes are turned over for collection to the county treasurer, who adds to each bill a 4 per cent collection fee, which, upon collection, he retains. Should this collection fee be considered a revenue of the city?

Question 10-3. A county's fee officers (sheriff, county clerk, etc.) deposit their collections with the county treasurer. Once a month, the county auditor determines the accounts to which such collections apply and makes the proper entries. Most of these collections apply to the general fund but some of them apply also to other funds. (*a*) Should these collections, pending their allocation, be handled through the general fund or a trust and agency fund? (*b*) Assuming they are handled through the general fund, what entry should be made in that fund (1) when the money is collected and (2) when the allocation is made? Assume $14,000 applies to the general fund and $1,000 to other funds.

Question 10-4. What is the difference between a nonexpendable trust fund and an agency fund?

Question 10-5. Classify the following as to whether they are expendable trust funds, nonexpendable trust funds, or agency funds:

a. A fund established to handle tax collections by this governmental unit for other governments.

b. A pension fund.

c. A loan fund.

d. A fund whose principal is to be held intact but whose income must be expended for bravery rewards.

e. A fund established to handle deposits.

f. A fund established to handle that part of the proceeds from the sale of property for taxes which is to be refunded to the property owner.

g. A fund whose principal and income are both to be used in granting scholarships.

Question 10-6. Classify the trust funds in Question 10-5 according to whether they are public trust funds or private trust funds.

Question 10-7. According to the terms of A's will, the city is to become the owner of an apartment building. The net income from the building is to be added to the policemen's pension fund. (*a*) Is this an expendable or nonexpendable trust fund? (*b*) Suppose that, in computing net income, the city does not take into account depreciation. Is the fund expendable or nonexpendable?

Question 10-8. What is the difference between a special assessment fund and a private trust fund?

Question 10-9. In what respects are a pension fund and a sinking fund similar and in what respects do they differ?

Problems

Problem 10-1. The following is a trial balance of the firemen's pension fund of the City of Z:

CITY OF Z
Firemen's Pension Fund
Trial Balance
January 1, 1955

Cash	$ 6,000	
Investments	52,000	
Interest Receivable on Investments	450	
Pensions Payable		$ 150
Pension Fund Reserve		58,010
Unappropriated Surplus		290
	$58,450	$58,450

The following transactions took place during the year:

1. Required contributions from employees amounted to $22,000 and from the governmental unit, $22,000; required earnings amounted to $1,000.

2. The required contributions became due from the general fund ($38,000) and the special assessment fund ($6,000). One half of these amounts represents the employees' share of contributions.

3. The general fund paid $30,000 and the special assessment fund $4,000 of the amounts due from them.

4. Securities were acquired for cash as follows:

(a) First Purchase	
Par Value	$20,000
Premiums	300
Interest accrued at date of purchase	200

(b) Second Purchase	
Par Value	$15,000
Discounts	150

5. The general fund and the special assessment fund paid over the balances due from them.

6. Interest received on investments amounted to $3,000, including interest receivable on January 1, 1955 and accrued interest purchased.

7. Premiums and discounts in the amounts of $50 and $30, respectively, were amortized.

8. Pensions paid, including pensions accrued at January 1, 1955, amounted to $800.

9. Pensions accrued at December 31, 1955, amounted to $190.

Required:

(a) Prepare journal entries, including closing entries.

(b) Post to "T" accounts.

(c) Prepare a balance sheet as of December 31, 1955.

Problem 10-2. The following is a trial balance of Child Welfare Principal Trust Fund as of January 1, 1955.

Cash....................................	$ 98,000	
Land....................................	70,000	
Buildings...............................	162,000	
Reserve for Depreciation.................		$ 65,000
Accrued Wages..........................		110
Accrued Taxes..........................		1,800
Due to Child Welfare Earnings Trust Fund		15,000
Child Welfare Principal Trust Fund Balance		248,090
	$330,000	$330,000

The endowment was in the form of an apartment building. Endowment principal is to be kept intact, and the net earnings are to be used in financing child welfare activities.

The following transactions took place during the year:

1. Expenses and accrued liabilities paid in cash were as follows:

Coal...................................	$5,200
Janitor's wages (including $110 previously accrued)...........................	3,000
Painting and decorating.................	3,750
Repairs................................	1,500
Taxes (including $1,800 previously accrued)	3,750
Managerial commissions.................	4,500
Miscellaneous expenses.................	1,500

2. A special assessment amounting to $2,000 was levied by the municipality against the property and was paid.

3. Rents for 1955 (all collected) amounted to $45,000.

4. The amount due to the Child Welfare Earnings Trust Fund was paid over.

5. Expenditures of $15,000 were made out of the Child Welfare Earnings Trust Fund to finance the 1955 summer camp activities.

6. The following adjustments were made at the close of the year:

Depreciation...........................	$6,000
Accrued taxes..........................	1,800
Accrued wages.........................	110

Required:

a. Prepare a balance sheet as of December 31, 1955, and a profit and loss statement for the fiscal year ended December 31, 1955, for the Child Welfare Principal Trust Fund.

b. Prepare a balance sheet as of December 31, 1955, for the Child Welfare Earnings Trust Fund.

Problem 10-3. (Adapted from an American Institute of Accountants' examination.)

The City of *B* had not been operating a public library prior to October 1, 1954. On October 1, 1954, James Jones died, having made a valid will which provided for the gift of his residence and various securities to the city for the establishment and operation of a free public library. The gift was accepted by the town. The library funds and operation were placed under the control of trustees. The terms of the gift provided that not in excess of $5,000 of the principal of the fund could be used for the purchase of equipment, building rearrangement, and purchase of such "standard" library reference books as, in the opinion of the trustees, were needed for starting the library. Except for this $5,000, the principal of the fund is to be invested and the income therefrom used to operate the library in accordance with appropriations made by the trustees.

The property received from the estate by the trustees was as follows:

Description	Face or Par	Appraised Value
Residence of James Jones:		
Land..................................		$ 2,500
Building (25-year estimated life).........		20,000
Bonds:		
AB Company.........................	$34,000	32,000
C & D Company.....................	10,000	11,200
D & G Company.....................	20,000	20,000
Stocks:		
M Company, 6% preferred.............	12,000	12,600
S Company, 5% preferred.............	10,000	9,600
K Company, common (300 shares).......	No par	12,900
GF Company (200 shares).............	4,000	14,500

The following events occurred in connection with the library operations up to June 30, 1955:

1. 100 shares of GF Company stock were sold on November 17, for $6,875.

2. Cash payments were made for: (a) Alteration of the house—$1,310, (b) General reference books—$725, (c) Equipment having an estimated life of ten years—$2,180. The trustees state that these amounts are to be charged to principal under the applicable provision of the gift.

3. The library started operation on January 1, 1955. The trustees adopted the following budget for the year ended December 31, 1955:

Estimated income from investment.....................	$ 5,000
Estimated income from fines, etc......................	200
Appropriation for salaries............................	3,600
Appropriation for subscriptions.......................	300
Appropriations for purchase of books..................	800
Appropriation for utilities, supplies, etc................	400

4. The following cash receipts were reported during the six months to June 30, 1955:

Sale of C and D Company bonds including accrued interest of $80...	$11,550
Interest and dividends................................	3,100
Fines..	20
Gift for purchase of books............................	200
Total...	$14,870

5. The following cash payments were made during the six months to June 30, 1955:

Purchase of 100 shares of no-par common stock of L and M
Company including commission and tax cost of $42.50.. $ 9,655
Payment of salaries.................................... 1,500
Payment of property taxes applicable to the year ended
December 31, 1954, based on an assessment as of June 30,
1954.. 200
Purchase of books..................................... 900
Magazine subscriptions................................ 230
Supplies and other expense............................ 260

    Total... $12,745

6. On June 30, 1955, there were miscellaneous expenses unpaid, but accrued, amounting to $90. Also there were outstanding purchase orders for books in the amount of $70.

Assuming the town records budgetary accounts, prepare all statements necessary to show results of operation to June 30, 1955 and the financial position of the library as of June 30, 1955. Where alternate treatment of an item is possible, explain the alternate treatment and state the justification for your treatment.

Problem 10-4. The following is a list of the accounts of the trust and agency funds of the City of F:

Cash—Cemetery Perpetual Care Earnings........	$ 2,420	
Cash—Cemetery Perpetual Care Principal........	4,875	
Cash—Employees' Retirement Fund.............	88,953	
Cash—Returnable Deposits.....................	49,600	
Accrued Bond Interest Receivable—Employees' Retirement......................................	5,206	
Accrued Employees' Contributions Receivable.....	12,954	
Cash—Nash County Taxes.....................	13,500	
Cash—Doyle Park Endowment.................	2,100	
Cash—Doyle Park Income......................	750	
Due to City Treasurer—Employees' Retirement...		$ 15
Employees' Retirement Fund Balance............		618,989
Interest Receivable—Cemetery Perpetual Care Earnings.....................................	1,585	
Cemetery Perpetual Care Earnings Balance.......		3,450
Cemetery Perpetual Care Principal..............		77,435
Returnable Deposits...........................		49,600
Nash County Taxes Balance....................		105,100
Taxes Receivable for Nash County—Current.....	73,200	
Taxes Receivable for Nash County—Delinquent...	18,040	
Nash Park Endowment Principal................		110,789
Doyle Park Income Balance....................		875
Investments—Cemetery Perpetual Care Principal..	75,000	
Investments—Employees' Retirement:		
Municipal Bonds...........................	468,000	
Unamortized Premiums on Bonds.............	47,500	
Investments—Doyle Park Endowment..........	102,570	
Totals..................................	$966,253	$966,253

Required:

Prepare a combined trust and agency funds balance sheet as of December 31, 1954.

Problem 10-5. The following is a trial balance of the tax agency funds of the City of Q as of June 30, 1955:

Cash...	$ 90,000	
Taxes Receivable for City X.....................	22,500	
Taxes Receivable for City Y.....................	48,000	
Taxes Receivable for City Z.....................	69,000	
Taxes Fund Balance—City X.....................		$ 37,500
Taxes Fund Balance—City Y.....................		78,000
Taxes Fund Balance—City Z.....................		114,000
	$229,500	$229,500

The following transactions took place:

1. Cash to the amount of $89,400 was paid over as follows:

City	Amount Due	Collection Fee	Amount Paid Over
X...........................	$15,000	$100	$14,900
Y...........................	30,000	200	29,800
Z...........................	45,000	300	44,700

2. The collection fees were paid over to the general fund.
3. Taxes were levied as follows:

City	Amount Levied
X................................	$ 50,000
Y................................	100,000
Z................................	150,000

Required:

a. Prepare journal entries.

b. Post to "T" accounts.

c. Prepare a balance sheet as of November 30, 1955.

Problem 10-6. The City of M collects, in addition to its own taxes, those of other units. The following are the tax levies for 1954 and 1955:

	1954	1955
City....................	$220,000	$240,000
School District..........	150,000	160,000
Park District..........	100,000	100,000
	$470,000	$500,000

Collections during 1955 were as follows:

1954 levy........................	$ 67,000
1955 levy........................	464,000

The city tax levies are in turn distributed among the following funds:

Fund	Mills per Dollar of Assessed Value	
	1954	1955
General...............	9.83	8.86
Library...............	1.08	1.30
Debt Retirement........	1.09	1.34
Total...............	12.00	11.50

Required:

a. Compute the amount of the collection of each levy applicable to each governmental unit.

b. Compute the amount of the collection from each city levy applicable to each fund.

c. Prepare the journal entry to be made on the city's books to record the collection of taxes in 1955 (that is, the collection of 1954 and 1955 taxes in 1955).

d. Assuming that the municipality charges a fee of 2.5 per cent for collecting these taxes, prepare the entry to record on the city's books the collection of the fee and its transfer to the general fund. Prepare also an entry to record the transmittal of the money to the units for which it is collected.

e. Prepare the entries to be made transferring the city's collections to the proper city funds, and the entries in each fund.

Problem 10-7. The following is a receipts and disbursements statement of the Cemetery Fund of the City of Q for the year ended December 31, 1954:

RECEIPTS

Balance in Bank, January 2, 1954	$ 2,050
County Treasurer—Tax Collections for Cemetery	7,350
Sale of Lots	6,700
Grave Digging	2,300
Fees—Monuments and Markers	120
Lot Upkeep	75
Monument and Marker Bases	150
Interest on Endowment Fund	1,340
Cemetery Endowment Fund	410
Miscellaneous Revenues	40
Total	$20,535

DISBURSEMENTS

New Equipment—Includes Tools	$ 275
New Improvements	3,050
Transfer of Endowment Funds	750
Contract—New Paving	625
Salary—Sexton	3,500
Other Salaries and Wages	7,200
Salaries and Wages—New Improvements	75
Equipment Rental	250
Water, Light, Power, and Fuel	525
Maintenance of Buildings and Equipment	250
Insurance and Bond Premiums	130
Gas, Oil, and Transportation	210
Miscellaneous Expenses	230
Balance in Bank, January 2, 1955	3,465
Total	$20,535

Required:

Convert this statement into an income and expense statement on a cash basis.

Questions and Problems on Chapter 11

Questions

Question 11-1. In a certain state the question has come up as to whether the maintenance of one of the state office buildings should be financed by a single appropriation for such maintenance or whether maintenance expenses should be financed out of a working capital fund. If a working capital fund were established, the departments would be charged rent based on the amount of space occupied by them and they would obtain money from an appropriation made to each of them for this purpose. Which of these two methods would you recommend and why?

Question 11-2. Can you think of any methods, besides those given in the text, of disposing of profits or making up deficits of a working capital fund?

Question 11-3. A working capital fund was established through the sale of bonds. What disposition should be made of the current assets of the working capital fund if the fund is dissolved?

Question 11-4. Referring to Question 11-3, suppose that the bonds are being retired from the general fund. Should the charges to departments for services include depreciation on buildings and equipment financed from these bonds, assuming (a) these departments are all financed from the general fund and (b) these departments are all financed from funds other than the general fund?

Problems

Problem 11-1. The following is a trial balance of the working capital fund of the City of P as of July 1, 1955:

Cash......................................	$ 50,000	
Land......................................	55,000	
Buildings.................................	32,000	
Allowance for Depreciation—Buildings.....		$ 8,000
Machinery................................	26,000	
Allowance for Depreciation—Machinery....		5,000
Equipment................................	36,000	
Allowance for Depreciation—Equipment...		9,200
Due from General Fund..................	77,600	
Inventory of Materials...................	25,000	
Vouchers Payable........................		55,000
Capital...................................		200,000
Unappropriated Surplus...................		31,400
Work in Process Inventory...............	7,000	
	$308,600	$308,600

The following transactions took place during the year:

1. Materials were ordered and received together with an invoice in the amount of $63,000.

2. Payrolls were approved as follows:

473

Direct labor	$12,000
Indirect labor	3,000
Plant office	6,000

3. Electric bills for $4,000 were paid.

4. The city treasurer transferred cash from the general fund to the working capital fund for the amount due to this fund for past services.

5. Vouchers payable as of July 1, 1955, were paid in full.

6. Telephone and telegraph charges of $500 were paid.

7. Plant office supplies were purchased on account for $200.

8. The general fund was billed $95,000 for materials manufactured for and used by it.

9. Materials used by the working capital fund during this period, $60,000.

10. Insurance expenses paid amounted to $500, of which $400 is applicable to succeeding years.

11. A small secondhand machine was purchased for $700 in cash.

12. Repair bills during this period amounted to $1,200.

13. Depreciation charges:

Buildings	$1,600
Machinery	2,600
Equipment	3,600

14. Work in process on June 30, 1956 amounted to $7,000.

Required:

Prepare a balance sheet as of June 30, 1956, and an income and expense statement for the fiscal year ended June 30, 1956.

Problem 11-2. The following transactions took place during the fiscal year beginning July 1, 1955, in the working capital fund of the City of M:

1. Budget requirements for the year were estimated at $70,000 and an appropriation was made for this amount.

2. Materials were ordered as follows:

Sand	$ 6,200
Filler	7,200
Asphalt	16,400
Crushed rock	8,200

3. Telephone and telegraph charges of $300 were paid.

4. Plant office supplies were purchased for $100 cash.

5. The materials ordered were received together with an invoice. The actual cost of the materials ordered was as follows:

Sand	$ 6,000
Filler	7,200
Asphalt	16,500
Crushed rock	8,000

6. Payrolls were approved as follows:

Direct labor	$6,000
Indirect labor	2,000
Plant office	3,000

7. Electric bills for $2,000 were paid.

8. An order was placed for a small machine estimated to cost $280.

9. The equipment (machine) was received together with an invoice for $300.

10. Repair bills paid this period amounted to $700.

11. Additional materials ordered amounted to $15,000.

Required:

(a) Prepare journal entries, including closing entries, for the budgetary transactions only.

(b) Post to "T" accounts.

(c) Prepare a balance sheet for the budgetary group of accounts as of June 30, 1956.

Problem 11-3. The following is a trial balance prepared for the Central Stores Department of the City of M at December 31, 1955:

Sales to Departments....................		$150,000
Sales Returns and Allowances............	$ 2,000	
Purchases............................	100,600	
Freight In............................	1,000	
Wages...............................	25,000	
Office Salaries........................	6,000	
Office Expenses.......................	1,000	
Miscellaneous General Expenses..........	2,000	
Land................................	40,000	
Buildings............................	90,000	
Allowance for Depreciation—Buildings.....		12,000
Machinery and Equipment..............	65,000	
Allowance for Depreciation—Machinery and Equipment.........................		10,000
Cash................................	15,000	
Due from General Fund.................	48,000	
Notes Receivable......................	2,000	
Inventory............................	70,000	
Prepaid Insurance.....................	700	
Accounts Payable......................		13,300
Bonds Payable........................		95,000
Capital..............................		165,000
Unappropriated Surplus.................		23,000
	$468,300	$468,300

Adjustments:

Insurance expired, $400.
Accrued wages, $1,000; accrued salaries, $300.
Accrued interest payable, $3,000.
Closing inventory, $80,000.
Depreciation:
Buildings, 4 per cent.
Machinery and equipment, 8 per cent.

Required:

Prepare a balance sheet and an income and expense statement.

Problem 11-4. The following is a trial balance of a working capital fund (established to finance the operations of a central garage) of the City of J at January 1, 1955:

Land................................	$ 30,000	
Buildings............................	70,000	
Allowance for Depreciation—Buildings.....		$ 10,000
Machinery...........................	30,000	
Allowance for Depreciation—Machinery....		5,000
Equipment...........................	150,000	
Allowance for Depreciation—Equipment...		45,000
Cash................................	40,000	

Inventory:
Gas...................................	4,000	
Oil and Grease.......................	2,000	
Tires................................	6,500	
Parts...............................	13,500	
Due from General Fund.................	20,000	
Vouchers Payable......................		75,000
Capital..................................		228,000
Unappropriated Surplus.................		3,000
	$366,000	$366,000

1. Wages and salaries paid (all chargeable to 1955) were as follows:

Salary of superintendent..............	$ 6,000
Mechanics' wages....................	29,000
Garage office salaries................	4,500

2. Purchases (on account) were as follows:

Gas...............................	$20,000
Oil and grease......................	2,000
Tires..............................	16,000
Parts..............................	20,000

3. Departments are charged at a predetermined rate based on mileage. During the year 1955, billings to departments amounted to $150,000, all of which was payable from the general fund. At December 31, 1955, the general fund owed the working capital fund $25,000.

4. Other expenses were as follows:

Heat, light, and power, $10,000, which amount is still due to the utility fund.

Depreciation:
Buildings, 5 per cent
Machinery, 10 per cent
Equipment, 10 per cent

5. Vouchers payable paid amounted to $35,000.
6. Closing inventories were as follows:

Gas...............................	$ 6,000
Oil and grease......................	1,500
Tires..............................	11,500
Parts..............................	15,000

7. Accrued salaries and wages were as follows:

Salary of superintendent..............	$ 250
Mechanics' wages....................	830
Garage office salaries................	180

Required:

Prepare a balance sheet as of December 31, 1955, and an income and expense statement for the year ended December 31, 1955.

Problem 11-5. (Adapted from an American Institute of Accountants' examination.) The following account balances are taken from the books of the City of *M* on June 30, 1954, the close of the fiscal year.

1. Segregate the data into the applicable fund or account-group trial balances, supplying the needed account titles.

2. Prepare closing entries.

Accounts payable—general....................................	$ 6,000
Appropriations—general......................................	106,000
Bonds payable—general.......................................	300,000
Bonds payable—special assessment—District No. 1..............	25,000
Bonds payable—premium—special assessment—District No. 1........	1,000
Building—garage..	20,000
Building—garage—reserve for depreciation....................	5,000
Buildings—other..	300,000
Capital outlays for construction—bridge.....................	70,000
Capital outlays for construction—special assessment—District No. 1.....	26,000
Cash...	47,600
Contracts payable—bridge....................................	5,000
Depreciation—garage...	2,500
Encumbrances—bridge...	25,000
Encumbrances—general..	7,000
Equipment—garage..	50,000
Equipment—reserve for depreciation..........................	10,000
Equipment—other..	75,000
Estimated revenues..	100,000
Expenditures—general..	104,000
Garage—original appropriation...............................	60,000
Inventory of materials and supplies—garage..................	1,500
Inventory of materials and supplies—general.................	4,000
Labor—garage...	5,000
Land—garage..	4,000
Land—other...	20,000
Materials and supplies used—garage..........................	2,000
Overhead—garage..	2,500
Public improvements...	1,250,000
Receipts—interest on special assessments—District No. 1......	1,000
Reserve for authorized expenditures—bridge*.................	100,000
Reserve for authorized expenditures—special assessments†.....	25,000
Reserve for encumbrances—bridge.............................	25,000
Reserve for encumbrances—general............................	7,000
Revenues—garage...	12,500
Revenues—general..	102,000
Special assessments receivable—District No. 1 deferred........	18,000
Special assessments receivable—District No. 1 delinquent......	400
Surplus..	1,419,000
Taxes receivable—delinquent.................................	75,000

* Synonymous with "Appropriations—bridge" described in Chapter 7.
† Synonymous with "Appropriations—special assessments" described in Chapter 8.

Explanatory Data:

1. The city has deposited all cash in a single bank account. The fund segregation will require a separate account for each fund. The cash is owned as follows: garage, $2,000; bridge, $35,000; construction of pavement, $2,000; special assessment bond payments, $1,600; interest on special assessment bonds, $2,000; balance, general city.

2. $3,000 of the special assessment construction expenditures is from cash belonging to the general fund.

3. The city's share of special assessment construction unpaid is $5,000.

4. The municipal garage has supplied services in the amount of $1,000 for the general fund for which no settlement has been made.

5. The municipal garage was built and equipped out of general taxes. The surplus earned by the garage to July 1, 1953, is $3,000.

Problem 11-6. (Adapted from an American Institute of Accountants' examination.) Prepare working sheet showing balances of accounts of Municipal Garage Revolving Fund of the City of *W* as at December 31, 1954.

The City of *W* maintains a revolving fund for financial control of a municipally owned and operated garage serving several departments. It is the city's policy to operate the fund accounts so that the departments served will be charged their several shares of the operating cost for a fiscal year. Current billings are made to the departments for services based on charges for actual materials and supplies and actual direct labor plus estimated overhead. Differences between total overhead actually incurred and the estimated amounts billed to departments are adjusted through supplemental billing at the end of each fiscal year. Adjustments to physical inventories are handled through overhead.

1. Garage overhead for the fiscal year ended December 31, 1954, comprised the physical inventory adjustments referred to and the following expenses: superintendence, $3,000; office salaries, $1,300; office supplies, $200; garage depreciation, $2,000; heat and light, $620; miscellaneous, $80.

2. Accounts payable at December 31, 1954, amounted to $1,100. All payrolls had been paid.

3. The garage originally cost $50,000, financed by a capital advance from the General Fund, and, as at January 1, 1954, the accumulated depreciation thereagainst was $4,000. On that date, records of the revolving fund showed cash $3,000; inventories of gas, oil, and grease, $1,050; and of repair and maintenance materials, $2,250; a balance of $900 on account of services previously rendered the general fund; and accounts payable of $700; capital advances from the general fund of $50,000; and a current surplus account.

4. Physical inventories at December 31, 1954, were as follows:

Gas, oil, and grease.................... $ 890
Repair and maintenance materials....... 2,000

5. Summaries of certain transactions for the fiscal year ended December 31, 1954, appear in journal entry form as follows:

(A)

Due from General Fund.................. $9,740
Due from Highway Fund................. 7,045
Due from Police Fund.................. 8,280
Due from Fire Fund.................... 4,685
    Services rendered to departments........ $29,750

To record charges to departments for services billed, as follows:

Department	Total	Gas, Oil, Grease (at cost)	REPAIRS AND MAINTENANCE Actual Cost Materials	Direct Labor	Estimated Overhead (75% of Direct Labor)
General..............	$ 9,740	$ 3,950	$1,240	$2,600	$1,950
Highway..............	7,045	2,460	910	2,100	1,575
Police................	8,280	2,280	1,100	2,800	2,100
Fire.................	4,685	1,540	520	1,500	1,125
	$29,750	$10,230	$3,770	$9,000	$6,750

(B)

Cash................................		$29,900
Due from General Fund............ ..	$10,400	
Due from Highway Fund..............	7,000	
Due from Police Fund................	8,000	
Due from Fire Fund.................	4,500	

To record cash received for services billed.

(C)

Purchases—Gas, oil, and grease..........	$10,100	
Purchases—Repair and maintenance materials.....................	3,580	
Accounts Payable................		$13,680

To record purchases for the period.

Problem 11-7. (Adapted from an American Institute of Accountants' examination.) From the following information, prepare a work sheet for the City of *M* for the year ended June 30, 1955, showing opening balances, entries in the various accounts to reflect transactions for the year, and fund balance sheets at the end of the year.

The fund balance sheets of the City of *M* at July 1, 1954, are submitted as follows:

CITY OF *M*

Combined Balance Sheet—All Funds: July 1, 1954

General Fund

ASSETS		LIABILITIES, RESERVES, AND SURPLUS	
Cash....................	$ 50,000	Accounts payable.........	$ 30,000
Taxes receivable—delinquent	25,000	Reserve for encumbrances...	5,000
Long-time advance to revolving fund...............	15,000	Due to revolving fund......	5,000
		Unappropriated surplus.....	35,000
		Unappropriated surplus—advance to revolving fund...	15,000
	$ 90,000		$ 90,000

Transportation Revolving Fund

Cash....................	$ 10,000	Long-time advance from general fund...............	$ 15,000
Due from general fund......	5,000		
	$ 15,000		$ 15,000
	$105,000		$105,000

Transactions for fiscal year ended June 30, 1955:

1. Estimated total revenues are $200,000, including $75,000 of miscellaneous revenues.

2. Appropriations are $175,000.

3. The council levied property taxes in the amount of $125,000. Based on experience, the expected losses will be 5%.

4. Receipts from current tax revenues amounted to $85,000 and receipts from miscellaneous sources amounted to $80,000.

5. Delinquent taxes received were $23,500 and the balance is considered uncollectible.

6. General fund materials and supplies received and vouchered for payment amounted to $95,000, including $4,000 in complete fulfillment of all orders outstanding at July 1, 1954; budgeted orders placed amounted to $100,000, and orders outstanding at the end of the year amounted to $4,000.

7. Salary and wage payments amounted to $72,000, as budgeted; vouchered bills paid were $90,000.

8. Collections on taxes written off in prior years were $1,650.

9. Taxes collected in advance were $1,000.

10. In order to finance the construction of certain local roadways, the council voted to set up a special assessment fund and levied a special assessment of $75,000 on 1/1/55, collectible in equal proportions over a period of three years, with interest from date of assessment at the rate of six per cent per year.

11. Pending collection of special assessments, 5% bonds in the amount of $25,000 were sold at a premium of $200 on January 1, 1955. The amount of premium is considered too small to be amortized over the life of the bonds.

12. Construction contracts were let in amount of $50,000.

13. Contractors were paid $20,000 less 10% retained percentage.

14. Special assessments collected amounted to $23,000, representing $22,500 principal on current assessments due for the payment of bonds and $500 interest on deferred assessments to pay interest on outstanding bonds.

15. Outstanding bonds of $12,000 were paid, plus interest of $625.

16. The transportation revolving fund purchased trucks for $9,000 of which $5,000 remains unpaid on open account.

17. The transportation revolving fund charged the general fund for transportation services applicable to general fund activities in the amount of $3,000 at cost, including depreciation on trucks of $1,200.

18. The transportation revolving fund was paid $6,000 by the general fund.

Questions and Problems on Chapter 12

Questions

Question 12-1. A certain city, wishing to acquire a privately owned utility, had an appraisal made of the property. The appraisers valued the assets on the basis of original cost less accrued depreciation and arrived at a value of $400,000. The owners, however, refused to sell the plant for less than $425,000, and the municipality was forced to pay the full amount asked. Give the entry necessary to record the excess of the cost of the utility to the municipality over its appraised value.

Question 12-2. The utility of the City of A follows the practice of amortizing premiums on bonds, whereas the utility of the City of B does not amortize such premiums. (a) If construction costs and nominal interest expenses (that is, interest expenses before amortized premium is taken into account) are the same in both cases, will the fixed assets of the utility of the City of B be capitalized at a greater or smaller figure than those of the utility of the City of A? (b) Suppose the same situation is true with discounts; that is, suppose that the utility of the City of A amortizes discounts, whereas the utility of the City of B does not. Would the utility of the City of B, in that event, if construction costs and nominal interest expenses are the same in both cases, capitalize its fixed assets at a greater or smaller figure than the utility of the City of A?

Question 12-3. The condensed balance sheet of a utility or other enterprise fund is as follows:

CITY OF K
Utility or Other Enterprise Fund
Condensed Balance Sheet
December 31, 1954

ASSETS		LIABILITIES		
Fixed Assets (Net)	$148,000	Bonds Payable	$150,000	
Current Assets (Net)	30,000	Current Liabilities	30,000	$180,000
Sinking Fund	40,000	Reserve for Retirement of Sinking Fund Bonds		40,000
		Unappropriated Surplus	$ 3,000	
		Less—Loss, 1954	5,000	2,000*
	$218,000			$218,000

* Red.

On January 2, 1955, a contribution of $10,000 was made to the sinking fund. Give the entries necessary to record this transaction.

Question 12-4. A pension fund is maintained through contributions from both

481

the utility and its employees and is administered by an independent pension board. (*a*) Should such a fund be shown as part of the utility fund? (*b*) Would your answer be different if contributions were made by the utility alone?

Question 12-5. A utility carries a pension fund as part of the utility fund. Should earnings on pension fund investments be included as part of the utility fund revenues?

Question 12-6. Comment on the following, which is part of an operating statement taken from a municipal water works report:

CITY OF *X*

Utility Fund

Operating Statement

January 1, 1954 to December 31, 1954

Operating Revenue:

Water Rates	$747,568.68	
Cisterns	30.00	
Damaged Meters	477.50	
Rental of Mains	123,453.80	$871,529.98

Deductions from Operating Revenue:

Shortage of Revenue from Rental of Mains	$ 61,153.80*	
Refunds	408.06	61,561.86
		$809,968.12

* Bills owing by the City for water for 1954 exceed the levy made by the City Council by approximately $61,153.80. This amount will remain unpaid until the City makes provision for payment.

Question 12-7. (*a*) A utility bills its customers separately for service and for sales taxes. Should billings for sales taxes be included among the revenues? (*b*) Suppose that the utility is not allowed to bill customers for the sales tax. However, rates have been raised approximately by the amount of the tax. Should the revenues be reduced by the amount of the sales tax? (*c*) Give the entries to show how the payment of the taxes by the governmental utility would be recorded in each of the above cases.

Question 12-8. A governmental water utility allowed a 10 per cent discount on each bill paid within ten days from the date of billing. Subsequently, it was decided to bill all customers net (that is, to reduce each bill by 10 per cent) but to add a 10 per cent penalty to all bills not paid within ten days. (*a*) If the total sales for the month in the first instance (when discounts were allowed) before deducting discounts were $100,000, and if 80 per cent of the amount billed was collected within ten days and 10 per cent during the remainder of the month, give the entries to record billings and collections. (*b*) If the total sales during the second month before adding penalties were $90,000, and if 80 per cent of the amount billed was collected within ten days and 10 per cent during the remainder of the month, give the entries to record billings and collections. (*c*) On the basis of (*a*) and (*b*) above, would you say that the change affected the accounting procedure? (Assume that metered residential sales are involved and use both general ledger and subsidiary accounts.)

Problems

Problem 12-1. The following is a trial balance of the utility or other enterprise fund of the City of *Z* as of January 1, 1955:

Cash...............................	$105,000	
Accounts Receivable....................	52,000	
Allowance for Uncollectible Accounts.......		$ 6,000
Inventory of Materials and Supplies.......	25,500	
Prepaid Insurance......................	600	
Interest Receivable.....................	300	
Land.................................	150,000	
Structures and Improvements.............	385,000	
Allowance for Depreciation—Structures and Improvements......................		75,000
Equipment...........................	157,000	
Allowance for Depreciation—Equipment...		72,000
Vouchers Payable......................		30,000
Accrued Salaries and Wages..............		4,500
Accrued Taxes........................		6,750
Interest Payable.......................		6,000
Bonds Payable........................		300,000
Governmental Unit's Contributions........		337,000
Unappropriated Surplus.................		38,150
	$875,400	$875,400

The following transactions took place during the year:
1. Total revenues billed for amounted to $250,000.
2. Equipment was acquired at a cost of $32,000.
3. Materials were purchased at a cost of $61,000.
4. Collections on accounts receivable amounted to $260,000.
5. Payments were made as follows:

Accrued salaries and wages...........	$ 4,500
Accrued taxes......................	6,750
Interest payable....................	6,000
Vouchers payable...................	110,000

6. Interest receivable amounting to $300 was collected.
7. Telephone and telegraph charges of $500 were paid.
8. Interest paid amounted to $15,000.
9. Taxes paid amounted to $2,000.
10. Interest received amounted to $550.
11. Total salaries and wages paid amounted to $90,000.
12. Bonds to the amount of $30,000 were retired.
13. A transfer of $10,000 was made to the city's general fund. (*Note:* This transfer was appropriated for.)
14. Adjustments were made as follows:

        (a) Accrued salaries and wages, $5,400
        (b) Interest payable, $4,000
        (c) Interest receivable, $520
        (d) Accrued taxes, $5,300
        (e) Insurance expired, $500
        (f) Closing inventory, $30,000
        (g) Estimated losses on accounts receivable, $510
        (h) Depreciation:

Structures and improvements	$22,350
Equipment...............	10,250

Required:
  a. Prepare journal entries, including closing entries.
  b. Post to "T" accounts.

c. Prepare a balance sheet as of December 31, 1955, and an income and expense statement for 1955.

Problem 12-2. The following is a trial balance of the budgetary accounts of the utility or other enterprise fund of the City of Y as of January 1, 1955:

Budget Requirements......................	$21,000	
Reserve for Encumbrances.................		$21,000
	$21,000	$21,000

The following transactions took place during the year:

1. Appropriations to the amount of $320,000 were made. (All expenditures, with the exception of depreciation and losses on uncollectible accounts, have been appropriated for.)

2. The materials ordered at the close of the previous year were received, together with a bill for $22,000.

3. Total salaries and wages paid amounted to $90,000.

4. An order was placed for equipment estimated to cost $60,000.

5. An order was placed for materials estimated to cost $40,000.

6. The equipment was received; the actual cost was $62,000.

7. The materials were received; the actual cost was $39,000.

8. Telephone and telegraph charges of $500 were paid.

9. Interest paid amounted to $15,000.

10. Taxes paid amounted to $2,000.

11. An order was placed for materials estimated to cost $24,000.

12. Bonds to the amount of $30,000 were retired.

13. A transfer of $10,000 was made to the city's general fund. (*Note:* This transfer was appropriated for.)

14. Adjustments were made as follows:

> (a) Accrued salaries and wages, $5,400
> (b) Interest payable, $4,000
> (c) Accrued taxes, $5,300

Required:

a. Prepare journal entries, including closing entries, to reflect only budgetary transactions.

b. Post to "T" accounts.

c. Prepare a balance sheet for the budgetary group of accounts as of December 31, 1955.

Problem 12-3. The City of S operates its own municipal airport. The trial balance of the airport as of January 1, 1955, was as follows:

Cash...................................	$ 35,000	
Accounts Receivable....................	49,000	
Allowance for Uncollectible Accounts.....		$ 2,000
Land..................................	200,000	
Structures and Improvements...........	700,000	
Allowance for Depreciation—Structures and Improvements.......................		50,000
Equipment............................	250,000	
Allowance for Depreciation—Equipment..		90,000
Vouchers Payable......................		48,000
Bonds Payable.........................		800,000
Governmental Unit's Contribution........		200,000
Unappropriated Surplus.................		44,000
	$1,234,000	$1,234,000

The following transactions took place during the year:

1. Revenues collected in cash: aviation revenues, $320,500; concession revenues, $90,000; revenues from airport management, $40,000; revenues from sales of petroleum products, etc. (net revenue, after deducting all costs relating to the sales), $10,000.

2. Expenses all paid in cash with the exception of $22,000, which remained unpaid at December 31, were: operating, $222,000; maintenance, $75,000; general and administrative, $73,000.

3. The vouchers payable outstanding on January 1, 1955 were paid.

4. All of the accounts receivable outstanding on January 1, 1955 were collected.

5. Accounts receivable on December 31, 1955 amounted to $30,000 all applicable to aviation revenues.

6. Accrued interest payable at the end of the year amounted to $3,000.

7. Depreciation charges:

Structures and improvements.......... $14,000
Equipment......................... 21,000

Required:

(a) Prepare journal entries, including closing entries.

(b) Prepare a balance sheet as of December 31, 1955.

(c) Prepare an income and expense statement for the fiscal year ended December 31, 1955.

Problem 12-4. The City of C has been donating property and services to one of its utilities, and the utility has in turn been donating services and property to the city. Beginning with January 1, 1955, the utility is to charge the city for all services and is to be charged for any services rendered to it by the city. Past donations of property and services made by the city to the utility or vice versa are to be credited or charged, respectively, on the utility's books to a Contributions from Municipality account.

These donations and services are as follows:

Donations to reduce debt service of City other than utility bonds and indebtedness.............................	$ 1,350
Services of City Comptroller unremunerated.............	4,252
Services of City Treasurer unremunerated...............	3,200
Services of Corporation Counsel unremunerated..........	19,525
Electric service rendered below cost....................	1,500
Engineering services rendered gratis in connection with fire alarm system....................................	500
Excess amount billed over cost for jobbing work done for the City......................................	135
Excess amount billed over cost of electric energy supplied for City...	88,217
Donation of cinders to Department of Public Works......	1,350
Donation of electric clock—City Council Chamber.......	42
Donation of land for street widening purposes...........	9,230
Jobbing work done for the City below cost..............	90
Rental of office space used by utility but not paid........	16,237
Donation of steam to storehouse of Department of Public Works...	7,510
Donation to City General Hospital....................	12,000

Required:

Prepare a statement showing how you arrive at the net balance in the Contributions from Municipality account.

Problem 12-5. The following is a list of the accounts of the electric utility fund of the City of *E* as of June 1, 1955:

Cash	$100,000	
Bond Fund—Cash	30,000	
Deposits Fund—Cash	2,000	
Bond Fund—Expenditures	100,000	
Bond Fund—Vouchers Payable		$ 40,000
Bonds Authorized—Unissued	50,000	
Accounts Receivable	77,000	
Deposits Fund—Interest Payable		350
Deposits Fund—Interest Receivable	400	
Deposits Fund—Investments	10,000	
Deposits Fund—Surplus		2,050
Deposits Payable		9,000
Sinking Fund—Cash	20,000	
Sinking Fund—Investments	50,000	
Sinking Fund—Unappropriated Surplus		5,000*
Unappropriated Surplus		139,000
Vouchers Payable		5,000
Inventory of Materials	10,000	
Allowance for Uncollectible Accounts		4,000
Appropriations		180,000
Reserve for Retirement of Sinking Fund Bonds		65,000

* Red.

You are given the following additional information:

The electric utility was formerly accounted for in the same manner as any other department. Beginning with June 1, 1955, the utility is to be accounted for as a self-supporting enterprise, and no formal records are to be kept of appropriations or other authorizations.

Fixed assets of the utility consist of the following:

Assets	Cost	Allowance for Depreciation
Land	$150,000	—
Structures and Improvements	320,000	$60,000
Equipment	105,000	30,000
	$575,000	$90,000

Bond fund expenditures consist of construction work in progress.
Bonds outstanding amounted to $300,000.

Required:

Prepare a balance sheet for the electric utility of the City of *E* as of June 1, 1955.

Problem 12-6. From the following information prepare a statement analyzing the changes in the Unappropriated Surplus account of the water utility fund of the City of *G* for the fiscal year ended June 30, 1955.

1. The balance in the account as of June 30, 1954, was $12,872,065.

2. A bond premium of $872,000 was realized during the year and was credited directly to this account.

3. Fixed assets of $102,700 were donated to this fund by the City of *G*.

4. The net income for the year was $2,917,000.

5. Other miscellaneous surplus additions minus deductions totaled $15,610.

6. Contributions by the water utility fund to other funds totaled $2,856,000.

7. The plant was appraised in December, 1954; the appraised value is $2,112,000 less than the net book value.

8. The allowance for uncollectible accounts was reduced by $82,650.

Problem 12-7. You are given the following data for the water utility of the City of *W* for the fiscal year ending December 31, 1955:

INCOME AND EXPENSE ACCOUNTS:

Operating Revenues (Control)*	$405,000
Operating Expenses (Control)**	309,000
Taxes	37,500
Customers' Deposits—Interest Revenues	7,500
Customers' Deposits—Interest Expenses	6,000
Interest Revenues	15,500
Sinking Fund Revenue	12,000
Interest Expenses	42,000

*DETAILED OPERATING REVENUE ACCOUNTS:

Private Fire Protection	7,500
Metered Sales to General Customers	267,000
Servicing of Customers' Installations	3,800
Interdepartmental Sales	3,000
Merchandising, Jobbing, and Contract Work	7,500
Sales to Other Water Utilities	15,000
Rent from Water Property	3,700
Public Fire Protection	30,000
Other Sales to Public Authorities	7,500
Interdepartmental Rents	4,500
Flat Rate Sales to General Customers	37,500
Customers' Forfeited Discounts and Penalties	1,500
Sales to Irrigation Customers	15,000
Miscellaneous Water Revenues	1,500

**DETAILED OPERATING EXPENSE ACCOUNTS:

Operation Supplies and Expenses—Source of Supply	2,200
Purification Supplies and Expense	12,000
Operation of Transmission and Distribution Lines	17,000
Maintenance of Other Distribution Plant	3,000
Miscellaneous Expenses—Customers' Accounting and Collecting	6,550
Insurance	7,200
Supplies and Expense—Power and Pumping	3,800
Maintenance Supervision and Engineering—Source of Supply	1,650
Operation Supervision and Engineering—Source of Supply	7,200
Maintenance of Purification Equipment	3,360
Maintenance of Structures and Improvements—Transmission and Distribution	340
Customers' Contracts, Orders, Meter Reading, and Collecting	13,450
Fuel for Power and Pumping	22,500
Supervision—Customers' Accounting and Collecting	3,600
Other General Office Salaries	6,000
Customers' Billing and Accounting	21,050
Expenses of General Officers and General Office Employees	1,400
Uncollectible Accounts	1,800
General Office Supplies and Expenses	970
Operation Supervision and Engineering—Purification	5,200
Legal Services	1,500
Supervision and Engineering—Transmission and Distribution	5,200
Operation of Meters	4,200
Maintenance Supervision and Engineering—Power and Pumping	400
Miscellaneous General Expenses	750
Services on Customers' Premises	2,700
Maintenance of Mains	10,500
Maintenance Supervision and Engineering—Transmission and Distribution	2,700
Maintenance Supervision and Engineering—Purification	2,000
Maintenance of General Property	1,050

Purification Labor...	22,590
Maintenance of Power and Pumping Structures and Improvements......	450
Maintenance of Source of Supply Plant.............................	18,500
Maintenance of Power and Pumping Equipment.......................	2,400
Operation Labor—Source of Supply.................................	45,500
Operation Supervision and Engineering—Power and Pumping..........	4,200
Maintenance of Purification Structures and Improvements.............	1,050
Operation Labor—Power and Pumping.............................	34,000
Salaries of General Officers..	7,500
Departmental Office Expenses—Transmission and Distribution.........	1,540

Required:

a. Prepare an income and expense statement.

b. Prepare a schedule of detailed operating revenues.

c. Prepare a schedule of detailed operating expenses.

Problem 12-8. (Adapted from an American Institute of Accountants' examination.) On the basis of the following information prepare:

1. A balance sheet of all funds after closing the books at December 31, 1954.

2. A statement showing the changes in the Unappropriated Surplus account.

3. A statement of income and expense of the water department for the year.

The City of *D* classifies its accounts under four different funds. The balances in the accounts of those funds on January 1, 1954, and on December 31 of the same year before closing were as follows:

	January 1	December 31
General fund:		
Cash..	$ 10,162	$ 21,215
1953 taxes receivable.............................	15,676	12,429
Accounts receivable...............................	2,325	3,545
Stores..	9,641	9,533
Permanent property...............................	3,154,695	3,154,695
1954 taxes receivable.............................		60,838
Estimated revenue from taxes......................		225,000
Estimated revenue from miscellaneous sources........		62,000
Appropriation expenditures for current purposes......		234,398
Appropriation expenditures for capital additions......		8,716
Appropriation expenditures for payment of bonds.....		25,000
Appropriation encumbrances (1954).................		5,842
	$3,192,499	$3,823,211
Accounts payable.................................	$ 2,826	$ 5,626
Reserve for 1953 taxes............................	10,200	10,200
Reserve for orders and contracts...................	3,286	5,842
Reserve for stores................................	10,000	10,000
Current surplus...................................	11,492	11,603
Bonds payable....................................	250,000	225,000
Capital surplus...................................	2,904,695	2,929,695
1954 tax anticipation notes payable.................		25,000
Reserve for 1954 taxes............................		24,766
Revenue from taxes..............................		222,894
Revenue from miscellaneous sources.................		64,325
Appropriations...................................		276,000
Estimated budget surplus..........................		11,000
Sale of old equipment.............................		1,260
	$3,192,499	$3,823,211

	January 1	December 31
Water Fund:		
Cash......................................	$ 6,126	$ 717
Accounts receivable.............................	7,645	5,573
Stores......................................	13,826	12,635
Investments of replacement fund...................	21,700	24,500
Permanent property.............................	212,604	214,204
Labor and material expense.......................		109,638
Interest on bonds...............................		3,000
Depreciation charge.............................		10,600
Accounts of prior years written off.................		1,097
Expended for additions to plant....................		12,460
	$ 261,901	$ 394,424
Accounts payable...............................	$ 4,324	$ 4,318
Customers' deposits.............................	1,500	1,600
Replacement fund reserve........................	21,700	24,500
Operating surplus...............................	21,773	21,773
Bonds payable.................................	60,000	40,000
Capital surplus.................................	152,604	154,204
Services billed.................................		146,867
Deposits lapsed................................		60
Interest on investments..........................		1,102
	$ 261,901	$ 394,424
Assessment fund:		
Improvement No. 50:		
Cash......................................	$ 4,653	$ 1,844
Assessments receivable..........................	46,829	33,414
Delinquent assessments receivable.................	4,826	2,010
Public benefit receivable.........................	5,632	4,516
Interest on bonds...............................		3,000
	$ 61,940	$ 44,784
Bonds payable.................................	$ 60,000	$ 40,000
Surplus.......................................	1,940	1,940
Interest on assessments..........................		2,844
	$ 61,940	$ 44,784
Improvement No. 51:		
Cash...		$ 851
Assessments receivable..........................		21,600
Public benefit receivable.........................		2,400
		$ 24,851
Bonds payable.................................		$ 24,000
Surplus.......................................		390
Interest on assessments..........................		461
		$ 24,851

	January 1	December 31
Trust funds:		
Cash..	$ 3,216	$ 31
Investments.................................	94,425	99,425
Premium on investments.....................		800
Accrued interest purchased.................		260
Cemetery maintenance......................		849
Cemetery expense..........................		2,976
Policemen's pensions paid...................		3,200
Firemen's pensions paid....................		2,400
	$ 97,641	$ 109,941
Cemetery endowment fund reserve............	$ 60,000	$ 60,000
Policemen's pension fund reserve.............	18,691	18,691
Firemen's pension fund reserve..............	16,824	16,824
Cemetery maintenance fund reserve..........	2,126	2,126
Profit on sale of investments................		600
Undistributed income.......................		4,800
Policemen's pension fund contributions........		4,160
Firemen's pension fund contributions.........		2,740
	$ 97,641	$ 109,941

It is the practice of the city to close out the unencumbered balance of appropriations of the general fund at the end of each year. Depreciation on the general property of the city is not entered, and accrued interest on investments or on outstanding bonds is disregarded. Income and profit on trust fund investments are distributed 62 per cent to cemetery funds, 20 per cent to the policemen's pension fund, and 18 per cent to the firemen's pension fund.

The cemetery maintenance fund consists of the income from the cemetery endowment fund and is used for cemetery expense. Excess of receipts over disbursements of pension funds are closed to the reserve accounts of the respective funds at the end of the year.

Attention is directed to the following facts and conditions at the close of the year 1954:

1. Taxes for 1953 in excess of the reserve against them are to be written off.

2. Because of the increased uncertainty of 1954 tax collections, the reserve on them is to be increased by 50 per cent.

3. Invoices on all orders and contracts outstanding at beginning of year have been paid with a saving of $111, which has been credited to current surplus.

4. The old property sold during the year was carried in the accounts at a value of $6,000.

5. Permanent property valued at $1,820 became useless and was discarded during the year.

6. Replacements of water department equipment costing $6,200 were made from the replacement fund during the year at a cost of $7,800.

Questions and Problems on Chapter 13

Questions

Question 13-1. What is meant by general fixed assets?

Question 13-2. A municipality was granted certain land for use as a playground. The property was appraised at $10,000. Subsequently, all land in the neighborhood rose in value by 20 per cent. Should the increase be reflected in the records?

Question 13-3. Suppose the same situation as above, except that there was a 10 per cent decline in the value of the land. Should the decline be reflected in the records?

Question 13-4. A municipality owns a fire station and is required to pay assessments of $10,000 as an owner of property in the benefited area. As a result of the improvements, the property has risen in value by $15,000. Should the asset be written up, and, if so, by how much?

Question 13-5. An asset was financed out of a special revenue fund and was carried in the general fixed assets group of accounts. Subsequently the asset was sold. To which fund would you credit the proceeds?

Question 13-6. Assume that the asset referred to in the preceding question was financed from a special assessment fund or a bond fund. To which fund should the proceeds from the sale of this asset be credited?

Question 13-7. What is meant by general bonds?

Question 13-8. A municipality's share of special assessment costs was $250,000. To finance these costs, the municipality issued bonds for a corresponding amount. Should these bonds be shown as part of the general bonded debt and interest group of accounts or as part of the special assessment fund?

Question 13-9. In 1936, general sinking fund bonds to the amount of $200,000 were issued. All were to mature in 1955. On December 31, 1955, the sinking fund had accumulated only $20,000, so that there was no possibility of the matured bonds being retired that year. Should the matured bonds be shown in the general fund or in the sinking fund, or should they continue to be carried in the general bonded debt group of accounts?

Question 13-10. Why should general fixed assets and general bonds not be shown in the same group of accounts?

Question 13-11. Why is it unsound to cancel inter-fund receivables and payables in a combined fund balance sheet?

Question 13-12. The legislative body of a municipality has established a relief fund through a special levy authorized for this purpose by the state legislature. The city also has a mayor's contingency fund set up by order of the mayor out of an appropriation made for his department. Can the mayor's contingency fund lend money to the relief fund? Can the relief fund lend money to the mayor's contingency fund?

Question 13-13. Can you see any reason for following a stricter accrual basis of accounting in some funds than in others?

Problems

Problem 13-1. The following transactions took place in the City of Y during the year 1955:

491

1. A contribution of $40,000 became due from the general fund to the sinking fund.

2. A lot, appraised at $50,000, was received as a gift from an individual for the purpose of establishing a playground.

3. (a) Furniture for the mayor's office estimated to cost $500 was ordered. (b) The furniture and a bill therefor were received; the actual cost was $525.

4. Sinking fund bonds amounting to $100,000 matured.

5. Sinking fund bonds to the amount of $200,000 were sold at a premium of $1,000.

6. The project financed from the bonds referred to in the preceding transaction was completed. Construction expenditures to the amount of $197,000 were closed out of the bond fund; proper disposition was made of the surplus.

7. (a) Special assessment improvements to the amount of $750,000 were authorized.

   (b) Special assessment notes to the amount of $550,000 were sold at par.

   (c) Assessments to the amount of $350,000 were levied on private property; the remainder of the cost is to be paid by the municipality.

   (d) The municipality authorized the issuance of bonds for the purpose of financing its share of the cost ($220,000).

   (e) The bonds were sold at a premium of $2,500.

   (f) The proceeds from the sale of the bonds, as well as the premiums, were transferred to the proper fund or funds.

   (g) The municipality authorized the issuance of special assessment bonds to the amount of $450,000.

   (h) The bonds were sold at par.

   (i) Construction expenditures at the end of the first year amounted to $100,000 and were closed out of the special assessment fund.

Required:

Prepare *all* journal entries needed to record the above transactions.

Problem 13-2. (Adapted from an American Institute of Accountants' examination.) The City of *M* has prepared its balance-sheet as of June 30, 1955, and shows therein a surplus of $258,216. The statement has been criticized as not giving a satisfactory reflection of the financial position of the city. You are asked (a) to revise the statement in accordance with acceptable methods of governmental accounting, and (b) to provide an analysis of the changes in current fund surplus for the year ended June 30, 1955. You may prepare your revised balance-sheet in columnar form if you prefer to present it in that manner.

The balance-sheet as prepared, together with a corresponding statement as of June 30, 1954, is as follows:

ASSETS

	Balance 6/30/54	Balance 6/30/55
Cash...	$ 20,485	$ 2,873
Taxes receivable..............................	54,200	36,690
Accounts receivable...........................	12,362	13,584
Investments..................................	42,000	42,000
Prepaid expenses.............................	6,487	5,374
Fixed assets.................................	696,565	710,465
Total................................	$832,099	$810,986

LIABILITIES

Warrants payable...........................	$ 30,900	$ 46,970
Bonds payable...............................	490,000	480,000
Reserve for depreciation..................	22,300	25,800
Surplus......................................	288,899	258,216
Total...............................	$832,099	$810,986

Additional information is available as follows: (a) Taxes levied for the year ended June 30, 1955 amounted to $64,300, of which amount $37,600 was collected and $650 abated. Abatement of prior years' taxes was $3,108. It is anticipated that an additional $1,350 of the 1954-55 levy will finally be uncollectible and that an additional $3,500 of 1953 and prior taxes will prove uncollectible.

(b) Revenue other than from taxes was $20,210, but of this amount $4,300 was collected for other governments and has not been paid nor set up as a liability, and $1,200 was from interest on investments. The investments are held in trust, the income to be used for library upkeep. Included in expenditures is $3,050 which is the cost of library upkeep for the year.

(c) Expenditures amounted to $153,400 during the year. Included herein is interest on bonds of $15,000, purchase of general fixed assets of $18,900, retirement of general obligation bonds of $10,000 and the abatement of this and prior years' taxes. The $10,000 of bonds and the $18,900 of assets purchased were also credited to surplus and debited to bonds payable and fixed assets.

(d) Included in fixed assets is $174,964 as of June 30, 1954 and $169,964 as of June 30, 1955 of property of the municipal water plant. The revenue of the plant and the expenses, including depreciation of $8,500 and bond interest on $90,000 of 3% bonds outstanding against the plant, have been netted, and the profit of $9,307 has been transferred to surplus. The reserve for depreciation, the accounts receivable and the prepaid expenses at both balance-sheet dates are applicable to the water plant operations. Also $5,025 in 1954 and $8,750 in 1955 of the warrants payable are applicable to this department. The cash arising from the department's operations, except for $500 of working fund, is used for general purposes of the city.

Problem 13-3. (Adapted from an American Institute of Accountants' examination.) The City of S uses budgetary accounts and maintains accounts for each of the following types of funds:

Symbol	Fund
A	Bond funds
B	General bonded debt
C	General fund
D	Property accounts (general fixed assets)
E	Sinking funds
F	Special assessment funds
G	Special revenue funds
H	Trust and agency funds
S	Utility funds
T	Working capital funds

The chart of accounts of the *General Fund* follows:

Symbol	Account
1	Appropriations
2	Cash
3	Due from other funds

Symbol	Account
4	Due to other funds
5	Encumbrances
6	Expenditures
7	Reserve for encumbrances
8	Revenues
9	Revenues (estimated)
10	Surplus receipts
11	Surplus (unappropriated)
12	1954 taxes receivable
13	Vouchers payable

The following transactions were among those occurring during 1954:

1. The 1954 budget was approved. It provided for $520,000 of general fund revenue and $205,000 of school fund revenue.

2. The budgeted appropriations for the general fund amounted to $516,000.

3. An advance of $10,000 was made from the general fund to a fund for the operation of a central printing service used by all departments of the municipal government. (This had not been budgeted and is not expected to be repaid.)

4. Taxes for general fund revenues were levied, totaling $490,000.

5. Contractors were paid $200,000 for construction of an office building. The payment was from proceeds of a general bond issue of 1950.

6. Bonds of a general issue, previously authorized, were sold at par for $60,000 cash.

7. Orders were placed for supplies to be used by the Health Department—estimated cost, $7,500.

8. Vouchers were approved for payment of salaries of city officers in the amount of $11,200. (No encumbrances are recorded for wages and salaries.)

9. The supplies ordered in item 7 were received and vouchers approved for the invoice price of $7,480.

10. Fire equipment was purchased for $12,500 and voucher approved.

11. A payment of $5,000 was made by the general fund to a fund for eventual redemption of general obligation bonds.

12. Of the taxes levied in item 4, $210,000 was collected.

13. Taxes amounting to $1,240 written off as uncollectible in 1951 were collected. No amount was in the budget for such collections.

14. $1,000 of the advance made in item 3 was returned because it was not needed.

15. Supplies for general administrative use were requisitioned from the store's fund. A charge of $1,220 is made for the supplies.

16. The general fund advanced $30,000 cash to provide temporary working capital for a fund out of which payment will be made for new sewerage installations. Eventual financing will be by means of assessments on property holders on the basis of benefits received.

17. Equipment from the Highway Department was sold for $7,000 cash. This sale was not included in the budget and depreciation is not funded.

18. The city received a cash bequest of $75,000 for the establishment of a scholarship fund.

19. Previously approved and entered vouchers for payment of Police Department salaries of $6,200 and for the transfer of $500 to the Police Pension Fund, were paid.

20. Receipts from licenses and fees amounted to $16,000.

Required:

Show for each transaction, by means of the appropriate numerals, the account or accounts debited and the account or accounts credited in the General Fund. If a transaction requires an entry in any fund(s) other than the General Fund, indicate the fund(s) affected by printing the appropriate letter symbol(s). If there is nothing to be entered for a transaction use the phrase "No entry."

Problem 13-4. The following is a balance sheet of the capital fund of the City of *I* taken from its audit report:

CITY OF *I*

Capital Fund

Balance Sheet

November 3, 1955

Cash in Banks:			Bonded Debt:		
Unexpended Bond Proceeds.............	$ 17,364.39		Maturing Within One Year:		
Bond Sinking Funds...	318,471.48		Public Improvement Serial Bonds......	$ 128,000.00	
	$ 335,835.87		Public Improvement Sinking Fund Bonds	20,000.00	
Amount Necessary to Be Raised by Taxation to Retire Future Bond Maturities............	$2,118,528.52		Maturing After One Year: Public Improvement Serial Bonds......	1,901,000.00	
			Public Improvement Sinking Fund Bonds	388,000.00	
				$2,437,000.00	
Land, Structures, and Equipment...........	2,710,316.77		Fixed Property Balancing Account..............	2,727,681.16	
	$5,164,681.16			$5,164,681.16	

The unexpended bond proceeds represent part of the money received from the sale of serial bonds. The project has been completed, and the money is not needed to finance construction, the cost of the project having been overestimated. Interest payable in future years, $950,000.

Required:

Prepare statements of (1) general fixed assets and (2) general bonded debt and interest accounts, respectively.

Problem 13-5. In beginning your audit of the City of *A*, you call for a balance sheet of each fund as of December 31, 1955. You are handed the following balance sheet:

CITY OF *A*

Consolidated Balance Sheet

December 31, 1955

All Funds

ASSETS			LIABILITIES		
Current:			Current:		
Cash....................	$ 120,500		Warrants Payable.......	$ 14,000	
Investments............	18,300		Interest Payable........	8,500	
Taxes (Less Allowance)...	94,900		Deposits..............	10	
Accounts Receivable.....	980				
Interest Receivable......	450		Total Current Liabilities	$ 22,510	
Assessments Receivable (Less Allowance)......	172,800				
Supplies—Inventory.....	10,050				
Total Current Assets...	$ 417,980				
Deferred Charges:					
Prepaid Insurance.......	$ 610				

			Bonded Indebtedness:	
Proprietary:			Outstanding Bonds......	$ 600,000
Land....................	$	92,000		
Buildings...............		105,000		
Equipment.............		495,000	Proprietary:	
Office Furniture & Fixtures		2,500	Surplus...............	$ 497,780
Autos..................		7,200		
Total Proprietary......	$	701,700		
Total Debits.........	$1,120,290		Total Credits.........	$1,120,290

A cursory examination reveals that the statement in question is a combined balance sheet of all funds in which no fund segregation has been kept. Upon further investigation, you discover that the City of A maintains the following funds:

Current fund (general fund)
Cemetery fund
Water fund
Interest and bond retirement fund
Special assessment improvement fund

The assets, liabilities, and surplus shown in the combined balance sheet are applicable to the various funds as follows:

1. Accounts receivable are distributed as follows: Current fund, $330; water fund, $650.

2. Fixed assets apply to the following funds: Current fund: land, $92,000; buildings, $103,110; equipment, $25,474; office furniture and fixtures, $2,500; automobiles, $7,200. Cemetery fund: buildings, $1,890; equipment, $338. Water fund: equipment, $469,188.

3. Assessments receivable belong to the improvement fund, and the inventory of supplies belongs to the water fund.

4. Of the total cash, $36,500 is applicable to the cemetery fund; $22,300 to the water fund; $51,200 to the interest and bond retirement fund; and $97,400 to cash for bond payments of the improvement fund. The current fund had a cash overdraft of $9,200, and the cash for interest payments in the improvement fund was overdrawn by $77,700.

5. The investments are applicable to the cemetery fund.

6. Warrants payable are distributed as follows: Current fund, $11,540; cemetery fund, $765; water fund, $1,695.

7. Taxes (less allowances) are applicable to the following funds: Current fund, $70,345; water fund, $1,902; interest and bond retirement fund, $22,653.

8. Interest payable is distributed as follows: Water fund, $4,686; interest and bond retirement fund, $1,967; improvement fund, $1,847.

9. Prepaid insurance is applicable to the following funds: Cemetery fund, $28; current fund, $540; water fund, $42.

10. Interest receivable is divisible as follows: Cemetery fund, $120; water fund, $330.

11. Deposits apply to the water fund.

12. Bonded indebtedness applies to the following: Water fund, $240,500; interest and debt retirement fund, $110,000; improvement fund, $249,500.

13. Inter-fund receivables are as follows: Due to cemetery fund from current

fund, $6,900, and from interest and bond retirement fund, $2,000. Due to water fund from interest and bond retirement fund, $9,000.

Required:

On the basis of the above data prepare a combined balance sheet as of December 31, 1955, properly subdivided between funds.

Problem 13-6. (Adapted from an American Institute of Accountants' examination.) From the following information, prepare balance-sheet working papers of each of the following funds of the City of M as of February 28, 1955:

(1) General Fund, (2) Special Assessments Fund, (3) Bond Fund and (4) General Fixed Assets (sometimes referred to as a group rather than a fund).

The City of M has established the above funds in its accounting system and in addition a Sinking Fund and a Bonded Indebtedness Fund (or group). Detail for the latter two funds is omitted in this problem and balance-sheet working papers of these funds are not required of the candidate.

The City of M keeps its accounts on the accrual basis, except with respect to interest receivable and payable not yet due. It makes provision in its tax roll for state road taxes, state school taxes, and county taxes which are collected by it as agent for the state and the county.

Ledger account balances as at February 28, 1955, are presented as follows:

	Balance
General Fund:	
Cash in depositories...............................	$ 125,000
Petty cash...	500
Taxes receivable—current...........................	215,000
Taxes receivable—delinquent........................	20,000
Taxes receivable for other units—current............	18,000
Interest and penalties receivable on delinquent taxes..	1,400
Vouchers payable...................................	130,000
Notes payable......................................	116,200
Due to special assessments fund.....................	8,400
Due to other governmental units—state..............	21,600
Due to other governmental units—county............	5,400
Unappropriated surplus.............................	44,900
Appropriations.....................................	921,800
Expenditures.......................................	900,000
Estimated revenues.................................	950,000
Actual revenues....................................	953,600
Revenues not anticipated............................	8,200
Taxes collected in advance..........................	14,800
Emergency note.....................................	5,000
Special Assessments Fund:	
Cash in depositories...............................	316,600
Special assessments receivable.......................	320,000
Due from general fund—municipality's share of assessment improvement costs........................	8,400
Special assessment liens............................	20,000
Improvements other than buildings—completed.......	75,000
Improvements other than buildings—in progress.......	28,000
Vouchers payable...................................	15,000
Notes payable......................................	90,000
Contracts payable—uncompleted contracts...........	130,000
Bonds payable......................................	350,000
Reserve for authorized expenditures*................	183,000
Unappropriated surplus—construction................	
Unappropriated surplus—interest....................	

Balance

Bond Fund:

Cash in depositories	120,000
Accounts receivable	15,000
Buildings—completed	120,000
Buildings—uncompleted	50,000
Bonds authorized—unissued	100,000
Vouchers payable	25,000
Contracts payable—uncompleted contracts	68,700
Contracts payable—completed contracts	60,000
Expenditures	390,000
Reserve for authorized expenditures*	560,300

General Fixed Assets (Balances as at March 1, 1954):

Land	1,200,000
Buildings	3,400,000
Improvements other than buildings	640,000
Machinery and equipment	325,000
Work in progress	
Investment in property	5,565,000

*Synonymous with "Appropriations" described in Chapters 7 and 8.

Your audit discloses the following:

1. Reserves for estimated losses against receivables after abatements in the general fund are to be provided for as follows:

Taxes receivable—current	10%
Taxes receivable—delinquent, and interest and penalties thereon	20%
Taxes receivable for other units—current	10%

2. Abatements of taxes not reflected are $4,900 for 1954, $710 for 1953, and $340 for 1952. Interest and penalties applicable to abated taxes were $80 for 1953 and $20 for 1952.

3. The state and county taxes, amounting to $36,000 and $9,000 respectively, were credited to unappropriated surplus as part of the entry setting up the tax roll. The current balance in the respective accounts—Due to Other Governmental Units—represent cash collected to date for these units. Such cash, which has not as yet been remitted to the units, has been credited to the account, Taxes Receivable for Other Units—Current account.

4. The taxes collected in advance of $14,800 were subject to a discount of $800, currently charged to expenditures account.

5. The emergency note was issued on February 1, 1955 to meet an emergency appropriation. Such note is to be retired through taxation during the fiscal year beginning March 1, 1955. Unappropriated surplus was charged for the amount of the appropriation, which equaled the amount of the note.

6. Unrecorded interest due on special assessment liens amounts to $540.

7. No provision has been made for retained percentages of $5,000 on uncompleted special assessment contracts.

8. The Reserve for Authorized Expenditures account[1] in the special assessments fund shows that on work completed to February 28, 1955, authorizations have exceeded expenditures by $1,400, an amount considered too small to be rebated.

9. Unrecorded commitments on unfilled orders for the general, special assessments, and bond funds amounted to $30,000, $45,000, and $18,000 respectively.

[1] Synonymous with the Appropriations account described in Chapters 7 and 8.

Problem 13-7. (Adapted from an American Institute of Accountants' examination.)

Part A:

Rearrange the following balance sheet of the City of X in acceptable form for municipal reporting:

CITY OF X

Balance Sheet

December 31, 1954

ASSETS

Current:		
Cash...............................	$ 50,000	
Taxes receivable (including special assessments $80,000).....................	100,000	
Supply inventories....................	10,000	
Investments of trust funds.............	30,000	$ 190,000
Fixed:		
Land...............................	$100,000	
Buildings...........................	800,000	
Equipment..........................	50,000	950,000
		$1,140,000

LIABILITIES

Current:		
Accounts payable.....................		$ 10,000
Fixed:		
General obligation bonds payable........	$350,000	
Special assessment bonds payable........	75,000	425,000
Fund Equities:		
General fund.........................	$ 35,000	
Trust funds..........................	40,000	
Bond fund...........................	25,000	
Special assessment fund................	5,000	
Capital fund.........................	600,000	705,000

Part B:

The City of X, for which the balance-sheet was prepared in Part A, will use budgetary accounts. You are to prepare the balance sheet for its general fund at the end of its first month of operation in its fiscal year starting January 1, 1955. The following events are to be considered:

1. A budget was adopted which provided for property taxes of $210,000 for general municipal purposes and for estimated revenue from fees, etc. of $23,000. Appropriations were $180,000 for current operations, $20,000 for debt service, and $35,000 for street and other capital improvements.

2. During January purchase orders of $9,400 were placed, $3,150 of which were received and vouchered at an actual net cost of $3,078. Payroll amounting to $5,185 was vouchered and $14,000 of accounts payable were paid.

3. The tax roll was not completed; but $21,000 of 1954 taxes were collected, $18,350 of which were special assessments. Also, $466 of delinquent taxes and

penalties were collected. These taxes had been written off and no amount was in the current budget for such collections. Miscellaneous fees, etc. collected amounted to $2,060.

4. Inventory of supplies at the end of the month was $10,400.

Questions and Problems on Chapter 14

Questions

Question 14-1. In a certain State, warrants are issued to payees by the State auditor, who requests the State treasurer to make payment to the payees named in the warrants. Although these warrants have no bank designated on them, they are accepted by banks and eventually find their way to the State treasurer for payment. The treasurer then writes a check for the amount of warrants presented by each of the banks. Should unpaid warrants be considered as a cash disbursement or should they be shown as a liability on the balance sheet? Give a reason or reasons for your answer.

Question 14-2. Suppose that the State auditor issues the warrant to the payee and that the warrant indicates the bank by which it is to be paid, but that the warrant is not valid until countersigned by the State treasurer. How should warrants issued by the auditor but not yet signed by the treasurer be shown on the balance sheet?

Question 14-3. The treasurer of the City of *F* does not consider a disbursement as such until the checks have cleared through the bank, whereas the treasurer of the School District of *F* considers disbursements as such as soon as the checks are issued, regardless of when they clear. Which treasurer in your opinion is following the more proper procedure?

Question 14-4. Why is it improper for an official to deposit government money to the credit of his own personal account?

Question 14-5. (a) Is it necessary to have a separate bank account for each fund? (b) What are the advantages and disadvantages of providing a separate bank account for each fund? (c) Under what circumstances would you recommend the establishment of a separate bank account for each fund?

Question 14-6. A city charter provides that the general fund shall make up all losses in the special assessment fund. Special assessment fund cash to the amount of $50,000 is in a closed bank, and it is estimated that only 60 per cent of this amount will be ultimately collected. However, the liability cannot be set up in the general fund until the actual loss is determined. How would you indicate these facts on the balance sheet prepared at the close of the year (a) for the special assessment fund, and (b) for the general fund?

Question 14-7. In a certain city checks must be signed by the mayor, the comptroller, and the treasurer. Do you think three signatures are necessary? If not, indicate how many signatures should be required and which of these three officers should sign.

Problems

Problem 14-1. The following are the opening cash balances and receipts and disbursements for special assessment districts 8, 11, 13, and 16 of the City of *F* for the year ending December 31, 1955:

| | DISTRICT | | | |
	8	11	13	16
Cash Balances:				
For Construction.............	$30,000	$45,000	$60,000	$ 15,000
For Bond Payments..........	15,000	22,500	30,000	7,500
For Interest Payments........	3,000	4,500	6,000	750
Receipts:				
Interest.....................	2,500	3,000	3,500	500
Sale of Bonds................	70,000	—	—	80,000
Current Assessments—For Construction.................	—	—	15,000	10,000
Delinquent Assessments—For Bonds....................	15,000	7,500	1,500	1,500
Delinquent Assessments—For Construction...............	2,000	2,500	2,000	3,000
Sale of Notes................	20,000	—	—	5,000
Municipality's Share of Cost...	15,000	20,000	10,000	15,000
Payments:				
Capital Outlays..............	75,000	56,000	80,000	110,000
Interest.....................	2,000	3,000	4,000	500
Bond Retirement.............	17,000	20,000	20,000	7,500

Required:

Prepare a statement showing opening cash balances, receipts, disbursements, and closing cash balances for each district and for all the districts combined.

Problem 14-2. The City of *F* maintains three bank accounts. On June 30, 1955, the balances according to the bank statements were as follows:

Loop National Bank.................	$175,900
U. S. National Bank.................	82,350
Best National Bank.................	51,410

The balances according to the treasurer's books on that day were as follows:

Fund	Loop National Bank	U. S. National Bank	Best National Bank
General....................			$62,000
Special Revenue.............	$51,950		
Sinking.....................		$40,800	
Utility or Other Enterprise...		44,200	

The treasurer considers disbursements as such as soon as he issues checks. The balances of cash according to the comptroller's books were as follows:

Fund	Amount
General............................	$72,500
Special Revenue.....................	42,750
Sinking............................	40,650
Utility or Other Enterprise............	33,500

The comptroller considers cash disbursements as such as soon as warrants are issued.

The following checks are still outstanding:

General Fund		Sinking Fund	
#3614........................	$ 450	#6112.....................	$ 130
4812........................	110	6997.....................	250
4813........................	270	6998.....................	875
4816........................	4,850	6999.....................	13,000
4822........................	2,000	7000.....................	2,000
4823........................	412		
4824........................	68		

Special Revenue Fund		Utility or Other Enterprise Fund	
#2190	$ 140	#1409	$ 75
2191	275	1416	42
2305	412	1512	97
2306	1,500	1513	1,500
2307	3,200	1514	110
2308	840	1515	67
		1516	143

Warrants issued for which checks have not yet been written are as follows:

Fund	Amount
General	$3,200
Special Revenue	750
Sinking	6,200
Utility or Other Enterprise	850

Interest credited by the bank but not taken up by the city is as follows:

Fund	Amount
General	$1,000
Special Revenue	350
Sinking	1,200
Utility or Other Enterprise	700

The following deposits were in transit on June 30:

Fund	Amount
General	$8,500
Special Revenue	2,000
Sinking	615
Utility or Other Enterprise	4,200

Exchange charged by the bank and not yet recorded on the city's books is as follows:

Fund	Amount
General	$ 35
Special Revenue	18
Sinking	16
Utility or Other Enterprise	42

Required:
Prepare a statement reconciling the cash accounts as shown by the bank statements with the balances shown on the treasurer's records and on the comptroller's records, respectively.

Problem 14-3. From the following information for the City of R, prepare a statement of cash receipts, disbursements, and balances properly classified by funds as of December 31, 1955:

CASH BALANCES, JANUARY 1, 1955:

Electric Fund	$ 42,520
General Fund	22,915
Pension Fund	14,630
Public School Fund	14,650
Special Assessment Fund	26,885

RECEIPTS OF 1955:
Electric Fund:

Sales..................................	462,350
Accounts Receivable Collections..........	22,620
Public Street Lighting...................	19,840 (a)
Rents.................................	3,575

General Fund:

Current Taxes.........................	405,500
Taxes Paid by Electric Fund.............	12,360 (b)
Parking Meters........................	5,702
Dog Licenses..........................	3,508
Police Fines..........................	10,650
Interest Earnings.......................	1,200
Concessions...........................	3,700
State Gas Tax.........................	18,300
Weights and Measures..................	4,650
Clinic Fees............................	3,420
Golf Fees.............................	7,810

Pension Fund:

Taxes.................................	32,720 (c)
Employees' Contribution..................	37,000
Interest on Investments..................	5,436

Public School Fund:

Taxes.................................	151,000 (d)
State Appropriation.....................	75,500

Special Assessment Fund:

Installment Collections..................	24,680
City's Share...........................	8,000 (e)
Interest Collections.....................	6,270

DISBURSEMENTS DURING 1955:

Electric Fund...........................	489,139*
General Fund...........................	472,210†
Pension Fund...........................	55,800
Public School Fund......................	190,287
Special Assessment Fund.................	51,630

* Includes item (b).
† Includes items (a), (c), (d), and (e).

Problem 14-4. The following data were taken from the treasurer's report of the City of *Y* for the fiscal year ended December 31, 1955:

CITY OF *Y*

Statement of Cash Receipts, Disbursements, and Balances
for Fiscal Year Ended December 31, 1955

Fund	Opening Balance	Receipts	Disbursements	Closing Balance
Current....................	$1,271,432	$4,305,206	$4,271,431	$1,305,207
Capital....................	31,009	75,743	54,692	52,060
Local Assessment..........	103,597	298,385	386,072	15,910
School....................	325,196	2,194,825	2,505,247	14,774
Pension...................	2,128	17,144	15,724	3,548
Water Works Improvement..	69,155	172,873	179,370	62,658
Sewage Disposal...........	1,237,825	615,412	1,104,383	748,854
Central Fire Alarm........	—	50,000	21	49,979
	$3,040,342	$7,729,588	$8,516,940	$2,252,990

The following transfers were made during the year and reflected in the comptroller's records but not on the treasurer's books:

Transferred from	Transferred to	Amount
Local Assessment	Capital	$ 8,125
Current	Sewage Disposal	62,350
Current	School	844,068
Sewage Disposal	Current	13,500
Current	Central Fire Alarm	1,275

Required:

a. Prepare a statement showing receipts, disbursements, and balances according to the comptroller's records.

b. Prepare a statement reconciling the cash balances according to the comptroller's records with the cash balances according to the treasurer's books.

Problem 14-5. On the basis of the following data, prepare a statement reconciling the receipts and disbursements as recorded by the county clerk of the County of F and as shown on the books of the county sanitorium:

According to the records of the sanitorium, it received $110,000 during 1955, whereas on the county clerk's books the sanitorium was charged with receipts of $110,233. The sanitorium received money from the sale of farm products in December to the amount of $967, which was not recorded on the county clerk's books until January, 1956. On the other hand, the county clerk recorded the receipt of $1,200 from the state for the benefit of the sanitorium, but the sanitorium did not receive the money until 1956 and therefore did not record it as a receipt of 1955.

According to the county records, the sanitorium disbursed $121,375 during 1955, whereas according to the sanitorium records, it disbursed $122,300 during that period. However, disbursements of $925 were charged as such on the sanitorium's books in December, 1955, whereas they were not recorded on the county clerk's records until January, 1956.

Problem 14-6. The following transfers were made between a state's funds during the fiscal year ended May 31, 1955:

The general fund transferred money to other funds as follows:

Administration Fund	$ 20,000
General AT Tax Sinking Fund	50,000,000
General BT Tax Sinking Fund	45,000,000
Sinking Fund	4,103,125
Liquid Fuels Tax Fund	5,000,000
School Employees' Retirement Fund	312,200
Motor License Fund	4,200,000
State Stores Fund	7,500,000
Flood Control Fund	275,000
State Employees' Retirement Fund	415,000
Liquor License Fund	1,200,000
Veterans' Compensation Sinking Fund	4,962,349

The state stores fund transferred $2,250,000 to the liquid fuels tax fund.

In addition to the transfer from the general fund, the state employees' retirement fund received money from the following:

Fish Fund	$ 5,350
Banking Department Fund	19,575
State Stores Fund	172,500
Game Fund	12,400
Manufacturing Fund	7,425
State Workmen's Insurance Fund	11,600

The general fund received money from the following funds:

Administration Fund	$ 20,000
Motor License Fund	18,752,000
State Insurance Fund	1,000,000
Liquid Fuels Tax Fund	5,510,000
Federal Rehabilitation Fund	259,000
Federal Vocational Education Fund	697,880
Liquor License Fund	1,000,000

Required:

Prepare a statement analyzing the inter-fund transactions.

Problem 14-7. The Village of *P* operates on an accrual basis with respect to both revenues and expenditures. It maintains two bank accounts at the Grovers State Bank, one for the general fund and one for the bond fund. You are asked to prepare from the following data (1) a statement reconciling the balances per bank with the balances of cash for each fund per comptroller's books on December 31, 1955, before any correcting entries are made, and (2) journal entries necessary to correct the comptroller's records.

1. Balance per bank statement: (a) general fund, $76,500; (b) bond fund, $32,700.

2. On December 30, 1955, the treasurer wrote check G112 for $95 in payment of a voucher chargeable against the bond fund. The comptroller caught this error but the check had already been cashed. To date no action has been taken on this matter.

3. Bond accounts receivable to the amount of $300 were collected on December 31, 1955, and reflected on the records, but were not deposited until January 2, 1956.

4. Due to an oversight general fund money received on December 31, 1955, ($250 from taxes receivable, $50 from fines, and check B904 described below) was not recorded until its deposit on January 5, 1956. The total deposit on that day, which included also January, 1956, receipts, was $2,000 and the entire amount was recorded as a January 1956 receipt on the comptroller's books.

5. The bank made service charges of $75. Of this amount $35 was chargeable to the general fund and the remainder to the bond fund. These charges have not been recorded by the city.

6. Check G108 was for $250 but was recorded in error on the comptroller's books as $230 because the voucher payable was for that amount.

7. Check B904 is a payment in lieu of taxes made to the general fund and turned over to that fund on December 31, 1955, but not put through for collection by the general fund until January 5, 1956. (See 4 above.)

8. The following checks were outstanding:

General Fund		Bond Fund	
G114	$210	B901	$ 75
G115	350	B902	15
G116	400	B903	92
G117	150	B904	1,000

9. Checks G116 and G117 were written on December 31, 1955. Check G116 was mailed on that day while check G117 was not mailed until January 5, 1956. Both were recorded by the comptroller as December disbursements.

Problem 14-8. The Z City Council on January 3, 1955, created a library fund by levying a special tax in the amount of $145,000 and appropriating $120,000 for library purposes. The amounts received by the city from this levy for each month during the year were as follows:

January	$10,145	July	$10,220
February	13,440	August	11,361
March	15,670	September	12,446
April	10,492	October	11,756
May	11,170	November	10,660
June	14,240	December	12,008

The following vouchers were certified, and the following warrants were issued each month:

	Vouchers	Warrants		Vouchers	Warrants
January	$ 7,147	$ 7,147	July	$14,875	$14,272
February	9,610	9,810	August	12,950	13,124
March	10,340	10,460	September	9,236	9,140
April	10,620	10,787	October	10,520	10,620
May	11,750	11,490	November	8,560	7,475
June	13,680	13,684	December	7,250	3,926

The city treasurer during the year paid warrants amounting to $109,376.

Required:

a. Set up "T" accounts as they should appear on the books of (1) the comptroller, and (2) the treasurer.

b. Prepare a statement reconciling the comptroller's cash with that of the treasurer.

c. Prepare closing entries and post to "T" accounts.

d. Prepare a balance sheet as of December 31, 1955.

Questions and Problems on Chapter 15

Questions

Question 15-1. In a certain governmental unit, homesteads are exempt from taxation up to $2,500 of their assessed value except taxes levied for the payment of bonds issued prior to enactment of the homestead exemption law and for the payment of the interest on such bonds. The assessed valuation of the municipality in 1954 was $100,000,000, out of which properties with an assessed value of $20,000,000 were entitled to the exemption privilege. The tax levy for 1954 was as follows: (a) for all expenses excepting interest and bond retirements, $700,000; (b) for interest and bond retirements, $100,000, out of which $70,000 is applicable to bonds issued prior to the enactment of the homestead exemption act and $30,000 to bonds issued after passage of the act. Calculate the tax rate or tax rates of the governmental unit in question.

Question 15-2. Referring to Question 15-1, assume that taxpayer A resides in a homestead with an assessed valuation of $10,000. What is his 1954 tax bill?

Question 15-3. Is it more proper to consider discounts on taxes as direct deductions from revenue or as expenditures?

Question 15-4. Is it more proper to consider estimated losses on taxes receivable as direct deductions from revenue or as expenditures?

Question 15-5. The law in certain states does not provide for the payment of taxes in installments. Small taxpayers, however, desire to start making installment payments long before the taxes are due or sometimes even before the taxes are levied. How should these installments be handled on the records?

Question 15-6. A municipality removes from the general fund all taxes delinquent more than one year. As these taxes are collected, the proceeds are transferred to the general fund. (a) What effect will the removal of the delinquent taxes have on the financial condition of the general fund? (b) How will the revenues of the general fund be affected by the collections of delinquent taxes?

Question 15-7. In certain states, uncollected city taxes are turned over to the city sheriff, who proceeds to collect them. Give the entries to be made on the books of the city and on the sheriff's records (a) at the time the taxes are turned over to the sheriff, (b) at the time the sheriff collects these taxes, and (c) at the time the sheriff turns the money over to the city treasurer.

Problems

Problem 15-1. The 1953, 1954, and 1955 tax rates for the City of K are:

| | RATE PER $100 OF ASSESSED VALUE | | |
	1953	1954	1955
General Fund....................	$1.00	$1.10	$1.20
Library Fund....................	.09	.09	.09
Municipal Bonds—Redemptions....	.20	.18	.16
	$1.29	$1.37	$1.45

The total assessed value for 1955 was $88,400,000.

Required:

Compute the amount of taxes levied for each fund for 1955.

Problem 15-2. In the City of K (Problem 15-1), collections were made in 1955 as follows:

1955 levy................	$1,000,000
1954 levy................	100,000
1953 levy................	50,000
	$1,150,000

Required:

Compute the amount of collections applicable to each fund for each year.

Problem 15-3. On the basis of the following facts, determine the assessed value of the County of Z:

Kind of Property	True Value
Real Estate:	
Homesteads on platted property up to $4,000.........	$ 18,000,000
Homesteads on unplatted property up to $4,000.......	3,200,000
Homesteads on platted property in excess of $4,000....	3,500,000
Homesteads on unplatted property in excess of $4,000..	100,000
Other real estate.................................	192,300,000
Personal Property:	
Household goods and furniture......................	32,510,000
Livestock, agricultural products, stocks of merchandise, and so on..	72,490,000
Other personal property............................	17,500,000
Money and Credits.................................	175,000,000

Basis of Assessment

Real estate is assessed at 55 per cent of true value. Homesteads on platted property up to $4,000 true value are assessed at 30 per cent of true value, and homesteads on unplatted property up to $4,000 true value are assessed at 25 per cent of true value. Homesteads on platted property in excess of $4,000 true value are assessed 52 per cent of true value, and homesteads on unplatted property in excess of $4,000 true value are assessed at 40 per cent of true value.

Household goods and furniture, including musical instruments, sewing machines, wearing apparel of members of family, and all personal property actually used by the owner for personal and domestic purposes or for the furnishing or equipment of the family residence are assessed at 30 per cent of true value.

Livestock, poultry, all agricultural products, stocks of merchandise, together with the furniture and fixtures used therewith, manufacturer's materials and manufactured articles, and all tools, implements, and machinery which are not permanently attached to and a part of the real estate where located are assessed at 40 per cent of true value.

Other personal property.is assessed at 55 per cent of its true value.

Money and credits are assessed at 98 per cent of their true value.

Problem 15-4. On the basis of the following data, prepare a statement similar to the one illustrated in **Figure 84**:

CITY OF *T*

Statement of Tax Levies and Tax Collections
January 1-January 31, 1955

Year	Total Tax Levy for Year	Uncollected Beginning of This Year	Amount Collected This Month
1946	$1,000,000	$ 60,000	$ 3,000
1947	950,000	70,000	4,000
1948	925,000	80,000	6,000
1949	900,000	70,000	5,000
1950	930,000	90,000	8,000
1951	960,000	90,000	9,000
1952	1,000,000	100,000	10,000
1953	1,000,000	110,000	20,000
1954	1,100,000	120,000	20,000
1955	1,100,000	1,100,000	400,000

Problem 15-5. On the basis of the following data, prepare a statement similar to that illustrated in Figure 85:

CITY OF *B*

Statement of Tax Levies and Tax Collections
for Fiscal Periods 1946-1955

Fiscal Period	Total Tax Levy	Collection of Current Taxes During Fiscal Period	Collection of Delinquent Taxes During Fiscal Period	Accumulated Delinquent Taxes
1946	$1,427,315.71	$1,389,195.28	$26,716.03	$ 87,070.23
1947	1,436,788.34	1,393,933.07	34,292.51	95,632.99
1948	1,418,678.05	1,371,841.33	42,809.66	99,660.05
1949	1,441,288.72	1,372,060.94	52,716.33	116,171.50
1950	1,267,183.83	1,174,818.47	55,140.92	153,395.94
1951	1,095,953.92	1,034,642.38	73,807.71	140,899.77
1952	1,081,375.23	1,028,771.11	56,725.53	136,764.82
1953	1,153,631.75	1,121,232.23	56,965.77	112,198.57
1954	1,162,104.72	1,138,005.55	38,949.86	97,457.88
1955	1,215,650.32	1,193,508.49	32,885.76	86,713.95

Problem 15-6. Prepare journal entries to record the following transactions:

1. Property *A* was sold for unpaid taxes covering 1953 and 1954 levies and interest and penalties, as follows:

Levy of	Taxes	Interest and Penalties
1954	$7,500	$750
1953	6,200	940

The cost of holding the sale was $65, and the property was sold for $17,500.

2. The taxpayer redeemed the property.

3. Assume the same facts as in the first transaction except that the property was sold for $12,000.

4. Assume the same facts as in the first transaction except that the governmental unit itself bid in the property. (*Note:* Set up an allowance for estimated losses on tax sale certificates through debiting Allowance for Uncollectible De-

linquent Taxes, $750, and Allowance for Uncollectible Interest and Penalties, $65.)

5. The governmental unit decided to use the property for recreational purposes. The taxes all belonged to the general fund. (Assume salable value of property is 85 per cent of the amount of the tax sale certificate.)

Problem 15-7. On the basis of the following data, prepare a statement for the Village of *J* analyzing the changes in the Tax Sale Certificates account during 1955:

Tax sale certificates canceled..................	$20,000
Transfers from taxes receivable...............	90,000
Property transferred to general fixed assets......	42,000
Payments received..........................	55,000
Interest, penalties, and costs on taxes transferred	5,000
Balance, January 1..........................	43,000

Problem 15-8. From the following data, prepare a statement analyzing the changes in the Taxes Receivable account during 1955:

Tax collections on current taxes were $900,000 and on delinquent taxes $225,-000.

Taxes levied amounted to $1,725,000.

Taxes to the amount of $200,000 became delinquent.

On January 1, the balance of current taxes receivable was $215,000 and of delinquent taxes receivable, $855,000.

Taxes canceled on the current year's levy amounted to $8,000 and on delinquent taxes to $12,000.

Problem 15-9. (Adapted from an American Institute of Accountants' examination.) The following is a balance sheet of the City of *C* at December 31, 1954:

Current Fund

ASSETS

Cash...	$ 15,482.34
Taxes receivable:	
Year 1951.....................................	1,917.66
Year 1952.....................................	7,308.14
Year 1953.....................................	8,133.11
Year 1954.....................................	123,170.65
Deferred charges:	
Overexpenditures of 1954 appropriations..........	437.10
Taxes canceled—1954..........................	850.00
	$157,299.00

LIABILITIES

Tax revenue notes:	
Year 1952.....................................	$ 7,000.00
Year 1953.....................................	8,000.00
Year 1954.....................................	123,000.00
Accounts payable..............................	17,601.00
Surplus revenue...............................	1,698.00
	$157,299.00

Capital Fund

ASSETS

Cash...	$ 17,810.95
Improvements in progress.........................	39,152.62
Deferred charges to future taxation for cost of completed improvements.................................	25,380.00
	$ 82,343.57

LIABILITIES

Serial bonds.....................................	$ 26,000.00
Notes payable...................................	49,000.00
Accounts payable................................	7,343.57
	$ 82,343.57

The governing body of the city adopted the following budget for 1955:

APPROPRIATIONS

Department of Public Works........	$ 275,450.00
Department of Revenue and Finance	48,500.00
Department of Public Safety........	535,375.00
Department of Public Affairs........	190,000.00
Department of Parks and Public Property..........................	60,000.00
Interest on bonds.................	3,500.00
Retirement of bonds...............	7,000.00
Interest on notes..................	4,500.00
Overexpenditures of 1954 appropriations	437.10
Taxes canceled—1954..............	850.00
	$1,125,612.10

ANTICIPATED REVENUES

General licenses...................	$ 10,700.00
Liquor licenses....................	63,000.00
Interest on taxes..................	22,000.00
City clerk's fees...................	700.00
Building permits..................	2,500.00
Bureau of health fees..............	5,400.00
Police court fines.................	3,000.00
	$ 107,300.00
Amount to be raised by taxation....	1,018,312.10
	$1,125,612.10

The actual amount of taxes levied for the year 1955 was $1,018,603.75.

During the year 1955, improvements in progress costing $30,000 were completed. The notes payable issued to finance the improvements were retired from the proceeds of a serial bond issue, which was sold at par.

A statement of receipts and disbursements for the year 1955 follows:

RECEIPTS:

1951 taxes	$ 1,012.75
1952 taxes	5,475.63
1953 taxes	6,125.47
1954 taxes	115,245.78
1955 taxes	787,375.62
General licenses	10,754.00
Liquor licenses	63,125.00
Interest on taxes	21,900.00
City clerk's fees	725.00
Building permits	2,530.00
Bureau of health fees	5,350.00
Police court fines	2,925.00
Miscellaneous fees	250.00
Tax revenue notes—1955	215,000.00

		$1,237,794.25
Serial bonds		30,000.00
		$1,267,794.25

DISBURSEMENTS:

Department of Public Works	$ 270,680.00
Department of Revenue and Finance	47,350.00
Department of Public Safety	525,250.00
Department of Public Affairs	187,325.00
Department of Parks and Public Property	59,100.00
Interest on bonds	3,500.00
Retirement of bonds	7,000.00
Interest on notes	4,300.00
Tax revenue notes—1952	7,000.00
Tax revenue notes—1953	6,000.00
Tax revenue notes—1954	114,000.00
Accounts payable—current fund	16,751.00

		$1,248,256.00
Improvements in progress	$ 5,900.00	
Notes payable	30,000.00	
Accounts payable—capital fund	7,343.57	
		43,243.57
		$1,291,499.57

The following bills applicable to the year 1955 were unpaid at December 31, 1955:

Department of Public Works	$4,000
Department of Revenue and Finance	1,000
Department of Public Safety	9,500
Department of Public Affairs	2,000
Department of Parks and Public Property	700

Required:

Prepare a work sheet showing (1) the balance sheet at December 31, 1955, (2) the changes in revenue surplus, (3) journal entries, and (4) cash transactions.

Questions and Problems on Chapter 16

Questions

Question 16-1. Why should depreciation not be computed on general fixed assets?

Question 16-2. An asset costing $10,000 was transferred from the general fixed assets group of accounts of a governmental unit to the governmental unit's utility or other enterprise. What effect would this transfer have on the surplus of the general fund and the utility or other enterprise fund, respectively?

Question 16-3. A utility's engineers claim that no depreciation charges should be made during 1955 on certain machines, because these machines are operating with 95 per cent efficiency. Are the engineers' claims correct?

Question 16-4. The engineers of a municipal utility claim that, in view of the fact that the city is spending money for maintaining the plant, depreciation should not be charged. Is their claim correct?

Question 16-5. State to which asset, (a) land, (b) structures and improvements, or (c) equipment, you would charge the following expenditures:

1. Cost of demolishing structure (less proceeds from sale of salvage) for purpose of clearing site for construction of new building.

2. Cost of preliminary engineering surveys.

3. Cost of transporting equipment purchased.

4. Purchase of tools at 50 cents each.

5. Broker's fees in connection with acquiring a lot on which new city hall is to be erected.

6. Cost of installing equipment.

7. Special assessments levied on governmental property located in special assessment district.

8. Legal expenses incurred by governmental unit in connection with perfection of title.

Question 16-6. What is the effect of undercharging depreciation during a particular year on the current year's income and on future years' income?

Question 16-7. Why is it not necessary to segregate an amount of surplus corresponding to the amount of assets set aside in the replacement fund? (Note particularly that this procedure is contrary to the practice followed in the case of a sinking fund, where an amount of surplus corresponding to the addition made to the sinking fund is segregated.)

Question 16-8. It is sometimes claimed that to include depreciation among the expenses and to provide money out of earnings to retire bonds which were used to finance the acquisition of the assets being depreciated is to overcharge customers. Through retiring the debt, the customers are paying for the old plant, and through depreciation charges they are paying for a new plant. Is this claim correct?

Question 16-9. Explain what is wrong with the following condensed balance sheet:

CITY OF *K*

Lighting Department

Balance Sheet

December 31, 1955

ASSETS

Fixed Assets (Less Allowance for Depreciation)...................		$419,055.17
Current Assets...		57,647.80
Miscellaneous—Reserves:		
Depreciation...	$41,874.08	
Compensation..	3,890.04	
Fire..	6,084.67	51,848.79
Work in Progress..		2,618.08
		$531,169.84

LIABILITIES AND SURPLUS

Liabilities..	$ 1,166.63
Donated Surplus..	105,774.49
Surplus..	424,228.72
	$531,169.84

Question 16-10. A municipal utility owns fixed assets costing $200,000 and estimated to have a life of 20 years. For 10 years the municipality has been transferring to the general fund at the end of each year all profits earned during that year. But, in determining the amount of profit earned, no cognizance had been taken of depreciation. It is now recognized that, unless provision is made for depreciation, the plant will be completely depreciated at the end of the next 10 years, with no provision made for its replacement. How much depreciation should be charged each year over the remaining 10 years, if the straight-line method of depreciation is to be used?

Problems

Problem 16-1. Give the entries necessary to record the following transactions in all funds and accounts, including subsidiary accounts:

1. Office equipment was ordered as follows:

Organization Unit	Estimated Cost
Mayor...............................	$ 750
City Clerk...........................	300
Election Board.......................	450
Commissioner of Finance...............	1,500
Purchasing Department.................	300
Police Department....................	3,000
Library..............................	7,500
Parks Administration Building..........	1,500

The purchase is to be financed out of the general fund.

2. The office equipment ordered was received. The actual cost was as follows:

Mayor...............................	$ 770
City Clerk...........................	340
Election Board.......................	360

Commissioner of Finance..............	1,500
Purchasing Department...............	270
Police Department....................	3,000
Library..............................	6,200
Parks Administration Building.........	1,500

3. General fixed assets (equipment) financed from general fund revenues were contributed to the governmental unit's utility from the following departments:

	Book Value	Estimated Accrued Depreciation
Department of Public Works............	$ 7,000	$ 1,500
Department of Health..................	4,000	750
Department of Fire.....................	12,000	10,000

4. A machine costing $12,000 and carried in the general fixed assets group of accounts was sold for $1,500.

5. Upon taking an inventory, it was discovered that general fixed assets belonging to the Police Department and costing $3,500 were missing.

6. A fire truck costing $7,500 was traded in for another truck. The price of the new truck was $8,600, but $2,200 was allowed on the old truck.

7. A playground shelter was torn down. The cost of dismantling the building was $2,200, and $900 was realized from the sale of salvage. The building cost $20,000 and had been financed from a special revenue fund.

8. A library building, which had been financed through the issuance of bonds, was torn down. The cost of building was $75,000 and the cost of dismantling, $4,200. Cash of $7,300 was realized from the sale of salvage.

9. Telephone switchboard wires costing $55 were removed.

10. The telephone switchboard, costing $1,000, was retired.

Problem 16-2. The following transactions took place in the Municipality of P during the fiscal year ending December 31, 1955:

	FUND		
	General	Bond	Special Assessment
Assets purchased...................	$65,000	$ 70,000	—
Assets constructed.................	—	120,000	$150,000
Work in progress at end of 1954 completed............................	—	65,000	70,000
Work in progress at end of 1955......	—	35,000	35,000

The balance of completed fixed assets at the beginning of the year was $210,000.

Assets disposed of amounted to $65,000.

Required:

Prepare a statement showing the opening balance of general fixed assets, additions, deductions, and the closing balance.

Problem 16-3. The following is a list of the fixed assets of the City of L as of June 30, 1955:

Parks—Land......................................	$23,491,420
City Hall—Structures and Improvements............	7,510,000
Fire Department—Structures and Improvements.....	1,587,826
Fire and Police Signal System.....................	1,593,850
Library Equipment................................	2,158,669
City Hall—Land..................................	2,500,000

Playgrounds—Land...............................	11,818,973
Public Works—Equipment........................	11,815,189
Public Works—Structures and Improvements........	1,239,900
Attorney—Equipment............................	73,000
City Hall—Equipment............................	62,500
City Planning—Equipment........................	13,636
Coliseum—Structures and Improvements............	1,450,000
Controller—Equipment...........................	44,694
Council—Equipment..............................	36,358
Department of Health—Structures and Improvements	22,500
Fire Department—Equipment......................	2,922,384
Fire Department—Land...........................	612,500
Library—Land...................................	4,198,914
Library—Structures and Improvements.............	4,392,000
Mayor—Equipment...............................	22,335
Bureau of Budget and Efficiency—Equipment........	8,299
Civil Service—Equipment.........................	27,000
City Clerk—Equipment...........................	50,629
Purchasing Agent—Equipment.....................	6,392
Sewer Maintenance—Equipment...................	35,122
Social Service—Equipment.......................	8,762
Street Sweeping—Equipment......................	188,785
Building and Safety Department—Structures and Improvements...................................	69,000
Building and Safety Department—Equipment.......	74,357
Fire and Police Pension—Equipment...............	6,943
Garbage and Refuse—Equipment..................	170,939
Humane Division—Equipment.....................	22,400
Municipal Art—Equipment........................	4,237
Parks—Equipment...............................	812,000
Playgrounds—Structures and Improvements.........	2,631,337
Police Department—Equipment....................	743,790
Public Works—Land.............................	5,529,688
Department of Health—Equipment.................	77,601
Department of Health—Land......................	11,500
Police Department—Land.........................	355,600
Police Department—Structures and Improvements...	1,239,900
Public Defender—Equipment......................	2,055
Humane Division—Land..........................	9,000
Humane Division—Structures and Improvements....	32,500
Parks—Structures and Improvements..............	4,696,066
Playgrounds—Equipment.........................	512,000

Required:

Prepare a statement classifying the fixed assets by function and organization unit.

Problem 16-4. The following is an inventory of fixed assets of the City of *G* at January 1, 1955, and additions made during the year:

	Inventory at Beginning of Year	Additions
Schools...........................	$102,765,000	$500,000
Public Works......................	215,760,000	450,000
Lighting..........................	37,945,000	100,000
Art...............................	7,694,000	300,000
Fire..............................	22,542,000	300,000
General Administrative Departments	585,000	75,000
Health...........................	7,320,000	100,000

	Inventory at Beginning of Year	Additions
House of Correction................	3,156,000	62,000
Airport.........................	3,500,000	75,000
Building and Safety Engineering.....	12,000	3,500
Welfare..........................	3,180,000	102,000
Zoological Park...................	3,650,000	120,000
Motor Transportation.............	2,372,000	70,000
Parks and Boulevards.............	65,757,000	300,000
Planning.........................	9,500	2,000
Purchasing.......................	3,000	1,500
Recorder's Court..................	82,000	5,000
Recreation.......................	3,506,000	97,000
Police...........................	6,253,000	70,000
Libraries........................	7,697,000	67,000

Assets of the following departments were disposed of during the year:

General Administrative Departments..	$ 35,000
Fire.............................	12,000
Lighting..........................	16,500
Motor Transportation..............	42,000
Parks and Boulevards..............	12,000
Police...........................	45,000
Health...........................	60,000
House of Correction...............	42,000
Libraries.........................	45,000
Public Works......................	32,500
Recreation........................	12,000
Schools...........................	105,000
Welfare...........................	90,000
Zoological Park...................	78,000

Required:

Prepare a statement classifying the above general fixed assets by functions and showing for each asset its value at the beginning of the year, additions, deductions, and the balance at the end of the year.

Problem 16-5. You are given the following data concerning equipment owned by the City of H:

Cost..............................	$135,000
Transportation Expenses.............	2,500
Installation Expenses................	12,000
Estimated Net Salvage Value.........	15,500
Estimated Life.....................	10 years

Required:

Prepare a schedule showing annual depreciation charges, the accumulated allowance for depreciation, and the net value at the end of each year for the life of the asset.

Problem 16-6. You are given the following transactions:

1. (a) A machine financed from a utility fund and costing $60,000 was sold for $2,500. The accumulated depreciation allowance was $60,000. A fund had been established for the replacement of the machine. (b) The asset was replaced at a cost of $72,000. Up to the time of the sale of the old machine, the replacement fund had accumulated $65,500.

2. General municipal equipment costing $35,000 was destroyed by fire; the

same fire destroyed utility equipment costing $25,000. The accumulated allowance for depreciation on the utility equipment was $12,500. The equipment was not insured against fire.

3. A machine owned by the utility, costing $25,200 and having an accumulated allowance for depreciation of $10,000, was traded in for another machine. The new machine cost $28,000, but the utility was allowed $5,000 on the old machine.

Required:

Prepare *all* the entries necessary to record the foregoing transactions.

Problem 16-7. Utility equipment costing $10,500 is estimated to have a scrap value of $500 and to last five years. It is decided to set up a replacement fund to replace the asset when it becomes worn out. A sinking fund table shows that, if the replacement fund assets are assumed to earn 4 per cent, the required annual contribution to the fund is $1,846.27. It is assumed further that contributions to the fund are made at the end of each year and are invested immediately at the beginning of the following year, and that earnings are received at the end of that year. For example, if the contribution is made on December 31, 1954, the money is invested on January 2, 1955, and the full amount of interest thereon for 1955 is received before December 31, 1955.

Required:

a. Prepare a table showing the amount to be contributed annually to the fund (assume the first contribution to be made on December 31, 1954), the required earnings, and the total required contributions and earnings.

b. Prepare for each year the entries necessary to record (1) depreciation charges, (2) contributions made to the replacement fund, and (3) earnings of the replacement fund. (You are to assume that earnings are per requirements.)

Problem 16-8. From the following data, prepare a statement classifying the assets of the water utility of the City of *F* by function and showing the book value of assets at January 1, 1956, additions, retirements, and book value of the assets at the end of the year.

	Beginning of Year	Additions	Retirements
Intangible Plant:			
Organization Expense..................	$ 75,000	—	—
Tangible Plant:			
Water Rights........................	135,000	—	—
Reservoir Land......................	42,000	—	—
Power and Pumping Land..............	33,000	3,000	—
Purification Land....................	52,000	—	—
Transmission Land...................	32,000	12,000	—
Standpipe Land......................	4,000	—	—
Distribution Land....................	7,500	—	—
Office Land.........................	6,000	—	—
Stores, Shop, and Garage Land.........	30,000	5,000	—
Collecting and Impounding Reservoirs...	95,000	—	—
Wells and Springs....................	122,000	14,000	3,000
Other Water Source Structures.........	84,000	2,000	2,000
Power and Pumping Structures.........	52,000	—	—
Purification Buildings.................	33,500	—	—
Distribution Standpipe................	30,000	—	—
Office Buildings......................	10,000	—	—
Stores, Shop, and Garage Buildings......	21,000	800	—
Boiler Plant Equipment...............	30,000	4,000	8,000
Steam Pumping Equipment.............	150,000	5,000	34,650
Electric Pumping Equipment..........	60,000	46,900	12,000

	Beginning of Year	Additions	Retirements
Purification System....................	195,000	20,000	—
Transmission Mains and Accessories.....	235,000	7,000	2,000
Distribution Mains and Accessories......	295,600	48,975	18,600
Services.............................	60,800	1,400	600
Meters..............................	78,600	3,300	750
Hydrants............................	74,500	2,500	1,500
Fire Mains and Cisterns................	19,900	100	1,000
Office Furniture and Equipment.........	65,300	1,600	100
Transportation Equipment.............	15,500	1,500	2,000
Stores Equipment.....................	7,800	—	—
Shop Equipment......................	5,500	500	—
Laboratory Equipment.................	3,200	—	—
Communications Equipment............	6,000	—	—
Miscellaneous Equipment..............	21,900	—	—
	$2,188,600	$179,575	$86,200

Problem 16-9. Classify the following fixed assets of the electric utility of the City of *M* by function, and show for each asset the balance at the beginning of the year, additions during the year, withdrawals, and the book value at the end of the year.

Note: Classify as general plant all properties which you cannot group otherwise.

	Balance January 1, 1956	Additions During Year	Withdrawals During Year
Operating Fixed Assets:			
Land...............................	$ 74,123	—	—
Structures..........................	501,781	$ 374	$ 1,144
Boiler Plant Equipment...............	652,117	5,818	1,419
Turbo-Generators—Steam............	649,822	85	3,199
Accessory Electric Equipment—Steam	160,081	1,075	—
Miscellaneous Power Plant Equipment—			
Steam.........................	4,322	1,242	—
Transmission Overhead Conductors....	1,746	1,696	—
Transmission Underground Conductors	39,696	2,399	—
Poles, Towers, and Fixtures—Distribution..............................	265,453	15,264	12,714
Underground Conduits—Distribution..	102,312	—	—
Distribution Substation Equipment....	218,227	17,714	190
Distribution Overhead Conductors.....	347,558	7,818	9,431
Distribution Underground Conductors..	21,490	404	506
Line Transformers....................	300,696	26,368	22,193
Overhead Services....................	129,414	2,422	3,059
Underground Services.................	—	412	—
Consumers' Meters...................	152,147	19,462	18,909
Consumers' Meter Installation........	61,319	424	999
Other Property on Consumers' Premises	2,492	—	—
Street Lighting and Signal System Equipment........................	185,917	1,327	475
Office Equipment.....................	13,945	4,088	1,328
Stores Equipment....................	1,935	72	—
Shop Equipment.......................	1,514	—	—
Transportation Equipment............	17,089	2,423	1,291
Communication Equipment...........	140	—	—

	Balance January 1, 1956	Additions During Year	Withdrawals During Year
Laboratory Equipment...............	6,864	406	—
General Tools and Implements........	3,748	105	45
Miscellaneous General Equipment.....	214	—	—
Total Operating Fixed Assets......	$3,916,162	$111,398	$76,902
Nonoperating Fixed Assets:			
Land.............................	$ 1,830	$ 4,169	—
Structures........................	15,856	—	—
Total Nonoperating Fixed Assets...	$ 17,686	$ 4,169	—
Total Fixed Assets.............	$3,933,848	$115,567	$76,902

Questions and Problems on Chapter 17

Questions

Question 17-1. Many states prohibit the sale of bonds at a discount. Can you see any justification for such a prohibition?

Question 17-2. Recast the following balance sheet so that it will reflect the true financial condition of the City of K:

CITY OF K
General Fund
Balance Sheet
March 31, 1955

ASSETS

Current Assets		$ 300,000
Fixed Assets		8,196,000
		$8,496,000

LIABILITIES AND SURPLUS

Liabilities:			
Current Liabilities		$ 350,000	
Bonded Indebtedness:			
Not Matured	$3,300,000		
In Default	100,000	3,400,000	$3,750,000
Surplus			4,746,000
			$8,496,000

Question 17-3. A city has an assessed valuation of $100,000,000, out of which $25,000,000 is homestead property exempt from taxation for all purposes except bonds issued prior to 1954. Total bonded indebtedness is $1,000,000, out of which $500,000 consists of bonds issued prior to 1954. What is the ratio of bonded indebtedness to assessed value?

Question 17-4. (*a*) A municipality has issued bonds to the amount of $200,000 for the purpose of financing the acquisition of a utility or other enterprise. The municipality has agreed to pay the principal and interest on the bonds without specifying any particular source from which they are to be paid. Should such bonds be shown as a liability of the utility or other enterprise fund? (*b*) Suppose that the amount of surplus transferred annually for the past few years from the utility or other enterprise fund to the general fund has been more than sufficient to pay both the principal and the interest that becomes due each year. Should the bonds be shown as a liability of the utility or other enterprise fund? (*c*) Suppose the bonds are to be repaid primarily from utility or other enterprise earnings but that, in the event that the earnings are not sufficient, the municipality guarantees the payment of the bond from general revenues. Should the bonds in that event be shown as a liability of the utility or other enterprise fund?

Question 17-5. Explain what is wrong with the following statement:

CITY OF X

General Fund

Balance Sheet

December 31, 1954

ASSETS

Cash..		$82,000
Taxes Receivable.........................	$100,000	
Less—Allowance for Uncollected Taxes........	100,000	—
		$82,000

LIABILITIES AND SURPLUS

Tax Anticipation Notes..............................	$80,000
Unappropriated Surplus..............................	2,000
	$82,000

Problems

Problem 17-1. Give the entries to record the following transactions:

1. Warrants payable of $150,000, together with interest thereon of $2,000, were paid.

2. Tax anticipation notes of $310,000 were sold.

3. Taxes receivable to the amount of $225,000 were collected. Of this amount 65 per cent represents cash which must be used to retire tax anticipation notes.

4. General bond anticipation notes to the amount of $150,000 were sold.

5. General bonds to the amount of $150,000 were sold at par, and the money was used to retire the bond anticipation notes.

6. Judgments to the amount of $15,000 were rendered against the city on account of accidents.

7. Cash to the amount of $75,000 for payment of bonds was transmitted by the governmental unit to its fiscal agent.

Problem 17-2. On March 1, 1953, School District X sold an issue of bonds amounting to $100,000 at a premium of $2,280 plus accrued interest. The bonds are to run for five years and bear a nominal interest rate of 4 per cent, payable semiannually on June 1 and December 1. Bond tables show that bonds sold on this basis yield 3½ per cent (that is, the effective interest rate is 3½ per cent).

Required:

a. Prepare an entry to record the sale of the bonds.

b. Prepare a table similar to Table 2, page 136. (Column 2 should read "Interest Paid," and column 6 should read "Par Value of Bonds.")

c. Prepare the entries to be made when interest is paid on (1) June 1, 1953. (2) June 1, 1955, and (3) December 1, 1957.

Problem 17-3. Assume that the bonds referred to in Problem 17-2 were purchased by the City of Y for its sinking fund and that the bonds are to be held over their life.

Required:

a. Prepare the entry to be made on the city's books to show the purchase of the investments.

b. Prepare the entries to be made when interest is received on (1) June 1, 1953, (2) June 1, 1955, and (3) December 1, 1957.

Problem 17-4. On March 1, 1953, the City of N sold an issue of bonds amounting to $100,000 at a discount of $2,720 plus accrued interest. The bonds are to run for five years and bear a nominal interest rate of 3 per cent, payable semiannually on June 1 and December 1. Bond tables show that bonds sold on this basis yield 3.6 per cent (that is, the effective interest rate is 3.6 per cent).

Required:

a. Prepare an entry to record the sale of the bonds.

b. Prepare a table similar to Table 3, page 137, showing the amortization of discounts over the life of the bonds. (Column 2 should read "Interest Paid," and column 6 should read "Par Value of Bonds.")

c. Prepare the entries to be made when interest is paid on (1) June 1, 1953, (2) June 1, 1955, and (3) December 1, 1957.

Problem 17-5. Assume that the bonds referred to in Problem 17-4 were purchased by the N School District as a sinking fund investment and that the bonds are to be held over their life.

Required:

a. Prepare the entry to be made on the school district's books to show the purchase of the investments.

b. Prepare the entries to be made when interest is received by the school district on (1) June 1, 1953, (2) June 1, 1955, and (3) December 1, 1957.

Problem 17-6. A municipality sold bonds with a par value of $150,000 at a premium of $3,000. The bonds are to run for ten years with $15,000 maturing each year. Interest is payable semiannually. Set up a table showing the amount of premium on bonds to be amortized at each interest payment date on the basis of the bonds outstanding method (see Table 4).

Problem 17-7. Assume the same facts as above except that the bonds were sold at a discount of $2,500. Set up a table showing the amount of discount on bonds to be amortized at each interest payment date on the basis of the bonds outstanding method.

Problem 17-8. On the basis of the following data, prepare a statement of bonds payable for the City of M as of December 31, 1955, similar to that illustrated in Figure 98:

General Sinking Fund Bonds

Fire department building bonds of $100,000 were issued January 1, 1940, and are due January 1, 1964. The interest rate is 4 per cent. Actuarial requirements to date are $50,564; the amount actually in the sinking fund is $50,710.

Municipal hospital bonds of $200,000 were issued November 1, 1943, and are due November 1, 1968. The interest rate is 4 per cent. Actuarial requirements are $68,308; the amount actually in the sinking fund is $68,100.

General Serial Bonds

Maumee River Bridge bonds of $500,000 were issued December 1, 1947, with maturities of $20,000 each year for the succeeding 25 years. The interest rate is 4 per cent.

Park bonds of $200,000 were issued September 1, 1953, with maturities of

$10,000 each year for the succeeding 20 years. The interest rate is 3½ per cent, and the amount authorized is $300,000.

Water-front boulevard bonds of $100,000 were issued April 1, 1954, and are due $5,000 each year for the succeeding 20 years. The interest rate is 4 per cent.

You are to assume that, unless otherwise stated, the full amount of bonds authorized was issued.

Problem 17-9. From the following data, prepare a statement of legal debt margin of the City of T as of June, 30, 1955:

Bonded Debt:

General bonds	$ 4,450,000
Water plant bonds	1,265,000
Gas plant bonds	522,000
Special assessment bonds	470,000
Sewage disposal revenue certificates	900,000
Assessed valuation	120,715,000

Debt margin, 5 per cent of assessed valuation.

Deductions allowable:

Gas plant bonds	512,700
Water plant bonds	1,416,000
Sewage disposal revenue certificates	900,000
Sinking fund	10,450
Special assessment bonds	410,000
Amount of general bonds without limitations by special legislative acts	1,712,000

Problem 17-10. From the following data, prepare a statement of legal debt margin of the County of L as of June 30, 1955, for (a) the electoral debt, and (b) the debt which may be incurred by the county commissioners:

Bonded debt created by vote of electors	$ 5,200,000
Bonded debt created by vote of commissioners	5,650,000
Floating debt created by commissioners—tax anticipation loan	700,000
Assessed valuation	175,350,000
Debt limit: Commissioners, 2 per cent of assessed valuation; electors, 5 per cent of assessed valuation.	
Sinking fund assets applicable to electoral debt	735,000
Sinking fund assets applicable to commissioners' debt	1,115,000
Other credits deductible from commissioners' debt	1,212,000

Problem 17-11. On the basis of the following data, prepare a statement of debt service requirements of the County of Y for the 20 years ending December 31, 1967 (see Figure 101):

Date of Issue	Rate of Interest	Amount Issued	Interest Due	Principal Due Date	Principal Due Amount
Jan. 1, 1938	5%	$200,000	June 30, Dec. 31	Dec. 31	$10,000 each year
July 1, 1940	4½%	150,000	Dec. 31, June 30	June 30	15,000 each year
July 1, 1944	4	300,000	Dec. 31, June 30	June 30	10,000 each year
Jan. 1, 1947	4	200,000	June 30, Dec. 31	Dec. 31, 1966	Sinking fund contribution of $6,717 on January 1 of each year beginning with 1947
Jan. 1, 1948	4	100,000	June 30, Dec. 31	Dec. 31	$ 5,000 each year

Problem 17-12. From the following data, prepare a statement of direct and overlapping debt as of June 30, 1955, for the City of *S*:

Assessed valuation of city...................................	$ 79,100,000
Assessed valuation of school district...............	80,250,000
Assessed valuation of county.......................	112,195,000
Net bonded debt—city...........................	950,000
Net bonded debt—school district..................	1,916,000
Net bonded debt—county.......................	1,536,000

Problem 17-13. From the following data, prepare a statement for the City of *T* showing (a) the ratio of net bonded debt to assessed valuation, and (b) net bonded debt per capita:

Year	Population	Assessed Valuation	Gross General Bonded Debt	Less General Sinking Fund
1947...............	72,500	$88,998,895	$2,175,500	$225,515
1948...................	74,200	94,300,000	1,962,000	65,348
1949...................	63,210	84,752,644	1,856,700	68,838
1950...................	59,370	82,350,000	1,712,877	—
1951...................	84,510	71,512,000	1,546,307	—
1952...................	82,740	72,565,000	1,297,259	—
1953...................	89,500	68,624,694	1,265,300	—
1954...................	96,270	68,400,758	1,017,500	—
1955...................	98,540	70,228,644	1,005,200	—
1956...................	100,27C	70,990,01C	972,300	—

Questions and Problems on Chapter 18

Questions

Question 18-1. In the course of an audit of the books of a municipality, you find that the financial statements, when prepared on the basis required by law, do not reflect the true financial condition or financial operations of the municipality. What would be your procedure?

Question 18-2. In making an audit, how would you ascertain that expenditures were properly appropriated for?

Question 18-3. You are called in to audit the books of a municipality for which taxes are collected by a county. How would you verify that taxes receivable controlling accounts are correct?

Question 18-4. In your audit of the taxes receivable of a county which collects both its own taxes and taxes for other units, how would you verify that the taxpayers' individual account balances, as reflected in the records, are correct?

Question 18-5. A municipal golf course charges 25 cents per hour for games played during regular hours but only 15 cents for games played during the twilight hours. It has been found that the clerk has been charging players at the rate of 25 cents an hour but recording the receipts as twilight hour receipts and pocketing the difference. What steps would you recommend to insure that all receipts will be properly accounted for hereafter?

Question 18-6. Describe briefly the contents of the audit report of a governmental unit.

Question 18-7. A municipality requires auditors to submit bids as to how much they would charge for the annual audit. The audit contract is awarded to the lowest bidder. What is wrong with this method of hiring auditors?

Problems

Problem 18-1. In connection with the audit of the City of Z, you are handed the following analysis of the changes in the Unappropriated Surplus account of the general fund. The municipality is required to keep its accounts for both revenues and expenditures on an accrual basis.

CITY OF Z

General Fund

Statement of Changes in
Unappropriated Surplus
for Fiscal Year Ending June 30, 1955

Unappropriated Surplus, July 1, 1954.....................		$ 75,000
Add—Excess of Revenues Over Expenditures:		
Revenues.................................	$350,000	
Less—Expenditures........................	305,000	45,000
Unappropriated surplus, June 30, 1955..................		$120,000

Among the revenues are included $15,000 estimated revenues not realized and $335,000 actual revenues, consisting among other items of cash receipts from the following sources: (1) collections applicable to the 1956 tax levy, $3,000; (2) sale of fixed assets carried in the utility or other enterprise fund, $2,500; (3) special tax levy made for the purpose of establishing a working capital fund, $75,000; (4) sale of general fixed assets which were financed by a general sinking fund bond issue still outstanding, $3,000; (5) sale of fixed assets originally financed 75 per cent from special assessments and 25 per cent from general fund revenues, $1,500; (6) a transfer from the sinking fund to the general fund, the money transferred to be used to retire sinking fund bonds, $150,000; (7) tax levy for the retirement of serial bonds, $15,000; (8) borrowed from the utility or other enterprise fund, $750.

The expenditures consist, among others, of the following items: (1) payments on account of the retirement of sinking fund bonds, $127,000; (2) payments for the retirement of serial bonds, $14,550; (3) repayment of a loan made from the trust fund, $450; (4) city's share of cost of special assessment project, $3,000; (5) purchase of general fixed assets, $10,000.

Included also among the expenditures are unliquidated encumbrances of $22,000 outstanding on June 30, 1955, as well as expenditures of $5,000 for which encumbrances amounting to $5,500 were outstanding on July 1, 1954.

Required:

Prepare a corrected statement analyzing the changes in unappropriated surplus and showing separately each item and amount by which the revenues or expenditures should be increased or decreased. Show also any other adjustments needed to reflect the correct balance of unappropriated surplus on June 30, 1955.

Problem 18-2. The following statement is taken from a state's financial report. (References are to schedules carried in the report but not reproduced here.)

Capital Balance Sheet
Property Assets, Investments, and Liabilities
June 30, 1954

CAPITAL ASSETS

1. Sinking Fund Assets... $ 23,528,921.16
    Consisting of:
    (a) Cash in State Treasury (Schedule A1)... $ 774,144.82
    (b) Investments and Bonds (Schedule B1)...   12,707,000.00
    (c) County Notes Receivable (Schedule B2)   10,047,776.34

2. Investments in Railroad Stocks (Schedule B3) (*Assume they apply
    to a trust fund.*)..   5,233,584.00

	Par Value	Market Value
(a) *X* Railroad Stocks........	$3,000,200	$ 4,410,294.00
(b) Atlantic and *X* Railroad Stocks.................	1,266,600	823,290.00
(c) Miscellaneous Stocks......	775,080	—

3. Fixed Assets:
    Consisting of:
    State Highways, State Institutions, Departmental Buildings,
    Real Estate, Equipment, and other fixed assets.......... $290,171,055.22

        Total Capital Assets............................... $318,933,560.38

        Balancing Totals.................................. $318,933,560.38

CAPITAL LIABILITIES

4. State Debt (Schedule B4)................................. $167,360,000.00
   Consisting of:
      (a) State Highway Bonds.................. $97,171,000.00
      (b) General Fund Bonds.................. 54,979,000.00
         (Funding, refunding, public improvement, permanent improvement for Educational and Charitable Institutions)
      (c) Special School Building Bonds......... 12,710,000.00
         (Reimbursable by Counties)
      (d) World War Veterans' Loan Bonds...... 2,500,000.00
         (Redeemable from Loans to Veterans)

         Total Capital Liabilities........................ $167,360,000.00

5. Capital Surplus.. 151,573,560.38
   (Value of Fixed Assets in excess of Funded Debt of State)

      Balancing Totals.................................... $318,933,560.38

Required:

Recast this statement so as to show the true financial condition of the state. You may split up this statement into as many statements as you think desirable. Assume actuarial sinking fund requirements of $23,520,800.

Problem 18-3. In connection with the audit of the accounts of the City of X, you are handed the following balance sheet which has been prepared by the city comptroller.

CITY OF X

Balance Sheet

December 31, 1955

ASSETS

	General Fund	Sinking Fund
Cash.......................................	$ 58,000	$ 82,000
Taxes Receivable............................	155,000	17,500
Amount to Be Provided for Retirement of Bonds		168,000
Total................................	$213,000	$267,500

LIABILITIES, RESERVES, AND SURPLUS

	General Fund	Sinking Fund
Bonds Payable.............................		$250,000
Vouchers Payable...........................	$ 81,000	
Reserve for Uncollected Taxes................	155,000	17,500
Operating Deficit...........................	23,000*	
Total................................	$213,000	$267,500

   * Red.

Upon investigation you discover the following additional facts:

1. Estimated losses on taxes receivable are $10,000 in the General Fund and $1,000 in the Sinking Fund.

2. Actuarial requirements of the Sinking Fund at December 31, 1955, $110,000.

3. Of the total bonds payable $100,000 represents serial bonds payable (not matured); $15,000 represents matured serial bonds; and the remainder is represented by sinking fund bonds payable which have not yet matured.

4. Matured interest payable on sinking fund bonds, $2,700, and on serial bonds, $2,100.

5. Interest payable in future years on sinking fund bonds, $10,000, and on serial bonds, $30,000.

Required:

Prepare a columnar balance sheet on an *accrual basis* containing separate columns for the general fund, the sinking fund, and any other funds or groups of accounts that you think it desirable to list separately. Your balance sheet should conform to sound municipal accounting principles.

Problem 18-4. (Adapted from an American Institute of Accountants' examination.) A governmental authority was constituted about July 1, 1954, to carry out certain recreational activities for which the authority was to buy or construct the equipment.

It was decided that the accounts of the authority will show budgetary estimates as well as actual income and expenditures in an approved manner, and that the transactions will be recorded in the following funds:

> General operating fund
> Working capital fund
> Sinking fund for redemption of bonds
> Property fund

From the following information, prepare a columnar work sheet recording the transactions of the authority so as to show the asset and liability and budgetary accounts for the year ended June 30, 1955:

1. An advance of $50,000 was made by the government creating the authority to finance the initial construction and activities, to be repaid out of operating revenues.

2. From the working capital fund thus created, $10,000 was transferred to the general fund for current operating expenses until revenues could be realized.

3. A budget of recreational activities for the year was adopted as follows:

REVENUES

Licenses	$ 50,000	
Fees	100,000	
Sales	30,000	
Miscellaneous	10,000	$190,000

EXPENDITURES

Administration	$ 10,000	
Bathing pavilion	65,000	
Boating	25,000	
Park maintenance	54,000	
Interest on bonds	6,000	
Sinking fund requirements	20,000	180,000

4. Purchases of supplies were made for central stores to the amount of $36,000 and paid in full.

5. A bond issue of $200,000 for improvements was authorized as of July 1, 1954, bearing interest at 3 per cent per annum, payable semiannually. It was disposed of on August 1st at par and accrued interest of $500.

6. Contracts amounting to $165,000 were let for improvements. Work was completed and contracts paid to the extent of $156,000, which included $1,000 extras, leaving $10,000 in progress on June 30, 1955.

7. Additional construction work was supplied through the working capital fund to the extent of $34,000, which included $18,000 labor paid in cash, $14,000 material from stores at cost, and $2,000 overhead. The working capital fund was reimbursed in full for this service.

8. Other services (labor only) supplied to authority activities and paid for by the working capital fund were as follows, including 10 per cent or $920 for overhead:

Bathing pavilion	$3,300	
Boating	1,100	
Park maintenance	5,720	$10,120

Of the above, $2,200 for park maintenance was incomplete and not billed as of June 30, 1955. Otherwise, reimbursement to the working capital fund was completed.

9. Revenues collected during the year were as follows:

Licenses	$ 48,500	
Fees	101,400	
Sales	29,200	
Miscellaneous	9,400	$188,500

In addition there were $1,600 of licenses billed but not collected, on which possible losses should not exceed 20 per cent.

Of the fees collected, it was necessary to refund $210.

Of the licenses collected, $500 represented advance payments on account of the following year.

10. Supplies were issued to authority departments by the central stores as follows, the figures in each case including 10 per cent or a total of $1,050 for working-capital-fund overhead:

Administration	$ 330	
Bathing pavilion	2,640	
Boating	1,650	
Park maintenance	6,930	$11,550

Transfers were made to the working capital fund to the amount of $10,600 on account of these items.

11. Contracts and orders issued during the year for operating expenses totaled $83,000. These were liquidated to the extent of $81,160, leaving $1,200 for bathing pavilion, and $640 for boating, or a total of $1,840 outstanding at June 30th.

12. Vouchers approved during the year for payrolls, invoices, and miscellaneous, including those covering contracts and orders liquidated, as well as other items, were as follows:

Administration	$ 9,450	
Bathing pavilion	59,160	
Boating	21,600	
Park maintenance	41,000	
Interest	6,000	$137,210

Treasury warrants were issued and paid in settlement of these items to the amount of $135,610.

13. Transfer was made to the sinking fund for $18,000 of the amount due it from the general fund, leaving the remainder as still owing. Securities costing $18,000 were purchased for this fund, and income thereon was realized to the amount of $300. Among the securities purchased were $5,000 bonds of the authority, which were immediately retired.

14. The sum of $5,000 was repaid to the working capital fund on the advance made to the general fund.

15. Purchases of office and general equipment to the amount of $20,000 were made from the working capital fund. This equipment is to be written off by charges to overhead at the rate of 5 per cent per year, beginning with the current year.

16. Overhead expense of the working capital fund paid for the year was $2,600. The physical inventory of stores at the end of the year was $12,300. Stores and overhead surplus were carried to the surplus account of the fund. The sum of $1,000 was repaid to the central government to apply on the advance made to the authority.

17. Among the invoices paid during the year from the general fund were items totaling $16,540 for park maintenance equipment.

Problem 18-5. (Adapted from an American Institute of Accountants' examination.) From the following municipal trial balance at the close of a fiscal year but before closing the books, prepare a balance sheet, properly subdivided into funds, after giving effect to necessary entries of the general fund and the sinking fund as of the close of the year and to settlements of all inter-fund balances other than permanent advances:

	Debit	Credit
Accounts receivable, general fund	$ 3,321.74	
Appropriation balances (unencumbered), general fund		$ 1,117.09
Assessments receivable	72,621.70	
Bond fund cash	2,005.60	
Bond fund balance (unencumbered)		678.00
Bonds payable, general capital account		250,000.00
Bonds authorized and unissued	8,000.00	
Contracts payable, bond fund		4,700 00
Due stores fund from bond fund		1,227.60
Due stores fund from general fund		1,593.96
Due stores fund from other funds	2,821.56	
Estimated revenues	1,500.00	
Fixed property	897,640.00	
Fixed property (income-producing, trust fund)	62,000.00	
General fund cash	1,842.10	
Income account, sinking fund		1,960.00
Interest account, special assessments	620.00	
Loan from general to stores and service fund	25,000.00	
Public benefit receivable (assessment fund)	6,400.00	
Reserve for encumbrances, general fund		2,827.10
Reserve for working capital		25,000.00
Reserve for retirement of bonds		160,000.00
Reserve for uncollectible taxes		2,875.00
Sinking fund cash	1,450.00	
Sinking fund investments	160,000.00	
Sinking fund requirements	1,000.00	
Sinking fund surplus		490.00
Special assessment bonds		80,000.00

	Debit	Credit
Special assessment fund cash......................	1,872.65	
Stores and service fund working capital (loan from general fund).................................		25,000.00
Stores and service fund cash......................	1,408.22	
Stores inventory.................................	15,942.80	
Surplus receipts, general fund.....................		896.00
Surplus, special assessment fund...................		1,514.35
Surplus invested in fixed assets...................		647,640.00
Taxes receivable, general fund....................	6,972.61	
Temporary loans, general fund....................		3,000.00
Trust funds balance.............................		96,320.00
Trust fund cash.................................	6,820.00	
Trust fund investments..........................	27,500.00	
Vouchers payable, bond fund......................		3,400.00
Vouchers payable, general fund....................		1,327.30
Work in process, stores and service fund...........	4,827.42	
	$1,311,566.40	$1,311,566.40

Questions and Problems on Chapter 19

Questions

Question 19-1. Name three differences between the accounting procedures of hospitals and those of municipalities.

Question 19-2. A county hospital derives its revenues solely from a special tax levy made for this purpose. Would the accounting procedures outlined throughout this chapter apply to such a hospital? If not, indicate the fund or funds in which the financial transactions of the hospital should be recorded.

Question 19-3. The funds used in hospital accounting are the general fund, temporary funds, endowment funds, and plant funds. Indicate the corresponding municipal fund (or funds) that is designed to account for the same type of financial transaction.

Question 19-4. In your opinion should depreciation be charged on the fixed assets of a hospital, if these assets have been financed from contributions but are intended to be replaced from hospital revenues?

Question 19-5. Referring to Question 19-4, assume that the conditions are the same as described in that question except that the replacement of the fixed assets is intended to be financed from contributions. Should depreciation be charged on such fixed assets?

Question 19-6. What is the advantage in showing billings at standard rates and showing allowances (such as those made to hospital plan groups) as deductions from gross revenues rather than showing the net amount billed as revenues without disclosing the amounts of deductions?

Question 19-7. Referring to the income and expense statement illustrated in Figure 104, why are contributions shown in the last part of the statement?

Question 19-8. The following entries appeared in a hospital general journal:

1. Provision for Depreciation of Buildings (General Fund)........ $10,000
   Reserve for Depreciation of Buildings (Plant Fund)......... $10,000
   To reflect depreciation charges.

2. Capital—Invested in Plant (Plant Fund).................... 10,000
   Unappropriated Surplus (General Fund)...................   10,000
   To reduce capital invested in plant fund by amount of depreciation charges.

(a) What is wrong with these entries? (b) Prepare corrected entries.

Problems

Problem 19-1. The following is a trial balance of the general fund of Hospital *D* at January 1, 1955:

Cash.....................................	$10,000	
Accounts Receivable......................	35,000	
Due from Temporary Fund.................	3,000	
Accounts Payable........................		$12,000
Allowance for Uncollectible Accounts........		500
Unappropriated Surplus...................		35,500
	$48,000	$48,000

534

The following transactions took place during the year:

1. Bills rendered to patients: $500,000 for routine services and $1,000,000 for special services; of these billings $5,000 is estimated to be uncollectible.

2. Accounts receivable in the amount of $1,480,000 were collected.

3. Expenditures for salaries and wages and for materials (all paid for in cash) were as follows:

Department	Amount
Administrative and general	$139,000
Household and property	291,000
Professional care of patients	737,000
Outpatient and emergency	28,000
Dietary	205,000

4. Bills in the amount of $10,000 were rendered to the temporary fund for its share of the cost of recreational activities.

5. Accounts payable outstanding on January 1, 1955, were all paid.

6. The $3,000 due from the temporary fund on January 1, 1955, was received in cash.

7. Mortgage interest in the amount of $3,000 was paid.

8. The cafeteria paid to the general fund $20,000 representing its net income for the year.

9. The following liabilities and accruals remained unpaid at December 31, 1955:

Accounts payable (for materials and supplies used; to be charged to professional care of patients)	$ 5,000
Accrued interest on mortgage	1,000
Accrued salaries and wages chargeable as follows:	
Administrative and general	3,000
Dietary	1,200
Household and property	4,800
Professional care of patients	13,000
Outpatient and emergency	1,000

10. Annual depreciation charges:

Buildings	$30,000
Equipment	50,000

11. Cash equal to the depreciation charges on equipment was transferred to the improvements and replacements fund.

12. Closing entries were prepared.

Required:

(a) Prepare journal entries.

(b) Post opening trial balance and journal entries to "T" accounts.

(c) Prepare a balance sheet of the general fund at December 31, 1955.

(d) Prepare an income and expense statement of the general fund for the fiscal year ended December 31, 1955.

Problem 19-2. The trial balance of the temporary fund of Hospital *D* at January 1, 1955, was as follows:

Cash	$5,500	
Due from Improvements and Replacements Fund	1,000	
Due to General Fund		$3,000
Fund *R* Balance		3,500
	$6,500	$6,500

Following are the transactions which took place during the year:

1. A donation in the amount of $25,000 was received in cash to be used for recreational purposes only.

2. The temporary fund was billed $10,000 by the general fund for its share of the cost of recreational activities.

3. Expenditures (paid in cash) for the year amounted to $1,000.

4. The $3,000 liability to the general fund at January 1, 1955, was paid.

Required:

(a) Prepare journal entries.

(b) Post opening trial balance and entries to "T" accounts.

(c) Prepare a balance sheet of the temporary fund at December 31, 1955.

Problem 19-3. The trial balance of the endowment funds of Hospital D at January 1, 1955, was as follows:

Cash.....................................	$ 46,000	
Investments............................	110,000	
Endowment Fund A Balance.............		$ 81,000
Endowment Fund B Balance..............		75,000
	$156,000	$156,000

Following are the transactions which took place during the year:

1. A donation of $75,000 was received in cash for the purpose of establishing an endowment fund (hereinafter referred to as endowment fund P) the income from which is to be used to provide special services for patients.

2. The money was invested in bonds which were purchased at par.

3. Stocks with a market value of $100,000 were donated to the hospital for the purpose of establishing an endowment fund (hereinafter referred to as endowment fund Q), the income from which is to be available for general purposes.

4. Bonds with a par value of $3,000 were sold at a loss of $300.

5. Stocks with a book value of $5,000 were sold at a profit of $500.

Required:

(a) Prepare journal entries.

(b) Post opening trial balance and entries to "T" accounts.

(c) Prepare a balance sheet of the endowment funds at December 31, 1955.

Problem 19-4. The following are the trial balances of the plant funds of Hospital D at January 1, 1955:

Improvements and replacements fund:		
Cash.................................	$ 15,000	
Investments.........................	6,000	
Due to Temporary Fund..............		$ 1,000
Fund Balance........................		20,000
	$ 21,000	$ 21,000

Investment in plant fund:		
Land................................	$ 90,000	
Buildings...........................	840,000	
Equipment...........................	370,000	
Mortgage Payable....................		$ 160,000
Allowance for Depreciation—Buildings..		10,000
Allowance for Depreciation—Equipment		30,000
Investment in Plant.................		1,100,000
	$1,300,000	$1,300,000

The following are the transactions which took place during the year:

1. The cost of constructing and equipping a major addition to the hospital was financed by cash contributions of $1,250,000 and a mortgage of $100,000. The cost is distributed as follows: land, $80,000; building, $950,000; equipment, $320,000.

2. A donation of $10,000 in cash and $10,000 (market value) in stocks was received. The donation is to be used to finance improvements and replacements.

3. Dividends on stock in the amount of $500 were received in cash.

4. Equipment costing $6,000 was purchased for cash.

5. Annual depreciation charges:

Buildings	$30,000
Equipment	50,000

6. Cash equal to the amount of depreciation on equipment, namely, $50,000, was received from the general fund.

Required:

(a) Prepare journal entries, indicating for each entry whether it applies to the investment in plant fund or to the improvements and replacements fund.

(b) Post the opening trial balances and journal entries to "T" accounts.

(c) Prepare a combined balance sheet of the plant funds at December 31, 1955.

Problem 19-5. Prepare a consolidated balance sheet in sectional form of all funds of Hospital D at December 31, 1955, using the individual balance sheets prepared for problems 19-1, 19-2, 19-3, and 19-4.

Problem 19-6. (Adapted from an American Institute of Accountants' examination.) The City of E built a municipal hospital on land previously owned by the city. The building was completed on March 1, 1955. Since that date the hospital has been under the control of a superintendent. He has rendered monthly reports to the town mayor, but these reports have been on a cash basis and have not shown separation of amounts by funds. You have been employed by the city government to prepare financial statements for the ten months ending December 31, 1955, and to do certain other work in connection with setting up an accounting system for the hospital operations. The city wants the financial statements to be on an accrual basis, to the extent such basis is appropriate, and to follow usual fund accounting practices. From the information presented below, you are to prepare statements showing income and expense and financial position.

(1) The total contract price of the buildings was $240,000. The contractor was paid in the following manner:

(a) Cash of $120,000 which was a contribution by the Federal government toward the hospital cost.

(b) Cash of $25,000 contributed by the county government toward the cost.

(c) Hospital bonds issued by the city to the contractor in the amount of $100,000. These bonds are 5% bonds dated 1/1/55, due in ten years, interest payable semiannually. They are general obligation bonds of the city but the city wishes to treat them in the hospital fund.

(2) Equipment was initially obtained as follows:

(a) Purchased by the city for cash—$35,300.

(b) Purchased out of cash donations made by citizens for that purpose—$9,800.

(c) Donated equipment which had an estimated value of—$11,000.

(3) The statement of cash receipts and disbursements, exclusive of items described above, for the ten months was as follows:

Received from patients:

Rooms and meals...............................	$105,314
Fees..	6,170
Out-patients....................................	4,201
Miscellaneous income from meals, etc...............	515

Received from estate of James Johnson, M. D........... 25,000
Miscellaneous donations............................. 10,410
Received from Beulah Jenkins....................... 32,500
Donations from churches............................ 1,850
Received from county for county charity patients—room
   and meals....................................... 940
Income from rents.................................. 2,000
Income from bonds................................. 2,125

Total cash received............................ $191,025

Payroll and taxes thereon paid...................... $ 96,200
Stores and supplies purchased....................... 34,180
Equipment purchased............................... 27,250
Expense of operating rented property................ 700
Miscellaneous expenses (including bond interest of $2,500) 4,170

Total cash disbursed............................ $162,500

Balance of cash 12/31/55...................... $ 28,525

(4) Investigation revealed the following additional information:
    (a) Patients' accounts on the books as of December 31, 1955 amount to $9,403 distributed as follows: For room and meals—$7,310; for laboratory and other fees—$1,095; for out-patients—$998. It is estimated that $500 of these accounts will never be collected.
    (b) As of December 31, 1955 accrued unpaid wages, etc. amounted to $5,234; unpaid supply invoices amounted to $6,810 and accrued utilities amounted to $174. The analysis of miscellaneous expenses shows that there is $330 of prepaid insurance. Kitchen and other supplies on hand amounted to $1,760 at cost.
    (c) It has been decided to charge current income with depreciation on general hospital property at the following annual rates based on the year-end balance of the asset accounts:
        Buildings—2%
        Equipment—10% and 20%
    All equipment will take the 10% rate except for $18,500 of minor items of equipment, which will be depreciated at the 20% rate. Depreciation is to be computed for a full year. The reserve is not to be funded.
    (d) The following facts were determined in respect to the donations:
        (1) The donation from the estate of James Johnson, M. D. was received July 1, 1955. It consisted of two houses and $25,000 in cash. The terms of the bequest provided that the cash is to be invested and that the income therefrom and from the houses is to be used for the purchase of surgical equipment. The houses had a market value of approximately $30,000 of which amount $5,000 was for the land. The estimated life of the properties from date of the gift was 25 years. The houses were rented and in addition to the $2,000 of rent received there was $150 receivable as of December 31, 1955. All expenses on the houses for the year have been paid and are included in the disbursements. No purchase of surgical equipment has been approved.
        (2) The miscellaneous donations were made for general purposes of the operation of the hospital.
        (3) The Beulah Jenkins donation received June 1, 1955 consisted of cash and of $50,000 face value of X Corporation 4¼% bonds. Interest dates are June 1 and December 1. The provisions of the gift were: "The amounts are to be invested by said trustees in accordance with applicable law governing trust investments and the income derived

therefrom is to be used to defray or help to defray the necessary hospitalization of such indigent women as the trustees shall designate upon application by their physician." The trustees were designated in the document. These trustees have accepted but have never met or transacted any business.

(4) The donations from churches are to apply toward purchase of an "iron lung." No order has yet been placed for such equipment.

Problem 19-7. (Adapted from an American Institute of Accountants' examination.)

Based on the data below, prepare:

a. A worksheet to record the transactions relative to the X County Hospital for the year ended August 31, 1955.

b. A balance-sheet of X County Hospital as of August 31, 1955, which reflects a general fund, an endowment fund and plant fund.

The Z Society, a fraternal order, which operated X County Hospital for indigent members of the community, donated it on September 1, 1954, to the Village of H, in which it is located. The gift included all of the securities in the endowment fund (the hospital's principal source of income), as well as the real estate, equipment and other assets. Since the village had made no appropriation for the operation and maintenance of a hospital, gifts from public spirited citizens supplemented the endowment fund income to provide for operating costs during the first year of its operation by the village, which coincided with the village fiscal year. No part of the principal of endowments may be used for operations. Before the end of the year preparations were under way for a drive to raise funds to enlarge and improve the plant. Since no money was collected in connection with this drive during the year under consideration, all expenditures for plant improvements were paid out of the general fund, but will be reimbursed from the proceeds of the drive.

The following transactions occurred during the first year.

Contributions and Receipts

1. Hospital site—value	$ 25,000
2. Hospital buildings—value	200,000
3. U. S. Treasury bonds contributed as endowment, principal amount	100,000
4. Accrued interest on U. S. bonds at August 31, 1954	1,250
5. Stocks and bonds contributed as endowments (no accrued dividends or interest)—market value	1,300,000
6. Equipment—value	60,000
7. Life insurance policies assigned to hospital as endowments—	
Cash value $ 5,000	
Face amount 150,000	
(Hospital to pay future premiums)	
8. Contributions from X County for hospital operations	10,000
9. Contributions from numerous individuals for hospital operations	20,000
10. Proceeds from sponsored charity bazaar	500
11. Interest received from U. S. Treasury bonds	2,500
12. Dividends from stocks	44,000
13. Interest from bonds, other than U. S. Treasury	12,000
14. Sale of stocks included in endowments at $27,000	52,000

Disbursements

15. Building improvements	$ 20,000
16. Equipment	15,000
17. Salaries	15,000
18. Food and dietary supplies	10,000
19. Medicinal supplies	20,000

20. Life insurance premium paid....................................	2,000
21. Property insurance...	5,000
22. Light, heat and water..	1,000
23. Expenses of charity bazaar, announcements, etc....................	15
24. Other operating expenses......................................	4,000

Other Information

25. Cash value of life insurance held for benefit of hospital at August 31, 1955.. $ 6,500
26. Contributions subscribed but not collected........................ 5,000
27. Prepaid insurance at end of year................................ 500

Balance in bank per bank statement at end of period............. 51,085
Outstanding checks amount to $3,300 and the last day's deposit of $1,200 is not included on the bank statement.

28. Upon completion of the $20,000 improvements to the hospital building it was appraised at $250,000.

Problem 19-8. (Adapted from an American Institute of Accountants' examination.)

The following balances appear on the books of Hospital *M* as of January 1, 1954:

	Debits	Credits
Cash on hand and in banks.........................	$ 143,866	
Accounts receivable—patients........................	48,740	
Sundry accounts receivable..........................	508	
Inventory of supplies...............................	17,583	
Prepaid insurance..................................	3,294	
Stocks and bonds..................................	3,702,010	
Other investments.................................	225,950	
Land...	25,000	
Buildings...	402,305	
Equipment..	106,500	
Allowance for loss on accounts......................		$ 10,385
Accounts payable..................................		29,227
Other current liabilities............................		38,014
Bonds payable—1st mortgage 5%....................		300,000
Advance payment by patients.......................		6,364
Balance..		4,291,766
	$4,675,756	$4,675,756

From the following information and summary of the transactions for the year ended December 31, 1954, you are to prepare work sheets showing by appropriate funds all information needed for (a) a statement of income and expense for the year and (b) a balance-sheet for each fund as of December 31, 1954. Changes in surplus accounts or in fund balances should be shown in additional columns unless all such changes are clearly identified in the balance-sheet columns.

(1) The stocks and bonds together with $112,808 of the cash belong to endowment funds, the income of which may be used for general purposes of the hospital. An additional $12,150 of cash belongs to specific expendable funds. Buildings and equipment are stated net of depreciation which has been charged to the current expenses of each year. There is no intention to provide a fund for replacement of assets, and as assets are replaced, payments are made out of general cash. The other investments belong to endowment funds for specific purposes. The income from these funds may be used only for the designated purposes.

(2) Cash income from endowment fund stocks and bonds amounted to $138,710. Income from other investments amounted to $11,765.

(3) Cash donations received amounted to $41,305, all except $10,500 of which was for current use. The $10,500 was expendable only for a designated purpose.

(4) Services rendered pay patients amounted to $930,480 which was all recorded through accounts receivable—patients.

(5) Cash collected from patients and prospective patients amounted to $925,428, of which $12,890 represented advance payments.

(6) Cash of $1,375 was collected on sundry accounts receivable.

(7) The allowance for loss on accounts was increased by $10,000. Patients' accounts totaling $6,302 are considered to be uncollectible and were written off.

(8) Depreciation on the buildings was $11,307. Depreciation on equipment was $18,541.

(9) The following vouchers were approved:

Storeroom supplies—$78,240; Insurance—$11,624; General operating expenses—$979,731; Maintenance—$7,448; Replacement of equipment —$11,432; Interest on bonds—$15,000; Retirement of bonds—$10,000. Other current liabilities were credited with $505,212 of these $1,113,475 of vouchers.

(10) The carrying value of equipment replaced was $2,710.

(11) Free services rendered during the year amounted to $108,000.

(12) Services rendered patients (see No. 4) were covered by advance payments amounting to $14,105.

(13) Cash disbursements were made of $502,701 in payment of other current liabilities and $610,043 in payment of accounts payable. Discounts taken on accounts payable amounted to $2,305.

(14) Storeroom supplies of $72,578 were issued for general use and $1,073 of supplies were sold to employees and charged to sundry accounts receivable. Insurance expired amounted to $10,445.

(15) Cash expenditures from specific expendable funds were $5,875.

(16) Cash receipts for the year included unexpendable cash contributions of $50,000, proceeds from sale of stocks and bonds of $502,164 and proceeds from sale of other investments of $52,125.

(17) Cash disbursements not vouchered consisted of $507,892 for purchase of stocks and bonds and $48,100 of the proceeds from sale of other investments which was invested in bonds.

(18) There was a loss of $7,354 sustained on the sale of stocks and bonds and a $9,978 loss sustained on the sale of other investments.

Questions and Problems on Chapter 20

Questions

Question 20-1. Name three differences between the accounting procedures of colleges and those of hospitals.

Question 20-2. The Main City College is financed solely from a special tax levy made for this purpose. The construction of the building was financed from the sale of bonds. These bonds as well as the interest thereon are also being paid from the special tax levy referred to immediately above. Would the accounting procedure outlined in the chapter also apply to this college? If not, indicate the fund or funds in which the financial transactions of the college should be recorded.

Question 20-3. The American Hospital Association recommends that depreciation be taken on all fixed assets of hospitals, whereas the American Council on Education recommends that, with certain exceptions, no depreciation should be taken on the fixed assets of colleges. Do you think there is a better reason for charging depreciation on the fixed assets of hospitals than on the fixed assets of colleges?

Question 20-4. As indicated earlier, the American Council on Education recommends the use of current funds, loan funds, endowment and other non-expendable funds, annuity funds, plant funds, and agency funds. Plant funds are in turn divided into improvement and replacement funds, retirement of indebtedness funds, and investment in plant funds. You are required to show for each of these funds the corresponding municipal fund or group of funds, if any, that is designed to account for the same type of financial transaction.

Question 20-5. A university income and expense statement is prepared in the following form:

A UNIVERSITY

Current General Funds

Statement of Income and Expenditures
for Fiscal Year

Income:		
Educational and general...........................		$4,550,000
Auxiliary enterprises.............................		1,041,500
		$5,591,500
Expenditures:		
Educational and general...............	$4,150,000	
Auxiliary enterprises.................	1,210,000	
Student aid.........................	115,000	5,475,000
Excess of income over expenditures.............		$ 116,500

(a) Is this statement properly arranged? (b) If not, rearrange it.

Question 20-6. Referring to item 3, on page 348, which do you think is the better procedure: to allocate to each fund its share of the income or to assume an arbitrary rate of return? Give reasons for your answer.

Question 20-7. Under what circumstances will the charging of depreciation on the fixed assets of an endowment fund fail to provide sufficient funds to replace such assets?

Problems

Problem 20-1. Part 1. The trial balance of the current general fund of X University on September 1, 1955, was as follows:

Cash..................................	$155,000	
Accounts Receivable.....................	30,000	
Allowance for Uncollectible Accounts......		$ 2,000
Inventory of Materials and Supplies........	25,000	
Vouchers Payable.......................		23,000
Unappropriated Surplus..................		185,000
	$210,000	$210,000

The following transactions took place during the current fiscal year:

1. Educational and general revenue collections amounted to $2,270,000 distributed as follows: student fees, $1,960,000; gifts and grants, $170,000; organized activities relating to educational departments, $115,000; others, $55,000.

2. Receivables at end of the year, $29,000, consisting entirely of educational revenues.

3. It is estimated that tuition receivable in the amount of $1,000 will never be collected.

4. Revenues collected from auxiliary enterprises, $300,000.

5. Materials purchased during the year for cash $500,000; on account, $50,000.

6. Materials used amounted to $510,000 distributed as follows:

Educational and general:		
General administration...............	$ 30,000	
General expenses.....................	5,000	
Instruction and departmental research..	305,000	
Organized activities relating to educational departments................	7,000	
Others..............................	53,000	$400,000
Auxiliary enterprises............................		110,000
		$510,000

7. Salaries and wages paid:

Educational and general:		
General administration...............	$ 170,000	
General expenses....................	63,000	
Instruction and departmental research..	1,212,000	
Organized activities relating to educational departments................	80,000	
Others..............................	85,000	$1,610,000
Auxiliary enterprises............................		90,000
		$1,700,000

8. Other expenses:

Educational and general:		
General administration................	$10,000	
General expenses.....................	2,000	
Instruction and departmental research..	53,000	
Organized activities relating to educational departments.................	3,000	
Others............................	7,000	$75,000
Auxiliary enterprises..............................		20,000
		$95,000

9. Interest expenses, all chargeable to educational and general, $3,000.

10. Vouchers payable paid, $40,000.

11. A transfer of $20,000 was made from this fund to the improvements and replacements fund for the purpose of financing plant additions.

12. The board of trustees of the university passed a resolution authorizing the transfer of $150,000 to a fund which is to function as an endowment.

13. The general current fund paid $20,000 for additions to the plant.

Required:

(a) Prepare journal entries.

(b) Post the opening trial balance and journal entries to "T" accounts.

Problem 20-1. Part II. The trial balance of the current restricted fund of X University on September 1, 1955 was as follows:

Cash...................	$32,000	
Vouchers Payable.......		$ 2,000
Fund Balance..........		30,000
	$32,000	$32,000

The following transactions took place during the current fiscal year:

1. Income was received in cash from endowments, $70,000; gifts and grants, $150,000; auxiliary enterprises, $130,000; student aid, $20,000.

2. Expenditures paid in cash:

Educational and general:		
General administration...................	$ 40,000	
General expenses.......................	30,000	
Instruction and departmental research.....	125,000	
Others................................	20,000	$215,000
Auxiliary enterprises................................		90,000
Student aid..		20,000

3. Depreciation charges on auxiliary plant carried as an endowment amounted to $15,000.

4. Cash equal to the depreciation charges, namely, $15,000, was transferred from this fund to the endowment fund.

Required:

(a) Prepare journal entries.

(b) Post the opening trial balance and journal entries to "T" accounts.

(c) Prepare a combined balance sheet of the current general fund and current restricted fund as of August 31, 1956.

(d) Prepare a combined income and expense statement for the current general fund and current restricted fund for the fiscal year ended August 31, 1956.

Problem 20-2. The following transactions took place in the endowment funds of X University during the fiscal year ended August 31, 1956:

1. A cash donation of $900,000 was received to establish endowment fund X, and another donation of $600,000 also in the form of cash was received for the purpose of establishing endowment fund Y. The income from these funds is restricted for specific purposes. It was decided to invest this money, to pool the investments of both funds, and to allow 5 per cent on the book value of pooled investments at the end of the year.

2. Securities with a par value of $1,000,000 were purchased at a premium of $10,000.

3. Securities with a par value of $191,500 were acquired at a discount of $2,000; accrued interest at date of purchase amounted to $500.

4. The university trustees voted to pool the investments of endowment fund Z with the investments of endowment funds X and Y under the same conditions as applied to the latter two funds. The investments of endowment fund Z at the date it joined the pool amounted to $290,000 at book value and $300,000 at market value.

5. Cash dividends received from the pooled investments during the year amounted to $70,000, and interest receipts amounted to $5,500.

6. Premiums in the amount of $500 and discounts in the amount of $100 were amortized.

7. Securities in the amount of $30,000 were sold at a profit of $2,400.

8. Each fund was credited with its share of the interest earnings for the year (see transaction no. 1).

9. Land, buildings, and equipment amounting to $800,000 were donated to the university, distributed as follows: land, $80,000; buildings, $500,000; equipment, $220,000. The donor stipulated that an endowment fund (hereafter designated as endowment fund N) should be established and that the income therefrom should be used for a restricted purpose.

10. Income from the property referred to in the preceding transaction is accounted for in current restricted fund N. This fund transferred $32,000 to endowment fund N, of which $10,000 represented depreciation charges on the building and $22,000 depreciation charges on equipment.

11. A trust fund in the amount of $350,000 was set up by a donor with the stipulation that the income was to go to the university to be used for general purposes.

Required:

(a) Prepare journal entries.

(b) Post to "T" accounts.

(c) Prepare a balance sheet of the endowment funds as of August 31, 1956.

Problem 20-3. The following transactions took place in the loan fund of X University during the fiscal year ended August 31, 1956:

1. A donation of $150,000 was received in cash for the purpose of making loans to students.

2. Cash in the amount of $50,000 was invested in bonds which were acquired at par.

3. Loans in the amount of $60,000 were made to students.

4. Interest on investments in the amount of $300 was received in cash.

5. Student loans in the amount of $1,000 were written off as uncollectible.

Required:

(a) Prepare journal entries.

(b) Post to "T" accounts.

(c) Prepare a balance sheet of the loan fund as of August 31, 1956.

Problem 20-4. The trial balance of the investment in plant fund of X University as of September 1, 1955, was as follows:

Land...............................	$ 200,000	
Buildings...........................	3,300,000	
Equipment.........................	1,200,000	
Mortgage Payable..................		$ 250,000
Investment in Plant from Donations....		800,000
Investment in Plant from Current Funds		650,000
Investment in Plant from Gifts........		3,000,000
	$4,700,000	$4,700,000

The following transactions took place during the year:

1. A cash donation of $40,000 was received from an individual for the purpose of financing additions to the educational plant.

2. The money was invested in securities which were acquired at par.

3. Cash in the amount of $20,000 was received from the current general fund for purposes of making additions and improvements to the plant.

4. Of the money received from the current general fund $10,000 was used to finance the acquisition of additional equipment.

5. Land, buildings, and equipment amounting to $800,000 were donated to the university, distributed as follows: land, $80,000; building, $500,000; equipment, $220,000. The donor stipulated that an endowment fund should be established (designated as endowment N in Problem 20-2).

6. The investment in plant fund was reduced by the depreciation charges of $10,000 on the building and $22,000 on the equipment referred to in transactions 9 and 10 of Problem 20-2.

7. A cash donation in the amount of $75,000 was received for the purpose of paying part of the mortgage.

8. A mortgage installment of $35,000 which became due during the year was paid from the above donation.

9. An uninsured piece of equipment costing $5,000 and financed from the current general fund was destroyed.

Required:

(a) Prepare journal entries.

(b) Post the opening trial balance and entries to "T" accounts.

(c) Prepare a combined balance sheet for the plant funds as of August 31, 1956.

Problem 20-5. (Adapted from an American Institute of Accountants' examination.) From the following information relating to Prep School, prepare a work sheet showing opening balances, transactions, also adjustments for the year ended June 30, 1955 and closed trial balances as of June 30, 1955, for each of the four classes of funds into which the general ledger is divided: viz., general fund, plant funds, endowment funds, and student loan funds.

The balances of the general ledger accounts as at July 1, 1954, are as follows:

Cash—for general use.	$ 1,000	
Cash—from alumni subscriptions for new dormitory	2,000	
Cash endowment.	45,000	
Cash—for student loans.	1,000	
Tuition receivable.	12,500	
Investments—temporary investments of general cash.	4,000	
Investments—endowment.	250,000	
Stores.	15,000	
Alumni subscriptions for new dormitory (due September 30, 1953).	8,000	
Student loans receivable.	3,500	
Education plant		
Financed from original and subsequent endowments.	600,000	
Financed from tuition funds.	50,000	
Financed from alumni subscriptions.	200,000	
Financed by grant from state and local government.	50,000	
Accounts payable for supplies.		$ 3,500
Unpaid expenses of alumni subscription campaign.		1,000
Balance.		1,237,500
	$1,242,000	$1,242,000

1. Endowment investments and $40,000 of the endowment cash represent principal of endowment funds held under terms providing that the income therefrom shall be used only for operating expenses of the school. The balance of endowment fund cash represents accumulated income not transferred from the endowment to the general fund.

2. Student population was 150 students. The tuition rate was $1,000 per school year per student except for six full scholarships and three partial (one-half) scholarships.

3. 90% of current tuition was collected and $100 of the balance is considered uncollectible.

4. Tuition receivable of prior years was collected in the amount of $12,000 and the balance is considered uncollectible.

5. Charges for operating expenses incurred and supplies purchased during the year totaled $135,000.

6. Inventory of operating supplies at June 30, 1955, amounted to $13,500.

7. Accounts payable for operating supplies and expenses amounted to $2,000 at June 30, 1955.

8. All temporary investments of general cash were sold on July 1, 1954, for $4,300 and accrued interest of $100.

9. Endowment investments having a book value of $25,000 were sold for $27,500, including accrued interest of $500.

10. Investments were purchased by the endowment fund trustees at a cost of $50,000.

11. Interest on endowment fund investments not sold during the year amounted to $20,500 for the year and was all collected in cash.

12. The endowment fund trustees transferred $22,500 to the general fund bank account.

13. As a result of the continued alumni subscription campaign, additional subscriptions in the amount of $65,000 were received for the purpose of providing a new dormitory. These subscriptions were payable one-fifth at the date of the pledge and one-fifth quarterly beginning January 15, 1955.

14. 5% bonds in the amount of $50,000 were issued for cash on January 1, 1955, to provide funds for immediate construction of the new dormitory. Interest was payable annually.

15. Contracts in the amount of $70,000 were let for construction of the new dormitory out of subscriptions.

16. The contract for construction of the new dormitory was 50% completed on June 1, 1955, and payment for one-half of the total amount, less a retained percentage of 10%, was made on that date.

17. All alumni subscriptions of the current year were paid on the due dates; those due previously were also paid in full.

18. Tuition receipts amounting to $5,000 were used to build additional bleachers at the athletic stadium.

19. A riding stable costing $4,000 and financed during a previous year from tuition receipts was destroyed by fire. Insurance recovery was $4,500; the building will not be replaced.

20. Student loans amounting to $3,500 were made.

21. Student loan collections amounted to $4,000, including $200 interest.

22. Expenses of the alumni subscription campaign were paid in full in the amount of $1,500.

Problem 20-6. (Adapted from an American Institute of Accountants' examination.) From the following trial balance of the accounts of the University of *R* and the additional information given, prepare a balance sheet in the proper institutional form:

	JUNE 30, 1955 Debit	Credit
Cash	$ 43,500	
Deposit accounts		$ 2,500
Income from endowment investments		85,500
Income from college operations		100,000
College operating expenses	195,000	
Interest accrued on securities purchased	500	
Inventories		
School supplies	5,000	
General	3,000	
Investments		
Bonds	875,500	
Mortgages	270,000	
Stocks	990,000	
Real Estate	100,000	
Mortgages payable secured by college plant		250,000
College plant		
Land	95,000	
Buildings	1,000,000	
Ground improvements	50,000	
Equipment	160,000	
Profit on sale of endowment fund investments		4,000
Prepaid college expenses	2,000	
Accounts receivable		
Students	3,000	
Miscellaneous	1,000	
Notes receivable	20,000	
Notes payable		2,000
Accounts payable		3,000
Reserve for doubtful accounts receivable		500

	Debit	Credit
Reserve for depreciation of buildings held as endowment-fund investment....................................		5,500
Reserve for contingencies...............................		5,000
Excess of assets over liabilities.........................		3,355,500
	$3,813,500	$3,813,500

Additional Information

1. An analysis of the cash account shows that the cash should be divided as follows:

Current funds		
Imprest cash......................	$ 1,000	
On deposit........................	35,000	
Loan funds..........................	2,000	
Endowment funds....................	4,000	
Funds subject to annuity agreements....	1,500	
	$43,500	

2. All the investments were made from endowment funds with the exception of $25,500 in bonds purchased from funds subject to annuity agreements. The income and principal of the latter funds are to be used to make certain definite payments during the life of the annuitants. Excess of annuity payments over income has been charged to the principal of the fund.

3. Notes receivable represent loans made to students from funds that are restricted to that purpose.

4. Memorandum records show that $11,500 of endowment funds are loaned temporarily to the current fund.

5. These records also show that $50,000 of endowment funds are invested in the college's plant which is in full accord with the endowment terms.

6. The income from $895,000 of endowment principal is restricted.

7. It was decided that the reserve for depreciation of real estate carried among the investments be funded.

Problem 20-7. (Adapted from an American Institute of Accountants' examination.) The following statement gives the account balances on the books of X College at the end of the fiscal year before closing:

	Debit	Credit
General current funds		
Cash...	$ 17,000	
Investments......................................	20,000	
Accounts receivable...............................	3,000	
Inventories.......................................	18,000	
Estimated income.................................	1,385,000	
Appropriations...................................		$1,360,000
Accounts payable..................................		2,000
Reserve for working capital............................		20,000
Unappropriated surplus (after entering budget)........		111,000
Educational and general expenditures.................	1,060,000	
Auxiliary enterprise expenditures.....................	252,000	
Other non-educational expenditures...................	26,000	
Educational and general income......................		1,070,000

	Debit	Credit
Auxiliary enterprises income..........................		315,000
Other non-educational income.........................		15,000
Transfer to endowment funds.........................	50,000	
Transfer to plant funds..............................	62,000	
	$2,893,000	$2,893,000

Restricted current funds

	Debit	Credit
Cash.......................................	$ 3,000	
Investments.......................................	58,000	
Accounts payable..................................		$ 1,000
Fund balances.....................................		60,000
	$ 61,000	$ 61,000

Loan funds

	Debit	Credit
Cash.......................................	$ 1,000	
Investments.......................................	5,000	
Notes receivable..................................	36,000	
Income...		$ 2,000
Funds principal, beginning of year...................		25,000
Gifts to loan funds, during year.....................		15,000
	$ 42,000	$ 42,000

Endowment and other nonexpendable funds

	Debit	Credit
Cash.......................................	$ 3,000	
Securities..	857,000	
Funds in trust....................................	100,000	
Profit on sales of investments.......................		$ 10,000
Endowment funds principal beginning of year..........		700,000
Gifts to endowment funds..........................		100,000
State tax collections for endowment funds............		100,000
Transfer from current funds (temporary)..............		50,000
	$ 960,000	$ 960,000

Funds subject to annuities

	Debit	Credit
Cash.......................................	$ 1,000	
Investments.......................................	99,000	
Fund balances, beginning of year.....................		$ 80,000
Gifts of annuity funds.............................		20,000
	$ 100,000	$ 100,000

Unexpended plant funds

	Debit	Credit
Cash.......................................	$ 4,000	
Investments.......................................	15,000	
Expenditures for plant additions.....................	360,000	
Replacement funds balances.........................		$ 15,000
Plant additions funds balances, beginning of year.......		50,000
State appropriations for plant additions...............		200,000
Gifts for plant additions...........................		50,000
Income on investments.............................		2,000
Transfer from current funds.........................		62,000
	$ 379,000	$ 379,000

	Debit	Credit
Funds invested in plant		
Educational plant, beginning of year..................	$3,100,000	
Bonds payable.......................................		$ 100,000
Investment in plant................................		3,000,000
	$3,100,000	$3,100,000
Agency funds		
Cash...	$ 2,000	
Investments..	8,000	
Fund balances......................................		$ 10,000
	$ 10,000	$ 10,000

Attention is called to the following facts and conditions which are disclosed upon examination of the records:

(1) Notes of loan fund amounting to $500 are found to be uncollectible and are to be written off.

(2) An annuity fund of $1,000 for current purposes has matured through the death of the annuitant.

(3) Included in the educational expenditures of the year from current funds is the sum of $14,000 for new equipment.

(4) Equipment included in the plant assets at the beginning of the year to the amount of $32,000 had worn out or other disposition of it had been made.

(5) Orders and contracts outstanding at the close of the year and payable from current funds appropriations amounted to $6,000.

(6) An analysis of endowment funds shows that at the beginning of the year $200,000 included therein represented undesignated funds temporarily functioning as endowments.

(7) A further analysis indicates that $100,000 of endowment funds has been expended for a residence hall, the value of which is included in plant assets but not in endowment funds.

(8) Income and expenditures of restricted current funds are included in the budget estimates and in the totals of income and expenditures carried in the general funds section.

You are required to do the following things:

(a) Make the necessary closing entries in all funds.

(b) Prepare a balance sheet after closing.

(c) Prepare a statement of current income, expenditures, and surplus for the year.

Questions

Question 21-1. What is the difference between general accounting and cost accounting?

Question 21-2. What is a unit cost standard and of what value is it in municipal cost accounting?

Question 21-3. Mention at least three factors which are likely to make the unit cost of collecting and hauling garbage in two cities differ.

Question 21-4. The City of A and the County of N share certain expenses jointly. The detailed arrangement is as follows:

The city pays the expenses of the sinking fund commission, the juvenile court, milk inspection, meat inspection, venereal disease clinics, and the city-county plaza. Once a month the city bills the county with its proportionate share of the cost (determined on a well-defined basis) and credits its own appropriation accounts in detail as to department, activity, character, and object.

The county pays for the following activities in which the city has an interest: the tax commission, the police radio, the fingerprint bureau, and the boys' reformatory. It bills the city for a share of the cost, which the city, in turn, charges to its own appropriation accounts.

It is proposed to allocate the cost of some of the functions entirely to the city and of others to the county, thereby obviating the additional accounting work involved. Would you approve of the proposed change?

Question 21-5. The City of K operates both an electric utility and a water utility. The electric utility uses water to generate steam, and the water utility uses electricity for pumping purposes. If both utilities make each year a sufficient profit from sales of services to customers to provide the money necessary for the retirement of bonds, should the charges made by the electric utility to the water utility (or vice versa) for services be sufficiently high to yield a profit or should they be limited to the cost of rendering the service (exclusive of profits)?

Question 21-6. A governmental water utility uses water in connection with the operation of pumps. Should the cost of this water be charged as an expense? If so, should the cost be limited to actual operating expenses, or should profits be taken into account?

Problems

Problem 21-1. The City of Y operates a central equipment bureau, renting out the equipment to various departments as needed. The following is a condensed statement of the expenses and miles or hours of use of each piece of equipment for the year ending December 31, 1955:

Equipment No.	Operating Expenses	Mainte-nance Expenses	Other Expenses	Miles or Hours* Used	Rental Rate per Mile or Hour*
1.................	$ 93	$ 71	$284	4,100	$ .1215
2.................	135	142	187	6,800	.0903
3.................	127	99	260	2,712*	.4464*
4.................	436	347	149	5,140*	.3600*
5.................	288	124	178	3,260*	.3402*
6.................	161	70	209	10,343	.0560
7.................	355	650	693	541*	2.0028*

The equipment was used during the year by the following departments, which were charged at the rental rates indicated above:

Equipment No.	Department Using the Equipment	Miles or Hours* Used
1	Mayor	4,210
2	Department of Public Safety:	
	Division of Weights and Measures	3,712
	Department of Health:	
	Food and Sanitary Division	4,100
3	Department of Public Works:	
	Division of Construction and Repairs:	
	Job B	600*
	Job C	300*
	Job D	1,500*
4	Department of Public Works:	
	Bureau of Streets and Alleys	5,112*
5	Department of Public Works:	
	Bureau of Streets and Alleys	1,210*
	Bureau of Sewers	1,712*
6	Department of Health:	
	Nursing Division	5,200
	Board of Elections	2,315
	Department of Law	3,625
7	Department of Public Works:	
	Bureau of Street Cleaning:	
	Street A	150*
	Street B	175*
	Street C	200*

Required:

a. Prepare a statement showing the cost of operating each piece of equipment, the earnings for each piece, and the net profit or loss, for the year ending December 31, 1955.

b. Prepare a statement showing for each organization unit the number of miles or hours worked for it by each piece of equipment, the amount charged to it on account of the use of each piece, and the total charges to it on account of equipment use.

c. Prepare a statement showing the amounts charged to the various construction and repair jobs and to the streets cleaned.

Problem 21-2. Counties X and Y operate a sanitarium jointly. Operating and maintenance costs, after revenues applicable to them have been deducted, are apportioned on the basis of the number of patient-days (the care of one patient for one day) attributable to each county. Expenditures for fixed assets, after rental income has been deducted, are distributed on the basis of the assessed value of the taxable property of each county. Settlements are made every six months.

You are given these facts for the first six months of 1955:

Operating and Maintenance Expenses		$73,000
Revenues Earned in Connection with Operations		1,000
Number of Patient-Days:		
County X	$17,500	
County Y	11,300	
Capital Outlays		400
Rental Income		560

Assessed Valuation of Taxable Property:

County X	$129,000,000
County Y	86,000,000

Required:

Prepare a statement showing the apportionment of sanitarium expenditures for the first six months of 1955 between the counties.

Problem 21-3. The County of X operates a quarry financed from a working capital fund for the purpose of obtaining rock needed for highway construction purposes. A small amount of rock is also sold to a municipality located near by. The operations of the quarry are financed through charges made to the county highway department and the nearby municipality.

The following is a summary of transactions taking place in 1955:

	Tons	Pounds	Per Ton
Sales to highway department:			
Crushed rock—from bins	3,173	1,100	$3.00
Crushed rock—from quarry	892	1,180	2.50
Rubble—from quarry	347	100	1.00
Rock dust—from quarry	71	1,500	.50
Sales to City of A:			
Crushed rock—from quarry	207	1,200	2.55
Rock dust—from quarry	145	100	.50

Expenditures were incurred as follows:

	Quarry	Crusher	Other
Labor	$5,351	$ 397	
Dynamite	82		
Repairs to machinery and equipment	147	1,328	
Building repairs	84		
Oil and supplies	124		
Tools	286		
Purchase of machinery and equipment	500	1,500	
Taxes, insurance, and royalty			$989
Freight on crushed rock			937
Labor unloading rock			229
Repairs and sundry expense			162
Power		225	

Use the short ton (2,000 pounds) in making your computations.

Required:

Prepare an income and expense statement for the quarry fund of the County of X for the year ending December 31, 1955.

Problem 21-4. On the basis of the following data, prepare a statement for the City of R for the year ending June 30, 1956, showing the total cost of refuse collection and the cost per ton or cubic yard, as the case may be (carry unit costs to three decimal places).

	Garbage	Rubbish	Dead Animals
BY CITY FORCES:			
Salaries and Wages	$512,000	$215,000	$4,100
Materials and Supplies	32,000	28,800	—
Equipment Use	116,050	70,500	2,200
Tons Collected	193,000	—	—
Cubic Yards Collected	—	312,000	—

	Garbage	Rubbish	Dead Animals
By Contract:			
Cost..............................	$ 81,600	$ 16,400	$3,300
Tons Collected....................	27,000	—	—
Cubic Yards Collected.............	—	26,000	—

Overhead is 12 per cent of total cost in the case of city force collection and 5 per cent in the case of collection by contract.

Problem 21-5. On the basis of the following data, prepare a statement of the City of K for the year ending June 30, 1956, showing the total expenses of the street cleaning division and unit costs for each activity (carry unit costs to three decimal places).

Activity	Unit	No. of Units	Total Cost
Ashes and Trash Collection.....	Cubic Yards..............	450,000	$230,000
Garbage Collection............	Tons.....................	7,000	57,000
Garbage Disposal.............	Tons.....................	9,000	6,200
Streets Cleaned by Hand Broom	M Square Yards..........	69,000 }	
	or		42,500
	Cubic Yards Sweepings....	15,000 }	
Streets Cleaned by Hand and Truck Patrol................	M Square Yards..........	97,000 }	
	or		21,000
	Cubic Yards Sweepings....	5,000 }	
Flushing......................	M Square Yards..........	43,000	4,500
Gutter Cleaning...............	M Square Yards..........	3,500 }	
	or		10,000
	Cubic Yards Sweepings....	6,000 }	
Alley Cleaning................	M Square Yards..........	700 }	
	or		3,500
	Cubic Yards Sweepings....	1,400 }	
Sweeping and Collection of Leaves	M Square Yards..........	18,000 }	
	or		18,000
	Cubic Yards Sweepings....	14,000 }	

Add overhead of 12 per cent of total cost in each case.

Problem 21-6. You are handed the following income and expense statement, which was prepared by the bookkeeper for the utility fund of the City of M:

CITY OF M

Utility Fund

Income and Expense Statement
for Year Ending June 30, 1956

Operating Revenues:

Sale of Water.........................	$ 44,000	
Fire Hydrant Rental..................	4,800	
Metered Sales of Electricity..............	107,700	
Street Lighting........................	12,000	$168,500

Less—Operating Expenses:

Fuel.................................	$ 21,000
Salaries and Wages....................	24,700
Materials and Supplies.................	3,000
Maintenance of Plant..................	15,500
Office Rent and Expense...............	3,000

Insurance...............................	4,600	
Interest on Deposits....................	200	
Meter Reading.........................	700	
Interest on Bonds......................	4,200	
Depreciation...........................	36,000	112,900

Net Income....................................	$ 55,600

Upon investigation, you find that the municipality operates jointly a water utility and an electric utility, both of which are financed from one fund, and that the above income and expense statement includes the revenues and expenses of both plants. It is desired, however, to allocate the proper share of revenues and expenses to each utility.

Upon further investigation, you find the following facts:

1. The cost of fuel is all allocable to the production of electricity.

2. Of the total salaries and wages, $2,800 is applicable to water.

3. Materials and supplies are distributable as follows: water, $800; electricity, $2,200.

4. Of the total office rent and expense, $1,500 is applicable to water.

5. Insurance expenses: water, $1,000; electricity, $3,600.

6. Maintenance of plant: water, $3,500; electricity, $12,000.

7. The interest on deposits and the meter reading expenses apply to electricity only.

8. Interest on bonds: water, $1,700; electricity, $2,500.

9. Depreciation: water, $5,600; electricity, $30,400.

The electric department has not included among its revenues the cost of current for pumping water, $6,200, nor among its expenses the cost of water used by it, $1,300. Neither did the water plant make any adjustments for services rendered to the electric plant or services received from that plant.

Required:

Prepare income and expense statements for the water and electric plants, respectively.

Problem 21-7. The public works department of the City of K has an agreement with the municipally owned electric utility whereby street lighting is charged to the department at the cost of generation, transmission, and distribution.

The total cost of generating, transmitting, and distributing electricity, exclusive of charges for use of equipment was $317,077 in 1956. The public works department charges the utility for the use of municipal equipment, such charges being based on actual cost of operation to the department. During 1956, equipment No. 3, 11, and 12 worked part of the time for the utility. Data regarding the number of hours operated and costs of operation are as follows:

Equipment No.	Cost of Operation	Total Miles or Hours* Operated	Miles or Hours* Operated for Utility
3	$840	15,000	10,000
11	966	4,600*	3,100*
12	600	2,500*	2,300*

The utility generated a total of 66,382,000 K.W.H. (kilowatt hours) which were disposed as follows:

Used by Utility Itself:

Station Auxiliaries........................	3,925,000 K.W.H.
Other Use by Utility.....................	565,000
Sales to Public Works Department...........	1,567,000
Sales to Other Consumers..................	54,525,000
Lost and Unaccounted for.................	5,800,000
Total.....................................	66,382,000 K.W.H.

Required:

Prepare a statement for the electric utility of the City of *K* showing the cost of electricity furnished to the public works department for street lighting during the year ending December 31, 1956.

Problem 21-8. (Adapted from an American Institute of Accountants' examination.) Four municipalities—Rose City, Copperville, Pineboro, and Coletown—formed the Spring Valley Water Commission for the construction and operation of a joint water supply. The project was estimated to cost $10,000,000 and to have a capacity of 100 million gallons daily (MGD).

It was agreed that the capital costs were to be apportioned among the participating municipalities according to the daily water allotments, but no municipality should be charged for the cost of any part of the project unless it were to receive benefit therefrom.

Capital assessment:

The four municipalities allotted the entire estimated supply of 100 MGD among themselves and agreed to an initial assessment of the estimated cost of $10,000,000 in proportion to these allotments, as follows:

	MGD	Assessment
Rose City...............................	30	$ 3,000,000
Copperville.............................	20	2,000,000
Pineboro................................	10	1,000,000
Coletown................................	40	4,000,000
	100	$10,000,000

All capital assessments were collected in full except that of Copperville, which paid only 90 per cent of its assessment.

Expenditure to Dec. 31, 1954:

At the close of 1954, Spider Dam and Crabtree Reservoir were completed, and pipe lines had been laid—namely, twin pipe lines from Spider Dam to the point where Rose City takes off the water and a single pipe line below that point. The cost per mile of the twin pipe lines was twice the cost per mile of the single line, and it was assumed that the twin lines were constructed for the benefit of all the municipalities. For convenience, the capital costs are identified by classes as follows:

Class A. Cost of Spider Dam and other costs at the headworks.

Class B. Twin pipe lines from Spider Dam and the headworks to the Rose City take-off—a distance of five miles. (In accordance with the agreement, the expenditures under Classes A and B are to be distributed to all of the four participating municipalities on the basis of the contract allotments.)

Class C. Single pipe line from Rose City take-off to Copperville take-off—a distance of three miles. (This capital cost is accordingly apportionable to Copperville, Pineboro, and Coletown.)

Class D. Single pipe line from Copperville take-off to Pineboro take-off—a distance of two miles. (This capital cost is apportionable to Pineboro and Coletown.)

Class E. Single pipe line from Pineboro take-off to Coletown take-off—a distance of ten miles. (This entire capital cost is chargeable to Coletown.)

The capital costs up to January 1, 1955, when operation began, were as follows:

Construction costs:

Headworks:

Spider Dam	$2,000,000
Pumping station	300,000
Power house	200,000
Total	2,500,000

Aqueduct:
$100,000 per mile of single pipe line.

Land, rights of way, etc.:

Class A	$1,993,100
Class B	447,800
Class C	198,900
Class D	104,200
Class E	256,000
Total	$3,000,000

Engineering costs:

Direct charges to classes:

Class A	$440,000
Class B	120,000
Class C	80,000
Class D	60,000
Class E	100,000
Total	$800,000

Indirect charges—$200,000 (to be apportioned to classes in proportion to direct engineering costs).

Administrative expenses—$500,000 (to be apportioned to classes in proportion to all construction costs up to January 1, 1955, exclusive of land and engineering costs).

Operating assessment 1955:

It was further agreed that the operating costs were to be apportioned according to actual water consumption, but in no event was the basis for any municipality's portion to be less than the contract allotment. The surplus or deficit resulting from each year's operations was to be credited or charged to the succeeding year's operating assessments.

In 1955 the average daily consumption was as follows:

	MGD
Rose City	40
Copperville	10
Pineboro	5
Coletown	25
	80

The 1955 operating expenses, estimated at $100,000, had been assessed as follows:

Rose City	$ 30,000
Copperville	20,000
Pineboro	10,000
Coletown	40,000
	$100,000

Rose City was the only municipality that paid its operating assessment in 1955.

Expenditure 1955:

The actual expenditures for 1955 were as follows:

Capital:
It was necessary to build a surge tank to prevent water surges from breaking the aqueduct. The tank cost $100,000 and was constructed halfway between the Rose City and Copperville take-off points. It was agreed that this surge tank was of benefit to all the participating municipalities.

Operating:
$71,000

In addition to the capital and operating expenses listed above, 1955 engineering expenses were $16,000, 50 per cent of which was to be apportioned to the capital division and 50 per cent to the operating division; and 1955 administrative expenses were $25,000, 80 per cent of which was to be apportioned to the operating division and 20 per cent to the capital division. The portions of the engineering and administrative expenses chargeable to the capital division are to be applied to the several classes of property on the basis of the engineering and the construction costs, respectively, to January 1, 1955.

Water sales 1955:

The Spring Valley Water Commission, in anticipation of the under-consumption of water on the part of some of the participating municipalities, entered into a contract with Glendale for 1955, whereby this municipality agreed to pay $30 a million gallons for water. The contract provided that Glendale would take a minimum of ten million gallons a day. Glendale paid the commission, $7,500 a month, on account; its consumption for the year was 3,300 million gallons.

There were no expenses chargeable to the water sales division except $30,000, representing the cost of connecting the pipe lines, which is not included in the above $71,000 operating expenses.

Profits from the sale of water to municipalities not participating in the project were to be apportioned annually to the participating municipalities on the basis of operating expenses charged to them.

General data and requirements:

The accounts of the commission are kept in three self-balancing divisions, namely: "capital," "operating," and "water sales." At the end of 1955, all inter-divisional balances are settled in cash to the extent that funds are available in the divisions.

Prepare a balance sheet (with supporting schedules and work papers) showing assets and liabilities of each division separately as of December 31, 1955, including the balances due from and due to the respective municipalities, and the equities of the participating municipalities.

INDEX